INTERVIEWS WITH CONTEMPORARY WOMEN PLAYWRIGHTS

KATHLEEN BETSKO
AND
RACHEL KOENIG

BTB
BEECH TREE BOOKS
A QUILL EDITION
New York

*For all the young men and women playwrights
of the future*

Copyright © 1987 by Kathleen Betsko and Rachel Koenig

All tapes, plays, reviews, criticism, and other research materials
gathered have been placed for preservation in the archives of
the Sophia Smith Collection at Smith College in Northampton,
Massachusetts.

Library of Congress Cataloging-in-Publication Data

Betsko, Kathleen.
Interviews with contemporary women playwrights.

Includes index.
1. Women dramatists—20th century—Interviews.
I. Koenig, Rachel. II. Title.
PN471.B48   1987   809.2'04   86-17489
ISBN 0-688-04405-0
ISBN 0-688-07033-7 (pbk.)

Printed in the United States of America

First Beech Tree Books/Quill Edition

1 2 3 4 5 6 7 8 9 10

BOOK DESIGN BY BETH TONDREAU

BIB

The word "book" is said to derive from *boka*, or beech.
The beech tree has been the patron tree of writers since ancient times and
represents the flowering of literature and knowledge.

ACKNOWLEDGMENTS

This collection of interviews would not have been possible without the generous support of many people. We are especially grateful to our editors, James Landis, Kristina Lindbergh and Jane Meara at Beech Tree Books for their faith in the project as well as their infinite patience. Novelist/translator/editor Marguerite Feitlowitz proved invaluable in shaping the final manuscript.

In addition, we received financial aid, and/or research assistance, moral support, and labor donations from the following organizations and individuals:

Bonnie Bursky; Mr. Huang Zongjiang, Xie Rong Jin, Zhang Xue Cai, and Chen Rong of the Chinese Theatre Association; Prof. Ruan Ruoshan of the Central Academy of Drama in Beijing; Su Hongjun of Fudan University, Shanghai; Prof. Constantine Tung of the University of New York at Buffalo; Martha Coigney, Elizabeth Burdick and their colleagues at the International Theatre Institute; Bob Thomas; Peter Landroche; Edward Langlois; Dick Polonski; Nancy Brown; the members of DWHE; Sue Morin; Eda Reiss and Jennifer Merin; Chris Carroll; Pat Truman; New York Public Research Libraries; New York University; Professors Helen Krich Chinoy, Len Berkeman, and Archivist Susan Griggs of Smith College; Andrew Harris, Grafton Nunes, and Simone Bloch-Wehba of Columbia University; Jane Gullong, Bill Hart, Morgan Jenness, Gail Merrifield, Joseph Papp and Ann Scott of The New York Shakespeare Festival; Julia Miles and the Women's Project at The American Place Theatre; The American Theatre Wing; Peggy Gold, Maggie Groves, and M. Kilburg Reedy of the Dramatists Guild's Committee For Women; The Dramatists Guild Fund; The Authors League Fund; Alberto Minero of the Center for Inter-American Relations; Francoise Kourlisky of UBU Repertory Theatre; The Writers Bloc; Ann Blumenthal at PBS, New York City; The Eugene O'Neill National Playwrights Conference; Mr. and Mrs. Leslie Wright; Mr. and Mrs. Arthur Rutter; Mr. and Mrs. Michael Rutter; Mr. and Mrs. John Braithwaite; Mr. and Mrs. Keith Braithwaite; Mr. and Mrs. William Braithwaite; Lee Hunkins; Jeffrey and Sheridan Sweet; Tanda and Elizabeth Marton; Anna Levine; Linda Edgerly; Ruth Josemovitch; Bonnie Greer; Sam Zygmunt; Kevin Geer; Lynne Brandon;

Deborah Perry and Women in Performance Magazine; Meryl Daw; Paul Minx; Sheila King; Jonathan Kalb; Bonnie Christianson; Jonathan Sand and Carol Reich of Writers and Artists Agency; Tim Wood and Chet Foley; Barbara Turen; Bettina Knapp; Rhoda Herrick; Elisa Ferraro; The Staff at the New York office of Gale Research Company; writer/editor Agnes Garrett whose advice, humor and common sense saw us through each phase of this book.

Rachel Koenig extends special thanks to:

Genevieve Salats, for saving a space on her bookshelf; The Brooklyn Women's Salon; Catherine Ruello, writer/translator and dear friend whose insights constantly challenge, shape and transform me; Dr. Catherine Johnson, writer and professor who first initiated me into feminist thought, and who encouraged my own beginnings; Michael Steinberg, Suzanne Slesin and Jake: together your laughter saw me through; Marielle Hucliez, whose wisdom, compassionate support and friendship are a blessing; Antoine Bootz, whose commitment, passion and imagination make everything seem possible. I thank him for his art, and for his unfailing confidence in mine; Doris and Jerry Koenig, whose artistic sensibilities, unconventionality, faith and nurturance inform my every endeavor.

Kathleen Betsko gives special thanks to:

Dr. David Magidson, Laura Rankin, Cathy Courtney, Lloyd and Barbara Richards, Alde Matteo, and Jean and Mary Jean Tibbils for their continuing faith in my creative efforts; to my children, Candy and Stephen Betsko; Greg; and my grandson, Aaron Marcus, whose efforts in the medium of Crayola suggest a bright, new artist for the future.

Ms. Betsko and Ms. Koenig have no adequate words to express their love and gratitude to playwrights Adele Ahronheim and June Calender and champion of the arts James Homan. Without their dogged labor and continuing commitment to documentation of the modern history of women playwrights this project would not have been possible.

CONTENTS

INTERVIEWS WITH CONTEMPORARY WOMEN PLAYWRIGHTS

Plays by Kathleen Betsko

BEGGAR'S CHOICE
JOHNNY BULL
STITCHERS AND STARLIGHT TALKERS

INTRODUCTION

Looking back over the interviews presented in this collection, Susan Griffin's powerful phrase "Every woman who writes is a survivor" comes to mind. For the woman playwright is a sturdy creature, one consummately dedicated to an art form which is entirely public, and to a vocation which requires absolute vulnerability. The living playwright is held accountable, and while the novelist's words must pass into print, into the hands of individual readers who may confront and reconfront the work at their leisure, the playwright's words must pass through a collective of artists who interpret the work for a collective audience in real time, an aspect of playwriting which heightens and increases the risk of misinterpretation—a decisive threat to any work of art.

And yet, these women bear up. And though all artists are in some way committed to putting themselves on the line, the woman playwright endeavoring to communicate her vision to the world is engaged in a radical act. One need not be familiar with the work of dedicated feminist scholars in every discipline who have so painstakingly documented the centuries of women's oppression to intuit and admit what is self-evident: the suppression of women's speech. Though women make up half the human race, women's words do not exist in equal numbers, nor do they naturally accrue over the centuries. If women's words were, or ever had been cherished, encouraged, or revered, we can be certain they would not have been lost to us, and those few fragments which did survive time and the elements would be more conspicuous, would need no special excavation.

One of the more obvious and simplistic observations one might make after reading these interviews, and more important, the work of the playwrights included, is the sheer number of words these writers have created to be spoken and enacted by women. This may be the most unifying and rudimentary element of the complex and multifaceted female voice in theater, and yet, the mere sounding of this voice, the speaking of women's words in public, as well as the invention and public presentation of male characters who were created from and who reflect a female viewpoint, is an act which has far-reaching consequences, for it is an act which challenges our age-old, one-sided notion of the universal, an act which

9

calls into question the very foundation and structure of civilization and power.

Despite the fashionable parry to the question of a female voice in theater—that "true" art is genderless—the fact remains that the woman playwright is a very real, very human agent. Her perceptions, dreams, memories, and visions are rooted in a female sentience. An integral and problematic component of the "true art is genderless" argument is its companion notion, "true art transcends gender," a notion which embraces the fallacy of the mind-body split. Rather than describing our human capacity to imagine as transcendent, imagination could be described as a bridge, connecting the known and the unknown, what is to what has been and what could be. Our leaps of imagination are a product of our astonishing capacity to form mental images of things which are not present to our senses, or of things never before wholly perceived or encountered in reality. Our sensibility, receptivity, readiness of feeling and awareness are what lead us to the foot of this bridge, and our ability to traverse the bridge of imagination, to guess at and form images to describe what the universe might have been or would be like *if* . . . does not exclude our bodily knowledge, and is, rather, an extension of our livingness, our sentience.

The woman playwright, who in her reveries can, as any human being, choose to traverse the bridge of imagination, nevertheless begins at its foot, and is, as are we all, rooted in and at one with her body. It is this female sentience, and the knowledge garnered there, which is threatening, which when extended into the world and made public through theater has been silenced and suppressed. For though a man may stand at the foot of the imagination's bridge, his leap is toward and not out of female sentience, and the woman playwright's public presentation of woman as her own subject boldly calls into question the entire history of the male playwright's previously unquestioned representation of female character. The woman playwright's creation of female character is a self-reflexive act which reifies female sentience. The male playwright's creation of female character is not and can never be self-reflexive. And while a male-created female character can and should ideally reflect her male creator's empathetic and imaginative leap toward female sentience, it seems she is much more frequently a substantiation of his idealization or his fear of women. Rather than contemplate what woman *is*, the male playwright often imposes upon his female characters his controlling values of what woman *should be*. Moreover, the audience, engaged in the suspension of disbelief, and aided by the actress and her performance, is given the illusion of authentic female character without the provisionary narrative cues which might enable them to discern a male modulation and inflection of female being.

Many of the richest periods in the history of drama resulted from the male playwright's impulse toward self-reflection, from his posing of the question "What is Man?," the implication being "What is human?" This powerful question reenters the drama with the advent of female self-reflection, and while the traditional question "What is Man?" is re-formed by the female dramatist who asks, "What is woman?," the implication —what does it mean to be human?—remains, and the cultural definitions arising from this reinvestigation of human nature now begin to reflect and include the previously silenced realm of female experience.

Theater is an art form which relies on sentiency; to begin with, the actor must engage with and embrace the playwright's words in a very physical and feelingful way. The playwright does not, as does the novelist, relate story through narrative, dialogue and imagery alone; the playwright's narrative is related through the animation and interaction of bodies in space; the speech of his or her characters is embodied by living, breathing human beings, and the imagery of the play must be expressed in stage terms. The components of fictive narration—action, rhetoric, and poetics—must therefore be transformed into a particular and living three-dimensionality, intended to confront the spectator in a very immediate and visceral way. In this sense, the female playwright's presentation of character is radically different from the female novelist's, for the audience must now bear witness to the actual *embodiment* of the female playwright's voice in both the male and the female actor. Returning for a moment to the self-reflexive nature of the woman playwright's creation of female character, it should also be pointed out that unlike the woman novelist, or the male playwright for that matter, the woman playwright in effect creates a character outside of herself who must be literally reembodied by one with a body similar to her own. The actress engaged in creating a female playwright's role is therefore involved in the same self-reflexive act as was its creator.

The diverse plays and artistic sensibilities of the women represented here reflect a complex, but always *resonant* relation to dramatic action, rhetoric and poetics. Immersed in these works during the course of this project, I began to hear this resonance, which seemed to me to originate in female sentience, in a very female consciousness, perception and apprehension of the world. These playwrights, each with her own prismatic aesthetic, each with her own cosmology, share a powerful impulse to illuminate and dramatize the multifarious spectrum of female experience. But aside from this, women are skilled in the art of attention, and have a strong tradition of listening, and not *only* to each other. For women are also the confidantes of sons, brothers, lovers and male friends, and therefore have intimate access to a particular and very vulnerable portion of the realm of male experience. The woman playwright also endeavors to re-create and dramatize her experience as practiced listener. An equally relevant aspect of female life experience is the fact that women have had access to and have studied and absorbed two thousand years of male literature. An empathetic engagement with male discourse is required of women as readers of and audience to male literature, and surely must come to bear upon the female dramatist's authorship and examination of male character. Beyond this, the analogous *lack* of a comparable body of female literature, history and tradition, as well as the devaluation of the act of *listening* to women's public and social discourse has perhaps correspondingly contributed to the literary misrepresentation and mythologizing of women by men.

In researching the reception of women's plays, as well as in listening to the women playwrights speak, it became clear that the censor, operant in the self and in society, was both attracted to and compelled to silence those elements of the work which were most deeply connected to female sentience and experience, those elements which either criticized or questioned male power and authority, or those elements which truthfully revealed male vulnerability. It also became evident that the plays most cherished by the playwright herself were cherished because they represented a successful rebellion against her own censorial impulse, cherished because of their daring, innovative, challenging, political nature. These plays were often described as underseen or unproduced, and were rejected (according to the rejection letters many playwrights shared with us) not because of any artistic shortcomings, but because literary managers— much like the television producers they apparently despise—felt compelled to protect their audiences from material they are not "ready" for. Those cherished, visionary plays which did manage to gain production were frequently the subject of vitriolic reviews, which in some cases effectively closed the production. It should also be noted that the publication of plays, and therefore their survival, is in this country entirely dependent upon the successful production of the play *during the playwright's lifetime.* In this sense, over-cautious literary managers, as well as virulent reviewers, can prevent a play from coming into existence as a piece of dramatic literature to be evaluated and/or produced by future generations. Play publication is the next and crucial step in the validation of women's voices and while it may be an encouraging sign that anthologies of interviews such as ours (as well as those which examine women's theater history) are now beginning to find publication, the reader should hold in mind the fact that these anthologies are *not* the plays, and that it is *only* through the publication and distribution of women's plays that the female voice in theater will survive.

As reader and audience to many visionary plays by women during the course of this project, I was both confronted with nonviolent dramatic conflict and positioned as a nonvoyeuristic spectator, asked not to passively observe a reenactment of a violent act, but to actively listen and evaluate valuable human testimony. Likewise I was witness to the lush landscape of female sexuality which when undistorted by the mythology of the pornographer's mind, bypassed the dynamic of sadomasochism so dependent on the hatred and denial of the "other" (the black, the woman, the child, the Jew . . .), and embraced nature, desire and erotic knowledge without fear. Thus I was confronted with new and theatrical imagery rich in the metaphors of female sentience, where blood could represent birth or the cyclical nature of life and death and *not* wounds and massacre. I saw mature women, married and unmarried, mothers and grandmothers who (like their creators) were not fragile or impassive, used up, or too old, but vivid, erotic, rebellious, *alive.* I saw women across the spectrum of age, race, and class taking action, bearing witness, responding to and making an effect upon the world. I saw the expression of female will and saw the exertion of this will go unpunished. I saw those who would wish to tame this will identified and cross-examined. I saw our ambivalence, our simultaneous and overwhelming fear and awe of nature reflected in the dramatic conflict between mother and daughter. I saw the split selves of a tortured psyche heal. A tradition of female action in the world was revealed to me, and I was given the chance to meet and observe relevant, remarkable women from many epochs who, once invisible, are now an ineradicable part of my vision of history. I saw regimes interrogated and presented in all their terrifying absurdity and wastefulness, I saw the notion of freedom considered and reconsidered, and I often saw its meaning redefined as embracing all human life. I saw continuity, the generations, the cycles of birth and death and rebirth, fertility and decay. I saw the shape of time transgress the linear beginning, middle and ending of all things. I saw dramas which described a purely feminine quest, dramas in which compelling, powerful women created their own destiny. I saw women avengers, and women survivors, but I also saw women succumb to a patriarchal siren song which, with ear-splitting intensity, obscured their own life force and lured and seduced them to commit self-destructive acts; but I came to see their death as unnecessary, and rather than passively accept their extinction, I was forced to mourn their fate, and therefore question and revise my own. I was held *responsible* for the horrors and atrocities of war, for the poisoning of the earth, for the passive acceptance of nuclear weapons which threaten the extinction of all living things. I was reminded that women, collectively and individually are *essential* to our survival. I saw that the abuse of women and children in a domestic milieu was inextricably connected to the international violence of war and I was shown that the nurture and protection and respect of children by feelingful women and men is a deeply heroic act, that in this act we are given the opportunity to resist the reenactment of the violence others may have unjustly inflicted upon us in our own childhood. I was given a glimpse into the dark side of human nature, but I was also given humor and hope, for in the enactment of these works I saw visions of the possible become actual. And I saw the agent of these visions, a dramatist, a woman, hold the power to shape the manifold of experience into new unities.

Once the central myth-making forum of society, theater arose to identify and map out a culture. And while the theater at present is debased in our film- and video-oriented world, it is still the most sentient, living and communal art form. It behooves us to re-create a theater which by dramatizing the key mythic questions of our own crucial epoch will once again function in an active and meaningful way. Despite the overwhelming obstacles set forth by our patriarchal society, despite the risks inherent in the communal art that *is* theater, women playwrights have demonstrated their capacity to pose and examine the imperative questions which are at present essential to our survival. By daring to challenge the "universal," by shaping the world into new unities, women playwrights are redefining culture, and in doing so they are broadening our sense of the range of human possibility.

—RACHEL KOENIG
Brooklyn, New York
February 1986

LILIANE ATLAN

Liliane Atlan was born in Montpellier, France, in 1932. Her plays have been produced extensively in theaters and at festivals in Europe and Israel. Ms. Atlan is the recipient of major French and Israeli literary prizes, the most recent of which is the Légion d'Honneur, reserved for French "national treasures."

For Atlan, the theater is ritual. That is, a theater piece binds—albeit with high-wire tension—the individual and collective consciousness, and individual and collective subconscious. Jewish history and practice, scholarship and mysticism have inspired and influenced Atlan. Throughout her career, she has sought to challenge traditional Occidental dramaturgy and conventional theatrical uses of time and space. Her most recent work, Un Opéra pour Terezin [An Opera for Theresien], takes the form of a Seder, lasts all night, and is designed to be relayed from country to country via satellite. The Messiahs should be staged in a planetarium: the Earth, the Galaxies, and the Planet of the Messiahs are characters in the drama. In France Atlan has pioneered the use of videodisk in theater. She emphasizes that her use of this technology is a new form of writing: "At first, men wrote on the walls of their caves, then on papyrus, then paper; why, in an age such as ours, should we not write with waves of sound and light?"

Three of Atlan's plays—Mister Fugue, The Messiahs, and The Carriage of Flames and Voices—are currently available in English, in Theatre Pieces: An Anthology by Liliane Atlan, The Penkevill Publishing Co., 1985. I had the great pleasure of working with Liliane on the final drafts of these translations. She took the opportunity of American publication to cut and/or revise with me parts of all of these plays, and considers the English versions definitive. During an especially difficult passage of Mister Fugue, we were racking our brains for a solution to what seemed then an unrelenting problem. Though the words were French, the syntax, strictly speaking, was not. The music I heard in the lines was definitely familiar, and yet was alien to the language to which, apparently, it was attached, and alien as well to the language of my translation. Suddenly, Liliane erupted, "But of course! This cannot go simply from French to English, because it is not written simply in French. It is a mixture of French,

Hebrew, Ladino, Yiddish—in short, it is written in a language of the Jewish subconscious."

Ms. Atlan's other plays include Les Musiciens, Les Èmigrants *(The Musicians, The Emigrants), 1976;* Même les Oiseaux ne Peuvent Toujours Planer *(Even Birds Can't Always Get High), 1979 and* Leçons de Bonheur *(Lessons in Happiness), 1982. Ms. Atlan has also written radio pieces and several books of poetry and prose.*

MARGUERITE FEITLOWITZ
Editor and Translator
Theatre Pieces: An Anthology by Liliane Atlan

Ms. Atlan began by discussing her new work, *An Opera for Theresien.*

ATLAN: I had from the beginning the desire to render tribute to the Jews of Europe interned in the ghetto of Theresien [Czechoslovakia]. They never stopped writing poems, plays for the theater, symphonies and even an opera. This opera is something I have to give, a kind of love for these people of the ghetto whom I've never known. I want to be in such deep mourning over their loss that I give something beautiful back to them in spirit. I would like everyone to grieve for the people of Theresienstadt [as the ghetto was known], that's my point. It is not to make a "nice play." In fact, the opera is not a play for theater, it is a Seder.

INTERVIEWER: You have been working for four years on this opera.

ATLAN: Yes, but I have been working bit by bit. The opera comes in little pieces, like a mosaic. I have to accept this as the truth of the process. Some months, I didn't work at all. It was part of my work to try and forget it. For many months I was waking two, three times a night, each time in Theresienstadt—I could not escape. For years I was afraid to even attempt this opera—I was afraid to go into that world, a world so fascinating that it would, perhaps, be impossible to escape. When I had the idea of making it a Seder, I suffered a big setback. It was [theater scholar and critic] Bettina Knapp who told me to go on. [See "Collective Creation from Paris to Jerusalem: An Interview with Liliane Atlan" by Bettina L. Knapp, *Theater*, Winter 1981.]

I am very lucky because I am not exactly French. I was born in Montpellier, France, but my parents are immigrants from Salonika. I was so disturbed by World War II and by the stories that my brother, who escaped from Auschwitz, told, that at a very early age I was compelled to study Hebrew and Hebraic tradition. I was influenced by the music of the Hebrew prayers. I remember the moment I knew that I needed to immerse myself in Jewish history, culture and tradition. I was sixteen, studying to be a French teacher—I was reading a poem of Lamartine and suddenly began to remember the stories my brother told me of Auschwitz. I felt such revulsion I became sick, I stopped eating and almost died. Then I discovered that I was not alone in my feeling— many Jewish students were revolted by the Western way of life and way of thinking that brought about the concentration camps and the horrors of the war. Then I found out about the Gilbert Bloch d'Orsay school where students were taught Hebraic tradition. We were twenty students each year, and theoretically we continued our regular studies at the Sorbonne, though they no longer interested us. We were taught to question: What does it mean to be Jewish? Okay, it means Auschwitz, but what else does it mean? How can one change life? How does one go about living? We discovered another life-style, an archaic life-style that was comforting. Instead of being taught abstractions, we were forced to incorporate our learning into daily life. We observed Jewish rituals which had been foreign to us, and in a strange language, Hebrew. Life began to take on a new spiritual and intellectual meaning, but after several years, this strangeness was no longer comforting to me. Though I no longer practice Jewish ritual, I feel lucky to have been nourished by the Great Hebrew texts: the Bible, the Midrash, the Kabbala, and to have received this knowledge not from a rabbi, but from a philosophy teacher who taught Jewish tradition as we studied the Talmud. We dreamed of changing the world. We didn't change it much, but our dreams gave us hope.

INTERVIEWER: Is your writing still informed by your Talmudic studies?

ATLAN: Yes. What I want to say with the opera is so strange that I am discovering a need to return to archaic form, to ritual. I am taking from the Bible, from the Talmud, I am inventing a literary form which corresponds to those archaic forms. So, the key conception of the opera is Hebrew. I am floating between cultures. Though I am not able to write in Hebrew, I do speak and often think in Hebrew. Even my French is not real French. The fact that I come to French from another world, and that I am nourished by another culture, makes the French language something else, and I think it brings something interesting to the language. I am French by chance, by accident, and that is why it is difficult for me here. I didn't want to live in Israel, although my play *Mister Fugue* [1967] was received well there, and I could have made a living from my writing. I need distance, and perhaps the mere fact of living in a hostile environment forces me to go further in my work.

The subject of my opera is Hebraic, it's Czech, it's everything but French! It is completely crazy, and yet it is good because I am obligated then, to be precise. For example, the opera is structured, as I said, around a Seder, the traditional Jewish Passover celebration. The fact that I must write about this in French, and that it *must* be read and understood by my French friends, and others who are strangers to these rituals and traditions, literally forces me to express it in such a way that it will interest them. I know I must go further in rendering the folkloric aspects of the opera. It is very important precisely because French is a language which is foreign to all this mysticism and spirituality. I have to write and write, and then pare it down to the essential. It is an extraordinary discipline.

INTERVIEWER: What disturbs you most about contemporary French theater?

ATLAN: What I find extraordinary and incomprehensible is that with all of the important events that have occurred in our century, most writers continue to use worn-out forms. [Playwright/director/filmmaker Armand] Gatti understood that the three major events of our time were Einstein, Hiroshima, and Auschwitz—now we can add Vietnam and others—but fundamentally everything was changed and affected by Einstein's new conception of space and time, and by Auschwitz, which gave to us a new conception of morality. These big events have become part of daily life, and I feel one cannot write as if they never occurred, or as if they have not affected us all in a personal way. I believe there is a collective mentality (masses of people) and a private mentality (individuals). It is difficult to capture the collective being, but because it *does* exist, it is necessary to create new forms of writing. . . . In our daily routine, we are in contact with many others through radio, television, newspapers. As a result there are collective stories and private stories. How can one encompass both realities? Certainly not with only three characters on stage! It is a problem. In the beginning I wrote plays which were impossible to stage because there were too many characters. To populate the stage is not a solution. I finally realized that I had to write in such a way that it would be possible to portray both the mass and individuals with thirteen characters at the most. That is why I am drawn to the use of music. Music within a play allows you to have chorus and solo, which are finally archaic and classical, but these conventions do serve to express the simultaneous existence of the mass and the individual.

INTERVIEWER: How do you penetrate the collective being? Through your dreams?

ATLAN: In the past my dreams helped me to explore a collective *unconscious*; now I am trying to explore and feel a collective *consciousness*, which may be more difficult. I would like someday to discover the *link* between the collective unconscious and the collective consciousness.

INTERVIEWER: Are you exploring this link in *An Opera for Theresien?*

ATLAN: Yes. For example, my opera is about a city. In this city there is personal history occurring, there is mass history and there is a connection between the two. So there are characters in the opera as well as the representation of an abstract character: the indistinct, undiscernible mass. The Jews of Europe interned in the ghetto of Theresienstadt tell us through their art the truth of what the Nazis did. They perceived, even if they were not aware of it, what was happening in the new contemporary history: the birth of masses and the advent of mass murder.

INTERVIEWER: I understand you are working from some drawings which were created in the ghetto.

ATLAN: There were marvelous painters there! I have spent days, months, studying their work which has helped me to understand, visually, this idea of the mass and the individual coexisting, and to visualize the lives of the people of Theresienstadt. The work of [Bedrich] Fritta has been especially inspirational.

INTERVIEWER: How have you gone about translating the visual imagery of the drawings into stage language and imagery?

ATLAN: I am attempting to extract the essence of the drawings. First I wrote stories without the drawings. In the beginning it was hard because I only had one book, *Requiem for Theresien*, I believe is the title, by Joseph Bor, and I did not want to simply dramatize his book. Later, when I went to Prague I discovered a book [about the ghetto] which was written in English because it was forbidden by the Bolsheviks for the Jewish Czechs to tell their stories in their own language. I was lucky to find the book—without it, it would have been impossible to work. It took me three years to learn the story, to forget it, to know what must not be done, and finally what I must do. Now I am writing stories *from* the drawings, using the history and details of my research. At first, I saw only details. . . . Later, I discovered that they had intuited this idea of the collective being and private being.

INTERVIEWER: What did you feel was imperative to avoid in telling their story?

ATLAN: I knew I couldn't write a realistic play, or for that matter a movie (though it would make an extraordinary expressionistic movie), because neither could give the idea or the feeling of the people who were there. To show the simultaneous existence of horror and joy is almost impossible. It was so hard for me to begin the opera—I tried to do something else to avoid it altogether, to fall in love or to write another book. It fell upon me, and I don't know why I am doing it, I only know that it is impossible *not* to. It was absolutely necessary for me to have friends and to have a steady private life to go through it.

INTERVIEWER: So it's important for you as an artist not to be completely isolated?

ATLAN: Well, I am completely isolated in the sense that all week long I am working here alone. It is important for me to make a life for myself, to set it up so that I can have all the freedom and loneliness I need to work and concentrate, as well as intimacy. Right now, I am in love with these people of Theresien. I don't have too much love to give to other people. When my friends come, I read to them and share my work. It gives me strength. I don't have the life of a nun or a sad, abandoned woman.

While I was married, it was difficult but I organized things in such a way that I could continue writing. I cannot be a housewife and be completely dedicated to my work. It was hard for my children in the beginning because my involvement in my work gave them the feeling that they were not the center of my world. For my daughter, it is still difficult—but they manage very well. Before I divorced, I thought the ideal solution for me would be to live alone, but it is not. When I was married, I always maintained an office and it was forbidden for anyone to enter it. I feel that the important thing is to write every day. Of course I dream about love! But even when I see my loved ones, I think back to my opera very quickly. When I am alone and suffering from it, I say to myself, "Either you live or you write! Do something! If you don't live, at least write," and I write.

INTERVIEWER: Do you think you will ever explore your relationship with your daughter in a play or a book?

ATLAN: After I finish the opera, I will take a rest, and then I hope I will write about it because I feel that if there is a future, change will come not through political ideas but through new links between children and mothers, links between men and women and children. I hope through this work to relate the historical-political to the mythic and world images I have explored in the past. I already have the title, but I have not been able to work on it at the same time as the opera.

INTERVIEWER: There is a common feeling in the States, born of American myths, that "The cream will rise to the top," that there are no such things as lost masterpieces. Do you agree?

ATLAN: If a work is not published, it is not possible to resurrect it. Perhaps some very strong works will survive and be known in the end, but that is not certain. Now you need money to bring your work into existence, and if your work is against the grain you might never find money.

Even though I am known in France, I was not able to find publication for *Even the Birds* [*Can't Always Get High,* 1979] or *Lessons in Happiness* [1982]; the publishers told me I was ahead of my time, and that I should wait some years. It's possible, but it's also possible that these texts will never exist in published form. Some people write what they know will find publication. I can't—it's mediocre. I'm not interested in making compromises in order to be recognized as a writer. So I must continue my work and hope that some day my unpublished works will find publication. It is absolutely possible that there will be an assassination of literature; that the true poets will write only for themselves knowing their work will disappear. I belong to a writers' union along with many published and known writers here in France. We were recently discussing our fears. . . . We all have the feeling that in a mass world, literature could be assassinated. For example, MATRA, a multinational corporation involved in selling arms, is also running Hachette, one of the largest publishing houses in France. I met with a man from MATRA corporation when I was seeking money for a project. This man, who was very handsome but completely cold, said to me, "Literature is not my business—I am in charge of arms." As I was leaving he informed me that he was soon to become one of the directors of Hachette publishing house. I said, "Will you be in charge of books about arms?" And he said, "No. Literature." This man had only a moment before admitted he knew nothing about literature! I was terrified by this experience.

To return to your question. If you had asked me twenty years ago, I would have answered like the Americans; I too, believed then that a strong body of work would inevitably be published. Deep inside myself, I still hope so. But I must admit I have anxiety about the future; the best way to govern masses is to use auto-da-fé, which begins with the burning of books. If you want control over the masses you cannot allow them to think because thinking leads to the desire for freedom. The only books that could exist in such a world would be comic books and mystery novels. I'd like to write a book on the phenomenon of the devaluation of literature: the last glimpse of a world wherein poetry was valued. When I am optimistic, I have the feeling that poetry could be preserved, not in a popular way, but by a few people like the manuscript copyists in the monasteries of the Middle Ages. These people, who were completely ignored by the public, saved the books. I believe there will always be a few such people writing. I tell myself I am writing because there are children—they are our hope—and I am writing for them.

INTERVIEWER: How do you support yourself financially?

ATLAN: My mother left me two very valuable chairs and some dressers when she died. Selling these enabled me to buy an apartment and I am able to live fifteen days a month on this investment. . . . It gives me the freedom to be outside the system.

I also received a grant from le Ministère de la Culture and Centre National des Lettres here in France, which allowed me for three years to devote myself entirely to my opera. If I did not have this financial aid, it would be difficult to continue writing. It also allowed me to travel, to research and to collect documents from all over the world. Now I have my documents with me, and so I am able to stay put in Paris. I have teaching credentials, but I don't want to teach because it tires me and uses up all my writing energy. I feel that I am at a point in life where I need to devote myself to my work. I am in great shape, I can work hard, I have acquired experience. I am not too old, I still have strength, though my eyes do tire. I'll have to hurry before I go blind! I have no time to lose on making a living.

I should also say that it is much more difficult for small theaters, which, like myself, are not in the mainstream. A director or an actor who wants to build a small theater company and who is working against the tide must find money and must provide a living for an entire community. It is much easier and less expensive for people to give money to a writer than a theater group. It is so difficult for those who are young and nonconformist. I like young struggling directors—I trust them, they have inherited the spirit of May '68. I prefer to work with them and I give them the rights to my plays for free.

INTERVIEWER: Bettina Knapp has described your play *The Carriage of Flames and Voices* [1971] as an exploration of "the double world of a soul divided." Is *Carriage* an "Everywoman" play? Is the fragmented character, Louli-Louise, an archetype of woman?

ATLAN: When I began *Carriage*, I had a vision of a woman literally cut in half [played in *Carriage* by two actresses]. I didn't ask myself who it was, though later I had the impression that this woman was me, or my friends. . . . If I had to discuss the symbolic meaning of Louli-Louise, I would say she represents our fragmented society rather than a precise woman or an archetypal image of woman. It is important that a character be *somebody*, in the flesh, lively, and not an archetype. In French, the word *archetype* is pejorative—it can easily mean that something is abstract, dry, without spirit—though I think in the States it is absolutely the contrary.

INTERVIEWER: Did the vision of a woman cut in half come to you in a dream?

ATLAN: At the time I was having horrible nightmares. I felt that I was going crazy. I finally saw a friend, a psychoanalyst, who referred me to a place where I might be cured. After seeing her, I went to my workplace, and sat in the room like a lost soul, telling myself in terror, "You are crazy, completely mad. . ." I had the absolute intention to go home, complain to my husband, then commit suicide. At that moment, I saw in the middle of flames a woman in white, viscerally cut in two. I saw her, not as on a stage, but floating in the space around me, like an LSD trip. I stood up and went to write without knowing what I was writing. I wrote fourteen pages and had the feeling that something was going on. I then went home, and showed my husband what I'd written and he said, "It's extraordinary . . . you should make something out of it." I had great confidence in his judgment, and I am grateful to him for encouraging me to continue because I did not understand what I was writing; I only began to understand *Carriage* for the first time this year. So the play was written in a weird, twisted way; it came from the deepest part of madness (which is difficult to see in a clear way). I was trying to find out what existed there. Finally, it occurred to me that madness was both a crisis and a gift, a shield which protects us under certain circumstances. At the same time I was writing *Carriage*, I was working on a book called *The Dream of the Rodents*. I even took the substance of *The Dream* and used it to nourish *Carriage*. In *The Dream*, I felt I was just writing about myself, whereas with *Carriage*, I had a fast feeling that even if I was starting with me, the play had a larger dimension. "I" was not important, and that's what helped me to write the play (the more personal work I was doing in *The Dream* was giving me again the desire to commit suicide). I felt *Carriage* was expressing the modern conscience. Louli-Louise are little pieces of something bigger which we can call conscience. I don't mean conscience in a dry, abstract way, or in a Freudian sense, which is difficult for the French to comprehend because they are so entrapped by psychology and always fall back on Freudian interpretation. It's more like an LSD trip—when you are on one, you know that you are just a little part of something bigger. This other form of conscience is concrete, simple, down-to-earth and very real. When you try to verbalize this feeling it becomes very philosophical, pretentious, and ridiculous. Perhaps it is not possible to understand except for those who have taken drugs or experienced visions.

INTERVIEWER: Would you elaborate on your statement that the French always fall back on Freudian interpretation of a work?

ATLAN: For instance, many people thought *Carriage* was a story of two lesbian women. In France, we either interpret literature in a psychoanalytic way or we look to the work as a way to enter politics. I felt all the time I was writing *Carriage* that it was through madness that one could rediscover a certain kind of wisdom; I saw madness as the opening in the system by which you could escape. Instead of expressing this feeling in political language, I expressed it through visions, extremity, and madness.

INTERVIEWER: In the orgy scene in *The Carriage of Flames and Voices*, you draw a distinction between pornography and eroticism. Do we live in a pornographic culture?

ATLAN: That scene was inspired by a dream I had. I was in a house full of people, and there was a complete absence of interest for each other. There was a meanness developing, and as a consequence, the house exploded. Everyone then found themselves in the water and someone said, "We have all become little sharks." I expressed the essence of this dream in *Carriage*. It is this total absence of interest for the other which we can call pornography. Nowadays, it seems nearly everyone has lost interest in each other. This began with Hitler—he dreamed of creating a new kind of man who would have pity for himself alone. In such a world, others become a currency of exchange, and have only commercial value. When we extend this, the other becomes merely an instrument of pleasure, and love becomes pornographic. This abominable tendency is connected to our loss of ideals. "Love your brother as you would yourself" has failed, and we haven't found something to replace it. So what is next? It is no wonder we are a society of consumption. We are entering a very dark period; even psychology embraces this philosophy of "My pleasure first and foremost." But there *is* hope: It is so impossible to be happy in this condition (unless we allow ourselves to be manipulated into becoming completely numb) that there will be, must be, a revolt.

INTERVIEWER: Would you describe your beginnings as a writer? I understand that you and your sister improvised plays to entertain each other while you were kept hidden during World War II.

ATLAN: I would say that my true beginning was when I was eight years old. I wrote a poem, and showed it to the woman who was taking care of my sister, Rachel. She was not at all dazzled by my effort, an awful, bucolic poem about steers! But I knew then that I wanted to write. Later, when I was ten, I was walking home from school one day (I loved school so much! I had the feeling that I was really living when I was learning about how languages, such as Latin, were forgotten, then resurrected) thinking about what extraordinary characters my parents and grandparents were. I recall telling myself, "But it is not enough to know they are extraordinary! I have to put it down somewhere. I must preserve it from death, and give this feeling its true intensity in writing." Of course, at ten, I was incapable of doing it—but I knew that was what I wanted most.

Then came World War II. My sister and I were, for the first time, separated from our family and sent into hiding in Auvergne, a province in the center of France. We continued our studies by correspondence, and it was quite boring. One day, to divert ourselves, we, along with another girl, decided to write a novel. It was a love story: There was a young girl, waiting at a window for a prince. We wrote one page, that's all, but I began a novel of my own, which was very mysterious and took place underground. I wrote fifty pages, but couldn't finish. Then we moved to Lyon. Rachel couldn't go out of the house where we were hidden because she really looked Jewish. This was a very large house, with a garden. In front of this garden was a bathroom (which was very dirty, nobody ever used it) with a terrace and a window. One day, I had an idea. I went to the window of that bathroom and began to act. That was the birth of our "theater." Rachel made beautiful costumes . . . we were very influenced by Molière, Racine, and the court of Louis XIV . . . Rachel played all the court, the princes and the princesses in the audience. She was my public, and I was the theater: the author, the actor, the stage, everything! The plays were always the same. There were many characters and they all died, one by one. The "public" would cheer and applaud and then the play was over. We laughed a lot, but it was tragicomic. Rachel could not go out. Every day she was trapped by that house with the little garden. She began to dream there were dead people in the house and she would bang her head against the walls. We knew that all of my grandmother's family had been deported.

INTERVIEWER: After the war, did you continue writing plays, or did you return to the novel?

ATLAN: In my twenties I wanted to write a novel, because the way theater was taught to me in school was insufferable; they only concentrated on the psychological aspects of drama, which didn't interest me much. I wrote poetry and began three or four novels which I was never able to finish, though they later nourished my plays. Now I am tired of the theater. What I write is not conventional, and theater in France is so conventional that it no longer corresponds to my writing or to our lives. The theater should be reserved to celebrate very exceptional moments that television, cinema, or novels cannot. The subject must be special, and the piece should be a celebration or a ritual between living people; otherwise, one should not make theater. What excites me is the prospect of videotexts: Then we could have the liberty of the book and the immediacy of a play.

INTERVIEWER: You utilized this concept of a videotext while you were creating *Even the Birds Can't Always Get High* with the addicts at Marmottan medical center in Paris.

ATLAN: Yes. *Even the Birds Can't Always Get High* is neither a film nor a theater piece. It was written with videotext in mind, though I realized that the actual videotext would not, given the present-day economics in France, be realized for some time. Home video has not yet become commercial here, it's expensive and therefore not available to everyone. I also wrote *Lessons in Happiness* as a videotext; I was able to raise money for it as a theater piece, but not as a videotext. That was an error on my part. Theater was not the place for *Lessons*.

INTERVIEWER: Would you be more specific in describing a videotext? Is it a book or a videocassette?

ATLAN: Both. A videotext would be designed to be either read at home, or seen on a screen, at one's own pace and leisure. I first had the feeling that videotext was a crucial new form when I was at the home of some friends. We were all lying on the bed watching a videocassette movie together. Suddenly we could all imagine looking, not at a movie, but to another form of literature which would provide all the space for poetry. Video is a great instrument—the cassette and the television are small and intimate. I am convinced that the new mode of communication is not the theater play, the novel, or cinema, but videotexts. And the mode of communication is of capital importance to a writer, second only to the content, the text. I often ask myself, "Is what I am writing good for the future?" If we are writing pieces which help to tell people what is good, if what we write can give them a weapon, awaken their enthusiasm, or help them to *act*, then we are successful.

INTERVIEWER: Have you been properly credited for innovating this new form of videotext?

ATLAN: It is not something superior to invent, it is banality. We invent when we don't have a choice. Either we invent, or die.

INTERVIEWER: You have also written for radio.

ATLAN: I came to radio by chance. Some of the people involved in radio made it a policy to hire theater writers. We are not paid for our work in the theater, but we are paid for radio, so I accepted. The first time, I suffered. The second time, I suffered less, and the third time, I had a good experience. We should write more for the radio, and we should write quality work so that we can move away from theater and come back to language, to the spoken word. When we return to pure language we are given great visions. I think we should either have the power of the word or the power of combined dialogue and image, but in the theater, we have neither, we have only chatter. Theater is rarely Great. Peter Brook is the best we have and still his work has never given me the enthusiasm that the lightning days of Beckett did. The days of Beckett and of the great directors like Jean-Marie Serreau and Roger Blin are over.

INTERVIEWER: Is it true here in France, as it is in America, that unfavorable critical reception of a play can close a production?

ATLAN: Yes, that happens here, too, and it has often been difficult for me. For example, people were disturbed by my play *The Musicians, The Emigrants*, because it was political—they didn't want to hear about Palestine, but I felt it was time. I wrote a play about the striking resemblances between Palestine and Israel. It was a very aggressive play, very cruel in a sense because it was not pro-Palestine and it was not pro-Israel. Perhaps the climate in America is different, but here it is so deteriorated. People hate Israel, and consequently if you speak in my way—which is meant to express not hatred but rather the wish to recuperate, to salvage our humanity—people misunderstand. That is one of the reasons it is difficult for me as a playwright to live in Paris—people believe I am a Zionist. Why? Because I love my people, I love Israel. It doesn't matter to them that I have written many times to *Le Monde* to alert public opinion *for* Palestine. France is very Cartesian, very analytical. When you are an intellectual or an artist here, it is to make an analysis of the situation or to give a political point of view, which can sometimes be clever or ironic, but is more often boring and dry, and this has nothing to do with poetry or imagination or artistry.

INTERVIEWER: You've said that you succeeded in reaching the addicts [at the Pierre Nicole Center in Marmottan, a post-curative home in Paris] "not by means of drugs—I had no experience in this domain—but through poetry." Would you elaborate?

ATLAN: Our sensibilities harmonized. Often we worked with improvisations—sometimes I gave them objects and metaphors, for example, a doll and an iron. The object of the improv was to inculcate moral principles to the doll with the iron. The participants took the doll, began to talk to her, to say fabulous things . . . then they put the iron in her sex, in her brain—you see, they understood that culture is like an iron hammer, that morals are pounded into us. I found their understanding so extraordinary and I loved them so much that I gave them my most intimate metaphors to work on.

INTERVIEWER: How did you find the experience of directing your own work, specifically, *Lessons in Happiness*.

ATLAN: I feel that my attempt at directing was a failure, though the experience was not a complete loss because through *Lessons* came the idea of using a Seder as a structuring element in the opera. I am not good with actors, and I didn't cast very well, but I also came to understand that my failure was partly due to the fact that I was dreaming of something other than theater when I created *Lessons in Happiness*. There is a special language used to direct actors. You must be able to restrain yourself from saying to them what you need or what you are trying for—the actors must come to these discoveries on their own. I don't have the time to learn this technique, and I also think one must have a lot of confidence to direct, which I do not. I am too anxious. A director needs to be objective, and as a writer, at least with my temperament, that is impossible.

INTERVIEWER: You once said, "My goal is to arrive at a nonegoistic type of writing: objective writing which would reawaken a love of life. I would like to be able to write from an *empty heart*, that is, emptied of myself—but filled with others" [as quoted in *Theater*, Winter 1981]. How do you discipline yourself into this kind of objectivity?

ATLAN: I think it is not a matter of discipline at all. I expressed my *self*, my subjectivity so completely in *Carriage* and in *The Dream of the Rodents* that I cannot go further. The opera is helping me to achieve this goal of objective writing because the Jews of Theresien are my people. I am giving myself, not to express myself, but to express what happened. I don't try to express my ideas or feelings about what happened—they are not important. Maybe I will want to do this later, in a book . . . maybe I will write about my parents, my brother, the d'Orsay school. But now I feel I am succeeding when I am for the opera, a scribe, a hand.

INTERVIEWER: Do you rewrite?

ATLAN: Yes. If *I* can read a manuscript or a scene a hundred times over without being bored, it is a sign that the writing works. I also believe in making a script so strong that the text itself will struggle with the actors and director, and still hold up. I recall that for a production of *The Musicians, The Emigrants*, the director wanted to make many changes in the script. The actors told him, "Look, even this *period* is so important that you cannot erase it!" That is my responsibility, to create a text which has integrity.

INTERVIEWER: Do directors in France often tamper with the text?

ATLAN: Do you know that a director once said to my translator, "Liliane should be dead, it would make things easier!" And another director expressed the same sentiment, simply because I was not happy with the cuts he made in the text. In France, it is very difficult for playwrights to keep creative control. If you want your work to be produced, you must play the game of the writer who needs to learn how to write from the actors, the producers, and the director of the theater. It's no worse for women writers than for men. Young people understand that it is best to connect with a theater company, and they are produced and published. I understand their reasoning, but in my opinion, a writer must also protect his or her solitude, and it is equally important to sometimes be in contradiction with others, which is not possible if one must maintain camaraderie within a theater company. I must give *everything* to the writing, and when I do, the writing is *alive.*

INTERVIEWER: Do you mind being called a "woman playwright?"

ATLAN: When I began writing I hated the idea that people might think of me as a "woman writer." So in the beginning, I took a pen name. I did it because at that time, I wanted to be sure that my poetry was not judged by the fact that I was a woman. Later, I was able to accept that I am a woman, to accept that I am Jewish and to accept that it gives the structure. A director of my play *The Musicians, the Emigrants* told me that it is not political theater. "It is true that it is not built as Brecht's plays," I told him. The play is written in an obsessional way, an Oriental, or perhaps Semitic way, with a circular causality. It is another kind of construction—which may be feminine. It is interesting to see that women enter my work much more easily than men, which makes things difficult because more journalists and publishers are men, or women who think like men. Children, adolescents, and women feel very close to my work. They seem to enter it and this gives me courage to continue and not to react in a sad way.

INTERVIEWER: American playwright Karen Malpede has written a book entitled *Women in Theater: Compassion and Hope,* as opposed to Aristotle's "pity and fear."

ATLAN: It's a Jewish idea. . . .

INTERVIEWER: As you said, your goal is to arrive at "a nonegoistic type of writing . . . which would reawaken a love of life." Would you say this desire is part of a feminine sensibility or approach to writing?

ATLAN: I would say that not "hope" but *vitality* is part of a female sensibility, vitality meaning the will to keep on going, and to create. This will, this vitality, is stronger than any ideology.

INTERVIEWER: Is there a female aesthetic in drama?

ATLAN: When I look at any work of art, I ask myself if the artist is creating in freedom, if he or she is going as far as possible in what they know and feel. I look for freedom and originality of perception and expression. I don't look for the masculine or the feminine elements; both exist in the world, and it is when we are not completely free that we are either too masculine or too feminine. It is true that when a woman shows her vision it seems completely new because there were not in the past as many women creating and because often the work of those who did create was not documented. True, a woman who allows herself to explore her femininity will discover new constructions: irrational forms with vitality and movement. But a man with an acute sensibility has the resources to find that also. If we are free enough, and have a very rich sensibility, we will have the point of view of the child, which is more integrated and holistic than a strictly female or strictly male point of view. We are *organic*; inside us are the elements—water, earth, fire, air—and there is also the unknown. We must transcend prejudice, and to make a separation between men and women is prejudice. I feel myself man and woman together. The difficulty, then, is to be truly free. When we are visionary, we feel ourselves part of a flowing stream—we are not only women and men, but thousands, billions of people, and we are also nothing. That we are nothing and everything simultaneously is what we must rediscover. At the same time, I know there is a prejudice in the way society is organized. This makes it difficult to be a woman and to write. Men have freedom in their sentimental life, and in their domestic life—they can come and go—but this is a question of private life and of social order, categories and systems built on prejudice. The stream of people and of *being* is amazing and frightening, and it is because we have lost our awareness of this that we have also lost our true identity.

INTERVIEWER: Do you agree with Bettina Knapp, who sees your work as "cosmic theater . . . cosmic in dimension though inhabiting the earthly plane; hallucinatory in its phantasms yet rooted in actuality. Embedded in history, in the event of the moment, in the second, her dramas, to use Beckett's words are 'time ridden.' They likewise transcend these limitations, their permutations diffusing into eternity."

ATLAN: Yes. Bettina invented this expression and I was very happy because it does describe my feeling and my aim. When I was young, I dreamt that I was not born of the earth, but from a stream of light. Later, I awoke one night with a feeling of "earth-sickness," and realized that I had again been dreaming of being part of this stream of light. I wrote about this feeling in my play *The Messiahs*, which was about some little messiahs lost in the immensity of the cosmos. Now there is cosmic dimension in travel—we have been to the moon. And there is the cosmic voyage of the inner self through psychoanalysis and drugs. Dreams and visions allow us to travel through these cosmic realms. [Gaston] Bachelard [French philosopher, 1884–1962] explored the power of imagination and poetry and expressed the bond, the relationship between the nature of imagination and the elements (to earth, water, fire and air, I would add *light*.) Yes, our imagination is something cosmic, and that is extraordinary.

—Translated by Antoine Bootz
Catherine Ruello

BAI FENGXI

Bai Fengxi has been a theater profes-
sional since her adolescence. She began her career as an actress shortly
after the founding of the People's Republic of China. As a playwright,
Bai Fengxi belongs to the post-1976, that is, post-Mao generation. Her
first dramatic work, a one-act verse play, praising the late Premier Zhou
En-lai (as countless poems, stories and plays did at that time), was published in 1977. The plays that fully and firmly established Bai Fengxi as
a serious and outstanding playwright are the full-length Mingyue Chuzhao
Ren (And a Bright Moon Begins to Shine, 1981) and Fengyu Guren Lai
(The Return of an Old Friend on a Stormy Night, 1983).

These two plays have proved thought-provoking in the People's Republic. And a Bright Moon Begins to Shine, in particular, caused great
controversy there because the play's heroine dares to defy the moral and
social conventions concerning love and marriage. The focal point of the
controversy is the love triangle comprised of the young heroine, her mother,
and the professor who is the mother's former and young woman's present
lover. (The mother had left the professor when both were students some
thirty years ago after hearing that he was politically unreliable.) After
painful soul searching, the young heroine determines to marry her professor.

Conservative critics attacked the play as immoral and antisocial. They
worried that the play's strong individualistic strain would create anarchist
chaos and confusion among the young audiences. Among other critics,
there was enthusiastic support for the courageous and iconoclastic heroine
who dares to break social and moral restrictions and taboos. This play
demonstrates the playwright's courage to take on issues in a way that
might provoke social, and even political, censorship.

Bai's second major play, The Return of an Old Friend on a Stormy
Night, is less controversial, but more insightful, introspective and illuminating. The play deals with a husband and wife in conflict over their
respective domestic and professional responsibilities. The play derives its
strength not only from Bai's superb powers of analysis, but to her sensitivity
to the unconscious, as well as conscious, desires and motivations of her
characters.

Bai Fengxi, as she expresses in the following interview, is interested in women's issues, and her plays deliver clear messages on this theme. But Bai's messages are not expressed with anger or frustration; her plays convey warmth and optimism for a future built on harmonious social and personal relationships between the sexes. The meaning of Bai's plays extends beyond feminist concerns. Bai's heroines' determined defiance of traditional values and moral standards is an unambiguous statement in support of individualism and the importance of critical thinking and acute judgment on the part of any individual seeking happiness and justice. Owing to their theatrical and literary excellence, Bai Fengxi's plays have an important place in contemporary Chinese drama.

—CONSTANTINE TUNG
Associate Professor of Chinese
State University of New York at Buffalo

We found Madam Bai with the generous assistance of Huang Zong Ziang of the Chinese Theatre Association in Beijing. I had met Mr. Huang in 1981 while developing my play *Johnny Bull* at the Eugene O'Neill National Playwright's Conference in Connecticut. He is one of China's foremost dramatists as well as a screenwriter and actor. When asked if there were many women playwrights in China and his opinion on their work, he replied: "They are far fewer in number than we men, but far better." Whether the latter part of the comment was fact or gentle diplomacy, Mr. Huang proved more than willing to help us find out for ourselves. He corresponded enthusiastically with us about our project as he sought out China's most respected woman playwright, Bai Fengxi, and arranged for our interview. Confirmation of her willingness to participate coincided with the news that playwright Corinne Jacker was soon to leave on a cultural trip to China. Rachel and I—in lieu of being able to travel to Beijing ourselves and feeling that personal contact was a warmer approach than written questions—asked Ms. Jacker if she would interview Madam Bai on our behalf. She was pleased to accept the assignment. Fengxi and Jacker met at the Chinese Theatre Association in Beijing in April 1984. Ms. Su Hongjun, a Smith College graduate student from Fudan University in Shanghai, kindly donated her time to the translation and transcription of the interview. A cultural exchange has begun: In the summer of 1985, Bai was a guest at the Eugene O'Neill

National Playwright's Conference and hopes to introduce contemporary plays by American women to the people of China; Ms. Jacker intends to produce and direct one of Bai's plays in the near future.

—K. B.

JACKER: Women playwrights in America have a much shorter tradition than the male playwrights. With a few exceptions, we have only been writing for the stage since about 1920. Is this also true in China?

BAI: Yes.

JACKER: What we are finding to some extent, in the United States, is that the concerns of women playwrights are perhaps of a more domestic and personal nature as opposed to the broader external concerns of the male work.

BAI: My plays have similar concerns to those of American women.

JACKER: Are you still acting?

BAI: Oh, you know about me? Yes, I have been an actress for over thirty years. I often play leading roles in the China Youth Theater. Now, how did I become a playwright? I myself did not at first intend to be a playwright.

JACKER: How do you feel your career as an actress has affected your work as a playwright?

BAI: In the past five or six years, I have written six or seven scripts, for theater and film, television and radio. The response has been un-expectedly good. I have received many letters from my readers and au-diences. They question me: "What kind of education have you received? Have you any specialized or systematic training in playwriting?" How do I answer them? I say: "I have neither the education that you might imagine nor the systematic training you may have expected. If you ask me how I have acquired my writing skills, I would say I owe these skills to my thirty-year life as a stage actress."

JACKER: I did not study writing formally, either.

BAI: So you can see we women writers share many experiences. I'd like to begin by telling you my experience as an actress. I can be considered fortunate. During the fifties and early sixties, I had the opportunity to play the leading roles in many plays. For example, in the early days after liberation I once played the role of the heroine, Liu Hu-lan. She is a very famous national heroine. She was executed with a big scythe by the enemy. To this day, the Chinese people cherish her memory. Later I played a role in the famous piece *Family*, by Cao Yu. A couple of days ago, I saw the American production of *Family* on TV.

JACKER: Yes, I saw that, too.

BAI: You've seen it? I played the role of Ming Fong in that. I have also played Princess Wencheng in Tian Han's *Wencheng Gongzhu* and Cherubino in Beaumarchais's *The Marriage of Figaro*. And, of course, I have acted in many other Chinese dramas. The point I am making is that I've been an actress for a long time. As I told you earlier, it is my thirty years onstage that has enabled me gradually to master the skills of playwriting.

JACKER: In my experience, it's the actors who have the true theater wisdom.

BAI: Yes, that may be so. I started to write plays after 1976. At the beginning, I did not expect that eventually I would be recognized by the audience. So I was in a dilemma as to whether to continue as an actress or pursue playwriting. My love of the stage is like my love for my mother: a love that grows with age—I'm in my early fifties now—and I am determined to devote all my life to the theater, no matter whether I go on acting or choose to write plays. I am determined to cultivate this land of Theatrical Art—the spoken drama. My first full-length play was a joint effort with Mr. Wang Qing-yu. At that time I was still wondering whether to act or write. While I was writing that play, I had to act at the same time. Then why have I not been acting these past few years? That's because I have been pretty successful as a playwright. Every time a play of mine was staged, I got very good—I can't say "appreciation"—but a very enthusiastic response from the audience. So I became more confident. My first play was in verse. It was written for the birthday of the late Premier Zhou. It's called *The Cave Lights Shine over Thousands of Families*. [At that time, when the revolutionaries took to the mountains, the lights in their caves gave inspiration to peasants in the valley below.*] The production was recorded and the text published. Some local operas also staged it in their own versions. We call this a "transplantation." That is, transplanting the content of a particular work to other performance forms. After that production, I decided to go on writing. I started to write a full-length piece, but wasn't sure I would be successful so I wrote my first full-length play in collaboration with Mr. Wang Qing-yu. It was called *Unveil Yourself*. It ran about one hundred and twenty performances and was well received. Later, during the theatrical festival at the thirtieth anniversary of the founding of the People's Republic of China, I received second prize for this play.

JACKER: Congratulations!

BAI: Thank you. *Unveil Yourself* really boosted my confidence. As a result, during the production, I began to write my own full-length play,

*Information provided by Su Hungjuan of Fudan University in Shanghai

called *And a Bright Moon Begins To Shine*. In this work, I posed a difficult task for myself: I tried to write without a single male character. I wanted to have a play with only women. I wanted to find out whether this kind of play could also possess interesting dramatic episodes. It is about three generations of Chinese women. There are sophisticated intellectual characters as well as ordinary farmers from the countryside.

JACKER: Was this unusual? Was it the first time this had been done?

BAI: Yes, it was quite unusual. It was commented on in many newspapers, including some foreign newspapers issued in Beijing. One article was entitled "A Love Story Without the Appearance of Male Characters." We have many plays without female characters, but we rarely have a play without male characters. For instance, plays about war . . .

JACKER: I wrote one [*Later*, 1978] with all women . . . two generations of a family without men. How was your play received? Was the audience surprised?

BAI: The work received heated criticism. It was very controversial. So far, I have collected some forty articles about it from all sorts of newspapers and magazines. Apart from the production in my theater, it has been staged by theater groups in other provinces and cities. Opinions published in the press in these provinces and cities were vastly different. Thanks to the controversy raised, productions sold out very quickly. I think this is very good. What do you think, Miss Jacker?

JACKER: I agree.

BAI: I think I raised questions that have aroused the interest of many people.

JACKER: If everyone likes a play, it cannot be very interesting.

BAI: I quite agree with you. At the time the newspapers were arguing their opinions of *And a Bright Moon Begins To Shine*, some of my close friends began to worry about me. They thought I was an actress, only a beginner in playwriting—like a newcomer to the battlefield. They wondered whether I could survive the critical controversy around my play.

JACKER: Do you find sometimes that your audience fails to understand your plays because you are a woman writing out of women's concerns?

BAI: Yes. This very issue relates to a play of mine that I am going to talk about in a few minutes. When you see the production of this play tomorrow, we will speak further on this matter. Naturally, some will agree with one's ideas, and some will not. This is very understandable. But one must write from one's *own* observations, from one's *own* understanding.

Playwrights are not supposed to give the answer to life. If someone expects otherwise of us, I would say that person is very impractical. We should raise issues about which the public has great concern, draw attention to these issues. In this way, we encourage our audiences and readers to think.

JACKER: A great American woman writer, Gertrude Stein, when she lay dying, asked her friend, "What is the answer?" Thirty minutes went by; no one spoke. And then Stein asked, "All right then, what is the question?"

BAI: Ah, of course. One cannot give an answer. But our plays reveal our preferences on the issues, don't they? In *And a Bright Moon Begins To Shine* my concern is with marriage customs and the way in which love is considered here. Because in China—I wonder if you know this or not—mercenary marriages and feudal ideas that marriage partners should be well matched in social and economic status still exist. This has made many young women miserable. I am making an appeal for these girls through my play. As you said just now, women playwrights often show more concern about women's problems. This might well be a natural affection.

The play I invite you to see tomorrow night is my new piece, *Return of an Old Friend on a Stormy Night*. The central idea of this story is summed up by a line from the play: *Women are not like the moon. They do not take advantage of others' "light" in order to show themselves.* In other words, women should have a strong sense of self-respect and constantly strive to become stronger. The raising of this question is related to Chinese history. China has developed from a feudal society. There are still ideas about women that I cannot tolerate. Although in the past few years there have been fundamental changes, I cannot say that we have eliminated the feudal attitudes in some people's minds. For instance, the idea that men are superior to women. In Chinese feudal society, there was a saying, "Talentlessness is the virtue of a woman." Of course, since the founding of the new China the position of women has improved considerably. But I can't say we have gotten rid of the residue of feudalism that hinders women in their professional development and limits the development of their talents. After the production of the play, I received lots of letters from readers and audiences. It was especially well received among women. I was really moved by some of their letters. They told me in great detail their own stories and difficulties. They often wrote that they wished to talk to me personally. So I wrote a newspaper article entitled I WILL USE MY PEN TO CELEBRATE HALF OF THE SKY.* In this article, I expressed my hope that more writers and playwrights would speak for women. There are many cases of inequality. I find my own

*Mao Zedong described women as "holding up half of the sky."

voice is too soft. I want more writers with me, so we can make a louder appeal on women's behalf.

JACKER: When you write for television, is your work different—less serious, changed in any way—from when you write for stage?

BAI: Of course, television writing is different from playwriting. I prefer to write for the stage. I have only written one television piece. It was for children and was aired on a children's program. Since then, the television station has been asking me to write more stories for them. But I have not written anything more for them.

JACKER: Why?

BAI: One old veteran playwright once praised me saying, "Spoken drama is the most difficult to write. Bai Fengxi has chosen the most difficult form." I am determined to go on with my playwriting.

JACKER: We also say that playwriting is the most difficult form.

BAI: We have so many feelings and ideas in common.

JACKER: Are you finding that you speak to the younger women who are coming up with a greater awareness of themselves and the need to find their own personal place in the world?

BAI: Yes. I don't have to work very hard to know people of my own generation, but I have to work very hard to understand and to know the younger generation. So now I am trying hard to make friends with young people, because the future belongs to them. Since their publication, my plays have been receiving strong responses from the young folks.

JACKER: Do you find, as I find in the United States, that we are the generation that stands as a transition between the old ways and what will be? For us, it's not a question of a revolution within our three-thousand-year-old culture, but the birth of an entirely new culture.

BAI: I myself have the same ideas on this subject.

JACKER: In a way, we have a responsibility—because of our role between the two ways of life—to show the new to the old, and the old to the new?

BAI: That is just what I wanted to say . . . I think people of our age are a very important generation. We should have a strong sense of responsibility and a sense of having an historical mission. This is where, in spite of difficulties and hardship, I get my inspiration and motivation in playwriting.

JACKER: In American literature, many women are beginning to find that not only do we deal with issues in the spoken drama that are unique to women—the domestic and ethical issues I spoke of—but that our sense of stage time is different; our sense of space and stage rhythms is even different. Do you find this, too?

BAI: I think, naturally, a woman playwright should be more exquisitely deep, more implicit. In that way, her plays are more touching. [To male interpreter:] Perhaps our talk now is a bit arrogant to a male listener. But I really think a woman's work should have those refined qualities.

JACKER: So the "action" is smaller, more implicit than the external drama of Tai-Chi or Kung-fu or any of the martial arts?

BAI: Exactly. I seldom put the story as it happened in life on stage. I walk around these stories, observe them and explore the meaning below the surface.

JACKER: One of the reasons this book is being written is to see if women playwrights are speaking with similar voices.

BAI: The characteristics of women writers are frequently commented on in the criticisms about my plays. So far, as you and I have been talking, I find that we speak the same language. We speak in one voice. Because we are women, we have more intense emotions than men towards women's concerns. I want to inspire my audience. I especially want my female characters to inspire the women in the audience to develop a strong sense of self-respect and to encourage them to work hard in their careers.

JACKER: To show them what's on the other side of the hill?

BAI: Yes.

JACKER: Have you found that your domestic life is sometimes in conflict with your writing life?

BAI: The play I am showing you tomorrow explores this issue. I think it is more difficult for a woman than for a man to have career achievements. I am fortunate. My husband works in my theater. He is a comedy director, and my daughter is an actress in the spoken drama. There aren't many domestic chores in this small family, so I can have more time and can exert more energy in my playwriting. Comparatively speaking, I am most fortunate.

JACKER: No difficulties?

BAI: My difficulties are that I had neither sufficient professional training nor a rich writing experience when I started to write plays. I began as an amateur. Although many critics think I am a talented, gifted playwright, I know myself best. I am neither clever nor gifted. I had many difficulties whenever I was writing a play.

JACKER: You come from the best possible training, the theater itself. It has been my experience that the most intellectually trained writers are furthest from their audiences.

BAI: Yes. My advantage is my thirty years as an actress. Are there many women playwrights in other countries who started in acting like me?

JACKER: Many. I began as an actress when I was a child. I acted from nine to fifteen years old. Then I was a stage manager and director.

BAI: Great! I think a playwright should know both directing and stage design, be an all-rounder in the field. In this way, he or she can produce better plays. Otherwise, when you read your play, it may sound okay and be well written, but it is only a written thing. When it is staged, it may not work so well as when you read it.

JACKER: "Good" writing can't be spoken. When I have good writing, I throw it away.

BAI: Me, too! And I always act out what I am writing in my plays while I'm still working on them. If I myself am not emotionally involved, how can I expect my actors and actresses to be emotionally involved in my plays? How could they move the audience? When I read aloud my new script, if I'm not moved by my words—or today I am moved by my play but tomorrow it doesn't affect me as it did the day before—I'd rather throw this piece away. I am only satisfied when the work can excite me and draw me into it every time I pick it up. Whenever my plays are staged, I sit in the audience and see the production for several nights. I watch the response of the audience carefully. Their responses have proved that the points in the play where I was intensely involved are also the moments when my audience was intensely emotionally involved. If I am not moved by what's on stage, the audience will not even notice the point I am trying to make to them.

JACKER: How long did it take you to write this play [Return of an Old Friend on a Stormy Night] that I will see tomorrow night?

BAI: This one was published in July 1981. I wrote two full-length plays within three years. This one took me about five months to write. I have a habit: I never tell anyone when I have finished a new play. I go to a few peers for consultation. I read my play to them, watch their responses, find out whether they are emotionally involved and interested, and then ask for advice. This is my way of discovering whether a play is ready to be staged or not. This process, between when I finish a play and when I finally hand it to my theater to be staged, is generally very long. I hate to publish a play that I'm not satisfied with.

JACKER: Who reads your new work first?

BAI: It often happens that my husband is the first listener of my plays. For instance, if I have finished one act when my husband comes home from work, I read it to him. At the same time, I watch his reaction. If he is not emotionally affected, then I know the piece is not good enough. You are an experienced woman playwright, Miss Jacker. I assume your career must have been smoother than mine?

JACKER: Oh, no. It seems very similar to yours. For me, playwriting is like climbing mountains. As soon as I gain knowledge of how to do one thing, there are ten higher hills ahead that I have to climb, but don't quite know how to do it.

BAI: I feel the same way. The excitement and joy I have after each success is always brief, while the hardship in writing is constant. For instance, I feel well rewarded by the success of this play but, at the same time, I am working hard at another new piece. So now I am very anxious. . . . In short: Joy is brief.

JACKER: Will you allow me to take a copy of the play home with me? I think it's important for Americans to hear the voice of a Chinese woman playwright.

BAI: Yes. I will write my inscription and put my seal on a copy of my play and give it to you tomorrow as a gift.

JACKER: Thank you. Let's talk about the critics for a moment.

BAI: It often happens in China that the more controversy that surrounds a play, and the more criticism a play gets from the critics, the more eager the public is to see it.

JACKER: A problem that women playwrights are having in my country is that often—because the works are dealing with more implicit actions—the critics don't seem to find their plays as important as the works that have larger, external actions, the large physical actions: the wars, the murders. . . .

BAI: Sometimes it's similar here. But what I have been writing are explorations of social issues with a background of family themes. My audience is more interested in such issues than in wars or murder. Of course, some people like murder and "exciting plots." But more people prefer serious drama like mine.

JACKER: Yes, I think our audiences do, too. It seems to be the critics who don't.

BAI: Do you mean that the critics in your country pay more attention to plays about murder?

JACKER: Not necessarily on the subject of murder, but subjects that contain larger physical and external actions rather than the implicit ethical action.

BAI: In China, one critic said in an article that my plays can be considered the beginning of a new genre called "ethic plays." Several years ago, the plays were about war and revolution. Ethic plays are still something new. So critics think that special attention must be paid. On my two most recent plays, I have collected many, many critical articles. So this sort of play is not being overlooked in this country.

JACKER: Your husband is a director. Does he direct your plays?

BAI: No, I don't think it is a good idea that he direct my work. He knows my work and my concerns far too well. It would be impossible for him to do something new and creative with my work onstage. My plays wouldn't develop as fully from the written form to production. My creations have better productions if they are directed by someone who knows nothing about them at all in the beginning.

JACKER: How do you work with actors during the rehearsal process?

BAI: I usually work with my directors. Since my plays are usually staged by my own theater, the theater organizes a group of people for the play, including directors, actors and production people. The director first invites me to talk with the group about why I wrote the play and how I developed the characters. They also like to know how the true stories which served as a point of departure are related to the characters. Generally speaking, I have a good working relationship with my directors. If the director needs a change in the script, he invites me to rehearsal to talk about it. We are very friendly to each other. Directors show great respect to playwrights and often come to us for advice. In return, the playwright respects the directors and shows gratitude for the work done to stage their images.

JACKER: So are you at the rehearsals and available all the time?

BAI: Sometimes I'm not there. If the director needs a change, he asks my opinion and we work out the change together. But I do the rewrite. The Shanghai Youth Theater is having a production of *Return of an Old Friend on a Stormy Night* at the moment. When I went to Shanghai, they invited me to come and talk about the play. Generally, we all work quite well together.

JACKER: Are there many women directors in China?

BAI: There are two in my theater. Nationally, there are many women directors now. The director for one of my plays, Chen Rong, is a very famous, established woman director.

JACKER: How many playwrights does your company have?

BAI: About seven or eight. Three or four of us began as actors. It gives us an advantage. It's very important for directors and playwrights to have stage experience. The director who directed the play you are going to see is a famous stage actor and has appeared in many recent films.

JACKER: We are back to what we were saying before that the more you know about the different aspects of theater, the various crafts, the more it will help you to write.

BAI: Yes. For example, when I wrote this play, I was thinking about the actress. She knows how to play violin, and so I put it into the script that this character plays violin.

JACKER: Of course. Shakespeare wrote for a company. It always helps to have an actor in mind. As real people help to shape our plays, I find the first actor who plays the role helps to shape that character.

BAI: Yes.

JACKER: There have been such enormous cultural changes in your country in the last few years. Have your audiences changed, too?

BAI: I have noticed great changes. There is a higher level of appreciation now. If we playwrights overlook the changes in our audiences, our plays will not be able to strike a response in the public. I seize every opportunity to talk with the audience, to have heart-to-heart talks with them. I have to find out what they are, or are not, interested in.

JACKER: In our theater we have a saying, "The most important character in any play is the audience."

BAI: I beg your pardon? I can't say that I understand this saying.

JACKER: The play is never the same because the audience interaction creates different performances on different nights.

BAI: The artistic creation of the actors depends on the reaction of the audience?

JACKER: That's right. Each audience hears the play differently from any other audience. What exactly are the changes that your audiences have gone through? Are you finding that your own material is changing? I have noticed that the things I want to write about now are different from the things I wanted to write about ten years ago.

BAI: Right. Similar changes are also taking place in China. A few years ago, there were more plays with a strong political message. Now the audience has changed. Now there is a thirst for knowledge. The plays should be educational and entertaining. They don't like plays that are too didactic and of a fixed pattern.

JACKER: Even the way we write about women's concerns has changed over the last decade. Ten years ago, it was enough for us to deal, in effect, with the politics of finding an equal place. Today this is not enough.

BAI: Yes. Therefore, as writers, we should be alert to the changes and have our finger on what we call "the pulse" of our time. I returned to Beijing because I was informed of your arrival. But I have been out in the biggest cities and the smallest villages in order to have a better knowledge of what has been going on in the people's minds over the last two years. I hadn't been out of Beijing for about two years, and the changes are really enormous. If you don't know the changes, then the plays you write will not be the kind that the people want.

JACKER: Yes, and it's especially true of the young people, who seem to change faster.

BAI: Exactly. It seems the changes—especially the psychological changes—of youth are universal.

JACKER: Do you find that the younger women come to your plays ready to share the things you're saying about career and home?

BAI: Yes. I received many letters from women about the present production of my play. It's a story about two generations of women, mother and daughter. Women like this very much. They respond strongly to the central idea of the play: Women are not the moon. They must not reflect the light of others. They can emit their own light. They are capable of making the same achievements in their careers as men. They should work hard and strive for independence. My women audiences feel the same way. They say the play has expressed what they want to say to society.

JACKER: It sounds as if, as your work continues, you will give a whole picture of the modern Chinese woman.

BAI: I'm afraid not. Critics have different interpretations of the theme and central idea. Some critics consider the message to be "anti-feudal." In fact, most of the critics think so. Some think the play is about mutual understanding between people, between men and women, between husband and wife. Still others say it is about the dilemma between a woman's devotion to her career and her commitment to family. Would you like to have a brief synopsis?

JACKER: Please.

BAI: It is about a famous doctor of gynecology and obstetrics. Her husband is a biologist who cannot understand her. She believes that a woman should strive to make contributions to her profession. He can't see this. He expects her to be a devoted wife. He doesn't approve of her ambition to be a famous doctor. For the sake of his self-respect, he divorces her. Later, the woman does become a world-famous physician. Although she has fulfillment in her career, she feels lonely in her private life. As a woman, she needed success in career *and* happiness in the family. . . . Twenty years later, her daughter is confronting the same dilemma. On the evening of her wedding, the daughter is informed that she did very well on a State exam and is now recognized as a genius in mathematics. The government has decided to send her to West Germany for further study and a Ph.D. Her mother is worried that her daughter will be made to sacrifice her personal life. The mother-in-law-to-be happens to be a former classmate of the doctor/mother; she insists that her intended daughter-in-law not study abroad—she knows of the famous doctor's divorce and wants to prevent her son and his bride from repeating this tragedy. She says something that hurts the respect of all women, "Your husband will be a scientist. You will be the wife of a scientist.

You will have the same honor." But the bride replies, "I don't want to be the *wife* of a scientist. I myself wish to be a scientist." This leads to a family dispute. The famous doctor realizes the mother-in-law has gone too far. She tells her daughter, "I don't want you to repeat my tragedy. I had hoped that you would make some sacrifice to the happiness of your marriage. But now I have changed my mind." That's where that line, "Women are not the moon. Emit your own light." comes in. At the climax, mother-in-law thinks of a plan. She invites the doctor's former husband to visit, hoping that he will be able to persuade his daughter on the basis of his own unhappy experience. She says, "If a woman is strong, there will be no peace in the house." In the final act, the doctor's ex-husband arrives. But he now feels differently. He says, "I am finished with the larger part of my life. In retrospect, I have come to understand this truth: The contradiction between family life and career are inevitable. But why should one half of the couple sacrifice herself to the other side?" He apologizes to his former wife and expresses his regret for what he has done to her. He begs her forgiveness. He says China was once a feudal society, that many people, including himself, still cling to the old ideas. He always expected his wife to be a devoted wife and mother. But he himself was not a devoted father and husband, he says, and this was unfair. He tries to persuade his son-in-law: "I was wrong when I was young. My attitude to women was wrong. Now the times have changed. You belong to a younger generation. Be more enlightened, open-minded, magnanimous. It has taken me half my life to reach this truth. Why are you still repeating my mistakes?"

The title [*Return of an Old Friend on a Stormy Night*] comes from an ancient Chinese poem, and it means an old acquaintance always comes back to help amidst the sounds of rain and wind. When the curtain falls, whether the son-in-law will let his young bride go or not, whether this older couple will remarry, are the questions that I leave to the audience. . . .

The reason I wrote this play is because more and more women here have received higher education. Then come the contradictions. In her career she must compete with and advance with men. This social problem has become very, very intense in China now. Traditionally, women are supposed to be submissive to men: "If the woman is strong, family happiness will not last long." But no one can stop the advance of history. Women's issues are unavoidable in present-day life.

JACKER: It's a very important theme.

BAI: I know little about the present situation in America concerning women's issues.

JACKER: Very much the same sort of problem.

BAI: I have seen the film *Kramer vs. Kramer.* I liked what Mrs. Kramer had to say. The Chinese title for the film was *The Quarrel Between Mr. and Mrs. Kramer.* Women's issues do seem to be of worldwide concern.

JACKER: In our country, it's a generally held opinion that a woman must choose between a career and an honest dedication to her home.

BAI: Will this go on to be a central concern of the future?

JACKER: Yes.

BAI: What do you think of my play? Some people like it. Others disagree with my ideas. They say: "No. If I am going to choose a wife, I want the woman who will take good care of me. Though I respect women like the famous doctor in your play, she can only be a good friend . . . never my wife."

JACKER: There is still guilt in many women in the United States that if they spend too much time on career they are, in a way, betraying their marriages.

BAI: Some women here have similar thoughts. However, I am against the idea that women are superior to men and should be taken care of by men. They should have their own independence and personality. Men and women should try to understand and respect one another. In my own family life, I try hard to achieve something professionally; at the same time, I try to better family life. For instance, I recently left home for a long period of time when I was studying the changes in our people. During this period, for one month, my husband never once cooked for himself. He knows how, but he has a man's idea that his wife should cook for him. He felt sad that no one was there to cook during my absence. When I came back, I found that he had not had good meals. I felt so sorry for him that I decided to make him a good dinner. When I started cooking, I cut my finger.

JACKER: This once happened to me with my husband. I have the same scar on the same finger.

BAI: You cut your finger, too? Isn't it amazing how much we have in common?

JACKER: Well, it shows the psychological split, you know, in all of us, unfortunately.

BAI: This split is the idea that my protagonist puts forward in the play. In her opinion, happiness in life and success in career are contradictory. It's impossible to have both.

JACKER: Yes.

BAI: One plus one does not always equal two. My character thought it was more rational to remain single. The younger generation says: "No. We want both to be successful *and* to live a happy family life. But when the young woman confronts life herself, she, too, will experience the contradiction. I don't think a writer can give the answer, or make a judgment as to which solution is right or wrong. All a writer can do is raise the question. In this way, we help the audience to solve the problems for themselves, and perhaps in a better way than in the past.

KATHLEEN BETSKO

K athleen Betsko has been selected three times to attend the prestigious Eugene O'Neill National Playwrights Conference for the production of her plays Beggar's Choice (1978), Johnny Bull (1981), and Stitchers and Starlight Talkers (1982). Beggar's Choice was adapted for radio and presented by Earplay on National Public Radio and was also aired in Australia. Johnny Bull was produced at the Mark Taper Forum Lab in Los Angeles in 1981 and received its world premiere at the Yale Repertory Theater in the spring of 1982. Subsequently, it has been produced at Horizons: Theatre from a Woman's Perspective in Washington, D.C., and at the Belgrade Theatre in Betsko's hometown of Coventry, England. Johnny Bull is published by Dramatists Play Service and was made into a television special that aired on ABC (Monday Night at the Movies, May 1986), starring Colleen Dewhurst and Jason Robards.

Ms. Betsko has written a television script on the life of Vivien Leigh for River City Productions in Los Angeles, and in 1985, she was selected by Embassy Television to work for a year in their Playwrights Development Project.

She was the recipient of a 1982 New York State CAPS grant and lives and works in New York City.

KOENIG: Do you consider yourself a British or an American writer?

BETSKO: I'm a British alien residing in the United States for over twenty-seven years. Neither fish nor fowl, really. I write mostly American stories about American working-class people and there's generally a British character lurking about. I suppose I write with English rhythms and humor—certainly an immigrant's sensibility. I was educated in the Old Country, a savage but fairly thorough grounding in the English language. I took "six of the best" almost daily with a willow cane for such subversive activities as writing dirty ditties about teachers and other vulgar enter-

47

tainments designed to amuse my fellow pupils. I remember the whistle of that slender weapon as it sang through the air. Before the last blow was delivered, I was already planning my next coup.

KOENIG: You were born in Coventry in 1939, just before the heavy bombing raids in World War II, and evacuated with other children . . .

BETSKO: Myself, two older sisters, and brother. We were separated and sent to different billets. We never saw each other again as children. Thousands of kids were put aboard trains with numbers round our necks and trucked out to rural villages or Wales or Scotland. It's something I want to write about. I've already begun the research, and have thirty-odd pages to date. Though I'm a passionate defender of the genre of social realism, I hope to try something a bit more experimental with this material. The canvas of Coventry under siege and what happened to the children is far too broad to be contained within the personal story of one main character or a single family.

When Coventry was attacked, I was very small. Over seventy percent of the housing was destroyed. I remember the whine of the incendiary bombs, the sky on fire. These are primitive sensory memories. But those air raids on my city were to have lifelong implications for me, my family . . . everyone in Coventry. Implications that reverberate to this day and tug at me to write. I must tell a side of that war that has rarely been told. Most war tales have been about male bravery. National history seen through men's militaristic eyes. I want to record the history of England's mothers at war . . . children at war. More precisely, I want to tell the story of a particular group of children, a "lost generation" of children that includes myself and siblings. Hundreds of kids taken from target areas to safety who, for a variety of reasons, were never returned to their families. These kids would be between forty-seven and sixty-three years old today. I need to find and interview them before they die without telling their experiences.

Though I've found some good sources of information, it's fruitless to go to the newspapers of the time for research. They're full of photos of happy children leaving and returning aboard trains, dangling out of windows with Union Jacks, waving cheerfully. Blatant propaganda— necessary, no doubt, to keep up public morale. One is raised to think of the stoic Brits shaking their fists at German airplanes, already putting the bricks back on top of one another, at the first wail of the "all clear" siren. There *are* many acts of individual and collective heroism on record. There *were* many children with happy evacuation experiences. But that is far from the whole truth.

KOENIG: In fact, there had been tragic governmental blunders, hadn't there?

BETSKO: Thousands of kids sent away. But the Germans pulled a fast one and never showed up. The kids were sent home. It was then that the enemy planes came with a vengeance. Throughout the autumn of 1940, over twenty-nine tons of high explosives, incendiaries, and oil bombs were dumped on our city. Coventry is the Detroit of England. All the car factories were converted to the manufacture of munitions and war-related machinery. It was the heart of the war industry and a prime target.

When my play *Johnny Bull* was recently produced in my hometown [The Belgrade Theatre, 1986], I visited the bombed-out Coventry Cathedral, St. Michaels's. It's a noble, medieval structure architecturally linked to a cold, ultramodern replacement. Standing inside this roofless shell—where they now sell hats with feathers to tourists—I experienced deep waves of emotion. I had an intense desire to finish what I'm writing, to make it bigger, to direct all the schoolchildren of Coventry in the re-creation of those massive evacuations. I could imagine the stories of the mothers dramatized as night draws in . . . the shadows of the Luftwaffe overhead . . . stirring music from Coventry's young composers and singers. November 14, 1990, will be the fiftieth anniversary of the most terrifying blitzkrieg. There ought to be some sort of commemoration; I don't know who one would have to persuade to allow a theatrical one but I may try to volunteer my services.

KOENIG: Do you subscribe to the theory that Winston Churchill deliberately sacrificed Coventry to protect the so-called Enigma Code?

BETSKO: I do . . . along with many of my fellow Coventrians. One thing is certain, he bloody-well knew there was a high probability of air attack on that infamous night . . . even had a code name for it: *Moonlight Sonata*. He could have slipped twenty-four hours notice, for the kids, for the hospitals to evacuate patients. But no. Most of Coventry's children were home. Hospitals, schools, churches were the first to go. More emergency evacuation schemes were hurriedly pressed into service, of course. But there was wholesale panic. Thousands of families streaming out of the city on foot, some still clad in pajamas, with mattresses tied onto bicycles, pitiful belongings tied up in tablecloths. A few desperately looted their neighbors' shillings from exposed gas meters. Some farmers sold space in their barns at exorbitant prices to victims seeking shelter for the night. We Brits don't like to think of ourselves this way.

In fact, these evacuations exposed already-existing deficiencies in England's Social Service systems. You can imagine those nice country homes—warm bread on the table, roses at the sill—suddenly invaded by hordes of urban kids infested with lice, malnourished, with impetigo, rickets, and other diseases. The lice and impetigo did not fall out of

German bombs. These conditions were the fault of our own government. The war merely exposed the horrors.

KOENIG: These urban children were a great burden?

BETSKO: In many cases, yes. They were emotionally traumatized. They pissed their beds, banged their heads against walls, tore up furniture and placid country schools, spread their infectious diseases to country children. No wonder the evacuees were upset. Some of them had stood on hills and watched Coventry burning, knowing their parents were still there.

KOENIG: What happened after the war?

BETSKO: A lot of kids were simply unclaimed. War places profound stress on even the most stable of families. Due to bombing deaths, marital split-ups, the general homelessness of many adults . . . lots of us kids were just left where we'd been billeted. We were kept or swapped or sometimes given away to elderly people in need of someone to run errands. My own mother lost four kids who had been dropped off in different villages and lost touch. She traced me, her youngest, when I was about twelve. But she never retrieved her other three children. She'd been bombed out of two homes, packed her share of parachutes, and other mandatory war work. She'd nothing left to bring us back to and lived in women's shelters until she moved to another town and remarried. There she worked long hours as a bus conductress before she died in 1967.

KOENIG: Have you written about her?

BETSKO: As is true of many women playwrights, I've not yet delved into the vortex of mother/daughter dynamics. I believe it is the last, dark continent to be explored in dramatic material. We've had centuries of father/son angst on stage and in literature. There are a few exceptions, but the love, savagery, and ambivalence between mothers and daughters is largely unexamined in theater. As you know, even Shakespeare didn't dare plumb those depths. It's a hot potato! Actually, I'm soon to have my chance. I've just been commissioned by a woman producer to develop a stage idea of mine called Starlings . . . about a radical feminist who has raised a conservative daughter. The mother character will be a composite of feminist friends of mine who sacrificed men they loved, had their children taken away from them (legally and illegally) or turned against them—women of considerable strength and achievement who struggled towards the ideal of women's equality with a collective conscience. The daughter character will be a lower-middle-class person, engaged to be married, employed, proud, and politically aware . . . someone who carries the pain of having been deprived of the traditional notion of "mother" . . . the homemaker with lots of time and warm cookie dough on her hands. Not that I'm against that. I'm for women having true choices, including full-time home, husband, and child care, if they so desire. This could well be one of the arguments put forth by the daughter: her right to return to tradition . . . even oppression . . . if she finds comfort and security in that. I may try to steer clear of humor in this play. That's risky. I write comedy well, but am tired of women being pressured to make their plays funny, to provide that "spoonful of sugar to make the medicine go down." Arthur Miller is not a laugh riot. I may want to get deadly serious, commit the heinous crime of talking politics right out loud in the theater.

KOENIG: Why the title *Starlings*?

BETSKO: I observed a tragedy once when in Baltimore, Maryland: the death and injuries of numerous starlings. My play will be set in a Baltimore hotel room where a mother is trying to provide a traditional Christmas in a transient setting for her grown daughter. Their conflicts will erupt into a serious, prolonged physical fight, which I don't think has ever been attempted on stage. Between prostitutes, maybe. But not between mother and daughter. Now, I'm not talking about child abuse, à la *Mommie Dearest*. I'm talking about lost adults, equals, driven nearly insane with unexpressed feeling. Along with the rage and disappointment, I'm hoping to reveal the foundation of love and the social, political, and familial need for alliance.

Starlings have a symbolic meaning to me. They've become a scourge in Baltimore. A once-beautiful bird, never meant to live in an urban setting, has proliferated out of control. Become a pest, a sort of flying rat, defecating all over public buildings. When they migrate around Christmastime, there is this frightening cacophony, the sky grows dark with their wings. In their terrible confusion, their need to survive, they accidentally hurl themselves into the windows of tall buildings and against brick walls. They fight for room to fly and then fall in great numbers to the pavement below. The sanitation department has to come and shovel them up. Others escape, of course, and fly off to a warmer climate. But they return after a respite to the city that despises them. No memory of those who died in the Exodus. And the cycle is repeated: shitting on public shrines, nesting, reproducing, rising up, escaping or falling. And then coming back for more. This is how I see the early women's movement and the more recent one. A lot of wounds and betrayals. I find the metaphor deeply moving.

KOENIG: Why and how did you become a playwright?

BETSKO: That's complex. As a working-class, urban street kid, there is not much in my background to explain how I ended up in this excruciatingly difficult, rather exclusive, male-dominated neck of the arts. It's all a bit too precious for me, and authoritarian. Attitudes that I hate. I think the theater should be a place to "get down and dirty" . . . passionate, visceral. Even unfair if necessary. Fairness is the opposite of passion. Perhaps it wasn't always so: this preciousness, this false politeness, this tiptoeing around in search of "the universal"—you know . . . theater as a place where only the sort of characters we'd be willing to bring home to brunch are acceptable: "sympathetic, well-meaning" men; "nice" women who don't swear. "Quiet" playwrights who take discreet notes in the back row. In our present-day rehearsal process, the most beloved playwright is a deceased one. Well, I ain't dead yet! I challenge the notion that anyone knows more about my script and my intentions as a writer than me. I don't want my thoughts delivered second-hand in some sort of tortured, secret code meant to manipulate the actor or stroke his or her ego. There is a popular notion that actors are children. I don't believe that. I respect actors as adults and am more than willing to learn things from other artists. But I'm not willing to let my specific knowledge of my working-class landscape go down the drain in the name of artistic harmony. I want a democratic piece of the action, of the *formal* rehearsal process. Not hurried luncheons as far away from the actors as possible. The phrase "collaborative medium" all too often includes only the actors and director. In terms of their scripts, writers are treated like idiots. Athol Fugard puts it this way: "The playwright is defenceless." Perhaps this is why he directs his own material, forges his own bonds with actors. Now, it is not that I haven't found much to respect in every single director that I've ever had . . . male and female. But I believe there is a blindness to the writer in the directorial process, an idea that the writer is an obstacle to overcome rather than a valuable resource. This suspicion of the writer may well have to be addressed by a playwrights' revolution. We may, all of us, have to learn how to direct our own first productions. I'm fed up with the way we playwrights whisper and weep to each other in bars after it's too late to assert our real intentions. We must put up a fight for what we mean even as others honestly strive to interpret what they *think* we mean.

KOENIG: So what are you doing in theater's benevolent autocracy?

BETSKO: Well, I started out as a raw poet . . . those dirty ditties I mentioned earlier. There are certain parallels between poetry and play-wrighting. One needs what [playwright] William Gibson once described [1974 interview, UNH radio station] to me as "an instinct for the jugular," a capacity to cut through the crap. Both poetry and playwriting require that skill. I have a natural crap-cutting talent. I like to challenge and be challenged. Playwrighting demands a bit of recklessness, a little combativeness. I may have a dash of those ingredients, too, qualities much admired in men but generally thought to be unpleasant and "unfeminine" in women. A play, I think, begins as a conscious or unconscious poem, an inner lyricism. I know there is poetry in me. It was first encouraged by a new young English teacher who appeared like a miracle in my school one day. All of my teachers to this point had been ninety-five-year-old females with warts and moustaches. They wore men's shoes and carried weapons. This new one wore lipstick and an engagement ring (suggesting to us kids that she had actually considered S-E-X, if not dabbled in it). I wrote my obligatory poem. Upon intercepting that saucy epic about herself, instead of caning me, she made me read it out loud. My fellow pupils (my first audience) were convulsed with mirth, as was I. Afterwards, this teacher discussed the work, straight-faced, in terms of iambic pentameter and the tradition of bawdiness in English literature. My punishment was to read Chaucer's "The Miller's Tale." I was instructed to write all the naughtiest bits three times over and underline the words I thought to be the most impressively vulgar. It was bloody hard work. Chaucer ain't easy. But I was on a hunt for the sinful and forbidden and because of that I enjoyed the assignment. My poems took a distinct turn for the better. Once out of school, creative writing was discarded. And I was thrown on the old treadmill experienced by many working-class kids.

KOENIG: You were in reform school for a while and later found yourself in an unwed mothers' home . . .

BETSKO: Yes. I had to be labeled "incorrigible" to qualify for the first and "immoral" to gain my invitation to the second. Both attributes one is said to need to be a playwright. Those kinds of institutions were especially grim back then. In the Luton Remand Home for Girls, our heads were shaved and we were put in isolation for long periods with nothing but a Bible. (Lots of ripe, naughty bits in that book, too.) And we were used by the local clinic as guinea pigs for snickering, upper-class, male medical students to learn the intricacies of gynecology. The unwed mums' home was nearly as dreary. But I remember that fondly. Long before the women's movement, I experienced true solidarity. All for one and one for all! A network of subversion against the "The Three M's" (matrons, moral welfare officers, and midwives). We laughed ourselves senseless during the day, and whispered and wept in the night. Such comfort. Great friends.

After that, I worked in shoe factories, and sold Wellingtons . . . eventually became a bus conductress like my mum. Still not writing, of course, but gaining experience: out in public, learning how to ring bells to stop and start a cumbersome doubledecker vehicle, leaping on and off of platforms while the bus was in motion, watching the damn thing drive off without me while I was trying to be humane and help a blind person across the road . . . much like being in the theater.

KOENIG: Then you married an American, thinking you might find Hollywood.

BETSKO: I thought I was going to escape British postwar poverty and live next door to Doris Day. I actually ended up beside a disused coal mine in western Pennsylvania with my coal-mining, Hungarian in-laws. Not a palm tree in sight. Perhaps that's why I frequently write about expectations versus reality. I was surrounded by hunting rifles, burgeoning unemployment, and the sort of domestic violence that often erupts when men are screwed out of their jobs, when they have nowhere to go but home with their frustrations after the beer garden closes. I had another child during that time.

KOENIG: You've used all this material in your plays . . .

BETSKO: I wrote *Johnny Bull* [a derogatory phrase used for the British by Hungarian miners] as a kind of apology to my mother-in-law who was very wise . . . for having to leave her, Pennsylvania, and her son. I've lived through some powerful family drama. Mind you, I soon learned in playwriting seminars to leave out the grittiest stuff, the worst bits. American audiences and critics can't take harsh reality written by a woman. One is thought to be a man-hater unless one makes male behavior palatable. The pressure on women to put "good guys" on stage is always overtly or covertly there.

KOENIG: You've had pressure to sweeten your male characters from directors?

BETSKO: Occasionally . . . even from women directors, sometimes. It was explained to me once that it was a feature of my own bitterness that one of my male characters threatens to shoot his wife if she leaves him. Well, just read the newspapers if you doubt the veracity of that.

Now, I have, I admit, occasionally succumbed to "sweetening" the men in my plays a bit. But [critic] Mel Gussow still accuses me of writing "brutes" or "louts." This sort of spiteful vocabulary reveals the attitude of the theater reviewer to working-class men, not mine. I don't think the men I write are "brutes." I like my characters. I don't approve of their view of women's "place" but I understand it. And I convey that understanding in my work. It's my job to write *authentic* characters, not to impose middle-class standards on working-class men, men who may behave badly when drunk or jobless. Wall Street executives have been known to beat their wives, too.

Rollo May [author and psychoanalyst] says that violence is impotence exploding. That comes in all classes and colors. Domestic brutality is on the increase and can't be ignored. But I have a right to treat it peripherally, too—as just *one* of the difficulties that impinge on my central characters, the women. It's a technical problem. Because critics are uneducated as to female metaphor and refuse to acknowledge political subtext in women's work, we are expected to endlessly "prove" that we are not anti-male when we presume to portray anti-social behavior in men. Women should not have to stop their plays and give a treatise on domestic violence in order to justify its presence on stage, to somehow let the males "off the hook." No one expects—least of all me—Sam Shepard to pussyfoot around violent behavior. The men I knew laughed and cried. They laugh and cry in my plays. I don't know what more I can do to humanize them. They had hopes for a better life, they dreamed of the mines and mills opening up again. They also carried guns, drank a lot of beer, and were often unreasonable. Having looked down the wrong end of a rifle once too often, I ran away with my babies, something I advise any wife in danger to do no matter how much she loves her man.

I landed in the textile mills of New Hampshire, where I worked the assembly line until President Johnson's War on Poverty cropped up. I've used that experience in the sweat shops in my play *Stitchers and Starlight Talkers* [1981]. After that came the late sixties. An era that some would like to pass off as a fashionable fad. But it was a very important time.

KOENIG: The Vietnam war was well under way, American youth was marching against it and demonstrating for civil rights, joining the Peace Corps . . .

BETSKO: And the VISTA volunteers. They came into our housing projects slinging a lot of fiery rhetoric. I liked it. It wasn't new to me. I come from a country where poor people voted for the Labour party, and called Churchill a warmonger. These idealistic college students re-kindled my old "underdog" mentality. I learned to yell, "Power to the People!" and ended up going to college without the proper credentials, just as American athletes have been doing for years. Packed up the kids and took them with me. At twenty-nine, I became the oldest full-time freshman on the University of New Hampshire campus. It took me six years but I graduated *summa cum laude*—without any academic dispensation—so no one will hear an argument from me against open admissions for "po' folk." I'm a product of it.

I began to explore creative writing. Fiction mostly. I had great teachers—male and female—who got all excited about my work. I began a novel, using all my "bleak" experiences, laced with generous helpings of humor, and made the students howl with laughter. Felt a fantastic sense of power from that. It was a good time to be in college [1968–74]. Debates were raging everywhere, newspaper editors being held captive in the lav while women took over the presses, students challenging teachers. I remember the glorious sense of freedom in letting down my teased hair and flinging off those spike heels, luxuriating in a new physical and mental freedom, free from fear. My rebellious nature was no longer an aberration—in fact, something that people admired. I was much in demand as a speaker, an articulate "Poor Person." I discovered that I had a theatrical delivery, could make students laugh and cheer while educating them about the realities of life in the factory and the humiliations of Welfare. Well, I switched my major from social service to theater in a hurry. So much for political purity.

KOENIG: Because you sensed the power of the stage?

BETSKO: Exactly. The power of words, the power to speak out. I became a pretty good actress. As the oldest student in the theater department, with a range of authentic British Isles accents up my sleeve, I was cast in major roles: Miss Jean Brodie, Meg in *The Birthday Party* . . . [parts in] Shakespeare, Greek classics. I was out of my mind with pleasure, learning to use power tools, to build and strike sets, to sew costumes. My kids were safe, happy, and running around with me in the Johnson Theater Complex. We didn't miss the housing project. But we did miss the friends we left behind . . . terribly.

KOENIG: This is a thematic element that threads through your work, isn't it? This grief at having to leave friends behind?

BETSKO: Yes. The women I left behind in the Pennsylvanian coal towns, the factory workers who helped me to get off the assembly line even though they were unable to leave themselves . . . singers and comediennes and kazoo players . . . fulla' hell and good cheer. Not people you had to watch your mouth around. Many are dead today from mohair-sweater dust in their lungs. Maybe that's the answer to your question . . . I ended up as a playwright so that I can carry my old buddies around in three-D, have them talk to me on stage, pee my pants laughing with them as I used to. Many of them were as talented as me or more so. But they had too many problems, or Brown Lung, or a pack of kids at their knees, or unemployed husbands they couldn't leave to race off and get an education. But they gave me their vital language, their down-to-earth philosophies on life, and I hope I carry it all on.

KOENIG: So you wouldn't agree with people today who claim that the early feminists were a bunch of well-to-do college girls who ran around whining about menstrual blood and writing victim poems . . . as compared to this generation of women who are doers and achievers?

BETSKO: Hell, no! We were doers and achievers *and* we looked out for each other *and* we watched one another's kids *and* formed house-cleaning teams to cheer up someone who might be depressed. We didn't burn our bras; we threw the suckers out until we learned that it hurts not to wear one if you have heavy breasts and then we threw them on again. We didn't give a damn for appearances. We had other ways to impress people.

When I first got to college and missed my gritty factory friends, I set about organizing other single, low-income mums to get an education. It wasn't an altruistic effort but loneliness. I had the pleasure of going through college with five women like myself. We had twenty kids between us, and were full-time students. We formed our own day-care center in a church basement, commandeered a chicken shack from the agricultural department, threw up some paint and curtains, and called it headquarters. We labeled ourselves Disadvantaged Women for a Higher Education [DWHE]. We loved the label. It made us visible. We were as proud of representing our social class in college as the black students on campus were proud of their race and heritage. We learned a lot from the blacks. We didn't want to join the mainstream. We wanted the mainstream to join *us*. I got remarried somewhere in the middle. Others got divorced, suffered miscarriages or deaths. But we stuck together and blundered on. We were delirious with learning, discovering art, growing in self-esteem, and still doing the laundry. Over a hundred mums and more than four hundred kids passed through our organization, in one way or another, in those years. The day-care center still remains and is acknowledged as one of the finest nurseries in New Hampshire. The original "dirty half-dozen" graduated with honors and made something of themselves. I've turned it into a treatment for a television series [*Daisy's Gang*, 1985], updated it. It's had quite a bit of interest in Tinsel Town but it's difficult to truthfully sell an army of defiant women hell-bent on an education to a TV network. I'll have to get Robert Redford or Jane Fonda on the case.

KOENIG: But there was a high price to pay for that education, wasn't there?

BETSKO: My son was stolen out of my legal custody across state lines by his father during my college years. There were no interstate laws covering child-stealing in those days. And I'd no money for private detectives, et cetera. He was twelve then and twenty-six now. My daughter and I still grieve for him. It's like a death. We don't know where he is. I know that he's become an environmental geologist and probably somewhere in Ohio. That's all. One of the reasons I write is in order to forgive. It wasn't an easy thing for me to "sweeten" that young husband in *Johnny Bull* in light of my loss. I forced myself to do it. I learned something. I learned to like and understand that character. The desperate adult man who stole the child was not the confused, violent teenager who couldn't find a job in Pennsylvania. I learned to care about my young male character on the page and on the stage, as I had when I married someone rather like him in life.

KOENIG: You were a professional actress for a few years before becoming a playwright . . .

BETSKO: I came to New York after I was divorced for a second time, after my daughter grew up and joined the Air Force. Now, there's gratitude for you. All that marching on the bloody Pentagon and where does she end up? Well, I support her in anything she wants to do. It's still one of the few ways a working girl can travel. She's a great kid and loves her old mum. But I threaten to drag my ancient MAKE LOVE, NOT WAR sign out if they ever try to send her off to battle. She's just presented me with a grandson. I write love poems to him. He's definitely a lefty: won't go to sleep, bites the hand that feeds him. My daughter, the patriot, says: "No Pinkos in the U.S.A.F., Ma!" Oh, well . . . I suppose I can wait till he's two to begin my ideological struggle for his heart and mind: "Say 'No Nukes' for Nana, Aaron. . . ." [Laughter]

KOENIG: You made it to Broadway as an actress within a year. Why did you change to writing?

BETSKO: I played the Nurse in *Equus* [Plymouth Theater, 1975]. Hardly a "tour de force." But I understudied The Mother and The Magistrate and got to go on stage in the more challenging roles several times during the national road tour. While on that tour for several months, I saw that a long run could be like the factory if you weren't careful: punch in . . . send it down the assembly line . . . punch out. I suddenly understood with blinding disappointment that I'd never get to do all those leading parts again that I'd had in college and regional theater. I thought it likely I'd end up playing English nurses and Scottish housekeepers for the rest of my life. I couldn't reconcile to that. After a vigorous year in New York City, I'd more than a good idea of the paucity of complex roles for women.

While we were sending *Equus* down the assembly line in Detroit, I bought myself a typewriter and began an endless saga called *Beggar's Choice*. That was in 1977. By 1978, I had this *War and Peace* epic that I sent off to the Eugene O'Neill National Playwrights Conference. It got selected for development. I couldn't believe it! Thanks to Lloyd Richards—someone who listens for new voices in theater more than perfection of craft, and a firm believer in my work now—I got to go and make a fool of myself in public. I've been at it ever since: Making a fool of myself and writing plays . . . both unavoidable when evolving into a professional playwright.

KOENIG: You often refer to yourself as the only working-class playwright operating in the American professional theater today. Is that true?

BETSKO: Probably not. There are plenty of Third World playwrights who maintain their class identification with pride. Among white playwrights, I could well be the only one. Actually, I just like to provocatively declare it because it's heretical in America to refer to oneself as "working-class" . . . unless it's a romantic reference to one's parents or childhood beginnings. I didn't earn much as an assembly-line worker but I make a lot less as a playwright. My gut feelings and alliances are still the same as before I obtained an education. I'm able to sneak past the cultural border guards a bit more easily now, that's all. If I'm wrong, I want all those other working-class playwrights, male and female, to send me their manuscripts. I'd like to edit that book: *American Working-Class Plays by American Working-Class Writers*. I might even get my American citizenship to celebrate *that* anthology. I strive to match the excellence of the middle-class writers I know and care about but I want to use any improvement I may manage in the craft, not just to entertain the average theater audience but to make the people my plays are about laugh and cry, too. I'd like to do *Johnny Bull* in front of a crowd of coal miners' wives in the Monongahela Valley; *Stitchers* for the women who sew sweaters in Manchester, New Hampshire; and *Beggar's Choice* for those English girls who think if they marry a Yank, they can nip over and borrow a cup of mascara from Farrah Fawcett. They're still there. Some of them are my nieces and second cousins. Still fantasizing about breaking free of the weaving looms and finding a touch of glamour, bless 'em, just as I did nearly thirty years ago.

KOENIG: Who are your major literary influences?

BETSKO: Shelagh Delaney, Alan Sillitoe, Alice Childress . . . and Mother Goose.

KOENIG: Now that we've come to the end of all our work on this book, what do you think? Is there a female aesthetic in the drama?

BETSKO: I believe so. We need hard research to prove it. We women are fragmented in our lives and fragmented in our structures. Professor Helen Chinoy of Smith College is investigating and documenting this fragmentation and mirror-imaging. The fragmentation is not necessarily poor craft. It is different craft. And we must challenge the critics— including some of the female critics—to examine the unconscious bias in favor of men in their writings and to begin to look for and identify the new forms, the new technical problems that we are struggling with that specifically arise out of women's experience and the different ways women have of evaluating and shaping their subject matter.

I don't think our "well-made" play efforts fit very well into Aristotle's old rules. In the traditional so called well-made play, the protagonist blindly takes action somewhere near the beginning, usually makes a terrible mistake that hurts himself and others, and—after observing the consequences of the mistake—learns something useful, fairly near the end of the play, that changes his life forever. I'm not a scholar but my feeling is that in women's attempts at "well-made" drama, the main character—when there is one—is usually female and she often takes the entire play to observe and learn and only then takes action. Almost the reverse of the traditional form. Perhaps that's why women are often accused of writing "passive" female characters. We may need to challenge the very definition of dramatic "action." Women tend to write shorter scenes, tend to share the text more generously between all characters on stage. And women may have a more intricate sense of "event" . . . such as that tendency we noticed to investigate violence, or the results of violence on stage, as opposed to aggrandizing a violent act as a dramatic event per se.

KOENIG: The French novelist and thinker Alain Robbe-Grillet said something about a new form always seeming to be more or less an absence of any form at all since it is unconsciously judged by reference to consecrated forms.

BETSKO: Right. Perhaps that's why women's plays are often referred to by reviewers as "nonplays." Remember how annoyed we'd get when we came upon that word *nonplay* over and over again in the criticism of women playwrights' work?

KOENIG: It's a refusal to admit that something different is going on within the work. Can you imagine anyone referring to "nonsculpture," "nonpainting," "nondance," "nonsymphony" . . . ?

BETSKO: Perhaps there's a new dramatic movement afoot: "Nonism." In my own opinion, women think and write differently than men because they have different experiences, different myths, different needs and desires and dreams and memories. As feminist scholars have pointed out, we exist as a separate culture within the dominant culture. A culture distinct from men's, no matter how intimately we may live with or love them. If content really does dictate form, then perhaps women will bring to splendid fruition what we feel is already going on: the development of different dramatic forms more suited to our own experience, that will reflect and enhance what may well be unique concepts of light, color, sound, time, and space. When women are free to be completely honest, the theater will be rocked to its foundations; far from destroying it, I think there'll be a glorious rebirth.

As for this confusion about whether we are feminists or humanists, I don't believe there was ever any difference. And, anyway, what ever happened to Mother Jones's famous challenge: "Get it right, I ain't a humanitarian . . . I'm a hell-raiser!" Of course, she was well known for her compassion for the oppressed, but she wasn't going to allow her righteous indignation to be defused by a more palatable word for what it was she was about: the eradication of injustice. One can't change things without a struggle. And one has to maintain vigilance over changes once they are made. In honor of Mother Jones, I prefer to keep the word *woman* in front of my *playwright* label, as a signal of solidarity with all women, kids, and the voiceless of either gender. It's a political decision. I don't think I'm didactic in my work but I know which side I'm on. I'll continue to use the phrase *woman playwright—woman anything* that women are not supposed to be—as an open invitation for men to abandon their fathers' competitive, often life-destroying culture and join our more civilized world. A world that holds hope for a new and infinitely more exciting form of love between men and women—a form that is good in and out of bed, on and off stage—equality between the sexes.

ALICE CHILDRESS

Playwright/novelist Alice Childress was born in Charleston, South Carolina, and raised and educated in Harlem, New York. Prior to her writing career, Ms. Childress was an actress with the American Negro Theatre both on and off Broadway. Her plays include The African Garden, Martin Luther King of Montgomery, Alabama, Mojo, Trouble in Mind, Wedding Band, When the Rattlesnake Sounds, Wine in the Wilderness and Gullah, as well as a children's play, Let's Hear It for the Queen. Her novels include A Hero Ain't Nothin' but a Sandwich (Coward McCann, 1973), Rainbow Jordan (Coward McCann, 1981) and A Short Walk (1979). Ms. Childress's numerous awards include a fellowship at the Radcliffe Institute for Independent Study, where she was playwright/scholar in 1968; the first Paul Robeson Award from the Black Filmmakers Hall of Fame, the Virgin Island Film Festival Award for Best Screenplay (the last two honors for the film adaptation of A Hero . . .); the Achievement Award from the National Association of Negro Business and Professional Women, the Actors Equity Paul Robeson Award and the Radcliffe Alumnae Association Graduate Society Medal for Distinguished Achievement. She also won the first Obie Award for Playwriting in 1954 for Trouble in Mind. Ms. Childress has been a councilmember of the Dramatists Guild, Writers Guild of America East, and is a Dramatists Guild Representative to the Authors League, as well as a member of the Harlem Writers Guild and the PEN Club. Ms. Childress is married to composer/musician Nathan Woodard, who created the music for Gullah.

———————

CHILDRESS: I wrote my play Wedding Band [1973] as a remembrance of the intellectual poor. The poor, genteel and sensitive people who are seamstresses, coal carriers, candymakers, sharecroppers, bakers, baby caretakers, housewives, foot soldiers, penny-candy sellers, vegetable peelers, who are somehow able to sustain within themselves the poet's heart, sensitivity and appreciation of pure emotion, the ability to freely spend tears and laughter without saving them up for a rainy day. I was raised by and among such people living on the poorest blocks in Harlem and have met many more on the boundary lines of the segregated life—the places where black, white, brown, yellow and red sometimes meet—in bus stations, train and plane waiting rooms, on lines where we pay gas, light and telephone bills.

Wedding Band kept coming at me from hidden, unexpected places, the characters called on my mind while I was trying to write something else, demanding attention, getting together, coming into being. It was a play I did not want to write, about people few others wanted to hear from . . . I thought. It somehow seemed to be answering back all the stage and screen stories about rich, white landowners and their "octoroon" mistresses.

Such stories meant nothing in my life. I am a black woman of light complexion, have no white relatives except on the other side of slavery, and have experienced the sweetness, joy and bitterness of living almost entirely within the Harlem community. I really did not wish to beat the drum for an interracial couple and yet there they were in front of me, not giving a damn about public opinion of this or that past day. It was like being possessed by rebel spirits, ideas clinging, taking over and starting my day for me. Instead of a joyous experience, writing the play became a trial, a rough journey through reams of paper. Characters know; they won't be fooled, not even by their medium, the writer. They *allow* you to write them, pushing you along until they're satisfied that they've done their thing to the utmost of your ability.

I was born in Charleston, South Carolina, and raised on 118th Street between Lenox and Fifth avenues in Harlem, New York City. My grandmother and her friends were not ashamed of living: "Got it to do!" they said. When people were ill, neighbors rallied and brought various home remedies to the bedside, seldom a doctor. Those days are almost gone, thank God. Who wants to live with one foot in hell just for the sake of nostalgia? Our time is forever now! Today our youngsters can freely discuss sex. Soon they will even be able to openly discuss one of the results of sex—life. I also remember death, funerals, just before it went out of style to have the last service within the home instead of at the undertaking parlor. In one corner of the kitchen, a big truckdriver of a man wept tears into a large handkerchief, his shoulders shaking with grief: "Why did she leave us? Only last week I was talking to her and answered real short: 'Shut up.' I said that to her . . . and now she's gone." And those there gathered answered him with healing words of comfort: "Well, God knows you loved her, don't take it so hard, you did your best." They brought him through that day. Other men, richer and smarter, had to go through three years of therapy to find the reasons why and why and why . . . and to know there's always another why. On our block there was prostitution, but we were so damned blind until even the prostitutes were called "Miss" Margaret or "Miss" Beatrice or whatever. And they did not beckon to men until our backs were turned, most of the time. Heroin was not yet King of the Ghetto and a boy would not dream of killing his grandmother or hurting his mama or her friends in order to pour cooked opium dust through a hole in his arm. But they weren't "the good old days." The only good days are ahead. The characters kept chasing me down. Men in love with "nothing to offer." Women who couldn't or wouldn't hold back their emotions "for the sake of the race." They tap at the brain and move a pen to action in the middle of the night. They are alive, they really are, pushing and shoving interfering creators out of the way. Now, in this slot of time, they return singing old songs about inner discovery. Other characters keep knocking at our doors, pushing, pulling, tearing at seams of life. Poets, novelists, painters, playwrights stand around shifting from foot to foot, trying to keep score. Ordinary people know more about how to live with love and hate than given credit for . . . even though they're never seen on talk shows.

INTERVIEWER: There was a difference between the white criticism of *Wedding Band* [a play whose central characters are an interracial couple; it premiered in 1966] and what the black critics had to say, wasn't there?

CHILDRESS: The white criticism was that the interracial couple needn't have stayed [in a Jim Crow state], that they could have gone away; they felt the male character, the white baker, should have turned his back on his mother and sister and escaped. Now, that's a very hard thing for poor people to do. It's easier for wealthy people. They can leave *and* send money home to their dependents. This baker *is* his family's livelihood. His mother contributed all of her money to his small bakery shop. For him to walk away from family and debts is almost unheard of in poor communities.

The black critics' objections were: Why talk about this interracial issue at all? Why couldn't I just write about a black couple? It may have sounded as though I were praising interracial love but, in fact, this was not my objective. In almost everything I write there are black couples, and there is also one in *Wedding Band*. But this was a true story my grandmother had told me, about a black woman named Miss Julia, who lived across the street from her in South Carolina and who "kept company" with a white butcher. I made him a baker in the play because I thought it would be more palatable for the audience than butchering.

Black critics felt that the character I based on Miss Julia should not have wanted to marry a white man, no matter that this situation often occurs in real life. The black audience would have been more comfortable if Julia had rejected her white lover. That was true even of the last production of the play at Joe Papp's theater [The New York Shakespeare Festival, Public Theatre, 1972]. It had been done earlier at the University of Michigan at Ann Arbor [1966] and in Chicago, where we had our greatest success. Black audiences in Chicago really liked the play. They sold out the whole six weeks, standing room only; you couldn't get tickets.

INTERVIEWER: The critical response was cooler in New York?

CHILDRESS: I don't know what it is about different regions. I think there were more Deep South people in Chicago to respond to a recognized Southern story. You see migrants from there landed in the Midwest.

INTERVIEWER: Did you find less resistance to your artistic vision in the publishing world?

CHILDRESS: Yes I did. I didn't have to fight and struggle as in the theater because, almost by accident, an editor [at Coward McCann] came to me who knew of my playwriting—the late Ferdinand Monjo, who was also a noted children's author. He said, "Alice, you've said so much about drugs in your writing, why don't you really put some time into it and do a book?" That's how I came to write *A Hero Ain't Nothin but a Sandwich*. He told me it had to be a young adult book because he was a young adult book editor, and young adults needed such a book.

INTERVIEWER: In *A Hero* . . . each chapter represents a different character's point of view: the boy on drugs, the boy's mother, the boy's teacher, and so on. Is this an instance of your playwright's training overlapping into your fiction?

CHILDRESS: Yes—theater and film. I was very impressed by the film *Rashomon* [by Kurosawa]. A woman was raped; she tells her story and the other characters tell their stories. Each one's version of the event is reenacted within the film. But all were *lying* except one, who was observing from a distance. And when he tells what happened, you understand why all the others lied. But I do an opposite thing. In my writing, all the stories differ, but I see that you can get ten *different* stories out of people *all telling the truth*. We don't all view things the same way, each perspective is different. Many-leveled narration is something I do well. It's true to theater. When I'm writing a character that I see as a villain, I try to take the villain's side and believe in the righteousness of the villainous act. In *A Hero* . . . we pondered long about cutting out the drug pusher's side of the story.

INTERVIEWER: Because it was a book for young people?

CHILDRESS: Yes. The drug pusher is so convincing about the rightness of his acts and the reader feels for him. Monjo was very helpful. After a great deal of talk about it, we decided to leave the character in.

INTERVIEWER: *A Hero* went as far as the Supreme Court in a book-banning case, along with books by eight other authors. Will you discuss censorship?

CHILDRESS: Nine books got to the Supreme Court, and mine was one of them. I don't know if I'm the first or only woman whose book got to the Supreme Court on a banning. They also banned Hawthorne's *The Scarlet Letter* because it was sympathetic to an unmarried pregnant woman. In one school, the authorities banned *Romeo and Juliet,* saying the Nurse was a poor role model because Juliet's parents had hired her to take care of their daughter, and there she was passing notes and arranging liaisons, covering up that Romeo and Juliet were seeing each other. Another school banned all of Shakespeare's plays *except Romeo and Juliet.*

Some people say, "I like this book, such a beautiful book shouldn't be banned." But they don't mind it when a book they *don't* like is banned. I feel we must be against banning regardless of whether we like a book. We do not have to accept its content and quality, we do not have to read or accept a book at all—but to ban it is wrong.

INTERVIEWER: Do you have any particular criteria you use to judge what is bad and what is helpful in criticism?

CHILDRESS: Yes. I weigh it and think about it. If ten people read or see a play at different times and they all zero in on the same trouble spot, the problem might not be *exactly* what they are expressing, but the playwright knows that there is *something* there that needs to be cleared up. I have an instinctive feeling when someone is giving me "wrong" criticism. I'm wary when I've labored over something for five years and someone comes over and tells me in five minutes, "Do this, do that, change this . . ." Well, you can't just trust and do what you are told. But at the same time, you must be open to "good" criticism. You have to get off by yourself and find out if it's merely your ego that is suffering. The viewer of a film or play doesn't have to spend all the years you've spent to know the ending is upsetting to them.

INTERVIEWER: Do you care if your endings are upsetting to the audience?

CHILDRESS: No, I don't, but I do care if the audience feels something is unbelievable or a lie. All fiction is tampering with the truth, but it bothers me if something seems like it's been thrown in just to make the script "work." I can't make a character do or say something that I don't think this character would do or say just because the audience would prefer it. But I do have to listen to a director or producer on whether a scene is too long, whether the progression of the play is being held up because of it. It's not only what the play has to say, but how it flows. If it's too long, it's too long. I don't care for lengthy plays—four, six, eight hours long. I don't want to go back the next night to see how it ends. I want to sit in one session, and see and hear a play all the way through. I want it all to fit, there and then. Some people criticize the "well-made" play, but it is not to be knocked. If you buy a suit you want it to be well made. You don't want the tailor to experiment; we want something dependable; well, *I* do.

INTERVIEWER: You don't approve of experimental theater?

CHILDRESS: When you know the traditional way, then you can destroy it and make a different form. Picasso could draw the human figure accurately, realistically. Some young artists want to skip over the conventional workings and start with the abstract. I think experimental theater should come out of first knowing how to write a well-made play.

INTERVIEWER: You've published several novels. Have they influenced your playwriting? Have you mastered something in your fiction that helps you to create the "well-made" play?

CHILDRESS: It's the other way around. The theater influences my novel writing. I feel each chapter is a scene. But when writing novels, I find description difficult. With plays, after we've described the set, we're free of that. We don't *have to* describe the sun rising or the sound of rain. Someone else brings lighting, set, costumes and sound to life for us. Playwrights are specialists in dialogue, situation and conflict; and they must make it all happen within a limited time and space. The novel is more permissive. When I'm writing a book, I visualize it all on a stage. I'm very pleased when critics say my novels feel like plays. I've learned to lean on theater instead of breaking with it. I came to theater first, acted for eleven years with the American Negro Theater and started writing out of that experience. When writing a novel or a play I act out all the parts. I've actually gotten up, walked around and played out a scene when I've run into difficulty with the writing . . . moved through all the entrances and exits. Making theater is more than how you feel and speak, it's how you move. You have to work it out, act it out, think it out, as if on a stage. I also think that way about a book.

INTERVIEWER: You were an actress first . . .

CHILDRESS: Oh, yes. I was in the original cast of *Anna Lucasta* [1944] on Broadway. I've also worked a little in television and movies. But racial prejudice was such that I was considered "too light" to play my real self and they would not cast light-skinned blacks in white roles. I realized I had to have some other way of creating. I love acting, the art of acting, but not the business of acting and auditioning. Most of the time, I didn't like the parts they wanted me to play. Unless one is lucky enough to get a lot of stage work, creativity is cut off or underexercised. I decided I'd rather create from the start, create good roles I'd like to play by writing them. I found, however, I wasn't interested in writing parts for myself. I've never written anything for me—though I've been tempted. When my work is presented, I feel I belong out front. I want to be the beholder, the audience.

INTERVIEWER: What exactly bothered you about the roles you played as an actress?

CHILDRESS: They were stereotypes, "packaged" situations. I don't necessarily mean derogatory stereotypes, but too predictable. "The black" would do one thing, "the white" another thing, and, of course, by the end they would all come together and resolve their differences—packaged solutions.

It's all very well to just take any old play and cast it from different races with no further comment—a nice exercise in democracy, a social service to one another—but I think there is something very particular about different races and religious backgrounds in America that has yet to be fully explored.

INTERVIEWER: Do you mean that in the effort to be "universal," we are losing something about the parochial?

CHILDRESS: Yes. Some of the greatest plays have come from Sean O'Casey, *Irish* playwright, who wrote *about* the poor Irish, *for* the Irish. Look at the works of Sholem Aleichem and [Isaac] Peretz—out of the blood and bones of Jewish tradition. The black poet, Paul Laurence Dunbar, works the same sort of magic about particular people.

INTERVIEWER: You're working on a novel about Dunbar now. Did you research extensively?

CHILDRESS: Yes. Writing about New York City in 1895, I have to find out what it was like here at that time, what products were being used, what clothing was in style. You try to get the underlying feel of the times. . . . My writing stops when I don't know what my characters would have done in certain situations . . . what they did in houses without bathrooms. . . . This often entails reading articles and books that have nothing to do with your story but which reveal the ambience of the period. I'm writing about African-Americans, but in my research have fallen headlong into the Jewish life of the late eighteen hundreds, immigrants coming from Europe, the teeming streets of the Lower East Side. All of these details help a story to bloom. Also, I try not to write in the past tense.

INTERVIEWER: Another feature of your theater training perhaps?

CHILDRESS: It's more theatrical to write in the present tense, and more interesting. I have Paul Laurence Dunbar and his sweetheart walking across the Brooklyn Bridge when it was two years old, when people were afraid to cross it. I have them talking about the newness of it.

INTERVIEWER: How did your interest in Dunbar evolve?

CHILDRESS: I'm writing about Paul and his wife Alice—their personal relationship. I read many published papers and correspondence they exchanged. I went down South and visited with their niece, and saw hundreds of original letters in faded ink. I decided to write about the four years they were married. Their union was turbulent. . . . Frightening. They were obviously in love but also tried to destroy one another. I liked the drama of it all . . . and the historical aspect.

INTERVIEWER: Will you bring the theatrical device of using many points of view to this novel as well?

CHILDRESS: Yes. I found myself writing mainly from his point of view, from hers and his mother's. I thought it so strange that these two people should have been together at all. Both parents—his mother, her mother—were against them getting married. I began to dig into her mother's life, too. And her mother's mother's life.

INTERVIEWER: If someone had offered you a stage for the Dunbar story, as Coward McCann offered to publish a book [A Hero . . .], would you have written it as a play?

CHILDRESS: That would have been delightful . . . but a play would have been more difficult. A book is more lenient than the stage, which has such space and time limitations I'd have to throw out half of my story.

INTERVIEWER: Why did you put your piece Gullah on the stage instead of into a novel?

CHILDRESS: It would have been simpler to write it as a novel. I felt moved to write a play. I started once on it—a big long thing—but it didn't hang together well. Then I tried again and that didn't work either. Sometime later, the South Carolina Commission on the Arts wanted a play specific to South Carolina. They only wanted an hour-long piece so that it could tour schools all over the state. Well, I said I'd boil down what I had, and make a short version. My husband, Nathan Woodard, composed music for it. We were quite pleased with the result and stopped worrying about it being full-length.

INTERVIEWER: Gullah is a name for a language, isn't it? A very musical language specific to certain islands off the coast of South Carolina. How did this language evolve?

CHILDRESS: It's a poetry of the people, and embodies their poetic expression and poetic feeling. During the time of slavery, Africans were often sold in mixed lots of different nationalities and language, because their owners didn't want them to communicate with one another. You see, there were about seven hundred fifty different tongues spoken throughout Africa. So the slave traders hit upon the idea of forming groups, "parcels," by selecting one slave from each nationality. The various groups were sold for labor on different islands off the South Carolinian coast, and a language evolved from the many African languages mixed with English and even a little German. Some people think the word *Gullah* came from people trying to say *Angola*. They became known as Gola or Gullah people. Island isolation helped preserve the Africanisms that blacks on the mainland soon lost through assimilation. My stepfather was born on one of those islands. After he died (on Edisto Island), some of his people came to visit us in New York. I could hardly understand a word. Now, of course, there are bridges, businesses have opened, property has been bought for homes and resorts. The South Carolina Commission on the Arts didn't want us to use the title *Gullah*. The word is sometimes spoken in a prejudicial way to mock country people and the way they talk. The play was called *Sea Island Song* down there but it sounded too Hawaiian, misleading, I thought. When we came back North I went back to the original *Gullah*.

INTERVIEWER: What's happening to the people and their culture?

CHILDRESS: They are being scattered and shattered. That's partly what *Gullah* is about. Their way of life is ebbing away. Their African baskets take weeks to weave. We live in an age of plastic and metal. They can't make a livelihood working with their hands. That's the problem.

INTERVIEWER: Is that true of all the arts these days, do you think?

CHILDRESS: It feels that way. The longer you take to make something, the less you are paid. If a publisher pays you an advance and it takes you six months to write something, that's what you make for six months' work. If it takes three years to write it, you still make the same amount of money. So some writers do tend to think about what they can whip together fairly fast. It's not satisfying; sometimes you have to let the work go with regret. I don't think I've ever really "finished" anything to my satisfaction . . . no matter how long I've worked on the material.

INTERVIEWER: You've said the less a writer understands the faster he or she can write . . .

CHILDRESS: Yes. And you're forgiven for what you don't know. But when you understand your material, you can't shove it along at great speed. When you "know," there is a pleasure in taking time, in stopping yourself, in choosing another direction. As my present editor, Refna Wilkins, once said to me, "Alice, you always pick the hard way." I ask myself if it's healthy, choosing the more difficult road. I guess the bottom line about writing is that it's a torturous process, but the beautiful part is there's a deep, indescribable, inexplicable *satisfaction* in having written. A feeling of elevation and joy afterward that is greater than the despair of sitting there and doing it. I don't enjoy the writing process. I like writing when I have completed it.

INTERVIEWER: What about the critics?

CHILDRESS: I've had some pretty good criticism along the way. The frightening thing about theater critics is the thought of them having to go to the theater every night. I've been on Tony Awards committees and had to see all the plays of a season. You get to the point where you hate the thought of going to the theater. You want to see a selection of the plays that interest you. You don't want to go every night. You don't want to review when you're tired or angry. If you've ever been around the offices of a reviewer and seen thirty or forty books waiting for them to report on, you can't help but wonder if the critic is tired, angry, or turned off by certain subject matter.

What I'm eager for is consumer feedback, which you don't get as much for novels as you do in theater. The reader may buy a book because the critics said it was good, but the writer may never know what the *reader* thinks, even if sales are good, though you do get letters from time to time. It's not as exciting as theater where every night the audience and the play are somewhat different and the response is immediate.

INTERVIEWER: Critics and public alike, these days, become upset if a female character stays with a "bad" man: "Why didn't she just leave the jerk in Act I, so we could all go home early?" In your play *Wine in the Wilderness* [1969], you go one further. Twelve years after the husband leaves, a woman calls up to ask Momma if she wants to come and claim his body. She does, saying, "A woman needs a man to claim even if it's a dead one." [laughter]

CHILDRESS: Well, I had in my mind so many stories I'd heard about men running off with other women, or disappearing from home for a while. People would talk: "You know, he turned up dead . . ." or "You know, she went down and claimed the body." There have been *kind* men who were better to women than the men who loved them. I think women need kindness more than love. When one human being is kind to another, it's a very deep matter. I think we underestimate words like *kind* and *pleasant* and *decent*. We live in a time of PR men, inflated reviews of movies. "Colossal" isn't good enough, it has to be "Gigantic, a *blockbuster*!" We need more touching tenderness. Tommy-Marie said it in *Wine in the Wilderness*: "If you live to be seventy, that's seventy chances to see springtime, seventy Christmases to celebrate." Life is a short walk. Why complicate it with everyday meanness? It behooves us to be *kinder*. People want to be *madly* in love and *passionately* desired. But what we remember longest are kindnesses.

INTERVIEWER: It's a widely held belief that a woman has never written a great dramatic masterpiece, and never will be able to write one. Why?

CHILDRESS: Who *wants* women to write great plays? Are the critics sitting there waiting? No. In fact, they are pulling against it. They're threatened by the prospect of a strong point of view publicly expressed by a woman. Now, I'm not saying that there aren't female characters that men in an audience admire more than others. No one will throw bricks at Florence Nightingale because she served men. She served *mankind*. But Florence had to fight men in order to do even *that*! Just to be able to serve and to give of herself, to raise the status of nurse above that of slop-jar cleaning. When women went into teaching grade school, it was a man's job. When they managed to press into the profession in numbers, men started flying out of it. It's a question of identification. It's the same with theater. There aren't any black critics who can close a white play. But in black theater, black experience has been fought against by white critics. The white critic feels no obligation to prepare himself to judge a black play. He simply has to ask himself, "Did it strike me? Did I enjoy it?"

INTERVIEWER: The critic assumes "universal" equals white?

CHILDRESS: The white reviewer's attitude is: "If I could interchange these black characters for white, would this story apply to white people? If not, then I don't like it." Most of what the black audience sees reflects *white* experience. And those black figures we do see in television stories and motion pictures, even some stage shows, are mostly roles that I would call "job opportunities," an effort to prove that there's *some* balance, that minorities are getting some chances to earn a livelihood. The public is now able to say, "Well, this story *sort of* concerns everyone." But it doesn't feel that way to most of us who watch these stories, discuss and evaluate them. They're stock characters, stock more often than stereotype. The black cop who's the sidekick of the white policeman. The beautiful complexity of our own experience is being avoided. If you speak to a white writer, actor or director about the difficulties of getting a black play produced, the response is frequently, "Well, it's hard for *me* to get work produced!" Which means, "I'm white and I can't. If I can't, what the hell do *you* expect?" That is to say, as long as there is a good white play that's not being done, we shouldn't complain. Well, that's not acceptable.

INTERVIEWER: Are there any parallels between the critics' attitudes toward women's drama and their attitudes toward black drama?

CHILDRESS: Oh, yes. There's always resistance to any oppressed group, and this resistance stems from defensiveness: "I fear your reaction to an unjust situation, so I must deny that it exists. I fear that advantages for you will threaten me." They must then claim that we have no fight—and say: "There's nothing about your problem that's different from mine!" But women, I think, have very special problems all over the world. And, in addition to sexism, the black woman is faced with the struggle against racism, which is the most bitter, painful experience in the world. Whatever concepts or ideas we have, we must feel free to express them, regardless of whether we catch hell or praise. I don't think we should have any less of an arena or any less access to the stage than men. But we're going to be judged by male critics for a long while because major newspapers employ few women as critics.

INTERVIEWER: What about the few women that *are* employed? Might they feel pressured to be harsher on women playwrights in order to impress their male colleagues with their impartiality?

CHILDRESS: Some do, the crafty ones. Women who haven't allowed their minds to go beyond their own lives, who have simply no idea about the condition of other women. . . . It's amazing they can't see a broader picture and say, "Well, maybe I've been very fortunate." There'll always be a few women who will be Uncle Toms or a more sophisticated version of the same idea. Kowtowing to the one who is holding them down. Being Master's and Mistress's favorite child.

INTERVIEWER: Many playwrights say, "I'm not a *woman* playwright, I'm a playwright," which would seem to imply that the struggle has been won, and that we now have an equal arena. . . .

CHILDRESS: Well, there are still some people who say, "I'm not a *black* playwright, I'm a playwright who *happens* to be black." Like they're some goddamned accident! You know? Happenstance. I am a woman and I am black. There were race laws in South Carolina. It was actually illegal to consider yourself anything different. It was against the law for white and black people to marry. Some of these laws are still on the books. Many people have said, "I wouldn't take you for black." You don't have to "take me" for anything! I am a black woman and I am a black woman playwright. I'm neither proud nor ashamed of it. This is our fight and our struggle. I'll take the responsibility on. I've heard young people say, "Oh, I'm so tired of hearing about black rights and women's rights." Well, people who are still fighting for these things are tired of it, too, but we go on working.

INTERVIEWER: You feel we must maintain a vigilance?

CHILDRESS: Of course. We also have to feel a sense of gratitude and admiration for what others have done, for those who have paved the way for us, and who are doing it even *now* in our time. The person who says, "I'm not a woman playwright," or "I'm not black, I'm a writer who happens to be black," et cetera, is deluding herself.

However, I am against the notion that women must be portrayed in an ideal light, that we are obligated to write glowing things about our mothers or sisters. This prevents us from discovering each other. Some feminists feel that a woman should never be wrong. We have a right to be wrong. I'm always a little puzzled by the idea that we, as feminists, should not write about men mistreating women because we are not supposed to portray women as victims. Who says I can't write victims? Men *do* mistreat women, all too often. But I feel too much of our writing advocates that women who are brutalized seek professional help, period. I don't object to teaching people to ask for assistance, but one must make distance first: The victim cannot afford to linger, stick around for social worker discussions; she must develop the drive to *get away*. . . . If man is compelled to turn his hatred against a woman, she doesn't need a psychiatrist or a counselor—she needs to *get out*—she needs a bus ride out of town . . . anywhere. If she hasn't much money, that's all right! She should travel without money! You have forty dollars? Take it as far as forty dollars will get you.

INTERVIEWER: Do you have any advice for young women who are thinking of becoming playwrights?

CHILDRESS: That's the hardest question. I can never think of anything to say, except *Write!* If someone takes up a musical instrument, he or she does not expect to master it immediately. People give up on writing too fast. I think sometimes the beginner may delay the starting procedure for too long as a means of avoiding the work. Don't worry about having perfect tools and proper conditions. You can start out with a crayon and a paper bag! Just put down what you see and think! Don't try to be perfect, just try.

CARYL CHURCHILL

Caryl Churchill, a British playwright, has written over thirty plays for stage, radio and television, including Owners, Objections to Sex and Violence, Traps, Vinegar Tom, Light Shining in Buckinghamshire, and Softcops. Her most well-known productions in the United States include Cloud Nine, Top Girls and Fen. Churchill's plays have been performed extensively on London stages, including The Royal Court Theatre, and have been performed internationally as well. Churchill has worked in conjunction with Britain's Joint Stock Theatre Company, and The Monstrous Regiment (a women's theater collective). She was the recipient of the Susan Blackburn Award in 1984.

On February 25, 1984, we interviewed British playwright Caryl Churchill in a restaurant across the street from The Public Theater, where her play *Fen* was in production. The conversation, due to the writer's time limitations, and her expressed reluctance to be interviewed, was all too brief. Later, on playing back the tape, we were distressed to discover that a significant portion of what we were hearing was the sound of our own voices attempting to answer Churchill's rapid and incisive questions on our research into the status of American women playwrights. The interviewers had become the interviewees. By the time we recouped, the playwright had escaped home across the Atlantic with most of her opinions on the craft still a secret.

In light of this error on our part, we were delighted when American playwright Emily Mann, on her way to England for a production of her play *Still Life*, agreed to try to extend our interview with Churchill. Since both playwrights in their separate sessions with us had expressed a deep respect for each other's work as well as a desire to meet, this presented a perfect opportunity for the two of them to get together. In addition, an interview between Mann and Churchill seemed to us consistent with Corinne Jacker's discussion, on our behalf, with Bai Fengxi in Beijing during Jacker's travels in China, and the generous gift of Maria Irene Fornes's questions and skills as interpreter in our lengthy session with Griselda Gambaro of Argentina.

The second part of the following interview is a result of the meeting between Emily Mann and Caryl Churchill, who introduced themselves in London on November 23, 1984, during the Riverside Studio rehearsal period of Mann's *Still Life*.

—THE EDITORS

INTERVIEWER: Is there a female aesthetic? And we'd like you to wrap this question up once and for all. [Laughter]

CHURCHILL: I don't see how you can tell until there are so many plays by women that you can begin to see what they have in common that's different from the way men have written, and there are still relatively so few. And we have things in common with male playwrights who are worried about similar things in their particular country and who have worked in the same theaters with the same directors. So it's hard to separate out and think of "women playwrights" rather than just "playwrights." Though I do remember before I wrote *Top Girls* thinking about women barristers—how they were in a minority and had to imitate men to succeed—and I was thinking of them as different from me. And then I thought, "Wait a minute, my whole concept of what plays might be is from plays written by men. I don't have to put on a wig, speak in a special voice, but how far do I assume things that have been defined by men?" There isn't a simple answer to that. And I remember long before that thinking of the "maleness" of the traditional structure of plays, with conflict and building in a certain way to a climax. But it's not something I think about very often. Playwriting will change not just because more women are doing it but because more women are doing other things as well. And of course men will be influenced by that too. So maybe you'll still be no nearer to defining a female aesthetic.

INTERVIEWER: Some of the playwrights we've interviewed suggest there are no "lost masterpieces" and that "the cream will rise to the top" in terms of women's writing for the stage.

CHURCHILL: Most theaters are still controlled by men and people do tend to be able to see promise in people who are like themselves. Women directors have pointed out to me how established men tend to take a young male director under their wing, and seem to feel more uncomfortable with a woman director because they can't quite see where she is, because they weren't like that at her age. I think the same thing can happen with writers: If you're at the stage where you are promising but not doing it all that well yet, it's perhaps easier for a man choosing plays to see the potential in a man writer. I don't know about "lost masterpieces" but people don't usually start out writing masterpieces and women may have less chance of getting started. Having productions does seem to make people write better.

INTERVIEWER: Has the political climate for women dramatists changed drastically since you began writing plays?

CHURCHILL: I began writing plays in 1958, and I don't think I knew of any other women playwrights then. Luckily, I didn't think about it. Do you know Tillie Olsen's book *Silences*? She says that at different times, whole categories of people are enabled to write. You tend to think of your own development only having to do with yourself and it's exciting to discover it in a historical context. When I began it was quite hard for any playwrights to get started in London. The English Stage Company had just started a policy of doing new writing at the Royal Court, but that was almost the only place. I had student productions at first, and then wrote for radio. In the late sixties and early seventies there was a surge of fringe theaters and interest in new writing, starting with the Theatre Upstairs and the Royal Court, and that was the first place to do a professional stage production of one of my plays, *Owners*, in 1972. For a while, a lot of writers were getting produced for the first time, though far fewer women than men. Gradually during the seventies the number of women increased, coming partly through fringe theaters and partly through women's theater groups. In the last five years there seem to be far more women playwrights and some theaters are more open to them, though others still aren't. At the moment, because of the financial cuts, it's again become quite hard for all playwrights. Theaters are having to do co-productions with other theaters because they haven't enough money to do a whole year's work on their grants, so it means one new play gets done instead of two. The Royal Court, for instance, can now only afford to do four new plays in the main house instead of eight. But I get the impression life is even harder for playwrights in the United States than in England because of there not being a subsidized theater.

INTERVIEWER: In Laurie Stone's *Village Voice* interview [March 1, 1983], you talked about women becoming Coca-Cola executives and you said, "Well, that's not what I mean by feminism." What exactly do you mean by feminism?

CHURCHILL: When I was in the States in '79 I talked to some women who were saying how well things were going for women in America now with far more top executives being women, and I was struck by the difference between that and the feminism I was used to in England, which is far more closely connected with socialism. And that was one of the ideas behind writing *Top Girls*, that achieving things isn't necessarily good, it matters *what* you achieve.

Thatcher had just become prime minister; there was talk about whether it was an advance to have a woman prime minister if it was someone with policies like hers: She may be a woman but she isn't a sister, she may be a sister but she isn't a comrade. And, in fact, things have got much worse for women under Thatcher. So that's the context of that remark. I do find it hard to conceive of a right-wing feminism. Of course, socialism and feminism aren't synonymous, but I feel strongly about both and wouldn't be interested in a form of one that didn't include the other.

INTERVIEWER: Do you think it's odd, given the fact that there is at best indifference, at worst hostility, political plays in America, that your works are so popular here?

CHURCHILL: Is it true that on the whole plays here tend to be more family-centered, personal, individual-centered?

INTERVIEWER: Yes, more psychological.

CHURCHILL: Whereas I've been quite heavily exposed to a tradition of looking at the larger context of groups of people. It doesn't mean you don't look at families or individuals within that, but you are also looking at bigger things. Like with the kind of work Joint Stock Theatre Group has done, where you go and research a subject and where you have a lot of characters, even if played by only a few people. It tends to open things out.

INTERVIEWER: The critics do ask, "Where are the American plays with the larger social issues?" Unfortunately, when one comes along our own critics usually turn thumbs down if the politics are overt. An overt political position is considered poor craft or preaching.

CHURCHILL: When I was in San Francisco I was talking to the people at the Eureka Theatre [where Richard Seyd directed a production of *Cloud Nine* in 1983] and they were talking about developing a school of playwriting which would break away from family-centered plays, and write about other issues.

INTERVIEWER: Could you talk a little about working with Joint Stock?

CHURCHILL: I've worked with them three times, on *Light Shining in Buckinghamshire* [1976], *Cloud Nine* [1979] and *Fen* [1983]. The company was started in 1974 by several people, including Max Stafford-Clark, who directed *Light Shining* and *Cloud Nine*. There's usually a workshop of three or four weeks when the writer, director and actors research a subject, then about ten weeks when the writer goes off and writes the play, then a six-week rehearsal when you're usually finishing writing the play. Everyone's paid the same wage each week they're working and everyone makes decisions about the budget and the affairs of the company, and because of that responsibility and the workshop everyone is much more involved than usual in the final play. It's not perfect, but it is good, and I do notice the contrast with more hierarchical organizations and feel uncomfortable in them. Because everyone is involved it's taken for granted that everyone will have good parts, so you can't write a couple of main characters and give everyone else very little to do. And usually because of the subject matter, the plays tend to have a large cast of characters, although the company is about six or eight, and the actors double. It's very pressured because the tour's booked and the posters printed long before the play is finished. It's a very intense way of working.

INTERVIEWER: Do you find collaboration difficult?

CHURCHILL: No, I like it. I'd always been very solitary as a writer before and I like working that closely with other people. You don't collaborate on writing the play, you still go away and write it yourself, so to that extent it's the same as usual. What's different is that you've had a period of researching something together, not just information, but your attitudes to it, and possible ways of showing things, which means that when you come back with the writing you're much more open to suggestions.

INTERVIEWER: Do you feel subordinate to the director in rehearsal? One writer we interviewed was actually ejected from her rehearsals by a well-known director.

CHURCHILL: No, I've always got on well with directors. But it depends on having someone with roughly the same ideas as you so you trust each other, and if you do work well together you keep on with the same people, as I have with Max Stafford-Clark and Les Waters. It's one of the things the Theatre Writers' Union has put in contracts, the writer's right to attend rehearsals, and it's very important. Though, of course, if you're having to invoke the contract you're already in trouble.

INTERVIEWER: Does the playwright have an obligation to take a moral and political stance?

CHURCHILL: It's almost impossible not to take one, whether you intend to or not. Most plays can be looked at from a political perspective and have said something, even if it isn't what you set out to say. If you wrote a West End comedy relying on conventional sexist jokes, that's taking a moral and political stance, though the person who wrote it might say, "I was just writing an entertaining show." Whatever you do your point of view is going to show somewhere. It usually only gets noticed and called "political" if it's against the status quo. There are times when I feel I want to deal with immediate issues and times when I don't. I do like the stuff of theater, in the same way people who are painting like paint; and of course when you say "moral and political" that doesn't have to imply reaching people logically or overtly, because theater can reach people on all kinds of other levels too. Sometimes one side or the other is going to have more weight. Sometimes it's going to be about images, more like a dream to people, and sometimes it's going to be more like reading an article. And there's room for all that. But either way, the issues you feel strongly about are going to come through, and they're going to be a moral and political stance in some form. Sometimes more explicitly, sometimes less.

London
November 23, 1984

MANN: How do you go about gathering research?

CHURCHILL: *Fen* is the most documentary of the plays, I suppose. We didn't use tape recorders. We went off to stay in a village and everyone would go out each day and talk to people and make notes or remember. The actors in the group would report back by becoming the person they met and saying the things the person had said; you could ask more questions and the actor would start to improvise and develop the character. Those of us who weren't actors simply described what had happened. So I was left with a lot of notes and quotes and things different people had said. But never a whole speech, just lines here and there. And I didn't make any characters who were based on a single person. For example, the old great-grandmother's speech on her birthday, practically every line is something that somebody actually said to us, but it's a composite of many different people. We met a woman who had been the secretary of the agricultural union, and the murder story, the Frank and Val story, was a newspaper cutting about someone she knew. A lot of the union references in the play were hers. There were a lot of things from one particular woman that went into the character Shirley, who's always working, about pride in working hard and not giving up, lines like "I didn't want my mother to think she'd bred a gibber."

MANN: You and the company started out with subject matter, an idea?

CHURCHILL: We started out very open—we were going to do a workshop in the Fens. But before we went, Les Waters, the director, and I had talked a lot about people having a bad time in the country; that's where the original sense of direction came from. We made a company of more women than men, so that was a decision affecting the subject of the play that was taken before we began the workshop. We read the book *Fen Women* by Mary Chamberlain before we went and during the workshop. And by the end of the workshop we had all focused on women land workers and knew the kind of issues it might be about.

But the difference between that way of working and what you've done, Emily, is that mine is an invented play, whereas you've written documentary things drawing on tapes.

MANN: You were making a completely fictional play, based on what you learned, from your response to being in the Fens and meeting all those people. In *Execution of Justice* I was working with the Eureka Theatre Company, and we talked and talked and talked and batted ideas around, then they gathered research for me, and I went out to San Francisco and did field work in the Castro district, and so on. The play is documentary, yes; that was a choice I made.

CHURCHILL: The only documentary play I've done was a television play about Northern Ireland, about a trial in the Diplock courts, which were introduced in 1973 because the government felt it was too hard to get convictions otherwise. There's no jury and only one judge. I had the transcript of a trial of a boy who was given sixteen years. A bomb had been planted in a British Legion Hall where some people were playing cards, and a boy walked in, put the thing down, and said, "Clear the hall" and they all went out. Half an hour later, a small bomb went off and nobody was hurt. The trial was extraordinary because there was no evidence to say the boy who was accused did it, except the police saying he'd confessed, which he denied. There was no signed statement by him. And there was an old man who'd been in the hall who said, "I don't know what boy it was but it was definitely not *that* boy." There was no positive identification at all, and it was hard to believe you would get a conviction in a normal court. So I did a play for television with Roland Joffe; it meant reducing the nine and a half hours of trial transcript. We put on a voice-over at the beginning and end of the program that explained the Diplock courts, and the BBC took it off because they said it was political comment, and put one of their own in different words, which they said was objective. We took our names off the credits as a protest. That was the only documentary I've ever done, and again it's different from what you've done because it was more specific and didn't involve so much research or so much material. Most of the plays I've written have been without any research, from what I already knew or what I imagined.

MANN: Let's talk about your play *Top Girls* [Methuen, London, 1982].

CHURCHILL: When I wrote *Top Girls* I was writing it by myself and not for a company. I wanted to write about women doing different kinds of work and didn't feel I knew enough about it. Then I thought, this is ridiculous, if you were with a company you'd go out and talk to people, so I did. Which is how I came up with the employment agency in the second act.

MANN: Are there specific characters in *Top Girls* that have their real life counterparts?

CHURCHILL: Quite a few of the things Win tells Angie about her life are things different people said to me. And of course the dead women at the dinner are all based on someone [from art, literature or history]. But apart from that, it's imaginary.

MANN: Tell me about the ways in which *Top Girls* has been misunderstood.

CHURCHILL: What I was intending to do was make it first look as though it was celebrating the achievements of women and then—by showing the main character, Marlene, being successful in a very competitive, destructive, capitalist way—ask, what kind of achievement is that? The idea was that it would start out looking like a feminist play and turn into a socialist one, as well. And I think on the whole it's mostly been understood like that. A lot of people have latched on to Marlene leaving her child, which interestingly was something that came very late. Originally the idea was just that Marlene was "writing off" her niece, Angie, because she'd never make it; I didn't yet have the plot idea that Angie was actually Marlene's own child. Of course women are pressured to make choices between working and having children in a way that men aren't, so it *is* relevant, but it isn't the main point of it.

There's another thing that I've recently discovered with other productions of *Top Girls*. In Greece, for example, where fewer women go out to work, the attitude from some men seeing it was, apparently, that the women in the play who'd gone out to work weren't very nice, weren't happy, and they abandoned their children. They felt the play was obviously saying women *shouldn't* go out to work—they took it to mean what they were wanting to say about women themselves, which is depressing. Highly depressing. [laughter] Another example of its being open to misunderstanding was a production in Cologne, Germany, where the women characters were played as miserable and quarrelsome and competitive at the dinner, and the women in the office were neurotic and incapable. The waitress slunk about in a catsuit like a bunnygirl and Win changed her clothes on stage in the office. It just turned into a complete travesty of what it was supposed to be. So that's the sort of moment when you think you'd rather write novels, because the productions can't be changed.

MANN: I don't know whether we're safer in the theater or not. . . .

CHURCHILL: With a play you do leave more room for other things and that's one of the attractions, that people can keep coming to it fresh and doing it differently. Lots of times I've liked foreign productions. I liked *Cloud Nine* in New York, [at Lucille Lortel's Theater De Lys, directed by Tommy Tune, 1981] and it was very different, though in many ways it wasn't as different as you might have expected. I was at rehearsals and Tommy Tune had seen Max Stafford-Clark's production in London. But still it was different.

MANN: What were the big differences?

CHURCHILL: Two main differences. It was broader, so it was more farcical in the first act and more emotional in the second. Tommy [Tune] talked about "permission to laugh" and thought the American audience might not realize at the beginning of the play that it was meant to be funny if the colonial thing was played as straight as it had been in England. And the other difference—which ties in with the more emotional feeling of the second half—is the moving of Betty's monologue and the song to the end of the play, to make more of a climax. It was sort of wonderful—the emotion of the end of the play in the American production—but I didn't really like it as much because it threw so much emphasis onto Betty as an individual, while the other way seemed to be more about the development of a group of people, in the same way as the first act. The New York version also meant that it ended with her very solitary, having the self-discovery that she enjoys sex in masturbation, but without taking her on from that to anything else. Whereas that monologue originally came earlier in the scene so you know from that that she's a sexual person and then you see her make her first move out toward someone else, even though it's a completely ridiculous and wrong move, trying to pick up her son's gay lover, but you know she'll have another go another time and it will work.

MANN: This is incredible, how much this changes what the play is about. Was it Tommy Tune who changed it? Or did you agree to it?

CHURCHILL: Moving the monologue was an idea of Tommy's that he had when I wasn't there, but I was quite glad and interested to try it. And I knew he wanted very strongly to make more of a climax at the end of the play. In the original production there's a song before the last scene of the second act and it's as if during it things change, because in the last scene everyone has moved on a bit and things have got better. But Tommy felt having the music there would make people think that was the ending, because we had a sort of climax with the music and then the last scene where people had changed and it ended more levelly and coolly. He wanted a different song, more uplifting, whereas the original one was a bit more ironical, and he wanted the music and climax right at the end. So it had quite a different shape and feeling to it.

MANN: So the difference for you is Tommy Tune changed your structure and in so doing changed the broader-based contextual look at the whole society.

CHURCHILL: Yes, they took it more to an emotional, personal point. And I suppose we could then launch off into the idea that this is one of the differences between the kind of work that comes out of a company like Joint Stock, which tends to deal more with groups of people and society as opposed to the personal. . . .

MANN: Yes.

CHURCHILL: You find lots of works which are just about people and their feelings in England, too. It isn't as if everything here was socially based. But there is a stronger vein of that, in this country, I think.

ANNE COMMIRE

Anne Commire is the author of Shay *(published by Samuel French, 1980),* Put Them All Together *(published by Samuel French, 1982, and cited in* Best Plays of 1978–79, Dodd Mead, *ed. Otis L. Guernsey, Jr.) and* Melody Sisters. *Her plays have had productions at ACT in San Francisco, Playwrights Horizon and the WPA in New York City, The McCarter Theatre in Princeton and the L.A. Public Theatre, among other theaters. She has also had residencies at The Eugene O'Neill Theater Center National Playwrights Conference in Waterford, Conn. Ms. Commire has written for television and film as well as theater. She has received a CAPS Grant and a Rockefeller Grant (fulfilled by serving as playwright-in-residence at Yale University, 1980–81).*

INTERVIEWER: When were you first aware that you were gifted as a writer?

COMMIRE: When I was younger there were always two voices bumping around inside me. One said I'd conquer Kilimanjaro; the other was right behind it, a little giggle that said, "Who, you?" They've always been there. The first voice is proud that I've learned a craft—like cobbling shoes. You just cobble and cobble and find, in time, you get better. But I don't know about "gifted." The gift might be persistence.

I was a nonfinisher all my life. I'd start to paint a chair, finish an arm and get bored because I already knew what the other arm was going to look like. So I never finished the chair. Whereas playwriting taps everything. You don't know what the second act's going to look like. You can write plays the rest of your life and never totally know the secret of writing a play. I think we all have gifts. Maybe some of us are lucky enough to trip over them, and then, lucky enough to have the opportunity to pursue them. Or maybe you just have to be neurotic enough to pursue them in the face of a lot of "Don't bothers."

INTERVIEWER: When did you trip over your ability?

COMMIRE: In 1968. I'd never seen a play until I was twenty-one; then I started working at a theater, Meadowbrook. It was a bona fide Equity theater in the wilds of Michigan, run by refugees from the Royal Academy in London. I was wardrobe mistress. I'd always wanted to write. I'd done my share of short stories, my share of Dorothy Parkers, but I was never in control of the writing—it was in control of me. Whatever I set out to say came out like so much Swahili. The prose simply would not respond to my feelings. It was stilted; it didn't have flair. So, writing was just this glorified dream, way out of my reach, until I had the opportunity to listen to Chekhov every night on the greenroom squawk box. This felt like something I could control, or at least get a handle on.

I found it much easier to break down a play and make it less awesome. I had never learned how to make a short story less awesome—I think it had something to do with paragraph density. But a play was like poetry —a lot could be said with well-chosen words. Even if the play never quite said everything I wanted, there was always a feeling that if I worked on it long enough, I could lick it. Maybe that's why I do so many rewrites. A feeling that if I'm willing to go over it and over it, by sheer labor, I can get it right. If I'm willing to dig as deep as I can into that unknown interior, I'll find out what it is I'm trying to say. Much more fun than painting a chair.

INTERVIEWER: What was your first play?

COMMIRE: *Shay* [1972], about a woman who's afraid to go out of the house. It was written long before agoraphobia was ever heard of—at least, I'd never heard of it. Nor had my mother, the "partial agoraphobic" [in the play].

INTERVIEWER: You've directed *Shay* [1983] and *Melody Sisters* [1984] yourself at the L.A. Public Theatre. How do you feel when you're in the audience, when you've had that glorious experience of directing and writing? Do you sense the power that you have to move people?

COMMIRE: When I watch the climactic scene in *Put Them All To-gether* [1978], I don't feel like I wrote it. I watch the power of that scene and every night I get caught up along with the audience. Every night *I* stop breathing. There's an odd feeling that it was written *for* me. That the subconscious had a field day. Funny, if I have any pride in my writing, it's not in what I wrote. It's because I dare to write, dare to face my demons and that enormously frightening machine daily. After fifteen years, I still face that machine with fear. Dreading there'll be nothing there. Dreading that today I'll find out I don't have an original thought left in my brain, that I squandered it on postcards to friends.

INTERVIEWER: Why is it often said that people are more deeply affected by the theater than by film?

COMMIRE: It's the immediacy. TV and movies can't compete with a live audience, live actors. The audience contributes to the creation. It's a major ingredient to theater magic and has a highly underrated impact on the success or failure of a play on any given night. Unless two people see the same play on August twelfth or January twenty-sixth, they are discussing two different entities. Theater risks every night. It has the possibility of soaring in the air or landing on its ass. People come for the spectacle, for the danger. Some with holly in their hearts; some like spectators at the Colosseum, rooting for the lion.

You can sense an audience; they're either bubbly and cohesive or very disparate people who are too intimidated to laugh out loud, locked into their own cooking pouches. The latter are especially difficult for comedy. Three minutes into the show, the actor usually compensates for the lack of audible response by pushing: Subtlety's gone, and we're all headed for a disastrous evening. An audience walks in with a sense of community or they walk in very isolated.

INTERVIEWER: Is there a difference between an East Coast and a West Coast audience?

COMMIRE: There's a different kind of audience every night, wherever I've been. Some more sophisticated than others. The matinee ladies are great laughers but sometimes miss the point. I have a scene in *Put Them All Together* where a mother's only refuge from a hyperactive son is to go to the airport and scream under the sound of the jets. Two women walked out of a matinee in L.A. One said, "Why did she scream at the edge of that runway?" The other said, "I think she thought the plane was going to hit her."

INTERVIEWER: Do you believe there's a female aesthetic?

COMMIRE: I'm not sure exactly what you mean by that, so I'll just amble. One thing that hit me very strongly was women's response to the review Mel Gussow gave to *Put Them All Together* when it was done at the McCarter Theater Company in Princeton in 1979. He didn't review the play in terms of craft or narrative, he reviewed the topic. It was a play written from somewhere deep in my vitals about motherhood, an attempt to explore the enormity of the task, the frustration, the twenty-four-hour duty. Mariette Hartley played the lead, rehearsing with a five-month-old daughter in a Snugli on her back, because she believed so much in what the play was saying. And Gussow wrote, "Anne Commire has taken a serious subject—child abuse—and has written about it in a manner that could be described as antichildren and antimotherhood." ["Stage: McCarter Presents New Anne Commire Play," *The New York Times*, January 30, 1979].

A lot of women were very angry [at Gussow's review—Ed]. I mean *very* angry. I was too busy being stunned. A friend of mine, a lit teacher, called me; "I've spent my life being asked to understand and empathize with men in war, male impotence, male bonding and male balding. I haven't been handed much literature where I've been given the chance to identify with myself, my own needs." Gussow stopped the play from coming to New York with his review. So, in essence, it was censored out of town. My favorite letter was from Tina Howe, which said in part, "I don't know you and I don't know your play, but I feel I must reach out to you. . . ." [Howe commented that her experience with her own play *Birth and After Birth*, which she felt dealt with similar themes, impelled her to write to Commire.]

When I was little I was starving for information from women about women, I spent my entire youth reading. Talk about escape. The library was on the absolute other side of town—I lived at Twenty-third Street, and the library was on First. I would go there every Saturday, check out a book, and walk home reading, knowing instinctively where every curb was, barely looking down. I'm amazed I'm not a traffic statistic. I read Hemingway and Dostoevsky and Williams and Steinbeck. Wallowing. Sometimes I'd find an author like Carson McCullers and go nuts because I was so greedy for a woman's role in plain sight. Before, it had always been digging through and getting the leavings. Lady Brett was fascinating, as was Grushenka, but it was like playing telephone. Now I could read about F. Jasmine Adams and Kelly in *Lonely Hunter*. . . . I died and went to heaven. When I was about twenty-four, I was on a real kick, reading all the women I could get my hands on: [Flannery] O'Connor, [Eudora] Welty, Muriel Spark, Margaret Drabble, Shirley Ann Grau. I was working with a couple of women in a publishing firm—both Phi Betas—and could feel that my reading habits were making them question my intelligence level. They felt I had a problem: reading the lessers. There was an attitude that what I was reading was not heavy literature, that I was wasting my time, that maybe something was wrong with me that I had such a need to read these women writers. Fraternizing with B-movies and minor leagues. I was tempted to hide the books behind my hardcover Kafka—just as my mother hid her movie magazines.

INTERVIEWER: Is there a gender bias in theater criticism?

COMMIRE: We're being reviewed through male eyes or women with male-oriented eyes—women who want to "write like a man." It's not some great conspiracy. Most men are uncomfortable with a woman's mind. They're uncomfortable with all that emotional life, with that passivity. They don't want to know they have that much power over women. They don't want to know that their authority scares the hell out of us. Or if they know, they have contempt. Thurber's "war between men and women" has been going on in every restaurant and every boudoir for years. That frustrating attempt to understand each other, to scrutinize the inscrutable, to find a common meeting ground. We all know the chasm exists, and yet we ignore any discussion of it in conjunction with literary criticisms. We'd like to pretend it's not an issue between (man) critic and (woman) writer. Check out the male critic's relationship with Mom and you'll see a direct connection to his receptivity toward women's themes. Books have been written *ad infinitum* on male-female misunderstandings. Most of Hollywood's success is based on it. And yet we've never dealt with that on a level of male critic/female writer. We pretend that it's not even going on.

INTERVIEWER: What about female critics who come down hard on women's plays? Do you think they have to bend over backward to prove to male editors how "impartial" they are?

COMMIRE: The female critic who caters is not ignorant; she is deceitful. That's even hard to forgive. With the male critic it's delusional, but not deceitful.

INTERVIEWER: Would you want a world where only women critics criticize women's work?

COMMIRE: We don't need it. We just need everyone to admit that they may not be experts.

INTERVIEWER: In reviews of women's plays, one criticism crops up repeatedly: "Well, why didn't she just leave this man?" Isn't it a sociological/cultural fact rather than a craft problem that women tend to stay in bad relationships?

COMMIRE: Oh, God, don't get me started. I could write a textbook on this one: "I don't believe she'd stay with him." "I don't believe she wouldn't see a psychiatrist." "I don't believe she'd kill herself with her mother in the house." I love the arbiters of human behavior. *They* wouldn't behave that way; therefore the playwright's basic premise is wrong. A play I wrote about my mother was reviewed thus: "I don't believe a woman would act that way." The only thing you can do is sit there holding the newspaper and laugh—it's either that or cry. We are being told by someone with a totally different emotional life whether or not ours is valid. It's what I call the critic's ceiling. I can only go as high as their reality, their perspective.

When I wrote the screenplay for the autobiographical *I'm Dancing as Fast as I Can*—the first of many versions—one of the main problems in the book that every critic went after was, "I don't buy that she would stay with this guy. . . ." Thus the middle of the book was invalid. Okay? Well, the fact is, in real life, she did stay with him. So we'll start with that. I, in my finite wisdom, didn't blink over this peculiar behavior.

Because I knew *I* would have stayed, too. I'm going to make him better, right? I'm going to be so loving and so different and so forgiving from anyone he's ever been near he will undoubtedly change overnight or at least by next Thursday. It becomes obvious in the book that he's a psychopath. (See Karen Horney, chapter and verse.) The problem with many psychopaths is that they are charming. And even though there's violence beneath the surface, you don't see it most of the time. What woman's going to even admit to herself that it's there? And when it does surface, there is remorse and the ingratiating, "Oh my God, I didn't mean to do that, I love you dearly. Pass the toast." Well, any woman stays right in there toe-to-toe with that one, right? Maybe it's not Willy Loman, but it's just as tragic.

I get the same review over and over again on *Put Them All Together*: flawed but powerful. And the basic flaw, they say, is that Maggie doesn't reach out for psychiatric help. I've been told many times that I could get that criticism off my back if I'd send Maggie to a psychiatrist; but that, to me, would be the flaw. Most people in Michigan won't go to a psychiatrist until they run naked across the front lawn.

Most women are not Noras. They don't slam the door. Sometimes they're lucky if they work up enough aggression to burn the supper. It's a different psychology.

INTERVIEWER: Our experience and vision may require new forms, a redefining of action. But then can our work be called Drama with a capital *D*?

COMMIRE: First of all, I'm not railing because reviewers are saying I bore the audience, or I fail dramatically, or my plays do not engage. I rarely get reviews like that, but if I did I could do something about it— I could cut, I could rewrite, I could quicken the pace, restructure. But when I get the other kind my only option is to lie. It certainly has been tempting. It's Drama with a capital *D* if it can hold an audience. Period. And believe me, if the play is not honest, it generally won't hold an audience. Unless it is considered a trifle in the first place.

INTERVIEWER: In an earlier play, *Put Them All Together*, you used traditional structure, moving toward the inevitable act of violence that provides the climax, followed by denouement. The rewrite of your play *Melody Sisters* demonstrates that you're placing more faith in the subtlety of women's action now than in the past.

COMMIRE: I don't want to feel that I have to utilize the "male climax," in terms of a gun going off or a punch in the nose. I would love to capture something I once saw Maya Plisetskaya do in the Bolshoi Ballet's *Swan Lake*. The power of the stage to me was exemplified when that swan died and I saw *from the balcony* at the Masonic Temple in Detroit—which is about twenty-eight miles from the stage—her wrist flick. Just that. In the power of that moment, I became addicted to theater. Minimalism. That's the direction I'd love to go in. That's what Athol [Fugard] did in *Master Harold and the Boys*. The power of that ballroom dancing scene! And the moment when Zakes Mokae pulls down his pants to show his "black ass," the climax of the play. What mastery Athol has to take you to that. Nobody got killed. He just pulled down his pants. And the audience wept for this man in that moment. That's brilliance.

INTERVIEWER: All due respect to Fugard's brilliance . . . But he *is* living in that South African culture where the issues are so much more severe and clear-cut. Isn't it dramatically easier for him to write a simple powerful play when he has the cultural given of world-acknowledged injustice and racism?

COMMIRE: He does have "the advantage" of South Africa, but for a different reason, I feel. It gives his plays distance. That distance, that exoticness, helps him enormously. Just as Southern Gothic writers have that distance. Tennessee Williams has that touch of the exotic. Because you're not dealing with as much cliché in dialogue. I played with phrasing in *Melody Sisters* much more than I did with *Shay*. Midwestern speech is *so* clichéd. I try to decide which colloquialisms I dare choose and which ones are going to look like bad writing.

INTERVIEWER: Were there any difficulties writing *Melody Sisters*? I know it was based somewhat on your own mother and her five sisters. Did you find that your ear had a good "memory"?

COMMIRE: Dead on. I hadn't seen my aunts for about fifteen years, but when my mother read an early draft, she said, "Why are you writing this? If Rowe sees this she's gonna think that I've been telling you." [Laughter] The same thing happened with *Shay*. There'd be whole sections, my mother'd say, "How did you know that?" I'd say, "I made it up." "No, you didn't." That subconscious is very busy. I drifted so far away from my family, and I'm realizing that I did adore them because they had such a sense of fun, a sense of silliness, a sense of wit. It's my love poem, I think.

INTERVIEWER: Ionesco has said there is nothing left to write about but the dream. Does dreaming play a role in your work?

COMMIRE: Absolutely. Literally as well as figuratively. When I first started *Shay* I would have a dream every night. It was of a painting, a portrait of someone sitting in a chair; but my focus was totally on its hand. And I was in the dream, standing outside the painting with a brush. And I was painting that hand, for hours. Shading it, stroking it, making it perfect. It was such a strong dream. Maybe that's what I was trying to say earlier about finally deciding playwriting was for me, because it was the only time I felt in control of making that hand as perfect as I could make it, whereas with other forms I felt I couldn't do that.

INTERVIEWER: That leads into the question of stage timing. You've said, as a director/writer, that timing is equally as important to you as text interpretation.

COMMIRE: It's what it's all about. If an actor has the timing, if he has the nuance, he understands the text. I know I join a long list of writers who think in terms of orchestration, in terms of music, while writing a scene, an act, a play. I think that's why I prefer to direct my own work.

INTERVIEWER: Will you talk a bit about the Eugene O'Neill National Playwrights Conference in Waterford, Connecticut?

COMMIRE: I love the O'Neill. It's the most painful place in the world. But that's because of the intensity of the experience. Each playwright has his/her week in the spotlight: open rehearsals, open discussions, meetings with directors, meetings with dramaturgs, meetings with actors. The play's presented. There is enormous support from fellow playwrights who have or are about to go through the same experience. All very heady. And leading it all, George White and Lloyd Richards, continually experimenting, enlarging. It's fun to watch the growth . . . like a child tying its shoes for the first time. No pretensions, no claims. Some of it works, some of it doesn't. No apologies. (Do you know how much that can infuriate some people?) I don't know how long it would have taken to get a foot in the theater world without the O'Neill. If ever. I love the support, the community, the friends made, the feeling that I can take myself seriously, which is very important, especially for a woman writer. We always feel we should be defrosting the refrigerator.

INTERVIEWER: You've been invited back three times now. Is each experience different?

COMMIRE: Very different. The first time, you don't even know who you are, or why you're there. I remember saying to [playwright] Frank Gagliano, "I don't know what the hell I'm doing here. My play is flawed." And Frank said, "So is *King Lear*." If you think I haven't used *that* to keep me going. . . . The second time, you're a little cockier. The third time, age and experience have weathered you. Back to humble.

INTERVIEWER: Does a playwright have an obligation to society?

COMMIRE: Yes. Not to bore it. That'll probably come back to haunt me some day.

INTERVIEWER: Do you mind being called a woman writer?

COMMIRE: Depends on the tone of voice.

INTERVIEWER: You have recently spent two years nursing a friend through a terminal illness. What difference has this made to your writing, your outlook on life?

COMMIRE: I watched my young friend, who had spent her life in television, trying to crack that exclusive male prime-time directors' club. There are only a handful of women directing in nighttime television. She'd directed soaps, she'd directed theater, she'd directed at the O'Neill, and she was good. The call finally came when we were in Houston at the cancer center. It wasn't for just another interview, just another carrot possibility—it was an offer to direct a nighttime show. An absolute offer. For one brief second I saw her excitement and then I had to listen to her turn it down, a job she had coveted for years. Because, at this point, she could hardly walk around the block.

I know that sharing that illness, sharing that death, is going to have a major effect on my writing. I don't know exactly in what way. I know that my priorities are different. That fact alone has to have an impact. What I deem important is different.

INTERVIEWER: What's important now that wasn't before?

COMMIRE: You're aware of the jetsam when you're dealing with death. Things that looked like "have to's" aren't. I don't know how to explain it. One is certainly more aware of love, and the depths of that emotion. Maybe that's where *Melody Sisters* comes from. It's fascinating to me that *Melody Sisters*—basically a loving look at a family—was written in hospitals, hotel rooms and chemotherapy wards. And it's the lightest, funniest play I've ever written.

GRETCHEN CRYER

*retchen Cryer was born October
16, 1935 in Indianapolis, Indiana. With composer Nancy Ford, Cryer
has written the musicals* Now Is the Time for All Good Men, The Last
Sweet Days of Isaac, Shelter, I'm Getting My Act Together and Taking
It on the Road, *and* Hanging On to the Good Times. The Last Sweet
Days of Isaac *won the Obie Award for Best Musical and the Outer Critics'
Circle Award in 1970. Cryer and Ford have recorded two albums of their
songs on the RCA label. In progress is a musical about Eleanor Roosevelt.
Ms. Cryer has three children, Rachel, Jon and Shelly.*

CRYER: I grew up in the country in Indiana, outside a town of two hundred
people. It was a very rural nineteenth-century area. There wasn't even
electricity in many of the homes; there were outhouses out back. It was
a primitive farming community with no cultural activities whatsoever. I
didn't see any professional theater. I actually wrote my first musical
without ever having seen one. Then I started working as a chorus girl in
theater the summer I turned nineteen, so I was suddenly inundated with
the live theater whereas before I'd had no experience with the arts at all.

INTERVIEWER: Is this where you met your collaborator, Nancy Ford?

CRYER: Yes, we were living in the same dormitory as freshmen at
DePauw University. By the time we had finished college and graduate
school we had written and produced three complete musicals. This opportunity was invaluable.

INTERVIEWER: What did you study in graduate school?

CRYER: I went to Harvard and studied English literature, but I was
also getting a teaching degree because I was going to be an English
teacher. Nancy and I had both married men who were going to become
ministers. So first both of us went, as wives, to Yale Divinity School.
While our husbands were going to school, Nancy and I worked as sec-
retaries right down the hall from each other in a chemical corporation.
And we kept writing together at night and on weekends.

INTERVIEWER: So you both put your husbands through college?

CRYER: Yes. Then both husbands decided not to go into the ministry and both decided to go into theater and both decided to go to school in Boston. So we all put our stuff together in a U-Haul truck and drove to Boston. It was at that point that I went to Harvard and then taught for a year because even though Nancy and I were writing at this time, we weren't considering the professional possibilities of our writing. It was kind of a hobby.

INTERVIEWER: How did the hobby turn into a career?

CRYER: We moved to New York after our husbands finished graduate school. I started working as a chorus girl on Broadway and began having babies while Nancy and I continued writing in our spare time. It took us five years to get our first professional show, *Now Is the Time for All Good Men*, produced [1967, Theater DeLys]. It was about a pacifist in Indiana, a teacher who gets thrown out of his job in a small town because of his political beliefs. I had been a teacher in my home state, so I was writing *exactly* out of my experience. As a matter of fact, at the same time that our show opened, there was a newspaper article about a teacher in Indiana who had been run out of a school for being a conscientious objector during the days of the Vietnam War. I clipped it out of the paper because I knew that New Yorkers didn't realize the frame of mind that still existed out there in the Midwest. The characters I wrote were straight out of my hometown. I put that actual dialogue up on the stage—things that came out of the mouths of people I knew in Indiana in the sixties. Critic Clive Barnes [*New York Times*, September 27, 1967] did not find the situation credible, but I think I knew that part of the country better than he.

INTERVIEWER: Do you think there may be a double standard at work in the media criticism? A different vocabulary used to review women's plays from that used for men's?

CRYER: Perhaps, although that problem did not figure in the *Now Is the Time* criticism. I think what happens with critics is that they have absorbed the dominant sensibility of the culture, which is primarily male. I've been reading a lot of history about the Depression and World War II while researching my Eleanor Roosevelt show. I've suddenly become overwhelmed with the fact that it's all about *men* and their doings. Franklin D. Roosevelt's first inaugural speech goes something like this: "What do the people of America want more than anything else? They want two things: work, with all the moral and spiritual values that go with it; and, with that work, a reasonable measure of security for themselves and for their wives and children." Okay, what have we got there? That the American *people* are *men* . . . who have the wives and the children.

When he said "What do the American *people* want?" he meant, "What do the MEN want?"

The language is so permeated, the messages so pervasive and so much a part of the culture that one doesn't even notice. The values we've absorbed are male-dominated values which are considered THE universal values. If a woman is writing from her own point of view, she is outside the culture. She is counterculture, a revolutionary, by definition; her point of view is from outside the system—unless she has absorbed a male sensibility. I must say there are a lot of women writers and playwrights who have adopted a male sensibility and therefore have adopted those values. But if you are a woman who does *not* accept those values, who, for example, may perceive as comic a certain kind of male behavior which is taken very seriously by men . . . then that's going to irritate a male critic because, on a gut level, he's going to feel *his* values are being laughed at. That definitely happened with *I'm Getting My Act Together and Taking It on the Road* [1978, N.Y. Shakespeare Festival]. When the show opened, the temper of the times was such that male critics were irritated by what it was all about. I think times have changed enough now that the play doesn't get as hostile a reaction from men as it did in 1978. But that's the danger, that's the risk women take if they write from an authentic point of view. Their subjects are going to be dismissed as being of secondary import; their subjects are not considered *universal*. Universal subjects are male. We may be accused of writing kitchen drama or soap operas.

Take the movie *Rocky*. Yes, it was exciting. It was about a man struggling to overcome great odds and finally going the distance. It was called "universal." If you write about a woman struggling to overcome great odds and finally going the distance, it's going to be called "feminist."

INTERVIEWER: Several critics complained that your male character, the manager, in *I'm Getting My Act Together* was no match for the female lead in terms of wit and strength. Many wondered why you, the playwright, had bothered to present the manager on stage at all. What upset them?

CRYER: I think they resented the nature of the male character's weakness and confusion—because he verbalized long-held male assumptions of privilege and rights that are emotionally felt by man as innate, inalienable. When the character was brought into headlong conflict with the female character, his assumptions seemed comic; and some men, some male critics, resent those assumptions being made fun of. That male character was a composite of a number of men I know. And he wasn't *all* that exaggerated. It was a man actually coming out and saying exactly how he felt about the relationship between men and women, verbalizing attitudes that are prevalent. Many men have *intellectually* accepted the idea of women's equality and say, "Well, of course women should be equal! That issue has become passé." But *emotionally* they're still back in the fifties and will not admit it because, *in theory*, they really believe women should be on an equal footing. But it's still hard for them to accept what equality means in the real world, emotionally. If a woman picks up the check at dinner, should that make them feel castrated or powerless? I've read all these articles recently about men who are now taking over some of the care of their children. The tone is definitely self-congratulatory. You'd think they should get a medal of honor. But let's face it, in the real world, equality may mean that a man takes care of the kids.

On the surface, we may have solved a lot of problems—people get pretty much equal pay for equal work. But on the gut issues of power and dominance, if women don't pay attention, gradually we may drift back to the old patterns without even realizing. Especially right now with a president like Reagan who insists that he believes in equality and behaves otherwise.

INTERVIEWER: Do you think there'll come a time when women's plays are better understood? And what can we do to improve their public interpretation?

CRYER: I don't know. In the past, I've used humor. *I'm Getting My Act Together* was very funny. After it had gained acceptance, people were able to sit back, relax and laugh. Even the men were able to laugh at themselves.

INTERVIEWER: What about the common complaint from the media that many women's plays are "non-plays."

CRYER: I haven't read as much criticism as you have. But take David Mamet . . . a wonderful writer. *Glengarry, Glen Ross* is a fantastic play . . . about realtors. It has been reviewed as universal, a struggle for primacy. Now, if we wrote about women hairdressers it would not be seen as primal. Three hairdressers competing would be called trivial one-upmanship, not a primal struggle. Media interpretation gives male playwrights the benefit of the doubt.

INTERVIEWER: Let's get back, for a moment, to your statement that women are now getting equal pay for equal work. In fact, they are not. Things have changed less than the dominant culture claims. Isn't it true that women still earn only 63 cents to the male dollar?

CRYER: Well, I know. The dominant culture says, okay, the battles are won, everything's fine, everything's equalized. I'm on the Dramatists' Guild Council and there are thirty-five members. When I was first elected, in 1974, there were four women members. Now, I think there are seven.

Marsha Norman was just elected, but still the numbers are imbalanced. I remember what the late [playwright and theater personality] Dore Schary said, about six or seven years ago: When I proposed that we start a committee for women in the Dramatists' Guild, Dore said, "What for? If women wanted to write, they'd do it." There was a lot of opposition to the idea on the council, originally. There isn't a committee for men at the Guild, after all. But the reason is, men already have the role models. At that time, we didn't even know why there weren't many women playwrights. Part of the reason for creating the Committee for Women was to investigate why there were so few women writing plays. Were they out there without our knowledge? If so, did they not know how to channel their work to get it seen? If they weren't out there, was it because there have been so few women playwrights in the past, that young women were not even thinking, when in college, of playwriting as a career?

There was a study done in the seventies that found in American federally funded regional theaters, only 7 percent of all the plays produced were written by women and only 7 percent of plays produced were directed by women. A few years ago, we were thinking of bringing a legal case against inequitable spending of federal funds but the following year, Reagan slashed the arts budget so there was no just way to pursue our own grievances when we were faced with the fight for *all* arts appropriations. There wasn't time to talk about affirmative action when the very life blood of the arts was being cut off.

INTERVIEWER: Was the gathering of statistics the main goal of the Women's Committee initially?

CRYER: Not specifically. It was to nurture women playwrights, to see what their needs were, to provide a basis for networking. We have about thirty or forty women coming to meetings now. And, more and more, they are starting to report productions of their work. Granted, it's often on a workshop level but that's a start.

INTERVIEWER: It would be interesting to compare the creative productivity of single, childless women dramatists to the output of women dramatists with families . . .

CRYER: The writer who has children is usually primarily consumed with being a mother. She is able to pursue a writing career at home if someone else—a husband, for example—is supporting the family. But if she is struggling for money, a woman can hardly justify sitting at home writing a play, if family survival dictates a second income. If she is a single parent, as I have been for the last twelve years, the struggle is even more difficult. There are a few playwrights who have husbands who are essentially patrons of the arts, husbands who support their initial efforts until they are established. But even so, there's always the problem of women having to spend their creative energy on the children and home. It means your output isn't going to be as great. I noticed an incredible difference the first year I had my kids out of the house and off in college. I've been able to focus on my work in a way that was never possible during the last twenty years. I've written a whole musical in five months! It's been fantastic. On the other hand, you find your experience has definitely deepened from having children. That's the positive part of it; the negative part is—compared to a man's life—you've been at home. Therefore, you're probably going to write about cloistered subjects . . . and then get criticized for writing kitchen drama. But still, there is a knowledge that comes from that experience. A lot of women who are just getting going as playwrights are perhaps in their mid-thirties . . . or over forty. And they consider themselves beginners. *I* feel like I'm just beginning. Yes, I've had a lot of work produced but after going through this last year's work experience . . . a whole new world is opening up.

INTERVIEWER: Is there any truth to the charge that women's committees in the theater world are network happy and so production oriented that there is little discussion of craft, or the development of new theories of the drama?

CRYER: In the Dramatists' Guild, there *have* been many symposia on the craft. Now, if you're talking about women dealing with craft in some different way than men, then that's another matter. Actually, we've had a symposium about that, too: whether or not there is a difference in sensibility between men and women writers that then influences the form their work takes.

INTERVIEWER: Is there a female aesthetic?

CRYER: I think, yes. The "well-made" play deals with certain structures which have to do with "building" conflicts, working to a climax, an orgasm. I think that women don't *necessarily* feel that a theatrical experience *has* to take that form. In film, adventure, action chases and that sort of thing seems to belong to a masculine aesthetic—a way of seeing the world. I don't feel life as a big chase or gun battle. If a woman is to write about what interests her, chances are she will not write about high adventure in the Andes.

INTERVIEWER: What if she *wants* to write about high adventure in the Andes?

CRYER: Then I hope that she would write it from an authentic point of view—not as a woman merely reflecting the values of a male-dominated society.

INTERVIEWER: You've said you're more interested in raising questions with your plays than resolving problems or providing solutions. When you start to work on a script, do you have the feeling of setting out on a quest?

CRYER: There's always a working through of some sort. *I'm Getting My Act Together* . . . was a kind of personal odyssey. The Eleanor Roosevelt piece is asking many questions that have to do with a powerful woman married to a powerful man. The ways in which Eleanor began to feel her own power happened in about three stages: Her husband had an affair that completely shattered her—to the point that she no longer cared to defer to him. Before that she'd been the mommy of six kids, intent on being the good wife of a young political hopeful. A divorce would have cut him off from his mother's money and ruined his political possibilities. Eleanor wasn't willing to damage Franklin's career. They made a deal, decided to stay together, but she wouldn't sleep with him after that. I think she loved him—probably always—but she no longer owed him anything. Two years later, he got polio. She had to go out and become his legs, eyes and ears all over the country . . . keeping his name alive politically. She became assertive *for him* and in doing so, gained her own power. Then, in 1945, during his presidency, he died. For the next fifteen years of her life, she made incredible contributions nationally and internationally. So you see, he had to betray her to set her free, had to become crippled to set her free, and finally had to die to set her free. But is that what it takes for a talented woman to truly come into her own power? That's a sad commentary, isn't it? That her potential could only be realized through his tragedy? But that's the way it was for her.

INTERVIEWER: Why is it that many women playwrights find it difficult to write about mother/daughter subject matter?

CRYER: I didn't know that women *were* finding it difficult.

INTERVIEWER: That's what we're hearing. . . .

CRYER: I haven't written a mother/daughter play. I haven't even thought about it. I've thought about my *whole family* situation. I'm sure I've got a lot of unresolved stuff hanging around about my own mother. I kind of closed her off, emotionally. She seemed to be very unhappy, so I identified with my very brilliant father instead.

INTERVIEWER: Do you mind being called a woman playwright?

CRYER: I haven't heard anyone call me that. But yes, it would bother me a bit.

INTERVIEWER: Do you have any objections to being called a feminist writer?

CRYER: No. I am a feminist; but I am not just a feminist. I consider feminism as part of a humanistic point of view. In other words, I'm not just speaking about women's concerns. I'm thinking about all of our concerns. I know there's no way that men can be whole unless women are, too. As long as men can shove off the nurturing on to women, they can assert, "Well, that's taken care of, I've got a wife to do that. I can go off now and fight gun battles and do car chases." Until men learn that nurturing is all part of the human condition, and that they have an equal responsibility to share in it, they are going to be stuck with their wars. So, it's in the interest of the human race that I'm interested in women.

In fact, it upsets me a great deal when women become separatists and, for political reasons, shove men out of the picture. Yes, you can say, "Okay, it would be so much easier to become homosexual," but I think if one is becoming homosexual for political reasons, that is an ego out. The severest problems lie in the area of heterosexual relationships. I remember the Wednesday-night discussion periods after *I'm Getting My Act Together* . . . a woman in the audience asked a question, "I don't understand why, in your play, you don't talk about women's relationships with women." I said, "Well there are scenes with women talking together but yes, they are talking about men." And she replied, "Well, we all know that you've had a lifelong relationship with Nancy Ford and so I don't understand why you aren't writing about women's relationships with women." I told her that a) I am heterosexual; and b) my concern has to do with sexual politics, with the relationships of men and women. This woman obviously was saying that one answer is for women to be just with women—that'll solve the problem. That doesn't solve it. Yes, perhaps for a little while; you *could* go off and have your female world where you could work and be just fine. But meanwhile the male population is still going to shoot things up. So what good is it to have your little female utopia? I think it's wonderful comical timing that women are now able to control their biological childbearing role, that they are getting out into the world to use their nurturing sensibility *just at a point* where we're really needing it. It's lucky happenstance that women's liberation came along just when it did so that women can participate in the world arena and rescue the planet. Just in the nick of time.

INTERVIEWER: Karen Malpede, American playwright, recently organized her students at Smith College to present dramatic work which dealt with their feelings about nuclear war. Her students' dream journals revealed that women are plagued with nightmares about nuclear holocaust.

CRYER: It's not only nuclear holocaust—though that is a very real and present danger—but the destruction of the ecological balance which comes directly from macho competition and the attitude of "I'm getting it for me and to hell with whether I will leave the world plundered behind me." You see, we have to think in terms of people being in a symbiotic relationship with the earth and nature and that is the important work that women are going to have to take care of. The male tendency is not in that direction. In the interest of "Defense" men tend to build more missile factories and more bombs. Of course I'm generalizing here because certainly there are many individual men who are working for world peace and some women, like Mrs. Thatcher, who are hawks.

INTERVIEWER: When you were having these Wednesday night discussions after *I'm Getting My Act Together*, did the men in the audience have any difficulty empathizing with a central female character?

CRYER: No. A lot of men identified with her, but were also able to admit they had the same attitudes as the male character. It was very touching sometimes; they would first deny it. One guy said he thought this was the most absurd character he'd ever seen. Three days later, we received his picture in the mail with a letter saying, "On second thought, I've decided I'm just like the guy in the play—and I want to audition for the part."

INTERVIEWER: I'm interested in how *you* felt in those open forums. You must have known how vulnerable the material was to criticism, as you were directly addressing the "battle of the sexes."

CRYER: Well, yes. But the audience response had been so positive up to opening night that I had no idea what was in store for us from the critics . . . no idea of the hostility the critics would show.

INTERVIEWER: How did you deal with it?

CRYER: At first I was crushed because I thought that meant the show would close. Then [New York Shakespeare Festival artistic director] Joe Papp—you know, he always loves to beat our critics—decided there was an audience for it and was going to keep it going. Two weeks later, when Walter Kerr's review came out saying how obnoxious and determined to look ugly I was (in the lead role) and how he hated my hair ["She also, quite deliberately, looks terrible. Asked what she has done to her hair, she replies, 'I just let it go, this is the way it is,' and the way it is is kinky-curly and, I would say, messy," *The New York Times*, July 9, 1978], the audiences—which had been good and strong anyway—were packing the house. That review was so personal! You never get descriptions of a male actor's physical looks in a review. I got up Sunday morning, read it, laughed, threw it on the floor and went back to sleep. The show played for six more weeks, then moved to another theater and ran for three years. We beat the critics . . . an interesting experience because they usually hold all the power. Mind you, the women critics hated it, too.

INTERVIEWER: In the smaller presses, there were one or two women who gave it an intelligent critique.

CRYER: Having a woman critic doesn't necessarily guarantee that you are going to get an authentic female perspective. Many of them, for survival's sake, have absorbed the male point of view.

INTERVIEWER: Aside from turning the audience away, do you feel that vicious reviews take a deep, personal toll on the artist?

CRYER: Of course! Of course, they do. a) You don't make a living. b) You have been publicly humiliated without recourse.

INTERVIEWER: But you kept on working. . . . What is your writer's routine like?

CRYER: Working on *Eleanor Roosevelt* has been unlike any other creative event in my life because it's a very different story now that the kids are gone. I work at my own rhythms. I get up at seven-thirty or eight A.M. and go out to a diner for breakfast because the fresh air wakes my head up. I start working at nine A.M. or so and work straight through— maybe just a bite of apple for lunch—until late afternoon when I go to the gym to work out for a couple of hours. I've found, after sitting, one really needs exercise. Then I wander the streets, have dinner and come back for work . . . go to bed at ten or eleven. In the past, my writing has been very limited: kids off to school, groceries, the house, laundry. Maybe I would get three hours writing a day in while the kids were out.

INTERVIEWER: When you are writing the book and lyrics for a musical do you work separately from Nancy Ford, the composer?

CRYER: Yes. After I finish a scene and lyrics, I give it to her. Then she works by herself. She shows the settings to me, then we talk and agree upon whether we like them or not. If I have reservations, she goes back and changes things. Sometimes she needs me to rewrite. But we work separately most of the time.

INTERVIEWER: Do you have a sense of yourself in the history of musical writing?

CRYER: I don't think of myself as a force. I've tried to be very original in my conceptions. I haven't written a conventionally formed musical since *Now Is the Time for All Good Men*—that was a traditional Rodgers and Hammerstein–type musical. In *The Last Sweet Days of Isaac* [1970], I was expanding the form. In all my work I've searched for different ways to use the musical form. In *Getting My Act Together*, what we've got is a *play* punctuated by a singer rehearsing the songs in her act. Those songs then take in a whole other level of reality. Very seldom have I written sung dialogue. I rebel at the idea that the book of a musical has to be less literate than a dramatic script. The conventional restriction is that you can't write real characters or naturalistic dialogue because if it's too real and naturalistic, the characters won't be able to leap into song. I've always known that I've been breaking rules, searching for other forms for the musical. Nobody has recognized that I'm doing that.

INTERVIEWER: The critics didn't credit you with *consciously* going after new form?

CRYER: In *Getting My Act Together*, the critics weren't looking at the form. They were mainly irritated by the content. They weren't concerned with craft, but with—as I've said—how unattractive my hair was.

INTERVIEWER: What inspired *The Last Sweet Days of Isaac*?

CRYER: Marshall McLuhan's *Understanding Media* got me thinking. Especially the second half of *Isaac* reflects McLuhan's influence. It deals with what happens to a person when she/he starts confusing the image with the thing itself. Ultimately, my message in *Isaac*, was that one's humanity is diminished in direct proportion to the extent to which she/he relates to once-removed images as if they were the things themselves. . . . *Isaac* had to do with the change in human sensibility from the primitive one where there was direct contact—one-to-one with a person or object—to the present society which deals with images as if they are the real thing. The critics never picked up on that one either. I got wonderful reviews and everybody thought it was hilarious but nobody took note of *what* I was writing *about*.

INTERVIEWER: Of the political implications of *Isaac*?

CRYER: Yes. Although, Martin Gottfried gave me more credit than I actually was due, saying that surely I was influenced by the work of Frank Stella's paintings because I'd juxtaposed very bold, primary images. I didn't even know Stella's work at the time.

INTERVIEWER: What were your artistic intentions with *Shelter* [1973]?

CRYER: That piece is about self-delusion. About a man building a structure of self-delusion. The man lives on a set in a TV studio with his best friend, a computer with whom he can program his entire environment. I wrote this in the early seventies before people had home computers. The central idea was that this guy could program his whole environment, pretend it was real. The main character is a TV writer who composes jingles for commercials. He's living on the set where they film commercials. The set has a living room, a bathroom and a kitchen that he treats as if it was his real home. He has a wife and kids out in the country and he has these illusions that he's a great husband and father. But he never goes home. An actress on the set falls in love with him and gets seduced into his world. She gradually starts treating the set as if it is a real home. Ultimately, she realizes that the relationship is not real and gets out. The critics didn't pick up on that one either. Maybe because it was a musical and people didn't look for much meaning in musicals.

INTERVIEWER: If you had not met Nancy Ford, do you think you'd be writing musicals?

CRYER: I doubt it. If I'd written anything, it probably would've been straight plays. I don't know what I'd be doing. I might still be an English teacher. I don't think I would have started writing lyrics. *That*, I'm sure, is directly because I knew Nancy. We just naturally collaborated.

INTERVIEWER: Does Nancy share the rehearsal process with you?

CRYER: Yes, she does. She works on the music, and of course, makes suggestions for the writing—the books and lyrics. Conversely, I can make suggestions about the music. We don't just stick to our own territory, although each of us has the final say in our particular area: she on the music and myself on questions about the book.

INTERVIEWER: If there is a disagreement with the director—if, for example, your intentions are not being realized on stage—do you and Nancy stick together?

CRYER: Yes. We nearly always have united creative opinions. But, there again, we have worked together since we were eighteen years old. Let me think! That's about thirty years.

INTERVIEWER: Any desire to write without music?

CRYER: I probably will. I might try straight drama sometime.

INTERVIEWER: Whom do you most admire among your contemporaries?

CRYER: Marsha Norman, David Mamet, [Sam] Shepard, [Tom] Stoppard, [Stephen] Sondheim and several others.

INTERVIEWER: Tell us about your new play.

CRYER: About four years ago, Nancy Ford and I wrote the songs for the book of a musical based on the life of Eleanor Roosevelt. The book turned out to be a very conventional linear approach to the story. And we didn't feel committed to it. We broke off our relationship to the guy who wrote that book and I decided I wanted to write it myself. So that's what I've done and I've taken a radically different approach. Except for four songs that we were able to keep, we simply junked the whole show for a totally new concept.

INTERVIEWER: Do you think women write from a different perspective than men?

CRYER: Well, I felt strongly that the way the male writer of the original book saw Eleanor was very external. It was based completely on the historic facts. There wasn't any effort to really get under her skin and discover what she must have been *feeling*. You just saw her as this sort of Victorian, uptight, do-gooder who had a highly moral sense of life and exerted her influence when she could. It wasn't meaty, it wasn't juicy. You couldn't connect with this character at all. So I've attempted to really get into her bloodstream.

INTERVIEWER: Did you read her journals?

CRYER: Letters. She wrote between a dozen and twenty every night. She was very passionate, so affectionate to her close friends. This is quite a different picture from that stately lady we get from the average history book. The new book is written from this perspective: There is a hundredth birthday party for her thrown by her cousin, Alice Roosevelt Longworth, after all the characters are dead. It is a gathering of their spirit selves, a settling of scores between Eleanor and Franklin and the close friends who made a difference in her life. One of the dramatic elements of the birthday party is that Albert Einstein has been invited, and he's discovered how to juxtapose moments from the past to the present. He's brought this discovery with him as a birthday surprise. He can just flash back and cut from the past into certain moments. Suddenly, at any point on stage, a moment from the past can materialize. But Einstein can't control all this very well, so sometimes there are embarrassing episodes. Gradually, you get the whole story of what she did and who she was through this device of Einstein's. It's almost cinematic.

INTERVIEWER: Do you have any desire to direct your own work?

CRYER: I'm not a director.

INTERVIEWER: Several women playwrights, Anne Commire for instance, are beginning to direct their own work. Irene Fornes and Emily Mann, among others, have directed their own work for years.

CRYER: Well, I'm overcome by the technicalities; there's no question about that. I don't know the technical side of theater. I never went to drama school.

INTERVIEWER: Couldn't you depend on a skilled crew for the technical help? Playwrights have told us that directing your first play is hard but after that, you become addicted to it.

CRYER: I can imagine getting addicted to it, if I ever once overcame the fear, because, you know, there are problems in the collaborative process. I think if I had the know-how, I would really like to direct. I haven't quite got the courage.

INTERVIEWER: Do we have to stop being "nice girls" in rehearsal?

CRYER: There is a certain value in encouraging people in a positive way, rather than in a negative sense, in order to get the best out of everyone. But you don't always know at what point you must stop being "positive" and "encouraging" and say: "No! That simply isn't right. You'll have to do something else." I know the value of positive reinforcement because I was a schoolteacher, initially. But at what point do you start putting your foot down? It's very delicate.

INTERVIEWER: When you are not acting in your own work, do you go to rehearsals daily?

CRYER: Yes, always.

INTERVIEWER: And do you sit behind the director?

CRYER: Yes. I've worked mostly with Word Baker. He and I have a very good relationship. It really is a matter of sitting behind him. It's been hard sometimes in the past, because when I performed in my own plays, I assumed the roles of both actress and writer. It was difficult to know whether to give notes directly to the actors or to the stage manager or go through the director. . . .

INTERVIEWER: Would you prefer to be allowed to talk directly to actors?

CRYER: Well, of course. I would like to be able to do that but that's stepping into the director's territory. He or she can't have control if the writer is going around talking to actors. You can't do that. And sometimes a director can bring a whole new slant to a play, something the writer may not have thought of, that adds new dimension to the performance.

INTERVIEWER: Couldn't the writer, by directing, discover her own new dimensions in rehearsal through the work with the actors?

CRYER: Possibly, but every writer is different.

INTERVIEWER: You don't feel the need for change, then, in the producer/director/actor/writer hierarchy?

CRYER: On a creative team, each collaborator yields different results. I have the freedom, for example, with Word Baker, to just say, "I think the actors should be doing this. Do you want me to talk to them?" He'll say, "Yeah. You go ahead and talk." We have that kind of relationship, now. But we've been working together for over fifteen years. It's taken a long time to build that sort of trust. It's different with every director and every writer so I can't generalize and say the balance of power should shift.

INTERVIEWER: Have you ever censored yourself as a writer?

CRYER: As I have gotten braver I have censored myself less. I've gone through different phases in my life. My teenage phase, before I was a writer, was very brave. Then I got married and deferred to my husband during the marriage. After I divorced, I returned to adolescence and an ability to say straight out how I felt. When I was married I was keeping myself to myself in some little secret place. I'm not casting my ex-husband in a repressive light. Not at all. He was encouraging and supportive of me. He didn't stop me from expressing myself in the writing. I did it to myself for some mysterious reason that I can't explain. I don't know why—other than a desire I had from an early age to protect men. I felt very protective of my father; I wanted him to be happy. I was always protective of men and their egos. I was very protective of my husband when I was married, and the result was to hide my own light under a bushel. Of course, I *was* working all that time. I'm not saying I was doing nothing but I really wasn't coming out. As for getting past the self-censorship . . . you see, writing is a kind of secret thing. You must do it by yourself. So I could always write more truthfully than I could speak out in my life. The reason that people were kind of surprised when *The Last Sweet Days of Isaac* [1970, Eastside Playhouse, NYC] came out was that, outwardly, it didn't *seem* as if Gretchen would have had that wry point of view about that kind of intellectual man. You would never have suspected that wryness from my smiling persona at the time.

INTERVIEWER: Do you have hope for the American theater?

CRYER: Yes, even though the current commercial situation on Broadway makes innovation very difficult. There is a great burgeoning energy in the regionals—that's our new hope. And the influx of women writers may infuse a whole new life into the theater.

DONNA DE MATTEO

Donna de Matteo was born June 24, 1941, in New York City. Her plays include The Barbecue Pit, The Paradise Kid, Animal Lovers, The Flip Side, Almost on a Runway, Rocky Road, and The White Pony, The Silver Fox, all of which have been presented at the HB Playwright's Foundation in New York City. Ms. de Matteo teaches playwriting at the HB Studios and has taught Contemporary Theater at The College of New Rochelle. She is married to Al de Matteo, with whom she has three children, Joe, Darren and Andrea.

———————————

DE MATTEO: For as long as I can remember, I wanted to be in the theater. First I thought I wanted to be an actress. I was sixteen at the time, but I had a father who was adamantly against a female child entering "show business." He swore he would disown me if I persisted in that direction. Because of that fear of both financial and emotional disownment, I tucked away my dream of a life in the theater, and tried very hard to convince myself that it wasn't what I wanted in the first place.

And so, I did the thing my parents expected me to do since the day I was born. I got married, and, strangely enough, stayed married. I married Al de Matteo when I was nineteen, and it was probably the best thing I ever did for myself, because he was the first man I came into contact with that not only didn't mind that I had a dream, but also nourished it. We'd been married about six years and had two sons, when one day I woke up and said to myself, "What the hell am I doing?" I had a terrific husband, two great kids, but something was missing, and I discovered that what was missing was *me*. Then a childhood friend dragged me to a creative writing class. And I decided to write a novel. I was naïve, positive I could get it published "just like that." Naturally, it was going to be very autobiographical, about my own family experience—like the whole world was waiting to hear about my mother and father. A terrific lady, Jean Fiedler, was teaching this class. She said the material I was

109

writing was good, but there was one thing wrong. "It's all dialogue! Where's the prose? You should really be writing a play!" A play? All my dreams of theater came back to me, and my father's words to boot: "The theater! You'll be surrounded by weirdos!" Then I asked myself, "Was there a day that you have ever felt normal?" Of course not. I was a weirdo myself! And besides, by now my father was dead. Which meant I no longer had to carry his fear of the world around with me.

So I started writing a play. I went to HB Studios, and took a class there with Dick Longchamps. Within a year, I had a production on, and I couldn't get over it! Oh, my God, I was finally doing something that I loved! The production was at a place called Theatre East [in 1969], a little Off Off Broadway house. The play was called *The Barbecue Pit*. It received some good reviews from the trade papers, *Show Business*, *Backstage*, et cetera. It was a very obscure family comedy-drama. I was so afraid that someone could point to me as being an autobiographical character, that I covered myself up in so many different disguises. In this particular play, I was a blind boy who was trying to get out of his family's clutches.

INTERVIEWER: Changing oneself into a male character seems common with women writers in their early work.

DE MATTEO: The character was a blind boy of eighteen years with a very strange situation going on in his household. I guess I made him blind because I didn't want him to see his family as they really were. I sent the play to William Morris, because I thought it was the only agency that existed! An agent there, Jane Chodorov, sent me a kind letter back: "It's a very nice play, but we're not quite interested in this work at this time. I don't know where I could place it. If you have any other plays, I would be interested in reading them." Damnit! I didn't have another play. So I immediately wrote one! It was called *The Paradise Kid*, which, lo and behold, was about an eighteen-year-old boy who's trying to leave home; however, this time I allowed him his eyesight! I wrote this comedy in about ten days; and again, I sent it off to Chodorov. She called me a few days later, and said, "I'd like to talk to you." And that's how it started. Jane became my first agent.

INTERVIEWER: Were you aware, back then, that the main character in *The Paradise Kid* was yet another Donna de Matteo disguised as a boy?

DE MATTEO: Naturally, but with so many trappings. Again, the character was someone trying to get out from under, fighting for independence, torn between family obligation and wanting a life of his own. When I spoke at the American Jewish Committee on a panel with Corinne

Jacker a few months ago, I brought up this play, because when I wrote it I was twenty-eight years old. And we discussed the boy in my play leaving the house at eighteen, and how it really took *me* ten years more, in real life, to make the break and get over the initial fear my father had instilled in me. It takes women a lot longer, at least women of my generation. It was much easier for the boy to leave home. He was brought up to believe that someday he would have to take care of his own family. I was brought up to believe that I would always be taken care of, with the proviso, of course, that I behaved properly.

INTERVIEWER: For many years, you have assisted Herbert Berghof in his famous playwriting unit. Will you talk a bit about what this experience has meant to you and your writing?

DE MATTEO: It's probably been the best of all creative experiences for me. The first time I applied to Herbert's class—he doesn't even recall it—he said, "No, no, no. Your work is not ready to be processed yet!" So I went into Dick Longchamp's class, learned more of the craft, and just when I was feeling comfortable, just when every scene I brought in seemed to work, Dick recommended me for Herbert's class. For the first few months with Herbert, I wrote scene after scene. . . . Of course, *none* of them worked. [Laughter]

INTERVIEWER: Were you aware of the craft problems at the time, or were you just trying to please him?

DE MATTEO: In the beginning, I guess I was trying to please him. I brought him what I thought he wanted to hear, not knowing, of course, that he *wanted* to hear what the playwright really had to say! I thought he was an "intellectual," so I was trying to write "intellectually." I felt scared. I felt I shouldn't be there. But then I thought, "So what? You fall on your face a couple of times. What does it matter?" And then, that wonderful day came, when I got over my What-Would-Mr.-Berghof-Like period. I finally brought in a scene that came directly from me, and he loved it! That particular scene developed into a full-length play, *Almost on a Runway.* The play was produced that same year at the HB Playwrights Foundation. Herbert Berghof directed it and Celeste Holm, Wesley Addy, Ben Piazza, Dolores Dorn-Heft, Steven Strimpell, Karen Leslie, Rosemary De Angelis, Rudy Bond, Shirley Bodtke, and Frank Gerace starred in it. It was truly a labor of love. No one was paid, we were rehearsing five days a week in one-hundred-degree weather in an un-air-conditioned theater.

INTERVIEWER: Berghof has directed nine of your plays. What is it like to work with this brilliant, but allegedly difficult, man of the American theater?

DE MATTEO: Contrary to popular belief, Herbert Berghof is not that difficult; especially if he is working with people who share the same work ethic he has.

INTERVIEWER: Do you have a favorite anecdote about him?

DE MATTEO: Well, once when we were rehearsing, I had to make a phone call. Marlene Mancini, his assistant, had called for us to take a two-minute break—the usual time Herbert allows during a five-hour rehearsal period—and I called home only to discover that my two-year-old daughter had swallowed some furniture polish and had to be taken immediately to a hospital. So, I ran back into the theater, and said, "Herbert, I have to leave!" "How can you leave? We're going to start the second act!" I say, "My daughter just swallowed poison!" "Oh, my God," Herbert exclaims, "That's terrible! Where is she?" I explain that my mother had just taken her to a hospital. Herbert says, "Oh, I'm so happy she's in the hospital already!" Then he lowered his voice and charmingly said, "But, uh, as long as she's already in the hospital, don't you think, before you go, that you could just rewrite these four lines in the second act? They're *little* lines!" [Laughter]

Another time, at another rehearsal, Herbert came back into the theater as the actors were finishing a scene and patiently let them go through it. We all noticed that he looked pale and was shaking. Naturally, we asked him what was wrong. Herbert replied, "Nothing much. But you have to excuse me for five minutes, my apartment is on fire." [Laughter] You know, he waited there at least five minutes to let the actors finish their scene while his apartment and all his worldly possessions were in flames!

He is a great man of the theater. I don't think we are ever going to see this kind of dedication and caring again. He's like a monk in the service of God, only with him it's service to the art of the theater. And to his own particular dream of what good theater is. . . . He was responsible for bringing Beckett's *Waiting for Godot* to this country and eventually directed it on Broadway. I mean, you can rest assured that when you work with him, you are not going to get a "pasted together" play that has just been thrown up there for the sake of a production, without knowing what the hell you have until you see it! I don't think you can put a play together that way. It's too fragile a thing. A new play is like a child.

INTERVIEWER: You've had some special actors in your work, over the years: Tony LoBianco, Donna McKechnie, Jerry Stiller, Vivian Blaine, the great Uta Hagen . . .

DE MATTEO: The best. Watching Miss Hagen during rehearsals is comparable to watching a superb musician playing a fine instrument. She is a master at her craft, very detailed, and patient in her approach to a character; but at the same time, she never loses sight of her instincts and emotions, and when you see her blend all of these elements together, it all looks so natural and effortless. . . . It transcends life. It's art at its best. Naturally, every actor approaches a role in a different way, and watching this process for a writer can be just as exciting as experiencing the result. When Tony LoBianco performs in front of an audience, he is like a stick of dynamite. Explosive! Magic!

INTERVIEWER: You've journeyed quite a distance from those early days of seeking approval as a writer. You've moved over a period of about fourteen years from comedy to serious drama. Were you aware of your societal concerns deepening?

DE MATTEO: I always had societal concerns. It's just that my approach in dealing with them changed. When I was writing mainly comedies, I was afraid of exposing any of the pain that I had really experienced in my life. . . . The comedy was a defense, a shield for the characters, and for myself. When I no longer felt that fear of exposure, my writing changed. But that doesn't mean to say my work is now devoid of comedy. Human beings in action are funny. They say one thing while doing the exact opposite. They are filled with contradictions.

INTERVIEWER: Although your experience with Berghof has been valuable, you've had less creative experiences, haven't you?

DE MATTEO: Yes, with another, more autocratic director, who just took my entire play and, well, it was my fault as well, because I let him. . . .

INTERVIEWER: You were passive in rehearsals?

DE MATTEO: Passive? Comatose would be a more appropriate word. The first day I walked into rehearsal all the proposed cuts were announced to me without even a discussion. This director and I had never sat down for five minutes before the first day of rehearsal to even talk through what the play was about. I figured, okay, so the man is busy, we will do it on the first day of rehearsal, but to my surprise and shock, it didn't seem to matter what I thought the play was about. At first, I quietly objected, but this particular director told me, "Look, this isn't Off Off Broadway. You're in the commercial theater now, and what works with audiences Off Off Broadway doesn't work here," meaning "If you want this production, you'll do it my way." I forgot to mention that this particular director was also one of the producers. Now, being a consenting adult, I could have just taken my play and walked. But instead, I tried to convince myself this person actually knew what he was talking about. I figured he'd been around much longer than I had, this was my first commercial production. He was a pro, and the owner of an institutional theater. I was a new writer. So, ultimately I talked myself into believing that what he wanted was correct. However, very late in rehearsals, I woke up and realized that I never should have entered this production, that I and I alone bastardized a play that I had worked on for a year, and for what? For a commercial production that doesn't represent the play I had written or myself? Of course I wanted the production. I would be a liar if I said I didn't. But the price was too high to pay.

INTERVIEWER: And you were afraid you wouldn't get the production if you didn't acquiesce?

DE MATTEO: Truthfully, I was afraid of everything. I was insecure. I was also afraid of "pulling" the play because people might think I was difficult to work with. Of course, the opposite was true. Everybody thought I was crazy to go along with this type of thing. One day, he wanted me to do *this*, the next day *that*, and before I knew it, I had a sitcom on my hands. By the way, the play was picked up after the production for a situation comedy. [Laughter] God!

INTERVIEWER: Can you be more specific about the *this* and the *that*?

DE MATTEO: I added two characters that weren't in my original play, that had no reason to be in the play at all.

INTERVIEWER: So, he, in effect, rewrote your play?

DE MATTEO: No, *I* rewrote the play. But yes, I executed his ideas.

INTERVIEWER: Under duress?

DE MATTEO: Under my own duress. No matter what, it all falls back on the playwright, anyway. You end up taking the rap. And the truth is, I don't mind taking the rap if I commit the crime; in this case, I was a willing accomplice. I mean, in one review, the reviewer quoted a line I had never written, something my director came up with because he thought it was hysterically funny. How is a reviewer supposed to know that was not my line? Nobody is going to know unless you put a prologue in front of the first act reading, "This play was written by committee! These rewrites are filled with clichés. They do not come from *my* sense of truth."

INTERVIEWER: Was all of this as evident to you in rehearsal as it was on opening night?

DE MATTEO: During rehearsals I knew, but I talked myself out of it. The truth is, you can't do that type of rewrite—completely pulling apart the structure of a play, adding characters, adding a lot of jokes—if you don't talk yourself into believing it. . . . You don't want to face it. You tell yourself it's all in your own imagination. . . .

I am happy to tell you I've changed, a little. Most writers prefer not to say anything negative about theaters because they feel they will never be able to work there again. I feel no such threat in this particular case because, even if given the chance, I would never work with this man again. The theater is supposed to be a place where an audience can come to see the truth of the matter explored onstage.

INTERVIEWER: How have you progressed as a playwright from your first play till now?

DE MATTEO: In the beginning, as I said, I was sometimes afraid of exposing too much of myself. Today, I have absolutely no qualms about exposing anything if it's the truth. Structurally, I think I have reached a place where I feel secure in the craft, where I can take a scene and pull it apart, and put it back together again.

INTERVIEWER: How does a play begin in your mind?

DE MATTEO: At first, I used to be motivated by a subject I felt very strongly about, or a story I had heard, but lately, it begins only after a feeling. The last play I wrote, *The Silver Fox*, was motivated by a song from *Cats* called "Memory." The first time I heard it was in my agent, Esther Sherman's, apartment. It brought up such emotional dregs in me, such a feeling of the past, a past that I had never dealt with before. After hearing it, I ran out and bought myself a copy and played it constantly, even though every time I heard it, it made me cry. I started to write the play a few days later.

INTERVIEWER: Do you think *The Silver Fox* would have happened without "Memory?"

DE MATTEO: I'd like to think so, but who knows? The wonderful thing about music is that it immediately evokes certain eras of one's life, brings you back to where you've been, even if you don't want to go there.

INTERVIEWER: "Memory" allowed you to write about family?

DE MATTEO: I had written about family before, but not about the harsher realities. The love and the hate. All those things we prefer to leave unsaid.

INTERVIEWER: The savagery of domestic life?

DE MATTEO: Definitely.

INTERVIEWER: You were instrumental in the formation of the Forum of Italian-American Playwrights. Will you talk a little about how this group came into existence?

DE MATTEO: In the beginning, our intention was to take younger Italian-American writers and provide them with an atmosphere where they could experiment and grow as writers. Secondly, the group was formed because the playwrights felt that the Italian-American images depicted by the media were negative; these images offered our people no sense of pride at all. They never focused on the Italian-American family as it really is. We do have our moments of intelligence and tenderness and, furthermore, many of us are educated; but one would never know it from the clichés depicted by the media. The women have been even more stereotyped than the men. You do see an occasional Italian-American man depicted as a lawyer, or a doctor, though nine times out of ten, even they are corrupt. The women, as depicted to the public, can barely string a whole sentence together, and they're usually chained to a stove, or being abused by some sadistic husband.

INTERVIEWER: Who was involved in the group in the beginning?

DE MATTEO: A lot of good writers: Leonard Melfi, Lou LaRusso, Gene Ruffini, Mario Fratti, Phil LoGuidice, Joanne Tedesco, Frank Gagliano, Ken Eulo. As in any group, we had our differences.

INTERVIEWER: What were the upheavals about?

DE MATTEO: Anything and everything. Some were artistic arguments. Some were personal arguments. The atmosphere was always exciting. There were arguments between the men and the women, but out of it all, a lot of good work was done. When the differences got too out of hand, the original group broke up and [the Forum] regrouped with the initial intentions for the organization intact.

INTERVIEWER: The original goal being the development of the youngsters?

DE MATTEO: Yes, we've gone through many different artistic directors. Now, we have Vincent Gugleotti, who is really dedicated and wonderful with young people. His vision is to help them get their plays on and to help them discover their writing problems at the same time. Vincent has just found us a new home on Forty-seventh Street and Ninth Avenue. There are about forty seats in the theater. You can put productions on there but they have to be simple ones, with small casts.

INTERVIEWER: I'm concerned about where the working-class writers are and where they're going to come from in the future. The Italian-American Forum seems to be finding more working-class writers than most groups of this sort.

DE MATTEO: Many of our young writers at the Forum stem from working-class families.

INTERVIEWER: Is that working-class experience being reflected on the commercial stage?

DE MATTEO: I think to some degree it is. Many Hispanics are dealing with the working class, as are many plays about the black experience. As far as Italian-Americans from working-class families are concerned, their parents are usually against them entering the arts. Most Italian-American parents work all their lives to make their children comfortable. They send their children to college so that they will *not* be of the working class, so they can be secure. So, when that same child comes home and announces that he is going to enter a profession as tenuous as playwriting! Well, all hell is liable to break loose. Most people in this country measure success in monetary terms, and Italian-Americans are no different on that count. Drama doesn't seem like a tangible profession to them. In the years that it takes you to get your play on commercially, you could probably become a neurosurgeon. Many of our young Italian-Americans are coming from families of construction workers, cab drivers, people who have really labored. They have worked very hard for whatever they have. They provide comfortable lives for their children. Sometimes this can be dangerous.

INTERVIEWER: Are you saying the kids become too comfortable?

DE MATTEO: To the degree that the child is not desperate enough to get out. These kids are not living in ghettos. They usually live in nice, secure homes.

INTERVIEWER: But from all that I've seen at the Italian-American Forum, no matter how protected those kids may be, they come in and talk, in vital language, about their working-class homes. There seems to be a certain class and ethnic loyalty.

DE MATTEO: Sure there is. There is a lot of affection and warmth in the Italian-American home. But there is also a lot of conflict in dealing with love-versus-obligation. Along with this kind of love comes guilt, and a feeling of overwhelming responsibility at an early age. And don't forget, the young people you are hearing have already taken that first step. What you hear them say in workshop and what you are eventually going to see in their plays as they grow older may differ.

INTERVIEWER: Is there a female aesthetic?

DE MATTEO: I don't think a man could write the same thing I write, but I don't think another woman could write the same thing I write either, not in the same way.

INTERVIEWER: If women continue to proliferate as playwrights, do you think we'll see more healing images on stage, as opposed to destructive ones?

DE MATTEO: I think so. In most cases, women do strive to make things better. They may do it late, but along the way they will take action for other people sooner than they will for themselves. Women, generally, are apt to put things together rather than tear them apart. Just to give you an example: Many years ago, we took a vacation in southern Portugal. There are miles of deserted beaches there. We were surrounded by clear ocean and clean sand. I was with my husband and my two sons, who were four and seven at the time. Seated not far away from us was another family with a little girl of about five. She asked my sons if they wanted to build a castle. My older boy got up and enthusiastically said, "Let's build it here!" For the next two hours, my sons and the little girl erected this monument. They all got along beautifully—one fetching water, the other sand, and the other digging. And when the group was finished, the parents ooohed and aaahed at the achievement. All was well until a fourth child, a boy of about seven, happened along and casually asked, "Whose castle is it?" My older son immediately says, "Mine." My younger son yells, "Yours? We used *my* pail and shovel." The little girl quietly says, "I did all the digging." And my older boy says, "But it was my sand!" My younger son screams, "But I sat on that piece of sand before you did!" My husband and I were stunned. They were actually fighting over sand when the whole beach was filled with it! Finally, my younger son, feeling cheated, angrily kicks in the castle, and says, "Now it's your sand!" My older son, also enraged, pushed his little brother into the castle, destroying the rest of it. The little girl walked back to her own blanket, quietly, in tears. Meanwhile, my husband was trying to break up the fight between our boys, when the kid who had caused all of this fury politely said, "I don't know what you guys are fighting over. Building a castle is a sissy thing to do anyway." My two boys nervously started laughing as if to save their dignity in front of this stranger. My older boy just said, "Race you both to the water!" And off the three boys went. . . . The little girl came back and politely asked me if she could borrow my son's pail and shovel. I said yes, and she started to dig on her own patch of sand. I looked at my sons, four and seven, jumping up and down in the waves, the sun beaming over their healthy bodies, and then I looked at the little girl starting to dig all over again by herself, and instead of feeling exhilarated in this idyllic setting, I felt fear for them all.

INTERVIEWER: Some women playwrights are accused of not observing their male characters well enough.

DE MATTEO: I think that the words "well enough" are sometimes a metaphor for a male character not being "nice enough." For instance, when a woman writes a male character that isn't, per se, what most other men would perceive as a "nice guy," we, as writers, are sometimes accused of wanting to show the male image in a negative way. Of course the opposite is true. If a writer, male or female, is interested in the exploration of truth in his character, whether the character is male or female, some- times, as in life, the truth is not nice; and if we try to soften up male characters for the sake of making them nice guys, we do them a great disservice by de-dimensionalizing them into what men *think* women should think of men, rather than what our own perception really is. I think the "make him a nice guy because I have to have somebody to root for" syndrome is a cliché; it has absolutely nothing to do with creativity, originality and truth. The writer's job is to stand behind every character in her play, not to judge her characters, but to understand them to such a degree that at the end of the play the audience will have the same understanding.

In *A Streetcar Named Desire,* could anybody classify Stanley Kowalski as a "nice guy?" If Tennessee Williams had been told to make him into a "nice man," there wouldn't have been a play. Instead, we have a full-blown character who is a product of his own environment. Stanley is trying as best he can, given his limitations of being uneducated and underexposed, to deal with a situation that is threatening his present existence. If everyone in real life were as nice as some people would prescribe for the stage, just think we'd have no need for government, the draft, the U.N., or nuclear missiles to protect ourselves from the rest of the "nice people." I could go on and on about this. I mean was Macbeth a nice guy? Or Othello? Hamlet? Crazy, yes. Interesting, yes. But *nice,* eh? These characters are, above all, human. A writer's job is to reflect the society in which he lives, to tell the truth about human problems. Trying to make your characters "nice" has more to do with Dale Carnegie's *How to Win Friends and Influence People* than with the real questions of the human condition in present-day society.

INTERVIEWER: Have you ever written a play where you have had this experience of having to make your male characters "sympathetic"?

DE MATTEO: I did once start writing a play that was a departure for me. It was a very "male" play. It was called *The Last American Convertible,* about a Cadillac salesman who marries the boss's daughter so he can someday take over the dealership. Although he is depicted as one person in the play, the character was really an amalgam of many men I had known. . . . My own husband had been a salesman at one time and knew that world. A good friend of ours had married the boss's daughter. And then I added to this character my own sense of wanting to be a success, my own sense of wanting to make it! I had only written the first act, and when I had it read, the criticism was that the men in this play were too brutal, that I was writing the main character in this way because I didn't like him, when the truth was that I not only liked him, I loved him. Sure, he victimizes other people: But why? Because he himself had been victimized, although he isn't aware of it himself. After hearing this first critique, just out of curiosity to see what would happen, I put my husband's name down on the title page, and proceeded to read it in an entirely different place. Since it was such a departure from my usual work, people believed that my husband was giving playwrighting a try. I wasn't so much interested in getting it on as I was in confirming for myself that when a male character who shows signs of brutality is written by a woman, *that* character is much less acceptable than if it had been written by a man. When the play was read with Al's name on it, it was critiqued and its apparent flaws discussed, but no one ever mentioned making the male character "nicer." [Laughter] I never did complete the play. I was too frustrated. Also, I knew I could never stand not having my own name on it.

INTERVIEWER: You write a lot of female characters that are strong, rather long-suffering, who take a reluctant stand occasionally. The Wife in *Flipside*, for example.

DE MATTEO: I don't think The Wife in *Flipside* is long-suffering. Although she does take a stand for herself, she is still behind the man, her husband, all the time. That does not mean to say that she is a wimp of a woman, but that she understands the problems that her husband is having so that she can aid him in trying to resolve them rather than adding to them.

INTERVIEWER: And Lynn in *Rocky Road*?

DE MATTEO: Well, she has different problems in taking a stand. Lynn has to take a stand in dealing with her own life once she's left by her husband who was the so-called center of her life. She suffers a nervous breakdown.

INTERVIEWER: That's what I was saying: Your women suffer a great deal before they take a stand.

DE MATTEO: Lynn stems from a generation of women that were brought up to believe that if you were married, you would always be taken care of.

INTERVIEWER: What about when theater critics say—as they often do—"Well, why didn't this woman just leave the jerk?" Why *does* Lynn stay, Donna? Why do women stick around in untenable situations on stage? Is it because they do in life?

DE MATTEO: That question was raised with my character Tina in *The Silver Fox*. . . . Why didn't she pick herself up? This is 1984, right? Intellectually, yes, we do have choices. However, intellect and passion have very little to do with each other. Tina is in a state of being in love with her husband. The tragedy in this case is that this couple are totally ill-matched. They shouldn't have been married in the first place. Her husband is a charmer—good-looking, worldly—and Tina is more or-dinary. If she'd married an ordinary man, she probably would've led a happier life. Naturally, the very things that attracted her to her husband also attract other women; her husband does cheat on her, and eventually outgrows her. In a sense, Tina is a prisoner of her own making. She takes the risk and she suffers the consequences. She is a woman who is very low on self-esteem. She has been brought up by a loving but dom-ineering mother. She has, for the most part, been fatherless. She has never really excelled at anything. She wouldn't know what to do with freedom if she had it. This particular woman wants to be part of her husband's life. She's obsessive. I would compare her to an alcoholic or a drug addict. Intellectually, these women know that their habit will eventually kill them; but they follow that road of self-destruction all the same, unless they find something else to take its place. Tina has never found that something else. And that was a very big problem for me to dramatize.

INTERVIEWER: How have you fared with reviewers?

DE MATTEO: After one production I walked into the bathroom. Naturally, you can't help but hear the comments. In there was a columnist who was going to interview me after the play for a local paper. She's talking to her friend and saying, "Well, what's wrong with this play is that the writer is not taking big enough risks." Ironically, what she didn't know was that the play had been watered down because the producers felt it might be too risqué for their audiences. You can't win, can you? Then this columnist goes on, "I probably could've written this play myself, that's how easy this play is to write. And I probably could've written it better." I didn't know it at the time, but she was also a critic. The *Chicago Sun-Times* gave the play a good review, but *this* columnist just tore me to pieces in the local gazette.

INTERVIEWER: Then you don't find women critics any more friendly than male critics?

DE MATTEO: This was the only woman critic I was every reviewed by. I don't know what makes a critic tick, but in the case of this particular woman, it was as if she was reviewing me personally, rather than the play. I mean, who even knows what the credentials of our critics are anyway? If you go back into history and look up critiques of certain plays, the works turn out to be classics in spite of the horrendous reviews. So who knows? It just seems that no matter what you write, from the time that it leaves your typewriter, it's all up for grabs, like it or not.

INTERVIEWER: Why do writers accept the life-and-death power of the critics? They're not that powerful in other countries.

DE MATTEO: Theater tickets are also not thirty to forty dollars apiece in other countries. Before anyone shells out that kind of money to see a Broadway play, they want some confirmation that they're going to see something that's been approved of. The same goes for Off Broadway these days. The tickets are high-priced. People want to know what they're getting. And anyhow, is there an alternative to critics? Do we have a choice? Or is everybody too afraid to change it? Or, if they did change it, what would it be changed to? Maybe the critics would like a change too. Very few writers ever get to talk to a critic. Dramatic criticism is so strange. For the playwright, it's almost like getting undressed in front of a doctor you've never met before and waiting for him or her to tell you you're in good shape. Or you have a year to live. You're going to get the best news or the worst news or mixed news, from a perfect stranger. But then again, when I go to my doctor and he tells me everything is fine, I tout him as being the world's greatest physician. If he would ever tell me there was anything seriously wrong with me, I'd have to get a second opinion!

INTERVIEWER: Unfortunately, in New York, there's only one "doctor" who counts, *The New York Times*. Pam Gems, the British playwright, says that we need to "unship" the critics.

DE MATTEO: Maybe the state of commercial theater as we know it should be unshipped. But then we'd all have to figure out what we would do in its place. [Laughter]

INTERVIEWER: On that note, perhaps we should move on to a discussion of comedy.

DE MATTEO: Comedy is the toughest thing to write. And probably the most frustrating.

INTERVIEWER: Are you aware, when you're writing, how funny your plays are?

DE MATTEO: Having been compared to Neil Simon [laughter], I humbly say, yes! What can I tell you? To define comedy is like trying to define how you happen to have dark hair. It depends on so many things. I mean, what is that ability to take a very tragic story and make it funny? I can tell a story about my father's death and have people in hysterics. Now, when it happened it was not funny. However, when I looked at the details of it, even that very night, when I heard this friend of my father's telling my mother that my father had died, I knew if my father had been there himself *he* would've been laughing.

This is how it started. A man, a friend of the family, rings the bell of my mother's home. He enters looking sad and pale and says to my mother, "Hello, Rae. Listen, I have some bad news for you." He didn't say, "I've got *bad news*." You see, that already isn't funny. "*Some* bad news" can mean anything. Plain *bad news* is really bad. And my mother, always a willing recipient for hearing "some bad news," perked up. My father's friend proceeds to tell her to sit down, not realizing that she was already seated. Then he goes on to say, "Uh, we were at the racetrack . . . and, well, Joe was sitting down . . . uh, just like you are now, and the five of us were eating steak. And the race started. So we all looked out the window of the clubhouse, you know, to see how our horses were doing. And all of a sudden I go to say something to Joe because his horse was winning when I notice that his head is in his plate! And his horse was winning! I said to the other guys, 'What's the matter with him!?' We thought he had too much to drink. So we started yelling at him, 'Joe, get up! Your horse is coming in!' Finally Tony lifted his head and said, 'Joe's dead!' And the other guy said, 'And he won!' Anyway, here's his two thousand dollars and we just came to tell you that he also died." And he paid my mother the two thousand dollars my father won at the track.

Now that is an incongruous story. Whether he told it in that exact way, I don't really know anymore; that's the way I perceived it. Whether he said, "Joe, you won," to my dead father, I don't know. The man did say, "And he won" to my mother. Now I preferred him telling the story in the third person. Whether he did or not, I don't know that either, because I was already imposing how I would tell that story after having received the original version of it.

INTERVIEWER: So comedy, for you, is a matter of fictionalizing your tragedies?

DE MATTEO: Immediately, I fictionalize everything. Was I there or did I just write it? You know, a guy held a gun to my head one day—we had an actual robbery. He was not a professional burglar and I think he was so scared himself that while he was holding the gun to my head, his hand starts to shake. When I saw his hand shaking, I wet my pants and it splashed over the floor. When the burglar started to get wet himself he backed away from me in disgust, and like a jerk—so embarrassed over the accident—I started apologizing to him for wetting my pants. "You know, I never do this," I said. "I'm so sorry!" After I got over the initial shock of being confronted by two strangers, I already started thinking it was funny even when one of them led me into a bedroom and tied me up. The other guy tells him to stay with me. I asked for a cigarette. He gave me one and lit it. But I couldn't smoke it because my hands were tied; so he kept taking it in and out of my mouth, and the other guy, busily ransacking, would pass by, see this and do a double take, cursing at his partner: "What the fuck are you doing? Do you think we're at the Boston Tea Party! Look for something!" [Laughter] They were *not* professionals. They were junkies, and they were calling each other by their first names; they came in with masks, then took them off, then put them on. . . . [Laughter] You know, "Joey?" "What, Bobby?" Bobby comes storming back into the bedroom only to see his lethargic partner sitting casually in a chair, still feeding me the cigarette. The more energetic of the two was furious. "You know, you're even a fucking lazy robber!" The other retorts, "Hey, I'm givin' this lady a cigarette. She's nervous!" And his friend says, "Look for something, you asshole! I take you on this job and you ain't even looking for anything!" And so, my patron of tobacco turns to me and says, "Is there anything in here I should look for?" And I heard myself say, "There's a mink coat of my mother's in the closet." He said, "Where?" I say, "Sweetheart, you have to open the door and look." He really *was* lazy. He did, however, carry out out a stereo. As I sat there after I heard the door slam, I wondered to myself where these two guys were off to now. Maybe they were going for a drink to relax. In other circumstances, I would've liked to have gone with them just to see their actions in a different situation. [Laughter]

INTERVIEWER: Do you mind being called a "woman writer?"

DE MATTEO: It depends on who's doing the calling.

INTERVIEWER: Do you feel "ghettoized" because this book will not include male playwrights?

DE MATTEO: I don't consider myself being "ghettoized" in this book at all. The thought would never have entered my mind. I don't know if I would go around calling myself a woman writer, the same way a male wouldn't call himself a male writer. But if someone does happen to say, "She's a woman writer," I certainly wouldn't take offense to it unless they meant it in a derogatory way.

INTERVIEWER: Many writers say they are not women writers, but writers who happen to be women.

DE MATTEO: You just can't happen to be a woman, can you? I mean, being a woman is a whole experience. How can you just happen to be a woman? It's like saying, "I happen to be a dog instead of a cat." Really? What are you talking about? Everything I *know*, I know as a woman. It is my gender. I am proud to be a woman. And I *am* a writer. I am something I never thought I could be.

ROSALYN DREXLER

Rosalyn Drexler is a writer and an artist. She has written over twenty plays, including The Writer's Opera and Graven Image, as well as several musicals that include Home Movies [awarded an Obie in 1964] and Starburn. She is the author of seven novels; her most recent, Bad Guy, published in 1982 by E. P. Dutton, received critical acclaim. She has also written many articles for leading magazines and reviewed movies for Vogue and The New York Times. Her paintings are in the collections of the Hirschhorn Museum and Sculpture Garden, Washington D.C., The Walker Art Center in Minneapolis, and the Whitney Museum of American Art in New York City among others. Her awards include an Emmy for TV work, three Rockefeller awards for playwriting, and three Obies; the most recent Obie was awarded in 1985 for Transients Welcome (two one-act plays). She was also awarded a CAPS grant in 1984 for fiction, an award from The Paris Review for her short story "Dear," and a Guggenheim Fellowship. Ms. Drexler is at present at work on a movie script, has a novel in the works, and a new play (A Matter of Life and Death [1986] formerly titled Green River Murders) in production at Theatre for the New City in Manhattan. In addition, she was commissioned by the same theater to write her most recent work, The Day Before Yesterday, a full-length play based on Franz Kafka's A Hunger Artist and on his life. Early in 1986, Ms. Drexler was awarded her fourth Rockefeller Grant.

INTERVIEWER: You frequently deal with incest in your plays; what's the fascination?

DREXLER: Well, incest is a furtive initiation into the world of pain; at first it masquerades as love, a victimless crime, but then its obsessional nature traps both participants. Usually the aggressor views himself/herself as impotent in the world, and impotent sexually (I'm not speaking here of children who have easy access to one another, and who experiment

125

in innocent curiosity). Forcing someone to do something, or being the one who is forced, creates wounds that seldom heal. It is this viciousness within helplessness, this need on the part of the aggressor to abuse and destroy those who trust him (transgressing upon what is almost a universal law), that fascinates me. Like rape, incest is not an expression of love or sex, it is evidence that something has gone terribly wrong.

INTERVIEWER: Are you using incest as a metaphor for something else?

DREXLER: Sometimes metaphors, sometimes semaphores . . . and sometimes a character just has a bug up his ass. Hey, why shouldn't something be itself? A pen is a pen, not a penis. A tunnel is a tunnel, not a vagina. But then again, a father fucking his daughter can be, metaphorically, a country fucking itself.

INTERVIEWER: You once said man, as poet and artist, likes to transform images, use them. What does the woman poet and artist do with images?

DREXLER: The same thing. *People* make art. Gender is only part of the artist's experiential stockpile: An entire history determines content, style, attitude. . . . I feel that you can tell from my work that I'm a woman, a particular woman: one who is strong, frank, sometimes vulgar, sometimes delicate. Take the way the character Susan in my play *The Writer's Opera* [1979], describes her body. She sees it plain; she knows her body, and talks about it:

> An appraisal of myself in flux: eyes bright . . . arms fleshy . . . spider-veined legs . . . soft breasts . . . soft stomach . . . broad thighs . . . painful knee . . . shapely calves . . . delicate ankles . . . toes in rows . . . expressive face . . . vaulted nose . . . slipped disk of the lumbar region.

Acknowledging the body is acknowledging what is real. It took Crystal Field, who played the part of Susan, a long time before she was able to do that scene. It was too close to home. When she finally accomplished it, she got wild applause. Colette, the famous French author, in *Chéri* and *The Last of Chéri*, was relieved when she observed the first signs of age creeping up: At last she could be herself, not *un objet d'amour*; she could spend time with her friends, gossiping, or working in the garden. It's such a strain, a struggle, to appear to be without physical blemish . . . to remain young as the relentless years add up. It's time consuming and emotionally depleting.

As a writer I'm more concerned with a *body of work*. . . . There's no perfection there either, but great satisfaction in trying. . . . I woke up this morning thinking about words.

INTERVIEWER: What were you thinking?

DREXLER: I was thinking that theater is like certain children in certain families, who are scapegoats and kept chained in the basement. I was thinking that words are now the scapegoat of the theater. They are trying to make theater multimedia, visual, no words . . . the director takes over. The writer is becoming less important . . . that madman Artaud, spawned on disease and disruption, first proposed this trend. In writing a movie script, the writer must surrender to the visual aspect—this is cinematic storytelling, this is different from theatrical writing. Here the writer is tolerated as a necessary evil, and her/his contribution immediately usurped by the director. Woody Allen erases this demarcation by being both writer and director.

INTERVIEWER: Do you want to talk about directing?

DREXLER: For twenty-five years I've been searching out this particular language: how to convey what you want to the actors. The important thing in directing is concept and imagination . . . there isn't too much of that around. I haven't directed myself, yet, but I'd like to. The process of directing is now demystified for me.

INTERVIEWER: Do you have much input during rehearsal?

DREXLER: Depends on who you're working with. I once made some suggestions to a certain (he shall remain nameless) director, and he said very loudly, "One more insurrection, and you leave the theater!" Amusing? A friend of mine was hit on the head with a chair by the director of his play when he ventured an opinion that was displeasing to the director. He stopped writing plays. The point is, when you're in rehearsal, and you don't have much time before opening, there's not too much you can do about it, or you won't have a show. This happens a lot: one is stuck with an inadequate cast, or with a script that needs additional rewrites, or the budget can't be budged for additional music, props, whatever. I can deal with the rewrites, but the rest is up for grabs. In this collaboration that is theater, the chances that everything will come together is a kind of miracle . . . *input or not*. The casting of my play *Delicate Feelings* [1984] was particularly difficult. We had to find a dwarf who could play the harmonica, wrestle, sing and act. We needed two young women who could wrestle, sing country blues, and act, et cetera. There was some nudity, a rape scene, and wrestling in the mud . . . we needed the music for thirteen songs! During the production I noted that the songs had a way of stopping the action. I've rewritten the play and taken out all of the songs except for the title song.

INTERVIEWER: What about your play *Starburn* [1983]? It was reviewed as a campy comedy, but I found it tragic, moving, very real. Was it difficult adapting it from your book to a play?

DREXLER: No more difficult than rolling a boulder uphill in a snow-storm. You know why I did it? My novels are out of print, unavailable except perhaps in some libraries. I didn't want *Starburn* to have lived in vain, I wanted to keep it alive somehow. . . . It's like a housewife saying, "Oh, this towel is ragged, now I can use it for something else, be inventive, make a doll out of it, make it wonderful.". . . In the *Starburn* adaptation I had to leave out a character, a retarded sister who was very interesting in the book, and the mother's relationship to the homosexual father. I also eliminated an absurdist court case in which a hypnotist puts the main character, Jenni Love, under, in order to help her remember the murder/abduction of a rock critic. I had to keep to a straight plot line, and not do riffs—stick to the story about a young woman who becomes a punk-rock star along with her group The Great Mother Goddess Cult, and who is suspected of murdering a rock critic. It became a mystery story.

INTERVIEWER: In *Starburn*, you have the critic cut into bite-sized pieces, bagged in plastic Baggies, and dropped into an ice machine. Does it make live critics nervous when they're out there in the audience?

DREXLER: Have you read the Gussow review of *Starburn* [*New York Times*, March 13, 1983]? I felt he *may* have taken it personally. On the other hand, I take it personally when he cuts me up. The critic and the artist are, in most cases, symbiotic adversaries.

INTERVIEWER: When you began writing plays, were you aware of other women playwrights in New York?

DREXLER: I didn't know anybody when my first play was done. In fact, I didn't even know how to write a play. I was isolated, bringing up my two kids. When my daughter was in school, I'd write in her room, the sunny one, and I'd laugh a lot while I was writing, amusing myself. I didn't think anyone would want to do this "play" . . . then I showed it to a friend, Richard Gilman [noted theater writer, critic and professor of drama at Yale University], and he said, "They might like this at Judson Church." And I asked, "Oh, what is Judson Church?" The rest is history. . . . Al Carmines wrote the music and Lawrence Kornfeld directed and the play was called *Home Movies* (my first Obie, 1964). It was the first play to go from Off Off Broadway to Off Broadway, to The Provincetown Playhouse in Greenwich Village.

After that Irene Fornes did *Promenade*, Barbara Garson was writing *Macbird*, Megan Terry was working on something with Joe Chaikin, Rochelle Owens and Julie Bovasso were turning out their special brands of theater . . . It was so exciting! I found myself in the company of exceptional peers. Willy-nilly there we were, defining the sixties in our plays. Then a bunch of us got together determined to produce our own plays: Irene was the president; I was the treasurer. We were going to have it all women, but then we realized that there were a lot of men around too who were writing at the same time, and that we should all be in this thing together.

INTERVIEWER: But it started as a women's group. Did it have a name?

DREXLER: Oh, we were all throwing out names and I said, "What about Stone Soup?" That's that fairy tale of the soldiers starving. The villagers were stingy so the soldiers just boiled up water and put a big stone in it. Then, after a while, the villagers started coming around and putting everything into it and the soup became really wonderful. Everybody contributed. And Rochelle said, "Oh, that's terrible. Everyone will think we're women and we're in a kitchen making soup." I said, "That's not the point. The point is: *Need* will make you invent something." We eventually called it the New York Theatre Strategy. I preferred Stone Soup.

INTERVIEWER: What were you attempting to do with that group?

DREXLER: We wanted to ally ourselves, we wanted to raise money. We felt there was enough talent to fill a theater every season with our work. We were all writing writers, we weren't one-play writers. Irene did a heck of a lot of paper work and contacting people. She's so good at that. But while she was doing it, it was very difficult for her to write. You can't do both.

But anyway we had The Strategy for a few seasons with both males and females. We did our plays at Manhattan Theatre Club before it was "Manhattan Theatre Club," you know, in quotes. Before it became a commercial trying ground for Broadway. Yes. We were aware we were around and we were proud of it. Then people say, "Where are the playwrights?" We are still out there. America is a throw-away society. Waste. There's no respect.

INTERVIEWER: Did the initial all-female group just happen or was there a feeling of discrimination?

DREXLER: I felt discrimination because of the kind of noncommercial work I do. Commercial has to do with if it looks good at the box office. I thought that was discrimination against me. The reason my plays never went anywhere—even after good reviews—was because they might offend people. *The Writer's Opera* got rave reviews, won an Obie. I didn't receive one offer from any theater around the United States. Maybe it's too difficult to do, the content too shocking. . . . That didn't stop Genet's career. David Mamet, Sam Shepard aren't penalized for "vulgar" content, are they? . . . Do you think it's because my form is different?

INTERVIEWER: Well, we think women have many unconventional structures that are not, at the moment, critically recognized. A phrase that crops up often in reviews is, "This is a non-play."

DREXLER: I suppose it's also a matter of pleasing the patrons who give money to the theaters: That's why *Our Town* and *Playboy of the Western World* are done so often.

INTERVIEWER: Have you had any response from the regional theaters?

DREXLER: Of course some, but on the whole nothing much. I'm happy to have Theatre for the New City to work in, to always have a home for my plays, to develop an audience that enjoys my work. Plays must be done, otherwise they die. I write with great excitement, already imagining opening night when the play first comes alive.

INTERVIEWER: You frequently deal with the subject of rape in your plays.

DREXLER: Did you see *Extremities*? At one point, the rapist is there with the women and one of them has to go out and get something. In the plot, if she's not back within a certain amount of time, someone is going to die. Well, when she comes back, a little late, she says, in effect, "Oh, I met a friend in the parking lot and we got to chatting. . . ." I mean, something like that, in the middle of a serious play, says to me: Here's a writer who hates women. You know? Something so important —like *life and death hanging in the balance*—but we women gab on. I said, "What kind of shit is this? That is just someone who wants to use violence and thinks the audience will enjoy it." Nobody's for rape, you know. But here he's going to *show* it! And there the woman is, in her panties, threatening the rapist whom she now has cowering, hammered into a sort of fireplace. It was very . . . how do you say? . . . peek-a-boo.

INTERVIEWER: Voyeuristic?

DREXLER: Voyeuristic. I thought it was just done for titillation. I didn't believe the writer for two seconds.

INTERVIEWER: You've written very honestly about rape—at the end of *She Who Was He* [1974], and in *The Investigation* [1966].

DREXLER: In *She Who Was He* [1974], Thutmose, Hatshepsut's husband, engineers her murder so that he can ascend the throne and become a conquering hero . . . Pharoah of Upper *and* Lower Egypt. He then attempts to erase her name from history, has servants chipping away at obelisks raised in her honor, removes her name from scroll and tomb . . . no one knows where she's buried to this day. But in my play, Hatshepsut becomes Egypt (a theatrical trick) and Thutmose rapes her before he has her killed . . . in effect, he is raping Egypt.

Hatshepsut spoke of herself as Egypt. Her lover Senmut, the architect, built temple Deir El Bahri for her. . . . But the thing is, she ruled for twenty years in peace and prosperity, and Thutmose wanted to make war. What I tried to do in *She Who Was He* was handle a bigger subject than women are normally given credit for.

INTERVIEWER: How faithful is this play to historical fact?

DREXLER: I researched it rather thoroughly: Hatshepsut's history, the ways of Egypt at the time . . . how they prepared bodies after death, the mother-daughter relationship and the coming of age of a woman. I hadn't seen this subject handled in any play, so I thought it was a wonderful subject to tackle.

INTERVIEWER: I wonder what a playwright expects from a production when her stage directions read: "The blue sky opens up and all fly into it" or "Hatshepsut becomes the map of Egypt."

DREXLER: I expect magic. The way we achieved it in one instance was a painted cloth was dropped over Hatshepsut's head and it flowed all about her . . . the whole map of Egypt—art plus ingenuity. When Hatshepsut was conceived, when the sun god, Ra, was having coitus with her mother, Ahmose, we had sparks coming out of his golden codpiece . . . it was very elaborate, a beautiful thing sparkling all over the place.

INTERVIEWER: Has it been difficult to juggle the roles of wife, mother, writer?

DREXLER: Of course it is, but I try to write early in the day, before other activities become imperative: the mail, shopping, phone calls, cooking. . . . New York is too distracting; one gets invited everywhere: plays, movies, art shows, dinner parties . . . Sometimes I just don't want to do all those things. So what if I'm not *au courant* constantly? I don't want my life to be gorgeously interesting, and falsely zippy. "I *vant* to be alone."

INTERVIEWER: Who do you show your first drafts to?

DREXLER: Actually I don't show first drafts to anybody. I tend to think of my third draft as a first draft. I just keep working on it. When I'm ready to let it go, I show it to either the director or the producer, and then take their ideas into consideration, and work on the script some more. During rehearsals I may throw out a scene or two and add a dancing horse instead. A playwright's work is never done.

INTERVIEWER: In *The Writer's Opera*, the life and death of the artist are very closely linked. Is there a link between the creative drive and fear of death?

DREXLER: I have a paperweight on my desk and all it says is *TIME!*

INTERVIEWER: There's a lot of death in your work.

DREXLER: Yes: Linda in *Room 17C*, death by fire and smoke inhalation; the rapist in *The Investigation* shoots himself; Amy in *Graven Image* [1980] incites her husband to shoot her; Susan in *The Writer's Opera* dies of old age; the father in *Starburn* is a suicide. In *Delicate Feelings*, Mike, the bar owner, shoots the woman who rejects him, then kills himself. In *The Green River Murders* [1985], the serial murderer strangles a hooker and also scares his mother to death with a knife. I'm a newspaper and TV addict. It's addled my brains. However, what's more dramatic than a great death scene? Shakespeare knew the value of a blood-curdling scream, and a corpse-laden stage.

INTERVIEWER: If you had to describe the genre into which Rosalyn Drexler fits best, what would it be? People have called your plays theater of the ridiculous . . . American absurdist . . .

DREXLER: I'm more real than real, I'm a super-realist. My plays are inside out . . . things that most characters only think are given voice and spoken in my work. Life is now more absurd than fiction. I have a facility with language. I play with words. I'm an artist; therefore, I can picture my plays as if they were paintings. I'm a singer/musician and feel the cadence of sentences, also where music might go, musical bridges, songs. Yes, I have an outrageous flare and an irreligious outlook on life . . . but where do I belong, in what category? Who knows?

INTERVIEWER: Has your work been done in London?

DREXLER: Charles Marowitz directed *The Investigation* [Open Space Theatre, London, 1969]. I didn't see it, but one of the London critics said something like "I hope America isn't like this." That was my first rape play. Max Stafford-Clarke directed *The Line of Least Existence* [1968] at the Traverse Theatre in Scotland. It had very loud rock music and people were holding their ears. I taped it, but I had a cold and so did my daughter who was with me; we were both coughing, and that's all I could hear on the tape. Joe Papp [artistic director, New York Shakespeare Festival] was going to produce *The Line of Least Existence*, but then he had a falling out with the director and the play didn't get done. It would have been the first play with rock music. . . . Actually Joe took me around the theater before the whole thing was constructed. He said he wanted me to feel that it was my second home. . . . He hasn't contacted me since. That was about twenty years ago. I feel like a prodigal daughter, or someone out of a Kafka novel: What's my crime, Joe?

INTERVIEWER: You were in Europe on a Rockefeller grant to study theater. What did you do there?

DREXLER: I saw theater, especially in England. Saw Brecht's *Puntilla*, acted by The Royal Shakespeare Company, went to Chichester and saw

Strindberg's *Miss Julie* with Maggie Smith, and other plays. . . . I stayed for a while with John Russell, the art critic, and met V. S. Pritchett at dinner. I saw a lot of art in London, Paris, Italy and went everywhere on a Eurail pass. I wrote on the train. I was working on *The Line of Least Existence*.

INTERVIEWER: You've been compared to Orton, Ionesco, Kafka, Jarry. . . . Do you feel flattered when compared to great writers?

DREXLER: I tend to believe it, and I'm more than flattered, I'm embarrassingly gratified. I like to be respected, to be taken seriously. . . . However, I'd like to earn a living from my work. I'm talking about being a writer among writers . . . yes, to be noted in history . . .

INTERVIEWER: Do you feel isolated?

DREXLER: Yes, even though I have a play on almost every season. I haven't had a financial success. I'm not written about. I'm writing now, doing my best work, but I'm referred to as a sixties playwright. This is odious. This is burying someone alive.

INTERVIEWER: In studying women playwrights throughout history, we see this pattern of erasure of women's dramatic writing. They were there but then forgotten. You explored this sort of thing in your play *She Who Was He*—this wiping away of a woman's accomplishments.

DREXLER: Yes.

INTERVIEWER: Do you think the answer lies in women's work being published and properly distributed? Why aren't more of your plays in the libraries?

DREXLER: I've tried to get more of my plays published, but I've been told that I need a big hit play (Broadway, Off Broadway) for it to be worth a publisher's while. I can't get *The Writer's Opera* published even though it won an Obie, did respectable business and was lauded highly. Also, the publishers want plays that amateur groups around the country would want to do, plays that are one set, few characters, uncomplicated, and slice of life. So you see, that lets me out . . . although there is a new publisher, young, adventurous Kip Gould of Broadway Play Publishing, who is putting out a book of three one-acts by me (called *Transients Welcome*). The plays in this book are about as real as I get . . . even he doesn't want to take a chance on my strongest work, my full-lengths. I wish the reading of plays would have a renaissance the way poetry has. Poetry is even reviewed in the Sunday *New York Times Book Review*. Do you think my *Transients Welcome* will be reviewed? I'll try, but lots of luck to me.

INTERVIEWER: What writers have influenced you?

DREXLER: I haven't been directly influenced, really. It might be obvious from my work. But I've *enjoyed* a whole range of authors. Particularly Colette for her detail and for knowing her milieu and knowing how every flower smells, knowing about cats, knowing about loving women, loving men, about relationships, mothers, husbands, work. She did so many things, I mean, like me. She was an acrobat, too. I was a weight-lifter. She had a perfume shop, she acted, she toured nightclubs. I've sung. I kind of relate to her. And she was from the provinces. Too bad about her first husband, Willy! But it's probably good he was such a bastard and locked her in her room even though he took credit for her novels.

INTERVIEWER: Why?

DREXLER: I often think it would be nice if someone just locked me in a room to write and I couldn't get out. [Laughter] I also respect Kundera; *The Unbearable Lightness of Being* was wonderful! And Elizabeth Hardwick is perfection.

INTERVIEWER: Is there a different kind of relationship between editors and authors than directors and playwrights?

DREXLER: A fiction editor has a more respectful, hands-off attitude toward the writer. He/she may suggest things, have questions, but a book is your "baby" and in the end you take responsibility for its success or failure (in artistic terms). A director is much more *auteur*, deals with the script in many ways, leaves her/his mark on the work and shares in the kudos or boos. Fate hangs in the balance when a director takes over. It is hard to tell the direction from the play sometimes, and often, one chance is all you get.

INTERVIEWER: Can writing be taught?

DREXLER: Writing and the ability to express yourself clearly can be taught. But that special thing, that extra thing, a turn of mind, a kind of wicked energy, intellectual seriousness and responsibility to the original impulse . . . that cannot be taught. It can be recognized, and the good teacher can help to keep the student open to herself/himself. The greatest stumbling block to being a creative writer (in the highest sense) is the writer herself, who self-edits too soon. A teacher must be careful not to set this censorship of self into motion. It is extremely delicate . . . all the junk and embarrassing stuff has to come out with the good . . . then comes the winnowing. As Hemingway once said, or was thought to have said, one must have a built-in shit detector. But to have that, one must have smelled shit at least a few times.

INTERVIEWER: When did your own writing begin?

DREXLER: As soon as I got a secretary to transcribe my stories: I was six or seven, and my mother was there with pad and pencil. She was very encouraging. My father wanted me to write his ideas. He said, "I'll give you a good plot and you'll be very famous. There are all these people on a plane, the plane crashes, and the people are stranded together for a week until they are rescued. While they are there we find out about all of their lives." Daddy was right. It's a good ol' plot. It's been done to death: The *Titanic* . . . *Airport,* many others. . . . When I began writing my own little stories and poems, Dad got very upset . . . he couldn't handle my subject matter, it embarrassed him . . . sex . . . death . . . I suppose he was frightened.

INTERVIEWER: How old were you then?

DREXLER: Oh, fourteen through sixteen I suppose. . . . I was kicked out of high school [The High School of Music and Art in New York City], where I was a voice major, for cutting gym. Funny, because later on I became an athlete. I was in the first Women's National Power Lifting contest [Nashua, New Hampshire]. Trained with the heavyweights, became a strong contender, got me an AAU card, just because I wanted to see if I could do it. . . . I was the oldest woman competing. I'm into decadence now.

INTERVIEWER: What about your career as a painter?

DREXLER: Now that's where I'm really being erased from history. . . . There are artists making mucho moola on things that I was doing: the stop-action figure, for instance . . . movie images and placement . . . men-and-machine series . . . paintings done in the sixties and early seventies. I was also doing paintings that I hid . . . the funky "bad" stuff that I thought no one would understand, also in the sixties . . . it's big business now . . . reputations are being made with this kind of work. I had my first show at the Ruben Gallery in 1959: eighty-two pieces of sculpture—then I became a painter, showed at Zabriskie, and for three seasons at Kornblee. I'm in numerous important collections. . . . I was the first painter to actually use photographs in my work, to blow them up, paint over them. . . . I was a so-called Pop painter . . . however, I was not asked to be part of the [1985] *BLAM!* show at the Whitney. Nobody acknowledges that I'm a precursor of certain painters.

A few years back, when Lawrence Alloway was a curator at the Guggenheim, he included me in a show of artists who were at the Ruben Gallery. It was at the top of the Guggenheim, and I showed the sculptures that I had done for the Ruben show. Lately I've had a show at P.S. 1 of paintings. July/August 1986 I'm having a major retrospective at Grey Art Gallery (NYU), in New York with a beautiful catalogue, and articles written about the work. September 1986 the show travels to Greenville County Museum of Art, South Carolina.

INTERVIEWER: Have you ever had any dark moments, periods when you were unable to write?

DREXLER: No. When I have my dark periods, that's when I steer towards what I love the most—writing. I write through the pain. I wipe everything else out, whatever the hell is going on: life, death, arguments, no money. . . . I will write, no matter what. I haven't ever had a so-called writer's block. I've been stuck sometimes, like for a week, taking time to think what I want to do next. But I'm never really empty or fallow.

INTERVIEWER: Did it help or hurt your career to win the prestigious Obie Award for your very first play?

DREXLER: It might have stopped some people . . . but I felt I had to go on and do more. It was encouraging. Although I actually didn't write plays for a while after that.

INTERVIEWER: Your play *Delicate Feelings* is about mud wrestling, isn't it? Would you talk a little about your own experience as a wrestler, as Rosa Carlo, The Mexican Spitfire?

DREXLER: Well, I used to go to a gym here on Forty-second Street, which no longer exists. It became a storage place for old pie tins. But at the time I went there, circus people and wrestlers worked out. They thought I'd be a good wrestler and introduced me to Billy Wolfe, who had a group of women wrestlers touring the country. So I went up to this hotel and talked to them for a while and they said, "OK, we'll give you a call." Later, when some women wrestlers were in a car accident, they flew me down to Florida and broke me in.

INTERVIEWER: Did you continue to write while you were doing this?

DREXLER: Not at the same time but I have always been a writer.

INTERVIEWER: Was it all rather scary?

DREXLER: Oh, yes, terribly. I mean, we wrestled in airplane hangars and all sorts of big arenas. I've wrestled in bigger arenas than any of my plays have ever been in, you know? There I was in the ring—grappling!

INTERVIEWER: Were you ever hurt?

DREXLER: No, luckily. I've been tied in the ropes. I've been thrown out of the ring. I've come back. I've gotten chest blows. I wasn't in the business very long. . . . It's Show Biz. It's burlesque. They exaggerate for publicity. But people *do* get hurt.

INTERVIEWER: Did you have a theatrical costume?

DREXLER: I had a bathing suit that was reinforced so that it wouldn't come off. And wrestling shoes. And a little satin jacket. Now it's all become more stagey. People come on with bongos and African outfits. They come on as Egyptians, Indian princesses, Greek goddesses. It's crazy time. However, mud wrestling is different. Another voyeuristic thing for men with sadomasochistic inclinations. I saw one bout—it was like a little play. Two assistants carried these two women into the mud as if they were dolls. And then the hair pulling and slipping and sliding began and getting all dirty. I've written about it . . . covering themselves with baby shit is what it was. It's degrading.

INTERVIEWER: Where do you think this tendency to sadomasochism in our culture comes from?

DREXLER: Giving and taking pain is probably more "natural" than sitting in the sun and having a great time. I don't like it but . . .

INTERVIEWER: Writers Karen Malpede and Susan Griffin, who make a clear distinction between eroticism and pornography, feel that pornography has its genesis in fear. . . .

DREXLER: It does come from fear. Male fear that they won't get it up. So they have to invent games. These games are like magic. I've seen an artist who applies clothespins or pincers to a woman's nipples and then paints her breasts.

INTERVIEWER: What about those who would say the model is consenting?

DREXLER: Sometimes women consent because other things are at stake: peace in the family . . . whether or not someone is going to get even with her . . . fear of losing someone. . . . This kind of politics goes on all the time. Sex is used that way. I object. I hate pornography: women or men in degrading tableaux. . . . No, pornography is *not* good; what men *see*, men *do* . . . no pornographic illustration or movie has ever prevented a man from enacting his own destructive fantasy on a woman. Pornography is not a safety valve, it is a writ of permission. When I was younger, I was personally victimized by this kind of thing . . . by men wanting me to play their games. . . . I could never understand what this kind of horror theater had to do with making love, or even sex. Sex is the most ordinary, natural thing in the world. Why make it so tediously, repetitiously, vicious and obsessional? I fear that what has once been regarded as kinky is now the norm, and is regarded as pictorial spice to sell underwear, or shoes. A mean expression, a dangerous environment is interpreted as the way to look, the place to be. The accouterments of hate and impotence have become the signposts of good taste and desirability. . . . As far as the producing of pornography for sale, there's so much money to be made there, so much profit from misery, that I fear it can never be stopped. But legislation against pornography could infringe on free speech; as a writer and patriotic American, I'm against that.

INTERVIEWER: What would you do with your life if you weren't a writer?

DREXLER: If I couldn't write and couldn't paint, I'd probably collect pebbles and look at how beautiful their colors are. I'd be a jazz singer. I love to sing. I sing all the songs from the twenties, thirties and forties.

I did a gig recently at SNAFU. My son played the trumpet. The owners gave me a present, a videotape, so I'll always have that moment.

INTERVIEWER: Is your husband an artist?

DREXLER: He's a painter . . . does beautiful figures painted on rocks—a modern paleontology—mysterious as cave paintings. His work is a revelation to me. Like all good artists, he creates a private, special world. It affects me deeply.

INTERVIEWER: You have a lot of work behind you. What's next?

DREXLER: You know, it's a funny thing. I feel as if I haven't begun yet, like I haven't really done what I wanted, like something *important*. I have a feeling there's some work I'm going to do soon that will be really satisfying . . . all the way . . . so wonderful . . . so beautiful . . . and soulful.

INTERVIEWER: Like good sex?

DREXLER: Much more adventurous than that . . . something un-common.

INTERVIEWER: We never really answered that question about whether or not true art is genderless. Is there a female aesthetic?

DREXLER: The female aesthetic is to be *un*aesthetic. When I think of *aesthetic*, I think of something too finely placed, too much in good taste. Women are trying to be a little sloppier, changing forms, getting stronger, letting ideas come in—and that is unaesthetic.

LAURA FARABOUGH

Laura Farabough, playwright, director and designer, is the artistic director of her own theater company, Nightfire, based in Sausalito, California. She began the company in 1980 as a radical step in redefining her artistic language after eight years as the director of Snake Theater. Since its inception in 1980, Nightfire has produced eight works, including Liquid Distance/Timed Approach, which was performed at the 1984 Los Angeles Olympics Art Festival, Obedience School, which played at San Francisco's Magic Theater and New York's Performing Garage, and most recently, a location piece, Under Construction, performed at Pier 3, Ft. Mason, San Francisco. Ms. Farabough works in multimedia; her plays are innovative and challenge traditional notions of theater. She received a National Endowment for the Arts Playwright's Fellowship in 1982, and was artist-in-residence at the Bay Area Playwrights Festival in 1981–82. Farabough has reconceived her play Femme Fatale: The Invention of Personality as an opera, and is working on the libretto with composer Kim Sherman. Femme Fatale . . . is at present in development at the Minnesota Opera Company, and will be performed in the spring of 1988.

————◆————

INTERVIEWER: When did you begin writing?

FARABOUGH: I learned how to read and write at age four, and as a child I always wrote plays and stories. I made puppet shows, and my playmates and I would stage backyard extravaganzas with dancing and singing and cardboard sets. I liked to dance and sing and playact. I also liked to paint and to make things. I don't think of myself exclusively as a writer or a playwright. I am also a painter and sculptor, an actress, dancer, and stage designer and director, and as a child I had the same multiplicity of artistic interests. I loved elementary school. My favorite activity was when the teacher read stories to us, but even better was when we got to write and read out loud our own stories. I also liked it when the teacher would play music and ask us to draw pictures that went with the music.

INTERVIEWER: Was there a particular moment when you knew what you wanted to be when you grew up?

FARABOUGH: Oh yes, I knew very clearly when I was ten what I would be. My parents had a good library and I read all their books about theater, essays, history, criticism, and plays. Tennessee Williams was an up-and-coming playwright then, and I liked him. I especially liked *Suddenly Last Summer*—this is when I'm about eight or nine—I liked the sensationalism, the lobotomies, and the cannibalism of it all. And then, on TV, when I was ten, I saw A *Member of the Wedding*. And it affected me profoundly. I was very moved by Julie Harris's performance. I wanted to be an actress. And that's when I realized that I would devote myself to theater. So I told my teacher the next day what my plans were, and he said, "Great, why don't you write the sixth-grade class play?" And so I did. It had to incorporate our studies of early California history and I think I called it *Party at the Pueblo* . . . sort of a juvenile Mexican-flavored *Suddenly Last Summer at The Wedding*. I also directed it. I was not the lead actress, which disturbed me at the time. At any rate, in my autograph book, my teacher wrote a request for two tickets to my first play on Broadway.

INTERVIEWER: Did your parents encourage your writing?

FARABOUGH: Yes. They encouraged all my artistic endeavors. I started taking ballet, tap and acrobatics when I was five and my dancing lessons continued till I was about twelve. I also went to art classes. But the most important activity when I was young was horses. I started riding when I was six. And from ten to seventeen I was in the junior horse-show circuit riding thoroughbred hunters and jumpers. I trained every day after school and all day on weekends getting ready for the next show. It was a very rigorous and disciplined schedule for a young girl.

INTERVIEWER: What did your parents do?

FARABOUGH: My father was an anesthesiologist, and my mother was a housewife who wanted to be an artist, I think, but never pulled it off. Actually, they both wanted to be artists. My mother and a friend opened an art gallery once. It was fun. It was probably one of the first art galleries ever in the San Fernando Valley. Hundreds of artists came by with their work. My father hated being a doctor. He was an outdoorsman and an inventor. He belonged to a motorcycle club, scuba dived, flew airplanes. He and I used to go on camping trips; I had a little motorcycle, and we'd take bows and arrows and shotguns and shoot at rocks and at trees. It was make-believe hunting. He built an airplane in the backyard and a boat in the front yard. He used to weld sculptures in the garage, and we were big model-airplane builders. He was a lot of fun, but also scary because he lived at such a reckless pace.

INTERVIEWER: Were you an only child?

FARABOUGH: No. I have a brother, John Ross, who's five years younger. He's a computer designer and inventor and very interested in the medical uses of computers. Science and technology, the mechanics of how things worked, was a family pastime. I remember when my dad became interested in medieval warfare. We turned the entire backyard into a city under siege. We had trenches everywhere, and catapults. In the trees we suspended baskets that could be pulled across wires to another tree in case your first tree came under attack. We had water warfare, canals, and we would make miniatures of villages and indicate their lines of defense and then flood them out. My introduction to location theater.

INTERVIEWER: Why did you move to Texas?

FARABOUGH: Well, in 1963, a month after President Kennedy was assassinated, my father was killed in a car accident. There is a five-hundred-acre farm forty miles north of Dallas that has been in my mother's family for about a hundred and fifty years. Growing up, whenever there was talk about catastrophes, or the need for my family to change life-styles, the "ranch" was always brought up as the place we would go. It was always the symbol for escape, making new beginnings. Well, the catastrophe happened, and my mother moved us to Dallas. I was fourteen. I became an extremely rebellious teenager. I was very unhappy. And my own deep sense of loss and disillusionment was also reflected in American social concerns. The national mourning for JFK, the magnitude of racial injustice being addressed by the civil-rights movement, the rumblings of the free-speech movement, the revelations of the war in Vietnam. I was just old enough to grasp the meanings and implications of all this turmoil, and it made me afraid and angry. I became wild. I ran away from home several times. And finally, I was sent to a boarding school in Arizona. My mother thought she was doing the best thing. But the school had its own problems, and in 1965 it was busted for drugs. We moved back to California the next year. I went to public high school for a while, but simply could not relate. I was too independent.

INTERVIEWER: Why did you drop out of high school?

FARABOUGH: I wanted to go to art school, to be a painter. I left home when I was seventeen, and supported myself as an artist's model. I married my boyfriend, a Greek-American hillbilly who was a painter, and we moved to New York. We lived in an abandoned fifth-floor walk-up just off Tompkins Square Park. We literally starved and froze. We lasted about eight months and then moved back to Los Angeles. We got involved with older painters, and we had a couple of good years. Being around serious working artists was wonderful. Even though I was very young, they took the time to talk to me and listen to my ideas about art and aesthetics.

INTERVIEWER: How did you make the transition from painting to theater?

FARABOUGH: I had given up on theater. I had no access to it. I had grown into a very shy young woman, and theater is a social art. And I was happy painting. Painting is a very difficult art as well. It took a lot of time. I was working, still, as a model, and also at a radical bookstore which put me in touch with writers, but not playwrights. When I was twenty-one, I left my husband and got a little house in Venice Beach. There I started writing seriously. Then, one day, Chris Hardman stopped me on the street, a total stranger, and started talking to me about Bread and Puppet Theater in Vermont. I was all ears. I loved the whole idea of huge masks, big paintings, banners, folk stories and political parables in the street. It made complete sense. It was a type of theater that used every art form, was heart-wrenchingly simple, and possible to make one-self. Chris and I talked nonstop for a week. Then he went back to Vermont. I decided to start writing plays. I had to teach myself dramatic structure and visualization. I spent a year totally absorbed in playwriting. Then, in 1972 Chris moved back to California. We got together and decided to make a theater.

INTERVIEWER: Was that the beginning of Snake Theater?

FARABOUGH: Yes, it was. But our first name was Beggar's Theater. We worked hard and had a lot of fun. We enlisted our friends, neighbors and family. We started a mask-making business that supported us and other members of the theater and every dime we made we put into the plays. In 1973 we moved to San Francisco, and then in 1974 we moved to Sausalito. There is a great deal of history that is wonderful and worth telling, but I'm going to skim over it pretty fast. We were Beggar's Theater from 1972 to 1976. We did about thirty different plays, parades, street shows, political skits in that time. Our style evolved from being an im-itation of Bread and Puppet to something that was more uniquely ours. In 1975 we were invited to tour Mexico by the Instituto Nacional de Bellas Artes. We toured the country for three months with two shows, both performed in Spanish. When we came back we became politically involved with our waterfront, houseboat community. It was under siege by developers and being threatened with destruction. We organized a variety of events and plays. During that time, we became close friends with another waterfront couple, Evie Lewis, a dancer, and Lary Graber, a composer. In 1976, Beggar's Theater became Snake Theater, and Evie and Lary became our main collaborators.

Snake was a quantum leap above Beggar's. Our plays were no longer lost in space, they were fixed in a modern time frame and [were] local . . . set in California. Snake Theater existed from 1976 to 1980. We did a lot of location shows. *Somewhere in the Pacific* was performed at Ft. Cronkhite Beach just a mile or so up the coast from the Golden Gate Bridge. It was a large and beautiful landscape. Essentially, it was about a sailor lost at sea during World War II and a love letter he sent to his girlfriend back home. One of my favorites was *Her BLDG*, 1977, that we did at Sausalito City Hall. It was performed outside, with the City Hall as a backdrop. It was a play of soft paranoia about a woman who has an appointment with a building. That was the first time we used video. Another play was *Auto*, 1979, that was performed at an abandoned gas station in Sausalito. We had matched yellow Mustangs, and a huge White 1936 eighteen-wheel truck. The play was about a family trying to leave town who get stuck in a gas station when their car dies due to neglect. And the last play we did was *Ride Hard/Die Fast* which was okay, but strange for me. It was the first play that I hadn't co-written, it was Chris's play which I directed, and I really didn't like it very much. At any rate, we toured it around Europe in 1980, and that was it for *Snake*.

INTERVIEWER: How did Snake Theater become separated into your company, Nightfire, and Chris Hardman's Antenna?

FARABOUGH: Recently I was doing a radio interview and was asked this, and I was starting to give my answer which I wanted to say as "Well, I think both Chris and I," et cetera, but what came out was "Well, I think both I and I . . ." and I heard what I said and laughed, but that slip is a good hint as to the problem. There was just no distance or separation between us; we did everything together all the time and we'd been living and working like that for nine years. Our personal and professional relationship just buckled beneath the strain. A few years earlier we had put into practice a decision-making mechanism that worked for quite a while: who had the last word. And we alternated that responsibility with each show. But in the last couple of years that system broke down and I had the last word on all the shows, which was very frustrating for Chris, to say the least. Along the way as the shows became larger and more complex, our working roles became more defined. We'd start out together and write the shows, and then I'd go out and get it cast, secure the location, and start rehearsing, and since I was directing the shows I had the last word, and Chris sort of got trapped in the workshop building the props and sets for the shows and didn't have as much access to the play's development. At that point each of us was equally strong in all aspects of theater, but I wanted more chance to design, and Chris wanted more chance to direct, and each of us wanted to write our own plays. Lary Graber, Snake's composer, wanted Snake to stay together. So we decided we would take turns at the helm, I'd write, design, and direct, and then Chris would, and Lary would do the music for each. It might have worked, but then, very suddenly, Lary got leukemia and died. That was in 1980. Chris and I then started our own theater companies.

INTERVIEWER: What did the separation of Snake mean in terms of physical space, assets, and other people?

FARABOUGH: The development of the two companies has worked out very well. In large part that success is due to the board of directors of Snake who protected both our interests and oversaw the separation of assets. Snake is our nonprofit corporation that both companies still operate under. We are both based in Sausalito, and we alternate use of our workspace facility. We use the same bookkeeper, since there must be a joint income report to cover Snake. Occasionally we go in on grants together. But that's it. Each company operates autonomously.

INTERVIEWER: *Femme Fatale: The Invention of Personality*, the first Nightfire production in 1981, was a bold departure from the style of the previous work of Snake, more complex in its conception and more elaborate in its staging, as well as dispensing with the use of masks which was the Snake signature visual element.

FARABOUGH: I think we're all familiar with the artist who develops a style, achieves some recognition for that style, and then gets trapped in it. To me, that's what had happened with Snake . . . it was a formula, and I felt like I could not learn any more from it, that any further work in that vein would be stale. *Femme Fatale* was my first play on my own and a chance to try something new and dangerous. I had a glorious feeling of creative power and vision. I felt dangerous. And I picked two dangerous women to make a play about, Mata Hari and Greta Garbo. And I chose to make a comparison between the development of their public personalities and the effect of their legends on their private lives and actions. The play is performed in parallel with both stories occurring simultaneously and intertwined. Mata Hari was a Dutch woman who had lived with her military husband for a brief time in Java. When she divorced him, she found herself alone and destitute in Paris. As a means of surviving, she invented an elaborate new identity as a Hindu Javanese princess and became an international sensation as an exotic dancer. She performed at the Opera House in Paris, the composer Massenet was one of her many lovers and she danced in his production of *Salomé*; she performed at La Scala in Milan, all over Europe. Her story was never questioned. She began to have a hard time herself distinguishing between what was real and what she had made up. She believed herself to be invincible. She was arrested by the French as a German spy and executed in 1917. A true femme fatale. Greta Garbo is quite different. A girl from Sweden, she chanced into drama school and was discovered by a Swedish movie director. It was his ambition to create a star who would sweep the world. He had already picked the name for this woman should he ever find her—Garbo. He shaped Greta Garbo from scratch, and molded her public personality as a woman of ice and fatal beauty. Garbo was never comfortable with this image. When World War II broke out, her style was no longer popular, it was the time of the Ooomph Girls, bouncy, bubbly blondes. Her last movie, *Two-Faced Woman*, has Garbo playing two roles. One is a young, married country girl, a professional ski instructor. Her husband is a newspaper critic. She suspects he is having an affair with a woman playwright in New York, so she decides to disguise herself as her own "twin sister" and win back her husband. In this disguise, Garbo is made to act like an Oomph Girl. It was a disaster, it killed her career. The meeting place in my play for these two women, is the movie *Mata Hari*, made by Garbo in 1926.

INTERVIEWER: *Femme Fatale* mixes documentary material and fiction? Will you describe the visuals?

FARABOUGH: For the original production I painted twenty paintings, each eight feet by eight feet. These were on frames that could be rolled across the stage. Sometimes the paintings were used like backdrops and could suggest locale, and other paintings were suggestive of the inner conditions of the women. I had two favorite paintings. One was a huge face of a woman, her hair is on fire, and there is fire in her eyes; she's holding up her hands as if about to strangle you, but her wrists are chained together, and furthermore, her hands are trapped in blocks of ice. The other painting I liked—and I made two of them—is of a sleek dog that has the face of a beautiful woman, running across the floor of a hotel lobby.

INTERVIEWER: Do you have any future plans for *Femme Fatale?*

FARABOUGH: I've always conceived of this play as an opera. If all goes well, it should be produced [by the Minnesota Opera Company] in 1988.

INTERVIEWER: How would it be performed differently?

FARABOUGH: Well, the structure of the play will remain. I will cut down enormously on the amount of text, and rewrite it as a libretto, in close collaboration with the composer. Mata Hari and Greta Garbo will be played by two mezzo-sopranos, and the other twenty-six roles will be played by six other male and female singers. I will also want to work with live and prerecorded video, as I've been doing lately.

INTERVIEWER: In many of your plays you've cast people who have the same profession as the characters they portray. Why?

FARABOUGH: I often write plays for a specific location and for specific people. *Surface Tension*, 1981, was the first time I did that. I decided to do a swimming-pool show, and I had a high school pool available for use. It had a high diving board and I realized the play had to have a diver, a young man. So I asked around all the college and high school diving teams and found a young man, seventeen years old, who was a good diver and was studying acting in high school. I wrote the play for him and for myself. He played a high school boy who's a lifeguard in the summers. I played a woman, thirty, who worked at a carnival shooting gallery.

INTERVIEWER: Why did you go back to acting in *Surface Tension?*

FARABOUGH: I thought it would be fun, and useful; I'd been directing for so long, I wanted to be inside of a play and get the feel of performing again to help me be a better director. Also, I got in great shape, swimming every day for months to build up my strength and endurance for the show.

INTERVIEWER: Why a swimming pool?

FARABOUGH: I love water. It's not a stage illusion, it's the real thing.

INTERVIEWER: There must be a lot of technical difficulties to solve.

FARABOUGH: There are enormous technical difficulties. But I think they're worth it because the environment gives so much in return. But I don't know if I'd ever try touring a location show again. We toured *Surface Tension* to swimming pools up and down the West Coast. What a riot! We had this massive installation to set up, usually in a matter of hours. Lights, sound, projectors, underwater props. Plus, the show was physically dangerous. I was so exhausted one night after a setup in Portland that I went out there and about fifteen minutes into the show I made a really stupid move and broke my leg.

INTERVIEWER: Did you finish the show?

FARABOUGH: Oh yeah. I was in shock, it seemed much more terrifying to stop than to just keep going.

INTERVIEWER: Did having a broken leg affect your playwriting?

FARABOUGH: Yes. And much to my own good. I was in a cast and on crutches for eight weeks in the beginning of 1982. I was living on a tiny houseboat and I couldn't get up to shore except at high tides. So I had a confined and enforced schedule for writing, and that's when I wrote *Obedience School*, a play about conquering fear.

INTERVIEWER: How does a play begin in your mind?

FARABOUGH: I carry around a visual idea, often for a couple of years, that I know is going to develop into a play. Since *Nightfire* only produces plays written by me and we do about two new plays a year, I have to have ideas bouncing around two to three years before I sit down and write the play.

On the average, I usually have about two months of actual writing time and then we go straight into production. So I write under a great deal of time pressure. I have to produce. Now I've always worked this way, and it's something I set up myself, so I must need that kind of schedule. But I wish I had more time. So when I am at last ready to write I will do anything to get the ideas flowing. I talk to friends, I talk to myself on a tape recorder, I draw pictures, I read enormous amounts of books about my subject, I make lists of dream images, I make outlines and try to find a structure, I make up stories about the characters. It's a frantic search for the focus, the meaning of what the play will be. It's very hard on me physically and emotionally. And then, it comes, I have it, and I know what it is. Then I just write it. It usually comes very fast and clear.

INTERVIEWER: How do you present your ideas to your collaborators and performers?

FARABOUGH: I have worked with a lot of the same people for years. So they have been hearing about the "next play" for a long time, and we've talked about it long before I start to write. Often I know who the performers are going to be in advance, so I write their parts for them. As soon as I have a solid outline and description of characters and a description of the thematics, I give everyone a copy of the first draft.

It's important to get the composer, the set builder, the lighting designer, and especially Ron Blanchette, who is Nightfire's video director, to work as soon as possible. So, I make special maps or guidelines for each of them, and we discuss the function of their art form in the play, and then they go to work in their own domain. I visualize every aspect of a play. I try to solve the technical problems as I write. I have to, my plays would never happen if I didn't.

INTERVIEWER: Do you rewrite?

FARABOUGH: I do and I don't. Rarely do I rewrite a scene, or in any way change the structure of the play. But the dialogue usually changes a great deal. A creative, inventive performer is very good at improving my written dialogue. I'm getting farther and farther away from prerecorded dialogue, and so I notice that by using live voice, either over live video or through wireless mikes, my plays are having more intimacy and variety of sound. Also, it lets the performers have more rehearsal time to develop and create their characters' vocal styles.

INTERVIEWER: How have you changed or developed your movement and vocal styles over the years?

FARABOUGH: I've moved from a very robotic style to one with much more individuality, character, nuance and dynamics. Snake used masked performers somewhat as animated props. All the dialogue was taped. In the first plays of Nightfire, I got rid of the masks but still kept using recorded dialogue. *Femme Fatale* used recorded voices for all of the characters except Greta Garbo and Mata Hari, who spoke live through wireless mikes. All the dialogue was recorded in *Surface Tension* and *Obedience School*. Recorded dialogue is usually monotone.

What opened up the dimensions of live voice, for me, was the use of video. Having a live camera the performer would go to in the course of the play, and deliver their character's most intimate thoughts. I still had the distancing effect, but there was now animation and an immediacy. I now use a combination of prerecorded dialogue, prerecorded video, live video and live dialogue with the use of wireless mikes. I have, in large spaces, to use amplification because I have an amplified music and sound element to balance, and an unmiked voice will not be heard. In *Beauty Science*, which was performed in a small beauty parlor in Sausalito in 1983, almost all of the dialogue was live and unmiked, but I rarely work in places that small.

As for the development of movement, more and more I work with dancers who have a distinct personal style. In the pieces that have a large number of performers, I will group choreograph for them.

INTERVIEWER: You've taught at the Bay Area Playwrights Festival. Do you feel that your approach to writing plays can be taught?

FARABOUGH: I don't teach writing. I teach playmaking. What I try to do is teach all the aspects of seeing an idea through from its conception, production, and into performance. I try to impress upon people that there are alternatives to language through which to express ideas: images, movement, lighting, technology, repetition. You can come up with an idea and introduce it at intervals so that an accumulation of information comes across.

INTERVIEWER: Do you ever bring back an old show? Or do you imagine anyone else could produce one of your plays?

FARABOUGH: I've never brought back a play. I'm always too busy getting ready to do the next one. I don't really think anyone else could stage my plays. Although I have received requests to produce some of my location ones. So far I've said no. I am protecting my aesthetic, I suppose. It is the goal of the opera production of *Femme Fatale*, however, that another opera company could mount a production.

I would like to produce *Under Construction* again. I miss that show very much.

INTERVIEWER: What about *Liquid Distance/Timed Approach,* which you performed at the 1984 Los Angeles Olympics Arts Festival?

FARABOUGH: That show was performed at The Beverly Hills High School swimming pool. It's a very interesting building. It's indoors with a stadium configuration seating fifteen hundred people. It's a combination swimming pool/basketball court, and has a two-part movable floor which opens to reveal the pool. It also has one- and three-meter hydraulic diving boards. To my knowledge there is no other pool like that operating in the country. It could not be restaged in a different kind of pool since we made a whole scene around the opening of the floor.

INTERVIEWER: How did you like the festival?

FARABOUGH: We didn't get to see any of the other theaters because we were working so hard and our performances overlapped with the other groups. I don't think the festival promoted us correctly. Their PR made it sound like we were doing a water ballet. We're accustomed to a younger, artistic, ethnically mixed crowd. On opening night, fifteen hundred white people over sixty-five years old walked in. We were probably the most controversial group at the festival. I would have liked to cut it down by about twelve minutes, but I couldn't make any cuts because of technical restrictions; it would have meant reediting the music, dialogue and videotapes, and there wasn't the opportunity. I had an excellent company of athlete/performers who worked together with superb precision. The premise of the piece was an exploration of the fantasies swimmers use to keep up their momentum and determination when in competitive training . . . fears of drowning.

INTERVIEWER: Were there any creative breakthroughs for you in producing *Liquid Distance/Timed Approach?*

FARABOUGH: Yes. Ron Blanchette and I discovered how to seamlessly mix live video with prerecorded and edited video. Also, we made the cameraman a part of the action. We improved and refined that technique in *Under Construction.*

INTERVIEWER: *Under Construction* was a monumental work. What were your goals in producing it? As a playwright and as a designer?

FARABOUGH: I had been thinking about making a show for big machinery for a number of years. In particular I've been fascinated with Paris cranes—those are the enormous cranes used to build skyscrapers. I had seen a number of them outside my hotel window in Munich once and they looked anthropomorphic, like graceful dancers. I tried to get a site in a construction area but the insurance costs were sky high, so I had to change my approach. I was able to get Pier 3 at Ft. Mason in San Francisco by sheer good luck. Once I had secured the location, I then set about getting performers. I wrote the play for Ernesto Sanchez, who played The Architect, Deborah Marcom, who played His Wife, and Wayne Doba who played The Master Builder. I have worked with Ernesto off and on for twelve years and with Deborah steadily for four years; I'd never worked with Wayne but had admired him as a performer for a long time. At any rate, with the location and the performers in mind I then set about writing. I wanted the play to have an accessible story line. To have a clear linear drive and momentum. Sometimes I write plays that are circular, or that have no story line at all, but this time I wanted a very clean plot. What developed was a play about The Architect who has a vision of heaven with His Wife The Queen of Heaven. He decides to build her a monument, a Pyramid. And the play ends with the Pyramid built and His Wife locked inside. The Architect ascends to "Heaven" . . . we lifted him in the air on a rope attached to a crane. The Master Builder is left alone and with a new longing for art, not just craft.

INTERVIEWER: You worked with an architect in constructing the installation?

FARABOUGH: Yes. A young architect, Robert Hayes, built huge wooden sculptures for the piece. The pyramid was twenty by twenty feet and was rigged so that one wall at a time came down. He also built a series of wooden doors that were rigged in such a way that when they were closed they were twenty feet long and only about two feet wide, and then when they were opened they became ten feet wide. Very beautiful. We covered the floor with fifty tons of sand and five tons of gravel. It was a beautiful texture and shimmered in the lights. We raked the sand into patterns every night before the show. Our playing space was two hundred feet long and eighty feet wide. We sat the audience in two long rows, one on either side of the area. This seating arrangement was important to me. . . . Everyone was in a front-row seat, no one sat in front of anyone, and this allowed the audience to take in an enormous area. It was an intimate feeling, actually. We then set up ten TVs on either side in front of the audience. When it was time for live camera, the cameraman would walk into the set and the performer would go and talk to him. At other times the live camera would "spy" on a scene that was taking place.

INTERVIEWER: What are your responsibilities as artistic director of Nightfire?

FARABOUGH: My primary responsibility is to write, design and direct plays. Oh, and to try and stay within a production budget. With the scale I work in, my plays are getting more and more expensive, and I don't really have enough money to do what I do. Probably I should be making movies. My other responsibilities include planning for the future, establishing production schedules about two years in advance, and generally overseeing the company, making sure everyone is working towards the same goals and getting the support they need. Nightfire operates with a small staff: an executive administrator, an accountant, a fundraiser/grants-writer, and a promotional director. I can't afford, yet, to keep my artistic collaborators on a yearly salary, but it is a definite goal.

INTERVIEWER: Do you have your own theater space?

FARABOUGH: No. I have an office and a workshop. I need a rehearsal space, a place to dance and work on movement.

INTERVIEWER: What are your goals as a playwright?

FARABOUGH: To get more personal about my work, in terms of text and subject. Much of my material comes from my dreams.

INTERVIEWER: How do you feel about being called a "woman playwright?"

FARABOUGH: It depends how it's being used. Generally, I don't like it. Do people call Sam Shepard or Richard Foreman a "man playwright?" I find less and less do people need to dwell on the fact that someone is a woman artist. Unless the woman herself insists on the point being made because of the political or feminist nature of her work. My work does not address itself to those concerns. I am an artist and I like to invent my own world with its own logic, rhyme and reason, and fortunately, I have been able to do so for many years and shall continue to do so in the forseeable future.

INTERVIEWER: Have you had any restrictions or problems as a woman artist?

FARABOUGH: Not really. I've had no problems professionally. I notice that it's sometimes a problem for other people, though. Especially men who are a particular type of frustrated artist, the ones who just can't and probably never will be able to do it. But that's really their problem, not mine. I have been lucky in my career generally. I work with many very talented men and women and my work is informed by both a male and female sensibility.

INTERVIEWER: How is your work received by the feminist press?

FARABOUGH: I have sometimes been criticized for presenting imagery that, to their tastes, is too erotic or too violent . . . somehow not politically correct. On the other hand, I've read that my work can only really be understood by women because of feminine symbols and imagery. A lot of my imagery is from the iconography of mysticism, such as a young girl bleeding from her hands, as in stigmata, and filling up wineglasses with her blood that two older women then drink as an act of rejuvenation for them and a sacrifice to womanhood (i.e., the beginning of her first menstrual cycle) by her. That's from *Beauty Science*.

Or the tent scene in *Under Construction*. The Master Builder has just torn down the house of The Architect and His Wife to make way for the Pyramid. His Wife wants to know where they are supposed to sleep. A tent appears. They go there to sleep. His Wife wants to make love with her husband, but he's afraid to. He thinks if he holds her she'll disappear (she is his artistic muse). He leaves the tent. She has stripped. She calls after him, "Please come back. You can do anything you want to me." He says, "I can?" He reenters the tent and says, "Well, I've always wanted to try this," and proceeds to wrap her up as a mummy. It's very weird, erotic in a bizarre way and hilariously funny. As he wraps her up he keeps thanking her, asking if she's okay. When he's done he wonders what it means. Why has he done this, he wants to know. He leaves her and runs outside to ask the computer. It's a wonderful scene. But, if you're a staunch feminist, I suppose, such imagery can be disturbing. Maybe it's good for them to be disturbed.

INTERVIEWER: What do you think about the way you present women in your plays?

FARABOUGH: In *Obedience School, Beauty Science*, and *Under Construction*, there is a woman who has a direct link to her dream world, which I usually call Heaven, and she gets power from that place, from the Angels. Often my women have a problem integrating who they are and what they have learned from their dream world and the circumstances of their day-to-day lives, particularly with the men in their lives. The women in my plays, because of their access to Heaven, the dream world, are very powerful, but they don't realize it or know what to do with their powers.

INTERVIEWER: Will there come a day when women playwrights will be accepted on equal terms and referred to as "artists?"

FARABOUGH: Absolutely. That has already happened, for the most part. I think I am accepted as an artist. I don't ever want to set myself up as a "woman artist," because I don't want to take advantage of being a woman. You know the idea of "if you want it you'll get it because you're a woman and women artists are so hot right now." I was hesitant about being included in this book because I don't like the ghettoization of women artists.

But, maybe I'm too defensive, like reverse snobbery. The artists I admire the most are women: Frida Kahlo, Marguerite Young, St. Hildebrandt, and contemporary artists like Pina Bausch and Ariane Mnouchkine and a host of others. Artists whose work has affected me deeply emotionally, intellectually, spiritually, and aesthetically. A strong woman artist who is not afraid of herself, her sexuality, passion, symbols, language, who is fearless, willing to take any and all risks, often produces work that is staggeringly beautiful and at the same time frightening, dangerous, something to be reckoned with.

MARIA IRENE FORNES

M*aria Irene Fornes has had a long career as both playwright and director. Her plays include* Tango Palace, Promenade, The Successful Life of 3, Molly's Dream, Evelyn Brown, Mud, The Danube, Sarita *and* The Conduct of Life. *A collection of Ms. Fornes's plays,* Promenade & Other Plays, *was published by Winter House, Ltd., 1971. A more recent collection,* Four Plays, *was published in 1986 by Performing Arts Journal. Fornes has earned six Obie Awards, one of which was for sustained achievement in the'theater, as well as many prestigious grants. She conducts writing workshops at INTAR and at Theatre for the New City in New York. She is at present at work on a book on creative methods for writing.*

INTERVIEWER: You came to America from Cuba when you were a young girl. What were your initial impressions of this country?

FORNES: I arrived here in 1945. It was three months before World War II ended. It was a great time, a lot of excitement. Everybody was happy that the war was over. There were many young men in uniforms arriving in New York and going home. Apartments were difficult to find, like now. I went to school for a month, and then I started working in factories and in offices. I had many jobs and I didn't like any of them. After I was here for two years, I began to meet people in the Village, and that's when I became a bohemian. I was seventeen. I started painting when I was nineteen, and then when I was twenty-three I went to Europe. I came back and eventually gave up painting, because I realized I was really not a painter. I had to push myself to paint . . .

INTERVIEWER: Did you see your first plays in Europe?

FORNES: I'd seen some plays here, but I didn't go to the theater often because it was expensive and I didn't like to plan things. Sometimes I would buy the ticket in advance and miss the play! At that time, there was something peculiar to me about going to theater, something forbidden. The first play that amazed me (I thought it was the most powerful thing of all—not only in theater but in painting, film, everything!) was Beckett's *Waiting for Godot*. I saw the play in Paris and I didn't understand a word of the French, but I left the theater as if I'd been hit over the head. I understood every moment of it. That play had a profound influence on me. When I returned from Europe, I started writing. That was 1959.

INTERVIEWER: Had you done any writing previously?

FORNES: In a way. I had been translating some letters that I brought over from Cuba. Letters that had been written to my great-grandfather from a cousin who lived in Spain. These letters told the whole story of their lives. At first I was just translating them for myself, not for anyone else to read. I wanted to understand something about that whole world. Then I became completely obsessed with the idea of writing a play. I thought about it day and night. It wasn't as if I thought, "I want to be a playwright"; it was just something I needed to do. For nineteen days I did nothing but write the play. Each day I called in sick to work. I would wake up in the morning and go directly to the typewriter. That was *Tango Palace* [1963]. I had never experienced such an obsession in my life. Never. I could not eat . . . there wasn't anything that I preferred to do. It was like a door opened, and I entered into a world. If anything, I was afraid I would never come back. I could not *stop* writing. I loved it, it was such a thrill. I started writing late; I was around thirty. I had never thought I would write; as I said, I was an aspiring painter. But once I started writing it was so pleasurable that I couldn't stop. Then it became more difficult.

INTERVIEWER: Why did the writing become difficult?

FORNES: I began to get a little lazy, I had to push myself. It was a question of discipline. It was hard to get started. Once I got going it was okay. Then I discovered that when a day passed without work, the next day was harder. If I stopped writing for two days, it was even more difficult. Then there was a period when I was running the New York Theatre Strategy, a group of avant-garde playwrights. I didn't write plays for six years. People kept saying to me, "You should write," and at the time I was offended. Looking back, I don't understand how I ever could have given up my writing to put on other people's plays, or why I didn't accept it as a compliment when people said that I should be writing instead. Finally I hired other people to coordinate Theatre Strategy, which ran for a few more years. I worked on *Fefu and Her Friends* [1978]. My work habits were erratic at that time. The only reason I would write was because I was under a deadline. I promised to have a play ready on a certain date so I had to finish it. It is still so; to a degree I need deadlines. I have no sense of time. Days pass, months, and I still think I have plenty of time. For the past three years, I have been conducting a writing workshop at Intar which we call The Lab, because it *is* a laboratory. Sometimes I call it The Sanitarium [laughs]. My work habits are now excellent. People who come to visit The Lab are always amazed at how peaceful it is and how beautiful the light is. I designed this workshop which is for ethnic, underprivileged or minority writers.

INTERVIEWER: What happens in your "laboratory?"

FORNES: It is a place where we do many experiments on writing. So far, they have been very successful. Unlike most workshops and classes that exist in universities, where you go home and write, bring your writing to class, have it read and get criticism, the Lab is all about inducing inspiration. I have never felt that criticism was the way to teach writing. In painting classes you paint *together*; you don't paint, bring your work to class and have it criticized. There is a model and everyone is working together. The important thing is to teach how to *work*, not how to criticize a finished piece. There is something about the atmosphere in a room full of people working. Each person's concentration is giving you something. Once you've experienced this phenomenon in the practice of another art form, you have a knowledge that it exists. If you've been exclusively a writer, I don't think this way of working would ever occur to you. In fact, most writers say, "I have to be alone to work." That's nonsense! They usually need to be completely alone because the other people around them are *not* writing. But if you experience working in a room with people who are also writing, there is no distraction. There is an exchange of energy and you know the other writers are not there for you to chat with. Even if you wanted to talk, you would be interrupting, so there is no temptation. No one is waiting for you, distracting you, and yet others are there. It has something to do with having all the advantages of being alone, without the isolation. One of the writer's problems is being alone. When I think of all the people who could write, and who have time to write, the only ones who actually do are those who can bear being alone. There are probably many talented people who are not writing simply because being alone is something that they are not willing to go through.

So working in this manner in the Lab, first of all, we are not alone; and secondly, there is a kind of mental communication. It's not anything we pursue, but we've discovered people often write about the same thing at the same time. It happened the other day. There were twelve people in the Lab, and two of them were writing in very different ways and for different reasons about a devil disguising himself as a man. Separately, these two writers came up with the image of a devil's tail showing from beneath baggy pants. It's such a strange image. It was remarkable. So there is, as I said, a kind of mental communication. That's why our tables have to touch. We sit in a circle and write by hand, and when I see a gap between tables, I immediately feel, "Close that gap!"

INTERVIEWER: Do you use exercises in the workshop?

FORNES: Yes. Partly because I am more experienced than the other writers and partly because I am trying to discover a Hispanic sensibility. The people in the workshop are so different—the mental attitudes, the taste, the kinds of plays they're writing, the level of education, of sophistication . . . the variety is incredible. Yet when we are working in this way, it doesn't matter. I try first to have the students avoid writing any particular play with any particular characters, which leaves things completely open. Then for a period of two or three months I give exercises and they work with whatever imagery or characters emerge. You begin to notice that certain characters reappear and that there are certain elements that grab you in a more serious way than others. That will become the play. I must say that the exercises I use in the Lab have also helped me. They are a kind of meditation, but a meditation for writing. We begin with a half hour of yoga, which gets us into a state of inner awareness (it's also good to move, to be physical so that we can spend the rest of the day sitting down and not get bad backs). Then everyone goes to their seats and closes their eyes and I guide them to an inner concentration. Then I give an exercise which each person applies to their own work. It's incredible how the writing pours out. Sometimes I look around and each person is in their own world, you feel that they are miles away . . . it's incredible, the power. I make them explore and explore until they have explored so much that they are masterful.

INTERVIEWER: Criticism is never a part of the process?

FORNES: Not at all. I give criticism, when, for instance, I see that a person is blocked or in a rut. But I feel more like a coach for a sport who gives instruction, like telling a swimmer his elbow is not moving enough. This year, for the first time, we also give Monday-night cold readings of first drafts and I will give criticism on a first draft. During the summer the students do further work on their plays and in September we have another reading.

INTERVIEWER: Before you began the Lab workshops, did you utilize exercises in your own work?

FORNES: Since I began writing I have always played games. The very first time I sat down to write I looked around and saw a recipe book. I opened the book and using those ingredients I wrote a crazy story. Before that, when I was upset I would write a letter to a friend. The letter became something else, it was a way of writing. That writing was always personal.

The first thing I wrote that was not a personal outburst was a game that I had set up for myself with words. My first play, *Tango Palace*, was an idea that came from something very personal: a feeling about the relationship between a mentor of some sort and a student. That came from my inner energy, I didn't need any provoked inspiration. But my next play, *Promenade* [1965], began by my putting some characters and places on index cards. I played a game with the cards and this made it easy for me to write. I have a playful nature; I have never been able to do things because it is my duty to do them. If I can find a way to do my duty by playing a game, then I can manage.

INTERVIEWER: You once said that the novel is more delicate in structure than a play. Would you elaborate?

FORNES: I never said that. I don't know anything about the structure of a novel. I do think a play has to have a tough structure in the sense that people are always messing with it. You hand a play to a director and he or she interprets, then the actor interprets, the audience interprets, and the play has to stand up through all of this. Maybe that's what makes novels different, but I don't think they necessarily have a more delicate structure.

INTERVIEWER: When did you discover that it was essential for you to direct your own work?

FORNES: I didn't know I had to direct my own work right away, but I did find out immediately that the position of the playwright is unbearable. I went to the very first rehearsal of a work of mine. And as the actors started moving around with the script, an actress stood behind a chair, and I said, "Oh, wonderful!" Then I jumped up from my seat and said to her, "Here . . . try this!" I went on stage to where she was standing, positioned her, and said, "Oh, yes!" Everyone stared at me. I had never been to a rehearsal of anything in my life. I had simply seen something that I wanted the actress to push a little further; they all looked at me as if I had committed the worst crime. The director came to me and said, "Irene, I am very happy to hear any comments you need to make. Bring a notebook, write everything down and at the end of rehearsal we'll meet and you can tell me what your thoughts are." I thought he was insane. Then I thought he must be right because everyone around seemed to accept what he was saying to me. No one intervened or said, "Gracious, why are you telling her to do *that*?" We did meet afterward for coffee. He never understood a word I was saying and if he understood, he said, "No, I don't agree." I thought, "How could you not agree? Who are you not to agree?" I had been dealing with these characters for months and he suddenly wanted me to accept that I didn't know anything about them, to say, "Of course, you people know much more than I."

To me it was a world of madness. I learned as a playwright you "behave." You learn how to give up your play to people who "know better." I know there are many writers who do not direct, but to assume that just because you are a playwright you *can't* direct! And people do. I just received an award for directing, but people still say to me, "Imagine what your play would have been like if it had been directed by someone else. You would have had an objective eye." The stupidity of that statement. I think people simply feel that the playwright has too much power.

INTERVIEWER: In what sense?

FORNES: The creator is like God in relation to the creation. The playwright has a lot of power, but at the same time, the playwright is very gullible and naïve. I love playwrights, they are like angels really. When they are mistreated, when they are told, "GET OUT!" they go, poor darlings. Playwrights are told they don't know anything about theater. How can they write a play if they don't know anything about theater? It is true that there is a technique to directing actors, but a playwright can learn to deal with that. In fact, I have always felt a liaison with the actors, because the lines have to go *through* the actor. The actors must say the lines you have created until something begins to trigger inside them; in that sense, the actors are much more connected to playwrights than to directors. I have watched directors make wrong choices in rehearsal, and often the actors begin, instinctually, to say things as I thought I had written them. Then the director sometimes says, "No, no. That's not it." Often I wanted to go to the actors afterwards and says, "I think you are doing right," because I felt a connection, an alliance. I never did so because I thought it should be done in the open or not at all. I thought I could be helpful in a different way. At some point, I just decided that I would direct my own work or my work would not be done.

INTERVIEWER: Do you feel that playwrights should educate themselves about directing and acting techniques?

FORNES: I think every playwright needs to. First of all, you are not a good playwright unless you do all of those things. There are many reasons why playwrights, given the opportunity, might not *want* to direct: Perhaps they don't like dealing with so many people, or they're impatient; maybe they prefer somebody else to do it. If it's the playwright's choice and they prefer not to direct I don't think they have to. But to say they cannot direct! At the Padua Hills Theater Workshop where I go every summer you don't need to ask permission to direct your own play. On the contrary, if you don't want to direct, you have to *find* a director. We don't tell people, "You must direct" . . . they just do. It's like making your own sandwich. Because of this, the students see from the start that they *can* direct their own plays.

INTERVIEWER: Are women playwrights more intimidated by the idea of directing their own work because of the traditional notion of the director being the "father" of the production?

FORNES: I don't think so, because the playwright is the "woman" of the theater.

INTERVIEWER: Whether the playwright is male or female?

FORNES: Yes. The playwright is the woman and the director is the husband. Lanford Wilson pointed that out to me. I was explaining about how, as a playwright, you feel that someone is taking you out to have a "nice day" in a "nice place." The idea is "You be a nice girl and I'm going to take care of you." I thought that was because I am a woman, and Lanford said, "I feel the same way. I feel I am a girl; I have to be nice to this guy who is going to do nice by me; he's going to choose the right actors for my play because I don't know what I'm doing. I am very talented, but I don't really understand anything." I thought, "Well, perhaps it is because Lanford is not forceful enough." But then I was on a panel with another playwright who had had several plays on Broadway, and who had done quite a lot of commercial work. He looked like a business man, a big-shot executive. The panel was discussing the position of the playwright and this man, who was so masculine, so firm and definite with his white shirt and proper suit and strong voice, said that he understood the position of women in society because as a playwright, he was treated as a woman. So I am assuming that the playwright is the woman of the theater.

I do think it's more difficult for women directors than male directors. First of all, a producer has to believe that as a director, you will be in charge, that you will be able to control the cast, the crew, the production. In my case, they never would believe that I could control anything, and it's true. I don't have any control over anything *except* my art. I never say, "*You*, go there!" But I work with people who believe in my work and then I have a power that is almost hypnotic.

INTERVIEWER: Any advice for playwrights who are interested in directing their own work?

FORNES: Do it. You don't know how to talk to an actor? Take acting classes, find out what the actor needs. Technique is not a language of the gods. I think it has always been difficult for playwrights to take that control because it is hard enough to get your play produced without coming in with conditions. You learn to direct in the same way you learn to write plays. Work as a stage manager, watch how other directors work, find out about the elements of theater and how to deal with light designers, set designers, space. You cannot go into a theater expecting to direct merely because you wrote the play. You would not be doing a service to the play. By the time I insisted I would direct, I had taken acting classes at Actor's Studio, I had done costumes. I had been involved enough in theater so that I felt I could put together a reading. My first directing experience, *Molly's Dream* [1968] at New Dramatists, was essentially a reading—there were no reviews or publicity, and only five performances. It wasn't until later that I directed something finished, and then I had to work with lighting designers, etc. But I do have a good eye, and that's important. I was able quickly to ask for what I wanted and when the light designers would show me something, I knew whether it was good or not. I remember what a surprise it was to work with them.

INTERVIEWER: Did your new understanding of the technical side of theater affect your writing? Did it open your imagination?

FORNES: Yes. For instance, you have to find out what lights are all about or you may destroy scenes. But you see, I was a painter before. The stage for me is a very beautiful place, nice to look at. And space is very important. I'm very picky with actors. I will keep on positioning them—a little to the left, no, three inches more . . .—because for me, it's as important as focusing a camera. You reach a point, pass it, go back a little and ZING! it's in focus.

INTERVIEWER: Is this how the photographic freezes between scenes evolved in your play *Mud* [1983]?

FORNES: I did the play in Padua Hills, outdoors, and I could not have blackouts because I had scheduled myself in daylight time. The freezes were a way to change scenes. I kept them in the New York production because there was something about the freezes that I liked.

INTERVIEWER: What about the monochromatic quality? . . .

FORNES: The drab color also had to do with the original daylight production, which started when the sun was about to set and ended when the light became gray. The light changed during the performance, and the audiences always felt that it was deliberate because later in the play, everything becomes gray. The direct sunlight also created a quality. In the New York production, the clothes were drab and the set was white. The costume designer made the character Lloyd's clothes streaky, dirty. At some moment in rehearsal I felt he looked like a painting. I said to the designer, "Let's go with this . . ." and she gave Harry and Mae's costumes the same look.

INTERVIEWER: Would you discuss the eroticism in your work?

FORNES: That really began to happen with *A Visit*, which was an attempt to do something erotic. There is sexuality in the earlier work, like *Successful Life of Three* [1965], but it's more cartoonish. I don't like *A Visit* too much now, because it was composed from other people's writing and I violated their intentions. It was something I did in a playful way, almost like a party piece for friends. People have wanted to publish it and I have had some offers for productions, but I have refused. I was using material from Victorian novels, and I found there was something hot about the emotions in them. I took sections and made a collage of other people's writings. This completely changed the authors' meanings. I turned their Victorian words into something erotic. The men wore porcelain phalluses and the women porcelain breasts. The designer who made them put a little blue line around the tip of the penises and nipples. It was mischievous, playful, and I think it was my way of breaking through a kind of shyness about erotic things—because one always feels shy. To do something all the way out, like A Visit—which was completely erotic and completely bold, although it was in good taste because I don't like pornography—freed me.

I think, too, that as you get older you become freer sexually. When you are young you are afraid if you write something like A Visit people will call you on the phone and say, you know . . . [laughter]. But when you get older, you don't care. First of all, nobody calls you on the phone [laughter]. I feel that the older I get, the more shameless I feel. And in a sense, more pure. For instance, I am more interested in my work now. When I was younger, I was more interested in romance. The hours and hours I would spend being tormented by somebody or trying to pursue someone, fantasizing or imagining what the words meant. Now I watch that in others and it seems like rather odd behavior. Not that I am indifferent to love or romance. I am just not obsessed. I have more time to concentrate. I watch young people and it's endless, constant, they are like little animals, like dogs in heat. I think my writing is more passionate now, because when you are younger there is a fear of exposure and you protect yourself.

A play is so hot, so passionate; the Greeks, Shakespeare, opera have hot, hot passions, but very little sexuality. Today, sexuality is dealt with in pornography, in a cold, obscene way. The possibility of sexual drama is something unexplored. I am freer to examine these passions now because of the workshop. Many of the exercises, the meditations I do, are intended to work in a visceral way. I employ exercises to root the writer into their own organism, their own humanity, rather than the intellect. Writing is an intellectual process, so it is good to *root* the process into your stomach, your heart, your bowels. It is difficult sometimes for the younger women in the workshop. They are in a room of Hispanic men. Because of my age, I set an example: Whenever something erotic comes up in my own work, I read it. At first they all go, "Whoo . . ." It may be better for the younger women not to read when something erotic comes up in their work because it's true, when women are younger, they have to put up with the guys saying "Hey, baby . . ." But when I read my erotic passages aloud as an example, as a possibility in writing, at least I have given my female students permission to be fully *present* as writers, even if they choose not to read that material out loud. It may be that because of these exercises my own writing is becoming more erotic. Even so, I don't think, "Oh, here comes the erotic scene." I just write a scene of Harry [*Mud*] eating soup one day, and a scene where he is sexually aroused and masturbating the next.

After I had written the erotic scenes for *Mud* and *Sarita* I realized that the sexuality is very unconventional. They are not scenes that represent a typical sexuality, they are special moments, and those moments are theatrical. I probably owe—and I say *owe* because I think it's something important that has come into my writing—those strong sexual scenes to *A Visit*.

INTERVIEWER: Do you believe there is a female aesthetic in drama?

FORNES: How could there possibly not be? Not only is there a women's aesthetic, each woman has her own aesthetic and so does each man. It's like saying "Is there a Hispanic aesthetic?" Of course there is. Your aesthetic is different from mine—each person has their own universe—but how could we, as women, have nothing in common? That's not possible. We are different from a man, who is not a woman, who has never had a menstrual period in his life.

INTERVIEWER: Do you feel that a gender bias may exist in theater criticism, are women's plays often accused of being poorly structured "non-plays" when the playwrights may have intentionally broken form?

FORNES: You have to remember that we are dealing with theater and theater is the backward art. Theater is one hundred, two hundred years behind the times. There was an American girl living in Paris who wanted to translate *Promenade*, and have it produced in France. She came to New York to meet me and during her visit she went to [the] Lincoln Center [Branch of the New York Public] Library to read some old reviews of the play. She was amazed when she discovered that *Promenade* was considered an avant-garde piece. I told her, "It's because we are backward in the theater." If *Promenade* connects to anything, it's with movies of the thirties, popular art from the thirties—which is commercial! When the play was done in 1965, and then again in 1970, it was called "The musical of the seventies" to warn people that they were going to see something odd. I am sure people *still* consider that play odd.

I have a discussion every night after the performance of *The Danube* at The American Place Theater [1984]. I love doing it because I like to hear what audiences think. It's not pleasant, often the response is "What does it mean?" or "Why didn't you make it clear?" or "I'm *depressed*."

The triumph came just last night. A woman (one of those who said earlier that she did not understand the play) said, "Frankly it is excruciating. Could you tell me why anyone would produce this play?" I was glad that [artistic director] Winn Handman was there; I let him explain why he produced it. After a few more comments, the discussion closed and the same woman said in praise, "This is really an important play and I have to tell you that the images are so powerful." She was quite honest, even though what she said was contradictory. I think at first she felt, "If this doesn't tell me a clear story it is not theater. If this doesn't conform to everything I've seen previously in theater, then the playwright must have made a mistake." Perhaps when she heard the other comments she realized that her notion of theater was not necessarily what theater is; other things count also.

INTERVIEWER: Are the public discussions required by The American Place Theater or do you routinely attempt after-play discussions with the audience?

FORNES: They are set up by The American Place. Usually the playwright is asked to participate in a few of the discussions, but writers often feel as if they are being attacked, they feel defensive. There are times when the criticism is unanimous and harsh, and I have also felt from time to time like saying "You didn't like the play? Too bad!" But for the most part I like to hear what the audience has to say because you seldom get a chance to find out what people think about your work. For instance, I used to assume that when people liked the play they saw it in exactly the same way I see it. But that's not always true. I think it's very important to find out what people see in your work. I like to explain things, too. It helps me formulate my ideas, to put even the obvious into words.

INTERVIEWER: What do the more conventional critics find disturbing in your work?

FORNES: I was thinking about it just today. I wanted to discuss it with my students. I was thinking about what makes conventional theater. Let's say you were interested in doing a play that would be accepted by large numbers of people. What is it, then, that you should concentrate on? I realized that what makes my plays unacceptable to people is the form more than the content. My content is usually not outrageous. I think it's mild! *The Danube* is a play about a nice family that is being destroyed. Why don't nice middle-class people feel, "Oh, those poor darlings! That nice boy Paul and his girlfriend Eve, they were so good to their father and he loved them and this thing came along and destroyed their nice home . . . how terrible." That is the story of that play. I think people are sometimes afraid and suspicious. They don't know what bomb you have planted in your play. There is no reason for that. *Fefu and Her*

Friends, although it has very profound things in it, is a middle-class play. It is about nice middle-class girls from Connecticut, not about people saying "Let's destroy the world." It's mild. What makes people almost vicious must be the form. Because there are many plays that have outrageous things going on, but they have a conventional structure so people don't care. Isn't that curious?

INTERVIEWER: In a recent *Performing Arts Journal* symposium, you stated, "We have to reconcile ourselves to the idea that the protagonist of a play can be a woman." Would you elaborate?

FORNES: Even women are not aware of how important that is. Some women feel they must write plays in which there is a feminist statement, that they must attempt to clarify a situation in which there is prejudice against women. But they want to see situations where a woman is at a disadvantage and then becomes a victor. They are not interested anymore in seeing cases of women who suffer or succumb. I see their point. It's nice to see the person you are rooting for win all the battles, but at the same time, it is a little childish. I don't believe that the artist, the creator, is saying, "This character has perished, therefore all humanity will perish." I am very sad when I see a film or read a story in which the character I'm identifying with dies. But I don't feel that something has been killed inside of me because the character died. My ability to see their death as unnecessary is intact regardless of the pain I may feel about their death. I believe when you portray an unnecessary death, you are speaking on behalf of the person's life, the person's prime.

INTERVIEWER: Would you discuss that in terms of the female protagonist in *Mud*, who is shot by one of her lovers at the end of the play? One critic said the message of the play was directed towards women: "Don't try, they'll never let you get away with it." This critic felt it was quite a despairing play.

FORNES: I see Mae differently than many people did. I love her very much, I'm completely identified with her, but she is *not* an angel. I wrote the last scene just the way I saw it. At the end of the story, Mae is after something; she is learning, and that is so dear you cannot blame her for it. *Mud* is not an anti-male play that says men are pigs. It is also not a feminist message play about how Mae tries to liberate herself from these two men who will not let her develop. They are not keeping her down. She can leave any time she wants. It isn't that she is a brilliant woman. She says that she has a difficult time remembering things, she can't pass the tests at school. I think if she had got away she would probably have come back to Harry and Lloyd. She loves them, they love her, that's their life. When Lloyd shoots her it is not because he doesn't want her to get away and develop herself. It's because she is leaving and he would die without her. He must not let her do this. I think that when you write you must really open your eyes and see: Is it true that they would not let her get away? Does Lloyd's response grow out of the play? Of course it does. Of course Lloyd is very annoyed in the beginning that she is pursuing her studies. But it is not this annoyance that leads him to kill her. I don't think Mae really would have improved herself if she got away. What's wonderful about Mae is her love for knowledge. Knowledge is the beloved thing. She is not an artist, she worships art and wants to go where she can visit museums, et cetera. There is something noble and beautiful in this aspect of her character and I don't think it has been dealt with in plays or in fiction. Mae is a pursuer of angels, it doesn't mean she wants to *be* an angel, to grow wings and have magic powers.

In terms of the question about the female protagonist, I feel that what is important about this play is that Mae is the central character. It says something about women's place in the world, not because she is good or a heroine, not because she is oppressed by men or because the men 'won't let her get away with it,' but simply because she is the *center* of that play. It is her mind that matters throughout the play, and the whole play exists because her little mind wants to see the light, not even to see it because she wants to be illuminated, but so she can revere it. It is because of that mind, Mae's mind, *a woman's mind*, that that play exists. To me that is a more important step toward redeeming women's position in the world than whether or not *Mud* has a feminist theme, which it does not. The theme is just a mind that wants to exist and has difficulties. The difficulties have nothing to do with gender, but the fact that this mind is in a woman's body makes an important feminist point. I believe that to show a woman at the center of a situation, at the center of the universe, is a much more important feminist statement than to put Mae in a situation that shows her in an unfavorable position from which she escapes, or to say that she is noble and the men around her are not.

INTERVIEWER: What did you mean when you said, "It is impossible to aim at an audience when writing a play?"

FORNES: It's impossible because you can never predict the audience reaction. People think they are writing a comedy and then nobody laughs. If nobody laughs, it's not a comedy. That's why many plays fail. People spend millions of dollars to put plays on Broadway. If people knew what would succeed, none of those plays would fail.

INTERVIEWER: You have said that you would be willing to spend your entire life in poverty and struggle in order to be a working playwright. Have you had to make sacrifices in order to devote yourself to writing for the theater?

FORNES: I haven't made sacrifices, really. It's not as if I chose writing as a career to make money. There *are* people who can write ad copy or soap operas, I couldn't, I would die. I might be able to do it technically, but I could not spiritually. I feel I've never had any choice. When I'm not doing something that comes deeply from me, I get bored. When I get bored I get distracted, and when I get distracted, I become depressed. It's a natural resistance, and it insures your integrity. You die when you are faking it, and you are alive when you are truthful. I consider myself lucky to have been able to survive financially doing what I want to do. Sometimes it's been very, very tight, and sometimes it's been scary because I've had to go into debt. Still, I don't consider it a sacrifice.

MARY GALLAGHER

*M*ary Gallagher is an actress and *director as well as a writer of plays, novels and stories. Her plays include* Fly Away Home, Little Bird, Father Dreams, Chocolate Cake, Buddies *and* Dog Eat Dog, *all of which have been published by Dramatists Play Service. Her first novel,* Spend It Foolishly, *was published in 1977 by Atheneum Press; her second,* Quicksilver, *by G.P. Putnams Sons in 1982. Ms. Gallagher is a member of New Dramatists in New York City, where she has done developmental work on all her plays, and of the Ensemble Studio Theatre, also in New York. She received a Guggenheim Fellowship for Playwriting in 1983 and in 1984 was awarded a Rockefeller Playwrights Residency Grant at Ensemble Studio Theatre to direct a workshop of her play* How To Say Goodbye.

INTERVIEWER: When did you first realize what a writer was, that a book was written *by* somebody?

GALLAGHER: Reading *Little Women.* I got that book for Christmas in 1954, when I was seven, and I just devoured it. So Jo was my first image of what a writer is, and I figured she was really the author, Louisa May Alcott. Jo is a great character, always in trouble because she's so stubborn, and has a terrible temper—she's very dramatic! She's the mainstay of her family, supports them financially with her writing. And she writes, directs and stars in her own plays. So I started doing that. The house we lived in had a little platform landing at the bottom of the stairs, and that became our stage. My parents and the little kids would sit facing the platform, and my oldest brother and sister and I would put on these extravaganzas. Kathy played the princesses and girlish parts, Tom played princes and henchmen, and I played the character parts: Captain Hook; Rumpelstiltskin, that was my favorite. It was always my idea; I herded everyone around and made them do it.

As it turned out, I've done all the things that Jo did as an artist—write

168

stories, novels, journalism, make theater in different ways, help support my family. Because homebound artists like her were my role models, I didn't realize, as a child, that being an artist could take me out into the world, whenever I wanted to go. I always wrote poems and stories, but I thought of it as just for *me*. By the middle of high school, I was an actress. My self-concept was all bound up with how I got approval, how I experienced the power to move people. And I loved being part of the theater world. The world where outcasts find a home! When I was a senior in college, I set my heart on acting. It was that silence . . . that would fall over the audience when *I* started talking . . . hooked me good. I *wanted* that!

So I went back to Cleveland, my hometown, spent two years at the Cleveland Playhouse, got into the company, got my Equity card, and got kicked out, because they had apprentice ingenues coming in the windows. But I was afraid to go to New York. Instead I got a shitty job, saved every dime and went to Europe by myself. I traveled for four months. Then I ran out of money, so I spent the winter in Paris as the live-in nursemaid to two rich, insane French children. I had a little high school French, on the order of, "The record player doesn't work." I was supposed to be going to French classes every day, but the parents paid me so little that I couldn't afford classes. So I pretended to go, and instead, for three hours every day, I wandered around wet, gray, lonely Paris. I always stopped in a café to get warmed up, and I had this new notebook, for my French classes, you see . . . and I started writing a story. I wrote every day, maybe an hour a day. And in four months, I wrote a novel. That was my first experience of writing as a throughline in my life. It saved me. And I still think that's the best way to write, set aside the same time every day, it doesn't matter how long a time, and write. When I started traveling again, I continued working on that novel, and I discovered that I could be happy *not* acting, that I *was* happy. That was very freeing. I had hardly any money, so I had to hitchhike. And I was afraid. But the morning I left Paris, when I stood by the side of the Autoroute and stuck out my thumb . . . that was one of the most significant moments of my life . . . because I felt that I was turning over so much control to the gods. . . . I learned that I could take care of myself.

So I moved to New York. I was ready to try to be an actress, because I didn't "need" it anymore. I started getting work right away, hooked me in, you see. First year in New York, I had eight months' work. Paid acting! Next year I didn't get diddly-squat. But by then I was so obsessed with getting acting work, I didn't think about anything else. But I kept writing . . . and without my being much aware of it, writing became a craft for me. Most of my jobs were in regional theaters—Stage West, the Meadowbrook, the Barter, Alaska Rep. . . . There I'd be after the show had opened, in some cheesy rented room with nothing to do all day but write. Rewrote my Paris novel . . . wrecked it! Lesson number one, if it's good, don't fuck with it. And my old friend, Bonni, a writer, had an agent. I wrote one story that we both felt was a *real* story. Outside of me, it had a validity, a life. She sent it to her agent, who became my agent. . . . A woman, yeah, both of my agents are women. And that story never sold. But the next one, "The Sublet," sold to *Cosmopolitan.* Well! Working actress, selling author . . . my personal life was a wreck, but for the next five years, I made my living acting, writing and directing. Published two novels. Started writing plays. And the acting became less and less compelling and the writing more and more so.

INTERVIEWER: Were you aware of that happening?

GALLAGHER: Yeah. Acting excited me, in a feverish way, but it never made me happy. To be good, you have to be more and more vulnerable, and meanwhile you're getting kicked in the teeth about twenty times a day. My pattern as an artist seems to be to focus on the kind of work that I get the most approval for. I'm an approval hound. *But,* it has to be approval for what I most want to say, the way I want to say it, and they have to pay me for it, enough to help support my family. So I had to be a playwright. [Laughter] But really, that *is* what I want: the life of an artist who lives by her real, true art. The outlaw life! *And* . . . a happy homelife, too. We're only here once. Why aim low? And see, I thought for a while that acting and writing stories for magazines might be the perfect balance. But that was because, with both, I had luck at the outset—the hook. The second story I sold was called "Leaving the City"; it was a very bleak picture of being an actress in New York, and it was *about* "the hook" . . . about how every time you get to the point of realizing that you're unhappy pursuing this goal and you don't have to do it anymore . . . you get a job or some other major reinforcement, and you recommit again. As with much of my writing, I wrote that story to figure out my own pattern for myself. And when *Cosmo* bought it, I thought, "This is great, I can write anything I want!" [Laughter] So I wrote three stories that my agent and I thought were good. We'd get notes back from the editors, you know: "Oh, we loved this one, we passed it all around the office; oh, we laughed and laughed!" But they wouldn't buy it. "Dog Eat Dog" was one of those. It was a story before it was a play. No one wanted it, said it was depressing. Then I sold a story to *Redbook* and they gave me much more grief than *Cosmo.* I was furious. I went to the Bagel Nosh every day for four days and wrote this story called "But You're Not Brian," about this complete twit who goes to a singles bar and falls in love with a handsome slime right out of a French briefs ad. We sold it in a week. And I thought, "Screw it, this is just too heartbreaking." I started directing then. And, just for me, I wrote another novel, about being an au pair in Paris. *Spend it Foolishly*. That was the first novel I got published, in 1977.

INTERVIEWER: Why did you stop directing?

GALLAGHER: Too many directors, not enough work. I did direct workshops of my first two plays. But you don't get reinforced for that.

INTERVIEWER: What was your first play?

GALLAGHER: I wrote a one-act when I was in college. But my first play that I wrote with real consciousness was *Getting Rid of It*, now known as *Little Bird*. I bought a new notebook, and wrote, "Act One. KELLY's apartment." Three hours later, my hand was falling off, but these people kept coming onto this page and arguing, and then the arguments would build, and they'd say these absolutely rotten things, and then there'd be these silences . . . and someone else would enter . . . and I thought, "Shit. I'm good at this."

Then I decided to get it on its feet. I called a bunch of good actors I'd worked with, and directed a workshop of that first act. We rehearsed in a church, and then I bought a slot in the Direct Theater's Directors' Festival, where you paid twenty-five dollars and got an hour of performance time and some minimal technical help. A good friend, Mary Moran, stage-managed—if you want to direct your own work, you have to have a healthy genius for a stage manager. We threw together the props from our own stuff. When we finally played it for an audience—Jesus, all these people came—I was standing in the back. It started. And the audience was listening. Then they were laughing. . . . My legs started to shake so hard I thought I would fall down. I got so physically, sexually turned on, it was like, you know, that ginger ale running through your body? I was practically hallucinating and hanging onto the wall. At the end of the act, it gets very emotional and violent, a fight between two sisters, with a lot of pain and anger, not violence, but the emotions of violence. The audience was dead quiet. Then it was over, and there was this huge applause. . . . Later on that night, we were all at a party at my place, and there was this Ouija board. When I put my finger on the little thing that moves, that spells the answers, it took off! Flying! What I felt was that I had released some force, some tremendous energy, inside me! And it was because of what had happened in that theater, what I had *made* happen for all those people!

INTERVIEWER: Something magical?

GALLAGHER: Yes! Yes, and more! I had a sense of power like I'd never had before. That I could create a *world* and people would totally go into it!

INTERVIEWER: Perhaps that's why women playwrights have lagged so far behind. Because creating drama is a godlike power. Who knows what dark forces we might unleash?

GALLAGHER: Yeah . . . And that experience brings up the question of directing one's own work. That was the last time I did it. Now, why did I stop? Was I afraid of that power in myself? I mean, most producers and directors will *discourage* you from doing it. They say you can't focus on the text, see if it works moment to moment, and at the same time stand back far enough to see all the elements of the production as a whole. I do think if you have to *rewrite* the play very much, you just don't have enough time or enough intellectual and emotional energy to direct it, too. But this new play I'm working on, *How To Say Goodbye*, I think I'm gonna direct a workshop of it.

INTERVIEWER: Perhaps masses of playwrights directing their own work will be the next revolution in the theater.

GALLAGHER: I'm worried about it. What if the producers and directors are right, and I don't have enough emotional resources to handle all those needs at once? But I'm also excited about it! And I know so many terrific actors I'm dying to work with! Damn. I'm gonna try it.

INTERVIEWER: After the workshop of your first play, *Little Bird*, what was the next step?

GALLAGHER: Eventually I sent a version to the Office for Advanced Drama Research, Arthur Ballet's outfit . . . and he wrote back and said, "Yes, you have a voice, we'd like to try to get you a production." Which they did, at ACT in San Francisco. April, 1977. In their little fifty-seat Playhouse Theatre, the Plays-in-Progress Series. OADR flew me out, gave us a real production budget. Delores Ferraro directed—she was terrific! She let me say anything I wanted in rehearsals, which most directors won't. But I'm an actress, I know how to talk to actors. And we talked a lot, more than I would today. I was absolutely mesmerized by the whole process.

INTERVIEWER: In *Little Bird*, you have two blood sisters arguing both sides of the abortion issue. Did you have any problems from feminists on that score?

GALLAGHER: Not then. Women who came to see it and talked to me about it were just very moved by it. You know, what *Little Bird* shows about abortion is that you can't have one without sadness, without pain. It doesn't say abortion's wrong. But these are scary times. If it were done now, I think some feminists might be concerned because the forces of the repressive Right Wing are very strong, and a play that shows the sadder aspects of abortion might be fuel for The Right. Barbara Schneider, friend and terrific playwright, was concerned about it in that way. It bothered her that my character, Prandy, who has the abortion, hasn't got the good arguments for it. But that's my point. Her reasons have to do with who she is. She's an emotionally precarious young woman, very self-destructive, in *no way* able to handle an unwanted pregnancy, not to speak of *raising* a child. The audience should realize that. And that's the *best* reason for abortion.

INTERVIEWER: Are you thinking of having this play produced again?

GALLAGHER: Under the right circumstances. You have to stand by your work and hope that most audience members will see the complexities you're showing. And I love that play. I rewrote it again this year. Unbelievable, seven years later and still rewriting! [Laughter] But now it's been published by Dramatists Play Service, so I have to stop. Publication is the only thing that makes me stop rewriting. My current fear is that I wreck my work rewriting . . . like spoiling the clothes by cutting pieces of the dress till there's nothing left. I'm learning not to throw out old drafts.

INTERVIEWER: Because that spontaneous first flood . . . may still be the purest writing?

GALLAGHER: Right. Also I feel that I've been working too hard for spareness, which is fashionable, when actually one of my strengths as a writer is detail. Plays get more like screenplays all the time.

INTERVIEWER: Do you think visual imagery is displacing language in the American theater?

GALLAGHER: In experimental theater, yeah. And I'm jealous of those people, because the good ones are so imaginative and nonspecific, the way dance and music and painting are nonspecific. You, the audience, receive nonverbal forms much more emotionally and purely than verbal forms, during which your brain is always asking, "Do I agree with that?" Most of my favorite theater experiences have been with nonspecific, visual, imagistic theater, because I can turn off my brain and just go with it. On the other hand, most of it is terrible. Just like verbal theater.

INTERVIEWER: I once asked a male playwright who is well funded by foundations, "What's the secret of getting all this grant money?" And he said, "Make sure they can't understand what you write." Do you agree?

GALLAGHER: Well . . . I think you're less at risk if people aren't sure what you're saying. But it's a major miracle to get a grant with a naturalistic play. Naturalism is yesterday's prom dress, we're supposed to be embarrassed by it. It's an idiotic definition, anyway. Nothing that happens in theater is purely naturalistic. If you dismiss any play that has characters that seem like real people, that deals with ordinary human problems, you're going to say "Fuck you" to 90 percent of the audience. I like to mess around with structure, but I'll always continue to tell certain stories for the stage in a simple, chronological way, with characters who seem real to ordinary people, because I want to speak to the people I grew up with, to my family and my oldest friends, and other people like them. I *can* speak to them now in a powerful way, and I won't give that up. But it's tricky. Because at the same time I also want to speak to my most demanding peers, and that requires surprises. In form, especially. Toughest question for the playwright: Who do you want to speak to and what do you want to say to them, and how do you hold on to what is really yours—your voice, your essence—and still communicate? I want to speak to everybody.

INTERVIEWER: Your play *Dog Eat Dog* [produced in 1983 at the Hartford Stage Company] was a larger-than-life look at the corporate executive in an economic recession. It didn't go down well in Hartford.

GALLAGHER: No. It scared them. The Hartford audience are the people the play is about, whose lives are entirely dependent on corporate jobs. And when the corporations fold in the play, and the characters have to fend for themselves . . . people in Hartford did not think that was funny. They'd say to me, "I'm sorry I didn't laugh more. It was just too close to home." Well, of course I wanted them to laugh *because* it was close to home! I wrote it for that audience. I wanted to say to those guys, "This is your fear, right? Let's look at it! Maybe it won't be that bad." But they didn't want to look at it.

INTERVIEWER: The woman in the play is a heroine. She organizes the neighborhood. And the play has hope at the end, because they're going to build a new community, however awful the world has become.

GALLAGHER: It's hopeful for the *people*, but it isn't hopeful for the system. The central question of the play is, are you willing to junk other people to survive? And in the end, the characters say no. They join forces, share everything, begin again together as a collective family. Well, that's communism! And it flies in the face of the current Reagan-Yuppy attitude that you can't worry about anybody but yourself if you want to get ahead. I didn't realize till I saw the play with that Hartford audience that it's a direct attack on the whole American society, a society dependent on the capitalist system flourishing. In the play, the system falls apart. And at the end, the characters survive by saying, "Junk the system. It ain't happening anymore. We're on our own. Where do we start? . . . A garden." Which is very radical, politically.

INTERVIEWER: Let's talk about politics in the American theater. We've all seen those articles in *The New York Times* that ask, "Where are the political playwrights?"

GALLAGHER: Oh, they're so full of shit.

INTERVIEWER: Are political plays being written but ending up in the theatrical wastebasket?

GALLAGHER: You bet they are. I go to readings of plays that are so political, so radical, they make my blood jump. Do they get produced? Hell, no. I got the best review of my life in the Friday [*New York*] *Times* [March 4, 1983] for Hartford's *Dog Eat Dog* production, eighteen months ago. Has anybody wanted to produce it since? Hell, no. We get the notes: "Best thing Mary's ever written. Can't produce it. Audiences just aren't ready." Get this image of the audiences packed in crates and being pumped with vitamins, getting 'em "ready." Shit!

INTERVIEWER: Yet political theater from other countries . . . South Africa, for example, is welcome here.

GALLAGHER: Aha! [Laughter] Aha! That's my favorite. Fugard gets done here. British plays attacking Britain's system get done here. Makes you feel good to be appalled by someone else's way of life. God forbid you should take a good look at your own.

INTERVIEWER: So you feel there is censorship, then?

GALLAGHER: Oh, absolutely. Censorship of the dollar. Censorship of the approval hound. Audiences gotta like it. Mustn't shake 'em up. Now there are some producers—Mark Lamos and Bill Stewart at Hartford [Stage Company], for instance who do look for plays that will shake people up. And there are theaters and companies that do exclusively theater pieces with social-political themes. But there's very little crossover between that ghetto of radical theater-makers and the mainstream audience. What I wanted to do with *Dog Eat Dog*—what a lot of playwrights hope to do—is write a political play for the audience that *doesn't* go to political theater and have that play be about *their* problem. Couch it in terms of comedy and fantasy, sneak it over on them. But the message was too scary. They backed off. I have hopes for the future of that play. When other work of mine has had more success . . . and if the political climate changes . . . that play will be done. In the meantime, thank God for Hartford Stage Company. Mary Robinson directed the play superbly. On shaping a text, she's the best director I've ever worked with. Hartford has many women in nontraditional jobs: production stage manager, almost all the stage managers, education development. And an atmosphere of great warmth, great support.

INTERVIEWER: Your play *Father Dreams* takes place in the mind of a character as he drifts in and out of sleep; it has a dream-like quality. What led you to subvert the form in this way?

GALLAGHER: Well . . . *Father Dreams* was my second full-length play. My father's a manic-depressive who's been in a mental hospital most of the time for the last twenty-five years. So the central psychological event of my growing up was my father's deterioration and disappearance into an institution. I knew I had to write *through* that, to come to understanding. But it couldn't be a novel or a naturalistic play; I had to have more structural control over it and I had to get in and out quickly, because it was going to be so painful. Then I read an article about dream research, saying that most people dream in a series of five dreams, orchestrated like a symphony. Each dream was a different length and explored a different aspect of the central problem or theme of the dream. And I thought, this is the structure for my play. The short dream structure would mean I had to get out at certain points, I couldn't wallow in the sadness. And I could explore, through the central character's dreams and fantasies, what I couldn't show in real time. Also I thought that making a play like a dream would *get* the audience, subliminally, like a dream does. For further distance and control, I made the central character the oldest son, and the center of the play was his trying to resolve his broken-off relationship with the vanished father. But it was still a very black time, writing it. I did the first draft in two weeks, I had to. But then I kept reworking it, over a five-year period, in workshops and productions. I could never direct *that* play myself. Too hard to be around it. But it works like gangbusters. The play began as a personal exploration but it ended up making a very strong statement about society's expectations, especially of men, and what that pressure does to them. All *good* theater is deeply political, revolutionary, when the society's values are as warped as our society's are now.

INTERVIEWER: Do you think, through writing your brother and your father, you've gained deeper empathy for your male characters?

GALLAGHER: Yes. I really came to terms with men. Growing up in a family where the men fell apart, I was very leery of men for a long time. Didn't trust 'em, didn't know what was going on inside 'em. Writing about men, walking around in their shoes, I found out what their problems were . . . how a lot of 'em got so fucked up! And as always with my characters, I came to love them. The other thing about actually writing as a man, being his voice, is that I find it freeing. A male character can't be as obviously "me." So I'm not self-conscious. I have more fun, I worry less about *explaining* feelings . . . I'm more lecherous. Of course this bothers me. I should be able to have that freedom in a woman character. So I'm working on that. Getting closer . . . Marina in *Dog Eat Dog*, for example.

INTERVIEWER: Tillie Olsen's book, *Silences*, talks about how women as writers avoid themselves. She warns against putting our boldest voices into male characters.

GALLAGHER: Well, it's a real temptation. That disguise, that freedom. Now I have to say that I have not avoided the "me" character. I've got what amounts to the Andy Hardy series for short, ex-Catholic girls. I need to concentrate on women characters who *aren't* me. *Chocolate Cake* was so much fun to write because it was about my guiltiest obsession, but neither of the characters was me. And there were no male characters, so everything I wanted to say was channeled through one of those two women . . . with a sense of freedom.

INTERVIEWER: Some of the most successful women's plays have no male characters in them. *Top Girls, Uncommon Women . . . , Skirmishes, 'night, Mother, Fefu and Her Friends. . . .* Perhaps it gives the critics less to criticize when they don't have to run interference for male characters.

GALLAGHER: Well . . . on the other hand, I've gotten the most affirmation from critics, grant people, playwrights' groups, et cetera, from plays with male protagonists. Which might piss me off, except I have to admit that those are also my most adventurous plays in terms of style and structure. So . . . there again, giving myself more freedom with a male character. In any case, if you write men well, you get affirmation from men. Which can also be a trap. Writing to please Daddy. Actually, I think women writers have done better by male characters, on the whole, than male writers have done by women characters. Women are bred to have empathy for men. You never hear a woman complaining about being mistreated by her husband or her boss without immediately adding, "But I *understand* why he's doing this." Right? Men have not been bred to empathize with women. That's only changing now.

INTERVIEWER: Do you think it's possible, as we women "infiltrate" the world of playwriting, that *we* will be the ones influenced? Might we lose those empathetic skills?

GALLAGHER: That's a frightening thought. No. I think it'll work the other way. It feels better to have empathy. Not *comfortable*. But you're much better off knowing *why* that guy is giving you a hard time—that it isn't aimed at you, it's *his* pain. Men have to learn to see that. And women have to learn that, after a point, it doesn't *matter* why he's doing this to you. You can't let him do it anymore.

INTERVIEWER: Are women playwrights influencing male playwrights? Do you think men are trying to write more complex women characters?

GALLAGHER: Some of 'em. And some male playwrights write terrific women characters. Mostly *not* hotshot playwrights. What still surprises me is that a play can be a huge success and have completely unbelievable women characters. But the greatest writers wrote great women. Most women fall in love with the theater through those plays.

INTERVIEWER: But aren't those magnificent characters—with a few exceptions, like Ibsen's Nora—usually dead, raped or mad in the end? I wonder whether you think . . .

GALLAGHER: Whether *healthy* women can be written by men? [Laughter] Well, I don't know how many healthy women *I* write, either. Healthy people aren't that interesting.

INTERVIEWER: Professor Helen Chinoy of Smith College has a theory that there's a certain fragmentation in the work of women playwrights, a duality. For instance, in writing seminars you are often taught to decide whose play it is, who's the primary character . . .

GALLAGHER: Oh, God. "Whose play is it?" It's mine!

INTERVIEWER: But frequently you do get this duality, this kind of split in women's drama, mirror images threading through . . .

GALLAGHER: Interesting. My work is full of that duality: Kelly and Maura, Prandy and Maura [*Little Bird*], Al and Marina [*Dog Eat Dog*] . . . all those pairs of characters represent conflicting responses to the same problem. Actually, all my plays are fundamentally about how the hell do you cope with the pain of life? How and where roads diverge is probably the central theme for me. And there *is* no central character, the *problem* is the center. Maybe that's how women see things. We don't see one person as the center of the universe. So our plays don't reflect that.

INTERVIEWER: Women playwrights don't need a protagonist?

GALLAGHER: Well, the best male playwrights don't go for that *one* central character bullshit either. You know, there are a lot of people, *not* writers, who are eager to beat you over the head with Rules For Writing. None of those rules apply once you take flight. Playwrights, regardless of sex, are the best supporters when you're having black doubts, too. They'll pull you out of the swamp. And I think women playwrights— because as women we've learned to squelch our sense of competition, because we're good at walking around in the other person's shoes—tend to bend over backward not to see another artist as competition, but to see her or him as a comrade in arms. So the new presence of women in playwriting circles is reinforcing the instinct of all playwrights toward mutual support. . . . The fellowship of artists, *us against the world*, that's very important to me. When I'm writing fiction I really miss the group dynamic. Now in screenwriting, there's almost nothing but group dynamic, most of which is useless . . . and the writer has no control. They can monkey with your story and your language any way they want to. In playwriting, you get the best of both worlds, the creative family and also the absolute right to say, when you're ready, "Okay, this is all great and interesting, but *these* are the words you'll say. These are the images, the ideas of the play. You can't distort them."

INTERVIEWER: So you've been able to put your foot down about that?

GALLAGHER: Oh, yeah. As a playwright, you always can. If you don't, if you let them do some other play, loosely based on yours, it's your own fault. Your play is what you say it is.

INTERVIEWER: Have you ever come close to pulling a play because your intentions weren't being realized?

GALLAGHER: No. For the most part I've had very talented and caring people working in all capacities on my productions. And if they go off the track, I keep nudging them till they get back on. I have pulled productions *before* we went into rehearsal, because a producer or director wasn't sympathetic to the play, or wasn't gonna do it right. If you feel uneasy about an actor or a director or a theater space . . . it ain't worth it. For a playwright, there's no bigger waste than a rotten world premiere.

INTERVIEWER: Let's talk about politics a little. Weren't you in Nicaragua recently?

GALLAGHER: Yeah. December 1983. For three weeks.

INTERVIEWER: How did that come about?

GALLAGHER: Well . . . fall of 1983 began a period of . . . I guess, reassessment, for me . . . I'm still working through a lot of doubts about my work, my artistic life. The first half of '83 was a turbulent time, big career changes, *Dog Eat Dog* and *Win/Lose/Draw* [a one-act series which included *Chocolate Cake*; the other two pieces were co-authored with Ara Watson], one after the other . . . and then I got a Guggenheim, a very generous living stipend for a year. So my husband and I moved out to the country. And I didn't write for six months. I realized that I had come to the end of a long cycle of using writing most often to explore my own emotional life. I wanted to open myself to a whole universe of influences and forces that I'd closed off before. I've had a pattern of literally shutting out any information about the outside world that was just too painful to handle. The war in Vietnam is the obvious example. This horrible embroilment, so laden with despair . . . I just couldn't think about it without getting . . . crazed, enraged . . . so I shut it out. For most of my adult life, I had kept the world at bay like that. Explored my inner world. But now, partly because of Reagan, because he speaks for everything that's antihuman, antilife, and he calls up those terrible forces in many other people . . . I felt that I had to face those large, painful issues and somehow deal with them. I was reading a lot about

Central America. And I read an article about an American nun, living in a village in the Nicaraguan war zone . . . and I could not get her out of my mind. She was about my age, she even looked like girls and nuns I'd known in Catholic school. I became obsessed with my old question of where the roads diverge: Why did I end up here, why did she end up there? I couldn't comprehend her bravery, and yet I felt that under different influences, we might have traded places. I wanted to write about her. And finally I decided that I had to go and see her. My husband and some good friends really didn't want me to go—Nicaragua *is* at war, with *us*—but three women playwright friends especially backed me up: Barbara Schneider, Ara Watson and Lynne Alvarez; Lynne loaned me the money to go. If I wanted to write about this woman's courage, I had to explore my own. I had that scalp-prickling feeling that if I just said I wanted to go to Nicaragua to enough people, I would go. Two weeks later, I was on the plane.

INTERVIEWER: Was the trip government approved?

GALLAGHER: Oh, no. The U.S. State Department doesn't want Americans going to Nicaragua, and they've been refusing visas to Nicaraguan spokesmen, preventing them from coming to the United States to speak. So the Sandinista government has been inviting groups of Americans, in all fields, but particularly in health care and in the arts, to come to Nicaragua and see the revolution for themselves.

INTERVIEWER: Who was in your group?

GALLAGHER: It was made up of theater artists from around the United States and Canada. We went specifically to attend a festival of Nicaraguan theater groups and then to go out into the countryside, the war zones and the cotton and coffee production zones, to see these theater groups performing for the people—soldiers, workers, campesinos. A.S.T.C.A., the Sandinista artists' union, had invited Victoria Rhue and Tony Gillote, who are both very involved in what one might call radical theater—by which I mean theater which is overtly political and experimental in structure—to assemble a bunch of theater people and bring them for this major event. They'd invited a lot of well-known and lesser-known people, and mostly what they got was *not* the obvious hotshots of nonprofit theater. We were mostly female, in our thirties or early forties . . . many were women who run or co-run theaters.

Since I've only worked in the dreaded *mainstream*, I felt like I had NATURALISM tattooed on my forehead. We'd jog along on the bus with people talking about how the personal story is dead, how the only valid theater is collective theater telling the collective story of a people . . . which was also what we were hearing from Alan Bolt, who's the maestro of the Nicaraguan theater movement. Well, since the personal story is my stock-in-trade, and since I was already having all these doubts about my work, hearing over and over about dead, bourgeois, naturalistic, inner-exploring theater was very painful for me. But then we saw the plays that Nicaraguan groups were making up and putting on. And they were in fact personal stories . . . which had social messages, political messages. Working from the need to convey a political message—Join the Revolution! Don't sit on the fence!—they still had to show personal detail, human nature, to express their feelings and beliefs and to communicate. Those of us who begin at the other end, with the need to express a feeling or belief, also wind up with plays that have a political and social message, any time we address a serious and complex issue. Good theater incorporates the personal, the social, the political, seamlessly. That's what I learned. And I must add that, rhetoric aside, our group was a resourceful, intelligent, kind bunch of people, many of whom I feel a real connection to now. And it was tremendously affirming to be in a country where artists are considered essential to the survival and the growth of a people. The theater brigades are a major tool for unifying the Nicaraguan people. Music, dance, poetry are taught in every community because the Sandinistas believe that Nicaraguans can't explore their national identity till they are making art. We spent ten days in Managua, seeing the groups from all over the country perform for the people in the neighborhoods and the other theater groups, who all critiqued each other in a very healthy way. . . . We were also meeting with a great many people in the Sandinista government, leaders of the artists' unions, people in the clergy, the public-relations officer at the U.S. Embassy, who did not trot out the expected line and was quite balanced in his assessment of what was going on. . . . We participated in a vigil, in front of the Embassy, by U.S. citizens living in Nicaragua asking the U.S. to stop interfering in Nicaraguan affairs. And then we went up and down the Pacific coast for another week, visiting the school where Alan Bolt trains the theater groups and seeing performances of some of the groups in village squares and cotton haciendas.

INTERVIEWER: Did you go into the war zones?

GALLAGHER: Yes. That was the best for me.

INTERVIEWER: Were you frightened?

GALLAGHER: No. Once I got to Nicaragua, I was never frightened . . . only *interested*! And exhilarated! Actually, I felt jealous of the Sandinistas. They're really creating a world. And they know it. What a sense of power! The young people in the artists' unions and the national arts movements, who are working eighteen hours a day for the revolution, for the survival of their own Nicaragua, are so full of joy and pride. National pride. It's a painful thing to be a U.S. citizen among them. We haven't felt that pride in our own country for a long time, chiefly because it's our country that's standing in the way of self-government for Nicaragua, and El Salvador, and many other struggling nations. And it was heartbreaking to experience the friendliness and openness of the people everywhere we went, and to have them ask us, "If the U.S. people really knew what we're trying to do here, what the revolution is about, they'd be on our side, wouldn't they?" Well . . . the U.S. people put Ronald Reagan in the White House. That doesn't speak well for our compassion or imagination. And you need both to understand another country's politics. When we went to the border . . . we were traveling with a group of Costa Rican students, and the bus was jammed with people and knapsacks and laundry hanging on these makeshift lines . . . we bumped along these paved roads, and as we kept going north, dirt roads with huge ruts . . . it's extremely beautiful and rugged country, rolling rich green hills, bright blue skies, volcanoes, lakes, hills thick with coffee trees, and the poorest huts you can imagine, with children barefoot in the dirt outside . . . then further out, thatched huts, open to the wind, with cooking fires, no lights, then nothing, for miles and miles. And then we reached this cotton hacienda, and a camp for workers where we spent the night. We got off the bus, and all these men and women and children stood around us, absolutely stunned to see a bunch of gringos and gringas get off this bus in the darkness. These workers and their families, and many students who were temporary workers helping to bring in the harvest, were all living in very cramped huts and tents, eating rice and beans wrapped in tortillas, working from four in the morning till almost dark . . . and their camp was completely surrounded by darkness, cotton fields and then the ocean . . . except that, far off in the distance, you could see very faint glimmering light. To the northeast, a little light . . . and to the west, a sprinkling of light. We were at the northwest tip of Nicaragua, maybe eighty miles from El Salvador, maybe a little farther from the border of Honduras. And the light in the northeast was the light from a U.S. military base. And the lights in the west were the lights of the U.S. warships off the coast. And here were the Nicaraguans eating with their fingers because they didn't have forks.

INTERVIEWER: Did you see a theater performance there?

GALLAGHER: Yes. A group made up of young teenage girls and one boy. We called it the "muchachas' group." They were very thrilled by the fact that our group was mostly women, too. They told us that they wanted to have men and women, but when the theater organizers asked for volunteers to start a group, mostly girls showed up. We told them that was often our experience, too. A number of kids in these theater groups have lost family in the war. But that's the given in Nicaragua.

Life is very hard there, apart from the war. The life expectancy is only fifty-two. Half the population is under fifteen years of age. The militia, the Popular Army, the theater brigades . . . they're teenagers. That's who we're fighting. Kids.

INTERVIEWER: Did you feel angry?

GALLAGHER: Enraged. I'm enraged all the time, now that I'm paying attention again. These times call up one's anger. But a lot of people are angry and are paying attention, thank God . . . . There was a group of Vietnam vets staying at our hotel in Nicaragua, and one of our group got talking to three of them one night about what we would do if the invasion came while we were in Nicaragua. We were there a month after the United States invaded Grenada, and the Nicaraguans saw that as a dry run for Nicaragua. Everyone was digging trenches. We saw the militias drilling in the evenings. And one Viet vet said if the invasion came he'd go straight to the U.S. Embassy and go home, because since Nam he couldn't even see a gun rack on a car without getting the shakes, and he knew he couldn't be around a war again. Another one said he would join the Sandinistas and fight the U.S. He had decided before he'd come to Nicaragua that he would fight on their side if the war started while he was there. And the third said that he would stay in Nicaragua but he wouldn't fight on either side, he'd avoid the areas of fighting, which he knew how to do, since Nam. Then the other two told him he was full of shit, because war is too random, especially jungle, mountain war, for anyone to just avoid the problem areas. All these guys hated the U.S. government and thought its policies in Nicaragua were pushing us toward another Nam. Which they undoubtedly are. I have a lot of questions about the Sandinistas, but there's no doubt that our government is bungling with its policies and instrumental in a lot of suffering.

INTERVIEWER: Did you meet the nun that you had gone to find?

GALLAGHER: Yes. She came to the vigil at the Embassy. We talked a little. And she said that she didn't want anyone to write about her, even in a fictionalized form. And I understood that. By then, it didn't matter. The questions and themes that her story raised for me continue to absorb me, and I'm going to be exploring them in some way, related to these larger political questions, very soon. What matters is that I have moved forward into this next cycle.

GRISELDA GAMBARO

Griselda Gambaro, one of Argentina's foremost writers, was born in Buenos Aires on July 28, 1928. She is best known in the United States for her play El Campo (In the Country), which was written in 1967 and produced in New York in 1983 at the Open Space under the direction of Fránçoise Kourilsky. Ms. Gambaro's other plays include El Desatino (Folly, 1965), Matrimonio (Marriage, 1965), Las Paredes (The House, 1966), Nada Que Ver (Nothing to Do, 1972), Solo un Aspecto (Only One Aspect, 1973), El Nombre (The Name, 1976), Decir Sí (To Say Yes, 1978), La Malasangre (Bitter Blood, 1982), Real Envido (Royal Bet, 1983) and Del Sol Naciente (From [the Land of] the Rising Sun, 1984). El Campo was published in English in 1971 by the University of Texas Press. Ms. Gambaro's novels include Nada Que Ver con Otra Historia (Nothing to Do with Another Story, 1972), Ganarse la Muerte (To Earn One's Death, 1976), Dios No Nos Quiere Contentos (God Does Not Want Us Happy, 1979) and Lo Impenetrable (Impenetrable, 1984). In 1977, Ganarse la Muerte was banned by the president of Argentina. With her family, Ms. Gambaro left the country to live in Spain and France until she could return to Argentina in 1980. Her work has been translated into French, German, Czech and Polish, and she has had productions throughout South America and in Europe. She has lectured and given seminars at a number of universities in the United States, including Florida International University, Yale, Cornell, Rice, University of Texas at Austin and Arizona State. Ms. Gambaro has won numerous awards and prizes for her work, including a Guggenheim Fellowship for fiction in 1982.

We interviewed Griselda Gambaro in April 1984, in New York City, and invited playwright Maria Irene Fornes to participate and to act as our interpreter.

INTERVIEWER: Did you start by writing for theater?

184

GAMBARO: No. When I was twenty-four, I published a book of stories that I don't want to remember. It was so immature, so full of the sort of imperfections that mar many first books. And then when I was thirty-four, I published again, three short novels collected in one volume entitled *Madrigal en Ciudad*. This manuscript won a prize, El Fondo Nacional de las Artes, which consisted of publication, in 1964. The prize I won for this book enabled me to enter the theater easily, comfortably. Nowadays young playwrights have a more difficult time.

INTERVIEWER: Was there anyone in particular who influenced or nurtured your writing?

GAMBARO: No. I come from a milieu where there were very few books.

INTERVIEWER: Are you from a working-class family?

GAMBARO: Yes.

FORNES: You weren't allowed access to books?

GAMBARO: There were no books. I am the youngest of five, and have four brothers. There weren't books because there were family needs that were more primary. One of my brothers—five years older than I—did buy books.

INTERVIEWER: In growing up without books, how did you discover literature and your own desire to write?

GAMBARO: I always had a deep love of the written word, even in early childhood. Once I started going to school, I discovered the public library in my *barrio*. Then I learned a lot by chance. I didn't see much theater, but I read plays by O'Neill, Chekhov, Pirandello.

INTERVIEWER: What were the occupations of your parents?

GAMBARO: Father was a sailor for a time, and then he became a post office employee. My parents were first-generation Argentinians and my grandparents were Italian.

INTERVIEWER: What's the population of Italian descendants in Argentina?

GAMBARO: I don't know the exact amount, but most of our population comes from Spanish and Italian descendants.

FORNES: It was always like that or did the immigration happen all of a sudden?

GAMBARO: At the beginning of this century there were big currents of immigration in Argentina and that kept going until about 1930. People came to Argentina because it was a rich, fertile country.

INTERVIEWER: What is the average size of the theaters in which your plays are performed?

GAMBARO: At the beginning, my plays went the so-called avant-garde circuit. They opened in an institute dedicated to avant-garde work. In

1972, I was produced at the Teatro Municipal, which allowed me to find producers, to open in good theaters (three hundred to four hundred fifty seats), and to work under good professional conditions. However, due to the commercial failure of my last two plays, *Real Envido* [*Royal Bet*] and *La Malasangre* [*Bitter Blood*], I'm back underground for the moment. My plays are being done by nonprofessional companies in smaller spaces.

INTERVIEWER: Have you been influenced by any particular Argentinian playwrights?

GAMBARO: Yes. H. Serebrinsky, who committed suicide this year. It pleases me that our work has points in common.

INTERVIEWER: Is Serebrinsky considered a political playwright?

GAMBARO: All of our theater is more or less political, and we are all political writers in one way or another. There is always implicit or explicit political content in our work, though it is not a *goal*.

FORNES: Is it an artistic choice that a political point of view is not the writer's goal?

GAMBARO: No. For me, it is a necessity. I don't know whether my plays seem political. But one feeds oneself with the information provided by one's surrounding reality. One transmits, transfers, this information into one's work. One pre-orders this information as well as one's own personal experience. When one transfers that information into a theater piece or a novel, that reality is political, in a wide sense, of course, not political from a partisan point of view. One lives in a *politique*, and in a politicized society; so necessarily, this will be *reflected* in the work of art, be that what it may.

INTERVIEWER: Do you have some material which would only be appropriate for treatment in a novel?

GAMBARO: I think one always writes about the same theme, with variations. In some themes I see a situation on a stage, but there are others which would work better in a novel. Novels are themes that take me a long time to develop—they are a longer meditation. I usually write theater rapidly, but a novel can take two or three years.

FORNES: How long does it take you to write a play?

GAMBARO: The writing *for me* is just a simple question of pages. I could tell you that a theater piece takes me thirty-five pages, while a novel takes two hundred. It has to do with my personal method of work. I think *a lot* beforehand, and I take a long time thinking. Once I know what I want to say, it takes me a month to write a play. When the structure is solved—though I might need some bridges, or to revise and make cuts—I let it rest. I ask for opinions and then I go back and revise, which takes another three or four more months of work. Then it's ready.

I know when a play or work is good or bad after that first month, when the structure is done—the beginning, the ending and the scenes.

INTERVIEWER: What inspired your play, *Información Para Extranjeros* [1972] [*Information for Foreigners*]?

GAMBARO: I don't have a copy of that play any more because at the time, it was risky, dangerous material to have in Argentina. It was published in Italy, so I now have the Italian version. It is a play I would like to revise, because it was the first time I used material from newspapers, which I treated as *true* information. Later, history proved that this information was false. So the play itself may no longer be truthful. That's why I want to revise it—I'd like to check history point by point against information I used.

FORNES: You weren't aware that the facts in the newspaper were false?

GAMBARO: No. The play was written in 1972, the beginning of the guerrilla movement in Argentina. I used the first *desaparecidos* and the first people taken to jail. The information was reported like police-blotter items, and came under the newspaper heading of "police information." For example, I remember a lawyer, Roberto Quieto. I wrote a scene based upon the information in the newspaper which said the police had detained a lawyer who had something to do with human rights. The real story was that Quieto was one of the chiefs of the People's Revolutionary Army.

FORNES: What is the reality?

GAMBARO: The reality is that he was a subversive and that he was disappeared. It's not that I would change my optic were I to rewrite the play, but I think that a new angle has been imposed.

FORNES: Was the play confiscated from you?

GAMBARO: No. There were raids, the army paid us "visits" during which they looked at all the material in the house [1973]. As *any* material was considered subversive—Marx, Freud—a big burning of books resulted. Everybody who owned books burned them.

FORNES: Was *Información* eventually presented in Argentina?

GAMBARO: Never. A theater in Germany wanted to perform it—but I refused permission. If this play had been done in *any* theater in *any* country, intelligence personnel connected to the Argentinian Embassy would have been informed. (This was to happen with *El Campo*; Intelligence even sent back newspaper clippings in which journalists drew parallels between what happens in the play and the military dictatorship in Argentina.) I was afraid for my family in Argentina, and besides, I was counting on returning there as soon as the situation permitted.

INTERVIEWER: Much of your work signaled the advent of a repressive regime well before the actual events took place. Were you aware of the prophetic nature of your material?

GAMBARO: Well, there were certain data floating around. . . . An artist has to have antennas. I think the artist has antennas that are a little more sensitive to reality than most.

INTERVIEWER: Why did the character of The Guide, in scene five of *Información*, react like a "drama critic" to the father's bedtime-story version of a kidnapping?

GAMBARO: Yes, Néstor Martins, an attorney, and his client, Nildo Zentero . . . It was one of the first kidnappings that happened. It was ten years ago, but seems so much longer. It is very difficult for me to know why things happen in my plays. To me it is enough to know things are coherent. I never know why they occur.

INTERVIEWER: How has the new democracy in Argentina affected the artistic community?

GAMBARO: The difference is lack of terror. We lived not only with terror, but with censorship and fear. It was a time of extreme risk, where the game was to survive—nothing else. And now, well, one feels that one can talk, that one can communicate with others. In the previous years, the entire culture was balkanized, broken down into particles. Each one kept working, writing—but each one did it in his own private margin and space. The communication among artists themselves was difficult, as was the communication between artists and audiences.

Through balkanization, regimes are able to employ horror and fear. The fact that everybody is isolated helps the purposes of any dictatorship. Every dictatorship is based on that principle. One starts being afraid of one's shadow. In Argentina, if your name was in the personal agenda book of anybody who was related to some [political, social] activity, you began to get scared. You knew that by the simple fact of your name in someone's address book, you would be considered guilty, too. Which didn't mean just being taken into detention! One could not have said, "No, that man has my telephone number because of x reasons. . . ." It meant to be disappeared. That's why it was so hard to deal with The Fear. [The National Commission on Disappeared Persons (CONADEP), appointed by Argentine President Raúl Alfonsín in December 1983, has estimated that eleven thousand people had been abducted by the armed forces, and that they have almost certainly been murdered.]

INTERVIEWER: Did artists continue to work during those years?

GAMBARO: Yes. People worked with censorship and self-censorship. But only when the military government had become deteriorated at the end of 1981 did Teatro Abierto, "open theater," occur. Teatro Abierto was a movement that united all playwrights, directors and actors. It was decided that in two months Teatro Abierto would present twenty-one plays: three one-acts each day on seven different programs. Everyone worked free of charge and there was a very low ticket price. The festival had an extraordinary response from the audience. For the first time, theater people got together to talk more or less freely, and the response was a massive one.

FORNES: Was that before the Falklands War?

GAMBARO: I believe so. It was during the military government, September–October 1981.

INTERVIEWER: Did the Falklands War effect changes in the military government?

GAMBARO: Yes. But at the same time, the government was already *so* deteriorated. In fact, during the first week of Teatro Abierto they [the paramilitary police] put a bomb in the theater and destroyed everything. But the festival had already created a need in the people. People had already lost their fear. Though the majority of the plays were political, a press conference was given after the bomb, and two other theaters offered their spaces. It wasn't that the festival had a big theatrical value in itself, but from the political point of view, it was an important event.

INTERVIEWER: Were there any victims of the bombing?

GAMBARO: No, it was in the early hours of dawn. The costumes caught fire and they were all burned. The press helped very much by giving the incident so much publicity—and, of course, the government had to keep from stopping the festival, to prove that it wasn't *that* dictatorial. But the government was already deteriorated. It wasn't the government of 1977—we could not have done a festival like Teatro Abierto *at all* if it were anything like 1977. The government had deteriorated because of the political and economic situation. And because of the situation, they had to allow a wider margin of activity.

FORNES: Was the political response of the theater people larger than those in the other arts?

GAMBARO: Theater artists were more engaged than the people in the cinema, for instance, who couldn't do anything in those times, because of the cinema's commercial infrastructure. There was a cinema institute, run by the government, but they would not give funding without first approving a script. Cinema people couldn't address anything; they made purely commercial movies. And television was *very* much under control.

INTERVIEWER: Did the Falklands War help precipitate the fall of the repressive government?

GAMBARO: I think the regime would have fallen anyway, but the cost of the acceleration of that fall was too great to pay. I don't think our people were thinking at that moment that the war would weaken the military regime. People were suffering, they were grieving for all the young people who were sent to their deaths. Many went to war unwillingly, it was not a choice. There were eighteen-year-old kids who were called up and sent to die.

FORNES: So the sorrow was more for the loss of life than the loss of the Islands?

GAMBARO: The Malvina Islands weren't ours. We lost them in the last century. We always fought to have them back, claimed them. They belong to us by right. By fact, the British are there.

INTERVIEWER: Why did you decide to leave Argentina in the late seventies?

GAMBARO: In March 1977, they banned my novel *Ganarse la Muerte* [*To Earn One's Death*]. I was in Buenos Aires and the prohibition came by decree of the Executive Power, President Rafael Videla. It was forbidden to sell the novel, it could not be sent by mail, and it was taken out of circulation. At that time, to have a prohibition, not from City Hall, but the *Executive Power* was very dangerous. One started to be a suspected person. As a result, I couldn't open a new play, I was not given interviews or publicity of any kind. My channels of communication were cut off. Aside from that, I was living in an atmosphere of terror. I went to Spain (with my husband and children) and stayed three years. I returned in 1980.

INTERVIEWER: A French theater journal noted that the official theaters in Argentina preferred to produce classics rather than new work, which only constituted one fifth of their repertory. Is this true?

GAMBARO: We have only two subsidized theaters: La Comedia Nacional and Teatro Municipal San Martin. The Municipal receives the largest subsidy and presents classics as well as original Argentinian plays. Still, there is a whole group of Argentinian playwrights who were never performed at the Municipal during the period of The Process. The most well-known, Roberto Cossa, Gorostiza (now minister of culture), Osualdo Dragun and myself, were prohibited playwrights.

FORNES: During the epoch of 'The Process?' What was that?

GAMBARO: We called the period of the military dictatorship 'El Proceso,' from March 1976 to the arrival of Alfonsín. It's a name the military gave to themselves; they called their government 'El Proceso.'

INTERVIEWER: What is the future of the arts in Argentina?

GAMBARO: We're going to see this year. It is too soon to tell. And Argentina is going through a tremendous economic crisis, which of course reflects in the arts. But already more things are being published, there are many new theatrical projects, and more cultural events of a popular nature are taking place, such as poetry readings, music in the squares.

INTERVIEWER: Would you tell us about the women in Argentina—of all religions—who have publicly gathered to mourn and protest their disappeared relatives?

GAMBARO: There is in Argentina a group called The Mothers of the Plaza de Mayo. I think these women have done something very important, from all points of view. They have proven that when women get together in numbers, we can change things. These women started in the middle of The Fear. Every Thursday they would walk around Plaza de Mayo at three o'clock in the afternoon. They were menaced, some disappeared [CONADEP reports fifteen Mothers—Ed.], but they finally made themselves heard, and not only in Argentina! It's a very important historic event in the world.

What began as a personal wrench—mothers searching for their own children—became a political act that gathered more and more weight. The women had to be very brave, they gathered to protest in plain sight in the middle of a military government. The Mothers of the Plaza de Mayo started with five women, then ten, then twenty. . . .

INTERVIEWER: You sometimes juxtapose acts of human violence with children's games. What is the association between violence and innocence?

GAMBARO: I think that only happens in *Información Para Extranjeros*. It's not my usual method of work. In that play, I used a children's game placed within the context of real violence and cruelty to give a different strength, more intensity to violence. I used it to create a stronger image. Children are violent. But I believe that theirs is a particular kind of violence, and that it can be channeled in ways which are less dangerous to others. Generally in the child, violence is not criminal. In the adult, violence is criminal. Those who have more means, more technology, can be more dangerous. The poor, vulnerable child is without those means.

INTERVIEWER: Critics have said that your artistic vision of man is "grim and absolute." Do you agree?

GAMBARO: No, I wouldn't even say that of my earlier work, though in my latest plays there is another optic. Not a view toward the world, but a view toward *people*, which is maybe a more compassionate optic. Even my darkest work has a positive side because it appeals to people's lucidity. It's a call to attention. My vision is not necessarily fatalistic. My message has never been "We have to be like this."

INTERVIEWER: Why do you write?

GAMBARO: The process of writing is still very much a mystery to me. I foresee a situation and I feel that I *need* to write about it. But why I write? Or why I need to write? I don't know.

INTERVIEWER: You were recently [spring 1984] on a panel of women writers at the Center for Inter-American Relations here in New York. What did you discuss?

GAMBARO: The other two outstanding writers on the panel, [novelists] Angélica Gorodischer and Luisa Valenzuela, were in agreement that what feminism means is to change our optic, our vision, which means we must also change our ethics. That's the most substantial thing they said.

INTERVIEWER: Is there a movement of women writers in Argentina?

GAMBARO: There have always been isolated movements, sporadic periods of women writing but they were never organic. Women in Argentina gained the vote many years ago and they made certain gains, but a feminist movement did not previously exist. Now, with the new democratic government which took office in December 1982, our feminist movement has gained strength. There are many new feminist groups in Argentina; we are hearing women's voices, and we have benefited. For example, the Women's House, Casa de la Mujer, opened last year. There is a café where women hold meetings and get-togethers related to feminist concerns. Casa de la Mujer offers various courses to women in photography, et cetera. There is also a group of women with their own television program, and though it is not billed as a "feminist" program, it always deals with the problems of women.

INTERVIEWER: Are there many feminist publications?

GAMBARO: There is a newspaper with a weekly women's supplement. The directors and editors are men, but it is dedicated to a feminist point of view.

FORNES: It doesn't just portray women as domestic?

GAMBARO: There is another magazine, *Women*, like that; it is a mixture of commercialism and the "feminine." You see, these magazines are not created by women; they are financed by newspapers and commercial publishers who have an eye on the market. Commercial publishers have realized magazines directed toward women can make a profit. The most singular development in Argentina in terms of women is the arrival of women in the arts: women filmmakers, theater directors . . . though of course we already had a tradition of women writers in Argentina. The first Argentinian women writers appeared in the nineteenth century: Juana Manuela Gorriti, Eduarda Mansilla, César Duayen. In the twentieth century, women's writing has gained great strength. Among poets I would mention Alfonsina Storni, Alejandra Pizarník, Olga Orozco.

From an extensive list of prose writers, I would mention Angélica Go-rodischer, Silvina Ocampo, Noemí Ulla, Libertad Demitropulos, Alicia Steinberg.

FORNES: Do you have a tradition of women writing for theater as well?

GAMBARO: No. No. Theater is very much connected with the society, with the social situation. It demands a different sort of aggressiveness, and that's why we only have a few playwrights who are women. Movies are also connected to society—we only recently began to have women working in the cinema, but not too many.

FORNES: Why do theater and cinema demand a different type of aggressiveness?

GAMBARO: Writing a novel requires an engagement, but it is not as immediate. A theater piece, of itself, demands a confrontation with an audience. It demands that you connect with other people; it demands a collective and social effort with the company and later with the audience. Theater writing is much more direct than novel writing. The contact is person-to-person in the theater *through* an object: the text. And theater is such a concise field, more concise than the other arts. I believe that all acts of writing are impudent, shameless, but drama especially, because one knows that one is going to be on the stage through the actors. That's why theater is more aggressive, it shows more—of whatever it shows. It is immodest.

INTERVIEWER: Do you believe there is a female aesthetic?

GAMBARO: Yes. I believe so. I think with time this will become more clear. Still among us (all of us, men and women alike) the vision is a little amorphous. As women, we should try to make our vision less shapeless. At least in my case, I'm trying to do that. We must make our vision our own and not something male.

INTERVIEWER: Have you ever directed a play?

GAMBARO: No. I think it is another area of creation, an area that belongs to the stage director. Sometimes when I see a play performed, I feel I would like to direct it myself. But directing is another profession, it involves another technique, one which I don't know about. When I write my plays, I do make my own *mise-en-scène*. I create the settings, and I act out all the characters. When the play must be performed on a stage, it demands the work of another person who has the craftsmanship to deal with physical theatrical space.

INTERVIEWER: Are there women theater directors in Argentina?

GAMBARO: Yes. My last play, *La Malasangre* [*Bitter Blood*, 1982], was directed in Buenos Aires by Laura Yunsen, who will also direct the next play I'm opening. And my two short pieces which are about to open,

Viaje de Invierno [*Winter Voyage*], written in 1965, and *Nosferatu* (1970), will be directed by another woman, Malena Lasala.

FORNES: Is that by chance, or because these women are especially interested in your work?

GAMBARO: I believe that they are very good directors.

FORNES: But do you think there is something in your work which requires the sensibility of a woman?

GAMBARO: I'd like to believe so, but honestly I think I could have worked with one or two male directors whom I consider good.

INTERVIEWER: Is it difficult for you as a playwright to hand over a script to a director?

GAMBARO: No, I feel expectations. I feel the birth of an enthusiasm. If I trust the person, I feel that person is going to re-create what I wrote in a better way.

INTERVIEWER: In *El Desatino* [*Folly*, 1965], why did you choose to have Alfonso's wife, Lily, never appear on stage except in a dream? And what were your intentions in the stage directions which describe Lily as "An exaggerated version of a movie sex symbol?"

GAMBARO: Well, that is a 1965 play. I think it is like that because it reflects the particular vision of the male character, Alfonso. Lily is his own vision of what woman is. Alfonso literally has restraints on his feet. He is very weak and dreams about a woman. That woman is the stereotype of what he has seen in the movies, or of what he thinks a woman is. In the dream, Alfonso says that Lily is his wife, but she isn't. In reality, that female character does not exist. She takes form on the stage. Alfonso does not reflect my opinion of all men. At the time I wrote *El Desatino*, I was consciously reflecting the vision of that specific male character.

INTERVIEWER: In your early work, the main characters are male. Have your women characters become less peripheral over the years?

GAMBARO: Yes. Beginning in 1976, my female characters started to be the protagonists. In my most recent plays, the main characters are women. And I believe that my women characters have become more dynamic, more active and that they have more ideological weight. That's a response to the fact that I myself am much more conscious and understanding of what it is to be a woman. Before, I wrote instinctively, without being conscious of what happens to women in the world or their position.

INTERVIEWER: How did your consciousness change?

GAMBARO: I wrote that banned novel, *Ganarse La Muerte* [*To Earn One's Death*]. The main character was a woman. I didn't think she reflected the state of women; I thought she reflected Argentina. But the novel was published in France by the Women's Press [*Gagner Sa Mort*, Editions des Femmes, 1976], and they invited me to France. I had the opportunity to meet the feminists of France, and I began reading about the specific problems related to women. I started to realize things which, before that time, I had only felt in an instinctive way.

INTERVIEWER: In *El Campo* [1967], the diseased and wounded artist, Emma, plays a concert on a dead piano while the audience insults her. Did you intend this image to symbolize the vulnerable position of the artist in the world?

GAMBARO: When I write a piece I pay attention to what it demands of me, to what the play and the characters propose. I'm simply following the characters on the stage. As in any work, one can later see it's charged with symbolism. I didn't think about it when I wrote the scene, but it may well represent what you say.

FORNES: So the theatrical situation actually *marks* the behavior of the characters?

GAMBARO: Everything influences one, everything is interrelated. How can they be separated? It's very difficult to separate the thread from the yarn.

INTERVIEWER: American academic critics have often written that you have been influenced by The Living Theatre of Julian Beck and Judith Malina; The Environmental Theatre of Schechner; Ionesco, and by the ideas of Grotowski and Artaud.

GAMBARO: No, I don't believe so. Who invented that? We come from Argentinian dramaturgy, a genre called *grotesco* [grotesque] created by a playwright named Armando Discepolo, [1887–1971]. We don't come from European absurdism, which is so metaphysical, which presents the world as a fact with inexplicable laws.

INTERVIEWER: In what era did Discepolo write?

GAMBARO: I don't exactly know, but the production of his works was 1935 to 1965. *Grotesco* has its roots in the theater of Pirandello. The Argentinian dramas of the immigrants—in which people speak in a certain way that we call "Cocoliche"—were influenced by Pirandello. But Discepolo and others who work in the same genre gave to it a very Argentinian characteristic. Ionesco's absurdism considers the world has inexplicable laws. The same holds true for Artaud. I don't see a clear connection with Artaud and our theater. Our theater is much more connected with a social element, and our plays deal directly with political and social content. We also believe that society is modifiable, changeable.

INTERVIEWER: Would you discuss your ideas about the relationship between your plays and the spectator? Critic Rosalea Postma said of

Información Para Extranjeros " . . . it attempts to involve the spectator in a dramatic experience that will also radicalize his perceptions." ["Space and Spectator in the Theatre of Griselda Gambaro," *Latin American Theatre Review*, Fall, 1980.] Was this your intent?

GAMBARO: I believe that all theater means to produce not shock but a response in the spectator. It could be an emotional response, or a rational, sensible response.

INTERVIEWER: If the twenty-one scenes in *Información Para Extranjeros* were to be, as you suggested in the stage directions, experienced in a different sequence by each of several audience groups, would the total effect of the scenes on each audience member be the same?

FORNES: This is the kind of question people ask me! I did a play, *Fefu and her Friends*, where I divided the audience into four different groups. Isn't that funny? I didn't know you had done that, too. Did you know that some productions of Chekhov have been staged this way? Though his plays, of course, were not written with that intention.

GAMBARO: What I thought was that *the director* would have to find out how to make the order of the scenes work. As a work of imagination, I *could* have done it but I never made a decision as to what the correct scene order would be.

FORNES: Does the audience go together to see each scene?

GAMBARO: No. The audience is separated and they see different scenes at different times. Only at the end do they come together. It is aleatory, meaning they see everything, but they see different things.

INTERVIEWER: What is the relationship between playwrights and critics in Argentina? Do critics illuminate a piece of work?

GAMBARO: In Argentina I don't think there is any good criticism. There are no good critics.

INTERVIEWER: Are your critics especially hard on women writers?

GAMBARO: No. Only one critic, at the beginning of my career, attacked me as a woman. He called me a "little, young lady writer."

INTERVIEWER: Does the financial success of a play depend on a good critical reception as it does here in the United States? Do your critics have the power to close a play or extend a run?

GAMBARO: Of course, the critic can help a play, but in Argentina, the critic cannot undermine the *existence* of a play. Good critical reception helps success, but does not determine it. In my case, I have been working in Argentina a long time. I've earned my own space and have entered that suspicious, dangerous category of "respectable" people. [Laughter]

INTERVIEWER: Is the playwright able to make a living from his/her work?

GAMBARO: With difficulty. And only if the plays are staged often and with success. If a play is successful it's profitable for the playwright. One can live well. In Argentina there might be three or four playwrights who can live off their work.

INTERVIEWER: Do they write drama or comedy?

GAMBARO: I'm talking about the serious dramatists. Those who write comedy can live on what they earn from writing, and so can those who write for commercial theater.

FORNES: Does a successful serious drama play only in Buenos Aires, or does it tour in the provinces?

GAMBARO: It can tour, but in the provinces one earns very little. The real market is Buenos Aires, or Uruguay if you plan a long tour.

INTERVIEWER: We've read that 90 percent of theater pieces in Argentina are presented by acting companies which are formed cooperatively.

GAMBARO: In Argentina, one might work with a commercial theater, but more often one looks for a producer and then forms a company which will perform that particular play. When it's a short-term production, we work *en cooperativa* [in a cooperative]; the actors start making profit once the play is running.

INTERVIEWER: Is it as important to have your dramatic texts published as to have them performed?

GAMBARO: Both are important. Publishing allows the text to tour, to be translated. It also makes other stagings of a play possible. Very few plays are published in Argentina. I don't have all my plays published, but my last three will be published in June.

INTERVIEWER: Are there any American playwrights that are particularly admired in Argentina?

GAMBARO: Yes. Arthur Miller has been played a lot. As well as Tennessee Williams and Edward Albee.

INTERVIEWER: Is there any subject that is presently obsessing you which you must write about soon?

GAMBARO: No, because when something starts to absorb me, I just put it in writing.

FORNES: And if, at this moment, an obsession came into your mind would you quit everything and start working?

GAMBARO: Here in New York? Impossible. The visual impact is so strong here.

INTERVIEWER: Are there any special difficulties in translating your work?

GAMBARO: The only translations I know are German, French and Italian. My work is difficult to translate into French because the French language is very rational. And in my case—especially in the novels—I stress the intensity of the verbs, and use idiomatic games which are very difficult to employ for the French, and hard to translate.

INTERVIEWER: How do the Argentinians feel about the success of *Evita*?

GAMBARO: Many people are not in agreement with the portrayal of Eva Perón. That provokes anger of a political nature.

INTERVIEWER: Because the play aggrandized Eva Perón or because it was not fair to her?

GAMBARO: Because the story was simplified. They made a slick interpretation.

INTERVIEWER: Is Eva considered a serious political person?

GAMBARO: Yes. With many contradictions. She herself was someone with enormous contradictions. Partly due to her class, partly because she didn't have intellectual capacity. In my opinion, Perón doesn't deserve any sympathy. I think Eva had more sincerity, more vivacity, and more bravery than [her husband] Perón.

INTERVIEWER: Do you have children?

GAMBARO: Two. A daughter of twenty-two and a son of eighteen.

INTERVIEWER: Has motherhood affected your writing?

GAMBARO: Well, I had less time. But my sister helped me tremendously, so I was always able to save the mornings for my work.

INTERVIEWER: Are you still a morning writer?

GAMBARO: Yes, I start at about eight-thirty. But when I am involved, for instance, in the writing of a play, I work the afternoons too—I work whenever I can—sometimes all day. As discipline, mornings are essential. There's no excuse for not having the discipline to work every morning. I write a page by hand, which I then type, because if not, I can't see clearly. And of course, once I pass a page or a unit of writing through the typewriter, I correct it many times. But the new, the original, is always handwritten. I believe there is a more direct communication with the writing itself when I write by hand.

INTERVIEWER: How does a play begin in your mind? Do you use journals, dreams . . .

GAMBARO: I don't keep personal journals, but I do use the material of dreams. I dream very little—that's my disgrace! I am very interested in the material that comes from dreams, and if I can remember them, I use my dreams. If, of course, they are useful.

INTERVIEWER: Are there any other art forms that influence you?

GAMBARO: Not in a direct way. I write with music playing all the time. I don't really listen to it, but I have it on cassette in the background.

INTERVIEWER: Do you want to say anything about your upcoming productions?

GAMBARO: The project that I'm most interested in is a play I wrote last year, *Del Sol Naciente* [*From the Rising Sun*]. In Argentina, we call Japan "the rising sun." It's a play that began as a dream. I dreamt that I had written a perfect play, with a Japanese ambiance. When I woke up, I thought, "Why not?" I wrote a play with a Japanese setting, but the theme is related to the Falklands War.

—Translated by Alberto Minero

PAM GEMS

P*am Gems is a British playwright.*
Her plays include Dusa, Fish, Stas, and Vi *(Edinburgh Festival, Hamp-stead Theatre, Mayfair Theatre 1976/77),* Queen Christina *(Royal Shake-speare Company at The Other Place 1977, Tricycle Theatre 1982),* Franz into April *(1977),* I.C.A. Lunchtime, *and* Piaf *published by Samuel French, 1983; produced at The Other Place, the Warehouse, the Aldwych, Wyndham's and Piccadilly Theatres, and on Broadway where Jane La-potaire won a Tony Award in the title role, 1978/81). She has also trans-lated Chekhov's* Uncle Vanya *(Hampstead Theatre 1979, National Theatre 1982) and Ibsen's* A Doll's House *(Newcastle Playhouse 1980). Her most recent plays include* Loving Women, Camille, *and a version of* The Cherry Orchard.

INTERVIEWER: Do you have the opportunity to see many American plays here in London?

GEMS: Yes, but it isn't satisfying to see American plays performed by British casts. We're brought up with American movies. Our English ears are better attuned to American rhythms than vice versa.

INTERVIEWER: Are you familiar with many American women writers?

GEMS: Only Lillian Hellman, who is very upper-class. It's so difficult to get copies of scripts of the new work—people like Marsha Norman, Beth Henley. When I was last in New York, I mentioned Tennessee Williams (this was before he died) and was amazed that he was not more revered—a great, great writer . . . the most superb dramatic line ever.

INTERVIEWER: Would you tell us about the Women's Playhouse Project?

GEMS: We have no theater as yet but our first production, *The Lucky Chance* by Aphra Behn, has been playing at the Royal Court Theatre, very successfully. Our aims are to have a theater run by women . . . and men, but practicing positive discrimination. We've commissioned new plays with the help of the publishers Eyre Methuen, and our next production will be a new version of *Beauty and the Beast*, by Louise Page. We are determined to find a theater, which we intend to name the Sarah Siddons Theatre. Women have been most influential in the theater in this country. I may mention Emma Cons and Lilian Baylis, who began what became the National Theatre, Joan Littlewood, Ninette de Valois, Marie Rambert . . . their names are hardly commemorated.

INTERVIEWER: Do you feel it would be possible for young women playwrights to be produced today had it not been for the struggles of their predecessors? Yourself, Michelene Wandor, Caryl Churchill . . .

GEMS: No. Such groups as Women in Entertainment, Monstrous Regiment, the Women's Theatre Company, and many smaller groups have been important in changing climate, most particularly among audiences. I accept that we're never grateful for the struggles of our ancestors. But so long as we don't renege!

INTERVIEWER: Are younger women in England more conservative than their predecessors?

GEMS: No. Here in England I would say not. It is fashionable to say in the yellow press, "Feminism is dead," but it is also fashionable to say that the only two growth areas at the moment are computers and feminist publishing. There has been a political swing to the right, but that is on the turn again now here. Some of them feel strongly the need for radical feminism to be sound on the need for solidarity . . . at a time of high unemployment, for men and women to fight is social suicide.

INTERVIEWER: Would you tell us about the publication of women's writing in England?

GEMS: A struggle. Women's books are published much more now, serious books of all kinds. But plays are a specialized market. They are, after all, blueprints.

INTERVIEWER: Do critics have the same power in London as they do in New York?

GEMS: No. Not in the same way. Is it as it was when Clive Barnes was king? Fatuous situation, that so many livelihoods could be in the fee of one man's liver. I wish the critics would get it right. When the notices are good they're for the wrong reason. Theater critics claim that they are there on behalf of the paying public, *in loco*. But you wouldn't have a golfing correspondent who knew nothing of golf. My complaint is of ignorance and ineptness. It's odd, books are reviewed differently. If a book is about fishing, the reviewer is a fishing expert . . . a new volume of poetry, ask [poet] Philip Larkin. I can't see why this doesn't obtain in the theater. How can a man, and here it's always a man, see four or five shows a week, year after year . . . it's insane human behavior.

INTERVIEWER: Do critics have a different vocabulary to review women's work than to review men's work?

GEMS: Yes, but it's a very complex thing. Apart from the fact that critics don't want to hand over any of their power, especially in the theater where there are very few jobs, *au fond*, men fear and hate women more than women fear and hate men (unless the women have been abused). Our first sanctions come from a woman, the mother. There's a very primitive hostility that comes from early power plays. I see it time and again as I get older, that resentful fear of the mother figure. There is a spiteful revenge in some criticism of women's work. I did a play, a two-hander, about Arthur and Guinevere, and fell over backwards to make the arguments fair and equal. I made Guinevere shallow, trivial . . . which Guinevere knows, and she knows why . . . it is because she, as a woman, has been kept out of the action. The critics, all male, dubbed the play unfair to men.

INTERVIEWER: Are there subscription audiences in London theaters?

GEMS: No. Not as in America. The Royal Shakespeare Company has a subscription system. A lot of us fear the system, as we feel it has an inhibiting and conservative effect on artistic policy.

INTERVIEWER: Has it become a matter of status to go to the theater in London?

GEMS: It used to be. It used to be a standard middle-class night out. This has changed because theater seats are expensive, eating out in London is expensive, parking a car is expensive, and there are muggers, or the fear of. The older, loyal theatergoer is dying out. The scene is more polarized with the advent of film, television, video, and some of us feel the need to sustain the young audience if theater is to live. People will come for the right product. Look at the thousands who will go to a rock concert by The Police. Of course, there you are guaranteed a visceral experience. Theater is chancy. One of the problems for theater in England is that we have excellent television programs. This not only keeps people at home, it uses up a lot of writers who might otherwise be writing for the stage.

INTERVIEWER: Have you ever made compromises in your writing for production?

GEMS: No, I never do. I can't see the point.

INTERVIEWER: Is life easier now that you have a name, less of a fight?

GEMS: No. The fight is with yourself. You have to break ground . . . make the voyage of discovery . . . surprise yourself. It's an arrogant act, to ask people to be quiet and listen to you for two hours (and pay you for the privilege). You have to try to honor the contract.

INTERVIEWER: Are women writers in England often accused of poor craft, of writing "non-plays," when in fact their works are often highly structured but in unconventional ways?

GEMS: Do you find that in America, too? We came across it early on with Michelene Wandor's early pieces. She wrote a number of poetic, tangential two-handers, and we couldn't get anyone to produce them. We gave them to Ed Berman of the Almost-Free Theatre, because he was putting together a series of plays by women. No way. He said they had no plot, no through line, no crisis. But in a group of thirty women attempting to choose plays for the season, the response to Michelene's plays was total. They spoke to us. We needed them. There was no problem for us.

INTERVIEWER: Does women's work require new forms? Is there a female aesthetic in drama?

GEMS: This is an important question. It is precisely the job of women in this century to begin to try to find this out. We have been, through chemical mutation, so very recently rescued from the appalling perils of the childbed (how many children did Jane Austen, George Eliot, or the Brontë sisters have?). Until recently, a woman did well to remain chaste if she wanted any sort of life span. So, we've only just begun to have the time itself, let alone the leisure to investigate ourselves. Drama forms part of this investigation. I personally think that women are particularly well adapted to theatrical writing because theater is subversive, and women have traditionally had to be subversive in order not to get their heads knocked off.

Also, traditionally again, women have reared children. It's an awful generalization nowadays, but by and large men have been off, and the children have been at the teat and the heel, certainly for the first four years. Women, during these years, become sophisticated in the minutiae of emotional information, feeling and response . . . it's necessary for the survival of the infant.

To return to the question of form and aesthetic . . . Certainly in *Dusa, Fish, Stas and Vi*, and in *Piaf* I deliberately used a kind of dramatic shorthand, a very filmic way of working. This was deliberate, and related to the subjects. But I was accused of not knowing how to write a well-made play, of writing "non-plays."

INTERVIEWER: How do you feel about male playwrights attempting to create feminist characters?

GEMS: It's fashion. And I regard it extremely cynically. You get women like the lady in David Hare's *Plenty*, a most inaccurate play, where the woman purports to be a protagonist but is the old emblem, just as before . . . sexy, moody, mysterious, and a right old turn-on, with a plainer friend (this used to be the Una Merkel part). Spurious stuff.

INTERVIEWER: You have said you used *Piaf* as a metaphor for working-class women. Could you draw a distinction between emblematic and metaphoric use of character?

GEMS: Words can mean what you want . . . you context them, and make your meaning clear . . . you hope. I'm not too happy with *emblems* . . . perhaps it smells a bit reactionary as a word. If a theme interests you you take whatever you need as a setting . . . outer space, the Wars of the Roses . . . playwrights have always done this. It's not important. That's just the metaphor. All the stories have been told long ago. Your job is retelling. Relighting. You have a number of weapons as a dramatist . . . humor, suspense, sexual attraction . . . anything to make people come alive . . . watch . . . listen. Certainly women have been used as emblems throughout history . . . as objects of desire, worship . . . to be feared, guarded, protected . . . humiliated, enslaved, most particularly as property. Shaw's "new woman" purports to be a protagonist. But he gets off on her a little too much for my liking. I prefer Harley Granville-Barker, I only wish he'd written more.

INTERVIEWER: Do you believe that women playwrights are making progress in fighting discrimination? It's not the first time we've been in the public eye. In 1920 there were fourteen plays by women on Broadway. . . .

GEMS: That's very interesting! It was just after World War I and the Russian Revolution (before it all went wrong) . . . just after skirts went up. Great changes . . . modernism in clothes and art . . . fascinating. Why aren't there more women now, one asks? Partly it's for the reason that playwriting involves play production. You can write a novel at home, all it costs is the pen and paper, but a play's production is dearer and more complicated. There is another aspect, and this is to do with ambition. Women, often, in my experience, don't have the same drive to power.

This question of women and ambition brings to mind a brilliant woman novelist called Molly Keane who wrote West End plays in the fifties under the name Farrell, and then stopped. She's only begun to be published again now, in her eighties, because Peggy Ashcroft was staying with her and found a manuscript of a novel in a drawer. It interests me that Lillian Hellman stopped. There doesn't seem to be the same drive in women to maintain status. Very interesting this silence thing with women. Different patterns. I saw something fascinating on television. They've been doing research on infants, looking for sex differences. And they've found differences in response not only to sound—the sound of a known, and an unknown voice for example—but differences in response to light. There's a sexual difference in the rod and cone vision in the eyes. We are different. Women really do have to chart and explore their own history. Men have been talking to one another for thousands of years. We're dealing with thousands of years of race memory, perhaps, of patterning. We're not necessarily seeking to erase, but we may need deep societal modifications, to accommodate the other fifty percent of us.

INTERVIEWER: Do you feel that it was easier for you as a woman writer that you had your children first and then began writing plays?

GEMS: This is the sixty-fourer. How do we do both? How are we lover, confidante, nurse, cook, cleaner, shopper, intellectual equal, achiever, sharer of financial burden, sister, mistress, mother? There's no clear answer. So much of our lives is dominated by chance, call it luck, if you like. I think, speaking generally, that you can't afford to drop out, go into a dream of babies and puppies and baking nowadays. Not if you want to pursue an art . . . craft is different. It takes all of your time. But really, there's no general rule. I have always written, whether produced, published, or not.

INTERVIEWER: Did you always want to be a writer?

GEMS: I always was a writer, yes. Not that I expected to make a living at it, I didn't have that kind of self-image. I come from the working classes and was used to a world of weekly wages and the fear of the sack.

INTERVIEWER: What changed that self-perception?

GEMS: Accident. I came to live in London with my family to get specialized training for my youngest child, who is mentally handicapped. Because her preschool nursery hours were from ten to three-thirty I was free to go to lunch-time theater. The atmosphere was pleasant and informal, there was often food and drink on sale. I began to make acquaintances, and to write for the fringe. Having a handicapped child meant that I had no social life. This meant I worked whenever I had free time.

INTERVIEWER: Would you discuss language and playwriting? How do you develop language in your plays? How does a play begin in your mind?

GEMS: Usually sideways. Somebody asks for a sketch for a miner's benefit, and nothing comes to mind. But a sort of energy aggregates into coagulation, into a sort of restlessness. Then a lot of disparate themes seem to want to be put together, usually because they are an impossible mix . . . it's a game. I like authenticity, partly because, trained as a psychologist, I was never allowed to posit hypothetical cases, we were allowed only to work from factual data. I always take incident from firsthand. I do get more and more interested in the formal side of play-writing. I do logic problems a lot when I'm working on a play, it keeps my mind lively, and I play a lot of word games in my head. The formalistic side of writing plays is very important. For me it's a problem with many people's work, they seem unaware of the form they're attempting to work in. Great bouts of dialogue, windy generalized statements, often couched in heightened language . . . it's an amateur's notion of what drama is about. Drama is about us. Medea is a woman whose husband leaves her for another woman. The nature of the dramatic mode is the withholding of information, in the creation of a puzzle for the audience to solve. Clues.

INTERVIEWER: Subtext?

GEMS: Yes. The way we actually communicate, for much of the time, in real life.

INTERVIEWER: Is less exposition tolerated in the theater today?

GEMS: Well, an actress friend of mine said the other day, "I'm only doing this play, you realize, for the metaphor." Seriously, we do have a problem, not only because other people can stay at home . . . switch channels . . . but because whole generations are growing up accustomed to the quick elision of the visual mode . . . the quick transitions of movies and television. We have to elide. But a serious play is working at depth. So it ain't easy. You need surface value, in live performance. And something else, something more. Something that remains in the mind, something that is there when you lift your head from the pillow the next morning.

INTERVIEWER: What are some of the aesthetic problems that you have encountered and dealt with in your own writing? What do you feel you are pushing toward?

GEMS: More elision. Greater precision, clarity. A smaller tip to the iceberg, and I recommend the great French artist Marguerite Duras as the *maîtresse* in that sphere.

Everything is a trap, you make people laugh and that's pleasant and it's tempting to do it again. And again. I have to try something new every time, which is not a good idea if you want to be successful. People want you to cut a shape. And for you to become more and more famous, and make more and more money, and wear fur coats, and go to restaurants. I find as I get older that the only way to get myself going is to do risky productions. If I can't get a risky production I'll go to a smaller theater.

INTERVIEWER: Would you tell us something about the controversy over your play *The Treat* [1982]?

GEMS: We tried to do something very risky and inevitably some people hated it. We were a collective, and we were trying to *confront* the fact that (leaving aside gay men) men, primates, are attracted by secondary female characteristics. That is a constant. We felt that a lot of feminism was incorrect in its hostility to the phenomenon as such. Thus, given that women turn men on . . . what is permissible behavior between the sexes? And what isn't? So we did a play about a brothel where women turned men on. We wanted to say, "Yes . . . a turn-on, right? But hang on. What's going on now? Is this all right? It isn't? Why not?" A lot of people got it, and were deeply moved and respectful. A lot didn't and thought we were exploiting women . . . we had actresses displaying their bodies in the "brothel" in order to be "chosen." "Of course," said a young woman graduate, interviewing me for radio, "you set the play in the twenties because this wouldn't happen nowadays." I looked at this girl, a Cambridge graduate, who was totally unaware that there were two brothels within five minutes of the theater, where the women had given us data.

INTERVIEWER: Do playwrights have artistic control in rehearsal here in London?

GEMS: Very little. You have much more in America. I'll tell you . . . the classic story goes like this. Director: "Listen everybody, the writer's coming in this morning. Don't laugh."

INTERVIEWER: How do you get your artistic intentions across?

GEMS: By deviousness. Directors will work with you upfront and all seems sweetness and light. But they renege. Usually through thickness rather than bad faith, often through exigency. I've learned to be tougher because, in the end, when you've spent two years on a play, it isn't good to allow it to go by default.

INTERVIEWER: Do you ever take the actors aside?

GEMS: If necessary, but not lightly. A play is a director's production . . . his or her vision of the piece. Take that away from a director and you demote her or him to a Guvnor calling rehearsal schedules. But you have to smell the wind. Actors are usually obedient and willing at the top of rehearsals. But as they get nearer to production, to the day when they've got to go out there and risk themselves, they become demanding, and properly so. If necessary, you have to step in.

INTERVIEWER: Do you have such problems with both male and female directors?

GEMS: For me, less so with women, simply because I'm not frightened to talk with them. I'm not frightened of damaging their egos. The trouble is, there aren't that many good women directors. They don't get the work, so they're less skilled. . . . So, you say, "Am I a good feminist?" I've worked more with women than with men because it's important to support other women, and because I feel comfortable. But there have been failures. Of course.

INTERVIEWER: Do you find you are growing stronger as a writer in the rehearsal process?

GEMS: Well, the writer is weaker to begin with. His or her work has already been exhausting, for months or more. The director and designers have put in some work, the actors usually not much. A lot depends on the director, and the general conditions. The backup at the Royal Shakespeare Company is wonderful, but there is a special tension, the necessity for excellence.

INTERVIEWER: Do you still feel that you don't want to take commissions because it affects your work?

GEMS: Yes, although I'm less naïve. You can take the commission and do what you want anyway. It's not really a matter of choice, so much writing is involuntary. You set out to write one thing and find you've written another. Many writers say this.

INTERVIEWER: How do you know when the play is succeeding? Is it something you feel in your gut?

GEMS: I'll tell you what it's about. It's about silence. I have a bad eye, so that I often have to close my eyes in the theater. What you have to control, in the writing, is silence. You have to orchestrate that important member of the cast, the audience. Orchestrate, and conduct. One joke too many and they become flatulent, blowsy. One thought too many and they begin to move, restless, oppressed. The audience *must* be working, as hard as the actors. The audience must be alive, must create the play. Despite what Brecht said (but didn't do) we proceed by empathy. And it's powerful.

INTERVIEWER: How do your ideas come?

GEMS: Partly because I'm older, I've done a fair amount of living so that things flop out. I try not to be schematic. I fear the so-called committed theater, which can be fascistic. I am for Dionysus. Also there is this dirty word *entertainment*. Without descending to the groveling depths of the worst of Broadway, with grown humans trying to be cute for our favor, there is the need to engage. We are inviting people at the end of their working day. Brecht was a great entertainer . . . good songs by Kurt Weill and [Hanns] Eisler. Politics, direct statements, belong on the platform not the stage.

INTERVIEWER: Can politics and social relevancy also be entertainment?

GEMS: Yes. It's fashionable to say that Chekhov is not political. He is an extremely political writer. His plays are suffused with politics. Whatever you are writing is suffused with your own life, it can't *not* be, unless you are a liar.

INTERVIEWER: Would you discuss the sexuality in your plays, and, if possible, your ideals for sexuality, because it seems you are in some way recommending a different kind of relationship between the sexes.

GEMS: I don't think consciously about it; it probably slips out. I'm influenced by something I read about the nature of Celtic life, or more primitive life, before ownership. In England, when the Romans came and started to enclose land, we had plenty of rain, so we were like Ireland still is, a pastoral land, which meant that you had loose, tribal connections. Marriage was a formal contract, but as easily dissolved. The society was matriarchal, which meant that the relationship between men and the children was fraternal rather than paternal. I find I leapt on that with a feeling of great joy. It made me feel that there could be another way which has to do with the extended family notion.

As for sexuality, and its use in the theater, well, it's something to be used with precision, like humor, suspense, plot. It's a temptation to use a lot of sex or humor because it puts people in a good mood . . . it puts people on your side.

INTERVIEWER: Do you think women are pressured toward writing humor?

GEMS: I think we are. Because, of course, they've traditionally accused us of not being able to do it. And there's no doubt about it—laughter ringing around the theater is very pacifying. I'm trying to be more disciplined about it.

INTERVIEWER: In America, with the influx of British women's plays, we had the impression that women playwrights in England were having an easier time getting productions.

GEMS: It's sporadic. In relation to the number of men produced, it's still woeful. This is why we want the Women's Playhouse here. All of the literary managers here are men. There simply must be a way to provide opportunity. I remember reading a script by an older woman. It was long, it was demanding, it wasn't practical, her stage directions were naïve. I couldn't get anyone interested. But the wit, the perception, the wisdom. There was no way this woman's work was going to be produced; no one felt impelled to help her. If the Woman's Playhouse Trust does nothing else it can become a focus, a center, somewhere to share ideas, and put some things together.

INTERVIEWER: You said recently that the insights of a mature woman were rarely seen in the theater today. Would you elaborate?

GEMS: Because of movies, the focus of attention has moved more and more to the younger protagonist, to the central sexual attraction (even though the actors, particularly the men, may be unsuitably aged). In the movies it is regarded as an essential that the audience is mesmerized, in love with the protagonists. The semi-criminal, cynical, alienated figure is the model today. This iconoclastic figure is essentially young. So, in this day and age, people try to be young . . . they have their faces mutilated, they dye their hair, et cetera. Some of this is good, some humiliating. I'm inclined to believe that a healthy society respects maturity. But that's just a feeling. I do think that the women's movement is facing these sanctions and achieving. Film actresses used to be "over" by their mid-thirties. Now we have Fonda, Burstyn, Fletcher, Redgrave . . . parts are being written for people rather than sexual emblems.

INTERVIEWER: Do you mind being called a woman playwright?

GEMS: Well, it is fatuous since it's obvious by my name that I am a woman. And, as we know, men aren't called men playwright or male novelist. The day that the phrase ceases perhaps something will have been achieved!

BETH HENLEY

B*eth Henley was born and raised in Mississippi. She is the author of* Crimes of the Heart, The Miss Firecracker Contest *and* The Wake of Jamey Foster. *Her plays have been produced extensively, on Broadway, in American regional theaters and abroad.* Crimes of the Heart, *her first full-length play, won both the Pulitzer Prize in Drama and the New York Drama Critics' Circle Award for Best American Play in 1981, and was co-winner of the 1979 Great American Play contest sponsored by the Actors Theatre of Louisville. She is at work on a new play entitled* The Debutante Ball. *Ms. Henley graduated from Southern Methodist University. She lives and works in Los Angeles.*

INTERVIEWER: Why are you living in Los Angeles when most of your fellow playwrights are in New York?

HENLEY: Before I knew that I wanted to write, I wanted to act. It was either New York or Los Angeles. Some of my close friends were living in L.A., so I came out here. It was not a very calculated decision. The acting world was tough. I was on such a low level that I'd audition for anything in the paper. Right away they didn't like the way you looked or the way you talked. It was so much more difficult than writing.

INTERVIEWER: Having been raised in the South, did you experience any culture shock when you first moved to Los Angeles?

HENLEY: It was like I'd crossed over to the moon! In the South, everything is staid. Everyone knows you. Out here, it's real transient. Nobody knows anybody, you're completely anonymous, and in a way I like that. I like going places and not running into several people I know. In Los Angeles, everybody's out for themselves. But everybody's trying, everybody's got these *dreams*—some of them pathetic and unreachable —but at least they do have hopes and aspirations. In the South, you just know what you're going to do and you do it. It gets to be very suffocating when I go back there.

211

INTERVIEWER: What is a typical Beth Henley day like?

HENLEY: It depends. . . . Usually I get up late, piddle around my house, read the newspaper, have breakfast and give my dog a bone . . . then I go to my office and work all day, till about five-thirty. Then Belita, a friend, comes over to the office and we do our Jane Fonda exercises. After that, I go out to dinner with friends (I hardly ever cook) or have people come over. I usually stay up pretty late at night, either reading or writing.

INTERVIEWER: Tell us something about your creative process. . . .

HENLEY: I write excessive notes, character charts and outlines before I even start the dialogue. After the first draft, I usually don't need to do major rewrites, though I make a lot of minor changes and do some rewriting during rehearsals. I like to fix stuff that's not working. Though I used to write at night, I've taken to writing in the afternoons now that I have an office. I usually take my vitamins, pick up some lint on the floor, look out, look around, think about who I have to call, because I *hate* to make phone calls, I'm desperate about it. I always have to do *something* before I start writing. I don't think it's good to rush it. I do a certain amount of dialogue a day, which I reread the next day before I go on. I look over my notes. I always write out *What is this play all about? What are you writing? What does this mean? This sucks.* I've got all these notes on the floor. I have character charts and cross references . . . all these rituals are really more complex than I can explain. I mainly just do this stuff to keep busy so my mind can be left alone to figure it out.

INTERVIEWER: What is the rehearsal process like for you? How much input do you expect as a writer?

HENLEY: Equal to more input than the director on the script, and equal to less input into the production. If you work with someone you respect, you can always work things out.

INTERVIEWER: Do you talk directly to the actors?

HENLEY: Generally I don't like to talk to the actors. I prefer to speak to the director—to give him notes—because actors seem to get really hurt when the playwright says something negative to them, much more so than when the director says things.

INTERVIEWER: Do you sit through the entire rehearsal process?

HENLEY: If it's a first production of a play, I can't leave. I hate to get coffee or go to the bathroom. I love to sit there and watch, even if I'm just staring into space. I love to watch actors work and I love rehearsals. Watching the actors discover things is like watching a home run. I don't want to be out making phone calls or doing publicity.

INTERVIEWER: When you feel the play isn't coming across the way you intended, will you push for what you want?

HENLEY: Oh, sure. I always push for what I want. Only on a couple of occasions have I had arguments with the director. Usually, I try to be more manipulative, you know, say, "This is just wonderful, but I've just got this little thought . . ." I try not to get people on the defensive, I try not to say, "I *have* to have this idea," or, "This thing really sucks, why don't you fix it?" I'd rather try to deal with specific problems.

INTERVIEWER: How do you deal with opening night?

HENLEY: I sit in a bar across the street. . . . I'm talking about New York or London. . . . The thing is, it's a false night for the actors and for the playwright because the critics are there. I mean, I'm not going to sit in the theater with people who have note pads and are writing down criticisms of my plays. It makes me too sick. Besides, that's the great thing about being a playwright; you don't have to sit in the theater. I've sat in the theater and died a million deaths. So my advice is to leave. It saves you the misery and the terror.

INTERVIEWER: Do you remember the first time you saw a production of one of your plays?

HENLEY: I remember I was real cavalier about it. I'd written *Am I Blue* as a sophomore in college [1972] and they pulled it out for production when I was a senior. I had my name down as Amy Peach. . . .

INTERVIEWER: You took a pseudonym?

HENLEY: Yeah. I remember I saw the play first in a preview. It wasn't very good and I was real embarrassed. But after a while, the show improved. I saw it later in Hartford, [Hartford Stage Company, 1981] and then again in Dallas. I recall being moved by the play because it reflected so clearly who I was when I was eighteen. When I wrote *Am I Blue* I was so emotionally covered up that I didn't even realize what I was saying about myself or about life or loneliness, family situations. I just thought it was a kind of funny piece that I wrote to pass playwriting class. When I went back to it, I was so glad I'd written it down because I'll never be that innocent again . . . with that point of view, knowing nothing about life. At eighteen, I was simply terrified that I was a failure.

INTERVIEWER: *Crimes of the Heart* [1979] is partially about sisterly love . . .

HENLEY: Oh, God. I have three sisters and the relationship with each is different. My littlest sister I've always just adored. My other two sisters were closer in age, so we always ganged up against each other. We had horrible, normal battles. . . . I don't know whether we loved each other more than most sisters, or whether we hated each other more than most.

[Laughter] We're still into each other, we talk on the phone . . . we criticize the other sisters, things like "I think she should lose weight" or "I can't understand why she is with that idiot."

INTERVIEWER: What was your family's response to all the Pulitzer publicity?

HENLEY: They were very surprised. On the negative side, I know my sister, C.C., felt pressured. She was in a dress shop and the woman who's done her alterations for years and years said, "C.C., I know you're just as smart as your sister, why don't you go out and get you one of those Pulitzer prizes?" C.C. said she felt like Billy Carter. Mississippi is such a small place. It's much more significant there to have had a show on Broadway or a Pulitzer than it would be in, say, California. Out here, you have to be a major-major celebrity, like Farrah Fawcett, to feel like a big deal.

INTERVIEWER: Did your father live to see you win the Pulitzer?

HENLEY: No. I'd written *Crimes of the Heart* and he had a stroke that summer. He'd read one of my earlier plays and didn't like it. It was a 1940s musical called *Parade*. He hated it because he'd been in World War II. He thought the work was completely abysmal and historically inaccurate. He didn't see me as a writer.

INTERVIEWER: How do you think he would have felt about your success?

HENLEY: Oh, he would have loved it. He loved the limelight. He would have loved to come up and criticize my plays and tell me what needed to be fixed.

INTERVIEWER: How did your home town react?

HENLEY: My mother says people are always claiming that they recognize themselves in *Crimes of the Heart*, and I haven't even met them! They've met one of my sisters and think they've met me. The play was done in Mississippi this spring and it was a big hit. It's like something you wish in high school, being so shy, not really making good grades, not even being in Advanced English. Then you come back, and people are your friends, they are so nice to you and you think, "Who am I? Why are they nice to me now? What's different?" I understand what's different, but at the same time, there are parts of me that are intimidated, or rebellious, or just confused.

INTERVIEWER: What was your own response to winning the Pulitzer Prize?

HENLEY: I felt so happy, it was just the moon. And it was really a surprise.

INTERVIEWER: What are the negative points, if any, to winning?

HENLEY: Later on they make you pay for it. I think the fate of *The Wake of Jamey Foster* is part of the cost of winning. They just make sure you don't get overwhelmed by it, they want you to feel like it's not a big deal. "They" meaning the fates, not necessarily the critics. Winning the Pulitzer also put pressure, as I have said, on some of my family and friends and I didn't like that aspect of it at all. Mainly it was great because it got me a lot of money and a car, which I'd never had before. A bit of power.

INTERVIEWER: Your mother is an actress.

HENLEY: Oh, yes. She acted in community theater. As a child I just loved going to the theater and sitting there in rehearsals, watching. I thought it was glamorous. She'd come out in this green dress and stand on stage and get kissed by a man. I thought it was the most wonderful thing for a mother to do.

INTERVIEWER: In a *Time* magazine interview with Richard Corliss [February 8, 1982], you said that you are always afraid you're going to die before completing a play.

HENLEY: Oh, yes. I always think about death. I can't get through a day without thinking about it because it's my fate. When I'm working on a play, that's what helps drive me to finish it. Before I completed my new play, *The Debutante Ball*, I was going nuts because I had to go to the Hartford Stage Company for *The Wake of Jamey Foster* [January 1982], and I was working on the *Crimes of the Heart* screenplay. These responsibilities were taking me away from working on *The Debutante Ball*. I kept thinking, if I can at *least* get through these notes for the play, then maybe someone could finish it if I die.

INTERVIEWER: Why do you write?

HENLEY: Writing always helps me not to feel so angry. I've written about ghastly, black feelings and thoughts that I've had. The hope is that if you can pin down these emotions and express them accurately, you will be somehow absolved. I like to write characters who do horrible things, but whom you can still like . . . because of their human needs and struggles.

INTERVIEWER: You don't cover up the ugliness, do you?

HENLEY: I try to understand that ugliness is in everybody. I'm constantly in awe of the fact that we still seek love and kindness even though we are filled with dark, bloody, primitive urges and desires.

INTERVIEWER: What is your fascination with the grotesque: swollen heads, dead and injured animals, burn victims, aborted babies and suicides?

HENLEY: I've always been very attracted to split images. The grotesque combined with the innocent, a child walking with a cane; a kitten with a swollen head; a hunchback drinking a cup of fruit punch. Somehow these images are a metaphor for my view of life; they're colorful. Part of that is being brought up in the South; Southerners always bring out the grisly details in any event. It's a fascination with the stages of decay people can live in on this earth . . . the imperfections. But I do feel that all my plays are extremely optimistic.

INTERVIEWER: And what about all the animal imagery in the plays?

HENLEY: I hadn't ever realized there was animal imagery until my friend, playwright Frederick Bailey, pointed it out to me. I don't know what it means.

INTERVIEWER: There is no intended symbolic value?

HENLEY: Well, humans are animals. We're mammals; I think we should stop pretending that we're not. In the set for *The Debutante Ball*, I've got a beautiful, lush, upstairs sitting room and bathroom. I show all the things that people do in the bathroom before they go out to make themselves not animals, like shaving their legs, plucking their eyebrows, vomiting, pissing, perfume. . . . That is what is fascinating about people, their strange mixture of primitive instincts, intellect and spiritual confusion.

INTERVIEWER: Your plays are very funny. Would you discuss your ideas on comedy?

HENLEY: I always feel so emotional and miserable when I'm working, like I'm writing something tragic. Then everything manages to come out funny . . . and I'm glad.

INTERVIEWER: So you don't set out to write a comedy?

HENLEY: No. Not at all. All these things that I feel inside are desperate and dark and unhappy. Or not *unhappy*, but searching. Then they come out funny. The way my family dealt with hardships was to see the humor or the ironic point of view in the midst of tragedy. And that's just how *my* mind works. I don't think the plays are hilarious, though I'm glad they're not somber because that could be real boring. My comedy comes out of the situation and the characters rather than in funny lines. However, I *do* understand about making the rhythm of the line a *comic* rhythm. I know I can take one word out, or put two words in and it will get a laugh.

INTERVIEWER: Marshael plays the violin, though not very well, in *The Wake of Jamey Foster*. Babe, in *Crimes*, looks forward to improving her saxophone playing in jail. Are the musical instruments a metaphor for the creative impulse?

HENLEY: They must be. Growing up I never had a musical instrument because I didn't play. So for me, just to be around musical instruments means something special. Part of the reason I like to use musical instruments in my plays is so that they will be onstage, so that I can play around with them, pick them up when nobody is looking! They represent something beautiful, all this music and magic that I can't touch, can't grasp. I love saxophones and trumpets. The notes go so high, it's almost like the most exalted thing a human being can do, to play those wild high notes. It's like the musicians are straining, reaching for something beyond knowledge or the stars but they can't quite reach it.

INTERVIEWER: When we hear the saxophone playing at the end of *Crimes of the Heart,* are we to believe that Babe is condemned to prison?

HENLEY: No. No. The saxophone is more of a freeing image. The sisters are able to have this wonderful moment, despite impending doom, despite the fact that everything isn't sorted out, straightened up and made right. The idea is you've got to grab what you can, because when is life ever perfectly happy?

INTERVIEWER: If you were to write a sequel, would Babe be in prison?

HENLEY: I've changed my mind on that a couple of times. I think Babe probably gets off. They get people off for all sorts of things in Mississippi.

INTERVIEWER: The word *blue* seems to crop up frequently in your scripts—the color, as well as in reference to jazz and mood. . . .

HENLEY: I like the blues, I like jazz . . . colors pop up a lot. It scares you when you start writing your plays and they're all somehow the same play; they're not the same, but you use the same troubles and perceptions. It must mean you haven't sorted anything out . . . you're still stuck with the same fucking problems year after year.

INTERVIEWER: You were accused of writing another *Crimes of the Heart* when you wrote *The Wake of Jamey Foster.* Do you see them as the same story?

HENLEY: To me, they're different; they were dealing with different kinds of ghosts. I don't know . . . no one said, "Degas, don't paint any more ballerinas . . ." I seem to have been driven to explore different Southern families in different situations. *Miss Firecracker* and *The Debutante Ball* are also set in the South and they're about families, too. Maybe the plays are all variations on the same theme. I like dealing with similar characters. The Katty character in *The Wake of Jamey Foster* is something like Chick in *Crimes.* I was dissatisfied with the Chick character and I wanted to show the other side of her, to delve further. I have to write what is exciting to me and even if it may not seem very different to anybody else, it's exquisitely different to me—all glittering colors that I've seen but haven't dealt with fully before.

INTERVIEWER: Which of the characters in your plays is most like yourself?

HENLEY: All of them are different facets of what I feel. I think everybody writes autobiographically. You can't say that anything in my plays has actually happened . . . well, that's not true . . . *The Wake*, I guess is my most autobiographical play, as far as events. And *Debutante Ball* may be the most psychically autobiographical play I've written.

INTERVIEWER: Tell us something about your new play, *The Debutante Ball*.

HENLEY: I just had a reading of it in my house. It was beautiful. I have some actors that I always use because they understand the tone of my writing. It's about the debutante and her mother, about mother-daughter love. About the fragility of love, how people need love so badly that the need literally cripples them in their struggle to attain it. They are no longer able to seek love in a pure way. Instead, strange distorted devices are used to attain this balm, this love that they now seem to need in druglike excesses.

INTERVIEWER: Many of your characters are trying to break free of the labels that others have forced on them.

HENLEY: Yes, that's true. Particularly in *Miss Firecracker* and in *Crimes*. Both are about overcoming ghosts of the past and letting go of what other people have said you are, what they have told you to be. My other plays, *The Wake* and *The Debutante Ball*, are about what happens when you haven't overcome the shit . . . or have had more shit added on.

INTERVIEWER: Why did most of the reviewers sensationalize the fact that Babe, in *Crimes of the Heart*, says she shot her husband because she "didn't like his looks." Didn't she have deeper motives? Hadn't Babe been physically and mentally abused by her husband for years?

HENLEY: The press like something that's quick and funny and catches your attention, a catchphrase. That's all I can figure out, or else they just didn't get the point.

INTERVIEWER: Do you mind being called a 'woman playwright?'

HENLEY: No.

INTERVIEWER: Is there a female aesthetic in dramatic writing?

HENLEY: Probably in a general sense there is, just like there is a Southern aesthetic or an animal aesthetic. But it all sounds too much like school to get me very excited.

INTERVIEWER: Do you consider yourself a feminist?

HENLEY: Yes.

INTERVIEWER: Do you think the critics, in their rush to pin a label on you, overlooked the fact that your work has a profound feminist message? Not one said you were a feminist, but several called you a "Southern Gothic" writer.

HENLEY: "Southern" won out over "feminist," I guess. . . .

INTERVIEWER: Do you think this may have helped you escape some of the critical accusations often leveled at work with overtly feminist themes?

HENLEY: They're used to women writers from the South and so it's not such a big thing. There are so many women writers that are Southern, I guess critics allow them the right to write what they want.

INTERVIEWER: Do you think men's plays are critiqued differently from women's plays?

HENLEY: This is where my ignorance comes into play; I hate to read reviews. I have this hubris that always gets me in trouble if I ever read them. Like they sent me the reviews from the *Miss Firecracker* production in Chicago, a big package. I said, "I don't read reviews," and they said, "These are great. Read them." [Ms. Henley screams] I pulled out the only horrible one. It said, "It's certain that she'll never write anything as good as *Crimes of the Heart.*"

INTERVIEWER: I want to push you a bit on whether or not the work of male playwrights is evaluated differently.

HENLEY: Before *Crimes of the Heart* was a success, it was done in Louisville. I remember a review that said it was just "gossamer women" talking in the kitchen. And when *Miss Firecracker* was done out here, in California, they called it a petty play about a beauty contest. They wouldn't look for any of the deeper meaning or the spiritual levels in the play. Whereas if a man wrote a play about a baseball game, critics might be more inclined to find deep meanings about the Lost American Dream.

INTERVIEWER: Critics have often condemned women's plays for being too wordy, for not having enough "action."

HENLEY: I know I go home to Mississippi and we *talk*. No TV, we just sit around the kitchen table and pick something to talk about. It's exciting, always amusing and dramatic. I love to listen to conversations, to sit and eavesdrop. It's just so interesting, people's lives and the little things that conversations show. That's why I like playwriting.

INTERVIEWER: Language? Conversation?

HENLEY: Yes, and as a human being, I also find it fascinating to think about what the world is going to be like when people won't talk anymore. There are probably brilliant people, geniuses, alive today who don't even know how to say, "Hello, how do you do?" because their minds are absorbed with electronic images. I've been reading a book, full of little bitty things from around the turn of the century in Wisconsin. Clippings from a newspaper in a small town: They use big words and twists of phrases that are poetic and much more literate than newspapers today. I'm astounded when I think of what a dive we've taken in such a short time.

INTERVIEWER: Is *Miss Firecracker* an indictment of beauty contests?

HENLEY: It's a story about wanting to belong to the world. I didn't want to judge the contest. The contest is important to the character; winning it would make her feel like she is somebody. It's interesting to me what people do to make themselves special. It's exalting to me that they do these things.

INTERVIEWER: Would you discuss the recurrence of barren women in your work?

HENLEY: In *The Wake of Jamey Foster* I wanted to capture an image of all the women, to present different images of women in their state of fertility: Marshael, who has had children; Katty who wants to but can't; Collard who'd had the abortion; and Pixrose, the virgin who dreams.

INTERVIEWER: Is having children a present or future concern for you?

HENLEY: No, it makes me sad. I wish I were the type of person who wanted children, but I think I've got to admit I don't. I wish I could cook up a good spaghetti sauce, sling it out there on the table. But I'm not that type. My sisters have a lot of kids and I play with them and love to talk with them. They amuse me so, yet I know I have a fear of being tied down. My mother was. I know my fear is based on her being trapped in with all that talent she had, by kids and husband and the world. I purposely didn't take home economics; I didn't learn how to cook or sew or type. I finally had to teach myself to type. I'd refused to do things that would make me into something I didn't want to be. But it's sad, too, because you wonder and think that maybe you should commit yourself more to things. Something less completely selfish . . .

INTERVIEWER: Somebody's got to write our plays. . . .

HENLEY: Well, but now those assholes say everybody can write plays and have five kids and be gourmet cooks and all. Still, I've noticed that very few women writers throughout history had children. Because a kid's got to be more important that a fucking piece of paper. I know it could be so enriching to have a child. I am only speaking against it selfishly, in terms of writing. Sometimes I think, "Yeah . . . I could do all sorts of stuff . . . write during pregnancy . . ." Then I think, "What are you doing? You'd be having this kid as a kind of experiment, and that's despicable." I couldn't inflict that on a little child.

INTERVIEWER: Was it hard for you when *The Wake of Jamey Foster* closed so quickly [opened on Broadway, at the Eugene O'Neill Theatre, October 14, 1982, closed October 23, 1982], considering your previous success with *Crimes*?

HENLEY: Yes, very hard. But I don't think *Wake* was a flop artistically. And at the time it was running, it was exhilarating. I felt much happier after *The Wake* opened than I did after *Crimes* opened. The day after *Crimes*, I was completely drained. I was stunned after *The Wake*, but as a woman from the South, I was ready for it. . . . I thought, "You can overcome this! You can live with this! Fuck what everybody else thinks. You're alive!" When people praised *Crimes*, I felt like I had to be so self-effacing it wasn't any fun. I felt I had to say, "Ah . . . it's really nothing. I didn't mean to write that . . . I was really writing a grocery list." When you have a flop, you can fight. I must say I did love *The Wake*. I was exalted the whole week it ran after the reviews came out.

INTERVIEWER: Is there still discrimination against women playwrights in the American theater?

HENLEY: Yes, I think there is. Simply because there are still a lot more men than women in charge of our theaters: producing, directing, managing, fund raising. That's where the power and the money are in this country. Men generally can't help but be more moved by a man's play because they relate to it in a personal way. Women are more used to identifying with men, because they're raised on it, they've got to be. Men aren't used to identifying with women. And all writing is creating or spinning dreams for other people so they won't have to bother doing it themselves. In terms of the people who make decisions about play production, the closer these dreams are to their version of themselves, the more chance they'll want to sit through a play or to find money to produce it.

INTERVIEWER: Why don't we see more broadly political plays in America?

HENLEY: I can only speak for myself. . . . I like to write about people. The problems of just being here are more pressing and exciting to me than politics. Politics generally deal with the facades of our more desperate problems. I don't really feel like changing the world, I want to look at the world. That is fascinating and challenging enough—without saying, "I'm going to write a play to change this." And what is *this*? *This* is madness. So you change it? So you get a Republican in, so you get a Democrat in? You're still in hell. What is amazing to me is the existential madness that we—everyone—are born into. There's a sense of power-lessness in the world. I have a moratorium on watching the news since Reagan's been president. I know I am burying my head in the sand but I just can't bear it. It's all such a game, such big business. People lie and cheat and steal. My father was in Mississippi politics for a while and he understood that people buy votes. I'm cynical—that's the word—cynical about politics. So now I think, "Don't be rude to people in stores, don't litter, remember to send your grandmother flowers on her birthday, enjoy the trees, write what you write—that's all you can do—try to be kind from day to day." I can't go out there with a banner, it's not my personality.

INTERVIEWER: Would you discuss the difference between writing for the stage and screenwriting?

HENLEY: I love writing for the screen. I like to zip from one image to another and the fact that you can go on and off the stage, have tons of characters, lots of scenes. One problem is that the writer doesn't have shit to say. They can take what you've written and change it any way they want. And another problem: I haven't been able to get a movie made yet. Also in the movies you have no control over casting. With a stage play you have the freedom to do your play and see it like you want. In Hollywood, they can fire your director, fire you, not do the movie, take the idea, which might be one of your only ideas—I don't have that many ideas that I can be throwing them off and selling them to movies. I've also written for TV. You go in with a committee of people and each one gets one of their own ideas in. It's like nailing them all together and trying to patchwork the thing. And it comes out brown dishwater: nonspecific, bland. I mean, they *work* at getting things bland for TV. Now I'm spoiled. I tell my agent I've got money from *Crimes of the Heart* coming in from the national tour, and I don't want to write for TV. Lots of times there *are* some good working situations, but I love having the control to just go anywhere in my mind. It's too great a freedom to give up just for money.

TINA HOWE

*T*ina Howe was born and raised in *New York City. Her plays include* The Nest, Birth and After Birth, Museum, The Art of Dining, Painting Churches *and a number of one-acts she wrote as a high school drama teacher for her students in the sixties. Her published works include* Birth and After Birth *in* The New Women's Theatre *(Honor Moore, ed., Vintage, 1977) and* Three Plays by Tina Howe, *published by Avon Books in 1984. She is the recipient of a 1983 Obie Award for Distinguished Playwriting, the John Gassner Outer Critics Circle Award, a Rockefeller Fellowship and, most recently, an NEA grant for playwriting. She teaches playwriting at NYU. Ms. Howe is married to the novelist Norman Levy, with whom she has two children, Eben and Dara.*

INTERVIEWER: After the critics had castigated you for *The Nest* [Howe's first Off Broadway production, 1969], how did you find the courage to write as volatile a play as *Birth and After Birth* [1973]?

HOWE: There is something in my makeup, a perverse tic. When I'm attacked, it just emboldens me to be more outrageous. Of course, when you're twenty, it's easier to bounce back. As you get older, you need more stamina. I really understand how playwrights who've been at it a long time become dispirited and take to drink or bodily harm.

INTERVIEWER: So you have strong recuperative powers?

HOWE: Yes, I do. I think it's because I am so solitary. I live a very rich life in my imagination. I don't deal much with the outside world.

INTERVIEWER: In *Birth and After Birth*, you juxtaposed the rituals of primitive societies with those of the modern American family. What were the connections you saw between the cultures, and what did you hope to achieve or expose in the play?

HOWE: When you deal with childbirth and raising children, you're in a murky, primitive place. One of the reasons I wanted to write the play was to try and put that arena on the stage. We've seen family life portrayed theatrically a million times, but the child is almost always an adolescent. I wondered what would happen if I put a child on the stage who wasn't verbal yet, who still inhabited that mysterious world of pre-speech. And what would happen if I added a harassed mother and a father who is losing his job. How would they respond to this inarticulate id? Once I got into the area of childrearing, its horrors and its glories, a whole new primitive landscape opened up. Middle-class families tend to shut it out—but any woman who's had a baby knows that when you're on that delivery table, grunting and pushing and you feel this creature slither out of you like a huge wet pimento, something mysterious and ritualistic happens. I don't think you can write about birth without going back into that strange, misty harbor.

INTERVIEWER: You've said the play was derived from your experience of living in suburbia. . . .

HOWE: Yes, we were living in Columbia County [New York] at the time. I had just had my second child and was eager to get back to writing a few hours a day; so my friends would babysit. I was part of this circle of women whose situations were similar to mine because we all had small children—but they didn't share my need to try and make sense of it all. They were much more besieged. Young mothers inhabit rather wild territory. Their emotions range all over the place.

I think the best work comes from the imagination. The most exciting moments in the play are those I made up. It was tremendously difficult to write. It took three years. I kept fooling around with all these fancy metaphors. I was trying to deal with the media, and the way we use tape and film and camera to record family life. It was getting very high-flown and aesthetic. It took me a long time to finally distill everything. I was really experimenting with dramatic form.

INTERVIEWER: The play has a dreamlike quality. Has this quality been captured in production?

HOWE: It's never been produced. It's so incendiary I'm afraid critics would stone me to death. I've had a hard enough time with my elegant pieces, *Museum* [1976] and *The Art of Dining* [1979]. Even though *Birth and After Birth* precedes those plays, I've always felt the only way I would slip it through was by having a certain measure of credibility as a play-wright. It is not the kind of work you just casually put on. There was interest in the play after *Museum*, but by then I was on to different preoccupations. I was also afraid that with the whole Women's Movement exploding, everyone would come down on me—the men, the feminists, the nonfeminists—so I held off. Maybe when I finish my new play, I'll go back to it. It needs more work. The first act is pretty good, but the second has a lot of loose ends.

INTERVIEWER: So professional credibility is a major concern for you?

HOWE: Yes, after I first showed *Birth and After Birth* around, everybody was appalled by it. They threw it on the floor and shouted, "This is disgusting, unworkable!" Even the agent I'd had for two years said, "I can't represent you any more, Tina, it's just too exhausting!" I finally realized that if I wanted to have a life in the theater, I'd have to put different kinds of things on stage. So I deliberately set out to fashion something that was less threatening. I paid attention to the plays that were successful. They all tended to be escape plays, set in these fantastic settings. The curtain rises, and you're at the beach . . . or a changing room . . . or backstage . . . or in Hamlet's court.

INTERVIEWER: Have we inherited this escape mentality from television?

HOWE: It has to do with the fact that modern life has become so difficult. Audiences don't want to be hurt anymore. It's enough dealing with the daily bruises. They want to be transported when they're at the theater. So I tried to think of exotic settings—the last place on earth one would expect a play to be set—and I came up with a museum. Nothing happens in a museum. It's a temple of silence. When you are most moved by a painting, you just stand there and look at it. My challenge was to somehow animate this hallowed environment. It was a very deliberate choice. *Museum* led directly to *The Art of Dining*, which has the same kind of large landscape, but it goes deeper. I went further into the pain of the characters. It was another deliberate move, which is surprising for me because I am not naturally intelligent. I'm much more instinctive. I suppose, that's the one time I really surpassed myself—sitting down and actually making that conscious choice. I'm not reflective, I don't figure things out. I have a very low IQ. It's so low that when it was announced in high school, everyone came rushing up to me with, "Do you realize just *how* low your IQ *is*?" So that moment of figuring out a design beforehand was a kind of breakthrough. I had to do something drastic in order to survive. It was that simple.

INTERVIEWER: *MS.* magazine describes you as a *highly* intelligent playwright.

HOWE: When they gave me the Obie they said I was intelligent, too. I think it's because I love words and like to swim around in them. But that's not the same as being intelligent. That's being flashy. I'm not very logical. I can't do algebra or read contracts. I never did well in school. I didn't realize until college that there was any correlation between what was done in class and what was assigned as homework. I was the class clown. For years and years, the only way I could have an identity was by making people laugh. I was always being thrown out of the classroom. I spent most of my time in the principal's office being told what a low IQ I had. My family was highly intelligent, so I was the black sheep. All the Howe men went to Harvard. So I took the territory that was left— being ridiculous.

INTERVIEWER: Would you discuss the positive and negative aspects of having a famous father [Quincy Howe, a world-renowned television and radio newscaster]?

HOWE: Well, the positive aspect of growing up with someone who is not only famous, but intelligent, is that you have a model. My father was always talking about work. He felt it was through work that you find yourself and make a contribution. "You have to use yourself," was his constant refrain. His father was a man of letters, a poet and biographer who published over fifty books, won a Pulitzer, and lived until he was ninety-six. My father's brother and sister were also big achievers. At Thanksgiving the conversation was invariably, "What have you done? What are you publishing? What are you planning next?" The highest value was placed on achievement, not money.

What was difficult for me was that I grew up in a very East Side, old-world atmosphere. I went to elitist private girls' schools, but had a father who had been a radical in his youth and was the only Democrat among the parents of my classmates. My sympathies were liberal and avant-garde, but I had to maneuver in a narrow, suffocating social world. I was hopeless at it.

I suppose the negative aspect of coming from a well-known family is that you can never live up to the expectations. My biggest neurosis is insecurity; I've never felt successful. I've never felt I've "arrived" in any way. It's always uphill. I have periods when I feel so inferior and homely I can't even go out. I just stay home and hide under the furniture. A lot of that comes from having grown up in a rather rarified household with all these expectations whirring around. I spend much too much time feeling sorry for myself. It's much better to get on with the work. But I think most artists feel insecure. It's just a bit extreme in my case. The reason to pick up the pen or the paint brush is to fight back.

INTERVIEWER: What gives you the greatest pleasure as a playwright?

HOWE: My greatest joys come from those moments when I solve a problem at the typewriter—unravel the darkness and find the image. You get so involved in this imaginary world, groping for the right phrase and gesture, that finally when it comes, it's like the heavens parting. Public acclaim is the gift that comes afterwards. It's finding the missing link that really sends you into the stratosphere. But then the awful thing is the moment you've solved one problem, you stumble headlong into the next one. So you go right back to feeling miserable and bereft and lost. When you finally finish the first draft, you think, "This is it," then God help you, you read it, and you're miles off. So, the thrill of success is very momentary. The rewards are so elusive in the theater, that unless you really take pleasure in the writing, you have to be mentally deranged to be a playwright.

INTERVIEWER: In *Birth and After Birth* you were saying that the barren woman is a pariah in our society. Do you think things have changed since you wrote the play in 1972–73?

HOWE: I had my children late. We were childless for five years. My fertile German sister-in-law used to harangue me, "You're not a woman, Tina, until you have children!" This was a refrain that had been ringing in my ears ever since I got married. What I was trying to show in the play is that you lose either way, in a sense. If you have children, you're certainly homebound at the beginning. But if you don't have children, there is always this suspicion that you're missing something important. I really didn't take sides in the play. I was trying to show how threatening women on either side of the fence can be to each other. I do think times have changed. It's terrific now, because women can wait for children until they're ready. They can have careers until they're thirty, taste the full range of their independence and then have their babies. They can have it both ways.

INTERVIEWER: Why do you think some feminists reacted negatively to *Birth and After Birth?*

HOWE: Well, when I wrote it in the early seventies it was the feminists who hated it the most. Probably because the setting was so blatantly domestic. When the Women's Movement was starting, I think women really wanted to get out of the home. They wanted to find their roles outside the house, and then perhaps return . . . or perhaps not. This was a little too close for comfort, I guess.

INTERVIEWER: Would you discuss the father-son relationship in *Birth and After Birth?*

HOWE: I felt tremendous sympathy for the father, because when a woman has a baby, she is totally wrapped up in it, often to the exclusion of her husband. I've always preferred men to women because my father was very gentle and mild. The men in my family tend to be that way, while the women are much larger and more flamboyant . . . a little scary at times. So I felt a real sympathy for my character Bill. He's left out. All he wants is somebody to love. There's a constant vying for position in the play. At one moment, the mother and the child are allied and the father is left out, then the father and child are allied and the mother is left out, and so on.

INTERVIEWER: Would you describe the play as impressionistic?

HOWE: I would describe it as absurdist. It's extreme. I take a familiar reality and lift it about six feet off the ground. God help me if I ever write a realistic play. Oh please, don't call *Painting Churches* [1983] realistic.

INTERVIEWER: It's certainly more realistic than *Birth and After Birth*.

HOWE: No, it's quite off-center. One of the reasons I chose The Second Stage City is that they do this kind of work so well. They are one of the few theaters in New York that really lift you out of your seat. They take risks; they don't present the same old formula stuff. The acting is always impeccable, the design is right-on, they are masters at presenting heightened reality. And of course, Carole Rothman [co-artistic director, The Second Stage] is a very gifted director. She is extremely tolerant. She accepts a work on its own terms. She completely enters its spirit, which is rare.

INTERVIEWER: Do you feel more comfortable with a woman director?

HOWE: I keep trying to figure out why I like working with Carole so much. Is it because she's a woman, or because she's Carole? I think it's a combination of the two. What is most striking about her is the way she works. She's direct. There are no power plays, no circuitous maneuvering. She's totally honest and wants what's best for the play. Once you've sorted out all the values, she's committed to illuminating them. Her style of working is very clear, and that is where I've usually gotten into trouble with directors. To have a woman who's not only sensitive to my point of view but who is also completely workmanlike is astonishing. I've gone through many more scenes of hysterics with male directors than with women directors. My feminist friends had been asking for years, "When are you going to work with a woman?" But having had this large, often cruel mother, and having gone to all-girl schools as a child, I thought, "Oh, spare me. I don't want some menacing woman with red talons and streaming hair coming in to humiliate me. Give me a soft, sensitive man." I was in a time warp. Now suddenly, I find all of these bright, creative women all over the place, and it's marvelous.

INTERVIEWER: Do you rewrite during rehearsals?

HOWE: I try not to. I try to have the script pretty tight. Some writers need the actors to liberate the script. But I am such an internal writer I get thrown. If the actors start taking the script apart, I can't put it back together again.

INTERVIEWER: Have you ever written prose?

HOWE: Oh, a hundred years ago. That was what I always wanted to do—write a novel—and for a few years I tried desperately, but I was too self-conscious about the language: "He flew into the room; he danced into the room; he tiptoed into the room; he spun into the room . . ." I could never get on to what was happening. My prose was so self-conscious and syrupy, it was embarrassing. There is something thrilling about a novel. You don't need people to interpret it. You don't need lights and scenery and costumes and wigs. I have a tremendous respect for novelists. I mean, it's a ludicrous argument, but I would much rather be Virginia Woolf than Lillian Hellman. What I do isn't really writing, it's charting emotions, gestures and images. Dramatic imagination takes precedence over gorgeous language. Except for Shakespeare, of course. He is that sole dazzling exception.

INTERVIEWER: How long does it take you to write a play?

HOWE: It depends. *Museum* took six months; *Birth and After Birth*, three years; *The Art of Dining*, a year and a half; and *Painting Churches*, four years.

INTERVIEWER: Did you consider the production values when you wrote *Museum*? It has a large cast, and an elaborate set.

HOWE: No. I probably should have, but I just plunged in with an idea and let the producer worry about how to pull it off. My ultimate fantasy for *Museum* has been to have it actually staged in a museum. You could commission the artists, get [Robert] Rauschenberg to lend five of his white paintings, and someone like George Segal to do the soft sculptures, and then use their real names. In the daytime, the set could be a real art exhibit, and at night, bleachers could be brought in—there'd be this wonderful confusion of people saying, "Have you gone to the museum to see *Museum*?" Joe Papp was intrigued with the idea, but found out that the price of insuring important art works was prohibitive. Still, it's an old dream of mine, because I've always conceived of the play as a work of art.

INTERVIEWER: Is there a connection between the speech about the artist gnawing on bones for raw material and the image of the culture vultures tearing at the carcass of the exhibit?

HOWE: No, a connection never occurred to me. The speech about gnawing on the bones is really about the artist's descent into his work. Museums are such temples of beauty I felt it was important to show the anguish an artist goes through in order to create. It is one of the few private moments in the play. It was a note I wanted to sound. But basically, *Museum* is a comedy of manners.

INTERVIEWER: Will you discuss that scene during which the museum-goers ravage the art works?

HOWE: It's a scene about people's desire to possess what's beautiful and immortal. If you've ever been to the Met to see a popular show—it's terrifying—you take your life in your hands what with the thundering hordes. These aren't wicked people; they want to bathe in beauty for a while. The viewers in my play get a bit carried away. What I was trying to show was just how passionate people can become. It is a play, remember, a confection, not real life. I have an obsession with art. It runs through all of my plays. I loved those characters in *Museum* because they were all aspects of myself. It was great fun to write. *Museum* is architecturally the most complex of my plays. I don't know how I put it together.

INTERVIEWER: Were there difficulties in rehearsal?

HOWE: Yes, but once the cast got the rhythms, they had a ball. The actors kept saying, "I've never had so much fun." It was a fantasy come to life.

INTERVIEWER: Were you upset that the critics called it a "non-play?"

HOWE: Yes, I was very upset. It has a definite beginning, middle and end. It's just not a *traditional* play. The design was always clear to me.

INTERVIEWER: They were disturbed because you did not present a central protagonist in *Museum*.

HOWE: In a certain way, *Museum* is a play *about* criticism. Everybody entering the museum had a very strong point of view. I was making fun of that. I think it made the critics feel very self-conscious. But you can't second-guess them. If you try to, you're doomed. Which doesn't mean that they can't hurt you, break your heart, or even kill you. The most important thing is not to think about them while you are working. That is one of the reasons I am a recluse.

INTERVIEWER: Is *Art* the protagonist in *Museum*?

HOWE: I don't think about plays that way. Each play has its own dynamic, its own energy which propels it forward. *Museum* is hinged on rising menace. That note is sounded from the very beginning with the announcement that there has been a violent attack on a painting in Europe. Next come these small encroachments, steady little acts of violence that are clues. I knew at the end there would be a massive act of destruction, so I consciously set it up.

INTERVIEWER: Did you feel the same rapport with the material and environment in *The Art of Dining*?

HOWE: Not at all. The world of haute cuisine is intimidating to me. I'm a terrible cook, and I've never liked food. I find eating terrifying, particularly in public. *The Art of Dining* was a real leap of the imagination. I turned my own fear and distaste for food into the opposite. The thing that's crucial is having very strong feelings about whatever you write. They don't necessarily have to be positive, that's all.

INTERVIEWER: What is your fascination for anorexic characters? Elizabeth in *The Art of Dining*, Mags in *Painting Churches* . . .

HOWE: For every artist there is always a strong sensual element in the work. For some it's sex, for others it's food, and for some it is a love of violence or danger. This goes for all artists, from the most abstract painters, to musicians. I think you have to go back to your own traumas. I always seem to end up with food. The trials of eating and having to have good manners at the same time. Obviously it's something very private with me. I was never anorexic. It was never that severe. But it *is* a neurosis of mine. I think everyone has neuroses. One of the joys of being an artist is finding the craft to release them.

INTERVIEWER: You seem to associate the anorexia with the woman artist. Elizabeth is a writer, Mags is a painter.

HOWE: They're not anorexic. They're just neurotic. It's true they're both women. But then I'm a woman. It's the gender I know best.

INTERVIEWER: Cal, Ellen's husband in *The Art of Dining*, is constantly stealing her ingredients. Would you comment on your intention?

HOWE: He's jealous of her success and abilities. I think he wants to be a part of her. It's not so much sexual hunger, as the hunger of someone who feels ignored. My weakness has always been writing strong men. With Cal, I was finally able to trust myself.

INTERVIEWER: Both Mags in *Painting Churches* and Ellen in *The Art of Dining* have a deep need for approval of their creations. Is this a particular vulnerability of the female artist?

HOWE: Anybody who puts their work on the line needs a nod every now and then. I write about women because that's what I know best. I don't see my heroines as a vehicle for any particular point of view. I'm not making a political choice.

INTERVIEWER: Do you have a favorite of your plays?

HOWE: For a long time *Art of Dining* was my favorite. I like its denseness. *Painting Churches* is the most touching, I suppose. It was certainly the most painful to write. It took a lot out of me.

INTERVIEWER: Because it was dealing with parental issues?

HOWE: Yes, I was dealing with relationships that were close to home. But it is not autobiographical. If there's anything I've discovered, it's that being inventive is much more daring than exposing the truth. When you invent, you are left naked. *Painting Churches* is probably my deepest play and I feel very close to it. But I still like the big messy ones. I love silliness and slapstick and people falling down.

INTERVIEWER: Not a single review mentioned that the woman chef in *The Art of Dining* was a metaphor for the female artist. Playwright Honor Moore has stated that the critics, who are mostly male, have difficulty identifying with a central female character's experience as a metaphor for their own lives.

HOWE: Honor and I have these discussions all the time. I hate to think that it's men against women. I keep trying to avoid the issue because I find it so frightening. Most of the critics *are* men. What can I do? I write what I perceive.

I knew that *Painting Churches* was my last chance after the reviews of *The Art of Dining*. I was very aware of "Two strikes and you're out." The Elizabeth character led me directly to Mags and her family [*Painting Churches*], but I think there was some other, very primitive survival instinct at work that said, "You better put a play in a conventional setting. You've got to stop all this fancy horsing around and settle down." I'm sure that conservatism was at work in the back of my mind, because your spirit does get eroded, and you *do* despair. I have this *will*, you see. . . . More than anything I want to make people laugh. It's so simple. I don't have any great message, or terribly profound contribution to make. Maybe it's having been raised on Marx Brothers movies—howling in the dark with my rather staid parents—it was such an incredible release. So unexpected and hilarious.

INTERVIEWER: Were you surprised by the warm reception that *Painting Churches* received in New York?

HOWE: Yes. Genuinely. What moves people is the sheer fantasy of it. In real life, we all know perfectly well there's rarely that moment when our parents finally say, "You are a wonderful artist, and I admire your work." What moves the audience is that split second when the three of them are finally reconciled. It lasts for one heartbeat, and then is gone. We all know it's a purely theatrical moment, which is why it's so precious. The play particularly seems to affect people who have recently lost their parents.

INTERVIEWER: Are your parents still alive?

HOWE: No. I couldn't possibly have written it had they been alive; but I wonder if they were, how they would have felt about it. I like to think they would have been pleased. My father would have said, "Awfully clever, Teen . . ." I think my mother would have really been shaken.

INTERVIEWER: Do you feel that your less conventional work would be more appreciated in Europe?

HOWE: I've always felt that my work is more European in style. The writers I identify with are Ionesco, Beckett, Genet and the true-blue absurdists before them, Pirandello, Cocteau and Giraudoux. They are my heroes.

INTERVIEWER: What are your work habits?

HOWE: I write in the dining room, at my desk. My schedule is one that has developed over the years. I sit down the minute the children leave for school. The only way I can get work done is every day from nine A.M. till one-thirty, and often seven days a week. I've got to have the clatter of my typewriter keys! I do battle when I write. Every six months I have to have the entire machine overhauled. I rend it into jewelry. For years I used my father's pre-World War II Royal. He wrote eight very large books on it, and I have a tremendous attachment to it. I wrote all six drafts of *Painting Churches* on it, even though the ribbon spools wouldn't feed properly. Now I use a Hermes I bought for my husband in 1965. I type to Glenn Gould's Bach recordings. And I drink a lot of soda. The heavy sugar intake coupled with Gould's ecstatic playing really gets me going.

INTERVIEWER: Many of the playwrights we've interviewed have said that their work has a musical architecture. . . .

HOWE: Theme and variation is the technique I use most often. I studied piano for seven years but wasn't very good. I go to concerts more than I go to theater. My first love has always been music.

INTERVIEWER: Did you ever study painting?

HOWE: No, my mother was a painter, though. She was a watercolorist and my son is a wonderful artist. I go to art shows all the time. The visual arts are so much more experimental and exciting than theater. I've always been drawn to the experimental. I wish I had the courage to be more avant-garde. I think I'm getting a little too tidy. But my heart is always with the anarchists.

INTERVIEWER: How many plays had you written by the time your children were born?

HOWE: None. I couldn't afford to write. I put my husband through college and graduate school. It wasn't until he began teaching that we could afford for me to stop working. I did write a one-act while I was at Sarah Lawrence. I was in a short story class. It was embarrassing, I was so bad. I had to try to save face somehow. So I wrote this preposterous little one-act play about the end of the world. My friend [actress] Jane Alexander, loved it and said, "Let's put it on." Jane directed it; then the leading lady got sick, so she took over the part. It was a great success. Everybody began screaming AUTHOR! AUTHOR! I found myself tearing up to the stage and throwing kisses to everybody—I behaved outrageously! Something happened in that moment of acclaim. I graduated in the spring, and my father offered me a choice between a year of graduate school or a trip to Europe. I immediately got on an ocean liner to Paris. Jane was going to Edinburgh, and we crossed the Atlantic together. In Paris, I really began writing. I suddenly began taking myself very seriously. I fell in with a group of expatriate American and English writers. We were all self-conscious, but there were enough real writers around to give us credibility. I had a little room over the Seine. I was euphoric. I never ate or slept. I just wrote around the clock. It was during that year in Europe that the infatuation began.

My understanding of craft developed when I started teaching high school. I managed to talk the principals of both schools I taught at to let me run the Drama Department, on the condition that only my plays be done. I was given the incredible luxury of suddenly having my own company. High school kids will try anything. I began writing plays for my students. If you can hold an audience of a thousand teenagers who couldn't care less, that is really a trial by fire. I learned the craft in those years of writing plays for students. I began to see what worked on stage. It is vital to have that connection to real theater, whether it's at a public high school, Circle Repertory or the Joint Stock Company. It's almost impossible to find your voice without a willing company of actors.

INTERVIEWER: Do you consider yourself a philosophical rather than a political playwright?

HOWE: Neither. My preoccupations are mainly artistic. I'm fascinated by culture, and the way people entertain themselves. My concerns are much more aesthetic than they are social or political. I'm certainly against nuclear war and will continue to march for world peace, but that's hardly a measure of political sophistication these days.

INTERVIEWER: Do you have any opinions on the relationship between the arts community and the present Reagan administration?

HOWE: I don't think there *is* a relationship right now. Reagan has turned his back on the artistic community. We're all on our own. What's striking to me is how very apolitical we've become. People are so disheartened, the malaise is so extreme . . . Artists are becoming introverted again and less socially-minded.

INTERVIEWER: Is this withdrawal from politics evident in the work of your playwriting students at New York University?

HOWE: Yes, they're very frightened of the world at large. They don't have many defenses, and who can blame them? Their work tends to be confessional, but wonderful in its innovation, which is of prime importance to me. I am more concerned with their ability to flex in the form than I am with their having a heightened social awareness. And it has been said that in times of political despair artists move inward and very exciting work is done as a result.

INTERVIEWER: Many playwrights have suffered political despair and still managed to look outward. Brecht and Trevor Griffith and . . .

HOWE: It *would* be exhilarating if an American playwright with a real political conscience were to take on the big picture. I would cheer for that. But there's also the new cry that life is so unjust and out of sorts now that art can't possibly imitate it. I hear this from my students who say, "How can we possibly write plays that can compete with the horrors around us?" I don't know how to answer them. I'm not a social historian, but it seems to me that in times of political chaos, many artists go inward because the outer landscape is so appalling.

INTERVIEWER: You once said, "If a woman really explored the areas that make her unique as a woman, was radical in her femininity, the commercial theater would be terrified. I keep a distance from my more radical female feelings, partly from my fear of being stoned to death, and partly because I'm not so sure I can handle them. Though I think it's high time someone did." Have your feelings changed?

HOWE: No, I still feel much the same way, but I'm trying to face my own femininity. I do think it's tremendously dangerous, but I'm trying anyway.

INTERVIEWER: When you say it's high time someone did explore this territory, we wondered if there is anyone who you feel is capable?

HOWE: Of the women writing now, I think Caryl Churchill comes the closest to the kind of theatrical originality I love.

INTERVIEWER: And you feel you are pushing in a similar direction?

HOWE: Now I am. The time has come to be strapped to the stake and let them pour the kerosene on . . . (laughing). I believe if we put all our darkness on stage we'd blow everyone away. I've always thought women were much more dangerous than men. Women are really awesome. Maybe that comes from having had a mother who was a good foot taller than my father—two feet taller with her hat on! Also, when you look at dramatic literature, who stands out? Clytemnestra, Medea, Lady Macbeth, Hedda Gabler, Blanche Dubois . . . you can go on and on. I think that's partly why I write female characters. They are capable of tremendous passion.

Women playwrights are finally coming out of the woodwork, and it's about time. Look, I mean . . . look at the contributions our sex has made to the novel and poetry! We're still in our infancy as playwrights. We've just started to pick up the bright tools of the trade. But wait until we master them. . . . Wait until we yoke our delicate touch and way with words with the darker impulses of theater. All I can say is when that moment comes . . . LOOK OUT BELOW!

CORINNE JACKER

Corinne Jacker lives in New York City and has been writing plays and nonfiction for over twenty-five years. Her best-known plays include Bits and Pieces, Harry Outside, Terminal, My Life, Later, After the Season and Domestic Issues. Her plays have been published by Samuel French and included in theater anthologies. Several of her theater works have been adapted for radio. Ms. Jacker's television work includes several episodes for various miniseries, including The Best of Families (PBS) and Loose Change (NBC); Virginia Woolf: The Moment Whole (Cine Golden Eagle award) and a segment of The Adams Chronicles for National Educational Television; The Lie, an American adaptation of an Ingmar Bergman drama for CBS; The Jilting of Granny Weatherall, an adaptation of the Katherine Anne Porter short story for the Public Broadcasting System and Overdrawn at the Memory Bank for American Playhouse, PBS. Ms. Jacker was head writer for NBC's Another World 1981–82, and received an Emmy Citation for her work as story editor on the CBS miniseries, Benjamin Franklin. Ms. Jacker received a Rockefeller Grant for playwriting in 1979. She is a member of the New York Writers' Bloc and is presently working on a science fiction teleplay.

INTERVIEWER: Of your contemporaries, whom do you most admire?

JACKER: I've got favorites but I won't list them. It seems to me that every time we make a list of bests we give tacit approval to the idea that writing's some sort of horse race and someone's going to come in first. But it's really all about competing with ourselves, isn't it? If I woke up and had to face the fact that I'm not as good as William Shakespeare, why would I go on writing? What keeps me moving on is finding that I did a little better on plot, or wrote a useful moment of conflict, or a line that's got a good sound to it. It's like swimming—today you swim ten lengths of the pool, tomorrow you do eleven, next week you improve your stroke or your breath.

Chekhov influenced me more than any other writer, I think. I adapted *The Sea Gull* when I was eleven, and I've tried to make my plays spare, the way he does.

I was lucky enough to go to public school, so I was never subjected to a real "education." I got my library card at our branch library, and I started to read; I started with fiction, the A's, then the B's, then the C's. So I read all the Dostoyevski in the library, and then I read all the Lloyd C. Douglas. I loved both writers.

INTERVIEWER: Is there a female aesthetic?

JACKER: It's true that women tend to think of domestic, encapsulated incidents as crucial. We look at the microcosm rather than the macrocosm. Emily Dickinson writes, "A fly buzzed when I died." Women do seem to understand global significances by looking at smaller events. And I think we are more interested in interior life than exterior life—this makes our sense of language, of time, of event, different. All of which means an audience has to learn how to hear us. Perhaps women find their metaphors in domestic experience because we are still new to the world of action. And plays are about people who act. So we often have to use men as our central characters. *My Life* is about a well-known, nuclear-particle physicist, and if I had used a woman, I would have had to deal with the fact that this was unusual and presented unusual problems. The same problem arose with *Harry Outside*. Where was I to find a female architect who would have begun working in the nineteen-thirties who was of [Piero] Soleri's or [Frank Lloyd] Wright's stature?

INTERVIEWER: You've said that although you don't believe in autobiographical plays, *My Life* is probably the most autobiographical play you've written, that you and the main character, Eddie, were ". . . grappling with the same problem."

JACKER: I gave Eddie my problems—but he's a male particle physicist; he's a white Anglo-Saxon Protestant; his family is very different from mine; and what happened to him did not, in a literal sense, ever happen to me. But we both had to make similar decisions—whether to hide in a very comfortable set of past memories or put them aside and risk a great deal on the present.

INTERVIEWER: Writer Tillie Olsen feels that women should be cautious of casting female profundities and revelations into the mouths of male characters. Any comment?

JACKER: Eddie's revelations aren't female. As I said before, I didn't want to set up a "peculiar" circumstance by using a woman physicist—I didn't want to make being a woman in a male-dominated field a part of Eddie's character. It would have muddied the issue of Eddie's craziness. It would have confused the audience.

INTERVIEWER: Do you feel limited by the level of the audience's perceptions?

JACKER: I'm not trying to fulfill the audience's expectations. In fact, I'd rather surprise them. But I don't want to raise issues and then not deal with them. If it seems to me that if a character is a man, I don't *want* to write him as a woman—why should I? Eddie isn't literally me, he doesn't have anything like my experience. I think if it would have been important to make him a woman, I'd have written him as a woman. We do have a choice. And we don't put masks on our characters and dress them up in drag if we've got any respect for our work. You see, a writer's got a predicament: We can only write what we are able to imagine, to hypothecate out of what we've experienced. But what I've learned after a lot of struggle is that men are human, too. I did a series about people who lived in New York at the end of the nineteenth century. I wasn't there. I have no firsthand knowledge of what life was like then. But I can extrapolate from my experience—love is love; greed is greed; and so on. So, create as authentic an environment as you can, and put the character in it. When I wrote *Harry Outside*, people frequently asked me whether I'd based Harry on Piero Soleri or Mies Van der Rohe. Harry's based on my father, who was a plumbing contractor. But he's an architect, a credible one. Where's the autobiography, where's the fiction, and what difference does it make if the event in the play is solidly there? For quite some time, I was afraid to write men and it took me a long time to get over that fear. I felt like I was trying to enter an "alien" consciousness. How could I pretend to know how a man thinks and feels? In the opening monologue in *My Life*, Eddie talks about some of what it's like to have an erection. For a long time, I felt I couldn't write that; then I realized that if I used honest imagination, I could do it. If you are honest to the circumstances, the environment and the character, then you can write about how that particular human in that particular environment is going to respond. It was when I learned that men are as human as women that I was able to write men.

INTERVIEWER: William Gibson once said that he wrote female characters with the female side of himself.

JACKER: Sure. And to write men, I use the male side of me. That's frightening. Can we admit to ourselves that we *are able to imagine* what it's like to be a man? It's a kind of schizophrenia. When we're writing we have to deal with all these characters in our heads who talk to one another and take over the action without even consulting us. We are possessed by our characters. And that's terrifying enough. But when it comes to writing men, there's another, even more terrifying surrender —to my other self. Can I keep my femaleness if I recognize my "maleness"? This confuses people, too. Because I wrote five science books, how can I enjoy knitting so much? Because I'm so crazy about computers—my first book was about computers—how can I like cooking so much? As if there is a contradiction between "female" pursuits and intellectuality.

INTERVIEWER: What inspired the scene in *My Life,* in which your characters Laura and Margaret mirror each other?

JACKER: An epiphany in my own life. Probably one of the most terrifying moments I've lived through. For a variety of reasons, my life with my mother was very difficult. By the time I was out of my teens I hated her. She represented everything I disliked about women. And one night, when I was twenty or so, I was in my room, dressing. I was in front of my dresser mirror, putting on a necklace—I turned my head away from the mirror as I was fastening the necklace and when I turned around, I caught a glimpse of myself in the mirror, and I had my mother's face on—the mouth, the look in the eyes—I couldn't deny it. Of course, she was gone in a moment, but I was shocked.

INTERVIEWER: You have often been criticized for leaving things open at the end of your plays. Pinter and Shepard get away with leaving the audience to figure things out for themselves, why not Corinne Jacker?

JACKER: People assume that the theater will supply a resolution and an answer. If there is a moral statement to be made, people want *you* to make it; they don't want to make it themselves. However, I think there is a large difference between asking an audience to "figure it out," and leaving a play open ended. Sometimes, I want to write a play that has no closure, that just stops. And I think that's my own individual concern, not just because I am a woman, but because of the relationship I want to establish between the play and the audience. They've begun a conversation that may go on for a while longer if the lights in the auditorium come up and the play hasn't totally terminated. The plays end because there doesn't seem anything more to say. There may not be a complete resolution, but the dramatic action is over.

INTERVIEWER: Do you have any idea as to why you were so harshly criticized for your play *Domestic Issues* [1981]? Was it the subject matter, the fact that you were dealing with left-wing politics?

JACKER: No, not that, but *where* the politics were played out. It was a play about terrorists, but it didn't happen on the barricades; it happened in a very respectable suburban Chicago kitchen. There was a life or death battle that was being fought between two brothers, two pairs of husbands and wives. The play's called *Domestic Issues* because I think our world of large, political actions actually revolves around what happens in domestic situations.

INTERVIEWER: Politics for you are inextricably connected to the personal?

JACKER: Yes, of course. And the great male writers have realized that women have this view of the world. *Antigone* is more concerned with family honor than political law. The action of *King Lear* is precipitated because a woman was perceptive enough or stupid enough to use the need for salt as a metaphor for the love she has for her father. That's a woman's sensibility, and a perfect example of an entire kingdom going awry because she refuses to rephrase her statement in a more traditional way.

INTERVIEWER: Do you mind being called a "woman writer?"

JACKER: Yes, sometimes. I'd like to be taken seriously as a playwright, and I think when the word's modified by "woman" the evaluation drops a couple of notches. On the other hand, I like being a woman; I write from my female experience. And I certainly don't want to deny what feminism has given me. The women who now refuse to join any feminist organization are acting out of fear, I think; they don't want the bull-dyke, aggressive feminist-separatist label. They don't want to risk any possible taint of lesbianism or antimaleness. I can't accept separatism. I have to recognize that men are a part of my life. I can't, don't want to, exclude them completely. I write about women and women and men and men and women and men and the conflicts that arise between them.

INTERVIEWER: It seems that some women who've reaped the benefits from feminist struggles have become what playwright Caryl Churchill describes as "top girls."

JACKER: It's easy to be committed to feminism when you've only got a quarter in your sock; but when you've got a hundred dollars, you begin to think about what you've got to lose. So, the women who are beginning to find economic success because of the political struggles of the early feminists are now discovering that a public commitment to feminism can jeopardize that money. They don't want to make waves.

INTERVIEWER: Should women try to formalize their feelings about how womanhood affects their work?

JACKER: Not if it is going to be a complaint, an accusation that critics and producers don't take us seriously enough. But somewhere there may be a woman who can begin the formidable task of developing an aesthetic. Is there some inherently different form our plays take because they are written by women, and is the audience able to hear us? If we could get women together to talk about that, we'd be breaking new territory. Because I think the truth is that there may be a women's *Weltanschauung* that isn't being perceived. Yet of all the women's organizations that have seminars and panels about how to get women's plays produced, I haven't yet found a conference that tried to grapple with whether or not women have identifiably different senses of time, event, objectivity, character, action, and so on.

INTERVIEWER: You often write about slow evolution. Does this relate to your concerns about the audience being able to "hear" women's writing?

JACKER: Time is all I know how to trust. The special theory of relativity was written in 1905. Nonscientists have accepted it now. But this is eighty years later; relativity theory has to be tempered with quantum mechanics, and even Einstein couldn't accept that. We have to allow at least fifty years for an original idea to make its impact. That's true in the sciences and it's true in the theater. We still can't do Chekhov successfully most of the time. We don't know how to listen to him, and we don't know how to show what he's saying to the audience. Eighty years and we still can't hear this great artist. If we want immediate response, I think we give up quality for impact.

INTERVIEWER: How did the issue of giving up quality for impact affect your writing for *Another World*?

JACKER: That's what I wanted to find out. So we experimented with how seriously a soap opera could take itself. We wrote the first labor strike on daytime television. One of our central characters was a black woman who was losing her identity because she was living and working in an all-white world. But I didn't think of the soap opera in the same way I think of a play, or a nighttime TV film. Serials aren't dramas. They don't have endings; they aren't supposed to. There's no resolution; before one plot moment ends, three others are beginning. That was very unsatisfying to me as a writer. But we had individual scenes that were rich and moving.

INTERVIEWER: You said that your character, a black woman working in the white world, was losing her identity. Do women writers entering a male-dominated profession face similar dangers?

JACKER: Yes. The solution is to be as honest as we can. We are all in danger of losing our identities. I'm trying to locate solutions to my own problems, and the more I feel unique, the harder it is for me to solve my problems. Men and women have to deal with "selling out"— how far do we go before we lose our integrity? That's an economic issue; but for women, it goes beyond economics; it becomes a question of how much you are willing to give up in order to be considered a "serious" person. Don't you often hear women complain that they aren't taken seriously? When my first play, *Pale Horse, Pale Rider* [1958] (it was an adaptation of the Katherine Anne Porter story), was reviewed, one of the critics said Porter and I wrote in eyeshadow. It was such a damnation of the fact that we were both women. I couldn't deal with it. I stopped writing plays for ten years. I wrote science books instead.

INTERVIEWER: You said in an interview with Lloyd Richards [artistic director, Yale Repertory Theater, Dean of the Yale Drama School] that to think of those ten years of prolonged grief broke your heart.

JACKER: That sense of failure was terrible. I was a fool to believe what I read, and not what I wrote. Why was Walter Kerr more important than Tennessee Williams or William Saroyan, who both saw and were appreciative of the play? You see, I'd let the marketplace run my life. I felt that I'd failed not only the theater, but Porter as well. If I'd stayed away from the reviews, it might not have taken me ten years to get back to work.

INTERVIEWER: So it is dangerous to read one's own reviews?

JACKER: I don't think there's anything more deadly. It's like asking for an injection of cancer virus. A good review will never be good enough, and a bad review can be fatal.

INTERVIEWER: Were the ten years of writing science books useful?

JACKER: Yes. My writing became much less disguised, less obscure. I had to make myself clear to the reader. I learned a lot about craft because my emotional investment wasn't as great. I think I was using difficult metaphors, a kind of intellectuality as a way to hide from things I couldn't or wouldn't say.

INTERVIEWER: Do you have a sense of when you are writing something "taboo"?

JACKER: I used to think so. But that came out of a smug security, a sense of believing that I could predict an audience's sensitivities. But *Domestic Issues* managed to offend a lot of people to my amazement, and it made me look back at my other plays and face the fact that I really never paid much attention to the issue.

INTERVIEWER: You once said the metaphor of a white, empty space was for you a means of discovering form.

JACKER: If we think of the stage in Peter Brook's term, as an *empty space*, we can discover what seems to me to be the central difference between writing a stage play and other kinds of writing. When we read a poem or a novel or a book about traveling down the Nile, we imagine the space the book's events happen in, and we seem to exist in two different time frames: our real time—the time it takes to read the book —and the "real time" in which the events we are reading about happen. It may take half an hour to read about something that took place over a period of twenty years, or we may read *Ulysses*—the whole book happens over the course of a day—over the course of a week. But a play happens in real space, and every scene happens in real time. The play is, in the most abstract terms, a series of vectors that travel through the empty space. For me, as more and more vectors leave their trails, like colored tracer patterns, I can begin to understand what I am doing.

INTERVIEWER: Is there a central theme which runs through all your work?

JACKER: If I knew what the general theme of my work was, I could stop writing. But, after one has finished a certain number of plays, it's possible to locate images, important actions, that sort of thing. A friend of mine once threatened to write a thesis, "Eating and Drinking in the Plays of Corinne Jacker." There are almost always several deliberately "bad" jokes in the plays. And, especially in the early plays, there was always a character who needed to be a member of the club. I'm a woman, and as soon as we leave our domestic environments, we have a residual sense of not belonging. Women playwrights certainly don't belong; we are excluded from the "old boys' club" in the same way as many women scientists. I remember reading an article by a woman physicist at MIT called "What's a Little Girl Like You Doing Trying to Teach These Great Big Men?" And that, for me, is reinforced by other things that have made me feel "outside": being a Jew, certainly; and the fact that when I was twenty-five, I was ill and spent more than a year in bed.

INTERVIEWER: Would you describe your writing process? Your plays have very complex and innovative structures. Do you write scene by scene?

JACKER: I rewrite. A lot. *Bits and Pieces* [1974] went through fourteen full drafts. The first six were just efforts to find the right beginning. Then the rest was just shaping the wholeness of the play. I can't fix a little piece, I can't pull one thread out, I've always got to start on page one, with the first line, and fix till the end. I don't even know the beginning for a while. The first thing I knew about *Harry Outside* [1975] was that something blew up; then I found out it happened outside; then a couple of lines appeared. So, to solve the mystery, I wrote the play.

INTERVIEWER: Is there a musical structure to your work?

JACKER: Yes. When I was head writer on the soap opera I spent about a month laying out the plot in sonata form. The producer knew what I was doing and didn't seem to mind. *Harry Outside* was originally called *Duets, Trios, and Quartets*; and *Later* [1978] is a meditation on women and water, the music of water.

INTERVIEWER: Does your feeling about the "wholeness" of a play make it difficult for you to make line cuts in rehearsal?

JACKER: Well, I'm more and more interested in being considered a dead writer, one who can't rewrite from the grave. If it has to be done, I want to do it, but I want to be sure it has to be done. Lately I've gotten a better hold on structure, so I want to see how much of what I think is the finished play I can keep.

INTERVIEWER: How do you behave in rehearsal?

JACKER: I am very well behaved. I was taught the decorum of the theater when I was very young and I am still an obedient practitioner. I talk only to the director unless I am told I can speak directly to the actors. I don't badmouth people I am working with; I don't call the actors on the phone at midnight to redirect a scene or to explain the meaning of a line; I don't interrupt rehearsals, not even to explain something; and I hope I can learn to misbehave before I'm too old to go to rehearsals.

INTERVIEWER: What if your artistic intentions are not being carried through?

JACKER: That is where I'm an abysmal coward.

INTERVIEWER: You've never taken on a director?

JACKER: Maybe a little sparring match, never mortal combat. I know I should, but I haven't yet. And I have lost plays because of bad direction . . . oh, the guilt . . . knowing I actually helped to kill this living thing.

INTERVIEWER: Returning to the plays, your female characters are often on quests. Are you secretly a medievalist?

JACKER: Probably. At least I think they—my women—are looking for a Holy Grail, a cup that if they drink from it, they'll discover the mystery.

INTERVIEWER: Many of your plays end in a conjugation of being. Harry's [Harry Outside] last line is "I am." Eddie [My Life] asks, "What do you do when you've just been born?" You create a moment of extreme presence through the characters and their language.

JACKER: Yes. The "now" is the kernel at the heart of the mystery I was just mentioning. The now, and the joy to be discovered in a kind of meditation on it.

INTERVIEWER: You've identified the character, George, in Harry Outside, as Harry's counterpoint. George thinks if he sleeps with the appropriate person, he'll find out who he is. Whereas Harry finds his sexuality through his clear definition of self. Is this amorphous aspect of George connected to the fact that he is one of the generation of men that was so quickly confronted by the sexual revolution?

JACKER: Yes. But for me, it's not the sexual revolution that terrified George; it's the technological and political revolution. I don't know how people of George's age survive; how could you manage to go on breathing, much less worry about who you are and what you want, when you believe the world might blow up tomorrow. I haven't met anyone under the age of thirty-five or so who doesn't carry that ghost around all the time. And what's so moving is that they don't talk about it, they don't dwell on it, yet it shapes their lives. The Bomb has taken our power away from us —the mysterious hand belonging to a nameless person, poised over the red button. In a sense that red button has eradicated a sense of motivation from daily life. I have a friend who needs to know where her lover is all the time; that way, if the missiles are launched, she can still make a phone call and say good-bye—and she won't be completely alone at the end. But we are all alone; no one can share our dying with us. There's nothing inherently horrible about being alone, but I, too, have feared it. I lived with my parents, and then I lived in a college dorm, and then I got married. And before I was divorced I was living with someone else. I was forty years old before I lived alone and discovered that it isn't frightening at all. In some ways I was more lonely when I was living with another person. Sooner or later, even if it's only at the moment of death, we have to face the fact that the universe isn't connected to us. That umbilical cord was cut when we were born.

INTERVIEWER: Are you optimistic about the future?

JACKER: Playwrights are like some Indian tribe, the Hopis, I think: We have a word for the past and a word for the present, but no word for the future. It seems to me that the novelists write about what will be. We hold a mirror up and show the audience what is.

ADRIENNE KENNEDY

Adrienne Kennedy's short surrealistic plays have been translated into several languages and performed and taught all over the world. Her works include Funnyhouse of a Negro, A Lesson in a Dead Language, The Owl Answers, The Pale Blue Flower, A Rat's Mass *and* Sun. *Kennedy's collected plays are forthcoming from Harvard University Press. In the last decade she has focused on commissioned work for Juilliard—reworking the Greek classics* Electra *and* Orestes—*Brown University and The Mark Taper Forum among other institutions. She has been a visiting lecturer at Yale, Brown, Princeton and the University of California at Berkeley. In the spring of 1987, Alfred Knopf will publish a memoir of her childhood and early years as an artist called* People Who Led to My Plays. *Ms. Kennedy has two sons, Adam and Joseph.*

INTERVIEWER: When did you begin writing?

KENNEDY: I really started to write when I was a senior at Ohio State University. The year I was a junior, I took a course which was very inspirational; we studied Faulkner, Fitzgerald, D. H. Lawrence, T. S. Eliot. That course fired something in me. I suddenly found myself writing short stories instead of studying.

INTERVIEWER: You once said that you were disappointed with college.

KENNEDY: It was an ordeal. There were twenty-seven thousand students attending Ohio State, and southern Ohio was almost like the deep South in those days, much more bigoted than northern Ohio where I'd grown up. I majored in education. I expected to be a teacher like my mother. Then I majored in social work for a while. All the women—black women, especially—I knew majored in education and a few wanted to be social workers. I was a poor college student, I found college extremely boring, something to just get through. But there were these few English courses; when I was a senior, I had a couple of credits left over

246

and took a survey course in twentieth-century drama. I did better in that than I did in any course the whole time I was at Ohio State. Looking back, it was important.

INTERVIEWER: Did you pursue a profession in social work?

KENNEDY: I managed to graduate and got married a month later. From then on, I wrote. My husband went to Korea, and while he was away I gave birth. I lived with my parents and when I wasn't taking care of the baby, I wrote. After my husband returned, we came to New York. I remember the exact date, January 4, 1955. We drove in the snow from Cleveland. Joe worked while he was in graduate school, and I had a certain kind of energy; I would stay up all night and write. You have to do that when you have a baby! I wrote parts of plays . . . then I started taking courses, which I did for ten years, at various places such as Columbia University and the American Theatre Wing. I was always in a writing course. I wrote my first play about a year after I came to New York.

INTERVIEWER: Did you write as a child?

KENNEDY: I always kept diaries on people in my family. My mother used to sneak into my room and read them. I really owe writing to her in a sense, because my mother is a terrific storyteller and I feel that all my writing basically has the same tone as the stories she told about her childhood. She used to tell funny stories, but they always had this terror in them, a blackness. I was the only daughter, and we were very close. I feel that my writing is an extension of my relationship with my mother, of talking with her.

INTERVIEWER: How does she feel about your writing?

KENNEDY: It makes her edgy. My writing has a lot of violence in it. As a mother myself, I would find it disturbing if my sons were writing that kind of violence and darkness.

INTERVIEWER: What attracted you to dramatic writing?

KENNEDY: Like most people at that age, I was always writing poetry and short stories. But I really admired Tennessee Williams because he was the leading playwright then, and I'd seen *The Glass Menagerie* when I was sixteen, and I'd read his plays at Ohio State. I saw a lot of theater in New York. I worked two years on my first play in my spare time and it was very imitative of Williams, of *The Glass Menagerie*. I still have it. I was twenty-three then, and I sent the play to Audrey Wood [Williams's agent], who wrote me a long letter which said she couldn't take me as a client, but that she thought I was very talented. That was a great encouragement to me. I had written the play in a course at the New School taught by Mildred Kuner. She said I wrote the best play in the class, and entered it in a play contest in Chapel Hill, North Carolina, which also meant a lot to me. Well, I didn't win. And that was a pattern I had for a long, long time. People would respond very enthusiastically to my writing, then it would fall through.

INTERVIEWER: How did you maintain the stamina to continue writing plays?

KENNEDY: I became discouraged from playwriting and went back to writing stories and a novel. I went to the General Studies Program at Columbia University where I met John Shelby, the former editor of Rinehart, who played a very big part in my life. I had written some short stories and part of a novel which Shelby read. I remember one cold winter afternoon, I went to his office and he said: "I don't know if you will ever have a big success, but I think you are touched with genius." He took the novel and sent it around. He felt the novel would definitely get published. It never did, though he sent it everywhere. Then he moved to San Francisco, but before he left he put me in touch with another editor who'd done some work for *The New Yorker*. I worked with him on my stories off and on for two years. We sent the stories around and an agent at MCA, Richard Gilston, decided to represent me. By this time, I was twenty-seven and had been writing for six years. Gilston sent the stories around, but he could never get them published. One well-known editor tried to get me to write a novel based on a character in one of the short stories. I was unable to do that, although I worked on it for nine months. It is hard for me to take another person's idea and write about it. I was very frustrated by this time. I used to get despondent, and I must confess my former husband was extremely encouraging. He had his doctorate by this time and was teaching at Hunter College. I became discouraged; it bothered me that I'd begun at twenty-one and by twenty-eight, nothing had happened. I stopped writing for a year or so, and then Joe got a grant from the Africa Research Foundation to do a study in Africa. We went to Europe first, then Ghana, Nigeria . . . we traveled for over a year and it totally changed my writing.

INTERVIEWER: In what way?

KENNEDY: In the fourteen months I spent out of this country, my writing became sharper, more focused and powerful, and less imitative. It was a tremendous turning point. I was exactly twenty-nine when I wrote *Funnyhouse of a Negro* [1964], which many people still consider to be my best play. The masks in the play were very specific. I would say almost every image in *Funnyhouse* took form while I was in West Africa where I became aware of masks. I lived in Ghana at a most fortunate time. Ghana had just won its freedom. It was wonderful to see that liberation. And I thought the landscape of Africa was so beautiful, and the people were beautiful—it gave me a sense of power and strength.

We lived in a huge house. I went into the bush and visited many villages. My husband went into the bush every day, and my son, who was five, went to school; I had a lot of time to write. More time probably than I'd ever had in my entire life. I tend to be restless in hot weather, so I'd wake up very early and could not sleep until very late. That combination produced some of the most powerful images I'd ever had. And we'd been to London, Paris, Madrid, Casablanca—it was a total regeneration. I couldn't cling to what I'd been writing—it changed me so. I didn't realize it was going to have this big impact on me. I think the main thing was that I discovered a strength in being a black person and a connection to West Africa.

INTERVIEWER: Did it bother you to be constantly referred to as a "new writer" in the *Funnyhouse of a Negro* reviews, even though you had already been writing for ten years?

KENNEDY: No. Finally being recognized as a writer was tremendously gratifying. But *Funnyhouse of a Negro* presented some other problems; it is such an intense play, and so very revealing of my psyche—if not me, personally . . . It was very dramatic. People who know me think of me as quiet, and to suddenly have this play staged which, again, is quite violent, put a lot of tension in my relationships. Also, to read about yourself in the newspaper is very anxiety producing. I found *Funnyhouse* created tremendous anxiety for me for at least two years.

INTERVIEWER: Was this anxiety solely connected to being in the public eye, or were there other factors which contributed to it?

KENNEDY: Well, it was also going through the production which, as you know, is always full of tension and hatreds and personality problems. To this day, I have fear when a production is started. I wonder how I will get along with the director, and how I will relate to the actors. Even though I had a great director, Michael Kahn, and was thrilled to be working with the people in Edward Albee's workshop, *Funnyhouse of a Negro* wasn't what I would call a good experience simply because I am a writer who is happier at the typewriter than in the arena. At that time, it was expected of me that I fully participate. I've subsequently worked on productions where it wasn't expected of me at all. I usually try to get out of going to opening night. I don't hear anybody talking to me a few days before . . . I am intolerable. I loved working with Joe Papp . . . he let me hide up in the balcony! I find the suspense of opening night just killing. What are the critics going to say? What are your friends going to say. . . ?

INTERVIEWER: Do you read your reviews?

KENNEDY: I try to make myself read them, but sometimes I put them away.

INTERVIEWER: It seems your work is either highly praised or harshly criticized.

KENNEDY: That's right. My reviews are always split. It was clear early on that many people hated my writing. The initial shock came at the Edward Albee workshop production of *Funnyhouse of a Negro* at Circle in the Square. Nothing has ever been as shocking to me as that particular night . . . many people hated my writing. Then, when it went on to a production at Actor's Studio [1964] and people said things like, "It's really nothing—you've just written the same lines over and over again . . ." Rumors went around that people were saying, "She's psychopathic." So you see, I got it all at once, and from the very beginning. Other people felt the play was very lyrical, et cetera. But I realized then that many people disliked my writing. When I said it took two years to recover from *Funnyhouse*, that was part of it. Even now, there is that fear—that's why I want to leave town on opening night. You never know when the critics will attack you.

INTERVIEWER: Was the darkness and violence evident in your early writing, the stories, the novel?

KENNEDY: Yes, but it was tempered. I censored my writing more.

INTERVIEWER: Because you felt your work might shock people?

KENNEDY: Oh, I don't think it had anything to do with what other people might think. I wasn't that sophisticated. When I would read my work over and write a second draft, I would censor things which I, personally—sitting there at the typewriter—found uncomfortable. I had a certain image—even my friends thought of me as quiet and shy, and because I am small, I was labeled "sweet" from the time I was a kid. My writing, quite naturally, turned out to be just the opposite. It was a surprise for me when I would write stories which were so dark. I was censoring my work all the time. In that sense, I owe a lot to Edward Albee. I joined his workshop at Circle in the Square several months after I returned to the United States with my husband. I had written *Funnyhouse of a Negro* in Rome and handed it in to Albee's workshop. There was a lot of suspense about which sixteen people Albee would select for his workshop. After they accepted me, I went through *Funnyhouse* and edited it, very carefully. When they were ready to do my workshop production, I gave Michael Kahn, who was then Albee's assistant, my edited-out version. I'll never forget sitting in Michael's office; he said, "Isn't there something different about this play?" I said, "This is the version I want done in the workshop." He said okay, but mentioned it to Albee. After class, Albee said, "I hear you've given Michael another version of your play." I said, "I don't want that original version done in the workshop, that would be too upsetting. I used the word *nigger* throughout and I'm worried about what I said about my parents, even though it's fictionalized. I don't want it performed." That was a very big moment. We were standing at the back of the stage, and he said, "I really think you should try—I know it's hard—but maybe we should try to put the first version on." Then he said, "If a playwright has a play on, it should be his guts on that stage. . . . If you really think you can't, it's okay. But you should try." I was in tears. But I made the effort. I was the only black person in the workshop. I became very worried.

INTERVIEWER: Did you ever get strong, negative response when your writing was more censored?

KENNEDY: People always liked my writing in those early workshops. It was softened, and highly imitative of Tennessee Williams and García Lorca.

INTERVIEWER: In an earlier interview, you said that during this imitative phase, you realized that Williams's style would not work for you. Why?

KENNEDY: The structure wouldn't work. I couldn't sustain a three-act play. It was a huge breakthrough for me when my main characters began to have other personas—it was in fact my biggest breakthrough as a writer, something I really sweated over, pondered. It was very clear to me that my plays and novels lacked something. I read my work over and over, and found there was a stilted quality. I kept intensive diaries. I can remember the room I was sitting in when I said to myself, "You are very drawn to all these historical people, they are very powerful in your imagination, yet you are not interested in writing about them historically." That's when I decided to use historical people as an extension of the main character, and also to give up the idea that I had to write a full-length play. I would say those were my two big realizations, and to me, they were *really* worth the ten years.

INTERVIEWER: Returning to the *Funnyhouse of a Negro* productions, we read that the play almost closed after twenty-two performances and then was extended by private funds.

KENNEDY: Isabel and Fredrick Eberstadt came to the last performance and decided they would like to contribute money to extend the run. It's hard to explain, but those in the theater really loved that play, and other people were alienated from it and felt that it was bad or offensive—which I still find amazing. It was catastrophic when it was a failure. . . .

INTERVIEWER: A box-office failure?

KENNEDY: Yes. When it closed, I thought it was the end of the world. But other things came out of it, like Rockefeller grants and a Guggenheim. And it gave me a feeling of affinity for people in the theater which has lasted to this day. I still consider writers my best friends. I trust writers.

INTERVIEWER: Were you surprised, then, at winning an Obie?

KENNEDY: Yes. Yes. It was a very strange period. I was barely able to handle the extremes. The play closed, I was very upset—almost suicidal—then it won an Obie. It was utterly confusing. I felt totally alone. I don't think anyone could have made me feel better. That's part of being a playwright. You are really in it by yourself after a certain point. Nothing is comforting. I just sort of hid in the house and talked to my children as much as I could. And there is some comfort in going to the A & P. I remember being in a taxi with Michael Kahn, who said, "Well, Adrienne, you've really had the whole theatrical experience." I told myself I never, ever wanted to have another play on. But *Funnyhouse of a Negro* did help me to realize I was a writer. In the whole decade preceding the play, people felt I would *someday* achieve something. They felt I had captured and illuminated something with *Funnyhouse*, which was what I had been trying to do for a long time.

INTERVIEWER: How did the black arts community react to *Funnyhouse of a Negro*?

KENNEDY: A lot of blacks hated this particular play and said it was pretentious and imitative. It was upsetting. People wanted me to be part of the movement but, frankly, I was always at home with my children. So apart from my temperament, the hours didn't exist.

INTERVIEWER: You were not outspoken in your politics?

KENNEDY: That's right. I remember there was an article written in the sixties that attacked my writing specifically and said that I was an irrelevant black writer. That sort of criticism was pretty pervasive at the time, so I built up a little resistance to it. I was criticized because there were heroines in my plays who were mixed up, confused. But I knew what my alliances were. My father was a social worker and went to Morehouse College, where Martin Luther King studied. He even had the same cadence in his voice, and was always giving speeches. I grew up in a house where people wrote and we were members of the NAACP and the United Negro College Fund. I knew my alliances.

INTERVIEWER: Would you discuss your symbolism, the repeated motifs such as blood, birds . . .

KENNEDY: I really don't know how to talk about that, except that I was a nonstop reader as a child. My mother taught me to read when I was three years old. I read all the books in the library when I was in elementary school, so they had to order some new books! I've always been drawn to the written word and have found solace in symbolism, even as far back as when I was eleven years old and read *Jane Eyre*. I have an affinity for symbolism as a way of surviving. What always impressed me, whether it was Brontë or Fitzgerald, T. S. Eliot or Lorca, was the way that writers took anguish and turned it into symbolism.

INTERVIEWER: Do you have a strong religious background?

KENNEDY: I was expected to go to Sunday School and church. I think all those stories at Sunday School played a big part in my imagination. And I am overlooking the influence of my grandparents, whom my brother and I went to visit every summer. They lived in Georgia, in a town of about five hundred people. I remember the red clay of Georgia, the white churches, going to prayer meetings with my grandmother on Thursday night and to church on Sunday morning. All of that was so powerful. Everybody in my family is very dramatic. I look exactly like my grandmother and express myself like her. The whole family is emotional; people tend to cry a lot. . . .

INTERVIEWER: Are you conscious of the religious imagery in your work?

KENNEDY: Oh, sure. I'm drawn to religious symbols. They are very powerful. Yet I did not have parents who were constantly preaching to me and I did not go to church more than the average person. I did grow up in a neighborhood which was at least sixty percent Italian. I did see people going to catechism in their white dresses [an image from A *Rat's Mass*, 1967]. So that and those summers in Georgia played a huge role.

INTERVIEWER: What is the source of the imagery in your work? How do you get in touch with it?

KENNEDY: When I was in my twenties, I studied the symbolism of other writers such as Ibsen, Lorca, Chekhov. And my dreams were very strong. I used to write them down in a few sentences: "Last night I dreamed I was running through white walls . . ." It appeared to me that those sentences had a certain power. I began to feel that my diaries had much more life than my work. I began to examine them. I started using the symbolism in my journals that came from dreams. Realizing that my dreams had a vitality that my other writing did not was another breakthrough.

INTERVIEWER: How did you begin to incorporate the dream imagery into your work?

KENNEDY: I had many recurrent dreams, so I started to write tiny stories based on them, never thinking that they could be a "work," and not really seeing how I could turn them into a short story. I started to let the images accumulate by themselves. When I made the breakthrough where I discovered that the character could have other personas, the images then seemed more indigenous. Another source of imagery which I am overlooking is the fact that my father used to read to me every night when I was growing up. Sometimes just two or three lines of poetry from Langston Hughes, Paul Laurence Dunbar, James Weldon Johnson. That, too, must have played a role in my development. There is obviously a lot of pleasure in having someone read poetry to you.

INTERVIEWER: Do you agree with critic Rosemary K. Curb's analysis of the menstrual blood in *Lesson in a Dead Language* [1964]: "A sign, almost the antisacrament of the inherited guilt of womanhood"? ["Lesson I Bleed," published in *Women in American Theatre*, Chinoy and Jenkins, eds., Crown Publishers, Inc., 1981]

KENNEDY: (Laughter) Let me tell you something, I get very upset when I read people's analysis of my work. I try not to read it. It makes me uncomfortable.

INTERVIEWER: More uncomfortable than reviews?

KENNEDY: Yes. Yes . . . to have people sort of dissect my psyche . . . I think I fear that it will inhibit me in my future work. I find it disturbing. Reading a review compels me because it concerns whether or not the play is going to run.

INTERVIEWER: Would you tell us about *Lesson in a Dead Language* in your own words? How did the play begin in your mind?

KENNEDY: Apparently—because it is hindsight—I just have this thing about blood. I had always wanted to write something about menstruation. To me, menstrual periods, no matter how long you've been having them, are traumatic—simply the fact that you bleed once a month. I wanted to write about the fear . . . the fear that you will get blood on your clothes. . . . I tend to forget that play, but I like it very much. That play has almost been lost because it was published so long ago. Gaby Rogers did an exquisite production of it at Theatre Genesis [1970]. She captured it.

INTERVIEWER: You have dealt with many "taboo" subjects in your work—rape, incest, domestic violence. How did you find the courage to reveal such volatile truths?

KENNEDY: I wouldn't use the word *courage*. I got the *impetus* from *Funnyhouse of a Negro*. In the decade after, I wrote many one-act plays in rapid succession. It was a confident period . . . I felt confident because I knew I had revealed my obsessions in *Funnyhouse*. Many people like Ellen Stewart at La Mama and Joe Papp [New York Shakespeare Festival] were very responsive and receptive to my work. I'm not sure I could write those plays now. I was riding an emotional crest. After all those years of rejection slips, people suddenly wanted to do my plays. I got letters from Paris, London, Germany . . . it made me very productive. Then, maybe twenty years later (I was about forty), I realized that although I had many first-class productions, apart from grants my plays did not seem to generate an income. That produced another set of conflicts. I had been living on grants, and hadn't quite realized that.

INTERVIEWER: Isn't that always true of experimental theater?

KENNEDY: Beckett and Ionesco make money.

INTERVIEWER: Tell us something about your experience living in London in 1966.

KENNEDY: London was a very pleasurable living experience because of the literary community there. I met writers. I lived there three years on my Guggenheim and two Rockefeller grants. I could write every day. And I met many people in theater. La Mama was touring Europe, as well as Joe Chaikin, The Living Theatre—it was a heyday for Americans in London. I met [playwrights] Edward Bond, John Arden—I met them all at the Royal Court Theatre's Thursday-afternoon teas. My son went to school a block away—it was a very easy way to live. That was also about the time that Jean-Marie Serreau did a production of *Funnyhouse* at Le Petit Odéon in Paris. Jean-Louis Barrault who ran the Odéon with his wife [Madeleine Renaud], came to rehearsals. In fact, partly what made me cling to being a playwright even when I was very depressed about it, was that I had a romantic feeling about meeting artists and the theater has a way of introducing you to people you could never meet any other way. Being black, but more than that, being black and from the Midwest, from *Cleveland*, what could I do to meet Jean-Louis Barrault, or to have Gian-Carlo Menotti call me up? Writers are embraced by many people. I'm positive that has been the biggest reward, for myself and for my children.

INTERVIEWER: Did you meet many women playwrights in Europe?

KENNEDY: I have never known many women playwrights. I met Lorraine Hansberry once, and at the Actor's Studio I met Eleanor Perry. Megan Terry was working Off Broadway. I met Maria Irene Fornes twice, and Rosalyn Drexler. There weren't that many women playwrights.

INTERVIEWER: Were you affected by the women's movement?

KENNEDY: No. First of all, I hate groups. Secondly, I'd been through all of those struggles . . . alone. I'd been through that decade from age twenty to thirty, 1955 to 1965, trying to write with babies, trying to be a wife, and then experiencing divorce.

INTERVIEWER: You once described your divorce as "a choice for writing. . . ." Would you elaborate?

KENNEDY: I don't know whether I ever said that. There were so many tensions and writing was a comfort. It was much more complicated. I think my husband and I had a typical marriage of that time. He was very busy and on his way "up" and tensions built between us.

INTERVIEWER: Because you were a two-career family?

KENNEDY: I didn't have a career. I was a housewife. I wrote on the side at night and my husband was constantly busy. Each year was a step and the tensions built. Looking back, I think that people put those words in my mouth, because the divorce was not that clear-cut. One paradox I've never quite recovered from is that I feel my former husband encouraged me to write more than anybody has since then. And he supported me financially, and wanted to, and enjoyed doing it.

INTERVIEWER: How did he feel about your success?

KENNEDY: I don't know. By that time there was a lot of sadness that we weren't together. I had known him since I was nineteen. We were married thirteen years. So it wasn't that clear-cut. I am not a heroine who chose writing over marriage. It's not like that at all. I think divorce is futile. I would never divorce again, not with children.

INTERVIEWER: What inspired *Evening With Dead Essex* [1973], which dealt with the Mark Essex snipings? [Mark Essex, a troubled black ex-Navy man left six persons dead and fifteen wounded after sniping from the tower of a seventeen-story New Orleans Howard Johnson's Motor Lodge in January, 1972].

KENNEDY: When I go through periods when I can't write, I'm glued to the television news. I was following the Munich Olympics, and the Mark Essex snipings happened around the same time.

INTERVIEWER: How did you come up with the multimedia dramatic form—headlines are read, slides are shown . . .

KENNEDY: I was trying to capture how you feel when you hear all that on television. Isn't that funny? I've almost forgotten that play.

INTERVIEWER: *Evening With Dead Essex* was the first play by a woman to be produced at the Yale Repertory Theater. Were there subsequent productions of the play?

KENNEDY: It was done at The American Place Theatre first, in a small space, directed by Gaby Rogers, who is brilliant. It did not work well on the main stage at Yale; the actors got lost. Then it was done by a theater company in Louisiana; but nothing ever happened to that play. Apparently, my plays are sometimes expensive and hard to put on. They seem to be taught more than they are produced.

INTERVIEWER: How did your unusual and imaginative use of stage space evolve?

KENNEDY: Martha Graham was very popular in the fifties. I was in my own way attempting to imitate her. I also had a fixation for Picasso. I read everything Picasso had written about his work. Then, in Cleveland, there was one foreign movie house where in my teens I saw all of the French surrealist films, by people like Cocteau, Buñuel . . . my writing is definitely influenced by French film, Martha Graham and Picasso.

INTERVIEWER: What, specifically, were you drawn to in Martha Graham's staging?

KENNEDY: There were always many things happening simultaneously. And everything seemed to come out of darkness. People played many parts, she used a lot of black and white—there was a fluidity and a deemphasis on the narrative. The narrative was being presented to you in another way. I want to say that I wasn't yet capturing this in my short stories or in my plays, though there is no doubt that from 1955, it was on my mind. I'm sure I was also influenced by O'Neill's long monologues about people's torments—by the use of interior monologue.

INTERVIEWER: Do you believe there is a female aesthetic in drama?

KENNEDY: Yes, I think we can make a special contribution to theater.

INTERVIEWER: Virginia Woolf said that however much we may go to the work of male artists for pleasure, it is difficult to go to them for help in finding a voice. . . .

KENNEDY: That is a fascinating statement. I remember reading the stories of Colette when I was young. We carry that around with us. Women writers do affect me differently than male writers. That is probably the female aesthetic at its height. You see, *Jane Eyre* is my favorite novel. I'm glad that Charlotte Brontë was a woman. I think if you can bring your woman's experience to something, it is really great. It's important not to censor or inhibit that experience. Alice Childress has also been a great inspiration to me.

INTERVIEWER: Do you teach the work of women writers in your courses?

KENNEDY: That is a problem. I taught an American drama course at UC [University of California at] Davis and used O'Neill, Sam Shepard, Lorraine Hansberry . . . many writers. The girls complained that there weren't enough women in the course and they complained about the female characters in the plays. I'm not sure what the answer is for that particular period. Not many women playwrights have had recognition. And they are not in the textbooks.

INTERVIEWER: How do you feel about being called a "Woman Playwright," or a "Black Woman Playwright?"

KENNEDY: Ten years ago, it might have bothered me because I would have felt that people were saying I was lesser than say, Norman Mailer. [Laughs] I am a woman writer and a black writer and that doesn't disturb me anymore.

INTERVIEWER: Playwright Wendy Wasserstein says that our cultural idea of a playwright is a white male—anything else is some kind of subset.

KENNEDY: In some ways I have made peace with that. But when I say I have made peace, it is crystal clear to me what is really the issue:

as a black woman, or as a woman writer, or as a black writer, I don't stand in line for the income and the rewards, and that bothers me a lot. The white male writer can take steps. He's Off Broadway and the next thing you know, he's writing screenplays for Sidney Lumet. He does stand eighty percent more chance of getting his writing career to pay off. It's that simple.

KAREN MALPEDE

Karen Malpede is a playwright and theater historian. Her plays are A Lament for Three Women, Rebeccah, The End of War, Making Peace: A Fantasy, Sappho & Aphrodite and A Monster Has Stolen the Sun. Her most recent book on the theater is an anthology, Women in Theatre: Compassion & Hope (Limelight, 1985). She also wrote People's Theatre in America (Drama Book Specialists, 1972) and edited Three Works by the Open Theater (Drama Book Specialists, 1974). She was a co-founder and coordinator of The New York Woman's Salon for Literature and co-founder of New Cycle Theatre. She lives in Park Slope, Brooklyn, with producer Burl Hash and their child, Carrie Sophia. She has taught theater at Smith College, John Jay College and New York University. She lectures and reads widely, and is an active member of the Executive Committee of the War Resisters League and of PEN. A collection of her plays is forthcoming [1987] from Marlboro Press.

—————

MALPEDE: Yesterday I was at the hospital visiting my good friend Julian Beck, who is quite ill [Julian Beck, co-creator of The Living Theater, died September 14, 1985] and I asked him about the book he is working on, *Theandric*. "It's a book with a very simple premise," he said, "which is that the purpose of the theater is to reveal the divine in man." That's my tradition, you see, with its inherent contradiction, because in order for me to reveal the divine in "man" I had to come to feminism. There was no other way, I had to come to an understanding of the divine in women. Now I can truly be one within a long tradition of people who believe that theater is a way to reveal the spirit, the deep essence, the unrealized desires, the true holiness of humankind.

INTERVIEWER: Who else would you say is part of this tradition?

MALPEDE: When I sent Joe Chaikin a copy of the script of *Sappho & Aphrodite*, I wrote on it, *For Joe, who taught me "Torah."* I feel quite the same way about Judith Malina and Julian Beck; these are the people

259

who taught me, through their example and their friendship, about dedication to an artistic vision which is also a political and a moral vision and which exists quite independent of commercial success. They taught me that the artist is one who commits to that which is highest and best in the human spirit; who puts oneself with the victims of oppression in order to understand resistance; who deals in imagery which extends the boundaries of the known; who explores precisely those areas which have been taboo in order to better understand our fears and our potential; who is brave and uncompromising; who listens to an inner voice and does what needs to be done.

INTERVIEWER: How did you first discover this tradition?

MALPEDE: As an undergraduate at the University of Wisconsin I stumbled onto the work of the Irish Literary Revival and became a student of W. B. Yeats, Augusta Gregory, John Synge and Sean O'Casey, great people of the theater, each one, because they tied their work in the theater to something larger, whether it was the mysticism of Yeats or the lyric populism of Gregory, O'Casey and Synge. They wanted a theater which spoke of all we might become. Augusta Gregory used to say, "A theater with a base of reality and an apex of beauty."

INTERVIEWER: What inspired you to write three books of theater history and theory?

MALPEDE: My books have been an attempt to document this tradition, as much for myself as for others. I felt I had to learn as much as possible about what had already been done in order to locate my area of work as precisely as I could. *People's Theatre in America* is a history of radical theater in this country from 1927 to 1972; it's a book written when I was twenty-five and twenty-six, a young person's book, and written right in the middle of the Vietnam War. It's peppered with sentences like "As I type these words, Nixon is bombing Hanoi." It's an angry and impassioned book. As I researched and wrote it I learned there was an entire tradition of theater in this country I had never learned about. I discovered Hallie Flanagan and Federal Theater for myself, no one had ever bothered to tell me about her, even at the School of the Arts at Columbia where I did my graduate work. Now, mercifully, Federal Theater is being written about and taught; but the Theater Union, the New Playwright's Theater, the early pageants and agitprop plays of the twenties and thirties are still relatively unknown—although Helen Chinoy is doing wonderful work documenting the thirties. What interested me most as a potential playwright (I didn't dare know I was a playwright yet) about the work I researched for *People's Theatre* was that the prevalent form of American theater, realism, seemed so completely inadequate for expressing the highest aspirations of people. I was interested in how the realistic form was being stretched or even discarded because I felt that here was the real area of exploration if one wanted to make a theater which would reveal the divine in us.

INTERVIEWER: How did you meet Judith Malina and Julian Beck?

MALPEDE: It was after *People's Theatre* was published that I first met Judith Malina, Julian Beck and, through them, Joseph Chaikin, though I had already written about all of their work. I was at a women's theater weekend at the Quaker Meeting House on Fifteenth Street in 1972 when Judith came across the floor, threw her arms around me and said, "Karen Malpede, I finished your book at four A.M. and I feel so close to you." For me it was love at first sight; I was already quite enamored of her work. That much openness and warmth from an older, established and great woman artist toward a young and unformed woman provides amazing sustenance.

INTERVIEWER: What inspired you to edit *Three Works by The Open Theater*?

MALPEDE: In 1973 The Open Theater was about to disband, so I wanted to document their final three productions. Joe had been an actor in The Living Theatre. He founded The Open Theater to continue to explore the actor's role in the nonrealistic play.

INTERVIEWER: When did you start writing plays?

MALPEDE: It was 1973, and The Open Theater had just disbanded. A group of directors, playwrights, and critics were meeting periodically with Joe [Chaikin], discussing the nature of our future work in the theater. It seemed to me that through their work with voice and physicality, and their destruction of the realistic play, the sixties experimental theater and primarily the Living and Open Theaters had made the ground ripe for a reintroduction of language into the theater, but a language which was imagistic, poetic, and which spoke the unrealized hopes and dreams of the characters. I said all of this at one of the meetings we had in Joe's apartment. Jean-Claude van Itallie [playwright] was sitting across the room from me in the circle and he looked at me coolly and said, "It's much easier to talk about it than to do it." I went home and began to write a play of the sort I had described. I had a lot to say in imagistic language because I had recently encountered feminism and I was looking at my entire life in a completely new way.

INTERVIEWER: How did feminism influence you?

MALPEDE: I suppose it's hard for people who didn't live through it to understand the absolutely cataclysmic force with which first the civil rights and the peace movements and then feminism entered our lives. We actually felt, and it's a feeling that has never left me, that some great change for the good is possible, that our lives *are* a constant process of creation and that whatever we can understand about ourselves, about the nature of our own vicitimization, our own oppression, our own fears and our own resistance can be transferred into social life so that we might actually be able to understand community, and be able to live together in a feelingful, compassionate way. It's this understanding that allows me to work for nuclear disarmament, that gives me the strength, as the wonderful Quaker activist Frances Crowe says, "to keep on keeping on."

INTERVIEWER: Were your parents politically active?

MALPEDE: No, I was not raised in an activist home, but I was raised as a mongrel and an outcast and I think that sense of never belonging anywhere which I had from very early on has contributed to the wish to create a world in which I might feel at home. I think what I do as a playwright is to create world after world and I feel at home in each one for awhile.

INTERVIEWER: Why did you feel like an outcast?

MALPEDE: My mother was and is a strikingly beautiful Jewish woman from an upper-middle-class family that had fallen upon hard times. She wanted to be an actress but instead married my father, who was an Italian Catholic from an immigrant working-class family on the West Side of Chicago, and shortly afterward had twins. My twin brother, John Malpede, is a performance artist. I think the fact of being a twin to a brother has influenced my writing and my life far more than I ever have acknowledged. There's a great deal of twin imagery in my work, a lot of pairing, a certain complexity of levels, a searching for the lost self, the unrealized part, there are role reversals, disguises. My brother and I lived a rich fantasy life together as children and that probably has something to do with why I'm a playwright instead of a novelist.

In any case, these Italian-Jewish-middle-class/lower-class twins grew up in a white-Presbyterian-Republican-middle-class suburb where no one had ever seen a Jew or an Italian. We had hardly ever seen a Jew or an Italian outside of our families and I don't think that either of us had the slightest idea of who we really were.

When I moved to New York in 1967, it was like coming home. I remember once crossing the street which connects the old Lower East Side to Little Italy and in the exact center of that street with one half of me in the neighborhood of Eastern European Jews and the other on the side of the Italian immigrants I felt for the first time in my life I knew where I belonged.

My father was a self-made man who had worked his way up from poverty to become an executive of a chemical company. He had left his religion which—as practiced by his family—was a brutal religion of punishment and fear, and his class, but he carried with him the machismo and a certain astonishing mixture of brutality and passion which was the dominant emotional reality of my childhood.

INTERVIEWER: Were you close to your father?

MALPEDE: As a child, I adored him; as a woman, I became appalled by the memories and the imprints of his brutality. He died of cancer when I was eighteen, after a gruesome two-year battle with that disease. And I think that the suffering I watched him endure, and the suffering which was inflicted upon him by the inhumane treatments for cancer in this country, showed me graphically, and with a lot of pain—because I loved this man—the fragility of the human body as home for the human spirit. Watching my father die of cancer, and watching the other people on his hospital floor die, was like going through a war. It was natural for me to become a pacifist. What more does anyone need to see than the reality of one person's suffering? Of course, the families of violent men often learn a passivity which is not pacifism, but merely acquiescence to suffering. Pacifism is an active, assertive way of being which, when used effectively, disarms. It has to do with holding to a sense of self and of community and with refusing to be part of the victor/victim scenario.

INTERVIEWER: Your first play, A *Lament for Three Women* [1979] is about three women who are losing a husband, a father and a son to cancer. . . .

MALPEDE: Yes. It takes place in the waiting room of the hospital and in it the three women, who come from different backgrounds, begin to tell the story of their relationships to these men who have been so central in their lives. The men are dying. The women feel helpless and bereaved, but as they speak they begin to hear the similarities in their stories, they begin to bond together and to take strength from one another. Finally they gather enough courage to go towards the men and to help them die with dignity. They return and lament together, but their lament is a song, a song of grief and also a song of new life.

INTERVIEWER: Was there a production of A *Lament for Three Women?*

MALPEDE: Yes, it was staged by women who were in or around the Open Theater. Tina Shepard was in it, Sybille Hayn and a wonderful older woman, Elia Braca, who went on to act at New Cycle Theater. We performed it in a loft; we had no budget. It was done in natural light, at sunset, so the play began in that wonderful golden glow and ended in dusk. It was later done at the Cummington Community of the Arts in Massachusetts and it was there I first met Ned Ryerson, a writer and educator who became a major patron of my work for many years, and without whose financial support and belief I certainly would have had an entirely different history.

INTERVIEWER: How did Ryerson support your work?

MALPEDE: Ned and the City of New York Department of Cultural Affairs were the two major funders of New Cycle Theater, which I opened in Brooklyn in 1977 along with producer/director Burl Hash. New Cycle Theater premiered four of my six plays, most recently *Sappho & Aphrodite* [1983].

INTERVIEWER: What were your goals in anthologizing women's writings on theater in your latest book, *Women in Theater: Compassion and Hope* [Dramabooks, 1983]?

MALPEDE: I wanted to collect writings by women who had been both great artists and great theorists of theater; women like Augusta Gregory, Hallie Flanagan, Judith Malina, Ellen Terry, Fanny Kemble, Susan Glaspell, Lorraine Hansberry, Gertrude Stein, Isadora Duncan. You see, I've been creating for myself a tradition into which I could fit, and to which I can hold on in the years to come. A tradition which hopefully my own work may help extend.

INTERVIEWER: What do you have to say to women who are offended by the term *woman playwright*?

MALPEDE: Because they feel that *woman* is a second-class term?

INTERVIEWER: Yes. Some feel that the commercial theater is not ready for the truth of women's lives, that they must gain their credibility before exploring these truths.

MALPEDE: As a Jew I have to remember what happened when Jews felt they were safely assimilated into the life of Germany. I think if you censor your vision in order to be more commercial, or if you forget who you are, you can call yourself anything you want, you might even call yourself a successful playwright, but you can't call yourself an artist because somewhere along the line you have betrayed the very essence of art, which is absolute attention to the inner voice, and absolute willingness to speak the truth as you perceive it. The great artist speaks a truth so personal it becomes universal. There's no way you can do that with one eye on the market place.

INTERVIEWER: But theater is a market place. . . . Is there any way to counter this commercialization?

MALPEDE: It seems to me the only way to counter commercialism in a country where money is held up as the only test of human merit, is for the artists to band together to create a community in which the art that is new and daring and totally unacceptable to the commercial world is created and explored. Sooner or later it will end up on Broadway, because the commercial theater has always been subsidized by the avant-garde and the experimental. Eventually, we get *A Chorus Line* or *for colored girls* or *Torch Song Trilogy*. . . .

INTERVIEWER: So the real problem now is that the artists are separated?

MALPEDE: That's one problem. It's up to us to create an environment fertile for the making of our art and we find ourselves at a moment in time when such an environment does not yet exist again—if you know what I mean—because this problem has been solved many times before. Ours is a complex and disheartening situation and I really don't know what to do. Somehow everyone has to find a way to keep on working. Young people must be encouraged, supported, taught and listened to. I do think that until the avant-garde and the serious theater in general shake off their fascination with violence we are not going to see the burst of new energy and new community we need to see.

INTERVIEWER: Would you elaborate?

MALPEDE: When Genet or Artaud, or for that matter the Living Theatre, put sexual or political violence on the stage they did it for a reason which transcended a mere fascination with violence. Often their theaters were closed and their plays were banned, but they had an effect upon the culture. They were not saying complacently, "See how bad we are." They were saying, "Look at what we have done to one another in the name of love, in the name of justice; we have practiced cruelty; we are locked together in a sadomasochistic bondage and we must escape so that our society can change." But today, I think the depiction of violence and brutality has become a shield to mask the fact that we are living in a moment of impending nuclear end.

Recently I read a rave review of a serious new play in which *The New York Times* reviewer said with highest praise the play "looks into the blackness of men's souls." It seems to me that if you are getting an artistic high from looking at the "blackness of men's souls," something is terribly wrong. We don't really need more information about how bad we are, we already know. We live in the bloodiest century in the history of the world. We've experienced the Holocaust, dropped the atomic bomb. Since Vietnam we've had war on television; we are beginning to admit to rape, child abuse, political torture. To me, a continued focus upon violence in the theater is no longer an exposé; it begins to seem gratuitous. We have to look at violence, yes, but with a new eye—an eye that tries to see its root causes and attempts to change them. This is a psychological question as much as it's a social one.

INTERVIEWER: Any thoughts as to why we are fixated on violence?

MALPEDE: I think artists, like most other people, don't want to face the fact that we are very close to our extinction as a species and we intend to take with us all the life on earth. Our rage at our own individual mortality—because we have not found a communal, spiritually renewing way of facing death—has run so far amok that many people actually say, "I have to die anyway, it might as well be in a nuclear war; I just hope I go quick."

INTERVIEWER: What is the result of the artist's inability to confront his or her rage at individual mortality, or the fact of possible extinction by nuclear war?

MALPEDE: Once artists become psychically numbed, art becomes increasingly the tale of the victims. I think that's what we are seeing now. The one who writes a play about the blackness of men's souls is a victim of the dross just as surely as the reviewer who praises it and the audience who has to watch it. Women can be particularly adept at telling the tales of the victims. Elie Wiesel said the nuclear arms race has turned the world into Jews. It's turned the whole world into women, too. I've noticed that recent serious plays by women which have won awards like the Obie or the Pulitzer Prize are plays in which the female characters who are about the age of the women who fostered the feminist movement all through the seventies do not survive. They kill themselves or are killed and the lesson is very clear: If you dare, you die. These plays can be protesting violence against women or holding up suicide as a triumph of sorts, but the result is the same: The women die a violent death when what they really wanted to do was to live a fulfilled life. These are the plays that are being allowed through the censorship imposed by the reviewers and by economics; they are not the only plays being written.

INTERVIEWER: How have you, in your own writing, moved beyond images of women as victims?

MALPEDE: If you put yourself inside a tradition which sees the theater as a place where the holiness of humankind can be revealed you are inevitably drawn back to Greek drama and Greek ritual. You are part of a theater of origins. The work I like to do in theater is the work that addresses the slim chance we do have for survival. The imagination is a powerful force. When we make images of survival, when we enact them, we increase both our knowledge of and our desire for survival. I also think the playwright has a responsibility to the people she works with, because whatever we write is going to become the life of the people rehearsing it. In every rehearsal period I've ever gone through, at a certain point you notice there is no difference between the life on stage and the off-stage life, each has assumed the color of the other. That's why the theater is such a powerful place. We build worlds and because we rehearse them, we can really experiment with human potential.

I do want to say that it's precisely because I don't have the answer about how we might survive as a living species on a living planet that the questions are so very compelling to me. I don't even have the answer about how we might truly and fully love the people closest to us and at the same time truly and fully realize our individuality, but I know these questions are related.

INTERVIEWER: Is your work autobiographical?

MALPEDE: My life and work are intimately connected. Sometimes the work invents the life and sometimes the life invents the work. I have faith in the human imagination.

INTERVIEWER: Your plays are mythic rather than realistic. How do you incorporate autobiographic elements in a play such as A *Monster Has Stolen the Sun* [written 1980–1985]?

MALPEDE: I began writing *Monster* while I was pregnant with my daughter. Pregnancy can be a tremendously creative time in the life of a woman; the body itself is tied up in the act of creation so it's easy for the mind and heart to be similarly engaged. Once a week during my pregnancy I visited a wonderful psychotherapist named Jean Mundy. She put me into deep relaxation states and rubbed my growing belly and spoke to me about the glorious creature who was growing inside. My close women friends, many of whom already had children, were delighted with my pregnant self; they, too, would lay a hand or a head on the belly. And Burl Hash, her father, was eagerly anticipating the child's birth. I was in ecstasy for nine months, and then gave birth to the child of my dreams, a wonderful baby girl. But I had fought a very bitter battle with myself over whether or not to have this child. Burl and I had almost split. I had made two appointments for abortions, by the time I decided to have the child I knew that I absolutely wanted her because I had already confronted many of my fears.

In *Monster* there is a scene in which two pregnant women talk to one another about their coming children. *Monster* is a play set in Celtic Ireland, just at the moment Catholicism was subsuming the older pagan religion, with its knowledge of herbal healing and, also, of abortificants. One woman, Etain, the wife of the lord, is pregnant unwillingly; she feels it is her fate and does not know how to escape. She is met by Macha, a woman come down from the mountains to the sea to bear a child she has joyfully and willfully conceived. The two women are drawn to one another, they sit alone in the afternoon sun and stroke one another's bellies and talk about their coming births. Macha sees Etain's fears and she tries to ease them. Etain begins to take an animal-like delight in her own full rich body. Then, suddenly, she returns to fear; what she fears is really her own sense of ecstasy, her sense of her physical prowess. The fear stops her; she grows rigid and furious with the mountain woman who tempted her out beyond the realm of her own reality.

I think this happens often—I know it happens often to me—a sense of liberation, joy, a sense of creativity, a sense of finally becoming the person you were born to be, is suddenly choked by fear. . . . Now the task is not to do away with fear—that is impossible. The task is to understand the cyclical nature of change and to learn to trust that when you are ready to take the next step the road will open. The Quakers call this "waiting for the way."

In *Monster*, Etain gives birth to a son, but dies in childbirth. Macha gives birth to a daughter whom she names Etain. This girl-child, who is much beloved, grows up to become in many ways the fulfilled spirit of the Etain who died. So you see, nothing is ever lost; all of the energy that the older Etain blocked is finally let flow free in her namesake. Nothing is lost, but only if life survives.

INTERVIEWER: *Monster* also deals with questions of power, with incest, with parenting. . . .

MALPEDE: Yes, and it is the play in which I come closest to understanding the relationship between the sexes. In the new play I am working on now I am hoping to go further with understanding a true mutuality, respect, love and nonpossessiveness between women and men to show the social significance of such relationships; I think we need images like this. That doesn't sound dramatic, but I'm speaking about experiment —not about what's known—as I think many women are. If you think for a moment about how difficult the practices of intimacy, trust and social responsibility actually are and if you think about what sorts of form, what language, what actions illuminate those difficulties then you are carrying on the tradition of experiment in drama. I've recently read four plays by Marguerite Yourcenar, a writer I very much admire, and she seems to me to be exactly in the tradition I describe. So is Nelly Sachs, the Nobel Prize [1966] poet, who wrote *Eli*, which is one of the great surrealist-verse dramas of all time. And, naturally, so is Gertrude Stein. You see, we have a tradition, and it is a lofty one.

I've been very inspired by Etty Hillesum's diaries, *An Interrupted Life* [Washington Square Press, 1985], and I very much want to make a play about them. Etty Hillesum was a woman determined to craft her own life and to follow her own unique impulses in the midst of the most horrible of conditions, the rise of fascism. [She died November 30, 1943, in Auschwitz]. To do so she had to turn increasingly inside; she had to find a relationship with herself, her circumstances and the man she loved, which was a sustained prayer. As her own chances for physical survival lessened, her inner resources increased and her inner life became more and more rich. Even though she was a highly assimilated Jew and really knew nothing about the practice of Jewish law or orthodoxy, I've begun to see Etty Hillesum as belonging to the tradition of Jewish, or Judeo-Christian, mysticism. I've realized, too, that in one way or another all of my plays attempt to document the history of what the publisher of the Hillesum diaries, John Gaarlandt, calls "radical altruism." I have been most interested in characters who make unusual decisions for the sole purpose of wakening themselves to a higher reality.

There is another theme in my work which might at first glance seem at odds with this one, and that is sexuality, or more precisely, eros. I suppose you might say I am interested in the world-shaping possibilities of eros.

INTERVIEWER: You have also explored relationships between women in your play, *Sappho & Aphrodite*. . . .

MALPEDE: Yes, and it's interesting that that particular play got me in trouble. When I was working on *Sappho*, New Cycle Theater was performing in an arts center which is also a church. The woman who runs the space went to the board of directors very alarmed because we intended to present a play about women who love women.

INTERVIEWER: What was the outcome?

MALPEDE: They finally had to let us do four performances there—we'd been there since the space began in 1980. We moved the play into Greenwich Village and lost our connection with this space. But the play exists and the production we did touched many people. The true artist is bisexual; I'm not necessarily talking about whom you choose to sleep with but about how deeply you can enter into both your own psyche and that of someone unlike you. I am appalled by the homophobia in our society, and especially by the fear of lesbians. Even women who won't call themselves feminists have benefited from the love of other women; it has helped to sanction them as creative human beings even if they ignore it or if they partake of it in secret. The love women have recently openly expressed for women has contributed enormously to the fact that so many women are now beginning to see themselves as playwrights.

INTERVIEWER: Did you have an idea while you were writing the play that it would cause people to react so strongly?

MALPEDE: I was terrified to write *Sappho & Aphrodite*; every play I write terrifies me and lures me with its terror. I was literally afraid that a play about all women, even a play about a great woman poet, would not be universal. As I worked, of course, this fear gave way to an entirely new sight. I suddenly found myself, for the first time in my work, writing about a community which was free of the threat of violence: there was no war, no murder, no duels, no gunshot, no rape and consequently the women in this play were neither victims of violence nor using all their energy to resist it. Since physical violence was not an issue I suddenly found myself in the richest emotional territory I had ever encountered as a writer. I was writing about the relationships between a great teacher and the students who alternately idolize and seek to depose her, about Sappho's rebellious teenage daughter, about the complex connection between human love and artistic creation.

INTERVIEWER: How did *Sappho & Aphrodite* begin in your mind?

MALPEDE: Using the invented human stories of Sappho, her students and her child, which I found by meditating on the contents of her poems, I began to explore the connections between creativity and desire and between eros and thanatos. In my preliminary notes to the script I wrote, "Eros and Thanatos, love and death . . . unlike the Freudian idea of these two forces, which sees them in opposition, at war, this ritual drama presents eros and thanatos as part of one cyclical experience of life. Love and creativity (eros) contain within them a constant attraction toward, even necessity for, death of love, loss of creative spark: death and loss prepares the ground for new love, a new understanding of old love, and for renewed creative energies."

With *Sappho & Aphrodite* I was beginning an exploration of woman as erotically autonomous; I wanted to look at a group of women who are all, by inclination and training, going to follow their own erotic impulses and write the words they want to write, create the art they need to create and be with the person they need to be with. I wanted to see how such a community might rupture and heal itself, because I think the dream of community like this is a valid human dream and one which Sappho's legend gives us access to.

INTERVIEWER: How did the language of the play evolve?

MALPEDE: I was working with nineteen or twenty of Sappho's poems and fragments which I put right into the text. I wanted to create a seamlessness between her verse and the words the characters spoke to show, in part, how in a time of high creativity the spoken language and that which is written or sung are not terribly dissimilar. Poetic language and dramatic action unite (to make the Greek theater, the Elizabethan theater, the theater of the Irish Literary Revival), whenever a society as a whole is striving to surpass itself. The popular theater never disappears, performance never ceases to exist, the traveling troupe of clowns and jugglers and social critics always make their way from town to town, but beautiful language joins itself to this tradition (and always the popular tradition, by the way, not to the staid, stodgy or commercial) only when the collective begins to perceive a new relationship between humankind and the cosmos, only when, that is, a people is attempting to come closer to that which is divine both inside and outside of themselves.

Sappho used many exquisite images that reflected both the natural world and the intimate erotic experiences of women. She saw women as a part of nature and saw the natural world, therefore, as a reflection of and a way of understanding women. Immersing myself in Sappho's verse, or I should say in Mary Barnard's elegant translation of it, allowed me to make a careful study at the "master's feet" of something I had been doing instinctively since I began to write plays, which is to use female imagery as dramatic, and that means universal, imagery. When the play was in performance a male friend of one of the performers told her that the line "the vulva-like folds of the sea" was not writing; one couldn't use the word *vulva* in a serious literary work. Now *vulva* is an absolutely beautiful word. I was very anxious one day and I went swimming in a sea which seemed to me to be full of vulva-like folds, exactly; I felt enormously comforted as I bobbed about there so the image stuck. The play is also full of tongue imagery. Now the tongue is both the way we speak, making words and hence the spirit intelligible, and it is a delicate instrument of enormous sensual pleasure. Recently I have been collecting tender and sensuous images of the phallus from male writers; Lorca frequently compares male sexuality to a flower, to a carnation, or to the grape; Rilke uses the conch shell as a wonderful image in the elegies. I think when you try to write about female sexuality with similar grace and love you run into two problems: the contempt in which women are held, and the general, societal fear of tenderness shared by women and men. Pornography is far more acceptable in this culture than eros. The erotic images are going to be censored. Lorca was shot by the fascists because of his gentle love for the male body.

INTERVIEWER: Would you discuss the difference between the two types of rituals in *Sappho & Aphrodite*?

MALPEDE: Plays often come to me in two ways simultaneously. Something in the emotional life of the community in which I live asks to be explored and at the same time a formal or structural question poses itself. I wanted to write a play which showed the function of ritual in a community. Sappho and her students worshiped the goddess Aphrodite. In the play, Aphrodite stands not only for the sexual lives of women, but for their creative lives. At the annual ritual to Aphrodite which ends the first act, the celebrants remember that their first duty is to their own desire, their own emotional and creative destinies, if they wish to be artists, that is. They perform this ritual every year and every year the ritual heightens and sometimes changes the course of their life. In the second act I wanted to explore ritual at the moment of its creation. Atthis, Sappho's lover and student, has been chosen to write the verse for this year's ritual. That means the play also takes place at the moment when the student is beginning to challenge and, perhaps, even surpass the teacher. This is an awfully sticky time, as anyone knows who has ever been involved in an intense student-mentor relationship; the feelings released on both sides are likely to be extreme. In the scene in the cave, which is a dance of death, Atthis reclaims her will to live, and Sappho experiences her utter vulnerability. Once Atthis can be strong and Sappho weak, their relationship can reestablish itself along new, more equitable lines; they can become friends who love rather than lovers caught in the mentor-student, mother-daughter bond which catches us all at one time or another.

INTERVIEWER: Having read the play, I found that all my previous conceptions of Sappho had to be altered. She had become more human, and consequently more accessible to me.

MALPEDE: It's interesting that you say that because, of course, Sappho's frailty in the play has led some women to criticize it most strongly. No, she is not a perfect mother goddess dispensing words of wisdom to her worshipers; she is a very foolish and also very great woman, apt to make a hash of her life at any moment and then to write a great poem as a result. And that's just the point. She is capable, too, of enormous growth as a person and so is Atthis because they are willing to risk following their own creative impulses. If they hurt, it is a kind of hurt that comes from deepening their awareness and not from a sort of brutal snuffing out of someone else's capacities. For a woman to assert her right to her own life and to her own body, her right to take lovers and to be a creative artist, all of this is world-changing.

INTERVIEWER: In what sense?

MALPEDE: If we look back at the emergence of Greek drama we see that men were at a point where they were consciously saying, "The next great evolution of human societies depends upon us; the history of our consciousness is going to be the history of the race." And they broke from women and from the female force, from the love of the mother and of the collective, as all the Greek tragedies show them breaking, in order to be free to discover their own individual destinies.

It's not until very recently that women have had a collective sense of being history makers. It's not until faced with nuclear disaster that the relationships between the sexes have seemed so inadequate to our future as a race that women in large numbers, and feelingful men as well, have had to break with history and assert ourselves as individuals and as culturally responsible people. At this moment, of course, you have an explosion of women working in the theater, because the theater is that place where a society in crisis asserts itself and explores new values.

We have to accept that we have invented weapons capable of blowing up the world. We have to ask: Why? What events in our personal and social histories have brought us here, to this impasse? We have to understand and *grieve* for what happened to us and then we can begin to discover harmonious ways of being fully ourselves alive in the living world. We will then render nuclear weapons obsolete. This is the true creative challenge; it is the function of theater in our time.

EMILY MANN

Emily Mann is playwright and director who stages her own, as well as others' plays. She has written (and directed) Annulla Allen: Autobiography of a Survivor, Still Life and Execution of Justice, all of which have had numerous productions in the U.S. Still Life was presented at the Avignon Festival, in Paris, at the Edinburgh Theatre Festival and in London. Ms. Mann has also written for television and film. Ms. Mann's directing credits include The Glass Menagerie, Ashes by David Rudkin, Reunion and Dark Pony by David Mamet, at The Guthrie Theater in Minneapolis where she was a resident director. At the Actors Theater of Louisville, Ms. Mann directed Kathleen Tolan's A Weekend Near Madison, Jeffrey Sweet's The Value of Names and William Mastrosimone's A Tantalizing. She also directed the world premiere of Michael Weller's Dwarfman: Master of a Million Shapes at the Goodman Theatre in Chicago and a production of Oedipus the King at the Brooklyn Academy of Music. Still Life won Obie Awards for Distinguished Playwriting, Distinguished Direction, Best Production; the three original cast members each won Obies for their performances. Still Life also won the Fringe First Award for Best Play at the Edinburgh Festival. Ms. Mann's other awards include a Guggenheim Fellowship, a National Endowment for the Arts Fellowship, a CAPS Award, the Rosamond Gilder award for Outstanding Creative Achievement in the Theater and a Playwrights' Center/McKnight Foundation Fellowship for Playwrights. She is a member of New Dramatists in New York City, a member of the Board of the Society of Stage Directors and Choreographers and Vice-President of the Board of Theatre Communications Group. In March 1986, at the Virginia Theatre on Fifty-Second Street, Ms. Mann became the first woman to direct her own play, Execution of Justice, on the Broadway stage.

INTERVIEWER: You often utilize performance elements in your plays: recorded dialogue, repetitions, slides.

MANN: I'm fascinated with live performance aspects of theater. It enables you to add another layer of perception to what you are presenting and gives you alternative ways to tell your story. You can stylize without being linear, without the traditional rising and falling action, where you watch one protagonist. The play can then be seen from different angles simultaneously. I did use some performance elements in the writing of *Execution of Justice* [which premiered at the Eureka Theatre in 1982], and I like that aesthetic. Some people called *Still Life* [premiered at the Goodman Theatre in 1980] a performance piece. I don't know if I would or not. But there are certainly performance elements in it.

INTERVIEWER: Simultaneity seems important to you as a playwright, and as a director.

MANN: Yes. Incredibly so. For example, when I was working on *Execution of Justice*, I kept telling the dramaturg, Oskar Eustis at the Eureka Theatre [in San Francisco], that I was hearing all this emotional *noise* throughout the play. I wanted to hear both the trial and the community breaking down . . . at the same time. It has to do with content dictating form. The sobs from the community had to be heard. I had been in many living rooms, offices, kitchens in that city hearing people's stories and I knew the people I'd been talking to had to have an opportunity to give testimony. In the theater you can hear many voices at once; it is a wonderful aspect of live theater that can't actually be reproduced in film.

INTERVIEWER: At what point, during the creation of *Still Life*, did you realize that you were not using standard dialogue?

MANN: When I realized that the dialogue I'd written, which I'd liked by itself, didn't have the muscle I wanted. It became a way to get information across, and the play began to seem like educational theater. The piece seemed very leaden; it didn't have any poetry, it didn't have any drive or electricity or tension in it. And it didn't have the traumatic element.

INTERVIEWER: How did you get the invented dialogue and the material from the transcripts down to the "muscle," the "poetry"?

MANN: First, I became obsessed with the material, the story, and with what needed to be said. Then I found the form. For example, when I was editing the court transcript of the Dan White trial for *Execution of Justice*, I knew this was the spine of the play. I felt that I had to get the material in the right order, so that the audience would understand the trial. But that was only one layer, and I didn't know what the next layer would be. I'd edited the trial down well but that was just the first step. The rest came to me when I went to San Francisco for a full month. Once I was there, I heard the community story, breathed it and lived it.

When I went back to the raw material of that first draft, voices started to come at me. That's when I discovered that emotional noise and began to let it be words and responses and needs.

INTERVIEWER: How did the structure of *Still Life* evolve?

MANN: It's not mystical at all. The first draft was a series of monologues in a particular sequence for each of the three characters [distilled from taped conversations with a Vietnam veteran, his wife and his mistress]. Everyone who read the first draft loved it, then I had a reading and it was dead as a doornail. I didn't know why. I talked to my husband, Gerry [Bamman, actor] about it, and he said that he felt each monologue in its distinct form was fantastic, but he was curious as to why I had put the monologues in that particular order. I said, "Don't you see the connections between this moment and this one? Or this and this?" I indicated points in each monologue and how they related to points in others placed close to them in the text. He said, "Why don't you put the connections closer together?" Then he literally handed me scissors and tape. That was the beginning. Then all of my personal connections became so trippy and ultraclear that it was like I was on speed. A whole different part of my brain was working. I didn't sleep or eat for five full days. Before that, each monologue was about ten pages long. When I read a monologue I would *hear* the response in my brain, but it wasn't on the page. Now the response was there as I heard it. It was the beginning of my work with simultaneity, juxtaposition.

INTERVIEWER: What about the line breaks in the monologues? Were the original monologues in poetic form, as they are in the published version [*T.C.G. New Plays U.S.A.*, Volume I, ed. James Leverett, 1982]?

MANN: Yes. Those monologues were distilled down to ninety pages from the eight hundred pages of interview transcript. Obviously, when I began to narrow them down, they found their own rhythm, which was, in fact, iambic pentameter. I never had any fat in those monologues, even in first draft. There was never a wasted word. I wanted to retain the actual rhythms of the way each person spoke, in real language, during the interviews. That came from my training in literature and from my work with Shakespearean texts with director Michael Langham. So much of Shakespeare's poetry is in the rhythms of real speech; that's what iambic pentameter actually is! Many powerful moments emerge when speech rhythms change, for example, the witches in *Macbeth*, or the songs in Shakespeare's plays. I also learned about soliloquy from working with Shakespearean texts—they are, after all, conversations between the protagonist and the audience. I know from coaching actors the power of direct address, and so it became clear to me that I wanted to use it in *Still Life*.

INTERVIEWER: Did you realize the power and the poetry of everyday American speech while you were conducting the interviews for *Still Life*, or did that occur later during the writing process?

MANN: I realized it during the interview process. So many surprising moments occurred. I had expected combat imagery from the marine, but when I heard combat imagery from the two women, I realized that they had shared imagery, concerns, and common language. When Nadine said to me, "I've been in the jungle so long that even with intimates I protect myself," I thought, "What war were *you* in?" The language they spoke was an inspiration to me.

INTERVIEWER: Edward Albee says that each play has its own musical architecture. Is this true of your writing?

MANN: Yes. A Washington reviewer understood that element of *Still Life* and talked about the play as a fugue. I'm very aware of the music and rhythmic structure as I'm writing; it's not just instinct. Before I went into theater, I had to choose between music and the theater. I used to play three instruments, though I don't anymore.

INTERVIEWER: Why did you choose theater over music?

MANN: I knew I could never compose. I didn't have the skill. I felt I could become a better technician, but never master the creative side.

INTERVIEWER: Has working with transcripts, for example, the interviews you conducted and edited for *Still Life* and *Annula Allen* [which premiered at the Goodman Theatre, 1978], as well as the court trial you utilized in *Execution of Justice*, helped you to develop your extraordinary skill with dramatic exposition?

MANN: Yes. But the skill has partly come out of my experience as a director. I have directed many so-called well-made plays. I loathed having to do Ibsen first acts, because you have to make that exposition seem like it's *not* exposition, and it so baldly is. You must make it seem as if it is all coming out of character. That is hard work for directors and actors. Exposition is THE hardest thing to write. You must get the story out without being heavyhanded. The audience needs the exposition, they need information in order to make judgments and to be able to fully experience the piece. You cannot make judgments without that information. And my plays are *about* asking the audience to face that information, and to actively question it. That is the form and content of *Execution of Justice*. It is a trial. The audience is the jury. The audience must have the information. But finally, the audience must have a visceral reaction to the *play*. All of this information, this exposition has to be made theatrical, rather than expositional. You could write a whole book about this! But I do want to say that you've got to make it *theater*. And that means you've got to make the play an active, live, gripping, in-the-moment event for people. From beginning to end, the audience must experience the information in a visceral way so that they don't notice they are using their intellect; they must be sucked in by their emotions and love for story, and then they must use both intellect and feeling to sort out what they've learned. It's very complex. Given that we're in a world where there is film and television where exposition is sometimes over by the end of the opening credits, anything that smacks of old-fashioned exposition always makes me uncomfortable. I hate it. From that hatred, I think, came a drive to get at it in my own way. A way that satisfied me.

INTERVIEWER: How did you become interested in the Dan White trial [*Execution of Justice*]? [On November 27, 1978, Dan White—former policeman, former member of the Board of Supervisors of the city of San Francisco—shot and killed San Francisco Mayor George Moscone and City Supervisor Harvey Milk, a liberal, outspoken homosexual. Many believed the murders were politically motivated. White was tried and convicted of voluntary manslaughter. His relatively light sentence touched off serious riots in San Francisco's homosexual community. After his release from prison, White committed suicide.—Ed.]

MANN: I went to California to see the Eureka Theatre Company's production of *Still Life*, which was brilliant. They are a political theater, and they had been producing mainly English plays; until *Still Life*, they didn't feel that they had really seen a political playwright in America. They loved working on the play and said it was the most important show they had done with their company. The artistic director, Tony Taecone, said, "We love your work, and whatever you write, we'll produce. Why don't you write something for our company?" That was a fantasy come true. There were several things I was interested in writing, but I felt if I was going to write for a company, I should write something that was specific to their group or to their community. Then Tony quoted British playwright Barry Keefe, who said, "What about the Dan White trial? My God, if this had happened in England there would be ten plays about it." I vaguely knew about the trial, but I didn't know the details. That week I read Randy Shilt's book, *The Mayor of Castro Street*, about Harvey Milk, and I was astonished. The Eureka put together material for me. I read everything I could about the trial, made notes, and asked to get hold of the court transcript. When I returned in May, the people at the Eureka had the transcripts as well as ten weeks of newspaper coverage. During the next fourteen months (I was working outside of New York) I lugged it around in two suitcases. The month my husband and I were in Thailand working on David Hare's movie *Saigon*, I edited the trial, and decided who I needed to interview. There were many possibilities of approach to this material: I could have done the life of Harvey Milk, I could have made a murder mystery; instead I chose to use the trial transcripts and interview the community.

INTERVIEWER: Would you describe the function of the uncalled witnesses in *Execution of Justice*? Were they based on actual people?

MANN: I did interview many people in San Francisco, but the uncalled witnesses are an amalgamation of people, real and imaginary. *Execution*, like *Still Life*, is theater of testimony. I wanted to find out what would happen if you took away the old Perry Mason Fifties realism idea of the courtroom drama. I wanted to show people giving testimony, people on trial, a community on trial *and* a nation on trial. I also wanted to show the people who were *not allowed* to give testimony, and that's where the uncalled witnesses came in. I wanted to find a way to visually break down the walls of a courtroom, and I also wanted to show that in a trial of national significance, the community *must* be heard from.

INTERVIEWER: Was there ever a temptation to slip into the conventional use of dialogue and of scenes?

MANN: Yes. You should see the outs. It was so hard to keep to the form I had chosen because much of the information could have been relayed in half the time and written in half the time if I had written scenes. I had to constantly reinvent the wheel and find new techniques. In fact, the chorus of uncalled witnesses came in late. I don't think I would have come to that breakthrough if I had not recently directed *Oedipus*. I realized that the chorus was the community that had been affected by the characters and their actions.

INTERVIEWER: What is the significance of the sound motif of high heels throughout *Execution of Justice*?

MANN: The high heels are the sound that I always hear when I think of Mary Anne White running to meet her husband in the cathedral. I knew he was alone there, waiting for her. I knew he must have heard her running to him, and I heard that sound in my sleep. It's a sound image that provoked a visual for me of that wife running to her husband who had just committed murder. Her life is shattered in that moment of his confession; his life is shattered; he destroyed an entire community and he destroyed a movement.

INTERVIEWER: The word *homophobic* is never used in the play. . . .

MANN: It did not come up in the trial either, but I would hope it is a word which rings in your brain as you experience the play. I had a whole speech about it in an earlier draft, but I felt it was agitprop and decided to try to say something about it without naming it. That was a challenge I gave myself and I think the point is made stronger.

INTERVIEWER: How do you behave in rehearsal?

MANN: I hope well! . . . I directed the original productions of both *Annula Allen* and *Still Life*. When I direct my own work, I try to stay open. If something's not working, I'll try to fix it. I like that I don't have to go through anyone else before I make changes in the script; I can just rewrite it. As the director I try to look objectively at the play. I don't try to wear two hats at the same time. I watch the play. If it's not working, I talk to myself, the writer, say, "Don't blame the director! You have a problem!" Then I seek out ideas; I talk to the janitor, the designer, the producer, the actors. If something rings a bell, I use it.

INTERVIEWER: Have you directed the work of new playwrights?

MANN: Yes. I find most new playwrights are often less willing to rewrite than I am. But I am very careful as a director. I don't want to write anyone else's play for them; I want the playwright's intention to come through. I'm probably less willing to cut and change a script than most directors because I'm sensitive in this way to the writer. Perhaps too much so. I'm less hard on them than I am on myself. I have to examine that.

INTERVIEWER: Do you allow the writer direct access to the actors?

MANN: It depends entirely on the actors and the writer involved. Some writers don't know how to talk to actors and inadvertently say something damaging. It's a tricky situation. I certainly don't go by the old adage of keeping the writer away from the actors and the designers. I like collaboration, I like free channels! But I also want to make sure writers who are not experienced in the theater understand the etiquette, otherwise they hurt themselves, their play and other people during the rehearsal process. I carefully set up rules so that we can communicate healthily.

INTERVIEWER: As a director, do you often have to deal with emotional explosions during rehearsal?

MANN: I expect them. Especially from the actors because we are often doing deep emotional work. You have to judge whether the outbursts are healthy or destructive. If someone had walked into a *Still Life* rehearsal, they'd have thought they walked into a looney bin! But the work was fantastic, these actors knew exactly what they were doing. The explosions were about the work. However, when anger surfaces on a personal level, and does not relate to the work, I stop it. Cold. It is destructive and must not be allowed. By anyone. The work is at stake. If the writer is going to explode, I make sure it is outside of rehearsal, and with me. If there is validity in the writer's dissatisfaction we can talk about it. Hopefully, fix it.

INTERVIEWER: Would you tell us what a brain specialist once pointed out to you about the structure of *Still Life*?

MANN: Yes. It had to do with traumatic memory. She said that the juxtapositions, the form of *Still Life*, reminded her of the way the brain works when you are remembering a trauma. She said the play not only mirrored that brain function in the sense that the characters are in the process of remembering traumatic events, but also, the play itself seemed to her to be *my* traumatic memory of hearing their stories during the interview sessions. *Execution of Justice* also contains that element—it is an exploration of a community which has been traumatized by an event.

Maybe part of my attraction to and discovery of that form has to do with being female. Women sit around and talk to each other about their memories of traumatic, devastating events in their lives. Even women who don't know each other well! Sometimes, perfect strangers will sit and talk like other people talking about the weather or sports, except that it's about their divorce. You know? We often see the pain in one another and then we talk about it (I want to write a play about this, called *Talking Shop*). Most of what I know about human experience comes from listening. That's why it's very natural for me to believe in direct address in the theater. It is an extension of listening: I hear the stories, then I let *you*, the audience, have the same experience I had as a listener. I don't actually reenact these stories, I let you hear them. Hearing is very powerful for me. When I put these stories on stage, the audience experiences a direct interaction which is in the moment.

INTERVIEWER: It's interesting that the critics in New York responded by *directly* addressing *you*. Several even used your name, as if they were having a conversation with you, or writing you an open letter. Do you think this direct response from the critics was a repercussion of the form, the direct address you used in *Still Life*? For example, one critic contemptuously speculated, "O my dear, liberal, radical, feminist, juvenile Emily Mann! These people [the true-life characters] would be just as dreary and hopeless if there had been no Vietnam" [John Simon: "Still Life," *New York*, March 2, 1981].

MANN: Yes. We hit a *nerve* with *Still Life*. I stand by that. With three years' distance, I can understand why the play received that response and I can feel that it was, as I said, because we hit a nerve. But when I got the "direct" attack, I was devastated, depressed, enraged. Looking back, knowing what I know—that it went on to twenty productions and rave reviews both here and in Europe—I do believe it was a tribute to the work. In hindsight only, though. We got people very angry *and* very moved—the positive and the negative. We disturbed them; that's the goal. You can't write a play like *Still Life* and expect to be loved.

INTERVIEWER: Does the playwright have a responsibility to society?

MANN: Oh my God, yes. In a word, yes. In two words, absolutely yes. My plays are contextual.

INTERVIEWER: Why are so many playwrights choosing to write relationship plays? Why are they ignoring the larger questions?

MANN: I don't know.

INTERVIEWER: Are political plays being written but not produced? Are playwrights censoring their political viewpoints?

MANN: I hope that the playwrights are editing themselves. But I'm afraid they don't have any politics, that they have nothing to say except about relationships. That's my fear. I do think the *potential* for political plays is out there. This potential must be nurtured so that political playwrights will develop.

INTERVIEWER: How can we nurture this development?

MANN: We have to consider what is happening to new scripts at the literary manager level, the reader level. Who are the literary managers and artistic directors in our theaters? What they bring to a play is totally subjective. *Still Life* was rejected at the reader level. . . . I can't tell you how many theaters turned that play down. Who are these readers? It wasn't until after *Still Life* won the Obies that the regionals showed any interest. I think it is important to have people writing about our work, we need to be in the public eye. Mel Gussow's article on women playwrights, "New Voices in the Theater," [*New York Times Magazine,* May 1, 1983] was very useful. A good start. It sounds shallow, but when the literary managers and artistic directors see something in print which singles out different writers as important voices, the reaction is inevitably "Find me these writers," and "When these plays come in, put them on my desk!" It's important for the people in charge of theaters to find out about the *issues* which concern us as playwrights and to find out about the evolution of our work.

INTERVIEWER: Is the work of women playwrights affecting the work of male playwrights?

MANN: That's a fascinating question. Certainly the work of women like Megan Terry, Irene Fornes, Rosalyn Drexler, Rochelle Owens, and Ntozake Shange revolutionized the theater in the seventies. These women radicalized our perception of and our consciousness about theater. My instinct tells me that women's writing has to have affected men's writing, but I would have to discuss it with male writers to find out how women's work has consciously affected them. Certainly many male writers come to me and ask whether I feel that their female characters are drawn truthfully. They seek me as a colleague, as a director, and as a friend. I am sure that male writers have been made aware that they have a responsibility to their female characters.

INTERVIEWER: Of the contemporary women playwrights, whose work has affected you most?

MANN: Caryl Churchill has been a great solace. She is a brave writer. When I saw the last scene of *Top Girls*, I cried. I thought, "If I could write that scene I would die happy." To see that kind of material on stage made me happy, I felt I had a comrade-in-arms. Churchill's play, *Fen*, influenced some of the writing in *Execution of Justice*. It helped me to have the courage to go ahead with one of my instincts, to present a strong, theatrical, extreme image at the top of the play. I certainly respect Marsha Norman's work, though it is totally different from my own. I love watching her development. I feel stimulated by what she has to say and how she says it, though she is not as direct an influence as Caryl Churchill is. Ntozake Shange is a master of monologues; her sense of language and rhythm, and her poetry inspire me. There are more.

INTERVIEWER: Some of the playwrights we interviewed feel that there are no lost masterpieces, that the cream will rise to the top. Would you agree?

MANN: Wrong. I was amazed that although I had majored in English with a concentration on dramatic literature I had never come across playwright Rachel Crothers until David Jones brought me *He and She*, which I directed [BAM (Brooklyn Academy of Music) Theater Company, spring 1980]. I believe things can and do get lost. And there is the question of the unwritten, which Virginia Woolf so eloquently explored in her essay, "A Room of One's Own." Woolf poses the question "What would have happened if Shakespeare had had a sister who was equally talented?" Lost masterpieces and the unwritten or silenced voices are two big concerns for me and worry me a great deal, though I have great faith. Women are doing their work. We have things to say that people need to hear.

INTERVIEWER: Why have women novelists raced ahead of women playwrights in terms of publication and securing a place in contemporary literature?

MANN: The woman novelist can finish her work in total on the page. Novelists do not have to find a producer who believes in the work, and a director, actors, a theater. I'm not saying that it is easy to find a publisher—but you can at least finish the work in isolation. When I've felt upset about the theater, I've often dreamed of writing fiction so that I could feel I had finished a piece of writing without having to depend on other people to realize it. But my sister is a literary agent, and I know the other side of writing books; there are novelists and poets who spend five years on a project and get slaughtered, as we playwrights do, by bad reviews. Or cannot get published. There's no safe place to be if you are a writer.

INTERVIEWER: But what about places like the Eugene O'Neill Playwrights Conference? Or Winterfest at Yale Rep?

MANN: Quite the opposite of safe! What's scary is that often plays are presented as works-in-progress but they are actually being judged by the Big Gang of producers, and at a point where they should *not* be judged, but rather, absolutely protected and worked on.

INTERVIEWER: Where is the safest place to develop new plays in this country?

MANN: Away from New York eyes. If there is such a thing as a safe place, it must be far away from the meateaters, the naysayers. I don't think of New York and the environs around New York as a place to develop work. New York is a place to bring work when it is *finished*, when it is worked out, syllable by syllable, gesture by gesture. Then, if the critics want to tear it apart, it doesn't matter—you already believe in the play and even if they destroy the production with bad reviews, you, as a creative person, will not be destroyed. And you may have established an audience for the play outside of New York. You will go on to the next play, and hope to keep the other going in the regionals or in Europe. You cannot put a tender and developing work in front of these guys; they don't understand what the development process means. If you've seen a play work in ten cities, in front of ten different audiences, you can say, "I know the play works and it was beautiful." At that point, you will not be affected by the negativity and blindness here. We can't let them have that kind of power. They are in the midst of destroying playwrights in this country and we can't let them do it. That means we've got to take the power back. We can't keep them from saying things that will close a commercial production, or that can hurt us personally, but we can work and we can keep the plays alive. There is a network of caring people in theater all over the country, and outside this country who don't care about New York reviews, but rather, care about important voices. I also believe that publishing our plays is *crucial*. You've got to get on the written record. We have to make people aware of the different artists by writing about them intelligently, as well as publishing the actual work.

INTERVIEWER: Are there any mother/daughter plays in your future?

MANN: I have an incredible relationship with my mother—but I don't know what that play would be. I haven't found the story yet . . . autobiographical or otherwise. It's a relationship that fascinates me as a director; the mother/daughter scene in Crother's *He and She* is the one that everyone remembers, and is the reason I decided to direct the play. Mother/daughter is an important relationship to write about and I'm hungry to put it onstage—I just haven't found it yet. *Still Life* was on one level a letter to my father who approved of the war in Vietnam, and who said if I had been a boy, he would have sent me to that war. *Still Life* was my response to him.

INTERVIEWER: Did your father see a performance of *Still Life*?

MANN: Yes. He had great respect for the work, though he disagreed with the politics. It brought us together with new understanding and great forgiveness. That was beautiful.

INTERVIEWER: In *Still Life*, you explored domestic violence between men and women, and drew parallels to the international violence of the Vietnam War. The characters tell the audience about their savage experiences—what led you to the artistic decision to have the violence spoken, rather than dramatized?

MANN: I wanted to show the *effect* of the violence rather than stage it. While I was writing the play I saw *The Godfather* again on television and during the scene where Gianni Russo beats up his wife, Talia Shire, I realized that it had been staged as a turn-on. I knew, then, that I did not want to perpetrate the myth that violence is sexy, I did not want to be a party to it. That's why when you see *Still Life*, you see a battered woman, not a woman *being* battered. You see what this brutality has done to both the husband and the wife, and it's not sexy, and it's not fun. It's rare to see violence between men and women onstage or in film which is not somehow erotic. I want to break down those clichés.

INTERVIEWER: What is it in our culture that perpetuates this false depiction of violence as erotic?

MANN: I'm not sure; all I know is that I want to keep addressing the problem in my work.

INTERVIEWER: Have we cultivated a taste for violence?

MANN: We have a lust for it in this society.

INTERVIEWER: Was there something about the subject matter of *Still Life* that caused it to be turned down at many theaters before it gained the sanction of the Obies? Is there, perhaps, a subtle censorship of women's plays going on at the literary manager level, especially those that link domestic and international violence?

MANN: The literary managers and the artistic directors who are choosing their theater seasons are worried about their subscribers and given the economic times, I understand why. But I feel they are selling their audiences short. If they were willing to put on a good new American play, their subscribers would come to see it. Look at what [artistic director] Jon Jory has succeeded in doing with the New American Play Festival at Actors Theatre of Louisville. That audience has learned how to watch new plays and they are open to different voices, many of which are women's voices. The ability to watch new plays and see new forms can be learned and developed. It's a mistake to rob that subscription audience of a woman's point of view. Certainly the issue of domestic violence in our society, and explorations of the disappointment and rage that men and women feel for each other, are relevant to audiences in any part of the country. I would say that fully half the women I know have experienced physical violence, not just emotional, but physical violence from their lovers at some point in their lives. It's not a pretty subject and there are not many people who want to deal with the anger, the disappointment, and the violence between men and women. But we must make these explorations, so that we can move beyond.

INTERVIEWER: How did you meet the characters of *Still Life*: Mark, the Vietnam veteran, Nadine, his mistress, and Cheryl, his wife?

MANN: A woman friend of mine brought the real Nadine to see my play *Annula Allen* at The Guthrie Theater. Nadine went wild for the play and called me, saying, "I want you to meet a friend of mine who wants to tell you his war story." I said, "No, God, please . . . I don't want to do anything more about war after *Annula*." (*Annula* is based on the life of a central European Jew, 1900–1977, drawn from an oral history I made of her in London, 1974.) Then I found out this person had been in Vietnam. I said to Nadine, "I was in the antiwar movement; that war really chewed up my life, I'm still so confused . . . I can't really deal with it." She said, "Just meet him." I met him, and for three hours he talked in monologue about every atrocity he'd seen in Vietnam. I was so shellshocked by the time I got out of that room, I told him, "I can't handle this." He said, "Well, the real casualty of this war is my wife." That terrified me. I told Nadine I was frightened of Mark and the project. She said, "He's the gentlest man I've ever known." So I met his wife and the first thing she said was, "I'm constantly scared for my life, living with him."

I thought, "Now here's a play: One woman says he's the gentlest man she's ever known, and the other is afraid for her life . . . what is going on here?" It hooked me. But I am telling you, after I went through that series of interviews, and the last meeting where Mark made his confession, I had to get help. I gave the tapes to some volunteers at The Guthrie Theater to transcribe and I didn't look at them for almost a year. I couldn't face what it brought up for me. The most terrifying moment was when he told me how he found out that he loved to kill, that killing was the "best sex [he'd] ever had." I called different veterans' organizations and they said, "Oh, that's very common." [See also: Lt. William Broyles, Jr. (Ret.): "Why Men Love War," *Esquire*, November 1984.] Then a friend sent me a beautiful poem, which goes something like:

The sad thing is
When we send our young men to war
The young men die
The sad thing is
When we send the young men to war
The young men kill
And the sad thing is that
When we send our young men to war
They learn to love to kill.

Greek. Two thousand years old.

EVE MERRIAM

Eve Merriam was born in Philadelphia and has lived most of her life in Manhattan. She has written plays, poetry, fiction and nonfiction. She has also written for radio and television. Her plays include Inner City, The Club, Plagues for Our Time, Dialogue for Lovers, At Her Age, The Good Life: Lady Macbeth of Westport, I Ain't Finished Yet and Out of Our Fathers' House. Ms. Merriam's directing credits include Woman Alive: A Conversation Against Death and Domestic Issues by Corinne Jacker. Among Ms. Merriam's awards are the Yale Younger Poets Prize, Colliers Star Fiction Award and the National Council of Teachers of English Award for Excellence in Poetry for Children. Ms. Merriam serves on the Council of the Dramatists Guild and is on the Guild Committee for its annual Young Playwrights Festival. Her works-in-progress include The Seven Ages of Women and Wedlocked.

INTERVIEWER: You've had a long and distinguished career as a writer. You've written for radio, TV, films, magazines, newspapers, fiction and nonfiction for children and adults; you've composed song lyrics, written plays and musicals; and you're one of America's most anthologized poets. Are you sometimes surprised at the sheer volume of your work?

MERRIAM: Absolutely. Right now I'm trying to coordinate my work; I'm sending it to the Schlesinger Library, which collects my material. My oldest son was helping me to organize my lifetime of work last evening, and I said it's very depressing and exhilarating at the same time, but mostly, I feel baffled. I feel as though I'm a boat, a stationary boat, and this river has just gone past me. I started to publish when I was still an undergraduate. Good Heavens, it's almost fifty years of work! Just the sheer massing of paper! I had no idea of the *amount* that I've published. You know I've never kept a record of the number of poems and essays that went into print. But by now almost fifty books have been published.

288

I'm working on a major project at the moment which I'm calling *The Seven Ages of Woman*, a collection of the personal poems of my life, and perhaps some prose. I want to take a look at that and see the person that I've become. It may turn out to be a theater piece, I'm not sure.

INTERVIEWER: After reading a mountain of your work, I've come to think of you as a 'group of people' rather than an individual. My notes say, "Sad, serious, hilarious, cynical, weird, strong, vulnerable, critical, at once childlike and deeply mature, bravely political, highly individual, totally absurd . . . Eve Merriam is a Flying Circus of Words." You've had a long, passionate affair with language.

MERRIAM: Oh, that's the key to everything. Behind language, of course, are the emotions. I knew from a very early age the joy of language. That may be why I never became much of an athlete. I did all of my ballplaying and rope jumping and kidding around with rhyme and with the sound of language. Language always delighted me.

INTERVIEWER: Why do you write?

MERRIAM: I can only answer you in a double negative, because I can't *not* write. I have this in common with all the writers I know. It is a compulsion, an obsession. And it's terrible and glorious at the same time. When I'm not writing, I'm a mess. I really feel that my ego is not complete. Writing is a way of holding on to the universe, to keep from falling off, spinning away.

INTERVIEWER: Making order out of chaos?

MERRIAM: Well, it's a way of holding on to other people, of making comparisons among the wonderful discoveries that you find, even if you're in a tragic state, feeling so alone, so miserable. If I can write it and get it out of my system, then the outside world becomes more connected to my inner person. So it's a way of getting in touch with my own feelings. No, I wouldn't say it's order out of chaos. All emotions are chaotic. It's selectivity, it's a kind of pinning down, but I never become orderly. Never. It's making communication. I won't even say making *sense*, because a lot of things are nonsense. When one uses a metaphor or a simile, that's a connection. For me, it's a *human* connection. If I can say something is *like* something else, that's a contact.

INTERVIEWER: You've mastered many forms of writing. Which form is most important to you?

MERRIAM: Poetry. All my life I have written prose for only two reasons: one, to make a living for myself and my children; and secondly, to reach a wider audience. And really, the prose book that I wrote, *After Nora Slammed the Door* [Cleveland, World, 1964], which was an investigation of the unfinished women's revolution, was merely putting into a more accessible form what I had already said in a book of poetry called *The*

Double Bed from the Feminine Side [New York, Cameron, 1958]. I would *never*, never write prose if I didn't have to. And the pleasure in my life, at this stage, is that I've given up prose. I gave it up about five years ago. I don't even do book reviews any more. I won't do an article, no matter how much it appeals to me. I just want to concentrate on my two loves, which are very connected: poetry and the theater.

INTERVIEWER: What is the connection between poetry and play-writing?

MERRIAM: They both have a tremendous intensity. Theater, like poetry, requires *enormous* compression. And what they have in common is that they are both really dealing with the unsayable. In the theater, where you're dealing with dialogue, we never say what we really mean! Everything is indirection. We can't say it, we're too shy to say it, we're too angry to say it, whatever. The glory of the theater is to find some way to convey what's going on. The theater is always on a double track, just as poetry is on a double track of the inside and outside life. In the theater, by a gesture, by a look, you can convey a whole vocabulary. At least the kind of theater that I am most interested in, which is the non-naturalistic theater.

INTERVIEWER: Your book *Family Circle* was chosen for publication in the Yale Series of Younger Poets [New Haven, Conn. Yale University Press, 1946]. That must have been a quite thrilling experience as a young girl.

MERRIAM: It was one of the supreme joys of my life. The Yale Younger Poets Prize was, and maybe still is, the most prestigious award for a poet. I won it on the fourth try. I remember just dashing across the street to tell a friend, and the light had turned red and I thought, "I don't care if I get killed." [Laughter] Yes, it was an enormous pleasure. Incidentally, that book, *Family Circle*, has been reissued [New York, AMS Press, 1971].

INTERVIEWER: Does it still have Archibald MacLeish's introduction?

MERRIAM: Yes, yes.

INTERVIEWER: You once said of MacLeish, "He was my hero. I used to sleep with a copy of his *Conquistador* under my pillow."

MERRIAM: That's true. In the dormitory at college. I was so afraid somebody would steal it from me! I met him many, many years later, and I told him about that. I think he was quite touched. He was the judge of the Yale series the time I won.

INTERVIEWER: He wrote in the introduction, "The poems of Miss Merriam are meant to mean and be forgotten; that is their quality and not their defect." Would you talk a little about your reaction to this statement?

MERRIAM: I was livid. [Laughter] It seemed like such a backhanded compliment to me: "They are meant to be forgotten and not kept." One always hopes that one has said something which will remain.

INTERVIEWER: Including Mr. MacLeish, I'm sure.

MERRIAM: Yes. In his famous poem, *"Ars Poetica,"* he says, "A poem is not meant to *mean* but *be."*

INTERVIEWER: The classic double standard.

MERRIAM: Well, he obviously liked my poems and he did choose them for the Yale award, but it was bitter for me, yes. Because one always hopes to be praised. What I think he was saying was: "She has energy, she has a lot of momentum; these are carelessly dashed-off poems." That because of my *energy* there were vivid images in them. But they were not the stuff of eternity.

I don't know how much influence that had on me. I think it had a lot, because one of my saving graces is that I've always considered myself a "minor" talent. I have never had grandiose ideas. That's helpful in going on. At the same time, it can be a detriment, because there've been many times in the course of my writing career when I've felt, "Oh, I can't do this. I'm not capable of it. I really don't have the talent." But underneath, at the center, there *is* that core of confidence.

INTERVIEWER: Did you ever decide you were going to prove MacLeish wrong?

MERRIAM: Not consciously. My compulsion to write, especially poems, is something that there was no stopping. I was not encouraged by my family. I had the standard "one good English teacher." But the drive is there. John Erskine [American educator and writer, 1879–1951] said, "If you killed off all the horses in one generation there would be no more horses. If you killed off all the poets, in the next generation you'd have just as many as ever." I've been very fortunate in that I've made a substantial career out of poetry.

INTERVIEWER: That's very unusual, isn't it, to be able to earn a living as a poet?

MERRIAM: Yes. I'm extremely lucky. A good deal of my income comes from my young people's poetry which is widely anthologized. *Inner City Mother Goose* [New York, Simon & Schuster, 1969] sold close to one hundred thousand copies. But you don't become a poet to make money; you do it only because you must. It is not socially sanctioned. And when I was growing up, it was not something that you told your dates. When I went out, I said, "I'm a writer." I did not say I was a poet. There was that feeling that a *real* person, a real man, doesn't write poetry. Women classically have been considered inferior to men, therefore if we were going to go by the rules of the white-male-governed society, the thing to do is hide that you're a poet. And then the other thing you do *not* have going for you as a woman is that the muse of poetry is presented in myth as a female. You're the goddess in the *house*, you're somebody who has *inspired* a poet.

INTERVIEWER: Are *you* your own muse?

MERRIAM: No. I've been in love many times. Poets always are. They are always writing love poetry throughout life. But I don't have somebody there encouraging me and saying, "Write for me." In that sense, I think I *have* been my own muse. Because I've had to have my own approval, my own standard for going at it. Yes, I think you're right. Maybe in some ways I *am* my own muse. I've never thought of it before.

INTERVIEWER: You once said that the act of writing a poem during moments of despair begins by deepening the sadness one might be feeling, but ends by transforming one into a state of serenity and healing. Do you feel the same way about plays?

MERRIAM: No. No, I don't. A poem is a short form, very intensive. A play is such a *long* process, it's mulling inside you for so long, and taking different forms. And then you get to that glorious moment when the characters say to you, "You can't make me do this. This is *my* tone of voice. By now, I am who I am." So, curiously, a play is a less intensely personal process. Poetry has no clothes on it. A play has some clothing, there's some public face that is presented. People who are exclusively playwrights may not agree with that.

INTERVIEWER: You've said that poetry is the truth of our feelings. Some playwrights feel that the drama is the least truthful of the arts. I'm just wondering what value an art form has if it is based on lies or half-truths?

MERRIAM: Well, poetry is the most direct, and therefore I guess it's the most truthful, because you're not layering it with any kind of fiction. You're not making up a character. The minute I make up a character and put a person onstage, I am departing from the kernel of truth. So to that degree, it's so. Every playwright, every writer, wants to present the truth as she or he imagines it from their relationship to life. It's a hard thing to talk about, without giving specific examples. Some people who are playwrights are more comfortable hiding behind other personas, just as actors are. The classic image of the actor is a terribly shy, withdrawn person in life who can go into *Oh, Calcutta!*, and be the most uninhibited character. It's taking on a mask, a persona. In poetry, you're always taking *off* the mask, you're taking off your skin and presenting the *bone*, the beating course of life, the bloodstream. And when you get away from poetry, you're dressing life up to a degree. One of the reasons I like the musical form is that it is stylistic, very artificial, in a marvelous way.

INTERVIEWER: You mentioned that you prefer nonnaturalistic theater. What's wrong with realism and naturalism for you?

MERRIAM: It doesn't give me any new insights. It doesn't teach me something that I didn't know before. It hasn't the kind of charge or excitement that another person might get out of alcohol or drugs or an epiphany. The realistic theater confirms what goes on. Yes, *people* are like that. Yes, *life* is like that, that's true. But I think the classic example is Arthur Miller. When he departed from the realistic play, it's not accidental that the result, *Death of a Salesman*, was his most successful piece. Lillian Hellman is someone who interests me enormously as a *person*, and yet her realism, her plays, per se, didn't interest me that much. I mean, I want to write a play about *her*! It's her persona that fascinates me. But the plays in themselves? They're first-rate as far as the workmanship goes . . . but they don't have that leap into magic that the work, say, of Mabou Mines has for me, or Joe Chaikin's Open Theatre, or The Bread and Puppet Theater. It's not coincidental that I love working with Tom O'Horgan because he sees the theater as a circus, as some kind of monstrous clowning that's very related to the rituals of religion. I find that larger-than-life, or smaller-than-life, if you include some strange miniatures, is what turns me on. Not the "well-made" play.

INTERVIEWER: How about the rituals of playwriting? What is your working day like?

MERRIAM: I'm very sloppy. I make a lot of starts. I have at least eight started-and-not-continued plays in my file. It makes me furious with myself. I keep dreaming of being a neat person, and getting one idea, just being obsessed by it and working undistracted. I find in working on a play that I get an initial idea, a situation or a conceit, and it doesn't work out so well. It really is best when one finds the character first. Because it's absolutely true, that if you start with a character who obsesses you—and you have to be obsessed, of course— something is going to happen. How do you unravel that person in relation to somebody else?

I think I've led myself up the garden path when I have made a situation or a scene or a saying first rather than a character. I once imagined a setting of a tag sale. I thought, "Isn't this a marvelous metaphor to use?" And I started to say, "I'll have my character do a tag sale for her whole life." And then after I worked on it, I realized it wasn't a play at all. It became an almost throwaway speech in A *Second Opinion*, the play that I'm working on now.

So these situations and metaphors aren't lost in that mental sewing basket with the little bits of thread or the needles and pins. Things stick in there, and they get used for other things. I'm obsessed by Lillian

Hellman. She led me to other strongminded, achieving, unusual women in a time of great men. For example, Georgia O'Keeffe. Somewhere, somehow, that's a future play. I have the title: *Daddy's Girl*. I've got the beginning and I've got the end. I will get back to it. And I have a big work that I have been making massive notes on for years. It's a subject that fascinates me that I have dealt with in poems: the idea of a women's Utopia, the lost Atlantis. We're always searching for a time when we were not the inferiors. Once I get *A Second Opinion* out of the way, I'm going to concentrate on this big utopian piece, which is called *Down the Manhole*. [Laughter] I'm good at titles.

Next year I'm not going to do any teaching. I don't want to pin myself down. I'm not going to do an enormous number of poetry readings. I want to have the time that a theater piece will take. It's a long process, and you can't be in an exalted state if you are correcting papers. So I'm going to work away from home; I'm not going to have a telephone, and I'm just going to go deep into myself. You have to go into pain and suffering. It's hard work. I must do that in order to produce. I found with *A Second Opinion*, I was determined to do something which would be without a collaborator, without working with a composer, something that would not be based on anything else I had done. Not based on poems, not based on any kind of documentary material. All made up out of my own little head. So I got scared! And I found that I had to go to a sister playwright for support. I talked with Janet Neipris [whose interview in this book begins on page 312]. She was working on something new; we were bolstering each other. We made a pact that by the end of June we were each going to have something to show the other. And that was very useful, that little buddy system. Talking it out loud to her, just telling her my general ideas, was helpful. There are times when you just have to take yourself in hand and do that. I go through hell—everybody goes through hell—but I do it in the most roundabout way. I make unnecessary phone calls. I make dates for lunch. I go to the library. I go shopping. I do anything! I overeat, I overcoffee, until I get to that stage of self-disgust. And there is nothing for it but to get down to work. Often my first couple of pages will take me forever. It's very disturbing to me if the tone of voice for the character is not exactly right. I can't go on. I have to go back and redo it.

INTERVIEWER: Hearing the author's voice rather than the character's voice?

MERRIAM: Right! It is so unfair to the characters!

INTERVIEWER: What comes first, family or art?

MERRIAM: We women were brought up to serve and not to be self-centered. So our work is not thought to be important. It's ludicrous! I have supported myself and my children all my life! We've *never* been supported by a man.

INTERVIEWER: Even so, it's difficult to remember sometimes that writing is your profession?

MERRIAM: It's my work! It's what pays the rent. And yet, when a man is around, there is that feeling, "Oh, *I* should be the one to plan the meals, go food-shopping, take care of laundry and all the daily chores." It's a devastating defect we have. I hope a future generation's going to get more selfish. [Laughter]

INTERVIEWER: The concerns of women writers all over the world seem similar: How much to give to career and how much to loved ones.

MERRIAM: Of course, the enormous strength of the Women's Movement was consciousness-raising. We discussed feelings we had never expressed out loud before. That bonding is *enormously important*. You only have it in depth with a minority group. When you're in charge, you don't require such deep, secret waves of communication in order to get around the group in authority. I think this is why white males don't have intimate friendships. They talk about cars, they lie to each other about their conquests with women. They don't even bother to challenge one another about whether they're lying or not. It's difficult to be a man in these times.

INTERVIEWER: Is it up to us to educate them?

MERRIAM: No. We are educating them. Our first allegiance is to ourselves, to comprehend ourselves, to present ourselves and our feelings to the world and let men comprehend as much as they can and in that way become educated. No. To teach them, we would have to do the same job we did before!

INTERVIEWER: Rochelle Owens hears voices when she writes. Maria Irene Fornes sees colors. Do you experience any extraordinary phenomena in the process of creating?

MERRIAM: I *see* the whole thing. I see every detail.

INTERVIEWER: As on a movie screen?

MERRIAM: No. On a stage! Now that's one of the ways in which I feel playwriting and poetry are linked. Because, while poetry deals with all of the senses, it is visual more than anything else. Most of my metaphors, most of my images are visual. A great compliment once paid to me was that my poems were very "painterly." I am a frustrated painter in some ways. I know I've dreamed paintings. One of my sisters is a painter and my son is a painter.

INTERVIEWER: Do you "paint" stage pictures?

MERRIAM: I think so. Because I *see* it. I absolutely *see* the scene, and I have a sense of what those characters look like. The scene and the action of what's going on occur to me directly as I am writing. And the only time that has not happened, interestingly enough, is when I have taken poetry material and transferred it to a stage. Then, because the poems themselves are full of visual images, I can leave it to a director as to what kind of nonverbal movement they want on the stage. But when I'm in control of characters, oh yes. I see the chair, I see the bolt on the door. But I don't see colors so much. Actually, now that I think of it, the set is more like a black-and-white movie. I don't see brilliant colors in it. That's funny. Maybe to see brilliant colors would get me too excited or take me out of it.

INTERVIEWER: Is the creative drive at all related to fear of death?

MERRIAM: It's *tremendously* related. In my case, it's so strong that it's the most powerful force that there is. I believe, superstitiously, that if I did not write I would not be alive. Writing is breathing for me. It's a life force, this need to pin things down. I've always been conscious of being on a spinning globe. I deal with words as a way of fixing something. I get a metaphor or an image and I must pin it down to keep from flying off that globe. Yes, when all is said and done, it's that vulgar and that direct: we create to overcome the fear of death. But it is a saving grace *not* to be too aware of that, you know, *not* to say while writing, 'This is my immortality. This is my stand against the unknown." Writing is the throbbing, moving, small "yes" against the great fixed "no."

INTERVIEWER: How do you go about building a visual poetic image on stage? Are there certain images that you would only render onstage because they need that specific dimension?

MERRIAM: Yes, very much so. A piece of mine that failed in its first incarnation, *Viva Reviva*, a feminist musical . . .I had an image in my head. We couldn't do it, because the director felt that it was complicated. They didn't have the money, and it couldn't be done. But this was a revisionist version of history. I took four characters: Eve banished from Eden, Ophelia coming back from the drowned, Penelope and Circe as two sides of the same coin with Ulysses, and Joan of Arc, who refuses to burn. And the image that I had from the very beginning is that I wanted the ruins of a Greek temple and I wanted four caryatids—you know, those pillars that have a woman's face on top? I carried around a photograph—I had never been to Greece, but I had seen pictures in *National Geographic* and on postcards—I knew what I wanted! I would have these four pillars, these four women, I was dealing with the four corners of the world and the four winds and the four everything. I wanted their faces somehow there in a ruined area, because this is what patriarchal society has done. There is this ruin, and yet the strength of them remains. Well, that's not a poem. That's a visual thing on the stage. It's not a movie, because it's not something that vanishes and disappears. I wanted it there throughout the whole piece, as the living subtext for all to see. That absolutely had to be a theater piece, it had to have that image.

INTERVIEWER: It was too difficult to create?

MERRIAM: Yes. It was the director's first time out; she had been a choreographer. She was using a lot of movement and the space was small; she said it was just going to take her whole budget. I think she felt the idea would somehow be cluttering.

INTERVIEWER: You gave in with good grace?

MERRIAM: Yes. Because the life of the play didn't depend on it. If it were a matter of deforming the text, I would fight. Ted Mann [producer] wanted me to change the ending of *The Club* [for the Circle in the Square production in 1976], and I refused to do it. Lyn Austin [producer, Lenox Theater Center] wanted me to change my work, too. At the risk of not being produced, I would not do that. With *Inner City*, [music by Helen Miller, 1971], which was my first experience, and on Broadway, the pressures on me were *tremendous*. And I would not give in *at all* on the text. I *love* Tom O'Horgan [director of *Inner City*], but he wanted to have a mask of Nelson Rockefeller, who was governor at that time, and I said "It's not *about* Nelson Rockefeller. And this will just be too specific." And he was desperately eager to have a first-act curtain that would have something powerful. And I said, "No, I won't!" When it's a matter of fighting for the text, I will fight. On a set you very rarely get what you want, and you don't always get the actors you want. I've compromised a *lot* on actors, and been miserable because of it. But those are the exigencies.

INTERVIEWER: Is there a difference in your behavior during rehearsal when you are the writer with someone else directing your work and when you are the director staging another playwright's work?

MERRIAM: Very different. When I am the playwright and someone else is directing my work, I tend to think of myself as the ideal playwright, because once the director has been selected I am totally respectful. I will not talk to actors directly, I will never interrupt rehearsals, as much as I may want to; I just take written notes and then talk to the director afterwards. Anything a director asks me to do, even if I disagree totally, I will try to do. If the director thinks that it needs something added here or there, I will do it. I think you have to trust somebody else's vision. It is unfair to a director to say, "No, I disagree." That's the way in which I consider myself ideal. Also I pride myself in having the fastest pen, because I love to rewrite during rehearsals, I'm very good at it. I'm completely involved in it, and whatever I am asked to do I do. You can criticize my plays, but as a playwright in rehearsal I'm top-rate.

When I am directing my own work, I think I have done a better job in at least one case than with another director. Because my vision is clearer. Another director came in and did the same piece and it became too cluttered. The other director couldn't stand to have empty space. She didn't trust the words as much as I did. So the piece was too busy. But, by and large, I don't want to direct my own work. I'm very strongminded, and if I both write and direct, somewhere something is going to get short-changed. I'm better off with somebody else having the vision.

When I direct another person's piece, I'm good in some respects and not so good in others. I'm meticulous about respecting a playwright's suggestions . . . in as delicate a way as possible. Because I am a play-wright, I comprehend the work. I am able to talk to the cast and give them the subtext, explain what the play is about in an articulate way. I'm a wonderful director vis à vis the playwright, vis à vis what the play is all about, but I think I have a *lot* to learn by way of dealing with actors' vocabulary. As a writer, I don't have that shorthand that actors and old hands at directing have. I believe in giving actors as much leeway as possible. I don't like imposing my will. I have ambivalent feelings about directing. I like the sense of power; it's thrilling for women to have that power. I'm a good director in that I can visualize the set; I'm good at working with a set designer, because I have my own ideas. I'm good at the costume design. I may be too strongminded, but I have a vision to bring. I know what kind of lighting I want. When I talk to a lighting designer, I talk in terms of music, because I don't know the technical terms. I want to do some more directing, but the highest priority is to write. I must say that a playwright who is not respectful of a director makes it hard. I have worked with playwrights who will interrupt and talk to the actors. You absolutely have to respect the chain of command in the theater. To do anything else is just not professional.

INTERVIEWER: So you don't believe in democracy in theater?

MERRIAM: Theater isn't a democracy. Theater is a benevolent au-tocracy at work. Once a director is chosen, until that person is proved absolutely incapable, I think you must go along. Just as when you have chosen a cast, you go with that cast. If you find, at some point, that your choices are ruining the play, *then* you make changes.

INTERVIEWER: Where are today's rebels and anarchists of the theater?

MERRIAM: Who knows? I don't think "daring" is any particular place. One can't say, "It is in regional theater." We know it's not on Broadway. I think that's *all* we know. In some ways, Off Broadway is becoming as rigidly classified and as expensive as Broadway is today. I don't know that the O'Neill Playwrights' Conference necessarily is the most adventurous.

You just can't afford to think about it. You just go ahead and do whatever your demons and angels force you to do.

INTERVIEWER: But where are the Clifford Odets and the Hallie Flanagans of today? Who's shocking us? Who's speaking for the underdog?

MERRIAM: Who's speaking for the underdog? I don't know! David Mamet's language is shocking to a degree, but of course that becomes stereotypical and one gets accustomed to that. It may not be any *one* person. We may look back and see that there *is* a body of work, that there is a sensibility that belongs to this era. There may be a women's sensibility which is not clear to us at this point. Certainly we've gone beyond self-pity. I don't know that one can say we are in a period of anything specific. There is no group of playwrights leaning any particular way. The Mabou Mines people still work productively together. I was very sad when Joe Chaikin's group disbanded. One always hopes for a satiric group to form, a group of writers and actors. But essentially this *is* a lonely craft, you do have to go your own way. The unfortunate thing is that you have to be a salesperson as a playwright. It's the most difficult craft, and once you have finished your work you still have the problems of working with other people and getting a theater to produce it. There have to be enormous gratifications or there wouldn't be so many people doing it!

INTERVIEWER: Is there a female aesthetic?

MERRIAM: Yes. I know it's not fashionable to say that. I think there is a female aesthetic. We women are more tuned in to our bodies, and I think our language sometimes reflects that. We may find a physicality in some women playwrights' work that you will not find in men's. The men may stay at the "fuck you" verbal level, but frequently women have an *erotic* quality in their work that often does not come through in the work of male playwrights. The longing and the attachment for another human contact may be more accessible to women playwrights than to men.

INTERVIEWER: When you say "erotic," do you mean as opposed to "pornographic"?

MERRIAM: Yes. I mean erotic art dealing with the body with two people on an equal level. Pornography is the slave-master relationship. I'm talking about equality and acceptance and the joyousness of the body, which is something the Women's Movement has brought about.

INTERVIEWER: Do you think women have more empathy than men?

MERRIAM: Yes. It may be empathy or it may be a kind of a strange narcissism, this putting ourselves in another person's place or injecting another person into us. Maybe it comes of not being out in the world as much. Perhaps we take that other person "into" us and therefore take on the characteristics of and comprehend that person more.

INTERVIEWER: You were one of the founding mothers of the modern Women's Movement, perhaps *the* founding mother; you were writing feminist material way before Friedan, Bird, Greer, et cetera. You collected these ideas together finally under the title *After Nora Slammed the Door*, and that was published at about the same time as Friedan's *The Feminine Mystique*, in the early sixties?

MERRIAM: *Nora* came out at the same time, but it had been written before. My book was principally based on a series of essays that I wrote: "Myths About Women in Our Time" [The Nation, 1958–1959].

INTERVIEWER: Even in the late forties you were touching on feminism.

MERRIAM: I had started to write in that field in the late forties, the "Myths About Women" were published in the late fifties. And *After Nora Slammed the Door* came out in the early sixties. So, yes, certainly as a public writer I was, I guess, the first in the wave of feminist writers.

INTERVIEWER: Yet you did not receive any of the publicity or credit that was accorded to Greer, Steinem and Friedan.

MERRIAM: No, but I think that's because I'm a poet. Even in my prose, I wrote in a kind of cryptic, ironic, heightened style. *After Nora Slammed the Door* had, in addition to the myths, a series of poems in it and cryptic, gnomic essays, so it didn't have the kind of accessibility that Friedan's work did. It was not as journalistic, and Friedan took one point and she addressed herself to a white-middle-class audience in the suburbs, and said, "You are victims. As women you are suffering malaise." It was the right book at the right time. My work, with a few exceptions, has always been too soon. I wrote *The Nixon Poems* [Atheneum, 1970] and dedicated it to the Constitution four years before Watergate. *After Nora Slammed the Door* was approximately ten years too early. *The Double Bed*, a collection of poems which I published in the early fifties, was a totally feminist book. I think the only work of mine which was on time target was *The Inner City Mother Goose*; it came out in the late sixties, dealt with conditions in the inner city and was the right book at the right time. The theater adaptation was too soon. *Inner City* was presented on Broadway [1970–71] when Broadway had not built up a black or non-middle-class audience. So that was too soon. Most of my work has been just in advance, but you can't control your own psyche. There's no way that I can say I have not had to overcome bitterness and envy at people who have achieved great recognition. And so it's been very good for my ego that my play *The Club* has gone as far as it has. I thought that would be a tiny little feminist work that would never get beyond a small feminist audience. But it's still going on all over the world. It amazes me. It's been done twice in Japan. It's been done again in Australia, and it will probably continue to go on. You just have to take your licks and go forward because, basically, you write because you *must* write, you hope to make a living at it, you do what you can, you get your head bashed in and you just pick yourself up and do something else.

INTERVIEWER: Your work always seems to create a scandal. Didn't you have some hate mail when *After Nora Slammed the Door* was published?

MERRIAM: Yes, I did, but I had received hate mail before. I wrote a book for children in 1960 called *Mommies at Work* [New York, Knopf, 1961], and I received hate mail from women who thought that mothers should not go out to work. It was ludicrous. And I attacked Philip Wiley's notion of Momism in *After Nora Slammed the Door*. I attacked a big sacred cow, Ashley Montagu's *The Natural Superiority of Women*, which I don't believe in. I don't believe in the natural superiority of any group. I felt that Montagu was really being snide. It was sort of a fancy Norman Mailer, D. H. Lawrence approach: "You're so wonderful; you can have babies. That's *your* creative effort, and *we* create in our *work.*" So I made some *men* uncomfortable by my feminism and I also made some *women* who were passionately devoted to the status quo uncomfortable. Because I said dirty things out loud! And then I said we are living in a money society, and when you are not in a position to earn money, you are necessarily dependent beings, you are inferior. Flat out. And that troubled people. It still does. And I still believe it. We're still living in this capitalist white male society, and so you have to earn your own way; if you don't you have to manipulate and be coy and cute. And inferior.

INTERVIEWER: Some people say "I'm not a feminist, I'm a humanist." Were these terms ever separable?

MERRIAM: Yes, they were. When I first began to write, the word *feminist* was a very dirty word in common parlance. There was no women's movement per se. Don't forget that the thrust of my work was in the nineteen-fifties and nineteen-sixties, and the organized Women's Movement did not begin until the late sixties. So I would go on interviews for books that I had written and there would always be that chip-on-the-shoulder television interviewer, and he'd say, "Oh. You're a *feminist.*" Meaning "And you're a *ballbreaker.* You're somebody who doesn't like me." And I would say, "No, I'm *not* a feminist. I am a humanist. I'm someone who believes in personhood for both sexes." It seemed a way of not offending men and trying to show them that there was something in it for them. There *is* something in it for them. But more and more I feel male privileges have to be given up in order for the Women's Movement to develop further. So I think it is a cop-out.

INTERVIEWER: To say "I'm a humanist"?

MERRIAM: Yes. I used to do it a lot. It made interviewers like me better. I have always been very conscious of the fact that I am the mother of sons and that I *do* want a better world for my sons. I'm uncomfortable sometimes with certain feminists who really cut off the world of men. I always feel *I'm* the man in their presence. But I am a feminist. I always have been one, and I expect to remain one.

INTERVIEWER: So you wouldn't be likely to soothe an interviewer anymore?

MERRIAM: No, no. No, no. But don't forget that I am at a stage of my life and career where there is a body of work that's established, and I am who I am. And I feel I can stand up for that.

INTERVIEWER: So you don't mind being called a "woman playwright"?

MERRIAM: Well . . . That's dicey, isn't it? I guess I do mind. Because I never wanted to be a "poetess." I guess there's still something pejorative about it. I *don't* want to be a "woman playwright," because I don't want to have my things done in a woman's theatre exclusively. It smacks of a certain kind of ghettoization, even if one chooses it. I have been lucky in that my work is in the main arena, and I like the fact that it's feminist work that's in the main arena. That that's where I want to be. I would never define myself as a woman playwright.

INTERVIEWER: Is there an equivalent label to "feminist," with all its positive and derogatory connotations, for male playwrights?

MERRIAM: Oh, no. No. Because that's the patriarchal standard. What would you say? Penis playwrights? [Laughter]

INTERVIEWER: I'm just thinking of plays like *Hurly-Burly* [by David Rabe], *Glengarry Glen Ross* [by David Mamet], which are about the concerns of men, and in which women are referred to negatively. Yet critics don't say, "Here's another 'Manist' play."

MERRIAM: By and large, male playwrights have been in the forefront. Since they're male, they have male concerns and that's what we get.

INTERVIEWER: What's been the effect of motherhood on your art?

MERRIAM: Profound. I did not have children until I was in my mid-thirties because I thought I could not reconcile my writing career and motherhood. And then when I *wanted* to have children, there was nothing rational about it, it just came on me. I was writing a short story and the story turned in my hand and became a story about a woman who wanted to have a child. Because I had sons rather than daughters, I became concerned about what life is like for a man. Some of my best work has been about reconciling motherhood and a career, of dealing with that continuing dilemma.

INTERVIEWER: Are your sons proud of you as a writer?

MERRIAM: They are! It touches me very deeply. Just last month I went to the University of Illinois; my younger son was getting a Master's Degree in Library Science and I was asked to come and give a talk on censorship. He surprised me because he gave the introduction and presented me. My older son, who is an artist, has illustrated a book of my children's poetry, and he's done posters for some of my theater works.

INTERVIEWER: Why did you write *I Ain't Finished Yet* [New York, Samuel French, Inc., 1982]? After using all white females from history in *Out of Our Fathers' House* [1976], did you make a conscious decision to concentrate on black women?

MERRIAM: No, what happened is that Vinette Carroll, the black director and producer, saw *Out of Our Fathers' House* on television [1980]. She called actress Cicely Tyson and said, "I know Eve Merriam's work and I think you should get her to do a piece for you dealing with black women, a sort of counterpart to *Out of Our Fathers' House*." So Vinette approached me, and I thought it was a terrific idea. Then I met with Cicely a number of times; she's from Jamaica and wanted me to use a Jamaican figure, which I did. I did a lot of research and there was a really harrowing sequence about women in the sugarcane fields in Jamaica being attacked by the boss. By the time it came around to being performed at the Manhattan Theatre Club [1981], Cicely was no longer involved in it. Sheldon Epps, who was the director, felt that it would be better to concentrate on the North American experience rather than using a Jamaican figure. So I gave in on that. I don't know. I would have liked the Jamaican sequence, it was *extremely* powerful. And I had stunning historical Jamaican music which would have added a whole other dimension to it. Originally the character of Ma Rainey was not in it. The Manhattan Theatre Club wanted more music, so they asked me to put in Ma Rainey, which I did. It's interesting to see now that August Wilson has written a play about Ma Rainey. I'm eager to see it.

INTERVIEWER: Why did you select characters such as Moms Mabley, Fanny Lou Hamer, Sister Tessie, Hannah Tutson, Ida B. Wells, when you might have chosen more famous black women from history?

MERRIAM: I didn't want to use anybody who was—as in *Out of Our Fathers' House*—part of the system. I wanted people who were non-accommodating. I didn't want to use Harriet Tubman or Sojourner Truth, because they were well known. Their stories had been told before. I knew the life of Ida Wells, because I have written a young people's book of biographies in verse and had used Ida. I *loved* her life. I knew that I wanted to use Fanny Lou Hamer because I had heard her powerful speech at the Democratic Convention in Atlantic City in 1964. Hannah Tutson's testimony about the Ku Klux Klan in the Reconstruction period came directly out of my book *Growing Up Female in America* [New York, Doubleday, 1971]. The anonymous ex-slave came from my friend Gerda Lerner. She had written a book about black women in white America. It seemed to me that was a marvelous beginning, to show slavery from the point of view of the daughter who was rebellious, to show how the mother had had to accommodate herself and how the daughter had *not*. From the first time I ever heard Moms Mabley I thought, "Oh, I've got to use her in *something*, I don't care what!" Sister Tessie was an amalgam. It was important to have one character who represented the church experience, because it is significant to black experience. I thought that was a good way to show black male domination and women accommodating, trying to get around it. Sister Tessie is an invented character, as is the anonymous ex-slave, although they are founded on true documentation. Maybe chronologically was not the way to do it, but I ain't finished yet with that piece. [Laughter]

INTERVIEWER: As a playwright, how do you view what is going on politically in this country and in the world at large?

MERRIAM: I think a lot of people would like perhaps to be writing more politically than they are.

INTERVIEWER: Why aren't they?

MERRIAM: Well, it's not just the fear that it won't be produced. There is the fear of not being competent, that one cannot encompass what is going on. There is so much shifting. I've got a mass of notes. I was going to do an opera about Dioxin. I have a whole file called *The Love Canal*. I must have half a dozen political projects that I haven't gone forward with. And I daresay an awful lot of people you're talking to have the same situation. Emily Mann is doing political things. I wanted to do something immediately and urgently about Three Mile Island, and in fact I spoke to The Public Theatre. I said, "Let's get six playwrights and we'll all sit down like beavers and just digest all of this material, get something on immediately, immediately, immediately." Well, it was unwieldy, it couldn't be done. And then what happens is that one's passion, unless there are other people around you supporting it, tends to diminish. It comes back to that desperate need of homes for playwrights. The Public Theatre is not really a home. It is Joe Papp. To do some East European plays, okay, that's good, but that's not paramount as far as I can see. I wish Joe Papp had a workshop. I wish he would invite me and two dozen other playwrights, and just say, "Come." You know, "Here, fall on your ass. Fall on your face. Do political things. We'll give you some actors, we'll work things out." And I don't mean sardonic little things like Jules Feiffer's. I mean *real* political stuff, in an ongoing way. And if, indeed, anything good comes out of it, to then show the public outside the Public Theatre! I *long* for that. Some woman called me a few months ago and said she wants to do a political revue: "Do you have anything in your files?" Everybody's just looking for little things, which will be jokes about Reagan and the Gipper, or jokes about Mondale and the ghost of Humphrey. That's not what's needed. One needs a group situation. For years I talked with the people at Symphony Space [in New York City] about getting together a political satirist group. I would like to be a part of that. It just doesn't exist.

INTERVIEWER: What do producers or the theaters fear from the artists grappling with the larger political issues?

MERRIAM: But artists are not grappling. See, we're saying, "Well, a producer's not going to put it on. Is a producer going to come along if I write a play now about nuclear power that says something new?" I have to have so much confidence in myself, be so monomaniacal that I'm going to do it come what may. Whereas if you're passionate about character relations, and they're not that dependent on any kind of political situation, you say, "Well, I can always deal with myself." Now anything which is going to be significant, you may say, must deal with characters. But it's not always so. Look at Brecht's plays. I miss him so terribly, because I look at situations and I say, "Brecht would be writing a play about this."

INTERVIEWER: Do you think that Brecht would have been overwhelmed in a world of impending nuclear doom?

MERRIAM: No. He had such a massive ego. He had genius. He would have confronted it. He would have done half a dozen plays about it. Look at Jonathan Schell's book [*The Fate of the Earth*]. He transformed people. Rachel Carson [*The Silent Spring*] transformed people. If the passion is there and continuing, it will transform people.

INTERVIEWER: Well, both of those writers dealt with their concern to save the world in a nonfiction way. What does it take to make that leap to the stage?

MERRIAM: I don't know. I think we're suffering a failure of nerve. When you do a play, you have to have that audience or else it doesn't exist! You need that family support. You've got to have buddies who say, "Come on! Come on! Yes, yes! You can do it! We can all do it together."

INTERVIEWER: Do you think that's why the British playwrights are more political?

MERRIAM: Oh, *absolutely*! There is no question about it. Well, first of all, they're smaller geographically, so they're a much more homogeneous group. They have a more cohesive theater situation. Here you have all of these regional theaters quite separate from one another. And then you get into a little hidebound thing where a few theaters have their little groups of playwrights and directors, and that's that. . . . So you have to go to the outside.

INTERVIEWER: Is there an outside now? You've lived through the whole Off Off Broadway movement, but it seems that movement is almost dead now.

MERRIAM: I did *Plagues for Our Time* at La Mama Experimental Theater Club last year [1983]. We had a budget of six thousand dollars. It was ludicrous! Twenty people in the cast, and so little money.

INTERVIEWER: Do you feel isolated?

MERRIAM: I feel extremely isolated. And yet I have so many playwright friends! But we talk about feeling isolated. I say to friends, "Don't be discouraged! Here's a list of twenty theaters you can go to, and use my name!" And yet when it comes to myself, I die a thousand deaths. I can't make one call on my own behalf. Yet the will to work is so strong that we do keep on writing.

INTERVIEWER: Is there a possibility that university theaters are the answer? A safe harbor for the development of political work?

MERRIAM: To a degree.

INTERVIEWER: Aren't these institutions underused? Hundreds of productions of *The Boyfriend* and *Charley's Aunt* on public money.

MERRIAM: Well, see then you run up against problems. When I was playwright-in-residence at Ithaca College [1979], there were tremendous protests about my play *Lady Macbeth of Westport*. There were terrible letters in the local paper, people saying they just were not going to subscribe to the university theater anymore, that my work was disgusting and blasphemous. Ludicrous! While the university stood behind it completely, I have no idea whether, on the next go-round, they might prefer to have something a little less "controversial."

INTERVIEWER: They're not going to risk you taking another swipe at the American middle class?

MERRIAM: Well, they didn't get funded again.

INTERVIEWER: Is that your fault?

MERRIAM: No, I don't think so, but nobody else has done the play.

INTERVIEWER: In *Lady Macbeth of Westport* [1972], the husband carries a bomb aboard a plane and blows himself up with eighty-seven innocent passengers to get the insurance money.

MERRIAM: Becomes a millionaire and gets his picture on the cover as *Time*'s Man of the Year because he supported his family in style. It's disgusting how relevant that piece still is. We talk about the consumer society. The "consuming economy" consumes *us* as people.

INTERVIEWER: You mentioned giving a talk on censorship at your son's university. Will you comment on the issue of censorship of writers in America? You've been a victim of it several times yourself. And others have been victimized because of your writing. For example, the teacher Clark Natwick, who lost his job for allegedly committing an "immoral" act: He loaned your book *The Inner City Mother Goose* to a student. Whatever happened to Mr. Natwick?

MERRIAM: He was dismissed. He fought the case; the Teachers' Union in California fought it. He became a printer in order to support his family. After seven years he was reinstated and he went back to work, I think for one day, and then he remained a printer. Interestingly enough, when I did a special new edition of *The Inner City Mother Goose* with an introduction detailing all of the censorship in it, I got Clark's firm to print it. We thought that was a certain kind of poetic justice. We're still in touch. I felt terrible. And there are a number of teachers who have been fired in connection with *Inner City Mother Goose*, and I feel awful for all of them.

INTERVIEWER: What was it about *Inner City Mother Goose* that created such a furor?

MERRIAM: There were police groups who didn't like things that I said about policemen in it, because I suggested that policemen—in certain circumstances, because they didn't earn enough money—might take a bribe. Some people found the living conditions I described harsh. They hid behind sanctimoniousness and claimed that I was teaching children to commit violence, which I wasn't.

INTERVIEWER: Was racism involved?

MERRIAM: In a way, yes, because no censorship ever came from black communities; the censorship all came from very far right-wing white communities, who just didn't like the kind of material the book dealt with.

INTERVIEWER: You were accused in print of plotting to destroy the entire city of Baltimore. . . .

MERRIAM: Yes. But I've written a whole essay on that [in revised edition of *Inner City Mother Goose*, 1983]. I'll talk about regular censorship in the theater and I'll talk about self-censorship, too. In the play *Inner City*, there was a monologue which dealt with a woman having made love during her menstrual period. A producer who wanted to do the show later was very troubled by that. I was new in the theater, and I just assumed that the theater was a place where you could say and do anything. I had also had a monologue in there during previews, which we later took out—this was in 1970—about a woman who talked about having to take birth-control pills and the side effects, and she said very blithely, "Maybe I'll make it with another woman. That way I won't have to worry about the side effects." And this was in a Broadway show. Now, *at the time* it seemed to me the cutting of that number was not because of censorship—the actress playing it had left the show and we didn't need a number for her anymore. But it is the sort of thing that did raise eyebrows in that era. I don't think my work in the theater has been censored overtly or directly by somebody saying, "Take this out because I don't approve of it."

INTERVIEWER: Are you suggesting that censorship in theater is covert?

MERRIAM: Yes, I think so. The theater has a reputation as a free institution, and it would be very hard for somebody to come out and say, "I'm censoring this because of the audience." I have dealt a lot with menstruation. I'm affected by blood. It's a thrilling image. For women blood means one thing and it means something else for men. It's quite marvelous. I use it a lot. Now I had one reading of *Wedlocked* [1984], and the director told me in advance she was going to censor it. She said, "For this audience, we're not going to do a piece about a menstrual period. We are not going to use the word *fuck* for this audience." She told me in advance, and I didn't feel that it was important enough to fight over. But that's censorship. Self-censorship, of course, is the most insidious and the most dangerous. I've engaged in it all my life. That may sound odd, because much of my work is outspoken. . . .

INTERVIEWER: You're said to be one of the most censored writers in the United States.

MERRIAM: Yes. What I want most of all is to convey the inchoate, the things that people can't say and are afraid and ashamed to say. A great quote of Thoreau's: "I know how despicable mankind can be, because I know myself." We are all despicable and we all have moments of grandeur, because we are human. I want to be able to bring that spottedness out into the world. So I don't want to censor anything overtly political or that could be considered disgusting. Of *Wedlocked*, there are feminists who have said to me, "You're holding a woman up to ridicule and to shame and you shouldn't do this." I will not censor myself in that area. I censor myself in doing political work because I discourage myself ahead of time. Self-censorship takes forms that are not necessarily in terms of "Will the Reagan administration pass this?" It's self-censorship in terms of the critics. I would dearly love to get rid of the Mel Gussow and the Frank Rich inside my head. So often I hear myself saying, "Oh, they won't think *that's* very original or clever." That's tremendous self-censorship! That's the worst: "What will the critics say?" I have been hit very hard by male critics.

INTERVIEWER: What do you think about that?

MERRIAM: Well, in some cases I think they're justified, and in a lot of cases I think they're not. I had a very severe criticism from Richard Eder on *Viva Reviva*. I felt that the things he said about it were correct. It *was* a bad production, and I think a lot of my writing in it *was* too polemical. Frank Rich's criticism of *I Ain't Finished Yet* was all wrong, because he wanted me to write a different play. He was not willing to take it on its merits. In Mel Gussow's review of *The Club*, he said that George Kaufman said the same thing better in a vaudeville sketch, *If Men Played Cards As Women Do* [Mel Gussow: "Stage: Eve Merriam's 'Club,' " *New York Times*, October 15, 1976]. He didn't realize that I was writing the *opposite* of that sketch! I was battered for *Inner City* by Clive Barnes [Clive Barnes: "Theater: The New York of 'Inner City,' " *New York Times*, December 20, 1971]. He said he didn't know whether I was black or white. If I was black the show was okay; if I was white it wasn't. A: He knew I was white, and B: It was a ludicrous thing to say.

INTERVIEWER: Barnes said that you "took nursery tinkles and transposed them to the knell of doom."

MERRIAM: That's fair enough.

INTERVIEWER: But what his review leaves out is the fact that nursery rhymes were frequently savage political commentary in their day, not "nursery tinkles."

MERRIAM: Right. It leaves out the context, true. But that isn't what bothered me. Clive Barnes savaged the score of *Inner City*, which was a very original rhythm-and-blues score, and he was generally unfair. I have been slammed by the critics a lot, and that leaves scars. I've been fortunate in that a good deal of my work has gone ahead despite media criticism. You come up against these critics who do have life-and-death power: They can either make a play go or not go. That causes tremendous self-censorship on my part. The second thing that I feel causes self-censorship is a desire to do something significant. That's a curse. That's why I'm shy at this point of doing anything political, because to me political and significant go together. I think I try to do something which will *not* be too significant and therefore won't scare me so much and I'll be able to go with the flow of it. I censor myself in various ways. That's why a "buddy system" is so important. You need the community of theater people around you.

INTERVIEWER: *The Club* was political and yet *extremely* successful.

MERRIAM: Despite the daily critics! Despite *The New York Times* and *The Daily News*. They just hated it. I think it made them unhappy and uncomfortable.

INTERVIEWER: What did you intend by putting all those women into male costume?

MERRIAM: To say: "You're a bunch of silly puerile asses. And, in real life, as you see by these men's lives on stage, you are dependent on women; yet you idiots can't get along with them. You are still insincerely putting women on a pedestal, telling these sexist jokes to bolster up your confidence. You're just like little boys whistling in the dark. And this is all silly behavior on your part." To hold the male power structure up to ridicule is unpardonable. And so *The Club* was unpardonable.

INTERVIEWER: It's produced all over the world now. Is that because the women critics were supportive of it?

MERRIAM: Yes, yes! The breakthrough came with Edith Oliver in *The New Yorker* [October, 1976], with Marilyn Stasio in *Cue* [October, 1976] and with Erika Munk in *The Village Voice* [October 25, 1976]. It was the women critics who helped it.

INTERVIEWER: Your play *At Her Age* [1979] is about the aging process of women—something of a taboo subject—and the societal indignities that the aging woman is subjected to. We don't have many plays on this theme.

MERRIAM: No. Well, that's a polemical piece, like *I Ain't Finished Yet* and like *Out of Our Fathers' House*. It was done for a purpose, commissioned by the New York Council on the Humanities to say something particular about women and their stereotypes as they age. I thought I sugarcoated it well. It's an extremely useful and amusing piece.

INTERVIEWER: One critic said: ". . . Smacks of the classroom. Both the play and the discussion [following each performance] are stilted and do not work. Theater should be in the theater and serious discussion belongs elsewhere" [Tammy Mitchell: "At her Age," *Our Town*, June 24, 1979].

MERRIAM: *At Her Age* was written for a Golden Age audience [Joseph Jefferson Theater for Older People/TOP, Christ United Methodist Church, June 1979] and for a school audience. It should not have been reviewed in the daily papers. It should have been taken as an information piece in *The Going Out Guide* [in *The New York Times*]: "Here is something educational which is being done at the Methodist Church. It is free. There are going to be discussions afterward dealing with all forms of stereotypes about women, and if anybody wants to come to it, welcome!"

INTERVIEWER: Yet the subject of women aging in a patriarchal society direly needs attention.

MERRIAM: Only when you don't threaten the male power structure can you get away with women's subject matter. As women become more adept, as we get more into the political process, more into the theater process, we are able to be more subtle and more complex. We're touching more nerves. And therefore the men are resisting more. Women are not satisfied! Women are not as scared as they were. More and more, you hear of women in their late thirties and their forties, even in their fifties, getting divorces, not being afraid to go out, and saying, "I will not continue in a relationship which does not give me a sense of my dignity as a human being." And it's the *men* who are being left. So they are having to rationalize their lives, and yes, they're fighting. I don't think it's that they're necessarily fighting *more*, I think they're fighting *differently*.

INTERVIEWER: Do you think that's because we're becoming, artistically and in other ways, more subversive?

MERRIAM: Yes. We're seeing more. We're daring more. It is up to women to shed our old habits, our old self-pity. We cannot any longer afford to waste our energies in "What will men think? How will they respond?" We have to do what is necessary to be done. We have to stop apologizing and stop being cute. We have to become *acute*.

JANET NEIPRIS

Janet Neipris (Wille) *is the author of* Statues, Exhibition *and* The Bridge at Belharbour, *a series of one-acts;* The Agreement, *also a one-act; and three full-length plays,* Separations, The Desert *and* Out of Order. *She is co-author of a musical,* Jeremy and the Thinking Machine, *and wrote music for Kevin O'Morrison's* Requiem *and incidental music for a recent production of* Death of a Salesman. *Ms. Neipris's plays have been performed extensively in regional theaters. She has also written a series of radio plays for the PBS series,* Earplay. *Ms. Neipris's television credits include three years as a major writer for* The Baxters, *which was part of the Public Service Series, and numerous documentaries. She is Associate Professor and Chairman of the Dramatic Writing Program at New York University's Tisch School of the Arts and a member of the Playwrights Unit at Circle Repertory Company in New York City. Ms. Neipris received a National Endowment for the Arts Fellowship in Playwriting in 1979–1980. She holds a B.A. in English from Tufts University, an M.A. in English from Simmons College and an M.F.A. in Playwriting from Brandeis University, where she earned a Sam Shubert Playwriting Fellowship. Ms. Neipris is currently at work on a musical.*

———————

INTERVIEWER: You've said one has to be wildly persevering to be a playwright.

NEIPRIS: It's difficult to succeed, to sustain confidence. There are so many things working in your disfavor: the economy, public taste, critics, incompatible production aesthetics.

INTERVIEWER: Let's talk about some of those obstacles.

NEIPRIS: Getting the play read at all can be a problem. Once the producer knows your work, it isn't; but what about young playwrights starting out? Then, there's the question of taste. One producer has always said to me, "I don't understand the world of your plays. I appreciate your talent, but I don't understand your work." So you lose heart, but then, there you are, back at the post office. Playwrights tell stories of sending plays around to dozens of theaters before they find that producer who connects with their work. That's only the beginning after the three or four years it's taken you to write the play. Should a theater read your play and want to produce it, you have to find the right director, the one who shares your vision, can cast the play, get it up on its feet with a direct relationship to the verbalized production concept. If *all* of this is operative, *if* the director holds the key to that particularized universe, magic occurs—an original vision is pulled in one continuous line, through the playwright's mind into the typewriter through the director's concept, the actors' interpretations, and placed, in fragile tact, on that stage. There is no play until someone discovers the total life underneath it. This ideal production, of course, presumes the raising of needed funds to finance the play. And then, what if it's not to the critics' taste? And sometimes it *is* taste. I grant the critics their intelligence. They know when a play is not working, but sometimes you get that fine line, the nonobjective connector between head and heart that has nothing to do with the best of analytical intentions.

INTERVIEWER: So you think personal taste is sometimes delivered under the guise of aesthetic criticism?

NEIPRIS: It takes courage to believe in some quiet voice which tells you that this is the way you want to write the play. If you listen to what the producers and critics want, it's all over, because then you've lost your honesty. My play, *The Bridge at Belharbour* [1975], is what initially got me going. It had a unique voice, a style; I didn't know a bloody thing about playwrighting. I was in grad school when I wrote that. It was a straight shoot from the heart, something about death and destruction, a very dark play. It had a courage because it was a hard play to write; it came from places I've yet to understand. After that, I began to learn what drama was *supposed* to be about. Then I went through a more controlled period and wrote a play called *Separations* [1978]. I've put it on the shelf because it was too dark, too grim. I should have gone further, but I started to get scared and I stopped writing for a while.

INTERVIEWER: What scared you?

NEIPRIS: The responses I was getting. People said *Separations* was too dark, that nobody would come to see it. The Arena Stage in Washington [D.C.] did it in a workshop. Well, they're courageous, always have been. *The Bridge at Belharbour* was very dark too, but the play ran on a double bill with either of two one-act comedies of mine, *Statues*, or *Exhibition* [1974], so the evening was more palatable. During performances of *The Bridge at Belharbour*, I'd hear strange noises, see isolated men in the audience crying. It terrified me. I felt like a witch. It frightened me that I had dug that deeply. I backed off from that, felt like I had manipulated people's emotions. But a playwright is a manipulator after all. So I went into what I considered a lighter period. *Out of Order* [1980], and *The Desert* [1979] were conceived as comedies . . . but, if you're an honest writer, you don't lose your voice. It sneaks up on you. It follows you like your shadow. Though the intention was to make those two plays comedies, they ended up being quite serious. In *The Desert*, I decided that instead of going in a direct line, I'd "come up and over," with comedy.

INTERVIEWER: Sounds quite subversive . . .

NEIPRIS: It's a style that works for me. The clearer my vision gets, the more absurd it becomes.

INTERVIEWER: Why do you persist as a playwright?

NEIPRIS: Because I can't give up writing.

INTERVIEWER: The journey your play, *The Desert*, has taken is a good example of the tenacity that all playwrights need.

NEIPRIS: The story of the life of that play is interesting. It shows that it often takes five years or *more* for a play to reach production. I have a strong belief that if a play is good, it's like cream—it can't help rising to the top. There's not a substantial playwright in this country who doesn't eventually get produced; other things may interfere, but they're an expected matter of "topography."

INTERVIEWER: So you don't feel there are lost masterpieces?

NEIPRIS: There are masterpieces in hiding, but never lost. It's just a long-distance run. *The Desert* was commissioned five years ago by National Public Radio as part of their *Earplay* series and directed by Emily Mann. After the radio production, not wanting to let the idea die, I rewrote it as a stage play. It was then done in workshop at the Milwaukee Rep, six months later in workshop at the Women's Project at the American Place Theatre, and a year later in a production at the Pittsburgh Public Theater, directed by Susan Einhorn, with strong support from the producer of that theater, Ben Shacktman. The next summer it was produced in Sharon, Connecticut, using actors cast across the season. The artistic director of the theater didn't want to use the actors who had been so well received in Pittsburgh, nor the director. It was a new ball game. During auditions, my director and I were casting against three other men, directors who had all gone to Yale together. It was an old-boy network and I was left out. They kept saying, "Trust us, trust us," and I thought, "Maybe they know something I don't know."

I'm not so old in this business, but if I've learned anything, it's that you've got to trust your own inclinations. My director had seemed to understand the script, but when we went into rehearsal, I thought, I'm not hearing my play. What I finally understood was that the director was going for the broad humor. That was his production concept, not mine.

If I get a director who relies only on the humor of it, it's all over. The work requires a director who understands the "chiaroscuro." Oh, the review. I went to the store for the Sunday [*New York*] *Times* like the innocent going for the killing. I can quote that vicious review word for word, and I only read it once. I just got literally ill and had to go to bed for the day. It undermined my confidence for months. But I wasn't going to throw away the play so easily. How could it have been good in one city and not in another? I thought, "People love comedies and this is a comedy so I'll write COMEDY on the front page and send it to the Manhattan Punch Line Theatre," which specialized in comedies and where Terrence McNally's play, *It's Only a Play*, had recently been given a wonderful production. The size of the theater, ninety-nine seats, was right for the intimacy of *The Desert* [title changed in 1985 to *Almost in Vegas*]. They wanted to do it, we had a successful reading, but the play was optioned for Off Broadway by an independent producer. Five rewrites up the road and countless Park Avenue dinners—we were into casting, due to open in the spring—and it didn't happen. A long story. Everyone's story. That's what I mean by *topography*—expect the bumps.

INTERVIEWER: You've said the success of a play is far more than the written word.

NEIPRIS: It's the pacing, the timing, the suitability of the actors in a particular role. It's a whole dance—a little like sex, isn't it? There's nothing more beautiful in the world, but there's a big price to pay to get to that place. [Laughs] "I'm getting old, but my feet still move." That's a line from *Separations*.

INTERVIEWER: What was the first thing you ever wrote?

NEIPRIS: I took *Little Women* and made it into a play. I put it on on my back porch. Growing up in a poor neighborhood, I couldn't charge admission, so I had to do the reverse, I paid people to come and see it —twenty-five cents apiece. Used my babysitting money.

INTERVIEWER: How old were you then?

NEIPRIS: Oh, in the fifth or sixth grade. When I was in high school and college, I wrote short fiction and poetry—some of it was published. But in the fifties, most women were hidden in the pockets of America's aprons and didn't think much about careers.

I eventually moved myself to Tufts on the trolley. Everyone else drove up in cars with parents. That was hard. Hard, but all right. Part of my scholarship money was given to me by The Women's Scholarship Association, founded at the turn of the century, to raise funds to send young women in the Boston area to local colleges. I became one of their little stars because I could write good speeches. So, in my senior year, they had an annual luncheon to raise money, and I spoke about what my scholarship meant to me. I quoted Robert Browning: "The best is yet to be." As it turned out, it was true. Ten years later, it was the seventy-fifth anniversary of the Women's Scholarship Association, and I volunteered to write a show for them. The subject was the history of women in education. One of my three children starred in it, and the other two worked backstage. Well, serendipity has a great role to play in this business, and serendipity came walking into the room that afternoon at the luncheon in the form of Eliot Norton, the leading drama critic in Boston. He was the guest speaker and had to listen to this bloody musical before he could get on with his speech. After the show, he encouraged me to become a special student of his at Boston University.

That's where it all began. But it wasn't a straight road. I started a play under Mr. Norton's tutelage. I didn't trust, at that time, that it was realistic for a woman with a family to be a playwright. And I certainly couldn't find any viable role models. The only woman playwright I knew was Lillian Hellman and I couldn't figure out where my Dashiell Hammett was. My life didn't seem to be anything like hers. I thought, "I can't really be a playwright. That's a ridiculous idea—a fantasy." So I decided to get my Master's in English at Simmons. In the process we had to write a thesis. I thought, "My God, I'm not an academic and I can't write a serious thesis, but I'll trick them! I'll write a play!" A lofty form of debauchery indeed. The chairman of the English Department, Wylie Sypher, was delighted. I'll never forget, he said, "Janet, anyone can write a thesis, but not everyone can write a play." So I wrote *Rousing Up the Rats Again*, based on Camus's *The Plague*. Camus says in the novel that the plague never dies; it may lie dormant but the time will always come when "it will rouse up its rats again." The play was written during the Vietnam era, and was about the twenty-fifth reunion of a group of Holocaust survivors. it certainly was ambitious—twelve characters. When I look back, I'm embarrassed with the craft, but it does reveal a kind of promise, the very thing I look for now in my students' work.

During that same time period, in Boston, my good friend Barbara Greenberg and I collaborated on a musical called *Jeremy and the Thinking Machine* [1977]. Barbara had written the story and I composed the music; we wrote the lyrics together. *Jeremy* ran for a year at the 13th Street Theatre in New York [1977–78], and was closed down, finally, because the fairy godmother—dear, sweet character—was doing it with a lot of T and A, so we later learned. Barbara and I collected a total of about thirteen dollars, not exactly fame and fortune. Still not believing the reality of becoming a playwright, I made plans to teach English at Winchester High School. I was living in a suburb, married to a doctor, and making dinner parties. Tremendous creativity was being channeled into making those parties. I used to do themes; I'd turn my house into El Mexico . . . or France . . .

One afternoon Barbara Greenberg asked me, "If you could do anything in the world you wanted to do, what would you do?"

"I'd leave the whole family; I'd go to Yale, and become a playwright. But I can't do that, so pour me another cup of coffee."

"Well, there *is* something else you could do," she said. "You could apply to Brandeis . . . they have a playwrighting program." She picked up the phone, *that minute*, called the playwriting department, and made an appointment for me next day. This was 1972. I was thirty-six years old and there were all these youngsters running around with long hair. The department head told me that they only took three playwrights a year. "Kiss that one good-bye," I thought. Well, they accepted me. I was sure there'd been some terrible error that no doubt would be found out. They gave me a cubicle there and I had a little blue Royal portable typewriter; people would laugh . . . it looked like a toy, it cost thirty-six dollars. I'd drop the kids at school and come to my cubicle with no windows, and be there from eight A.M.—the janitors would let me in—and write all day long until it was time to go home for the kids. I became very extreme. I grew my hair in a long braid, wore silver hoop earrings and a blue work shirt—a huge embarrassment, I'm sure, to my doctor husband. I wrote my first *real* play there, *Statues*.

All the other graduate students had a theater background. First week tech assignments were made: "Janet will be in charge of the flies." I didn't know what they were talking about! (Laughs.) I had to climb a catwalk! Terrifying! I'm very unmechanical. My children would come with me. I'd pack them up in the car, cereal boxes in hand, and they'd come up on the catwalk and help me. They were the support: "Okay, Ma, you're doing it!" Then I'd drive them back, half an hour, to Winchester, bring them to school, and get myself back to Brandeis.

They had this big ladder in the theater, ten feet tall. The lighting designer said, "Okay, Neipris, up the ladder!" And I had to climb. The whole class was watching. All these kids. I was scared, I could feel the tears starting to drip down. "What's the matter?" the electrician called up. I said, "I'm really frightened, and I have this back trouble." "First rule of the theater," he shouted up to me, "C.Y.A.—cover your (own) ass. Come down and don't go up that ladder again." But I did. I did the spotlight for *Macbeth*.

INTERVIEWER: Did you eventually find a role model?

NEIPRIS: I didn't know any women playwrights, except Hellman, and though I admired her work, I only saw her once, walking down the street in Martha's Vineyard. Strangely enough, my role model was a man, [playwright] Israel Horovitz. He was my professor at Brandeis, and was a single parent raising a family, as in his film, *Author, Author.* We became pals. We'd get together with my three kids and his three and go shop for sneakers. He'd write in the morning, then have to interrupt to take one of his kids to a dentist appointment. And I thought, "Oh, my God, that's like my life!" Israel was generous, he recommended my plays to the Goodman [Theatre in Chicago]. I've tried to pass on that generosity, that spirit, to my own students at NYU. My first production was at the Goodman, in 1975.

INTERVIEWER: How did it feel?

NEIPRIS: This is a profession of terror, isn't it? I had never been away from home, not even when I married, and suddenly I was in a new city, without friends, in a hotel room. Judith Ivey was in the two plays, *Statues* and *The Bridge at Belharbour.* Gregory Mosher directed. He introduced me to a young playwright out there, David Mamet, whose play had preceded mine at the Goodman. David took me all around Chicago. Lillian Hellman's newest book had just come out, *Scoundrel Time,* and we bought it. He shared his work. I admired it—the power, the language. He was off the streets like me. I identified with the material—not about kings. He wrote me wonderful letter later. He signed it, "See you next year at the Moscow Art Theatre." I still have the letter.

INTERVIEWER: Did you suffer any deflation when you returned to Boston?

NEIPRIS: Oh, yes. I lost my ties as a playwright. The whole world of graduate school and other playwrights disintegrated after graduation. Some of those writers and directors went to New York, and I went back to taking care of my family. But an actress I knew had a house in Cambridge and rented out a garret room for a pittance. It was twenty minutes away from my house. That's where I wrote *Out of Order.* It was unromantic. It was lonely. It was hard work. It was right.

INTERVIEWER: You were divorced by then?

NEIPRIS: Yes. I wrote *Separations* in that period. The plays were beginning to get on in regional theaters, slowly. It was a time when the regionals were gaining in strength. It's like an afghan, the pieces get stitched together, here, there. Montana, Arizona, Chicago, Baltimore —the pattern becomes a whole. And you don't see those stitches going in. Sometimes I worry because I've not been done widely in New York, and yet I've had a consistent career, always writing, productions every year . . . somewhere. There are a lot of playwrights in the country that are having careers like mine, out in the regions.

INTERVIEWER: But you've worked with the Manhattan Theatre Club here in New York?

NEIPRIS: Lynne Meadow wanted to do three of my one-acts, *Statues, Exhibition,* and *The Bridge at Belharbour.* I don't know if it was the right decision. Right or wrong, we did them all [1977]. She believed in my work early on. Zelda Fichandler [artistic director, Arena Stage] in Washington, too. They were pioneers out in the countryside. Manhattan Theatre Club was far away from midtown. The production in New York was not the best the plays had received . . . a lot of those things that can go wrong did. If it was disappointing, it was the theater, the impossibility of repeating any moment experientially. That's quantum physics too, you know. I didn't want the plays reviewed.

INTERVIEWER: Why?

NEIPRIS: I wasn't happy with the production. If the reviews had been favorable, it might have made my career, but I couldn't take a chance.

INTERVIEWER: Was that just an instinct, to forgo reviews, or had you been advised on this strategy?

NEIPRIS: Instinct. Now, experience has been added to instinct. The decisions are more complex the more you know. Lately, since I've gotten to know other playwrights, we're able to exchange information in terms of production.

INTERVIEWER: For example?

NEIPRIS: Do you know this director? Have you seen his/her work? Casting ideas. What does it mean they want to try it out in Albany first? Before this, I was working in a vacuum, living in a suburb of Boston, feeling dislocated. There was more work coming out of New York. I was doing some writing for television . . . comedy work. It was fun and it paid. Circle Repertory Company had asked me to join their playwrights' unit and that was further incentive to move. Then Zelda Fichandler and I—by then she'd done two plays of mine in workshop, we'd become friends—well, we sublet a studio apartment together in New York. We had a lot of fun there. Shades of *My Sister Eileen.* The shape of a life in New York began . . . friends, professional ties.

Eventually, I moved and remarried. My husband, Don, is an engineer and a writer, and he was able to transfer to New York, too. I had been teaching all along at Tufts and at Boston Goddard, but I applied for a job at NYU. The School of the Arts had just started a Dramatic Writing Program that was to play a large part in my life. Jacqueline Park, then the chairman, offered me a part-time position, and by November of that first year of teaching, had offered me a full-time appointment.

INTERVIEWER: You write a great deal about isolation, the loneliness of men and women in a rapacious society. What fascinates you about these subjects?

NEIPRIS: Alienation is a major American ailment. It comes from the struggle to survive today in a landscape besieged by change. The plays are also about fragility of connections—and disconnections.

INTERVIEWER: Does this account for your emphasis on maintenance of community versus isolation, for banding together against meaninglessness?

NEIPRIS: It's the only way. I'm saying that in my work, and in my life. That's why I love the work at NYU so much. . . . It brings together all those writers, students and faculty. We have these generous teachers—Tina Howe, Eve Merriam, Tad Mosel, Len Jenkin, Lavonne Mueller. Arthur Kopit came as a guest for a semester. What role models! I like connecting people to the right places, making opportunities possible. Someone has to be the door opener. Plays are about that too, connecting the idea to the audience.

INTERVIEWER: If things get crazy in the rehearsal process, do you pace in the back? Go to the nearest bar?

NEIPRIS: No; I think the boys go to the bar. I go to Bloomingdale's and buy myself a "pick-me-up."

INTERVIEWER: How do you behave in rehearsals?

NEIPRIS: When I first started out, I let some things go on during rehearsal that perhaps I shouldn't have. Through a lack of understanding of the directorial process—playwrights attribute magical powers to it, give it almost a blind reverence. The playwright should stand in respect of that directorial process, but because of an educated awareness. Through experience, it becomes clear what to fight for and what to relinquish gracefully during rehearsal.

INTERVIEWER: There have been few dramas that examine the mother-daughter relationship in depth. Any desire to explore this area?

NEIPRIS: That's strange. I haven't explored that subject because it's so central to my life, having three daughters (and all in the arts too, I might add). It raises an interesting question. It must not be a burning issue. It's probably a happy one and plays are not about happy people. (Pause.) Family life—maybe I will.

INTERVIEWER: As chairman of the Dramatic Writing Program at NYU what goals are you trying to accomplish in the classroom?

NEIPRIS: Keeping playwrights true to their visions, helping them to focus those visions and not lose courage. It's very tricky because you're teaching the general rules of the craft and at the same time you're telling the students to take risks. You start out by making them keep the rules and then you encourage them to break them. You do try to share the common fears. We all have the same disease. The students come in, one by one, you learn what their strengths are, their shortcomings. It's very individualized care, like being in an outpatient clinic.

INTERVIEWER: What do you mean when you say we all have the same disease?

NEIPRIS: The fear that you have nothing to say, the fear that you do have something to say but people won't be able to understand it, or the fear you won't have the stamina to say it . . . the fear that it will get on stage but not be done well, the fear that it won't be done at all, the fear that you have nothing NEW to say.

INTERVIEWER: Are American audiences and critics a bit too consumer oriented . . . lacking in patience for a play that's not quite working yet?

NEIPRIS: Yes. Yes. They've been too televisionized. They're looking for the end product rather than trying to understand the questions the playwright is raising. Plays posit questions, they don't give tidy answers.

INTERVIEWER: You feel that the playwright, in order to develop, needs the opportunity to fail?

NEIPRIS: Yes. But theater tickets are so expensive, and a playwright can't afford to get out there and fail . . . not in a large way.

INTERVIEWER: You mean commercially?

NEIPRIS: Yes. Americans are on a hook-up for instant happiness. Maybe the theater world, too. Success comes riding in on a very small boat. A renowned playwright once confided that at the beginning of his career, he thought when his play went really well, he would be hailed at the end of the performance, the audience would cheer and carry him around on their shoulders. What you want as a playwright is to have as many moments as you can make where the play quietly connects with the audience. That's it.

INTERVIEWER: Has the concept of The Great Playwright gone the way of the dinosaur?

NEIPRIS: Sometimes we get great plays. Sometimes we get unappreciated ones, like John Guare's *Lydie Breeze*. And Emily Mann's *Still Life*. Few of the critics liked that play, but it survived because of sheer passion and talent. I think a lot of people were threatened by the honesty of Emily's play.

INTERVIEWER: Will you describe your creative process? Do you need special conditions?

NEIPRIS: Chaos. A lot of noise. All those years I complained to my children that they were interrupting me . . . I used to have a sign on my study when they were growing up: OPEN THIS DOOR ONLY IN CASE OF BLOOD OR DEATH. Well, I didn't mean it, I see now. Life going on around is a comfort against the isolation of writing. I work every day in my own fashion, getting up at seven A.M. I used to be a night writer. But then I often had to—because of bringing up a family. My schedule's more flexible now.

INTERVIEWER: As a playwright, what is your greatest fear?

NEIPRIS: Self-indulgence, getting mired in one's own despair because of some of the difficulties of the profession we discussed earlier.

INTERVIEWER: Are women playwrights discriminated against in the American theater by literary managers, producers, critics, or audiences?

NEIPRIS: No, I don't think so at all. I think we've gone way beyond all that. Discrimination may have existed in the early days of theater. For the most part the theater has been generous in terms of recognizing ability. I've found no discrimination in my career. I've found incidents where I was outnumbered, an isolated incident where I didn't have a say because I *was* outnumbered. But then, I've had bad experiences in the theater that had to do with women, too. Women can sometimes be crueler to other women than men are. I don't know why. No, I feel that I've been given every opportunity.

INTERVIEWER: If the isolation throughout much of your career was not by choice, isn't that a form of discrimination?

NEIPRIS: It's a matter of arithmetic. Yes, there are more men in the theater than women and consequently more male playwrights than women playwrights. So of course you're in an isolated experience. When I went out to the Goodman Theatre, I was one of the few women playwrights at the time. But right after that it all started to change.

INTERVIEWER: Do you attribute that change to the Women's Movement?

NEIPRIS: Sure. Women got the idea they could *do* something. Didn't I do that? I was in the kitchen when I perceived the ideas precipitated by the Women's Movement. It was revolutionary.

INTERVIEWER: In what form did you receive those revelations? From books, the media, plays?

NEIPRIS: No. It was in the air. Society was changing and I was always a risk taker. I left my home of forty years, Boston, friendships, all our family, to come to New York. I remarried at forty-five. It wasn't easy to break all those ties. I left a life I knew that was considered safe, solidly middle class . . . I had to break through a lot of doors. Terrifying! It was like being finally born.

INTERVIEWER: Which playwrights have influenced you?

NEIPRIS: Initially, Arthur Miller blew me away. Well, I had a father who had dreams too. There was that connection with Miller's vision. He articulated the heart of loss for me. Then, Chekhov—and *still*, for character, for the juxtaposition of despair and humor, for his humanity—and O'Neill and Williams—oh, the sadness and tenderness in Williams. All my contemporaries cut their teeth on *The Glass Menagerie*. Longing—all the "longing playwrights." Albee and Ionesco, for grotesque absurdity. They certainly influenced the absurd edge in my work. Oh, Ibsen and Hellman—the "well-made play." Molière, without question, and Thornton Wilder. He had a straight line to the human heart. I admire the intelligence of Guare's work and Sondheim's courageous innovations have totally revolutionized the musical. Gurney's focused body of work keeps a commitment to a unique voice. [Arthur] Kopit's and Horovitz's whackiness has influenced. [Christopher] Durang. I admire Lanford Wilson for his accessibility. Tina Howe and Eve Merriam influence me daily by their lives, their work and their friendship. . . . The work, after all, reflects the person, the artist. Well, I love them for their clarity, honesty, passion. Eve has this enormous wit and irony. And Tina is just unique in sheer outrageousness combined with humanity.

INTERVIEWER: Is there a female aesthetic?

NEIPRIS: You mean does it come in the color pink? No. I know women playwrights who write in red, then one who writes in desert colors, another in black, maybe I write in blue. . . . There's a human aesthetic that both connects and separates all playwrights.

INTERVIEWER: Do you mind being called a "woman playwright?"

NEIPRIS: No, that's who I am.

MARSHA NORMAN

M*arsha Norman's plays include* Getting Out, 'night, Mother *and* Traveler in the Dark. *Getting Out* won *the John Gassner Playwriting Medallion, the* Newsday Oppenheim Award *and a special citation from the American Theatre Critics Association.* 'night, Mother *starring Kathy Bates and Anne Pitoniak, won the 1983 Pulitzer Prize, the Hull-Warriner Award and the Susan Smith Blackburn Award. Ms. Norman has also received grants from the National Endowment for the Arts and the Rockefeller Foundation, and has been playwright-in-residence at the Actors Theatre of Louisville and the Mark Taper Forum in Los Angeles. She is a member of the Council of the Dramatists Guild and serves on the Board of the American Theatre Wing.*

———

NORMAN: There aren't many good writers writing about the theater. That's the problem. Very few of our critics can write. And yet most people get their information about the theater from the critics, not from the theater itself.

INTERVIEWER: Why is that?

NORMAN: Because people can afford newspapers more than they can theater tickets. It's that simple. We don't have champions, and we don't have thinkers; we have consumer journalists. Too often, reviews answer one question, "Should you buy it or not?" When critics approach a piece of theater with a "buy it or not" attitude, our plays are reduced to products; why more of them don't understand and fight that, I don't know. The real problem is that critics know so little about the way theater is produced. Most of them can't tell the difference between the play and the production. If you can't do that you have no business reviewing, because you don't know what you're seeing. Also, they don't understand that the director is the author of the production. It is a myth that playwrights have total control. In every production, there comes a time when the playwright just walks away, when you know that if there is any hope here, it will be because of other people, not you. Of course, ultimately you end up taking *full* responsibility for the production.

INTERVIEWER: You're left holding the baby, as it were?

NORMAN: Absolutely. And if it fails, everybody but the playwright can go out and get new work the next day. Back to the critics for a moment, there are some inherent problems in the job. For example, only negative comments can be funny. And nobody wants to read seven paragraphs without something funny! It's not enough to present clearly and carefully what they've seen. They've been bitten by the entertainment bug, too, and they feel like they have to hold their audience.

INTERVIEWER: Was the move from Louisville to New York a difficult transition for you?

NORMAN: It was hard, but it was critical for both of us. My husband, Dann [Byck, producer], needed to know if he could make a new life for himself, and I needed to be in the world of living writers. There are more writers for the theater in Kentucky now than there were when I lived there, but it's good to be able to see [playwrights] Lanford Wilson, and John Guare, and Mike Weller . . . on a casual basis. I like seeing that there are some people who do what I do, who are still alive. [Laughter] That helps.

INTERVIEWER: What do you miss about Kentucky?

NORMAN: Oh . . . Well, I miss the quiet, I miss the green, I miss the space. I have dear, lifelong friends still in Kentucky, and you don't really replace those. The first year that we lived in New York it was very hard to go back there. People weren't sure yet whether we would do all right here, so they worried for us; and they were still angry, at being deserted. They felt that somehow there had been a contest between New York and Louisville and New York had won—that they had been judged to be less exciting and less interesting. Now we go back to Kentucky and it's thrilling, because people are comfortable about where we really live. But I do miss my friends; people don't have that many friends in the world that you can leave them all behind at once. And, of course, I have great ties to Actors Theatre [of Louisville].

INTERVIEWER: Has your family forgiven you for moving away?

NORMAN: I think so. They are, of course, very proud. I think sometimes the reason I agree to do so much publicity is so that Bubbie and Mother can read about me in the magazines! Bubbie is my eighty-four-year-old great-aunt. I simply adore her. I spent years and years with her as a little kid. My own mother's mother was dying as I was born, so I was turned over to Bubbie for safekeeping. The relationship between us is close. Whenever anything appears about me in any publication, seven of her friends will call her. It's her own little soap opera: Who has said what about my Marsha today? I tolerate the interviews because Bubbie gets hours of entertainment from them. I learned so many valuable things from her, so early.

INTERVIEWER: You began writing at five years old. Was Bubbie influential?

NORMAN: Well, they all read to me. Granddaddy was one of the world's best storytellers. He grew up in New Mexico, so he had many stories about growing up in the West. One of his proudest personal achievements was that he lived in three states as they became states. I had Granddaddy's stories and books, and the piano. What else do you really need?

INTERVIEWER: What did you read as a child?

NORMAN: I was recently talking with Heidi Landesman, our set designer for 'night, Mother [1983], about the books that we read as kids—like Nancy Drew—and I suddenly remembered the book clubs that Mother joined. It seemed like a new book came every day. One series that I remember was the continuing adventures of this fellow named Danny Orlis. Every week Danny Orlis would be solving yet another crime or saving someone from another disaster. I didn't have any friends, but I knew as long as I was reading or playing the piano I was safe. That's still true.

INTERVIEWER: What do you read now?

NORMAN: I used to read almost exclusively fiction, and then for about the last year I've been reading a lot of nonfiction, contemporary philosophy, whatever appealed to me. One of the things I've learned to do is just to pay attention to what I'm interested in, and not worry about why I'm reading it. In the last three months I've read *The Enigma*, the story of Allan Turing, the man who deciphered the Enigma Code in World War II, the man who did the original thinking on the computer. And *Frames of Mind*, Howard Gardner's book about multiple intelligences, and the new Daniel Boorstin book, about inventors.

INTERVIEWER: Are you pleased with the production of your new play, *Traveler in the Dark* [at American Repertory Theatre, Cambridge, 1984]?

NORMAN: I'm very happy with the work we did. It's a complex piece, and a real step for me in terms of risk. I wrote the play to find out whether it was possible to write a sympathetic smart person for the American stage. And, of course, what you do by way of developing a smart person is let them talk, which is heresy in the theater today. I'm interested in what it takes to support that talk. The answer is not to get rid of the talk, but rather to find something that is sturdy enough to hold it up. I've read all the reviews this time, and I gather when people say "The play collapses under its own weight," it means that people are not used to listening with the kind of seriousness this play requires. It's just not American. We do not have a literary tradition. So it may take a while for us to figure out how to do it. I have been amazed at how many reviews have said the play is too clever. Too smart. [Laughs] I didn't know there was such a thing! But I guess there is a point when people have to work so hard at following the language, that they just back off emotionally. People think that they have a *right* in the American theater to go on an emotional journey.

INTERVIEWER: As opposed to an intellectual journey?

NORMAN: Right.

INTERVIEWER: Are people more willing to listen to language when the play is European?

NORMAN: Absolutely. Because there's that tradition to count on. Stoppard can make speeches because he comes from Shakespeare, the land of big speeches! Also because he's brilliant, of course.

INTERVIEWER: Are critics and audiences even less willing to listen to "talky" plays by women?

NORMAN: I don't know. Caryl Churchill obviously gets away with it. I really think it's cultural. I'm not sure that it's male/female. Although it could be. I'm very reluctant to say, "This is because it was a woman writing," whatever it is. The reason *Traveler* has the particular shape it does is because I was after very specific things. I didn't want to try and write *'night, Mother* again. When I have a piece, like *Traveler*, that doesn't seem to be getting through to the audience, then I get real interested in "Well, why not?" I'm also always exploring the rules. I want to know which ones are breakable and which ones are not. I'm convinced that there are absolutely unbreakable rules in the theater, and that it doesn't matter how good you are, you can't break them.

INTERVIEWER: Do you care to list them?

NORMAN: Sure. It's real easy, you could put this on the back of a cereal box! You must state the issue at the beginning of the play. The audience must know what is at stake; they must know when they will be able to go home: "This is a story of a little boy who lost his marbles." They must know, when the little boy either gets his marbles back or finds something that is better than his marbles, or kills himself because he can't live without his marbles, that the play will end and they can applaud and go home. He can't *not* care about the marbles. He has to want them with such a passion that you are interested, that you connect to that passion. The theater is all about wanting things that you can or can't have or you do or do not get. Now, the boy himself has to be likable. It has to matter to you whether he gets his marbles or not. The other things—language, structure, et cetera,—are variables. One other thing: You can't stop the action for detours. On the way to finding his marbles, the boy can't stop and go swimming. He might do that in a novel, but not in a play.

I like to talk about plays as pieces of machinery. A ski lift. When you get in it, you must feel absolutely secure; you must know that this thing can hold you up. And the first movement of it must be so smooth that whatever residual fears you had about the machine or the mountain are allayed. The journey up the mountain on the ski lift must be continuous. You can't stop and just dangle. If you do, people will realize how far down it is, and they will suddenly get afraid and start grasping the corners of their chairs, which you don't want them to do.

INTERVIEWER: You've said the main character must want something. Is 'night, Mother, then, Thelma's play? It seems that Jessie, the suicidal daughter, has lost all desire.

NORMAN: Well, Jessie certainly doesn't want to have anything more to do with her life, but she does want Mama to be able to go on, and that's a very strong desire on Jessie's part. She wants Mama to be able to do the wash and know where everything is. She wants Mama to live, and to live free of the guilt that Mama might have felt had Jessie just left her a note. Jessie's desires are so strong in the piece. The play exists because Jessie wants something for Mama. Then, of course, Mama wants Jessie to stay. So you have two conflicting goals. And at that point it is a real struggle. It might as well be armed warfare. Only very late in the piece do they realize that both goals are achievable given some moderation. What Mama does understand, finally, is that there wasn't anything she could do. And so Jessie does win. Mama certainly loses in the battle to keep her alive, but Mama does gain other things in the course of the evening.

INTERVIEWER: For instance?

NORMAN: They have never been so close as they are on this evening. It is calling the question that produces the closeness.

INTERVIEWER: What happens to a woman like Thelma Cates after her daughter has committed suicide?

NORMAN: Well, what's very clear about Thelma from the beginning is that she lives in an intense network of both things and people. Her friend Agnes says, "You have to keep your life filled up." That's what Thelma has done. She is devoted to her candy and her TV Guide and her handwork; she loves talking on the phone to her friends. After Jessie's suicide, Thelma's physical life continues pretty much the way it always was. Thelma is not weak and sick and old. She has only seemed weak and sick and old so that Jessie would feel useful. Jessie, of course, saw right through that. One of the things I think is new in Thelma's life is the experience of this evening, which will belong only to her forever. Probably for the first time, Thelma has something that is securely hers, that she does not need for anybody else to understand and would not dare tell anybody. She has a holy object: this evening that they spent together. And that probably makes for some change in Thelma. But it's probably not a change any of her friends would notice.

INTERVIEWER: Is the holy object The Truth?

NORMAN: It's the moment of connection between them. Basically, it is a moment when two people are willing to go as far as they can with each other. That doesn't happen very often, and we are lucky if we have two or three moments in our lives when we know that, with this person, we have gone as far as it is possible to go. After a lifetime of missing this daughter, of somehow just living in the same space, they finally had a moment when they actually lived together, when the issues of their lives were standing there with them, in silent witness of their meeting. This is exactly the kind of meeting the theater can document, can present and preserve. In an odd way, writing for the theater is like nominating people for the archives of human history. As playwright, I select a person to nominate for permanent memory by the race. The audience, the world-wide audience, does the voting. Some of my nominations make it and some of them don't. But it seems that Jessie and Thelma are going to make it. They are going to be remembered for what they did that night.

INTERVIEWER: Writing for the theater is an attempt to immortalize your characters?

NORMAN: Preserve is more like it. We preserve valuable things because they will be needed, because they are the heritage of the people who come after us. We have benefited from that preservation effort up till now—I am grateful that King Lear was preserved, that he is here for me, and I can look at his life and know what he did. We all have a responsibility to preserve those people from our own time who deserve to be remembered or must be remembered for some reason. It's the struggle that makes them memorable. Because on that night, Thelma does as good a job as anybody could do. It's that effort that gives her a place.

INTERVIEWER: Why doesn't Thelma go a bit further? Why doesn't she attack her daughter physically to prevent the suicide?

NORMAN: Well, there is that final moment at the door, and it posed an interesting dilemma. At that moment in the script, Thelma is reaching for something to hit Jessie with. In the early versions of the script, there was a line that said, "I'll knock you out cold before I'll let you . . ." In my mind I saw Thelma reaching for the frying pan. Like, "I am going

to hurt you now. And we will straighten this out when you wake up."
[Laughter] Then Tom Moore, the director, pointed out that while it may
be tragedy to pick up a frying pan, it is farce when you put it down.

INTERVIEWER: You weren't willing then to risk humor at that point?

NORMAN: Right. And you can't leave Thelma standing there at the
door holding the frying pan.

INTERVIEWER: But did you try it that way during rehearsal?

NORMAN: We tried to make the fight as violent as we could. Thelma
only has one thing left to try and that is physical harm. But I don't know
if the audience ever understands that effort.

INTERVIEWER: Did the fact that you could not demonstrate Thelma's
passion in a physical way put more weight on her final verbal plea to
Jessie?

NORMAN: The struggle at the door is one of the most difficult moments
for both of them. The actress, Anne Pitoniak, as a human being inside
that character, realizes she must fight and she must lose.

INTERVIEWER: Does she let go of Jessie in that moment?

NORMAN: Thelma's crucial letting go has occurred earlier in the
piece. This fight is pure instinct. This has nothing to do with thinking
or feeling, this is just physical. This is that last moment when you realize
you're cornered, and you're not going to try to talk to the grizzly bear
anymore. . . . She *does* know that she has lost. Jessie is simply too powerful. But that doesn't mean that Thelma is just going to stand there.

INTERVIEWER: You've said it's important to you to confront life and
death issues. Many writers have done it through metaphor, while you
confronted it literally. Not that the play is without metaphor—but the
central issue is very concrete. How did you come to that decision?

NORMAN: Suicide is not a new issue on stage. I had seen a couple
of pieces that treated it obliquely. Pieces that did not have, for example,
the person that loved you most standing there across the room saying No
to you. I felt that if you were going to talk about suicide, there was really
no way to talk about it without having someone argue back. It wasn't
that I wanted to work in such a naturalistic way, it was that the issue
required it. We're talking about a real gun, a real fight, a real death.
One of the interesting attempts that I had seen was a play that a friend
of mine, Vaughan McBride, had written. Vaughan and I both had seen
a newspaper article about a man who knew that he had terminal cancer
and was going to commit suicide. This man went to stay with his friend
over a weekend, the idea being that they would spend this weekend talking
and being together; then on Sunday morning the friend would go off to
get milk and the paper, he would come back, and the other man would

have had his opportunity to kill himself. Vaughan showed the evening of talking, the going to bed, and the friend going off to get the newspaper in the morning. Then the man who was going to kill himself walked back up the stairs and the play was over. There was never a mention of the suicide or the friend's agreement to this plan. There was a note in the program that said the man killed himself the next morning, and this had all been arranged. I found it unsatisfying, because I wanted them to deal with it. I didn't want to read it in the program. What I came to with *'night, Mother* was a kind of final submission to the naturalistic form. I simply felt that the subject required that it be treated in a naturalistic manner.

INTERVIEWER: The play is due to go to Japan soon, where I believe that suicide is considered a civil right. I should think the audiences there will experience your story very differently than a Western audience.

NORMAN: It's going to be fascinating, isn't it? I thought the same thing. I have no idea. Americans have a life-at-all-costs attitude. It's a very privileged point of view, actually.

INTERVIEWER: Where else is *'night, Mother* playing now?

NORMAN: Australia, Germany, South Africa, New Guinea . . . all over the world. The only trouble we've had is that all the translators—literally all of them—called me and said, "I don't understand. This person who once owned a farm is a peasant, yes? But how can a peasant have a dishwasher?" It is an interesting problem.

INTERVIEWER: In *'night, Mother* Jessie lets her son, Ricky, go. Thelma lets Jessie go. But in *Traveler* there is a fight for possession of the child.

NORMAN: I'm interested in the way that things transfer generation to generation. In *Traveler* you have this religious man—the grandfather, and the cerebral doctor/scientist as his son. Then the grandson turns out to have a great capacity [in a religious sense] to believe again. Obviously, it is not possible to live your life in total rebellion against a parental stance, without somehow incorporating that stance. The parent's beliefs are the foundation of the child's new religion, rebellious though it may seem. Sam, the doctor, realizes very late in his life that he has practiced his father's religion but not worshiped his father's god. He's worshiped the god of intelligence instead.

I'm also interested in the issue of protection, that, in fact, it's not possible to protect each other. And the efforts to protect each other are often the most dangerous things that we do. One of the things that is critical for survival is to understand that you cannot protect the people you love. As soon as you understand that, you can begin to figure out what you *can* do. You can't say to them your world will be safe. You can't say things will always go well, and you will get what you deserve. That is *not* something we can do for each other; we cannot guarantee anything.

INTERVIEWER: Is it a human instinct to protect each other?

NORMAN: Sure. We don't want to see our loved ones hurt, and so we try to protect them. Carried to the extreme, if you are afraid that your child will fall, one way to keep the child from falling is to strap him into the bed. That happens in relationships of all kinds. In fact, learning to fall is one of the most important things people ever do. I once wrote a play called *Circus Valentine*, in which a young trapeze artist talks about what makes the trapeze difficult. She says, "It's all time, see, and learning how to fall." That is what I think about life . . . because as soon as you know that you can survive a fall, what is there to be afraid of? People who are afraid they will not survive a fall, consequently don't take the necessary risks. *Can't* take them. And live with this terrible fear of falling.

INTERVIEWER: How has your work with emotionally disturbed and gifted children helped you?

NORMAN: What I was able to see in those two years of teaching gifted kids was exactly what my own education had been. I taught in the same program that I graduated from. I could see exactly what had been put in and how. I could see exactly what my literary background was. I knew precisely what they read to us, how we were taught to see things, what the definition of success was, and what the relationship was purported to be between a smart person and the world. I really learned a lot about myself.

My work with disturbed kids was perhaps the most valuable work I ever did. What you cannot escape seeing is that we are all disturbed kids. Emotionally disturbed children make extraordinary efforts to survive and be sane. What *you* see as their disturbed behavior is simply *their* effort to stay whole in some way. They have to go to much greater lengths than everybody else, maybe even metaphorical lengths. For example, one boy I taught was aphasic. He could read but could not talk. In other words, he could decode the language but he couldn't encode it. He fully understood what the words meant coming back in, he just couldn't arrange them himself and send them back out. This guy was real strong and tall and was from time to time stung by imaginary bees. Now, when he was stung by an imaginary bee, you had to get out of the way, because he behaved as any of us would if we were stung by a real bee—he would destroy a whole classroom trying to get away from this bee. He would run so fast that you couldn't possibly catch him, and anything in his way would just be beaten down. That seemed like truly crazy behavior to many people. But I know that I have been stung by imaginary bees and

I did the exact same thing. The only thing to do when you are stung by a bee is get out of there, as fast as you can, and destroy whatever is in your way. Watching those children cope with their terrors taught me to recognize it in myself and everybody else. It's a funny thing about mental hospitals. The patients and the staff are there for the same reason. There is something about the outside world that they cannot handle. We were as institutionalized as the kids were, and at that moment in all of our lives functioning in the outside world was not possible.

INTERVIEWER: Any parallels to playwriting? Do we enter the theater because we can't function anywhere else?

NORMAN: In the theater, we have the luxury of fighting one monster at a time. Which is certainly the way disturbed kids and schizophrenics do see their world. They're up against one gorilla, and they can do mighty battle with him, in an intense, focused way that seems strange if you, as an outsider, cannot also see the gorilla. If you do see him, then suddenly you understand the battle. I saw these little kids fighting for their lives. I came away absolutely brokenhearted, convinced that there was not a thing I could do for them. And yet I understood that they had done so much for me. It was all about what you need to survive. For that one boy it was a clear path away from the bee. He perceived a problem, chose a method of attack and went at it with everything he had. That is a quality that really inspires me.

INTERVIEWER: A kind of faith?

NORMAN: Yes. Oh, I was going to tell you about the other valuable job I had. *Getting Out* [1980] had been running for two-and-a-half years before it finally made more money for me than this little piece of work: I was hired by Kentucky Educational Television to write a workbook that accompanied a remedial reading series on television. This was a great job for me, because it paid me sixteen thousand dollars. It was the job that actually allowed me to quit working and write. The series was written for seventh, eighth, ninth and tenth graders who read at fourth, fifth, sixth and seventh grade level. I had to write fifteen hundred-word passages at each of those four grade levels on each of sixteen topics. Grade level is a function of sentence length and number of syllables per hundred words. So you would write a hundred-word passage on Muhammad Ali, one of sixteen that had to do with the sports category, and count the number of syllables in the hundred words. Then you would count the sentences in the hundred words and plot that on a little graph. Then you would find out, "Oh, shit. It's *fifth* grade level." [Laughter] You'd think, "All right, what do I have to do?" But you could see by the graph what you had to do. You had to add seven more syllables or make an entirely new sentence out of the syllables you currently had. So you would go back into the hundred words with that task. I am going to make a new sentence using no more words. Or: I am going to add seven syllables to this. I learned about the language on a syllable-by-syllable level. . . . I actually learned the *weight* of one syllable in a hundred words. It was incredible training for me. I really think all aspiring playwrights ought to have to do this job. If you combine that with a music background, suddenly you have an understanding of the way the language works in sentences.

INTERVIEWER: How does a musical background play into comprehension of language?

NORMAN: Well, it's all *time*, see. All of those questions: rhythm and tone and . . . are all things you learn best through music, not language. *'night, Mother* is written in a sonata form. And works that way. On the other hand, in *Traveler* there are incredible arpeggios and deep chords that hold all the way through the arpeggios. It's amazing. Somebody will say a word, they will go *Bomm* . . . [sounding a bass note], and then the other person will go *Da-da-da-da-da-da-da* [sounding a treble phrase]. It's fuguelike. That music background simply informs everything I do. It is always there.

Actually, I'm only writing today because I'm not good enough to have a life as a musician! That is what I'd love to be doing. Making music with people is a lot better than talking. I am a better than average amateur musician. But that's just not good enough.

INTERVIEWER: Would you like to compose?

NORMAN: Well, you know, it's very funny. I almost enrolled at Juilliard in composition, but, instead, I sat down and wrote *'night, Mother*. That is the literal truth. I was so angry then. And I thought, well, all right. I'm going to do one of these two things. It doesn't even matter which one. To be able to compose would be the greatest joy in the world. And yet . . . composers certainly have a difficult life. I was privileged to meet Ellen Zwillich who's a composer, and listening to her talk about what she has to do to make money . . . of course now she's doing well. But can you imagine? That "starving composer" business is no joke. It's like poets. How do poets and composers live? I have no idea.

INTERVIEWER: Is musical composition a more emotional art form than dramatic writing?

NORMAN: Well, there are things that music can do that language could never do, that painting can never do, or sculpture. Music is capable of going directly to the source of the mystery. It doesn't have to explain it. It can simply celebrate it. If I'm listening to music, that's all I want to do. It's a great joy to have studied the piano for so long, and so seriously, as a kid. There are pieces of music that I go back to play, that I understand so much more about now. I certainly can't play them as well as I did when I was a kid. But the adult mind is better at some things. Such as understanding the structure of a piece.

INTERVIEWER: Were you aware of the musical structure of 'night, Mother as you were working on it?

NORMAN: Oh, yes.

INTERVIEWER: Which came first, the structure or the content?

NORMAN: When I realized that the piece had basically three parts, suddenly I recognized the musical equivalent was right there and ready. That's an instant occurrence. In each of the three movements of 'night, Mother, you'll see that it builds and then settles down and stops, there's a moment of silence, and then that second movement picks up. Instruments could do that; better, I'm sorry to say.

INTERVIEWER: Do you write during the daytime?

NORMAN: Yes. I can't write at night anymore. I used to be able to. It's just a function of age. But I'm really writing all the time, I'm afraid, even when I'm not at my desk. You'll notice there are little pads of paper everywhere? [Laughter] It works for me to write down the things I want to know. Regarding a character, the progress of a scene . . . Even before I begin to write, I will say, "These are the things I must know before I can start to write." I'll simply make the list of questions. Over the course of the next couple of weeks or months I'll get the answers to those questions. Even when I do rewrites, I just make a little question that says, "How is another way to say this?" Then I will put the paper away. It may be on the back of a grocery list, but once I write the question down, I never forget it. I do have a prodigious memory, and that helps. So I don't need to keep track of all these pieces of paper, I just need to have them around. The answer will end up on some other piece of paper. Gradually, in the course of getting ready to write, those pieces of paper collect, and pretty soon I have a whole box of them.

INTERVIEWER: Do you ever use the interview as preparation for writing a play?

NORMAN: I've done several interviews. I did interviews when I was working on Getting Out and when I wrote The Pool Hall [1978], which is the companion piece for The Laundromat [written 1980; published with The Pool Hall in Third and Oak, Dramatists Play Service, Inc., 1985]. I really do have a wonderful memory for exactly the way people say things. Rarely do I need to record an interview. I don't like to do interviews, actually, because I'm reluctant to ask people the real questions! I'm so respectful of their privacy that I won't ask them things that are really interesting.

INTERVIEWER: Do you need special conditions for writing?

NORMAN: Absolute quiet. And the feeling of being unobserved. I don't even like for anybody to watch when I'm thinking.

INTERVIEWER: Do you use a word processor?

NORMAN: I have an IBM PC. My attitude toward the computer has changed. In the first year I owned it, I was a true believer. I wrote articles and gave interviews saying it was our only hope as writers. Now I've gone back to the yellow pad. I do my original work in longhand, then transcribe it into the computer and run hard copies to do my revisions. The computer is the ideal editing tool. Every writer should have one. But it is no more than a tool. It is an appliance, as necessary as the refrigerator, but, like the refrigerator, it won't save your life unless you put something good in it.

INTERVIEWER: Why did you go back to the yellow pad?

NORMAN: Two reasons. One, my love for paper is why I'm a writer in the first place. I missed the sensual pleasure of the pen running across the paper. Two, I found I was having conversations with the screen, rather than with the audience, or with myself. The screen appreciates a very particular kind of talk. You might say I was talking head-to-head rather than heart-to-heart.

INTERVIEWER: In a previous interview you said that you always liked to write the more tender moments in handwriting, and the stronger, more brutal language on the typewriter. Do you have other schemes like this?

NORMAN: One of my favorite tricks, when I'm in search of a particular speech, is to take myself out to lunch without any paper—purposely without any paper—so that it doesn't seem like I'm determined to write this. And then I have to find something in my purse to write on. There's something about that search for this piece of paper, that may in actuality be the cat's registration papers or something, that's helpful. Tricks. Some things you can't make up; in the most clichéd way, it has to "come to you." So you have to make yourself available. You can't stand there and pound on the door and say, "What is it? What is it? What is it?" At that point, it becomes like a torture session. you know? *"Tell us this answer or ve vill murder you!"* [Laughter] The information that you give freely is much better.

INTERVIEWER: You've said you never thought that anybody would want to see *'night, Mother,* so you never felt that you had to compromise any part of it. Now that it has been so successful and received many awards, I wonder if you've felt an invasion of that privacy?

NORMAN: Yes. There is a certain kind of protection that you can do when you are writing, and then there is a whole other kind of protection that you can only do when people start to ask questions. I didn't protect *'night, Mother* when I wrote it, so I have to do that part now.

INTERVIEWER: What don't you want to answer?

NORMAN: The question I have never answered is "Was there someone in your life who killed herself?" I never wanted to answer that question because I wanted people to continue to think about Jessie, and not about the people in my life, of whom there are several, who have committed suicide. Jessie's story is Jessie's story. It's one that I've written, but it's not one that I have a claim on or can disclose anything else about.

INTERVIEWER: But in *Getting out*, Arlie/Arlene is partially based on a real person, isn't she?

NORMAN: Yes, well, it was much easier to say I knew a thirteen-year-old girl in a detention facility and I wondered what would happen if she ever got out. But I disclosed that before I knew the dangers of doing it. If I wrote *Getting Out* today I might not tell that information.

INTERVIEWER: Does the person on whom Arlie/Arlene was based know that she inspired you?

NORMAN: I don't have any idea. I only had an hour's worth of conversation with her in the entire time that I knew her. And that was mainly saying "Don't destroy the furniture" to her, and her saying, "Fuck you!" to me. [Laughter] That was the entire content of our relationship.

INTERVIEWER: Would you discuss creating the "nowhere that is everywhere" in *'night, Mother*? What does that phrase mean to you?

NORMAN: When you are even remotely from the South, there is always this judgment: People in the South talk funny and they aren't very smart, and they sit around on the porch all the time. One has to fight that. I want to give the characters a real chance at getting through to the audience. To do that, I had to get rid of all the things that stood in the way, like locale, accents, dialect. If I were writing *Getting Out* today, you would probably not be able to tell where it was taking place. As it is, it's very specific. What I want to present is the theatrical equivalent of *Once upon a time* . . . which lifts you up off the stage and sends you back into yourself for the reference points.

INTERVIEWER: What strikes us about *'night, Mother* is that you confront the unpopular issue of control between mother and daughter. In *Getting Out*, to a lesser extent, you do the same thing. You have examined female violence. Do you see your work as violent?

NORMAN: Oh, sure.

INTERVIEWER: We've found that some women playwrights avoid domestic brutality as subject matter, though they are deeply concerned about the issue.

NORMAN: I'm sure that's because most of us live in domestic situations. There do have to be some concerns for the people that we live with. There are some plays that are not written because they would cost the writer some sustaining element in his or her life.

INTERVIEWER: Any thought of exploring your own mother-daughter situation?

NORMAN: You don't think I've done that? [Laughter]

INTERVIEWER: I'm reluctant to pry directly into that, given what you said previously about disclosure.

NORMAN: Well, it's the funniest question I've ever heard. Do you think I got this mother out of the thin air? [Laughs] Do you think I made this mother up? [Laughs] My mother once, as a matter of fact, came to see *Getting Out*, saw the mother character walk in the door with the cleaning supplies and didn't recognize herself at all. My mother once broke into her sister's house in order to clean it! Broke a *window*.

INTERVIEWER: What about the issue of whether or not there is a female aesthetic?

NORMAN: Well, I will be real disappointing here. I probably don't have anything to say. But you're welcome to try.

INTERVIEWER: You just won a Susan Blackburn Award for *'night, Mother*. Do you think women writers need special encouragement?

NORMAN: There are a couple of things that I think. One, the appearance of significant women dramatists in significant numbers now is a real reflection of a change in women's attitudes towards themselves. It is a sudden understanding that they can be, and indeed are, the central characters in their own lives. That is a notion that's absolutely required for writing for the theater. It's not required for novels; you can indeed be an observer and write glorious novels, in which women may or may not be the central characters. But the notion of an *active* central character is required for the theater. Not until enough women in society realized that did the voices to express it arrive. What is perhaps responsible for so few of these plays being done—and we'll exclude for the moment the fact that it takes a long time to develop the skills and the craft and takes a very particular background to produce a writer of staying power and quality—is the problem that the things we as women know best have not been perceived to be of critical value to society. The mother-daughter relationship is a perfect example of that. It is one of the world's great mysteries; it has confused and confounded men and women for centuries and centuries, and yet it has *not* been perceived to have critical impact on either the life of the family or the survival of the family. Whereas the man's ability to earn money, his success out in the world, his conflict with his father—those are all things that have been seen as directly influencing the survival of the family. Part of what we have begun to do, *because* of the increasing voice of women in the world, is redefine survival.

What it means is the ability to carry on your life in such a way that it fulfills and satisfies you. With this new definition of survival, Mother looms large. What you hope for your life, how you define the various parameters of what's possible for you, those are all things with which Mother is connected. She is the absolute source of self-respect and self-image and curiosity and energy. In fact, Mother is where "going on" comes from. Producing, Making Money, Making Your Way are all things that Dad has historically taken care of. But going on, that business of "Here we are; yet another day with yet another mess to clean up" is Mom.

INTERVIEWER: Maintenance?

NORMAN: As women, our historical role has been to clean up the mess. Whether it's the mess left by war or death or children or sickness. I think the violence you see in plays by women is a direct reflection of that historical role. We are not afraid to look under the bed, or to wash the sheets; we know that life is messy. We know that somebody has to clean it up, and that only if it is cleaned up can we hope to start over, and get better. Just because you clean up one mess, that doesn't mean there won't be another one. There is no end to mess, really, but you can't stop cleaning. This fearless "looking under the bed" is what you see in so many plays by women, and it's exciting. It says, "There is order to be brought from this chaos, and I will not stop until I have it." The lessons of all those years of domestic training—centuries, millennia of it—show up in the writing of today in a very powerful way.

INTERVIEWER: You seem to be saying that this idea of "cleaning up the mess" is giving the audience a new way to look at their own lives, to have courage, and feel that things aren't insurmountable. Do you have any comment on that in terms of the tragic turn 'night, Mother took when compared with the more hopeful image of Arlie/Arlene's survival at the end of Getting Out?

NORMAN: Well, clearly you have your personal view of 'night, Mother. My sense of 'night, Mother is that it is, by my own definitions of these words, a play of nearly total triumph. Jessie is able to get what she feels she needs. That is not a despairing act. It may look despairing from the outside, but it has cost her everything she has. If Jessie says it's worth it, then it is.

INTERVIEWER: But suicide is not survival. That's what I'm questioning.

NORMAN: But see, by Jessie's definition of survival, it is. As Jessie says, "My life is all I really have that belongs to me, and I'm going to say what happens to it." . . . Jessie has taken an action on her own behalf that for her is the final test of all that she has been. That's how I see it.

Now you don't have to see it that way; nor does anybody else have to see it that way.

INTERVIEWER: Better death with honor than a life of humiliation?

NORMAN: Right. I think that the question the play asks is, "What does it take to survive? What does it take to save your life?" Now Jessie's answer is "It takes killing myself." Mama's answer is "It takes cocoa and marshmallows and doilies and the *TV Guide* and Agnes and the birds and trips to the grocery." Jessie feels, "No, I'm sorry. That's not enough."

INTERVIEWER: Do you think that art is genderless? Can you tell from an anonymous play whether the author is male or female?

NORMAN: Sometimes you know and sometimes you don't. My favorite saying is "All great art is androgynous." But I don't know. I know that there are certain plays, *Requiem for a Heavyweight* or *Marty*, for example, that come from a long life lived as a male. We all have secrets. There are things that you know, that you would have no way of knowing unless you had been there. Paul D'Andrea's plays could only have been written by a professor!

INTERVIEWER: Do you feel a need to identify with other women playwrights? Is there any need for women in our profession to stick together, help each other? Do you think that to call oneself a "woman playwright" rather than a "playwright" is to be ghettoized?

NORMAN: Tough, tough series of questions. Clearly in the theater you must have help from the best possible sources, whatever they are. I am not inclined to seek or give help strictly on the basis of sex. I am particularly comforted and find it a joyous experience when the best help, when extraordinary help comes from a woman. Then there is this great bonus of special understanding. A special peace comes from playing at your level with another woman. I am also finding in my own personal life a new route to understanding the women in my history—Mother, Bubbie, my various aunts—but that's only possible once my identity is established and it's clear to them and a source of joy to them that I am not living the life that they hoped I would live. The choices you make out of freedom are the best ones. I am that much of a natural rebel that if somebody said to me, "Marsha, you *must* or you *should* choose a woman to do the lights because it's important," you would have such a fierce rebellion out of me that it would be terrible. I would call off the whole thing. I really resist other people telling me that I *should*. . . .

INTERVIEWER: Has that happened?

NORMAN: Yes. People have said to me, "Marsha, you should choose women directors for your work because your work has the opportunity to be seen in prominent places and women directors need your help." I would love that special joy of working with a woman on a piece of mine, but I must be free to make the decision based on the needs of the piece. Not my needs. Who is best for that piece? I have been involved in the various women's political organizations, such as the League of Professional Women in the Theatre, New York, and I'm doing the big Center for Research on Women keynote address. I do a lot of that kind of work. But I can't go to meetings. I am valuable because of my work, not because I go to the meetings. I have found that I am not a valuable organizational person, but I am certainly there when those organizations need me. When I was a kid I did not know that writers for the theater were from Kentucky or were women, except of course for Lillian Hellman. Lillian Hellman was it, as far as I was concerned. She was my only indication that this kind of life was possible. And, of course, because of *me*, no kid growing up in Kentucky has to worry about that again. That's nice. I like to be able to do that.

INTERVIEWER: Would you tell us about your interview [*American Theatre Magazine*, May 1984] with Lillian Hellman?

NORMAN: I went to say thank you. I didn't really ask her very much, I just read to her, pieces from her work, and said "Do you still believe that?" Or "What did you think when you wrote that?" Or "What did that really mean?" The joy that she got from hearing her own work was amazing! That's what the Endowment [National Endowment for the Arts] needs to do next, send unemployed actors and playwrights around to read their work to these aging giants.

INTERVIEWER: Is playwriting a hostile act?

NORMAN: Mmmm. I don't know. There are certainly pieces of mine that are seen as hostile. There are people who actively hate Jessie for what she had "done to Mama." I don't understand that. And it never occurred to me. In *Traveler*, I think my character Sam is wonderful! I can't imagine that he makes people angry or that people find him arrogant. Of course, lots of people *are* finding him arrogant, and terrible.

I do think that if there were any other way to say what it is you're able to say in plays that you would do it. I only write plays because there doesn't seem to be any other way to address the issue. I can't talk about it in conversation with my friends; I can't go read books about it. A play should only be written as a last resort.

INTERVIEWER: How did it feel to win the Pulitzer Prize? Has the acclaim changed you life at all?

NORMAN: Sure. There is some extraordinary security knowing what your obituary is going to say. That is no small thing, to know that regardless of what happens from here on, you will always have the Pulitzer Prize. They can't take it back. The Pulitzer allows you to say *no* more easily.

INTERVIEWER: So you have more choice?

NORMAN: Yes, and you have your own time back more completely. You don't have to sell so much of it in order to finance this little hobby of writing for the theater.

INTERVIEWER: Does celebrity have a negative side?

NORMAN: Sitting on my desk is a stack of mail fourteen inches high. And you want to respond to many of them. Somebody sends you a letter from a playwriting class in Des Moines; all of the people in the class have signed the letter and they want to know the five things they have to know about playwriting. Well, you can't refuse to do that! Not if you're human, you can't. But you also know that you have to reserve most of your time for yourself. That prize is a great comfort. Some people feel that it has a negative effect, that after you win it you are constantly in competition with yourself and that you must always then try to write one that's better than this last one.

INTERVIEWER: Are you feeling that?

NORMAN: Success is always something that you have to recover from. The primary state you must be in in order to write is an anonymous, unknown, unseen state. Finding a way to preserve that in the face of obvious visibility is simply a trick that you have to get better at. I do it by not answering the phone and by being hard to find. I'm very careful about guarding my resources. Sometimes I am very extravagant with myself and give and give and give and give. But the day does come when I know that the primary responsibility is to that talent and it is time to retreat from the world.

INTERVIEWER: 'night, Mother is closing on Broadway. Is there any sense of loss?

NORMAN: Of course. But I also feel an incredible triumph. We had eleven months. That's ten-and-a-half months longer than anybody thought it would be there.

ROCHELLE OWENS

R*ochelle Owens is the author of many controversial and innovative plays, including* Emma Instigated Me, Futz, Beclch, Homo, Istanboul, The Karl Marx Play, He Wants Shih!, Kontraption *and* Chucky's Hunch. *She has had productions at major theater festivals in Edinburgh, Berlin, Paris and Avignon. Two collections of her plays have been published:* Futz and What Came After (*Random House, 1968); and* The Karl Marx Play and Others (*E. P. Dutton, 1974). She has also published nine collections of poetry, including* The Joe Chronicles (*Black Sparrow Press, 1979) and* Shemuel (*New Rivers Press, 1979). Ms. Owens edited* Spontaneous Combustion, *an anthology of eight new American plays (Winterhouse Ltd., 1972). Ms. Owens has received several Obie Awards and Honors from the New York Drama Critics Circle.*

———————

OWENS: I thought of myself as an artist at an early age. When I was about four I had a blackboard and I remember holding the chalk and feeling a sense of tremendous power as I drew and redrew the round circles of the heads of the figures that children like to make. I wanted the heads perfectly round. And when I believed I had accomplished my idea, I was quite pleased. Language and the poet's sensitivity and the affinity begin very early. I studied ballet as a child and I remember leaning against the exercise barre, totally absorbed in the sounds of the French words designating the various dance movements.

As a child I read a play by a woman playwright, Mary Caroline Davies, *The Slave with Two Faces*, which had been produced at the Provincetown Playhouse in 1918. It was an allegorical morality play in a fairy-tale setting. I was very moved by the work. As a matter of fact, Elaine Shragge, who wrote a dissertation on my work, suggests that Mary Carolyn Davies was probably an early role model for me. . . .

INTERVIEWER: Do you agree with that analysis?

343

OWENS: Well, certainly the play and being exposed to art and literature in general were part of the various forces at work that made me
very aware of the power of art. Another writer I discovered when I was
about nine was Eliza Cook, a nineteenth-century American who wrote
in a very traditional rhyme scheme. Her poetry was strong, quite sad too,
about poverty and death. It was protofeminist work because she was aware
of the double standard imposed on women.

INTERVIEWER: How would you describe your early writing?

OWENS: I'm glad you asked that question. I've been thinking about
my work, my concerns and aesthetic involvement, lately. I'm becoming
more and more interested in the poetic process, human creativity and
imagination. Recently, I reread a large group of poems and fragments of
prose poetry that I had written in the late fifties and sixties. They are very
experimental and have a highly charged linguistic energy. They remind
me of the multicolored patterns in a mosaic. They are often words and
short phrases juxtaposed in unique and unfamiliar combinations. It's as
if I was a chemist, an alchemist, mixing and playing around with fluids,
living tissue, vapors, always testing the viability of the matter—language.
It can also be compared to holding a multifaceted crystal cube, shifting
and altering the position in a vast endless variety of ways. Seeing the
effect of light, shadow, and pattern change continuously just as time
alters living matter.

INTERVIEWER: What drew you to the experimental aspects of language?

OWENS: Authentic poetry, art, comes from the self. To be able to
move, to create oneself. I was bored by the conventional metrics and
diction of W. H. Auden or Robert Lowell. I began to read poets like
e.e. cummings, Emily Dickinson, Dylan Thomas, others. As a play-
wright-poet whose selfhood constantly works through an inner challenging of outer reality, of private versus public, the dimension that eternally
confronts the artist, I must personally master the relationship of my art
to contemporary developments in science and technology. Art is meaning
made anew. Meaning which identifies and moves us outside restrictive
definitions and turns our focus from habitual notions to the essential
activity—awareness of expanding the domain of the meaning of things.
My business as a playwright, therefore, means challenging the established
categories of theater.

INTERVIEWER: Were you part of an artistic community in your early
years as a poet?

OWENS: I was one of the founders of the St. Marks Poetry Project.
We read in coffee houses like Les Deux Magots, Dr. Generosity and
other spaces. Among the people I knew as a young poet were Allen

Ginsberg, Barbara Holland, Diane DiPrima, many others. Later I became involved with the alternative theater world: wonderful places and people like Ellen Stewart, [founder and artistic director of] La Mama, the Judson Church, which housed the Judson Poets' Theater, the Becks of the Living Theatre, John Cage, Crystal [Field] and George Bartenieff of the Theater for the New City.

INTERVIEWER: Is artistic community necessary for revolution to occur in art?

OWENS: It depends what you mean by revolution. But I can certainly imagine neolithic artists walking miles and miles to see what other people were creating on the walls of their caves. A community shares experience and ideas and so I think a sense of community is very comforting for artists, certainly enriching.

INTERVIEWER: Did you pay a price in the early days for the outspokenness, the expression of primal anger and sexuality in your poetry?

OWENS: Not among the poets and writers who had similar aesthetic concerns. However, the double standard always exists and a woman who rocks the boat is perceived as peculiar, maladjusted, whereas the male writer is considered remarkable, a discoverer!

INTERVIEWER: Why were women able to catalyze the art world and the theater in the sixties and seventies?

OWENS: The continuity of civilization works toward resolving problems and the artist throughout human culture needs the leisure and freedom to investigate. Women, finally, for complex sociological reasons began to get a little share of the pie, very minimal but it was a start. We are still treated like orphans in comparison to the men. The sixties was a unique time politically and artistically. Women playwrights were groundbreakers for so many other factions which were defined later on as pop culture. We were all fairly young and it was a time of creative consciousness. I'm glad that I was part of the community of artists who were breaking ground for those who came later.

INTERVIEWER: Do you teach the work of women playwrights in your courses at the University of Oklahoma?

OWENS: Yes, there are several women playwrights that I have my students read. Adrienne Kennedy, Megan Terry, Irene Fornes, Rosalyn Drexler, my own work. We were the pioneers of the early Off Off Broadway movement in the sixties. My own concept and vision was always in opposition to conventional mainstream theater. I ought to say that it still is. Regarding the feminist revolution and my growth as a playwright and poet, I am able to reread my own work with more insight, as well as excitement, because of my developed consciousness. I am sensitive to the protofeminist domain that includes all of human experience that is in the writing. The more enlightened the reader and spectator become, the more meaningful art is.

INTERVIEWER: What are some of the ways in which the women playwrights of your generation influenced the work of male playwrights? Have men's plays changed as a result of your individual and collective innovations?

OWENS: The creative women of the experimental theater at that time were dealing with being undercut, diminished in a sexist culture, which provided perhaps a catalyst, a kind of extra defiance to their already radical imaginative mentality. When I look back at my early writing, I see what I would call protofeminist structure and dynamics. Protofeminist because it preceded the wave of political and sociological consciousness of the late seventies. Many women were writing incredible plays which pointed up a warped, sexist reality. These plays elaborated and commented upon that reality in multitudinous ways that were different from the ways in which men wrote about it. I think our work, beyond being avant-garde (that means getting rid of old structures, finding new meaning and creating new forms) also had an aware sensibility of the paradox and the inherent—almost genetic—cellular injustice between the sexes.

INTERVIEWER: Do you believe there is a female aesthetic in drama?

OWENS: On the one hand, it doesn't matter what the ideology of a gifted writer, man or woman, may be. But if you juxtapose a story of Tillie Olsen with a poem by D. H. Lawrence or Ezra Pound, you will see that Tillie Olsen will point up the world of women because she has a total awareness of their world, their reality. This kind of "extra information" only enhances a gifted writer. The same information in the hands of someone who is not gifted will not enhance anything, but rather become writing which is just sexist dogma, rhetoric. Lawrence and Pound are examples of a very rigid, authoritarian male world but they had an intuitive dynamic which helped them realize the injustice toward women. Though their main ideology was sexist, patriarchal and terribly romantic—all to the disadvantage of women—they had the intuitive prowess as poets and as creative writers to sometimes hit the mark of universal truth.

INTERVIEWER: Are you saying that the true artist intuitively develops empathy for the opposite sex?

OWENS: Empathy is a good word, yes. I would say that the message, the ideology is secondary to the power of the artist, the poet.

INTERVIEWER: What inspired *Emma Instigated Me* [1976], which deals with a playwright and her relationship to Emma Goldman, both as the character she is inventing and a historical figure?

OWENS: After I wrote *The Karl Marx Play* [1973], I began reading Emma Goldman's autobiography. I became excited about the idea of Emma Goldman describing herself as an anarchist. You see, the process of artmaking is linked with random and accidental happenings that the artist encounters, a state of confusion and disorder, which is what anarchy is. One creates out of the disorder. I identified with Emma Goldman because she was as contradictory as I am. She intrigued me. She was passionate, full of conviction and idealism, paradoxical and mercurial. Which is what I love art to be. The author in the play allows Emma to defy, fight and confront her. Writing the play was great fun.

INTERVIEWER: Walter Kerr said in his *New York Times* review of *The Karl Marx Play* ["It's No Way to Write 'Das Kapital,' " *New York Times*, April 8, 1973], "Hell, my own free-associations bore me. What do I want with Miss Owens'?" In *Emma Instigated Me*, the character of the director says, "No free associations!" Was that an ironic reference to Mr. Kerr's remark?

OWENS: Listen, only Beckett and Peter Shaffer or Sam Shepard are allowed to free associate! When I do it, it's called self-indulgent. Talk about the double standard! My play *Beclch*, produced in 1966, was described by a critic as the work of a housewife who writes plays. Imagine calling Arthur Miller a breadwinner who writes plays. Regarding the character of the director in *Emma Instigated Me*, I had him say the kinds of banal statements that directors sometimes say, and that theater critics often write.

INTERVIEWER: In your opinion, does a gender bias exist in theater criticism?

OWENS: Definitely! My play, *He Wants Shih!* [1968], was described by a chauvinist male critic as being the work of a dirty-mouthed poet! And yet this same critic uses elevated high-toned language to describe a male playwright's concerns. Women are treated as second-class. But it's important to remember that women literary or theater critics can also fall into sexist thinking. And a mediocre mind, even with a raised feminist consciousness, is still a mediocre mind.

INTERVIEWER: Do you feel, as Tillie Olsen does, that criticism can have a silencing effect on the artist?

OWENS: I don't think so. But certainly nonrecognition can be deadening. The theater is faddish and only a handful of male playwrights are consistently produced. My new play, *Three Front* [1984], is as yet unproduced, in spite of the fact that my play *Chucky's Hunch* won an Obie Award, and was widely reviewed and praised when it premiered [Theater For The New City] in New York in 1981. [*Chucky's Hunch* was subsequently produced in New York at the Harold Clurman theater in 1982.]

The theater is only worthwhile writing for if you can get your play produced successfully. Luckily, I have the urge to write poetry and because I'm involved with poetry as performance I can continue to explore "meanings made anew."

INTERVIEWER: Is that a particularly American phenomenon—that artists are not often given credit or distinction for having sustained a long career in the theater?

OWENS: In terms of my own experience as a woman playwright I think that the message from the critics (there are a few exceptions) is that they know little if anything about the achievements and body of work that the writer has produced. Although I've published nine books of poetry and three collections of plays, some of the critics are so uninformed that they take the attitude that one's recent play is one's first play! It's the critics' virgin complex, I suppose. Again, the standard is different for a favorite son like Sam Shepard or Arthur Kopit. Then of course the critic "knows" the body of work of the playwright.

INTERVIEWER: Your stage language is very poetic. Critic Linda Swenson feels it is a challenge to the actor.

OWENS: Yes, because the actor must pay attention to the rhythms and tonal meanings as well as the inspired imagery of the language. I'll never forget an incident when an arrogant young actor who was in a play of mine, *Istanboul* [1976], insisted on ad-libbing lines in my play! Can you imagine ad-libbing Shakespeare?! You cannot do that with highly charged poetic language.

INTERVIEWER: Would you describe some of the protofeminist elements in your first play, *Futz* [1958]?

OWENS: I tend to agree with some of the comments by graduate students and professors who recently viewed the film version of *Futz* at the University of Oklahoma. They remarked that the cruel truths of the characters of the women in the play were fixed in an extraordinary way. Feminist theater criticism would add a new dimension to the complexities of my dramatic literature. Before the feminist movement in 1968, even the more efficient and astute critics had been perhaps more narrow and rigid than they ever suspected when it came to the revelation of a world of outraged female protagonists who fill the landscapes of many of my plays, including *Futz*. In *Futz*, the character Mrs. Loop says, "A son and his mother are godly." That is a cultural, religious and mythic truth, from the Virgin Mary to Isis, "a son and his mother are godly." The line points up the invisibilization of the rest of the human race. Are a *daughter* and her mother godly? Many such paradoxes exist. Throughout the play the theme of sexual imperialism, as well as other social evils, demonstrate how people's attitudes toward sex and class are conditioned by cultural myth. *Futz* also embodies *active reacting* against brutalization of women. I wrote the play in 1958, which shows how the arts are always ahead of the times. But no critic explored these elements and because there wasn't any feminist criticism at the time, the feminist elements were totally neglected. In fact, the entire dynamic of women in the play was ignored.

INTERVIEWER: Were you aware of the feminist dynamic while you were writing the play?

OWENS: Yes, in an organic and intuitive way but not in the same way, needless to say, as a scholar or a critic or a theorist.

INTERVIEWER: In retrospect, what were you saying about violence between the sexes in *Futz*?

OWENS: That question leads me to other reflections. That I wanted to write a play about exposing the hypocrisy of a society which continually needs to find scapegoats. As to your question about violence between the sexes, it's general knowledge that women and children are the ones who are scapegoated in patriarchal culture.

INTERVIEWER: A recurring image in your work is that of the watcher, the voyeur: Chucky in *Chucky's Hunch*, Loop in *Futz*, the hooded figure in *Istanboul*.

OWENS: Yes, that's correct. You see, the audience begins to identify with the character who is watching, the observer in the play. They feel the same tensions and emotions the characters feel and at the same time they can retain an objectivity because they know it's only a play. They can see the irony of the situation, or the fatal consequence. It's a result of the play, the poem, reaching out for an active response from the viewer or the reader. In my play *Kontraption* [1970], the characters often relate to the audience.

INTERVIEWER: What inspired your play *Beclch* [1968]?

OWENS: I've always been interested in myth, ritual and social conventions. I had read some of the essays of the historian Arnold Toynbee. They triggered my imagination. Director André Gregory had asked me to write a full-length play, and that was how *Beclch* came to life.

INTERVIEWER: Critic Bonnie Marranca described the character Beclch as "a female Idi Amin" [*American Playwrights*, Volume one, Drama Book Specialists, 1981]. What does Beclch's scream symbolize at the end of the play?

OWENS: It's a rebel yell. Beclch is a rebel and subverts the society around her. *Beclch* has quite a bit of protofeminist rage in it. And *Homo* [1966] is filled with feminist symbols. The main thing is that artists have always been able to see the discrepancies and unjustness in social organization. Artists delve into these dynamics, and later on, the political consciousness, the psychological consciousness and the scientists catch up with what the artist has always known.

INTERVIEWER: Would you say that the character Beclch represents feminist rage incarnate?

OWENS: Yes. She is right in the swing of things. On the other hand, she is not a stick figure Amazonian. Another woman writer who explored and experimented, thought and reflected upon this was Mary Shelley. I think everyone should read *Frankenstein*. Talk about focusing in on feminist rage! We all know who that monster was: It was little Mary Shelley, and she was writing for all women. We all know who that unloved, lumbering Frankenstein monster was—it was the dark side of women.

INTERVIEWER: You confronted the negative aspects of technology in your play *Kontraption* [1970]. What are your present views on technology and on nuclear weapons?

OWENS: My new play, *Three Front*, explores some of those concerns. Technology for murdering people and poisoning the earth is a symptom of a grotesque imbalance, I suppose. A collection of my poems, *Salt & Core*, contains a poem about the naming of nuclear weapons after pagan gods. It means that the culture we are all a part of celebrates death. In an odd way, or perhaps it's not so odd, I think there are psychological similarities between the arms race and the overwrought competitiveness in the art world and in publishing.

INTERVIEWER: Would you elaborate on these similarities?

OWENS: I host a radio interview program which is connected with the University of Oklahoma, called *The Writer's Mind*. I speak to poets, fiction writers and scholars. Here in this part of the country, the Southwest, the poets—American Indian and white—do not have the same attitude about publication as poets who live on both coasts. They are not constantly self-promoting and longing to publish a book every year. Some of them happen to be remarkable poets, and I mean that. They are not caught up in quantity, numbers, the self-generating urgency to be "famous." The imperialism of self, they are self-imperialists, many poets and artists in New York and San Francisco. If you compare that monopolistic attitude with the attitude of an American Indian poet who is a wonderful poet, who comes from a culture that is not greedy, which instead is meditative and reflective, then you will understand that success is determined by one's own ambition, politics, and endurance. I think the psychological dynamic is similar—wanting to hoard weapons of destruction to wanting to publish excessively. The stock market in Tokyo and the entire Western world and Russia should be equated with the artistic imperialism of those countries.

INTERVIEWER: Would you discuss stage language? You have been compared to James Joyce in your mastery of dialects which you both invent and convincingly reproduce.

OWENS: Every play has its own unique language style, rhythm and internal flow. The characters develop their own personalities and seem to have free will in my plays. They move and speak and act autonomously, at least when the play is going well. Language for me is tactile, concrete, I can sculpt and control it, mold it to the emotional color and mood that is right for the world of the play.

INTERVIEWER: Do you hear the language as a kind of music while you are writing?

OWENS: It's more like a pattern of beats and breath sound, physical, very internal. But I also act out the parts aloud to hear how it all sounds.

INTERVIEWER: Why are many of your plays set outside of America?

OWENS: *Futz* and *Emma Instigated Me, Who Do You Want, Peire Vidal* [1968], and a couple of radio plays that I wrote take place in America. I'm interested in human nature. Primal drives are always the same in any human society. If I have a play happen in a foreign context it's to explore the uniqueness of the event of the play playing. To reveal the universality of the dilemma in the play.

INTERVIEWER: You have been called perhaps the most profound tragic playwright in the American theater. Do you see yourself as a tragedian?

OWENS: Tragedy, comedy, are the juxtapositions of events in life. I suppose I've written some plays that might be defined as tragedy. There is also humor and irony in my work, needless to say.

INTERVIEWER: You explored Oriental philosophy in your play *He Wants Shih!* What did you have in mind when you began to explore the dual sexuality of your character Lan? Once he has transformed himself into his feminine ideal, he is raped. Did you feel it was necessary for him to experience the vulnerability of rape in order to experience fully the vulnerability and powerlessness of women?

OWENS: That's a sociological and psychological insight and rather interesting. The play is concerned with spiritual awakening. If *Beclch* is about the doom of excess, then *He Wants Shih!* is about the doom of total renunciation, and excess, too, in a way. It's about relinquishing power, about giving up, letting go. Lan is the great no-sayer, and he is an incredible misogynist. I had great fun creating Lan because empathy means "sympathy with the devil," as the Rolling Stones put it. A writer must have sympathy with the devil; that is literature, and that is what is exciting about art. I explored the psyche of men who hate women through his character, his transformation. I was able to enter the cultural feeling of hatred, and of contempt, toward women.

INTERVIEWER: In your play *Chucky's Hunch*, Chucky, the failed artist, writes to his successful ex-wife, "I had more options than you twenty years ago . . . I was the artist and you were just a pretender. . . . But then the female spider does devour the male . . . how many men have you chewed up—you fat spider?" Were you saying that the creative woman is perceived by men as devouring, castrating?

OWENS: Men who hate and envy women will say and do anything to dehumanize us. Even compare us to spiders. Sexism should be equated with antisemitism and racism.

INTERVIEWER: Chucky says, "My own failings are enmeshed in the times . . ."

OWENS: Chucky is based on a type of self-pitying male that a lot of women recognize as having known, married or lived with at one time or another. These men always regard women as support systems of one kind or another; nurturer, mother, sex object, muse, and scapegoat, if necessary. The very last thing they want in a woman is a competitor. That they cannot tolerate . . . when and if it happens . . . the poison and spite is ejaculated from them . . . the woman is the target. During the run of the play, women would come up to me and say, "My lover was just like Chucky," or "My husband is like that."

INTERVIEWER: Were Chucky's paintings, which are a part of the set, intended to be good or bad paintings? Did you perceive Chucky as a gifted artist?

OWENS: The paintings were similar to Motherwell's, because that was what was being painted during the fifties, abstract expressionism. Chucky is no more or less gifted than many other artists.

INTERVIEWER: You once stated, "I write so that God will not hate you." What did you mean by that?

OWENS: It was a way to take upon myself a great sense of spiritual authority as a writer. To claim the authority as a benevolent and just right to express truth.

INTERVIEWER: And now, why do you write?

OWENS: To tell the truth. To feel the joy. To risk.

LOUISE PAGE

B*ritish playwright Louise Page has written* Salonika, Falkland Sound, Real Estate *and* Golden Girls. *Her plays have been produced in England at the Royal Court Upstairs and the Royal Shakespeare Company, among other theaters.* Salonika *was presented at the New York Shakespeare Festival Public Theater in 1985;* Real Estate *was produced at the Arena Stage in Washington, D.C. the same year. Ms. Page has also written extensively for British radio and television. In 1981,* Salonika *was a joint winner of Britain's George Devine Award.*

INTERVIEWER: When did you begin writing?

PAGE: I've always known I was going to be a writer. There was no exciting discovery. My life has been a series of plods toward writing. Apparently I told my headmistress at the age of five I was going to be an author. I don't know how I knew the word! At infants school, we had to write topics. I loved all that. And when we did plays I always made up the stories. Nothing was written down, but I told everyone what was going to happen next. When I was about ten I began writing novels. I started the first major one when I was on holiday with my family in the Lake District. I wanted something to do, because it rained a lot; writing was a way of amusing myself. I wrote wonderfully long, extraordinary novels in which nobody did anything other than kiss passionately. All the men were one's latest heartthrobs, all the women were one's latest crushes. The stories were always historic and the ladies had names like Charlotte and Cordelia and they were illustrated. I found some the other day and after a while, my spelling mistakes and bad punctuation had me so hysterical I couldn't go on. When I went to senior school, I started a huge tome written in three enormous exercise books. It's labeled PLEASE BURN WHEN I DIE. I worked on this novel for an hour every night. I used to take it to school and read it to my friends. Gradually, they started acting it so I wrote more and more dialogue.

INTERVIEWER: Were you encouraged to write by any particular teachers?

PAGE: I was encouraged by a wonderful English teacher in my fourth year of school, but before that, all my essays were marked "Please rewrite. You have not done your spelling corrections from the last time. You are still spelling this wrongly." If you can't spell, you develop appalling handwriting, deliberately, to cover it up. Because my spelling was so bad, I developed an all-purpose vowel shape. I think that's probably why I write dialogue, and why I went into playwriting.

INTERVIEWER: Poor spelling?

PAGE: Yes, because you hear dialogue in your head—you don't think about the spelling. There is far more scope for spelling mistakes in a novel. I'm sure my spelling problems have to do with the fact that when I was learning to read, my parents moved around; I changed accents several times. When I began to read, we lived in Liverpool and then we moved to Sheffield. The vowel sounds changed all the time and my parents' accent was southern. But that's me trying to rationalize the problem. My spelling has improved, but one has blocks. I know I can't spell *definite*, so I don't use it if I can use something like *certain*. I am aware of using words or combinations of words that I think I can spell. Then people say, "Don't you use strange combinations of words?" One has a different vocabulary, a vocabulary that one can spell.

INTERVIEWER: How did your stage language develop? Have you been influenced by other playwrights?

PAGE: I hope I evolve the language anew for each character in each play. One is influenced by people like [British playwrights] Edward Bond, Howard Brenton. I'm told I write very sparse, poetic drama, but it's not conscious. That is how I write language; it's not that I sit down and *structure* my stage language. I hear the language as I am writing. I tend to talk it to myself. Very often, I hear it with an accent. I write with a northern idiom, because it's the one most akin to my own. I hear it when I am writing. I am now becoming more aware of my language structures because people discuss the way I write. It's other people who have told me that I rarely use pronouns. I'm not all that sure of what pronouns are. I'm not writing total naturalism, because I don't think it can exist on stage. Not unless you observe the unities of time, place and action. All the eighteenth-century French plays I know like that are very boring. I don't think plays have a duty to be realistic. Their first duty is to communicate with the audience in the most accessible way possible, dialogue, monologue, song, whatever.

INTERVIEWER: Is there room for traditional realism and naturalism on the stage today?

PAGE: I think there is always room for anything that is good, with something original to say. There are financial constraints biting hard at plays which are expensive to produce, but I think imaginative writers can work a sort of path round that. I don't think a style for the eighties has evolved yet. I think it has to be the epic six-hander. That's a very difficult sort of play to write. The closest I've seen to it is *Summer* by Edward Bond.

INTERVIEWER: How do you research a play? Do you use interviews?

PAGE: Yes. Sometimes I am outright and tell people I am interviewing them for a play, and sometimes I do covert interviewing where I talk to people and use what they say. It's very difficult in a sense; one is always looking for a scoop, something really good that one could use. I do interviews because I believe that the writer must never get a thing wrong. You've only got to say something like, "When the war started in 1915," and you lose the audience—they start to think, "Now has the actor got it wrong or the writer?" It is very important to be accurate because theater is about truth in writing. I think art is really about truth: making it or showing it. If you want to show a truth, everything that surrounds it must be accurate, true.

INTERVIEWER: What inspired *Salonika* [1981]?

PAGE: I was commissioned by the Royal Court to write a play about old age, which was something I had wanted to do for a long time. I had a reputation for writing "nice, sympathetic" plays, and I knew the Court was expecting the play to be set in an old people's home with a nice, sympathetic nurse—then we'd all have our little cry and go home.

INTERVIEWER: The Royal Court felt you would write a "nice, sympathetic" play though you had already written *Tissue* [1978], which dealt with breast cancer in quite an unsentimental fashion?

PAGE: That's what I felt they expected me to write. I don't think many people had seen *Tissue* at the time. Anyway, for *Salonika*, I did most of my research on trains. British Rail had an offer for pensioners which made it possible for them to go anywhere for a pound. The trains were packed with old ladies traveling. They wanted to sit and talk because they were lonely; they longed to have a listener and would tell me the most extraordinary things about their lives. I wanted to write about a mother and a daughter because many of the women I'd met looked after their mothers. I met one extraordinary woman in Greenland who was seventy-three. This woman's mother had died two years previously, but up to that point, she had *always* looked after her. When I met her, she had sold up and had taken to traveling round the world. She had been tied up with that mother until she was seventy-one years old! That the break never came was horrific and frightening and extraordinary to me. Then I wondered how far away I could get from an old people's home for the setting of the play. I thought, "Old people on holiday . . ." because I knew they could travel abroad very cheaply in the off-season. I chose Salonika because of its associations with the Great War.

INTERVIEWER: Did your preoccupation with the Great War precede the play?

PAGE: My preoccupation grew out of my interest in the characters. There was no way I could discuss the experience of women of Charlotte's and Enid's age groups without discussing the Great War. Its effect was devastating for women of their generations. It's interesting to me that *Salonika* suffered dreadfully because it was put on just as all the ships were coming back from the Falklands. It was perceived to be more of an antiwar play than it was written. The play also became more antiwar than I had originally conceived because I was rewriting during the Falklands War. I was influenced. As a writer, you do get knocked off kilter by world events. I couldn't write a play that wasn't antiwar. But I've done such a spate. . . . I already had a reputation for writing about medicine . . . now it will be wars!

INTERVIEWER: Many of the London critics seemed a bit squeamish about the so-called geriatric sex in *Salonika*. Why did they react that way?

PAGE: Ask them! I think everyone is squeamish about the sexuality of older people. Even the director said, "Louise, do they really go to bed together?" I said, "Yes!" and he said, "Because I can't imagine doing it after forty." But older people who saw the play often said, "Thank God somebody actually talked about it." I do think there is a notion about women that at forty you physically dry up and it's all over, and that men at forty are Don Juans desperately trying to prove to themselves, and everybody else, that they are still young and virile.

INTERVIEWER: Did you know when you started the play that you wanted to address this mythology, or is it a theme that grew out of the characters?

PAGE: It very much grew out of the characters. I had done a lot of reading on old age and loneliness. But I want to say that I think *Salonika* is a play about memory and hopes and missed opportunity more than a play about old age. We all know people who are really young at eighty and also people who are incredibly old at fourteen. I was interested in saying people aren't on the scrap heap at sixty, which is what this society does to them. It's a society that works in terms of youth. The upper age is being pushed to about thirty-five now, but there is still that idea that after thirty-five it's all downhill. For women it is how long they can go on looking beautiful—as sexual objects—and for men it is how long they can continue to be successful.

INTERVIEWER: Do you feel that there is discrimination against women in theater?

PAGE: I'm more aware of it all the time. The first time I came across it was at Cardiff where I went to do a postgraduate degree in theater studies. There were two women on that course and twelve men. The men were always being offered the jobs as stage crew. I wanted a job because I needed money. But they wouldn't let women work as stage crew because they said women couldn't lift and didn't have the experience. I said, "If I prove that I can cleat flats will you let me have a job on the stage crew?" I was the only one who could do it; I had a drama degree and had done it all before. That was the first time I was aware of discrimination.

When I started writing, it never entered my head that women didn't write plays, though I'd never seen a play by a woman. It never occurred to me that I couldn't write plays because I was a woman. Therefore it was quite a surprise, coming out of university and having had plays produced professionally, to actually realize that women weren't expected to write plays. That was quite a shock, especially because I had a very strong mother. I wasn't raised with the notion that "women didn't do those things." Also, there wasn't much discussion of feminism when I was at university. I entered in 1973, we were the generation that went expecting the experience of university to politicize us because we'd all watched 1968 on telly. It didn't happen, which I realized after I left university. I was involved in rent strikes and protests, but there was no discussion or political analysis going on. We never studied women playwrights as such. We discussed Shelagh Delaney in the sense of "Here's a play by a woman." But it didn't strike me as exceptional. I was much too involved and centered in myself to notice. Then, just after I left university, men began to say, "Why don't you go and work with a women's theater group?" I began to think, "Why aren't the men letting me in?" And then I wrote *Tissue*. I began to hear "We've got a season of plays by men; you're a woman and we need a play by a woman. . . ." I think I was probably sometimes the only woman I knew who was writing plays. In a sense that worked quite well for me. I was getting jobs because I was a woman and people felt, "Gosh, we need a play by a woman in our season." That helped me in the beginning. I got jobs I probably wouldn't have otherwise.

INTERVIEWER: Would you want jobs like that now that you are an established writer?

PAGE: I certainly wouldn't. If I thought I was going to the Royal Shakespeare Company as a token woman, I would be horrified. I think, as a writer, one doesn't meet the discrimination as full-frontally as one does in some other areas of theater. It's much harder if you are a woman director or lighting designer because you meet it face to face. A writer is much more undercover—you send in your scripts, they are read and then people come back to you.

INTERVIEWER: What about discrimination against women writers at the literary manager level?

PAGE: I'd accept that there is discrimination in terms of subject matter but there are also very bad plays written by women. You have to be very careful to separate the two arguments. I don't think it's valid to put on a bad play just because it is a play by a woman. "My play was rejected because I am a woman" can become an emotional response to a rejection. It's an attitude we should be aware of. There is a problem for new writers of getting enough experience to develop. The assumption that writers leap forth full-fledged is an erroneous one. Becoming a playwright involves a very public learning process. You have to be brave to make mistakes in public. Women are educated to be social animals and playwriting is very, very lonely. As a career it's wonderful, but it's not always great fun. To be a woman who spends all day on her own writing is regarded, I think, as fairly extraordinary. But there is a notion of a man who sits all day in his office. Also, when you spend so much time writing you forget all the niceties of social intercourse. I find it terribly difficult to go into rehearsal after having been alone all day with my own thoughts. You suddenly have to interact with people. Having to say "What did you see on telly last night," or, "Sorry about your cat being run over" is much more difficult sometimes than sitting at home writing; one is not used to these games. But that is me, speaking as a woman who lives on her own; it may be different for women who live with others or have a family. I have to be very, very close to people if they are to be around me while I am actually, physically writing. There is something about the physical process of writing which can be quite erotic.

I think it's extraordinary when women choose to do things on their own for vast periods of time, like women painters or novelists. Because women are not brought up to do big things which require extended concentration. If you have the convention of a mother at home, as a child you see your mother spend ten minutes making the beds, then she has to answer the phone, then she polishes the floor, goes to the post office, then back to making the beds . . . there is never a concentrated work process going on that you are aware of and that you see.

INTERVIEWER: In *Plays by Women* [Volume I, London, Methuen, 1983], edited by Michelene Wandor, you stated that your feminism underwent some changes. Would you elaborate?

PAGE: I was more into the radical feminist movement in the beginning, though I hate the labels attached. By radical feminism, I mean any sort of separatist politics. I guess, in the beginning, I was being more radical about my politics—but the problem was, they were not my politics. They were politics I was picking up from other people. Ideas I was not thinking through, which is why I'm probably always going to be a little behind. By the time I've thought a thing through, it's moved somewhere else. But that has to do with being a writer. One has to investigate; one actually has to go where one thinks things are and find the sources. I would call myself a socialist feminist. Some people would call that a tame sort of feminism, but I think what's needed is a liberation of all people from preinformed ideology. Feminism is the liberation of women to be able to do what they want and be supported. You only have to talk to successful men to realize that the support systems they expect are nonexistent for women. For instance, if you talk to your women friends, you'll discover that the men say things like, "Okay. Go away and work for a week. But if I'm not here . . ." There is the notion "If you go off and work for a week, don't be surprised if I find someone else in that time." Hardly supportive. I think it is a peculiar double standard: it's also that notion of "Right. It's fine you're going out to work, but don't forget the milk." My life is chaotic. It is fraught with work. When you look at the male writers, you suddenly realize that they have support systems. Practically every time I take the train to go to Sheffield or come to London, I've got a loaf of bread, a half pound of butter, a pint of milk—because there is nobody at home to get those things for me. Whereas very often, the men on the train are going home to where those things will be provided for them, plus a clean shirt.

INTERVIEWER: Judith Barlow, in her introduction to *Plays by American Women 1900–1930* [New York, Applause, 1985], notes that playwright Rachel Crothers was accused of "Just missing the masculinity of structure," in her play *A Man's World*. Do you feel that traditional dramatic structure is inherently masculine?

PAGE: Everyone has to invent their own structures. The great plays break molds, define their own structure. I suppose it goes back to what I just said about the way women are expected to split up their time. The way women playwrights often break up time structures may well reflect that.

INTERVIEWER: Many people attribute our new sense of time structure to the advent of film and television, which are episodic.

PAGE: Shakespeare is episodic in that sense. He has tiny linking scenes. I meant time structures in which time is not linear. Time is a structure that scientists have defined. There are debates going on now as to the actual *shape* of time. The big issue of the moment is how one reevaluates the stage play. I think you have to be very big and very bold on the stage now, and women are taking those risks. They are not tied down to convention, and in a sense, can get away with something that isn't naturalistic because there is that slightly quirky thing of people saying "Well, you are a woman." It's an area in which perhaps we as women are freer for not having role models. You are judged here against standards by men. You are judged as a "woman playwright," which immediately implies that the norm for a playwright is male. Caryl Churchill is said to be one of our "best women playwrights," instead of "one of our best playwrights," which is actually what it should be. There is a put-down implied in saying "one of our best women . . ." and that put-down goes on all the time.

INTERVIEWER: Is that derogatory inference why some women are reluctant to be called a "woman playwright"?

PAGE: Absolutely. That's why I'm reluctant. I object to the way the word *woman* is used at the moment in British society. I'm not going to accept that inferior implication. I'll be a woman playwright if the men are all referred to as men playwrights. It's such an unusual concept it even sounds silly. We should all be called playwrights. I think it is terribly important as a writer to avoid every category you can. The biggest problem in theater criticism is that it rarely discusses the effect of the play on the audience which is what plays are about. I think theater critics lose their critical faculties because they go to the theater five nights a week. I do, after three plays, and I don't have to write about them. Critics don't talk about plays in terms of audiences because that is also a hard judgment to make. You are asking, "How does this relate to me?" and "How does this relate to other people?" It also depends on whether a critic thinks dramatic criticism is to sell the play or to make informed comment. There is a notion in theater criticism of "This is a play by a woman." That is why I want to reject the label of "woman writer."

INTERVIEWER: Do you feel that as a woman you have unique material to present? Is this material undeniably female?

PAGE: Well, of course, because I am a woman. One can't be a writer and be totally outside one's own experience no matter how much you research. Though you can take your own experience and extrapolate. And as a woman you do of course write women as your main characters because it is the conversation you know. Still, I think one of the best scenes in *Salonika* is the conversation between three men. I find it believable. And in *Real Estate,* the play I've just written [1984] the scene between two men in a kitchen making Swiss rolls is good. But nobody ever says, "This is a good scene between men," whereas they say about male writers, "What an extraordinary perception of women. How exceptionally well he writes women."

INTERVIEWER: You've said that it has never been one of your goals to work with women's theater companies. . . .

PAGE: Yes, because I've never been particularly interested in the notion of performing to women-only audiences. You speak to the converted. I can see the argument that there should perhaps have been women-only audiences for *Tissue,* but at the same time it is terribly important that men see that play. They, in a sense, were the more important people in the audience.

INTERVIEWER: Some women felt it was important to be separatist, at least at the beginning of the women's movement, in order to develop new ideas.

PAGE: Yes. But when I came into the theater in 1977 it seemed to me we were past that. You can't stay in that stage. I got knocked for going to work at the Royal Court Theatre, and there are various people now who might argue against my going to Stratford. But it seems to me the most important thing is that you go to the biggest possible spaces, and say, "Look, I am a woman and I am working in these spaces. Take me seriously." I am very ambitious and there is a notion within the women's movement here that to be personally ambitious is wrong. There may be a point at which you have to compromise to get into those spaces but the next time you are allowed into that space, the less you have to compromise. If you were commissioned to write a play for The National Theatre and you then wrote a radical feminist play, it would not be produced. I think if you are offered the space and the chance to get your play on you must go as far as you can go politically in your writing and get your play on. You don't totally compromise yourself. It's very hard because one hates making them for fear of compromising too far. But I do think there are points where compromise is actually justified. It is a collaborative business being a playwright. You have to release your work to actors and directors. There are times you go with decisions made by the director that you don't like—but there are also things the director can bring to a play that are simply wonderful which one wouldn't have thought of oneself. The same with casting; there are actors who, perhaps, are not your conception of the part when you begin rehearsal, but then you come round to it. There is give and take.

INTERVIEWER: Do you assert yourself in rehearsals when you feel your artistic intentions are not being fulfilled?

PAGE: Yes. But there are moments that one does accept because the rest of the director's vision is so clear that as a writer, you go with it. Perhaps you think it is wrong, but you accept it. As one gets older, and one creates more, one becomes more articulate about what one wants and ways of achieving that. I now know how to get certain effects. I know how to ask actors to do certain things. I have learned a lot about acting, particularly this past year doing *Falkland Sound* [1983] as a collaborative piece. It has been an absolute eye-opener. I have talked to actors about the way they see and read new scripts. I have gradually learned what actors can do. Giving actors all those words is a problem with writers when they first start out. You don't have to write dialogue like "I have never been in this room before." An actor can play that. What you begin to learn is that playwriting is a reductive art. Actually, you want to write as few words as possible. A play can be totally fulfilling and only last half an hour. If I could crack the five-minute play that did everything, it would be great! These are all things you learn. The problem for women is that we don't have that tradition of apprenticeship yet. In that sense, most of us are still serving our apprenticeship, in the terms of the traditional craft apprenticeship. I haven't even been working for seven years. There are quite a lot of male writers who have taken other male writers under their wings. There are very few female writers who do the same for other women.

INTERVIEWER: Why?

PAGE: It's difficult because there are still so few women writers and you come up against the same people for jobs all the time. It's such a tiny world.

INTERVIEWER: How do you know when a play is finished and ready to go out into the world?

PAGE: One does it when one wants some response. On the whole, I think one knows if a piece is good or not. But you see, the way I judge my work is totally different from the way anyone else judges my work. I judge my work in terms of whether or not I have progressed from the last script, rather than whether it is a good script in itself. I set technical exercises for myself all the time, because there are moments of crisis as a writer, when you feel you can't write imaginatively but you can write by using your technique. Technical exercises are really games one plays with one's own writing. For example, choosing in a play to write interior dialogue without using monologue. It's a way to develop technique and if things are going badly it can be something to hang on to.

INTERVIEWER: What are some of your latest goals in terms of playwriting? What do you want to improve? . . .

PAGE: Everything! Structure and plot. For instance, I am really keen to do a play about the politics of sport and it will be a challenge to find a structure for that play because I'm not interested in doing agitprop. I am interested in the well-constructed play; the play as "thriller," where you take in everything in order to get to the end of the story. It's like fairy tales in a sense; you know that the prince and princess have to marry at the end, and in order to get the emotional "fix" from people living happily ever after—you are willing to go through all the dragons. The notion of a good story is quite important to me.

INTERVIEWER: You are a very visual writer. . . .

PAGE: I am now. I think when you first start writing you think the words are all important, then you realize that the visual aspects, the imagery and the symbolism, have priority in the theater because it is easy to shut out words and very difficult to shut out an image. Images are what people carry away from the theater. You don't come out of *Macbeth* reciting "Tomorrow and tomorrow and tomorrow . . ."; you come out with a series of images, like the witches, the dagger scene. You leave the theater with your interpretation of the words, not the speeches themselves.

INTERVIEWER: Is it important to you as a playwright that your work be published?

PAGE: I think it is extraordinary to see one of your plays in published form. It is part of a strange distancing process that begins with seeing a script typed by somebody else and photocopied, and ends with publication.

INTERVIEWER: Is publication of special significance to women playwrights?

PAGE: Publishing is the answer because it opens up women's work and makes it available. *Tissue* [*Plays by Women,* edited by Michelene Wandor, Vol. I, Methuen, 1983] has now sold three thousand copies, which is phenomenal for a play in print. Publishing is a sign that you are being taken seriously. But it worries me that women's plays get lumped together, you know, "Five Plays by Women. . . ."

INTERVIEWER: There are many anthologies which are strictly male in bookstores; they are just not labeled as such. . . .

PAGE: Yes, although there is also a tendency to publish male writers individually.

INTERVIEWER: We had the impression, with the influx of British women's plays in New York, that women playwrights in England had bonded and formed a movement.

PAGE: No. We are very stratified because of the ways we write and because we have different political perspectives. It's the people on the outside who have given us a label. We're all individuals trying our best. That goes for all playwrights male and female. Our first duty is to write with our own voices.

NTOZAKE SHANGE

Ntozake Shange *is the author of* Mother Courage and Her Children, *for colored girls who have considered suicide/when the rainbow is enuf,* Spell #7, A Photograph: Lovers in Motion, Boogie Woogie Landscape *and an adaptation of* Educating Rita. *She has also written two novels,* Sassafrass, Cypress & Indigo, *1982, and* Betsey Brown, *1985. She has recently completed book and lyrics for* Betsey Brown, *a rhythm and blues opera commissioned by Joseph Papp for the New York Shakespeare Festival to be directed by Emily Mann. In January 1983 Shange accepted the position of Mellon Distinguished Professor of Literature at Rice University in Texas. She is also Associate Professor of Drama in the creative writing program at the University of Houston. Work-in-progress includes the following performance pieces:* The Jazz Life, Black and Blue Valentines, Bosoms and Mares: Riding the Moon in East Texas *and* Smoke Voices, *all of which incorporate art, poetry and dance. Ms. Shange has received a National Endowment for the Arts Fellowship, a Guggenheim Fellowship, an Obie for* Mother Courage and Her Children, *and for* for colored girls . . . *an Obie, the Outer Circle Critics Award, the Audelco Award and the* Mademoiselle *Award.*

INTERVIEWER: Would you tell us something about the impact of dance on your creative life and writing process?

SHANGE: Writing is for most people a cerebral activity. For me it is a very rhythmic and visceral experience. Dance clears my mind of verbal images and allows me to understand the planet the way I imagine atomic particles experience space. I am not bogged down with the implications of language. I am only involved in the implications of movement which later on, when I do start to write, become manifest in the rhythms of my poetry.

INTERVIEWER: You've said that Western culture, as opposed to Afro-American culture, promotes a split between mind and body. What are the differences between these two cultures?

SHANGE: I am not an Anglo-Western civilization person so I don't think I could describe it. But it would appear to me that there is a definitive split between the two—Western culture is very keen on specific disciplines as opposed to multidisciplinary approaches. That much I think I can say without stepping over my boundaries.

INTERVIEWER: Does the notion of the multidisciplined approach tie into what you said in the introduction to your play collection, *Spell #7*: "We should demolish the notion of straight theater for a decade or so, refuse to allow playwrights to work without dancers and musicians."

SHANGE: Yes it does. Though I haven't allowed myself to do it in theater I did start doing visual art, a natural extension of what I said about multidiscipline. I've done four installation pieces in the last two years, which included performance art, not continually, but at the openings.

INTERVIEWER: What kind of multimedia are you using in the installations?

SHANGE: One installation [1981] was made of sticks, cotton and a hanging—rope silhouettes of smiling black babies. On the other side there was raffia and lace and garlic and okra and orchids and a big huge black baby who had an umbilical cord of velvet and magnolias. Another piece was called "The Jazz Life: Wall Poems." I simply wrote all over the walls excerpts of love poems that I read at the performance, which included two dancers. It was a way to actually trap people inside a poem and it really did work. This was sponsored by the Women for Art Caucus in Houston at The Firehouse in 1984. At the 1199 Gallery, I did a piece called "Working Women—How We Work," which was seven frying pans, one for each day of the week, filled with different things like contraceptives, bill receipts, dirty clothes, pictures of the Virgin, beer cans, little plastic twenty-two caliber pistols. "On the Board" was a celebration of Junsteenth Day [June 19th]. I don't know if you know this, but the slaves in Texas didn't find out till three years later that they had been emancipated and we celebrate that on Junsteenth Day. I'm also trying to do my piece, "From Property to Personhood," in a local park. It is a graduated scale, from two feet to six feet, of different kinds of circles. At the beginning, you have to crawl to enter, and by the time you get to the end you are standing—you come out a free person. I wanted to do something around my daughter—something that couldn't be sold. I didn't want her to think in any way that I made money off her. So I make things for her, in her honor, that can't be bought.

INTERVIEWER: Are you moving in the direction of performance art and away from the other styles of stage work you've done in the past?

SHANGE: The theater work I did was to me an anomaly. I was a performance artist to begin with. So I am doing what I used to do before

I was in theater. I haven't stopped writing plays—I just feel more at home in performance because that is what I started out doing.

INTERVIEWER: Is performance art closer to poetry than the stage play?

SHANGE: It is much closer to poetry, and it is freer because I can use a lot of improvisation.

INTERVIEWER: Were you aware, as a young girl, that you possessed a gift?

SHANGE: [Laughs] I didn't think of it as a gift until about 1971 when I moved to Boston. I started working with groups of musicians, and I had my own band (Zaki & The Palm Wine Drunkards). During this time, I was also involved in different kinds of spiritual activity which directed my attention to those things that are given by the gods in various forms. It was my most intense journal-keeping period as well.

INTERVIEWER: Do you still keep journals?

SHANGE: Off and on. Journals keep me grounded in some kind of emotional and creative arena that's not tortuous. I can't always do it now, although I wish that I could.

INTERVIEWER: Has having a child changed your life as a writer?

SHANGE: I don't have much time . . . time to think thoughts that might lead to poems or dances or creative pieces. I have to get out of my house to work creatively and I don't like having a studio outside the house; as a very domestic person, that is dysfunctional for me. But I have to, so I do.

INTERVIEWER: What are the positive aspects of motherhood?

SHANGE: Oh, my [three-year-old] daughter is a lovely person. And it is quite an honor to be her caretaker. She has a lovely disposition, she is a good trouper, she is very flexible, has an excellent memory. She enjoys dance and music and paintings. Her father is a painter so she knows that a painting *is* a painting, as opposed to something on the wall.

INTERVIEWER: Who are your influences?

SHANGE: Early Le Roi Jones, Ishmael Reed, Susan Griffin, Thulani Davis, Jessica Hagedorn, Victor Hernandez Cruz and Pedro Pietri, Wopolhlolup. Then Latin writers: Cabrera-Infante, Miguel Asturias, Gabriel Garcia Márquez. C.L.R. James, of course, Leon Damas, Zora Neale Hurston, and Langston Hughes. Also Olga Brumas, Gloria Naylor, June Jordan, Emily Mann, Manuel Puig, Lydia Fagundes Telles.

INTERVIEWER: You were recently appointed Associate Professor of Drama at the University of Houston. Can writing be taught?

SHANGE: I don't believe you can teach writing. What you can do is help someone refine the skills and the talent that they have. A course can be geared toward assisting each student to find his or her voice and toward challenging a student who is good in one form to become better in the form he or she has chosen, as well as others. I keep assignments short because I think if you can write one concise page you are more apt to be able to write fifteen beautiful pages than if you wrote three stupid pages. I'm very happy with my students, and I feel committed to them.

I want to add Alice Childress to the list of people who've given me inspiration. She is instrumental.

INTERVIEWER: In what ways did she influence you?

SHANGE: Her family is from the same part of South Carolina as my family. It's helped me a lot with the novel to think about the work I've seen Alice do and then—not to steal from her—but to try and get the same ambiance that I feel in her work. Not that I couldn't have done it on my own, but I think that you have to give credit where credit's due.

INTERVIEWER: How is Houston, Texas, after the mad world of New York?

SHANGE: It's exactly what I needed. I can work on my own schedule; I can afford to live a life-style that I think is reasonable for a single mother. I have immediate access to alternative spaces. There is a large visual arts community here. There is a fairly small, but very supportive literary community. I am able to do things here that I couldn't do in New York: I can ride horses; I have the time to take Kundalini Yoga; I have time to spend with my daughter. The black community here ranges from middle class to poverty-stricken, but it is not separated in the same classist way as New York. Also, Texas is much closer to Latin America than New York is, so my traveling has become much easier.

INTERVIEWER: You have been spending a lot of time in Latin America. . . .

SHANGE: Off and on over the last seven years, yes: Curaçao, Aruba, Jamaica, Brazil, Mexico, Cuba, Nicaragua, Nassau, Bermuda, Martinique, Haiti, Trinidad, Tobago and Puerto Rico. My primary influences, and most profound experiences have come out of my travels in Brazil, Nicaragua and Cuba. [See See No Evil: Prefaces, Essays, Accounts.]

INTERVIEWER: Was there anything that particularly impressed you about theater in South America?

SHANGE: The rapport that the teatrista people have with their audience is so much more intense and intimate than it is here. What they call Teatro Popular—Popular Theater or vernacular theater— is geared toward, and part of, the community of what we would call the working class, the working poor people. The theater is very open to them and it is part of their lives, which is not true here.

INTERVIEWER: Does this Popular Theater grow out of the community?

SHANGE: In some cases, yes, and in some no. A theater group from Bogotá might be touring all around the country. So it wouldn't necessarily be growing out of that community in some small town in the mountains. On the other hand, it's not estranged from the people either. In Spanish- and French-speaking places, the arts have never been isolated from government or from revolution.

INTERVIEWER: How has your reception been in foreign countries?

SHANGE: Very good. I have not encountered hostile audiences except in the United States.

INTERVIEWER: Why are American audiences hostile?

SHANGE: It's not *all* Americans. If I had to say who my enemies are, I would say male chauvinists, and English-speaking black nationalists who resent my work with Latin American countries and my bilingualism, and who refuse to admit they live in the Western hemisphere which is predominantly Spanish-speaking.

INTERVIEWER: Do you work in commercial spaces in Texas?

SHANGE: The commercial theater here has a subscription audience so I still have to be in an alternative space. My work is not the kind that subscription audiences are used to or want to see. It doesn't bother me because I like working in alternative spaces, I always have and I believe in supporting them. I think to continually work in big houses—like on Broadway or at the Alley [Theatre, Houston] or at the Mark Taper [Forum, Los Angeles]—is dangerous for somebody who is trying to explore because you can only explore so much when all that money is being invested in you. It's not that I don't like working in beautiful theaters, it's that I have to keep my mind clear about why they're going to let me work there. I have very good relationships with all the theaters I work with, and with my producers, but I'm not robbing Peter to pay Paul. I work in alternative spaces whenever I can and I don't have to ask anybody about it. It's important to have power over one's work. Right now, I want to experiment and I don't want to spend a lot of money doing it. I also don't want a lot of people around telling me what works and what doesn't. I want the audience to let me know what works and what doesn't.

INTERVIEWER: How do you feel about being called a "woman writer"?

SHANGE: I have been a feminist writer ever since I started. When I was nineteen I worked for the Young Lords Party instead of the Black Panther Party because in the Young Lords, equality for women was part of the platform of the party. I decided I was a feminist at that point [1968–1970] and I've never stopped being one.

INTERVIEWER: Why do you think that some women, who at one point were quite proud to call themselves feminists, now say, "I'm not a feminist, I'm a humanist"?

SHANGE: I don't know. I don't understand it, either. The only thing I can think is that they have achieved what they wanted and now feel that they are no longer in the struggle; but, that's presumptuous on my part, because I don't really know why they say that.

INTERVIEWER: What do we women have yet to win in our struggle for equality? What are you struggling for in your work? What issues do you think need to be addressed?

SHANGE: A development of respect for a real feminist aesthetic, which is why I am on the board of directors at the Feminist Art Institute even if I don't do as much for them as I'd like. I also belong to Women Against Violence Against Women and Children and the Women for Art Caucus. I'm very disturbed about the proliferation of manufactured goods [e.g., powdered-milk substitutes—Ed.] in Third World countries where women should be nursing; instead their babies are starving to death. I'm very concerned about the liberation of South Africa and the need for an end to bombings in Angola and Mozambique. I'm concerned about the embargo against Cuba after twenty-five years and the pending embargo against Nicaragua which it seems is coming down the line. I'm disturbed about the invasion of Grenada. And I'm disturbed that we still don't have equal pay for equal work. As a black person, I know that black women get paid less per dollar than anybody. We also have a higher infant mortality rate than any other ethnic population in the country. Those things to me are still very real and must be addressed. Hopefully they are addressed in the essays I write, which is why we put together *See No Evil: Prefaces, Essays and Accounts 1976–1983* [San Francisco, Momo's Press, 1984].

INTERVIEWER: The majority of women writers are dealing with more personal material.

SHANGE: I think the dangerous mistake that women make is to assume the personal is not political. When I make a personal statement, it is to me a political statement.

INTERVIEWER: Why is it so difficult for male critics to interpret the artistic intentions of women playwrights?

SHANGE: It is impossible to enter the territory of someone you oppress with the knowledge that you have as an oppressor. Male critics have no vocabulary or understanding of our condition. The only way they understand it is if they are in control of it. If we are in our own arena they are not in control, and, therefore, they have no language and no tools to comprehend what is being said to them or created for them.

INTERVIEWER: You have said that theater is the weakest arena in American art.

SHANGE: There are fewer great plays written by American artists than there are great visual works or great dances or great music.

INTERVIEWER: Is theater the most conservative of the arts?

SHANGE: It's the most costly. And it also requires the most collaboration. Between those two elements, it's real hit-or-miss—there are too many people involved in the success of one piece and it costs too much money to hire them.

INTERVIEWER: How do you behave in rehearsal?

SHANGE: I'm always the assistant director, that's how I behave. When I am the director, I do a lot of improvs and subtext work. Then we put the piece together.

INTERVIEWER: Are you ever frustrated when working with another director?

SHANGE: Usually we talk it through. I'm not one of those writers who is resistant to making changes in the text or trying new things. If I do feel frustrated, then of course I won't use that person again. But generally speaking, I don't have bad relationships with directors.

INTERVIEWER: How important is it for a playwright to direct his or her own work?

SHANGE: In workshop it is very helpful. It helps me at least to find flaws in the script. Directing helped me rewrite a piece that was in trouble—now I'm really proud of it. I also like directing other people's work because it gives me a clearer sense of structure—even if a piece is traditional; directing gives me a clearer sense of how nontraditional my own structure can be.

INTERVIEWER: You once wrote, "We must learn our common symbols, preen them, and share them with the world" [epigraph to *for colored girls . . .*].

SHANGE: It's what I meant earlier when I mentioned a female aesthetic. That is part of the work that Andrea Dworkin, Adrienne Rich, Susan Griffin and I do, as well as many visual artists like Betye Saar and Judy Chicago.

INTERVIEWER: Will you tell us what you mean by a female aesthetic?

SHANGE: No. Because I've written it already and I don't want to mess with it. [See Shange's introduction to *for colored girls . . .*, Bantam, 1981.]

INTERVIEWER: Is religion important in your life?

SHANGE: In the black community, the church is the strongest major institution. For me as a so-called representative of the black community not to have something to do with the black church would be contradictory. On the other hand, I feel more akin to radical Catholic priests in Central

America than I do to missionary sorts of work. So I am an amalgam of two things. Ernesto Cardenal is a priest; he is also the minister of culture of Nicaragua. There are also a number of priests working with the junta in Nicaragua. I think there is a major role that the church in its myriad forms can play in the struggle of oppressed people all over the world.

INTERVIEWER: Karen Malpede believes it is important for the playwright to present healing images, much like your last scene in *for colored girls . . .*

SHANGE: I believe in that. I think my pieces do that. It's unfair to rupture and bring forth a wound without, at the same time, offering some solace. Not a cure-all, but a sense that there is something else that can be done.

INTERVIEWER: Does the playwright have a responsibility to society?

SHANGE: Yes. I think everybody does.

INTERVIEWER: Why aren't we seeing more political plays from American playwrights?

SHANGE: I think somebody's got to light a fire up under their asses. [Laughter]

INTERVIEWER: Got a match?

SHANGE: As a matter of fact, I do have a match and it's called my work.

INTERVIEWER: Do you feel you've paid a price for being so honest and so outspoken in your writing?

SHANGE: For a little while I paid the price of having no privacy. I paid the price of becoming self-conscious. I had never experienced that. Moving to Texas has helped me to get away from those two things.

INTERVIEWER: How did it affect your work when you became self-conscious?

SHANGE: I was lucky. It did not affect my work. It affected my life as opposed to my work. The two are not the same.

INTERVIEWER: Did your concerns shift when you moved to Texas?

SHANGE: No, my concerns had time to become fuller.

INTERVIEWER: Do you feel attacked by the media or theatrical establishment for being a political playwright?

SHANGE: No. I might be, but I don't read those things so I am not affected by them. One's enemies are interested on one's disappearance. I expect reactionary criticism.

INTERVIEWER: Was it difficult to work with publishers at first because you have invented a unique style/language?

SHANGE: No, at first I worked with small women's presses so I never encountered any difficulty. I didn't come to commercial publishing out of a vacuum, I came from a small press literary community that had served my needs up to that point.

INTERVIEWER: Will you tell us about your work day . . . your creative process?

SHANGE: It changes all the time. Sometimes I am very disciplined and sometimes I am not. It's a catch-as-catch-can experience right now because I have to get up early with the baby to take her to school. My day is very, very disrupted.

INTERVIEWER: What about when you are traveling?

SHANGE: I keep journals. My journals are becoming more specific —journals for Nicaragua, journals for Cuba, journals for teaching—as opposed to the general journals I used to take with me. That's because I don't have a lot of time and I have to make priorities about what I am going to talk about.

INTERVIEWER: Do you need special conditions to write? Some women can write with their kids running around. . . .

SHANGE: I can't write with a child running around anywhere. I need a clean house and quiet. A fresh pot of coffee, a bottle of Perrier water, about three packs of cigarettes and some flowers.

INTERVIEWER: Have your yoga classes affected your writing?

SHANGE: They make it easier for me to write when I am blocked because they unlock my chakras. I assume that dancing and yoga contribute a great deal to my creative energy flow. And horseback riding helps make me more aggressive than I might be because I am having to control an animal that is much bigger than I am.

INTERVIEWER: Tell us what the difference was between your intimate working experience with small presses and alternative theater and the huge commercial Broadway success you had with *for colored girls . . .*?

SHANGE: I've never been a playwright who wanted plays—I am a writer who wants books. I get much happier about a book than I do about a show, although that may not *always* be so. I am still very active in the small press arena simply because I like books. Right now I have books made of handmade paper with Bookslinger Press, and Toothpaste Press, as well as the *See No Evil . . .* book, which is also from a small press called MoMo's.

INTERVIEWER: Why are you less comfortable writing for the stage?

SHANGE: I make a great commitment to the work when I'm doing it but I also know in three weeks it's not going to run anymore. *Spell #7* did have an incredibly decent run in New York—it ran for nine months Off Broadway—but still, nobody in the United States knows about that play.

INTERVIEWER: We were able to read it in the published version.

SHANGE: Right, that's why I like books. Books are available to everybody. Plays [in performance] are not, because they cost too much. I hate to sound obsessed with finances, but they cost entirely too much money. And you have to deal with too many people. I've written two pieces that I desperately want up, but I'm not writing any more until these two go on. What's the point?

INTERVIEWER: Any ideas about what can be done about the high cost of theater?

SHANGE: I do performance art. That satisfies me. Now a lot of people who want to see theater are not going to be happy with that; they should go see a Sam Shepard play or something, I don't know . . .

INTERVIEWER: In your work, there are warnings to the women artist about the possibility of the creative spirit being crushed under the weight of relationships.

SHANGE: I think that's true. Men take up an enormous amount of time and they also distort one's perception.

INTERVIEWER: Self-perception?

SHANGE: Self-perception and perception of the world, because instead of seeing yourself as an individual in the world you see yourself as part of a unit. Not that there is anything wrong with that, but there *can* be something wrong with that.

INTERVIEWER: Do you have any special memories of W. E. B. Dubois?

SHANGE: The story goes that he hated children, but that he put me to bed one night and sang me a lullabye. That's the family folklore—how true it is, I don't know. I know that Paul Robeson used to come to our house . . . Dizzy Gillespie still does, as well as Lalo Schifrin, who is now a big Hollywood music writer. Mango Santa Maria—many different boxers were around all the time because my father is a boxing physician. I remember that my mother used to take me to see ballets, especially if there were black people in them, like Carmen De Lavallade and Arthur Mitchell.

INTERVIEWER: So you had a lot of artistic stimulation while growing up.

SHANGE: Yes. My mother was *extremely* significant, as was my father, in terms of the breadth of Afro-American culture. The two together, Mommy concentrating on English-speaking artists, and my father concentrating on the international sphere.

INTERVIEWER: Have you written about your mother?

SHANGE: She appears in some of the letters Hilda Effania writes in my novel *Sassafrass, Cypress, & Indigo* [New York, St. Martin's Press, 1982].

INTERVIEWER: Why do some women have a hands-off attitude toward presenting their own mothers in their work?

SHANGE: What Adrienne Rich says in *Of Woman Born* is true: It is difficult to embrace the very female who taught you to be an oppressed person. I think it's going to take a long time for us to learn how to do that. Luckily, I've been able to start—but I, too, had a very "hands-off" attitude toward my mother for years. It's just since I've been able to start writing mother characters in the novel that I came to see the beauties in her and could transmit them to my audience. Everybody I've talked to about *Sassafrass* . . . has said they saw the character Mama as the mother that everybody really wants to have. Mama is in fact an amalgam of my mother, my great-aunts and my grandmother—but particularly my mother.

INTERVIEWER: In your travels in South America and throughout the world, have you encountered the phenomenon of pacifist women gathering together in a collective attempt to bring peace to the world, such as the women at Greenham Common?

SHANGE: I've been seeing a lot of women who are cultural aggressors. . . .

INTERVIEWER: These cultural aggressors are women artists?

SHANGE: Yes. They are doing pieces that have to do with the affirmation and exploration of women's lives. And that's what I call cultural aggression. I want to write a book entitled *Cultural Aggression* and probably will someday.

INTERVIEWER: Do you have a sense of yourself in the history of literature?

SHANGE: No. That is what secondary-source people, scholars do. I'm just me. I'm here doing what I'm supposed to do. I have a baby, I write, I take care of my house, I go to church, I vote. If you want to know what *I* think I do—that's what I do.

INTERVIEWER: Would you discuss the sexuality in your work?

SHANGE: I'm very uninhibited in the plays and in my fiction, but I couldn't write an essay about women's sexuality.

INTERVIEWER: You are quite successful at presenting erotic, as opposed to pornographic, imagery.

SHANGE: I hope so. We need that. There is a lush quality to women's sexuality that we have ignored because of the stark realities of pornography and the way men treat us as sexual objects. Hopefully, my characters bring out some of the richness and the sensuality that I think is inherent in a female existence, in a female landscape.

INTERVIEWER: What aspects of your work have been misunderstood? Is there any particular criticism which has made you angry?

SHANGE: What makes me angry is that people think after *for colored girls* . . . , I died. That's an element of commercial theater and one reason why I don't like it.

INTERVIEWER: We *are* a "star" culture. . . .

SHANGE: Yeah, well, they can't do that to me. That's what they've discovered. That's part of the reason I'm living in Texas.

INTERVIEWER: Did celebrity change your life?

SHANGE: It was a very isolating, alienating experience and I don't really like to talk about it.

INTERVIEWER: You've said that there is a phenomenon of black, Latin and Asian artists being "one-shot"—do you have any thoughts as to why these voices fall silent?

SHANGE: It's not that they fall silent, it's that they are not continuous commercial successes. Frank Chin is still writing, Jessica Hagadorn is still writing, Alice Childress and June Jordan are still writing—but they are not commercial successes, and that is why you don't hear about them.

INTERVIEWER: Have you any advice for young women playwrights of the future?

SHANGE: The only thing I have to say to them is a quote from a poem I wrote:

> We can't be stopped
> our lips are too thick
> and the air is too strong

MEGAN TERRY

Megan Terry was born July 22, 1932, in Seattle, Washington. A founding member of The Open Theater and The New York Theatre Strategy, she is now Literary Manager and Playwright-in-Residence at the Omaha Magic Theatre. Ms. Terry has written more than sixty plays, including X-Rayed-iate, Family Talk, Porch Visit, Above It: Speculations on the Death of Amelia Earhart, Family Circus: Featuring Scenes from the Life of Mother Jones, Fifteen Million Fifteen-Year-Olds, High Energy Musicals from the Omaha Magic Theatre, Kegger, Objective Love, American King's English for Queens, Brazil Fado, 100,001 Horror Stories of the Plains, Babes in the Bighouse, Hothouse, Nightwalk (with Jean-Claude van Itallie and Sam Shepard), American Wedding Ritual, The Tommy Allen Show, Approaching Simone, Keep Tightly Closed in a Cool Dry Place, Comings and Goings, Calm Down Mother, Eat at Joe's and The Magic Realists. Ms. Terry graduated from the University of Washington, earned certificates in directing, acting and design from the Banff School of Fine Arts, and won a Fellowship to Yale.

INTERVIEWER: You've written a cornucopia of plays, had hundreds of productions world-wide and share administrative and artistic responsibilities at the Omaha Magic Theatre. When do you find time to write?

TERRY: Whenever I have to. Helping to run a theater is like running a small business, so the writing has to get squeezed in whenever it can. I used to write two pages a day when things were calmer, but sometimes I have to write ten. I buy pens by the gross.

INTERVIEWER: You still write by hand, then?

TERRY: I always have paper in three typewriters. Two down at The Magic Theatre and one at home. And I must have pens. I always seem to be on the move.

INTERVIEWER: Describe your creative process. How does a play begin in your mind?

TERRY: In many different ways. I was trained in fine arts and went into theater first as a designer and performer. Sometimes it's an image, or the entire set. Sometimes I draw the set first and then write scenes to go in it. Other times, characters start speaking and acting in my mind, and then I become like a secretary to the characters and type as fast as I can to get it all down.

INTERVIEWER: When you work on a topic that requires research, do you begin the research or the writing first?

TERRY: No set way. *Approaching Simone* [1970] took me fifteen years to get together because I had to do a lot of research. Many of her [Simone Weil's] books were out of print, and I had to comb rare-book libraries. The greatest thing that happened as a result of doing the play was that the publishers brought Simone Weil's work out again in paperback.

INTERVIEWER: Your play *Brazil Fado* [1977] is peppered with news reports. Are those taken from real incidents?

TERRY: Yes, from *The Omaha World Herald, The Christian Science Monitor,* and *The New York Times.*

INTERVIEWER: Rosalyn Drexler uses news clippings, current events, weird items in her work, too. Why do you?

TERRY: In *Brazil Fado* I wanted to say a few things about the continuing tragedies in Central and South America.

INTERVIEWER: It's a fascinating play.

TERRY: Can you tell me why nobody's doing it?

INTERVIEWER: You're making a connection in *Brazil Fado* between an American couple playing torture games and torture in the world at large. Do you think, in this conservative era, anybody wants to buy a play on that subject?

TERRY: Not even other women producers, unfortunately. But we have no problem producing such plays for our Omaha audience.

INTERVIEWER: In *Magic Dust,* the newspaper your theater publishes and distributes in the community, you reported on your attendance at the Open Theater Conference at Kent State University in December 1983. You say most students have never heard of Joe Chaikin and the Open Theater.

TERRY: Even the head of the Drama Department there managed to stay away! [Laughter] That was always the case, too, when we were on tour with the Open Theater. Very rarely did the drama people—the people who were teaching in theater departments—ever show up at our performances! Isn't that amazing? It's unbelievable to me that the Open Theater has stayed alive in people's minds as long as it has! . . . One of the problems is that many *critics* are looking through a rearview mirror. I think they only read *The New York Times* and each other. They don't know what's happening in the *world*. And they're so negative. Even the supportive critics think nothing's happened since the sixties. But almost everyone who was in the Open Theater is now running a company of their own today. People such as Jo Ann Schmidman, Paul Zimet, Ellen Madden, Shami Chaikin, Ray Berry, Ralph Lee, Tina Shepard, Sam Shepard, Jean-Claude van Itallie, Gwen Fabricant, James Barbosa and Barbara Van are all growing and developing incredible new work. But several critics who attended that conference think that the only new thing is performance art. They don't do their homework.

INTERVIEWER: What was the most important thing about the conference for you?

TERRY: I think we realized that we were all meant to be together when we were. We realized we loved one another and we respected one another. That the work *was* important, and it was still ongoing in our heads and in the work we're doing now. It was a *fabulous* affirmation. Some of us had not seen each other for ten years! So you can imagine there was advance trepidation. People wondered if some of the old friction would arise, but none did. We've matured. It *is* possible to grow up! [Laughter] We were so *young* then! And we were working in the dark! We were uncovering things that were extremely dynamic and scary. Some of the early problems we had were just part of the process. We cried for joy when we saw one another. It was very heady to realize we'd made a great contribution to the growth of our field and to the artistic development of one another.

INTERVIEWER: What do you think that generation of theater people learned from the fifties, from the early work of The Living Theatre? And then what do you think the seventies learned from the sixties?

TERRY: I've written a play which I haven't released that deals with the late fifties. Obviously, nobody's ready to even consider it yet. Theater is a conservative art necessarily because it deals with living human beings having to get along with one another to bring something about.

INTERVIEWER: Theater lags behind the other arts?

TERRY: Yes—it has to—because discoveries have to be made in the other art forms before they can be assimilated into theater. Since painting or poetry is a one-to-one thing, it can develop faster. It's my opinion that American painting, poetry and jazz reached their zenith in the fifties. And that had to happen before the theater could take off. The theater conserves and accumulates, and the sixties couldn't have happened the way it did if such exciting work hadn't arrived in the fifties in the other art forms. Witness the amazing success of the exhibit of late fifties and early sixties painting entitled *BLAM!* at the Whitney [Museum of American Art]. Young people are going to that exhibit and coming out reeling with energy and ideas from that time. For too long people have believed the conservative propaganda that nothing happened in the fifties but Eisenhower's golf swing. Also, the sixties would have been different had Kennedy not been shot. The assassination was a catalyst that brought together and then exploded an astounding energy in theatrical art.

INTERVIEWER: Are there particular people of that fifties generation that influenced you?

TERRY: The American musical theater . . . the Beat Generation poets, [Gary] Snyder, [Jack] Kerouac, [Allen] Ginsberg . . . the painters [Robert] Rauschenberg, Red Grooms, [Claes] Oldenburg, Jackson Pollock, Helen Frankenthaler.

INTERVIEWER: And of the musicians?

TERRY: Anita O'Day . . . Sara Vaughan . . . Lambert Hendricks and Ross, Kenny Berrel Trio . . . I was very into jazz and Elvis Presley rock 'n roll!

INTERVIEWER: What happened to theater in the sixties? What was breaking down, changing?

TERRY: Up until the sixties, the American theater for the most part was an imitation—except for musicals—of the European theater. The Oedipus complex vis-à-vis Mother England was very strong. People went to the theater to learn how to behave, so they could continue an upwardly mobile climb. How to dress, how to smoke cigarettes with *élan*, how to mix drinks while looking seductive, et cetera—how to look WASP. We in the Open Theater and other groups were not interested in "getting ahead" in the old way. We wanted to get somewhere with ourselves, our art and with each other. We wanted a richer, a "realer" life. I feel we democratized the theater. We began to put every kind of American on the stage. I wanted to write plays where it didn't matter what you looked like as long as you had the talent to play it. Also, we were a generation of people educated by those who had survived World War II and come back to teach. World War II gave us as a people a global view. Up to then, in spite of World War I, we'd been insular. We now belonged to the whole world.

INTERVIEWER: And now do we think the world belongs to us?

TERRY: I think the Russians have made a very clear statement, lately, about *that*. The world is split in two. What happened to the [1984] Olympics in Los Angeles is continuing evidence. [The Soviet Union refused to send competitors to the games.]

INTERVIEWER: How did the democratization of the theater during the sixties affect the seventies?

TERRY: In the late fifties, early sixties, people came from all over America to New York. And they weren't welcome in the existing Broadway theater. So people like Lanford Wilson, Joe Chaikin, Irene Fornes, Julie Bovasso and all the rest of us who had been told we weren't tall enough, short enough, or thin enough got fed up, and in American entrepreneurial fashion started our own theaters. All these young people were idealists! With fine training. The models in our head were those of the Moscow Art Theatre, the Group Theatre. The Group Theatre ideal evolved into the Actors Studio, and, because of their directors going into film, put Americans in *film* on a *global* scale. But there was, to our minds, no *real* American *theater*. Previously playwrights had appeared to the popular mind only one at a time. In the beginning was O'Neill. Then Tennessee Williams. Then Miller. Edward Albee was the last of the "lone" playwrights. The sixties was an incredible explosion of thirty-five talented writers showing up in New York. And nobody knew how to deal with them! Critics have a Messiah complex! Their brains are too tiny to hold more than one talent in their minds at a time. Michael Feingold [*The Village Voice*], Jack Kroll [*Newsweek*] and Sylvie Drake [*The Los Angeles Times*] are different. They love *theater*. They're in it *with* us. Unfortunately, many other critics seem bent on using the stuff of theater as raw material for their own careers in a way that demonstrates they're not *part* of the field.

INTERVIEWER: Why do you think they're always bemoaning the lack of political plays?

TERRY: Yet when one appears, they don't recognize it. They're always asking for "language." But when Stephen Berkoff arrived with *Greeks*, or Maria Irene Fornes with *Fefu and Her Friends*, they couldn't hear it! . . . I don't know why most of them think there can only be *one* writer at a time to sum up an age! America is *vast*. There are many Americas. If you tour this country, you find that out very quickly. Yet critics tend to put the playwright up on the cross. They allow one or two successes, and then they fire napalm. The pressure is horrendous. I'm fearful for Sam Shepard now. You *know* you have to worry when your face appears on the cover of a national magazine. [Laughter]

INTERVIEWER: Do you make a distinction between theater critics that review for the media and academic theater criticism?

TERRY: I just heard three marvelous papers at Stanford University. Dr. Margaret Wilkerson on Lorraine Hansberry, Dr. Beverly Beyers-Pevitts and Dr. Rosemary Curb on an array of writers. Their criticism is useful, even inspiring, to a writer.

INTERVIEWER: What elements of criticism are useful to you?

TERRY: To have the thoughts of minds of their caliber paying attention to writing and writers, their creative comparisons, turns lights on in my head; I see things I hadn't thought of before. New possibilities for plays form in my mind. It drives me forward. Whereas, the other kind of criticism makes me think, "*What* am I *doing*? I'm going to go back to crab fishing!" [Laughter]

INTERVIEWER: What about the regional critics versus the New York critics?

TERRY: I'm thinking of Richard Christianson of *The Chicago Tribune*, Chris Koyamo of *Chicago Magazine* and Joan Bunke of *The Des Moines Register*. They bring a terrific education, a love of theater, concern and a disciplined but considered point of view to their writing. Sylvie Drake, Dan Sullivan and John Mahoney of *The Los Angeles Times*, Bernard Weiner of *The San Francisco Chronicle*, Mike Steel of *The Minneapolis Tribune* and Helen Krich Chinoy and Linda Walsh Jenkins, academic critics, are people who are joining in a partnership with the writer. There is an attitude in New York that critics and playwrights shouldn't talk to one another! Weird.

INTERVIEWER: But you once traveled three thousand miles across country with a critic, didn't you?

TERRY: Elliot Norton of *The Boston Herald-American*. He had panned my play, *Approaching Simone*. Among other things, he called the play "pagan." It was a trip sponsored by the American Theatre Association. We ended up falling in love with one another . . . as human beings. He has a right to his opinion. We became friends because we saw one another in action, helping to teach young writers.

INTERVIEWER: You discovered your mutual concerns.

TERRY: Right. The future.

INTERVIEWER: Walter Kerr, in a [November 23,] 1966 article in *The New York Times*, lashed out at your antiwar play, *Viet Rock*, while heaping praise upon Jean-Claude van Itallie's *America, Hurrah* in the same article. The headline said, "One Succeeds, the Other Fails. Why?"

TERRY: He attacked me two Sundays in a row. That's when Jean-Claude and I were both playwrights in the Open Theater. But he couldn't kill the play. He closed it in New York, but it was translated into every major language and was proclaimed in every major, and many minor, cities all over the world, and it repaid its backers every cent.

INTERVIEWER: Do you think that the critical vitriol increased because you directed *Viet Rock* yourself?

TERRY: Well, I was picketed by a group of directors besides everything else! Because I wouldn't join the Directors' Guild.

INTERVIEWER: In addition, you kept the critics away on opening night?

TERRY: No, that was a bad move on the part of the producer. For the sake of keeping the play running. This producer told me if he had it all to do over again, he never would have let the critics come at *all*. [Laughter] He could have kept it running for a year. We had standing room only. The place was packed every night until Kerr's second Sunday drubbing appeared in *The Times*. Then the phones went dead. Before that, they'd been ringing off the walls; people were throwing themselves in my arms and the actors' arms crying every night after the show, but Kerr managed to kill it.

INTERVIEWER: If all producers united, kept the critics away for a month, would theater criticism as we know it—the "hit or bomb" syndrome—change? One critic of *Viet Rock*, Whitney Bolton [in the November 15, 1966 issue] of *The Morning Telegraph*, said, ". . . I cannot deny [the producers] their right to close the first performance here to us. For that matter, I would think that there is no existing law demanding that newspaper and magazine critics be admitted gratis to any production. Producers in their exercises of rights certainly can deny us admission on the customary cuff and can demand that we buy our seats when and if available. For all producers to follow this pattern would be to send us (the critics) to the showers and that might not be a bad thing."

TERRY: Well, maybe it could be done. But reviewers—I'm not talking about critics—feel that they have to protect the public. Especially as the costs of tickets rise. So they're on the side of the public, not the side of the writers. You've got to remember that. Broadway is just a showcase for television now. Broadway is no longer the place I was taught about when I went to college, i.e., the place where The Theater was kept alive, the Theater of Ideas. A place where one could be in touch with human feelings, where you could see yourself, where society could see itself. Broadway is now a place for the tourists to go and be beguiled by stagecraft. They're giving standing ovations to strobe lights!

INTERVIEWER: Will you talk a little bit about Florence James, who she is and how she influenced your career?

TERRY: She's past ninety now and in a nursing home, though her mind is still extremely sharp. Until five years ago, even though she was blind, she still went to the theater where she worked and gave notes. She'd won a scholarship as a young woman to the Moscow Art Theatre, where she met and studied with Stanislavsky and was influenced greatly by Vaktangov and Meyerhold. She shared all her education with us in the theater she and her husband, Burton W. James, founded in Seattle.

I joined as a teenager and was especially swept away by the staging ideas and constructivist sets of Meyerhold. Mrs. James was our director and acting teacher, and her husband was a great actor. She was a powerful director and a powerful intellect.

INTERVIEWER: Do you think that having a great woman as an early role model was helpful to you?

TERRY: Definitely. But it wasn't only Florence's influence. It was my mother, my grandmothers, my aunts, my great-aunts, my mother's cousins. Fantastic women. I love to be with them. I go home several times a year just so I can hang out with them! They're all beautiful and bright, witty, full of the devil. Terrific singers.

INTERVIEWER: We read that your great-grandmother crossed the country with her seven children.

TERRY: Yes, by covered wagon, without her husband. He was on the job elsewhere as an Indian scout. I only found out about it recently. You see, I come from a pioneer culture, so I'm kind of different from people raised in the East. Women worked side by side with the men. I was taught to build houses. I worked alongside my father and grandfather. We built several houses together. My grandfather was a great engineer who built bridges and railroads. I grew up using tools. I think that's important. Not enough women get to use tools, not even kitchen tools! There's too much isolation among women nowadays. The culture I grew up in, the women were always in the kitchen together. Incredible co-operation, preparing family reunions with lots of joking and singing at huge parties. There was a conference in Kansas City a couple of weeks ago where Dr. Marlene Springer was speaking about a prairie diary she's editing with her husband. It described how the women in Kansas would hurry up and get all their housework done in the morning so in the afternoon they could go porch visiting! They'd sit and rock and pass the time. Then along came the telephone and the porch visiting stopped! And women missed the physical presence of one another. They were seeing men but only hearing each other on the telephone. When there was a special event in the community and all the women would see one another, there'd be an incredible reunion, they'd just rush to hug, and then exchange passionate letters afterwards. Some people have misinterpreted or inferred sexual significance to this, but actually they were just starved for the plain sight of one another! There also had been many instances on the prairies of women committing suicide because of isolation and loneliness. We tend to forget the important reinforcement that physical presence can bring. I find that's an extra dividend of writers' conferences for women. We can give strength and reinforcement to one another. We're going to work with the Springers on creating a new play out of their diary findings for next season, and of course we're calling it *Porch Visiting*.

INTERVIEWER: What do you say to those people who say that by holding women's conferences we're excluding half of the population?

TERRY: Men were free to come. Several men were featured speakers. There were only three men in the audience, but it certainly was open to them. I wonder why the other half of the population isn't where *our* action is.

INTERVIEWER: You teach playwriting. Are you spreading the word about women dramatists?

TERRY: Constantly. Recently, I taught Emily Mann's *Still Life* at a university in Minnesota. My students were *outraged* that they'd never heard of this play, nor the work of Maria Irene Fornes, nor Roz Drexler, Rochelle Owens, Adrienne Kennedy, Sybil Pearson, Caryl Churchill, Pam Gems, Ntozake Shange, Julie Bovasso, Jo Ann Schmidman, Tina Howe. They knew none of these people, and they were getting their master's degrees! They were really angry by the time I finished with them. [Laughter]

INTERVIEWER: You mentioned earlier that the theater world had been used to plodding along with one significant playwright at a time. Then, suddenly, in the sixties, thirty-five new ones flooded the scene. Was that the group Fornes told us about? The New York Theatre Strategy?

TERRY: Yes, there were thirty-five of us—men and women.

INTERVIEWER: It started out as an all-female group originally, though, didn't it?

TERRY: We couldn't raise any money! Foundations said we had no track record. And we said: We women have five hundred seventy-five thousand years of track record! They didn't give any money until we got the men in there, though.

INTERVIEWER: You said that you had always wanted to write for women, yet you began writing long before the Women's Movement.

TERRY: [Laughing] I'd been an actor! I gave directors a hard time because I would change my lines. I'd been trained via the Stanislavsky method; I always wrote interior dialogues for my characters and elaborate descriptions of what my character was doing before my entrance. Often I'd substitute my lines for what was in the text—but only for writers who, in my opinion, hadn't written well enough. However, I was more than happy to learn my lines when I was playing Shaw, O'Casey or Synge. But I didn't get to play them often enough. Finally I decided, "The hell with this! I'm going to start writing!"

INTERVIEWER: And that's where your playwriting began?

TERRY: Partly. I'd watch actors do great improvisations in workshops and acting classes at the Seattle Repertory Playhouse. Many times their work seemed better than the lines they were trying to learn. But I really started to write when I saw most actors couldn't repeat a great improvisation unless they were also writers. Some actors are great storytellers, and this gift could be transferred into writing.

INTERVIEWER: How did you manage to harness the spontaneous vitality of the improvisation and translate that into a text?

TERRY: I was trained in improvisation as an actor and so I internalized that way of working as a writer. Also, I've been a painter, sculptor and theater designer; laying down ideas, then ripping them up or moving them around was part of my method of work, so I didn't get lost in the linear.

INTERVIEWER: So how many drafts do you normally go through before you publish a text?

TERRY: Some come out perfect the first time . . . *Comings and Goings* [1966]. Others, like *Hothouse* [1971], take ten years of drafts.

INTERVIEWER: When you said earlier that you always wanted to write for women, did you mean parts for actresses? Or did you mean write for the women in the audiences?

TERRY: Both. So many of the interesting roles are for the men. These roles may show many facets of a character—thus the men playing these roles may stretch themselves and show their power as the character and themselves—while the women characters may have only one aspect to project. This may be all the play requires, but the actress does not get a workout and the audience sees only a one-sided woman.

INTERVIEWER: Do you think Aristotelian rules are at all relevant to women dramatists?

TERRY: Yes, know them and then you can play with them. You don't have to be controlled by them. They're there to use, like building blocks, and you can move them around in any way you want to.

INTERVIEWER: So you don't think women's experience demands new forms of writing?

TERRY: No. But I personally love new forms and I've created some new forms. I'm essentially a fan of the new, but the oldest form can be just fine—if you fill it with the truth as you see it. Put your experience into any form that's comfortable, or create one that's perfect for you.

INTERVIEWER: Do you see your work as influencing the writing of male playwrights?

TERRY: Tom Eyen told me after he saw *Calm Down, Mother* [1965], he ran home and wrote *The White Whore and the Bit Player.* Many other writers have told me that my work gives them courage.

INTERVIEWER: What did you mean when you said, "Theater is like medicine: It was started by women and usurped by men"?

TERRY: Storytelling. Mothers telling stories to babies. The first teaching was, is through storytelling. Kitchen sink drama didn't become "art" until men started doing it. Women were writing domestic dramas for thirty, forty years before John Osborne.

INTERVIEWER: Even Joe Papp has said he doesn't want any more "kitchen sink" drama in his theater [New York Shakespeare Festival]. Just as we are becoming more prolific, our most common settings—the kitchen, the bedroom—have become *passé*.

TERRY: And men have been out in the "real" world. Look what trouble this so-called real world has brought us.

INTERVIEWER: No woman playwright has ever been considered a literary "great." Why?

TERRY: The day *that* happens playwriting will no longer be called an art. The same thing happens in business. The minute women infiltrate a job, men turn their backs on it. It no longer has currency.

INTERVIEWER: Will you describe what The Omaha Magic Theatre is doing in terms of self-publishing of plays?

TERRY: We published our plays for ten years, and we've been recently rewarded for this industry by attracting Broadway Play Publishing, Inc., of New York City. They bring out our work now. It was a mind-bending experience learning the mechanics of self-publishing. But we did it!

INTERVIEWER: You've been trying to encourage women playwrights to send you their bibliographies so that you can drop them off at theaters around the country?

TERRY: Yes, also so that we can keep in touch. In addition, I do many seminars at universities where I can share this information. There is no such thing as substantial book royalties for a playwright. Photocopying has done away with that. All you can hope for is production royalties. That's why I've asked other writers for their bibliographies— that news is essential to send out into the world—to the young and to potential producers.

INTERVIEWER: Perhaps this book can carry the message to women playwrights to get those bibliographies to you.

TERRY: Someone should publish a bibliography of all the women writers and give them free to libraries. Then the young people, and we who care, can find out what each other's doing.

INTERVIEWER: What will it take to stop this state-by-state isolation in America? Do you think that New York will always be the heart of theater?

TERRY: The theatrical energy is no longer in New York, except when it's residing in writers like Irene Fornes and Ping Chong, or writer/performers like Meredith Monk. The energy now is Chicago, San Francisco, Omaha, Minneapolis, Los Angeles, Seattle.

INTERVIEWER: And Louisville?

TERRY: Once a year. But the theater is decentralizing. The next century belongs to the Pacific Rim and the Hispanics. Asia is rising. The Spanish are rising again. We're split into two worlds now, clearly. Maybe that's what happened with men and women, too? But we must work to bring about a balance.

INTERVIEWER: There are some people who feel that there is a renewed but more covert war going on between men and women now . . . a deeper malaise setting in, separating us.

TERRY: I think that men are negative because women are positive and on the rise! It's driving the men crazy! Martha Boesing, [playwright and founder of At The Foot of the Mountain Theater] was telling me that in the thousand plays she receives each year, most have hopeful endings! [Laughs] Women are feeling positive and forward-looking. Plays men are writing often end with everybody dead, dying or neurotic to the point of no return.

INTERVIEWER: What can we do to heal this polarization?

TERRY: Live your life as if the revolution had been a success!

INTERVIEWER: You certainly do. Tell us about the touring aspect of the Magic Theatre.

TERRY: We tour the Midwest six months of the year, and we take our other plays with us to sell as we go. We've sold the work developed at our theater by mail order, too, all over the United States and, in fact, the world.

INTERVIEWER: Has the Magic Theatre been addressing the issues of nuclear war?

TERRY: Jo Ann Schmidmann, our artistic director, wrote a marvelous piece called *Velveeta Meltdown*. We staged it in Central Park here and more than five hundred people came. The people of Omaha turned out for Mondale yesterday. When he said he was for a nuclear freeze, a cheer went up through the park that I'm surprised you didn't hear all the way back in New York. We have the SAC Air Force Base here. Omaha is the A-number-one target. Nebraska and Wyoming were told to accept the MX missiles.

INTERVIEWER: Are they torn between having jobs and getting rid of these weapons?

TERRY: No. Farm people don't want their land wrecked, nor do they want to be targets.

INTERVIEWER: You've opened up dialogues between your theater and the community. Your play *Kegger* [1982] discussed teenage alcoholism and toured Nebraska. What were the results of this particular effort?

TERRY: We're catalysts in the community. Communities keep in touch with us via our touring network. Everyone is working now to find ways to have chemical-free fun. They've formed positive peer-pressure groups within the schools to let kids know it's okay *not* to drink. One of the things that the Magic Theatre Company learned—doing research with neurosurgeons, neuropsychologists and biologists—is that people under the age of twenty-five lack an enzyme to deal with alcohol. That's why kids deteriorate so fast when they get heavily into booze and drugs. What might take eighteen *years* to ruin an adult will take eighteen months for a kid. But it takes a while to get this information through to kids. We were asked to take *Kegger* into a Lutheran college, a very conservative school, because they found their students were having keggers every night! The kids were coming to class drunk. After another performance of *Kegger* at a large state university, some of the professors came to us afterward and said, "You know you've really opened our eyes. We didn't know why the kids were sleeping in class, or why their grades were falling off." It never crossed their minds that they were drunk or hung over! It's a long education process. One of the big causes of this drinking is that kids don't think they're going to *see* [age] twenty-five. Many of the young people I interviewed really believe that we're all going to blow up, and that they might as well have their good times while they can!

INTERVIEWER: Are your playwriting students politically aware?

TERRY: You might get one out of fifty who sees the bigger picture. When they're under twenty-one they're still having a lot of problems with interpersonal relationships, with their families. . . . They have to work their family play out of their systems first. And some of the students I met are working three jobs.

INTERVIEWER: Is this despair in the young—drinking, and so on— stopping the kids from writing?

TERRY: At no time in history have so many people been writing plays. I had ten in a recent university group, and all ten of them could write. They had me working overtime to prepare for them. They were all bright; some were in a kind of negative despair, but not all. There is no lack of talent. We've just got to give kids a better world to live in.

INTERVIEWER: Do you feel that there's a necessity for regional theaters and playwrights to start forming the sort of alliances that the Omaha Magic Theatre has created with Nebraska communities?

TERRY: More theaters are willing to do that than a lot of writers may realize. I belong to the American Theatre Association, and I find a lot of community theaters are looking to affiliate with writers. Many universities are eager to produce new works of playwrights who are willing to work with their students. I think too many writers are sitting around waiting for Godot. The National Endowment for the Arts has done everything it can to encourage new works in the last ten years. And these efforts have paid off. Every proposal I've read from theaters all around the country has a new play production or development program. It's up to the writer now to go get affiliated or start her own theater. If you don't like the way a theater does things, then start your own, Babe! This is the land of entrepreneurs. If you read the tax laws, they're all written for the small business people. If the writer can see himself or herself as a small businessperson, the sky's the limit.

INTERVIEWER: In the Magic Theatre's Statement of Purpose, we see that you're not separating art from business. You are encouraging everyone to learn the business side.

TERRY: If you don't, you go under! Besides, if you don't know where money comes from, you get arrogant and begin to think the world owes you a living.

INTERVIEWER: Where would playwrights go to gather these entrepreneurial skills?

TERRY: You can start by starting. You can go and offer yourself to a small theater company. Every small theater company in this country needs talent. Learn it by doing it.

INTERVIEWER: And that would include learning to write a grant?

TERRY: *That* is the biggest pain in the neck. Everyone with writing skills should be learning to write grants and helping out that way. At The Magic Theatre we share the chore around so that everyone gets to learn what that "pain in the neck" is and sees where their salary comes from.

INTERVIEWER: When were you first able to earn a living from your plays?

TERRY: Strangely enough, with *Viet Rock* in 1966.

INTERVIEWER: Did you see any of the foreign productions of that play?

TERRY: No, but they sent me photos of it, from Tokyo, Germany . . .

INTERVIEWER: *Calm Down, Mother*'s being translated into Cantonese.

TERRY: Yes, it's being produced in Hong Kong. I can't tell you what a high that's given me. I have been intrigued by China since I was a child.

INTERVIEWER: Do you have any plans to go to China?

TERRY: Yesterday, we got a call from Korea. They want us to come to their next International Theater Festival. If we get to Korea, then perhaps we can tour China.

INTERVIEWER: Would you talk about the theme of dominance and submission that crops up so often in your work? Why is this subject so compelling to you?

TERRY: Well, I think you have to *submit* to art. [Laughter] One must submit the ego to the work, or the work never gets done. That's the positive side of submission. The only utopias that ever lasted very long were those where people submitted to an idea greater than the individual.

INTERVIEWER: Isn't that surrender rather than submission? Is there a difference?

TERRY: Yes. Surrender used that way implies bliss as well as loss of self. Submission, on the other hand, means against your will you do thus and so because you are forced by either superior strength or psychological power. Sorting this out is important for mental health, and I believe my plays have healing powers.

INTERVIEWER: Your work constantly addresses the power struggles of human beings. Where does this obsession come from?

TERRY: It started in grade school, being very bright in class. There were two boys as bright as I, and we were friends. I had one of those rare experiences of going to school with the same friends from first to the eighth grade. But by the eighth grade the teachers stopped calling on me, even though they knew I knew the answers. When I got into high school, that was it. It didn't matter how bright the girls were, only the boys were called on; you could see them being groomed for leadership.

INTERVIEWER: Did you feel angry about that?

TERRY: Oh, yes! But I was still very naïve when I was a freshman in high school. The other members of the freshman class urged me to stand up in an assembly and criticize the student council! Which I did. And there was an incredible silence. Later I found out—when I was a senior—that all the boys in the Student Council were offended and they collectively agreed *never* to take me out! [Laughter] They'd made a pact. I found out at an early age that when a woman opens her mouth there are consequences!

INTERVIEWER: Was that the theme you were dealing with in your play *Attempted Rescue on Avenue B* [1977]?

TERRY: If you show your power you'll get killed.

INTERVIEWER: How have you protected yourself?

TERRY: I think being Irish provides a certain protection, and strong women to look to in my family. My family has always been behind me one hundred thousand percent. My mother always told me I was beautiful and brilliant. She still does.

INTERVIEWER: What were the factors that led up to you leaving New York and divorcing yourself from the commercial theater?

TERRY: I saw that there were two worlds and I didn't have to live in the negative one. And I also realized I didn't have to be "the woman" behind "the man."

INTERVIEWER: Yes. That subject is also dealt with in *Attempted Rescue*. What kinds of sacrifices are necessary for women artists, do you think?

TERRY: I don't think one has to make any. It's all in the way you look at the world. It's just a matter of organizing your time.

INTERVIEWER: Are you organized?

TERRY: I must be, because I get *enough* done; but I feel that I only accomplish one-tenth of what I'm capable of.

INTERVIEWER: So a women doesn't have to sacrifice her personal relationships to be a committed artist?

TERRY: Not at all!

INTERVIEWER: Chinese playwright Bai Fengxi might disagree, I think. She bases much of her work around this very question. Can a woman have a full-time career as well as a happy marriage and family life?

TERRY: Perhaps her traditions place intolerable burdens on her. But we're a young country, and women raised here should be able to shrug off a lot of society's pressures.

INTERVIEWER: How different an experience was it for you to go off and work with someone like Jo Ann Schmidman in Omaha after the New York scene?

TERRY: It was very different. Because she liked everything I wrote! That was *really* different! I mean, reinforcing! It took me a long time to believe her, because she was so accepting with her generous policies and attitude. Plus she's a great director! I'm a pretty good director, but after I saw her directing I had sense enough to back off from directing and write more. She's also an amazing performer. She's the only actor Joe Chaikin ever put directly into the Open Theater without a probation period. She's the first director I've worked with who has been raised totally on television. She's visually literate. She physicalizes my work in ways that I would never have dreamed of! I have a terrific ear, but she has wonderful visual sense.

INTERVIEWER: So you have a true collaboration, then, between writer and director?

TERRY: Yes. We also write together. This piece we're working on now, *X-rayed-iate* [1984], is really her child. I wrote most of the text, but the concept, the structure, the movement of it is hers.

INTERVIEWER: Here in New York we sense a growing barrier between playwrights and directors.

TERRY: The director is a recent phenomenon, you know, in the last hundred years.

INTERVIEWER: You've described yourself as a benevolent dictator. Are you autocratic as a director in the rehearsal setting?

TERRY: In the sense that we have to open on a certain date, on time, you know. I expect people to be punctual at rehearsals and pay attention. I was involved in too many situations in the past where there was excessive talking and not enough action. Sometimes you can talk something to death and never get any work done. In that sense, you need to know when to be a dictator, to make sure that the work gets done. A director constantly has to strengthen the self-image of the actors. There's been something rotten going on in American theater for a long time. Artists don't believe in their own talents! One is constantly having to reassure them. I mean, it was true in the Open Theatre, and it's still true with these kids coming out of school, today. They don't know how to work, they don't know where to work. Not only do they not know how to work on a role, they don't know how to pick up a hammer! The culture that I was raised in, the work ethic of the pioneer culture, has disintegrated. You spend two thirds of your time teaching people how to work. If actors came knowing how to work, if they had a sense of themselves, that they had a right to work, it would be peaches and cream.

INTERVIEWER: Staying on the subject of director autocracy, what about playwrights like Susan Yankowitz, who was barred from rehearsals of her play *Knife in the Heart* at Williamstown. Isn't that taking dictatorship too far?

TERRY: I said *benevolent* dictatorship. I didn't know that was still going on. If it is, then direct your own work. Shaw did it. Irene Fornes is the best director of her own work. I know that in the old days a director used to take the writer across the street to the bar to get him drunk! [Laughter]

INTERVIEWER: Do you believe that there's a female aesthetic in playwriting?

TERRY: A female aesthetic could only happen if the next generation of women were raised all together on a desert island. We've been taught by men!

INTERVIEWER: So you don't think the innovations of women are in any way organic?

TERRY: I really don't. How would you measure it?

INTERVIEWER: We don't know. That's why we're asking women playwrights this question. What we do know, after reading tons of women's plays and hundreds of their reviews, is that there are certain elements common to all: Many of their plays are woman-centered, with a much higher percentage of female roles than plays by men.

TERRY: This will probably continue until the balance is redressed. But after there's a balance, and we have female characters living up there on the stage that we haven't had for a long time, that may all change.

INTERVIEWER: Tell us why you decided on cross-gender casting in *Babes in the Bighouse* [1974]?

TERRY: We thought that was a very clear way for men to learn how to empathize with women. After the performances, men said, "Now I understand what you women are talking about!" By putting a man in a dress, in the same constraints as the women characters in the play, it became clear to the men in the audience what women were up against. Earlier we'd learned, while playing a boys' high school, that the boys in the audience only paid attention to what male characters said. Men are socialized to respond to a male body and a male voice; from an early age they seem to be trained to discount what women say. There were terrific laugh lines that women had in the play, but the audience would only laugh if a male character said something funny. That's how we found out boys wouldn't pay attention to what women said. By having men play women in *Babes*, we got men to pay attention to what the play was saying. But we didn't have to change the writing. And this was in 1974!

INTERVIEWER: Will you tell us a bit about your experience bringing theater to inmates in prison?

TERRY: Any time we need an ego boost, we can play a prison and become reenergized. There are no masks. If they like the show, they're with you all the way—talking to the stage, calling out terrific, appropriate, additional lines and giving our performers standing ovations at the end. Then we have amazing discussions. They have a lot of time to think in jail, and they sincerely want to help solve society's problems.

INTERVIEWER: Do you have any problems getting your Nebraska audience to accept the sexuality in your plays?

TERRY: We don't have any trouble with people out here! They are farmers or they've been close to the farm. They deal with animals, pro-creation, the elements and nature. I think that people are too rarified in New York. They've been too long away from animals and plants and trees.

INTERVIEWER: Megan, do you think the voices of the black women playwrights have fallen silent in the last few years?

TERRY: There's nothing silent about [Ntozake] Shange. Some new writers are writing realistic plays—choosing Lorraine Hansberry as their model rather than Adrienne Kennedy or Shange, who are poets as well as playwrights.

INTERVIEWER: Shange's experimenting in performance art. She feels that's a viable way to keep her poetry alive. But she's had some difficulty getting some things produced.

TERRY: It seems to me *Spell #7* is an even stronger piece than *colored girls*, but Shange said the same men who produced *colored girls* didn't get behind her second play. Women are going to have to put one another forward. There's got to be more support among women for women's work. I think black women have a hard time getting hold of each other's work and need to find a way to share their work faster.

INTERVIEWER: Will you explain what happened when Actors Equity Association forbade its members to appear in showcases of your work?

TERRY: That was a result of a series of misunderstandings. There was a showcase of my play *Hothouse* [1974], in which ten actors took part. The Showcase Code states that if a play is moved from Off Off Broadway after its twenty-one performances the original actors must be retained in the cast or paid two weeks' salary. Then it was done again, produced by several of the original actors but with five or six replacements, at The Truck and Warehouse Theatre [in New York's East Village]. The actors begged me to sign a paper that they said was only a formality. They said they loved the show and wanted to do it again because they thought it would bring them to the attention of agents and producers. By this time about sixteen different people had been in and out of the play. The play was picked up by the Chelsea Theatre; they intended to give it a first-class production. The problems arose because the Chelsea management wanted to cast their own people in the play. I was happy with the first group who had played it at the Circle Rep Workshop. Barbara Rosoff had directed and Arden Fingerhut had created a stunning lighting design. But now there was a new director, a new producer, and they had their own vision. I argued and persuaded, but the Chelsea group would allow the retention of only one of the original actors. That person they fired after four days. Naturally, that person and those other actors were distressed, and so was I. Some of those actors complained to their union, and their union sent me a bill for over five thousand dollars and told me I was in effect blacklisted in New York City until that bill was paid.

I have not paid the bill. And I would advise playwrights not to sign a showcase form. It prevents subsequent performances of a play, because the play will become encumbered with this type of lien. Recently Equity has further complicated the code to make one pay not only theatrical salaries, but TV and film salaries, too, before they will allow the play to be performed. It seemed to me that if their union was a true union the new actors hired by Chelsea could have refused the jobs in favor of the creators of the roles. But this argument went nowhere with Equity. I offered to pay Equity twenty-five dollars a week for the rest of my life to help bring down this bill, but they wouldn't accept that. Where they thought I would dig up five thousand dollars just so I could have my plays done in New York City, I don't know. But I haven't had any problems getting productions in other cities.

INTERVIEWER: You once said that playwrights subsidize the theater.

TERRY: All artists have subsidized this culture since the beginning!

INTERVIEWER: Don't most people feel that it is the artists who are subsidized, and not vice versa?

TERRY: The average middle-class salary is thirty-five thousand a year, and the tiny percentage of artists who get five thousand are considered to be subsidized? There's been subsidy for artists only in the last fourteen years, anyway. The people at the National Endowment for the Arts, and some of the private foundations, work very hard to share money around, pitiful few dollars that there are. When I'm on one of those "deciding-who-gets-what" committees, I feel like I'm shredding pennies. Isn't it strange that this American culture has valued everything but the people who create something out of thin air? What is left when a civilization dies? Only its art and a few tool fragments.

INTERVIEWER: What's the playwright's responsibility to society?

TERRY: To critique that society, the perceived world and beyond. Beckett, for instance, critiques "being." You must always guard against being coopted.

INTERVIEWER: What was your first conception of a writer?

TERRY: I don't know, because I had such a miserable education. It was through other writers and painters that I learned to write. And through struggle. When you read what Lorca did and said before they shot him, when you think of the artists who made the effort to communicate with us. . . . Look what things they went through so we could open our minds. All the people who went to their deaths. . . . We owe them a lot.

INTERVIEWER: What do you wish to convey to the world through your plays?

TERRY: That life is possible. I'm always fighting against inertia. Art is about taking action. The essential core of theater is action. I believe in taking creative action. What else is there to do?

INTERVIEWER: What advice do you have for young women in high school and college who are thinking about becoming a playwright?

TERRY: Do it. See all kinds of performance, from polka dances to basketball games. Do you know what I miss in the world? Singing. There's a lot of noise, but there isn't enough singing lately. Don't you miss the women singers of the sixties? You have to turn on country music to hear a woman sing now. We don't have enough new singers. I'm still writing musicals, and I wish there were more singers.

INTERVIEWER: What contributions do you feel that you've made in changing the form of the American musical?

TERRY: I proved rock music worked on the stage. No one would believe it, or even allow it. Certainly I speeded up exposition. You don't have to sit for two acts anymore to get to the heart of a play or musical.

INTERVIEWER: You once said that the form of the play is the least important thing, that those who are obsessed with structure have received too much schooling. Telling the truth, you said, is far more important than form. Do you believe that content dictates form?

TERRY: I used to believe that, but I've been proved wrong. [Laughter] Because people have revitalized old forms! By putting another kind of content in it. If you're telling the truth, it grabs people. I think form is fashion. I just happen to love fashion.

INTERVIEWER: Is that why you've mastered so many different forms of playwriting?

TERRY: I love creating, and seeing if something will work. I like to keep building myself out on farther and farther ledges. I like to defy gravity.

INTERVIEWER: Would you say that your major concern as a writer is the continuity of the family?

TERRY: My biggest resentment about war, besides the obvious destruction, is how it wrecks families. Our family was destroyed by World War II, our extended family.

INTERVIEWER: Your play *Hothouse* dealt with this subject.

TERRY: I don't know if it dealt with it enough. Did it make the point?

INTERVIEWER (KB): It speaks to me personally, having been raised in Coventry, England, in wartime and having my own family torn apart by war.

TERRY: Maybe we can make other kinds of structures to take the place of the extended family. People these days seem to desire community more than romantic love.

INTERVIEWER (RK): Ideas of community were brought to a renaissance in the sixties and seventies. Now, as we move through the eighties, everyone has become more individual, more career-oriented. We hear many young women describe themselves as "post-feminists." Their goal is to make thirty thousand dollars a year when they get out of school.

TERRY: Young women are writing to me using the words *make it.* What does that mean? I don't know. I guess they are concerned about making enough money. For whom? In whose eyes? Wait till they make it and find out nobody cares. We're living in a kind of glitter time. You know what it reminds me of? Restoration comedy.

INTERVIEWER: Some of the women playwrights don't want to be aligned politically with women anymore. They say, "I'm not a feminist, I'm a humanist." Or, "I don't want to be called a woman playwright."

TERRY: They don't want to be ghetto-ized.

INTERVIEWER: How do you feel about being "ghetto-ized?"

TERRY: It's a danger. I told the feminists I wouldn't write their party line, either. I made a big speech to a large Midwest feminist group; I told them it was my duty to criticize everything, including them, and a whole bunch of people in hobnailed boots walked out.

INTERVIEWER: And yet no one looks at a book exclusively devoted to male playwrights' interviews—and there are many of them—and says, "Look at those poor guys—they're ghettoized. . . ."

TERRY: You're right. This came up last week at [a] Stanford University [conference on women in theater]. There were eight women's plays being presented. And there were no male characters in their plays. And one woman in the audience got up and said, "I don't like all this lesbian writing, where's love between the sexes?" Out of eight plays—only *one* had a lesbian character, and that play was an uproarious comedy. But this woman labeled all the work, work dealing with all sorts of female characters trying to solve many sorts of problems, in a pejorative way. On the positive side, I'm impressed that feminists can write so well. I witnessed some great writing there. But where were the male characters? This question took over the audience. It was like a mob psychology of the early seventies! After having this wonderful experience—fresh, funny, very moving writing—suddenly the whole audience took up what this woman was saying. Martha Boesing, [playwright] and I had to put a stop to it. Finally, I had to say, "Look. David Mamet just won the Pulitzer Prize, but you wouldn't think of asking him why there were no women in *Glengarry Glen Ross*." The minute a woman writes about what women are talking about when the men aren't around, people jump on them. Including other women. But I don't want to be perceived as writing only for women. I'm writing for the whole human race! I feel responsible for the past, present *and* the future!

INTERVIEWER: We see feminism as embodying humanism, not separate from it.

TERRY: I've noticed, at these conferences where some men have been speaking out, that a lot of American males perceive feminists as separatists. They want to dismiss all women's work if they think they're not going to be allowed to be an equal part of the audience.

INTERVIEWER: Isn't that male anger precisely why some women are reluctant to call themselves feminists?

TERRY: They're afraid of male retaliation. After all, who holds the purse strings?

INTERVIEWER: Are you talking about censorship?

TERRY: And grant giving.

INTERVIEWER: You've said you don't object to being called a feminist.

TERRY: Why should I object?

INTERVIEWER: So what does feminism mean to you personally?

TERRY: I want to redress the balance! If a Martian came here to visit our culture, it would think it was visiting a homosexual society. Men run everything.

INTERVIEWER: Your play *American King's English for Queens* [1978], explores sexism in the language of criticism. Do you think women's plays are critiqued with a different vocabulary than men's plays?

TERRY: I don't think the critics feel that they're doing this. They think they're being fair, that they're just applying a literary standard.

INTERVIEWER: If a man and a woman playwright, of equal craft, put a readily recognizable character on stage, why is the woman's character called a "stereotype" and the man's an "archetype"?

TERRY: How they take care of their own. Isn't it wonderful?

INTERVIEWER: Why is an angry play by a woman conceived of as "bitter"? Yet an angry play by a man is . . .

TERRY: A "blockbuster"!

INTERVIEWER: Are the women getting accused of bad craft when, in fact, it's the content that's upsetting to the critics?

TERRY: If you analyzed these plays, scene by scene, would the craft of the women's plays hold up?

INTERVIEWER: We think so. Especially in the case of a Caryl Churchill, an Emily Mann, Fornes, Drexler, Owens, Farabough, et cetera. A common critical term used to describe innovative women's work is "nonplay."

TERRY: They want a fried egg. A beginning, a middle and an end, with a rising climax. A male orgasm.

INTERVIEWER: Well, then, let's go back to your play *American King's English for Queens* and your attack on sexism in the language.

TERRY: Just go listen in the supermarket to how people talk to their children. It'll make your hair stand on end.

INTERVIEWER: The cruelty?

TERRY: Yes. Roles and attitudes toward the self are shaped within the family by how one is spoken to.

INTERVIEWER: What were the audience discussions like after *American King's English*?

TERRY: Exciting and intense, and that's where we got the idea for *Goona Goona* [1979], from the discussions after *American King's English for Queens*. We began to explore all the ways we talk to one another.

INTERVIEWER: But *Goona Goona* was about family violence. What's the connection?

TERRY: The violence in the language led to the discovery of actual physical violence going on at home. I mean this one door opened, and other doors just kept opening beyond that. Discussions after *Kegger* have led to our next piece, which will be about family communication. People found out that they're not only having a hard time talking to one another, they can't even talk to themselves in their own heads anymore. We've found a whole group of scholars who work with us, share their expertise and research to build plays for our audiences. The audience tells us what they want to deal with. We do one piece a year, which we think of as lending our skills to give voice to community concerns. The other seven plays we produce are for our own and our audience's artistic growth.

INTERVIEWER: The Magic Theatre, from what we've read, seems to be financially successful, too. You've combined art, community outreach and business rather well.

TERRY: And we've never had a deficit.

INTERVIEWER: If local corporations subsidize you or give grants— say, for instance, a place like Campbell's soup, which is based in your area—does that inhibit doing a play about the problems at a Campbell's soup plant?

TERRY: I understand that Campbell's soup is one of the best places for women to work. There may be difficulties in other places with other companies, but we haven't had any problems with corporations, because the things we've been writing about are the things that employees who work for them want to talk about!

INTERVIEWER: We heard you use these wonderful soft sculptures in your plays. Diane Degan designs them?

TERRY: And Sora Kim. We all design them. We have a large group of Midwest painters and sculptors who work with us on all our shows. We also have three composers in residence. When I designed *Goona Goona*, I designed the whole house as a gigantic quilt. I designed the costumes as a combination of puppets and football uniforms with padding so the actors wouldn't get hurt. They had to hit each other with baseball bats while depicting family violence.

INTERVIEWER: Do you get many requests from other states for your scripts that deal with family and community problems?

TERRY: Yes. The biggest difficulty right now is getting it down on paper fast enough to meet the demand. Right now I'm trying to get *Objective Love, Goona Goona, Kegger,* and *Fifteen Million Fifteen-Year-Olds* completed, so that we can share them around. We're constantly bombarded with requests for these scripts. We expect to have most of them ready by the end of the summer. In Xerox form. Our earlier plays have been brought out by Broadway Play Publishing, Inc.

INTERVIEWER: Megan, what message would you most like to send round the world?

TERRY: It's worth it to make a life in art. I want to tell everybody it's *possible* and it's worth it. I've lived long enough now to see what happens to people who don't follow their hearts.

MICHELENE WANDOR

$\mathbf{M}$ichelene Wandor was born in London in 1940. Since 1969 she has written poetry and theater commentary and criticism. And from 1970 she has written prolifically on her own for stage, radio and television as well as working in close collaboration with feminist and gay theater groups such as Monstrous Regiment, Gay Sweatshop and Ms. Worthington's Daughters. Her stage plays are published in Five Plays (Journeyman/Playbooks, 1984). Ms. Wandor is the author of Understudies: Sexual Politics and Theatre (Methuen, 1981), On Gender and Writing (London, Pandora Press, 1983), Strike While the Iron Is Hot (Journeyman/Playbooks, 1980), Upbeat: Poems And Stories (London, Journeyman Press, 1982) and editor of an annual anthology, Plays by Women (Methuen, 1982, 1983, 1984, 1985) as well as several other published works. Since 1978, Ms. Wandor has written extensively for British radio: Dramatizations include a three-part serial of Precious Bane by Mary Webb and an eight-part serial of The Brothers Karamozov by Fedor Dostoevski; among her features are pieces on writers Dorothy Richardson, Jean Rhys and Antonia White. Ms. Wandor has a BA Honours degree in English from Cambridge University (1962) and an MA in the Sociology of Literature from Essex University (1975). She has two sons.

INTERVIEWER: You are a poet as well as a playwright. Which of these forms did you discover first and are they related?

WANDOR: I think I was more conscious of my enthusiasm for the theater—I was obsessed with it from the age of about fourteen. Poetry became an interest at school and university; theater continued as an obsession in that I acted in plays all the way through university. There is a strong relationship between the two: both are concerned with voice, or voices—theater literally, poetry metaphorically. They are also total opposites—poetry potentially the most private and theater the most social and public of the arts. Anyway, I like a nice paradox.

INTERVIEWER: Many women playwrights began their careers as actresses. Why this shift from interpreting the written word to creating it?

WANDOR: In my case, I decided to marry and have children rather than pursue a career as an actress. Then, when I began to think about work again, my children were both too young for me to disappear and become an actress again. As you and the entire world know, writing is something you can do at home. So I sought a reinvolvement with theater through writing plays. I was helped very much by an extraordinary excitement about new theater in the late nineteen-sixties. Perhaps if the fringe had not existed I might have turned to a different fictional form. I also wrote poetry intensively at the same time as writing plays.

INTERVIEWER: You've earned your living as a journalist and critic as well as a playwright; are there any conflicts between the objective and subjective forms of writing?

WANDOR: There are no real conflicts between doing fiction and nonfiction writing. I have always felt a great need to do both. Generally though, it is always a little hard to switch modes. So a major nonfiction book usually means that I do virtually no fiction, and a major piece of fiction means that I minimize the amount of nonfiction writing. I can't give equal weight to both at the same time. It's to do with the difference between the nonfiction conscious need to be totally in control all the time, and the fiction privilege of being able to float, improvise, take risks and not always have to be totally conscious and in control, until the end of the process.

INTERVIEWER: You've devoted a great deal of time to the study of— and published several works on—the issues of gender and writing and gender bias in the theater. How did this investigation begin, and why?

WANDOR: I have always written fiction and nonfiction, so the books you're referring to were a natural extension of the reviewing and articles I wrote (mainly for *Time Out* magazine) during the nineteen-seventies. I am as interested in ideas, analysis, cultural theory as I am in the creation of new artifacts, so it is simply part of what I do. Also, an awareness of the desperate, urgent need for important cultural events (feminist and gay theater, to use a shorthand) to enter recorded history, to be in books, where people can refer to them and not forget. The anthologies of women's plays which I edit spring from an equally strong conviction and knowledge that only published plays enter the received and accessible history; and I also either kid myself, or am arrogant enough to believe, or am sure, that my opinions, judgments and perceptions are worth having. God knows what effect it really has. I am very grateful to the people, particularly students, who find my books useful; there has, however, been a resounding silence from both the theater establishment, and from theater workers, and also from the vast majority of feminists I know working in theater in England. I have no idea what they think of my work. Some people resent the fact that I haven't praised them enough. Tough. I don't think British theater is any less sexist now than it was in 1970, despite a scattering of more visible women writers, directors, et cetera. Nothing has permanently changed. I often think people don't know how to categorize me; either they seem to think I'm a critic who dabbles in writing plays, or that I am a playwright who ought not to be commenting on other playwrights' work. Either way I feel fairly paranoid and out on a limb. But tough to that, too. I suspect—and, of course, cannot prove—that theaters run by gentlemen may find it hard to work out what kind of animal I am. The rewards are when someone tells me they've found my work useful. The financial rewards are puny. But the work is important and will continue.

INTERVIEWER: Since 1982, you've collected, edited and published four volumes of *Plays by Women* (London, Methuen). What prompted you to begin this unique project? And what do you say to those who accuse you of "ghettoizing" women playwrights?

WANDOR: Originally, I wanted to do one fat anthology, because it seemed to me that there were some exciting plays by women writers which weren't commercially successful or trendy, and I thought they should be published. The publisher suggested making it an annual anthology (he was beginning to wake up to the fact that women "sell") and I jumped at the idea. The books sell very well—for that kind of thing— so it proves how much interest and need there is. If someone accuses me of ghettoizing women playwrights, I have two answers: one is unprintable, the other is that no one ever accuses the editor of an all-male anthology of plays of ghettoizing playwrights. Then, if I feel like it, I might launch into a spiel on the importance of making a positive space for women's work. As I say in the introduction to the third volume of *Plays by Women* [1984]:

> . . .a positive space for plays written *by* women; not always necessarily *about* women, and not, as is sometimes thought, written only *for* women. However it is true so far that on the whole women playwrights have tended to choose to write about their own sex—and actually, there is nothing at all unusual about that. Most male playwrights choose to write about their own sex—it is just that they rarely see that that is what they are doing.

The image of 'the writer' which is still very prevalent in our society, as being somehow transcendent of class, race or sex, conceals the reality of who it is that has power to determine subject matter and perspective. In the theatre, since men are dominant, as writers, directors and artistic directors, their gender bias is part of the fabric of unconscious thinking in attitudes towards plays. Therefore, when women write for the theatre, they too bring their own gender biases with them; but because as women we start from an urgent sense of being either inadequately represented or distorted on stage, it is easier for us to admit that we want to write about experiences which we don't see represented there, and which are close to our own—the lives, feelings and dilemmas of women—or rather, we want to put women in the center of the stage, instead of as frills around the edges. Every time a woman writes a play about women, then, she is implicitly challenging the men still at center stage. She may not be a conscious feminist, she may want to take no part in changing things for other women in the theatrical profession, but she will still in some way be justifying her existence as a woman playwright, and justifying the existence of her subject matter as valid.

INTERVIEWER: Women dramatists do not appear to have progressed at the same rate as women novelists and poets. Is this because theater is a public as opposed to a private art? Is there still resistance, on some basic level, to women voicing their opinions and perceptions in public?

WANDOR: Yes. Yes. Also the gentlemen who run the theater like women to stay in their place. They do not want to move over. They are also ignorant of the concerns of many women playwrights, and they are frightened of learning.

INTERVIEWER: Are women's plays censored somewhere between the typewriter and the stage? Do women playwrights practice self-censorship?

WANDOR: There are always pressures on playwrights to change plays. Most directors (male and female, I'm afraid) are often frightened of the text, and few writers have enough confidence and experience in the practical realities of working theater. Women writers may practice self-censorship—but then any writer does, if they are not working in conditions conducive to free exploration.

INTERVIEWER: You once said that it makes you see red when people say, "This character is not sympathetic enough." What angers you about the modern critical trend, this need, to "care" about every character in a play?

WANDOR: Too often, a crude emphasis on whether a character is sympathetic disguises a refusal to look at what the play is really about. A play is always much more than what one character represents; it is the relationships between characters rather than the characters themselves that makes theater different and exhilarating. The need to "care" is also a sloppy way of trying to pretend that theater is just about making you feel comfortable and confirmed in what you think and feel already.

INTERVIEWER: You've said that the idea for your verse play *Aurora Leigh* [1979] began with an article you read in 1972 by American feminist critic Elaine Showalter. What was it about this article that engendered a play?

WANDOR: It wasn't just the article. I was also getting interested in Elizabeth Barrett Browning myself. It was Browning's original of *Aurora Leigh* which inspired me to do the play, not the article. The article gave me a sense that this was a work of literature that had a place on a new kind of map.

INTERVIEWER: Your play *Aurora Leigh* went through many changes and traveled a complex journey before its production at the National Theatre in London in 1981. Why was the struggle to gain acceptance for this work so difficult?

WANDOR: When I first finished the play, I thought that the best location for it was in a theater where the company had a classical background—was not scared of verse. So I sent it to the Royal Shakespeare Company, the National Theatre, and the BBC Radio Drama Department. It came back from them all with either no comment (the Royal Shakespeare Company lost the script); or, as the BBC said, it was "not dramatic." The National said it wasn't Pushkin. Then Julie Holledge, a director who had started the company called Mrs. Worthington's Daughters—fringe and unfunded—wanted to do it. She was keen to take on the challenge of the verse, and also appreciated and understood the content of the play. When it was on, the cowards changed their tune: The BBC director said it was much better since I'd rewritten it (I hadn't) and another director later liked it, too. So it was done on radio and at the National. The paradox with this play, I think, was that the politicized fringe was put off by the verse (the form) and the cautious Establishment was frightened by the content.

INTERVIEWER: Verse drama is not exactly popular these days. Why did you choose this form for *Aurora Leigh*?

WANDOR: I wrote the play in verse because Browning's original text was in verse, because I am also a poet and wanted to bring poetry and drama together, and this was a marvelous way to do it. I also wanted to get under Elizabeth Barrett Browning's language and match it with my own. Not an easy task. The original epic poem is two thousand lines longer than Milton's *Paradise Lost,* and far broader in its concerns than I could make room for in my dramatization. It debates the social function of art, realist or escapist; it discourses on Christianity, socialism, Victorian philanthropy, republicanism, as well as feminism, economic indepen- dence for women, motherhood and (indirectly) sexuality. It was hard work, but tremendously exciting.

INTERVIEWER: You've supported and participated in separatist theater in the past. What are the positive and negative aspects of women writing only for other women and excluding men from the audience?

WANDOR: I don't think of myself as supporting "separatist" theater. It is not a phrase I use. I support, encourage, need women to become more active across the board in theater, and there are very many different ways of doing this. In England, no professional theater company excludes men from the audience. If a women's group wants to play to an all-woman audience (which happens rarely) or if a women's group wants to invite a theater to do its play for them, then why not? There are one or two women playwrights who are only interested in the reactions of women in their audience (that is not the same thing as writing for women), and if they say that, at least they are being honest, whereas some men writers would pretend that they cared about women's reactions, when in fact they only wanted approval from their male peers. All-woman companies, if that's what you mean, will continue to exist as long as women feel that they prefer, some of the time, just to work with women. There is absolutely no reason why women shouldn't do that if that's what they want. It's autonomy, not separatism. They're not harming anyone. In fact, they're usually challenging unthought-about assumptions that thea- ter is controlled by men.

INTERVIEWER: You scripted a play by the women's collective, Gay Sweatshop, called *Care and Control* [1977] and published it in your anthology *Strike While the Iron Is Hot* [1980]. This play dealt with the judicial practice of removing children from the legal custody of lesbian mothers, didn't it?

WANDOR: No. *Care and Control* dealt with the way in which mothers—lesbian and heterosexual—who do not conform to the stereo- type are penalized by the state. It was not just about lesbian mothers.

INTERVIEWER: *Care and Control* was researched and devised collec- tively by Gay Sweatshop and then you were called on to script the results. What were the pros and cons of working on material gathered by others as opposed to working on material that is all you own?

WANDOR: First of all, it was exciting coming in to work on material that was already there, and which the company was intensely involved with. They had worked out a framework structure and collected a lot of very interesting research about actual custody cases. They had also spent a lot of time improvising, and I sat in on some of these improvisations. I took away with me a lot of different kinds of material: verbatim improvs, research bits and pieces, and the plot which the company had worked out. I then had to do a job which involved editing, structuring, and writing in "filler" bits. I invented the beginning from an idea of my own, and also developed a simple end. I liked the company's approach in that it uncovered ironies and contradictions and prejudices in the state's attitude to motherhood, so that while the foreground, as it were, was about the particularly vicious prejudice against lesbian motherhood, it was against a background that demanded certain conformities of behavior from mothers in general in order to maintain a conventional family system. Those were all the pros.

The cons were that I had to stay within the brief of the characters and the improvisational style which the company had already worked on. From an aesthetic point of view, I thought they had two characters too many (they had six and I thought four was enough), and the first half of the play was over-naturalistic and a little unwieldy, I thought. But this was not a relevant objection in the context. I was scripting "their" play, and happy to do so. I still have the same criticisms of the first half, but the play stands. And I must say that despite those criticisms, I found the change of style between the first and the second half very exciting indeed—it was something I had done myself a few years earlier in a play about the Miss World Contest, a play called *The Day After Yesterday*— and I liked that idea of setting the audience up with one set of expectations, and then making them sit up and get used to a whole new style.

INTERVIEWER: We hear little in the U.S. of what happened to the playwright Shelagh Delany since her splendid beginnings with *A Taste of Honey* and *The Lion in Love*. Does she still write for the theater?

WANDOR: I can't comment on the status of Shelagh Delaney in British theater circles. I would guess that she's probably seen as someone precocious who wrote herself out. Whether that's true or not, I don't know. England treats writers like shit, and likes nothing more than to remove the work from the writer, make it a classic, and . . . well, I am venting some spleen. But the theater is full of men and women who are not kept in enough produced commissions to make it possible for them to continue writing plays. There is a very high fallout rate in playwriting. That's why it's important for women to be published, so that plays do not disappear and writers are not forgotten.

INTERVIEWER: In your monograph, *Understudies: Theatre and Sexual Politics* [1981], you claimed that the critics are "policing" the stage. What did you mean by that?

WANDOR: I think I meant that plays only reach public consciousness when they are reviewed, and the power of the critics is enormous and often unfair.

INTERVIEWER: In *Understudies* you explore gender bias in the theater. How does this issue manifest itself both on the stage and behind the scenes?

WANDOR: I can't possibly answer all that here. But I suggest people read the book, and its follow-up, *Orlando's Children*.

INTERVIEWER: In that same publication, you use a phrase, *parity of voice*. What does that mean in terms of the theater?

WANDOR: What it says. For every male voice which is given the space to express itself in theater, there should be a female voice. We should aim for a theater industry in which all jobs are as close as possible to a fifty percent male, fifty percent female ratio.

INTERVIEWER: In the hundreds of reviews of women's plays we've read, one word crops up with curious regularity: *non-play*. What do you think this word means?

WANDOR: No idea. Probably the equivalent of *nondramatic* or something. It probably means they don't understand what the play is about and don't want to bother. At the most simplistic level, anything at all could be a play.

INTERVIEWER: You've said that you don't believe there's a female aesthetic and yet you also say that you're not interested in an androgynous view of the writing process. The two statements seem to conflict.

WANDOR: No, I don't believe that aesthetics can be reduced to matters of gender, and that's precisely why I don't think one can talk either about an androgynous view of the writing process, since androgyny implies that there are sexual determinants which can be ignored or transcended. I think about it in a different way: There are different kinds of institutional cultural production, which produce different artifacts. The theater produces plays in performance. Theater has a complex history, a complex set of working relations (relations of production). These can be understood in relation to a number of different factors: class, gender, the state of the industry, the social and political configuration of the time. Any understanding of the aesthetics of theater can take any of these elements into account. And there is no single one of them to which aesthetics can be reduced. I think it polarizes the theater to talk about aesthetics as either male or female. It denies the contradictory complexity of form, audience response, all sorts of things. But women's relationship to the writing process, the way women enter into, or challenge the given aesthetics of a particular time—all that is crucially important.

INTERVIEWER: Women dramatists are often accused of writing passive characters. Their plays are frequently said to be static. Any comment?

WANDOR: I'm not interested in responding to that accusation of women's plays being static. I don't think it's any more true of women than men. However, there is not only a theatrical legacy, but also the empirical truth that, generally, women are secondary in life—so a play that merely seeks to reflect that will reproduce that passivity. Some define the meaning of action differently, but I think there are so many different kinds of action in all sorts of plays that, again, there is no division based on gender. In any case, there are a lot of plays now where women are active rather than reactive. Not enough yet, perhaps.

INTERVIEWER: Are women under pressure to use humor in presenting their concerns and ideas on stage?

WANDOR: Yes. If women write comedy, it confirms the image of women as frothy, unserious, not to be taken seriously. I feel strongly that we should be free to be as miserable as we like, as tragic as we fancy, as various and as unpredictable as we can; but it is certainly true that critics sigh with great relief when they see women making harmless jokes (they're not keen on hard satire) as long as those jokes are not about men. That the critics don't like at all. My guess is that commercial managements in particular are very nervous about anything that is by a woman and which can't be presented as comedy. I mean, Nell Dunn's *Steaming* . . . the material that wasn't written funny was made funny, and a lot of the funny lines were downright television comedy so it was safe. Nell Dunn says she didn't write it as a comedy. She thinks if it hadn't been seen as a comedy, it wouldn't have been so successful. It was the first stage play she'd written and it was very carefully packaged commercially and sold.

INTERVIEWER: It was not nearly so successful here critically. Walter Kerr of *The New York Times* panned the play, but then said something to the effect that the play's nudity was tasteful and therefore kept his interest ["The nudity in 'Steaming' is easily and naturally arrived at; you don't feel that anyone's being exploited. Of course I don't suppose as many customers would come if it all took place in the library." Walter Kerr: "Are These Feminists Too Hard on Women?" *New York Times*, January 23, 1983].

WANDOR: The nudity was tasteful and therefore completely unrealistic about how women might behave in a steambath where there's nobody but other women around. And yet it was taken as being a realistic portrayal—a funny double standard.

INTERVIEWER: When a writer is presenting an uncharted area of experience in the theater, such as naked women in a steambath, is there any way to avoid the trap of voyeurism?

WANDOR: It's terribly difficult. But I think you must always take risks. If *Steaming* had been given a very straightforward production as opposed to something comic and a bit sweet and "tastefully" nude . . . if there'd been an attempt to be realistic, the play could have been seen as shocking.

I think when there are naked people on stage, we are all voyeuristic to some extent.

INTERVIEWER: Is there an element of voyeurism to men watching women's experience—naked or otherwise—on the stage?

WANDOR: There must be. I think it makes some of them feel uncomfortable without quite knowing why . . . perhaps they feel "got at."

INTERVIEWER: Are women playwrights more concerned than their male counterparts with drama as art rather than business?

WANDOR: No. Not at all. Most women playwrights I know have to earn their livings from writing, and are very aware of the precariousness of their freelance situation. Perhaps that's more obvious here in England, where since 1975 playwrights have been vigorously organizing to protect their rights and get proper contracts through the Writers Union and the Writers' Guild. I think we know that all art is produced in some way, and that it is a business; it is work but it's also art, self-expression, creativity. The problem is that our abilities to develop creatively are so often hampered by not enough money or having to do other work to survive. But this is the condition of all freelance writers. It's just worse for women because, relatively, there are so few of them.

INTERVIEWER: Are contemporary male playwrights being influenced by the content of women's plays? Are they updating their stereotypes, selecting different subject matter?

WANDOR: I don't think that men writers are really much influenced by plays by women. Some of them are trying to write women better; most fail abysmally. Many of them find it genuinely hard, and actually, secretly, are not really interested in writing about women. I don't think there's anything wrong with that. I just wish they were more honest about it.

INTERVIEWER: You have expressed some strong views on form versus content.

WANDOR: Everything is given a form, there is obviously no content without form. And I don't take the view that there's a real difference between men's and women's forms. I really don't. I'm in the process of rewriting and updating Understudies and that's an issue I'm going to discuss more fully. There are differences in subject matter . . . in the way that women approach certain kinds of experience but that approach has to do with content rather than being an innate form. For example, take the fact that women playwrights have not, on the whole, done conventional tragedies. It's not because conventional tragedy is anathema to women or because we've got a better way of doing it. It has to do with the exploration, the establishing and the laying out of the field of the subject matter of women's experience.

This is a difficult thing to discuss. But, for example, plays in which women playwrights show women as victims or scapegoats—in a sense these are attempts to write modern tragedies. But I think that perhaps this way of asking the question is a little out of date; after all, the Greek or Shakespearean notion of tragedy comes from recognizing a fixed system of values in the world, and the thing about twentieth-century drama, by men as well as by women, is that we no longer work on that principle. So the great tragedy of the individual rebel no longer rings quite so powerful. I think the question of women's relationships to historical subject matter is an interesting one, and that brings up some of the questions which I suspect relate to the idea of tragedy.

As to what subject matter is unacceptable on stage, I would make the very sweeping generalization that any representation of women that counters dominant imagery will be threatening. It doesn't even have to be very radical.

INTERVIEWER: Quite a few American women playwrights are admitting to avoiding, consciously or unconsciously, mother/daughter subject matter as a *central* issue for their dramas. Have you entered this dangerous arena either generally or autobiographically?

WANDOR: That's a very difficult one. I agree with the importance of this. I think a number of women have brought *motherhood* into their plays . . . I have, in quite a few of mine; that is perhaps the way women are exploring it, rather than through mother-daughter relationships as such. I've done it in *Mal de Mère* [1973], *Care and Control* [1977], *Correspondence, Whores d'Oeuvres* [1978], *Aid Thy Neighbor* [1978] and *The Old Wives Tale* [1977].

INTERVIEWER: We perceive an increasing desire on the part of women to direct their own work. Any thoughts?

WANDOR: The director-writer relationship in theater is not good. In general, I think writers are scared of directors and directors often think they know better than the writers about the text. I have for some time been thinking that I would like to direct my next stage play myself, but I have worries about doing it without any professional experience. Perhaps I will overcome that. I think it would make a difference to the staying power of writers if they also knew how to direct.

INTERVIEWER: Do you have a sense of yourself in the history of women's literature? Do you feel you're coming out of a tradition of women's playwriting?

WANDOR: No. I feel that in many ways—style, tone—I have more obvious links to plays written by men, but this is not at all surprising. This is largely true for all of us, since we have virtually no role models from whom to absorb things. But there are new kinds of juxtaposition, uses of style, transformations, which are not at all linked to the things that men do. I certainly see my work as part of the very exciting spectrum of feminist writing, and hope it will be seen that way by others. But I also feel out on a limb in relation to radical feminist stuff—still, let a thousand flowers bloom, eh?

INTERVIEWER: In your book of essays, *On Gender and Writing* [London, Pandora, 1983], author Margaret Drabble says, "Women who feel they object to being called women writers show a lack of confidence in their own work." Do you agree?

WANDOR: Women writers have become used to the term *women* being meant as *secondary*, or as semi-abusive, and so they don't like being called "women writers" by other women or feminists. But I think that it is quite important to reclaim that description as a positive and polemical thing, in order to indicate that there are differences in the way men and women see their status as writers, and in the way they choose and write about their subject matter. I have no problems at all about identifying myself as a woman writer (though there are some situations in which the priority is to identify myself as a professional writer) because I'm always so keen to provoke people to think about the relationships between gender and writing.

INTERVIEWER: What do you say to those who claim they are humanist rather than feminist? Is there any difference?

WANDOR: I suppose writers take on labels when they want to indicate what is important to them. If someone calls herself a humanist, I want to know more. If a woman says she is not a feminist, then she may be right. I don't think all women are feminists, any more than all women are feminist writers. So it is complicated, because, as I said before, there are many different kinds of feminism.

INTERVIEWER: Describe your typical writer's day.

WANDOR: I don't have a typical day. I work incredibly hard.

INTERVIEWER: Is there anyone among the contemporary U.S. playwrights who interests you?

WANDOR: I don't see or read enough American work to be fair about that.

INTERVIEWER: Are British playwrights more political than their American counterparts?

WANDOR: British theater probably addresses itself a little more often to social and class issues than American plays, but then American plays are marvelous at getting under the skin of psychical experience, are more daring emotionally, often more fluid in language.

INTERVIEWER: What are the politics behind which English plays are chosen, or not chosen, for U.S. production?

WANDOR: I can't say. I suspect that it is often as crude as the Americans being prepared to follow the judgment of, say, the Royal Court Theatre and take a success because it is seen to be a success; perhaps, in some respects, it's that audiences respond to the same things.

INTERVIEWER: Has your work been produced in America?

WANDOR: I've had a few readings in America, but no production yet. Of course, I'd love to have a play produced there.

INTERVIEWER: What technical/technological changes do you envision for the theater in the next hundred years?

WANDOR: Frankly, I'm not very interested in technical innovations in the theater. I am, of course, delighted by any technical illusion that the theater can offer (holograms are very exciting) but the theater will always remain a labor-intensive medium, and it seems to me that technological changes will happen without struggle (they'll come about if theaters have the money), whereas other kinds of changes, particularly those affecting women, will happen only with a lot of struggle.

INTERVIEWER: Do you use a word processor?

WANDOR: I'm considering it; but I write directly onto the typewriter and often need to look at more than one page at a time. I'm a little nervous about the paraphernalia. When I rewrite, I generally rewrite the whole thing anyway, so the convenience of programming corrections may not be relevant to my way of working. Perhaps my way of working might change. I don't know.

INTERVIEWER: Have you any advice to offer young people who may be considering playwriting as a profession?

WANDOR: I'm afraid not. Although I would encourage young writers to direct their own work where possible. Not because I think directors are unnecessary, but because I think it's important for writers to know how to make writing work on stage. This gives them far more confidence and understanding of the process when they are working with directors.

INTERVIEWER: What is the financial outlook for noncommercial theater under the Thatcher government?

WANDOR: Pretty grim, I'm afraid. Subsidy is being cut—not massively yet, but enough to make it impossible for most theaters and companies to maintain the level of work of previous years, let alone expand. This means that lots of theaters who were commissioning plays from writers now are back to waiting till the right scripts drop on the doorstep, or taking in touring productions. It means less chance for new writers to try their hand, and fewer opportunities for writers who are already professionals to keep building their careers. It is obviously hard for everyone, but it will rebound on women writers as well, I think. We won't really be able to tell the full impact of it all until about ten years' time, and then we'll see who is still working.

INTERVIEWER: Do you think there is script censorship going on at the literary manager level?

WANDOR: Oh yes. First of all, few theaters have the luxury of a literary manager, and many theaters are dreadful about reading scripts and dealing with writers—it is partly that they are too busy, partly that they don't know how. I know one literary manager quite well, and he is really a kind of buffer between the directors and the writers. But he doesn't have the power to push writers who interest him, if a director doesn't already have an interest. So the literary manager mops up the scripts as they come in, but can really do very little. I've said before that very few people (including directors) really know how to READ carefully—and although lots of theaters do have script-readers, I don't have a lot of faith in the standard of their ability to read. But I have to say that this is true of publishing these days as well. Standards, as they say, are falling.

One of the most important things for women playwrights is to keep writing, to keep being produced. If you write a play and it's not produced, then there isn't much point in going on writing. That is one way in which women get silenced in the theater—someone writes a first play, gets patted on the shoulder, patronized, and then thrown aside for the next new writer. One of the things which has been happening in the past few years is that a number of young women writers in their early twenties are getting plays produced, which is very good news indeed. But it is interesting that theaters and companies all seem to be rushing toward those writers, as if they have forgotten that there is a generation of older women writers who are also still working. Theater goes for novelty anyway, and when women are seen merely as the novelty of the moment, then we know that we're not really progressing.

INTERVIEWER: Do you think there is excess pressure on the playwright to be universal?

WANDOR: Well, the idea of what is universal needs to be taken apart a bit. Of course, it is true that some plays can communicate to audiences across all sorts of cultural boundaries. But what is assumed in conversation to be universal or about a contemporary issue is usually in practice something which is about men's perception of what is important, since it is still men who make the main decisions in the theater. It seems to me that a powerful play is a powerful play is a powerful play—but there is a gender imbalance. While women can respond to the dilemmas in *Hamlet* or *Lear*, because we are so familiar with that tradition, men are simply not able to make the same imaginative leaps into plays from a female perspective. Women are somehow denied the privilege of being able to be universal. Male critics may compliment a woman if they think she is being "human," which is a way of their denying the specificity of the female experience on stage. But the truth is that women, like men, can be both gender-specific and write in such a way that their ideas or arguments can be seen to have a general application. Male critics also criticize the way women write male characters, saying they're "stereotypes" when they are oblivious to the way that men writers do the same to women. If anyone uses terms like *universal* or *stereotype* one has to break it down into something very concrete in order to know what it means. And a play, however surreal or weird, will always have socioeconomic clues—accent, vocal pitch, clothes, gesture, et cetera.

INTERVIEWER: Is there any public debate between women playwrights in England?

WANDOR: Not really. When there are public debates on theater, panels, or a festival or a conference, there's a bit of scurrying round to find the token woman, and mostly they go for someone who is pretty well-known to draw the crowds. I have found—in the very few situations where there has been public discussion with women playwrights—that many women themselves have a dubious or ambiguous relationship to feminism, and are simply not accustomed to public debate, or don't like speaking in public. Now I get nervous, like anyone else, but I love speaking, I like a bit of an argument, I like the performance aspect of those situations, and I am prepared to discuss my differences with other women. But that isn't very acceptable across the board, in life as well as in theater. Some women are also afraid to show disagreements between women, because they think we must simply be supportive. So they behave supportively in public themselves, but in private they operate their own circles of discrimination. One of the important ways in which we as women show that we are in control of our ideas and our work, is to show how different and various and vigorous we are, as well as how enthusiastically we share the same aims. But I often feel out on a limb in this, and am met with lame silences when I say it. So it's relatively safe to write it down. . . .

INTERVIEWER: Do you find that women avoid violence in their work?

WANDOR: Difficult one. I think there are particular difficulties for women in representing violence in fiction. First of all, we are very aware of having been the objects of violence, and knowing that violence against women is a source of pornographic pleasure in the media. We are very aware of the relation of voyeurism to women, and so we are faced with the danger that any violence we may represent will reproduce exactly what we're trying to avoid. I tried to have a go at that in my play, *Whore d'Oeuvres*, which is about prostitution and different kinds of violence. I wanted to represent violence in a way that would shock the audience through simulation, rather than representing it naturalistically. The simulation is both physical and in the language, and it is meant to shock both men and women—it is a difficult play to do effectively, I think—but those were my intentions. There are other reasons, which is that women writers often want to affirm the enthusiasm and the ordinary things about the way women relate to one another—and so it is less a question of avoiding violence than of having other priorities.

WENDY WASSERSTEIN

Wendy Wasserstein is the author of *the widely produced* Uncommon Women and Others, *which was published by Dramatists Play Service in 1978. Her other plays include* Sunset at Camp O'Henry *(stage conception, Gerald Gutierrez),* Miami *with composer and lyricist Jack Feldman and Bruce Sussman,* Tender Offers *and* Isn't It Romantic. *For the PBS Great Performances series, Ms. Wasserstein adapted John Cheever's "The Sorrows of Gin." She collaborated with playwright Christopher Durang on the film* When Dinah Shore Ruled the Earth. *Ms. Wasserstein is a graduate of the Yale School of Drama, a member of the Artistic Board of Playwrights Horizons and the recipient of a Guggenheim Fellowship.*

INTERVIEWER: Your plays are very funny. Will you talk a little about comedic writing in general, and then specifically about women's comedy?

WASSERSTEIN: Well, there's always that old Woody Allen joke: When you write comedy you sit at the children's table, and when you write tragedy you sit at the adult table. But I'm not sure that's true. It's very satisfying for me to hear the audience laugh. The audience is alive, it's *there*. What's interesting about my plays is that they are comedies, but they are also somewhat wistful. They're not *happy*, nor are they farces, which is odd because I've been given offers to write sit-coms for television, and I don't think I'd be good at it. There's an undercurrent in my work.

Christopher Durang is a very dear friend, and a brilliant writer. We've collaborated on a film [*When Dinah Shore Ruled the Earth*] and it's interesting how our voices merge at a point. Mine tends to be more warm, and his is more startling. There's a give and take, but I'm still interested in that warmth. Collaboration is also a matter of stretching oneself, trying to get out into other forms. Chris talks about moving toward more warmth, and I find myself moving toward something darker. When we wrote the movie, we met every day, and wrote the whole script on one notepad. The writing became *one* voice. It was very interesting.

INTERVIEWER: Do you think it is more natural for you to write "warm"?

WASSERSTEIN: I wouldn't say that. It's hard, talking about a female aesthetic. Best put, I once heard Marsha Norman say that women writing plays had secrets they wanted to tell. When I wrote *Uncommon Women and Others* [1976–1977], I wanted to write an all-woman play. Now given that, what am I going to write? My characters rafting down the Colorado River? It just happens that the men I've known have not gone to girls' schools for eight years. They have not had the pleasure of a course on "Gracious Living." They also did not grow up—and hopefully this has changed—with having to hear "Be a sweet girl, be a good girl." That's different nowadays. I was writing *Uncommon Women* from an experience I had. I don't know if that gets down to an aesthetic. When you're talking about an aesthetic, you're also talking about language.

INTERVIEWER: How would you describe your stage language?

WASSERSTEIN: The people in my plays talk circularly. They do not talk directly. I don't know if that's women or that's Wendy. It's probably Wendy. But Wendy is a woman writer, and *Uncommon Women* comes from a woman's experience. It's *about* women sitting around talking. It's reflective. I do agree with Marsha Norman in that I think there are stories to tell that haven't been told. But you're not only telling them for women, hopefully.

INTERVIEWER: You said that in working on *Isn't It Romantic* you were interested in the ways in which your characters became trapped by their own humor.

WASSERSTEIN: Janie Blumberg, the main character, is totally trapped by her own sense of humor. Some people seeing the first version of the play thought it was composed of very witty one-liners, but I felt it was how Janie talks. Janie is a character who has a problem expressing her feelings and she desperately wants to be liked.

INTERVIEWER: Is Janie's humor a way of protecting herself?

WASSERSTEIN: It's a protection, but it's a vulnerability as well. I think that may be very female. Janie in *Isn't It Romantic* tells joke, joke, joke and then finally explodes. Finally, she discovers her own strength. And furthermore, there is a strength in being comedic. It's a way of getting on in the world, of taking the heat out of things. Humor is a life force.

INTERVIEWER: It seemed that many of the critics missed the irony of *Isn't It Romantic* [1981] in its original production.

WASSERSTEIN: Women playwrights fall into a trap because the audience goes in expecting a "woman's play," with a feminist sensibility. Nobody goes into a man's play and thinks, "I want a man's point of view on this." They don't expect to discover the male playwright's political feeling about the sexes. That is never asked of men. For example, when Janie in *Isn't It Romantic* doesn't marry the doctor, it's not because she's a grand feminist, or because she loves her career, or wants to ride off on a tractor. He isn't right for her. As a playwright, first and foremost you must be true to your characters. It's the character's motivation; not me speaking for womankind. Even *Uncommon Women* doesn't say, "This is what I feel about women." Basically what it's saying is "I'm very confused." The characters are confused; they're also dear and kind and funny. The play asks: "Why are they so confused?" I want to *show* you their confusion. But it's not saying I have any answers. And what it's really not saying is "Fuck you."

INTERVIEWER: Didn't you once say that *Isn't It Romantic* is *about* being funny?

WASSERSTEIN: Janie Blumberg's humor gives her the ability to distance herself from situations. But she simultaneously endears herself to people by being amusing. The play is about her difficulty in communicating. She's so verbal, and yet she can't talk. It's a play about speech—about the ability to speak and not to speak at the same time, which comes from the pressure women are under to be a good girl, a smart girl, and a warm girl, simultaneously.

INTERVIEWER: Is *Isn't It Romantic* about *the price* of being a good, smart, warm and funny girl?

WASSERSTEIN: Yes, I think so.

INTERVIEWER: Is Janie willing to pay the price?

WASSERSTEIN: Janie is strong, but she doesn't know it. Maybe she secretly knows she's strong and is frightened by it. It's not going to be easy for Janie, but she is able to move from feeling and that's interesting. In fact, that's character. Janie is stronger than her friend Harriet who has all the externals. . . . Harriet could be a cover on *Savvy* magazine. The girl who "has it all." You know, the person who gets up at eight o'clock in the morning, spends twenty minutes with her daughter and ten minutes with her husband, then they jog together, she drives to work, comes home to her wonderful life, studies French in the bathtub, and still has time to cry three minutes a day in front of the mirror.

What's troublesome, from my point of view, about the Women's Movement is that there are *more* check marks to earn nowadays. More pressure. What's really liberating is developing from the inside out. Having the confidence to go from your gut for whatever it is you want. Janie is able to do that.

The character of Janie's mother in *Isn't It Romantic* runs around saying, "I like life, life, life." She's a bit of a crackpot, but she *does* have a spirit. The comedy itself is a spirit. It's not an application form, a resume, it's life. This life spirit creates a current, a buoyancy, which, getting back to drama, is very important. It's important to reach the essence of that spirit in what you create. That, to me, is heroic.

INTERVIEWER: In the Phoenix production of *Isn't It Romantic* most of the critics were upset by the fact that in the end, Janie rejected the nice Jewish doctor as a husband.

WASSERSTEIN: If the Jewish doctor had been a creep, and Janie decided not to marry him, the play would be a feminist statement: Good for her, see how strong she is. I wanted to write a nice man. And the play's not about the fact that she doesn't marry. I don't feel one way or another about marriage per se, though I'd like to get married one of these days. . . .

INTERVIEWER: The doctor isn't really perfect, is he?

WASSERSTEIN: He's not perfect at all! He tells her he wants to make alternate plans, he calls her "monkey," he buys an apartment without telling her. If these are people's ideals, after the play they should see a marriage counselor. And Janie's not scared. He is a Jewish doctor, he is darling and funny and dear, but Janie has a right to her decisions. She has a right, even if that means she's going to be alone. Even if she's *wrong* in her choice. Even if she's going to sit in her apartment and cry every night, if that's what she wants to do. . . .

INTERVIEWER: Since the emergence of women's issues, men's behavior has been under close scrutiny. You seem to have taken an ironic swipe at the "new male" in drawing your character, Paul Stuart [*Isn't It Romantic*], whose behavior is old hat—despite his liberated rhetoric.

WASSERSTEIN: Things have gotten very confusing. It's true that men can exploit the new rhetoric. My character Paul Stuart is very smart when he says that when he got married, women didn't know they could have careers. He says, "Now you girls have careers and *you* want a wife." He's pretty much figured things out. The fact that *he* still gets to have a wife is interesting. . . .

INTERVIEWER: Your plays bear the message that women *can't* "have it all." Helen Gurley Brown [editor, *Cosmopolitan*] says that women *can* have it all, if only they learn the right strategies.

WASSERSTEIN: I've never been one for strategies, really. Because I can't make one for myself. What should you do? Take colored index cards for everything you want, put them on a bulletin board: baby on the pink card, job on the blue? I never understood how those things work. I know there are women who have careers *and* babies. They work very hard. More credit to them. But the whole notion of "having it all" is ridiculous. It's a ridiculous phrase. Who's determining what "it all" is? Helen Gurley Brown? That's not fair. No man has had the pressure during the past ten years of having a different article come out every two weeks dictating how he should live his life. It changes every two weeks!

There isn't any formula for happiness. The very basic expectations of being a "good girl," a "nice girl," and a "kind girl" are still being put upon us. This is confusing because there's nothing wrong with wanting to be kind, unless it hurts you, or keeps you from doing what you want to do.

INTERVIEWER: Who is responsible for this malaise? The media? The theater? The government?

WASSERSTEIN: I don't know. You *do* want to work *and* have children *and* be gorgeous. But until there's a dictum for men that says, "Have it all," it's not fair for women to feel they should. Even with all the media talk about the "new father" and "time-sharing" I've yet to see the male "have it all" article come out.

INTERVIEWER: As far back as *Uncommon Women* you seemed to have an awareness of the way the "new male" was absorbing the liberated woman's language. Rita says, "The only problem with menstruation for men is that some sensitive schmuck could write about it for the *Village Voice* and become the new expert on women's inner life."

WASSERSTEIN: I guess to be fair, things have changed. . . .

INTERVIEWER: Doesn't it sometimes seem things have regressed?

WASSERSTEIN: Well, I went back to Mt. Holyoke in 1979 to see a production of *Uncommon Women*. I asked some of the students there what they thought about the play. One of them said, "Well, we think it's a nice *period* piece." I said, "Who do you think I am, Sheridan?" I mean, I had been studying there only eight years before! Then the women told me that unlike my characters, they knew what they wanted: to go to business school, or earn Ph.Ds or get married. I did think to myself, "This is becoming like Amherst College during the fifties." What's so great about that?

INTERVIEWER: Can we go back to the critics for a moment? Not many of them were kind about your rather broad character, Susie Friend, the cheerful organizer in *Uncommon Women*. Shakespeare was allowed a few clowns, why not Wendy Wasserstein?

WASSERSTEIN: Lots of women I know have grown up with Susie Friends. Now that's a woman's story! There have always been these little organizers in women's colleges. Of course, now they're organizing in banks!

INTERVIEWER: Is it okay for her to be a little less than three-dimensional because she is a peripheral character?

WASSERSTEIN: Susie Friend was a device. If you see *Uncommon Women* as a spectrum of women: on one end, there's Susie Friend, and on the other, there's Carter, the intellectual. That's all.

INTERVIEWER: You've said that the character of Tasha Blumberg in *Isn't It Romantic* was close to your mother in some ways.

WASSERSTEIN: Well, she is and she isn't. When you base a character on someone in real life, you are always condensing, as well as trying to keep the tone consistent. Tasha is not totally like my mother. Although my mother *is* a danseur! There is also an assumption that every mother you write is your own mother. That's not necessarily true. You have different things to say about a mother-daughter relationship at different times of life and in different kinds of plays.

INTERVIEWER: You've also said that it was easier for you to write the character Lillian, Harriet's mother, in *Isn't It Romantic* than Tasha Blumberg. Why is that?

WASSERSTEIN: Harriet's mother is an intriguing character. She was a more interesting woman to write because, of all the women in *Isn't It Romantic*, she is the most modern.

INTERVIEWER: Some of the critics saw Lillian as bitter. Do you agree?

WASSERSTEIN: Lillian is not hard or bitter. She is not Faye Dunaway in *Network*. But she's tough. In terms of comedy, she was fun to write because her sense of humor is very different from the other characters I have written. She has a little inflection, she's very wry and dry, and that was good for me because sometimes all of my characters have similar senses of humor. Lillian knows of the world and her own life. She has made her choices and has come to terms with them. In her life, there was not room for a man. She could not "have it all." She did pay a price and what's tragic is that her daughter is now going to pay another price.

INTERVIEWER: What is the price for Lillian?

WASSERSTEIN: Lillian had a bad marriage with a selfish man. Maybe with a more understanding man, she would have been fine. Who knows what the problem was? But in her life, she could not work it out. It wasn't worth it to her. Lillian is not a romantic. Lillian is fair. She is modern because she faces herself. What she has to say is honorable: "You tell me who has to leave the office when the kid bumps his head or slips on a milk carton." If she has to go home, time and time again, then why should she be with a man anyway? From Lillian's point of view, there is no reason to have *two* babies, your husband and your child. What's interesting is that Lillian, in her own way, is also a "good girl." She is not doing anything wrong. She is very American. A good mother, a hard worker . . .

INTERVIEWER: Be more specific as to what was more difficult about writing Tasha Blumberg, the character most nearly like your own mother.

WASSERSTEIN: I'll tell you why she was harder to write than Lillian. I've always thought that *Uncommon Women* was me split into nine parts, in terms of characters. But the truth is, what was always the hardest in *Uncommon Women* was writing Holly, who, autobiographically, is closest to me, though there are parts of me in all of the characters. That play is twofold. First, it's a play about Holly and Rita, which examines the fact that the Women's Movement has had answers for the Kates of the world (she becomes a lawyer), or the Samanthas (she gets married). But for the creative people, a movement can't provide answers. There isn't a specific space for them to move into. Holly was the hardest to write because I thought, "That's Wendy," or people will think, "THAT'S WENDY! There's the hips, there she is." And I also didn't want to self-congratulatize when drawing that character. So I find it difficult to write autobiographical characters. There aren't good guys and there aren't villains in my plays. If I were to say there's a problem with my writing, it's typified by the line in *Uncommon Women* when one character says, "Sometimes it's difficult having sympathy with everyone's point of view." I have been accused of being too generous to the other, less autobiographical characters in my plays, but in fact, it is hardest for me to be generous to the character that is closest to me.

INTERVIEWER: You feel you have to humble yourself?

WASSERSTEIN: Yes. I think so. When someone said to me, "You're a playwright, why use a confused persona to represent yourself in a play? *You* know what you're doing. Why shouldn't the character?" I said, "I'm a playwright *because* I don't know everything. Because I am trying to figure things out." You do divide yourself up when you are writing. Marty Sterling, the doctor in *Isn't It Romantic* has the sweetest speech about marriage. Why doesn't Janie have that speech?

INTERVIEWER: So Tasha Blumberg was harder to write than Lillian because she was more autobiographical?

WASSERSTEIN: Tasha is closer to my mother, that is true. I find my mother very funny. My mother dances six hours a day. She's, as she says, twenty-one plus, and she has not gone to Mt. Holyoke, but she is very sharp. Sometimes I find her humor funnier than my own. I saw my mother on the street the other day. I was in a taxi, and I stopped.

She jumped in and said, "Oh, it's so wonderful to have children, honey. It's so wonderful to see you and I only hope that by the time you have children, you take a fertility pill and have five." Then she looked at me and said, "And that's going into the play, isn't it?" I thought, there is no way I could write anything as good as that. And she knew it. I haven't finished with my mother yet. That is the truth of all this.

INTERVIEWER: Will you write about it someday?

WASSERSTEIN: Maybe it's where my writing is going. I don't know. Although I am proud of the last scene in *Isn't It Romantic*, the play doesn't deal with the pain of that subject. The real reason for comedy is to hide the pain. It is a way to cope with it. A way of staying "up." It's a privacy. You are there, and you are not there. You don't share equally about every topic. That's the truth of language, the truth of dialogue. If you did, you wouldn't be writing language, you wouldn't be writing what you are hearing, how people really talk. . . .

INTERVIEWER: So humor creates subtext?

WASSERSTEIN: Yes and it is also part of the delight of writing itself. When you come up with a good line, you make yourself laugh, right there at the typewriter. It gives you pleasure.

I want to say that the other reason Lillian was easier to write than Tasha was that Lillian was someone on my mind. She is contemporary. She's an image that is closer to, if not me, then me ten years from now. She reflects a conflict that I think about a lot. Men and children. Having children alone, and whether or not that's possible. Tasha Blumberg—forget my mother—is from another world, a different time, which is harder to capture. Lillian is closer to my world. I have considered writing plays about the young Tasha at Radio City, the dancer. And at one point in *Isn't It Romantic*, Janie gets up and starts to tap dance. There is an image of a person alone, who dances. Janie's mother is a dancer, and that is the gift from mother to daughter.

INTERVIEWER: You studied dramatic writing at Yale. Were there other women in the playwriting program?

WASSERSTEIN: Susan Nanons was there, Sharon Stockard-Martin, Grace McKeaney . . . they are all very talented women. But no, the playwriting program was not overflowing with women.

INTERVIEWER: Did you take a lot of flak for writing *Uncommon Women*, a play with an all-female cast?

WASSERSTEIN: I made the decision to write a play with all women after seeing all that Jacobean drama, where a man kisses the poisoned lips of a woman's skull and drops dead. I thought, "I can't identify with this." I wanted to write a play where all the women were alive at the curtain call. And I had seen my friend, Alma Cuervo, whom I love dearly, have to play the pig-woman in *Bartholomew Fair*, a panda in *General Gorgeous* . . . I thought, What's going on?

INTERVIEWER: Were people shocked by *Uncommon Women*?

WASSERSTEIN: Well, the play was not in as good a shape as it is now. I do remember someone who saw the Yale production saying that I was a "subset" of Christopher Durang. Chris came to my defense and said, "When I write my play about an all woman's college, you can call me." It was shocking to me.

INTERVIEWER: You said in an interview that the point of view at Yale was that "the pain in the world is a man's pain."

WASSERSTEIN: Though women are often said to write "small trage-dies," they are *our* tragedies, and therefore large, and therefore legitimate. They deserve a stage.

INTERVIEWER: Why didn't *Uncommon Women*, with all of its success, move to Broadway?

WASSERSTEIN: We had one offer, which is an interesting story. The producer told me that at the end of the play things should be different. He said the play was too wistful. He thought, that at the end, when everyone asks Holly, "What's new with you?" she should pull out a diamond ring and say, "Guess what? I'm going to marry Dr. Mark Sil-verstein." I thought, "Well, she'd have to have a lobotomy, and I'd have to have a lobotomy too." So the play never went to Broadway. It does stick in my craw because *Uncommon Women* is a very good play and it had such an amazing cast. But sometimes you've opened a door, and when you go to the next work, people listen. Don't I sound old and wise? The play should have moved to Broadway!

INTERVIEWER: Is *Uncommon Women* a political play?

WASSERSTEIN: It's political because it is a matter of saying, "You must hear this." You can hear it in an entertaining fashion, and you can hear it from real people, but you must know and examine the problems these women face. It all comes from the time I was in college, which was a time of great fervor. There used to be pieces in that play that were very political. The most political part was when Mark Rudd came to Mt. Holyoke. In that version, Susie Friend had a strike speech and even organized a strike for Mark Rudd.

INTERVIEWER: Why did you take that out?

WASSERSTEIN: Well, I took it out because I thought that it would open the play up to all the questions of Vietnam, and that's another play. I really wanted to do something so that women's voices could be heard. I'm happy I did that. I can remember the 1969 Cambodia strike. Si-multaneously, Amherst College was accepting women for the first time.

There were twenty-three women and twelve hundred men. That was a glorious experience. I didn't go to the dining hall for two weeks. I was scared to death! The first night I was there, the men were rating us! I remember going to the student-faculty meeting and saying, "You have to let us stay here." The speaker seemed to think this was a very selfish issue. He said, "We have Kent State, we have Cambodia . . . what's the big deal about a little girl wanting to stay at Amherst College?" I thought, "This is one of the most important things happening in terms of long-range changes for women." In fact, Amherst College went coed two years later. That's just an isolated incident. I do think that that whole period has not yet been resolved. Maybe things *are* regressing. I try to find answers to these issues through my plays.

INTERVIEWER: Your character Leilah in *Uncommon Women*, says, "Sometimes I think I just need to live in a less competitive culture." How do you think that relates to being an artist in America?

WASSERSTEIN: When I was at Yale, I was frightened to death. I remember years later telling Christopher Durang that I felt like I was going from platform to platform, trying to catch the train to Moscow. I went from platform six to platform seven and I kept missing the train. I had no idea what I was doing at drama school. Everyone else I knew was going to law school or marrying lawyers, except for my immediate friends, who seemed as cuckoo as me. I really couldn't explain my feelings to anyone. If you tell someone you are a playwright, they say, "So what do you do for a living?" Or, if you're a successful playwright, they say, "Gee, isn't that glamorous?" You think, "Yeah, it's real exciting. I sit in a room alone every day and I write. Thrilling!" Either way, you are in an odd spot. It doesn't place you in the margins, but you are not in the mainstream of society. It certainly doesn't make for a secure life. But it does at least make for a life of doing what you want to do. I feel very lucky to be able to do that.

INTERVIEWER: You seem to make a plea for community in your work. . . .

WASSERSTEIN: Yes. Or at least, a plea to establish your own kind of family. Maybe my family is Chris Durang and Ted Talley and André Bishop. It could well be, but again, that's pretty marginal. You can't go to weddings and say "My family is Chris Durang, and Ted Talley and André Bishop. . . ."

INTERVIEWER: Would you tell us something about Playwrights Horizons?

WASSERSTEIN: I am very lucky because that theater is my home, and it has made a tremendous difference to me, having someplace that I know I can work out of. I've had a long association with the people there. Life is competitive, but Playwrights Horizons is not. It is a community, and that has always been very important to me.

INTERVIEWER: What happens when you are in rehearsal with a play? Are you able to maintain sufficient artistic control over your work?

WASSERSTEIN: It depends on the production and on the play. I was there through everything with *Uncommon Women*. I was at the [Eugene] O'Neill [National Playwrights Conference], the Phoenix Theatre, and when they did the television production for PBS. I had a good relationship with the director, Steve Robman.

INTERVIEWER: You felt your intentions were given enough attention?

WASSERSTEIN: Yes. But subsequently, I have seen productions of *Uncommon Women* around the country and I can't tell you the sort of horrifying things I've seen. It's unbelievable.

INTERVIEWER: How do you react to a bad production?

WASSERSTEIN: It depends on whether you've been involved in the actual production. Sometimes you just go to see the play. That's taught me that there is a point at which you have to let a play go. It was hard for me to let *Uncommon Women* go because it had such a short run in New York. I like to be able to go to a theater for more than a two-and-a-half-week run.

INTERVIEWER: You don't experience anger in rehearsal? You've never had to fight for your intentions?

WASSERSTEIN: Well, yes, sure I have. Rehearsal is a very important time to learn not to be such a good girl. I think you have to learn to speak up, because the point is, it's your play, and you *do* know something about it. It is very important to pick the right director. That is step one. And you can't be a good girl about picking a director either. You can't pick somebody just so everyone will like you. You have to pick someone you respect and who will be right for the play.

INTERVIEWER: Have you ever worked with a woman director?

WASSERSTEIN: Susan Dietz directed *Uncommon Women* in California [L.A. Stage Company, April 1981].

INTERVIEWER: Did you feel she brought any special insights to the work?

WASSERSTEIN: I did like the production a lot. I don't know how to answer that question because I was assigned Steve Robman at the O'Neill and he stayed with the production throughout. It wasn't a conscious choice for a male director or against a female director. It is very important that there be more women directors, and that more women directors are encouraged, which goes all the way back to the question of how many women directing students there are at Yale. I do think what you want is a *good* director.

INTERVIEWER: What did you mean, earlier, when you spoke of "letting go" of the play?

WASSERSTEIN: I told Chris the other night that I've had the sensation, with both *Uncommon Women* and *Isn't It Romantic* of waiting for the play to embrace me. I keep waiting for the play to give back what I've given. And it cannot happen. You can get depressed. Because if you're a good writer, you're generous and you give it everything and people laugh and applaud—but still, the play is inanimate. It cannot reach out and embrace you. That's hard to come to terms with. You can follow a play around the country waiting for that to happen. But it can't—and finally, you have to separate from it and just send it out.

INTERVIEWER: Is the closest you can get to that embrace hearing the spontaneous laughter from the audience?

WASSERSTEIN: Maybe. But during *Uncommon Women*, there was something special among those actresses and me. I can remember being in the dressing room with Swoosie Kurtz and Jill Eikenberry and Alma Cuervo, and Anna Levine, Glenn Close and Ellen Parker and there was the sense of embracing, a sense of all starting out together . . . again, that feeling of community. And I would say I feel it more at the laughter than at the applause.

INTERVIEWER: Why did you decide to study playwriting at Yale instead of attending Columbia Business School, where you had also been accepted?

WASSERSTEIN: You know, I even sent Columbia a deposit! When I graduated from Mt. Holyoke I came to New York and took writing courses at City College. I studied with Israel Horovitz and Joseph Heller. While studying playwriting with Israel, I had my first play done at Playwrights Horizons—this was back when it was at the YMCA on Fifty-second Street. I applied to both programs because I felt "I've *got* to make a living." I was living at home at the time. I thought I'd go to business school, then get a job in Chicago and everything would be fine. But when I got into Yale School of Drama, I thought, "Playwriting is something I really want to do. It's worth a shot." But it was hard. It took me a long time to take myself seriously. I mean, it still takes me a long time to take myself seriously. . . .

INTERVIEWER: Did Durang and Talley have difficulty taking themselves seriously?

WASSERSTEIN: I don't know. I don't think they thought something was wrong with them because they weren't in law school or married to a lawyer. I thought something was wrong with me. I thought I was a Ford Pinto. Now, I've gotten used to it. I'm used to living a life of eighty percent security.

INTERVIEWER: Does a Guggenheim Fellowship help with that feeling of eighty percent security?

WASSERSTEIN: Yes. That was the best thing since *Uncommon Women.* It is a certified "We believe in you." I have a funny story about that. In October, my father said, "So what are you doing?" I said, "Applying for a Guggenheim." He said, "What's that?" I told him it was a foundation that gives artists money to finish their work. Then he said, "No daughter of mine's going on welfare!" I'm the only person whose parents are going to disinherit her for winning a Guggenheim!

INTERVIEWER: Did you see *Uncommon Women* as a "non-play," as some of the reviewers did?

WASSERSTEIN: *Uncommon Women* is not a conventionally structured play. On a simple level, it moves through the seasons of the year. I do not see that play as presentational. It's like an odd sort of documentary. I am more interested in content than form. *Uncommon Women* is episodic. I don't know what actually *happens* in that play . . . they graduate.

INTERVIEWER: Quite a lot happens. . . .

WASSERSTEIN: But it is an emotional action. And I tend to go on big canvases. My favorite authors are Russian: Tolstoy, Chekhov . . . the whole idea of presenting a social life and a personal life interests me. I also love Ibsen.

INTERVIEWER: There's much reference recently to "The new woman playwright"—Mel Gussow's article in *The New York Times Magazine* [May 1, 1983], for example. Is it really that women are newcomers to playwriting, or is it the attention that's new?

WASSERSTEIN: I think it's the attention that's new. I do think there are women who open doors, like Marsha Norman. I don't know if her play *'night, Mother* could have won a Pulitzer Prize twenty years ago. So maybe there is a little more attention nowadays. But at the same time, when I saw that article, I thought, "Where is Corinne Jacker?" And that article also brings up the whole issue of whether women playwrights are a separate category. We are all playwrights. I think that is very important. But for now, any minority group must be labeled. Our idea of a playwright is a white male—then all the others are separated into subsets: black playwrights, gay playwrights, women playwrights, and so on. The point is, we are all in it together. But I listen to my plays, and as I hear them, I distance myself, and I still think, "A woman wrote this."

INTERVIEWER: Are female playwrights becoming less political than they were in the sixties and seventies?

WASSERSTEIN: It depends on what you see as political. Politics on the largest level is *from each according to their ability.* Nine girls taking a curtain call can be seen as political. It's important in terms of feeling legitimate. So is the fact that men can come to my plays and laugh, and that some girl from New Jersey comes to the play and says, "This is my story." And if my story can reach her, maybe *she* can tell *her* story. That is very important. Comedy does not segregate the political.

INTERVIEWER: Do you feel that British women playwrights are more likely to be overt in their politics?

WASSERSTEIN: That could be true. It could have to do with being brought up in a society where feminism has been connected to broader political issues. Maybe feminism has taken a different shape there. Caryl Churchill is a wonderful playwright. Her *Top Girls* was great. The way she took the larger political scope and then looked at the personal was fantastic.

INTERVIEWER: Can you give us a summation?

WASSERSTEIN: It is very important that women keep writing plays for many reasons. The theater is the home of the individual voice—at least in dramatic form. It is not in movies or television. I think the work of women in America is evolving. For myself, I am trying to work on structure, on comedy, and on being able to create a feeling of community. That can only happen in the theater.

INTERVIEWER: Are you optimistic about the state of American theater?

WASSERSTEIN: Oddly enough, I am. Because you do not write by committee in theater. The way that artists are discriminated against does have an effect on your pocketbook. Getting a Guggenheim helped this year, but you know, I am not making millions. The Guggenheim is not the money you would make as a first-year lawyer. That's how our society works. It makes you feel marginal. But, as somebody who believes in the individual voice, I still believe in the theater and what can happen there. I believe in comedy, in its spirit, and in its ability to lift people off the ground. I also think there are stories to tell, and as a woman writer, I want to tell those stories, to work out those conflicts. I want to take these conflicts from the political down to the personal. And the personal level, to me, is somewhat comedic. I hope to write a play that is going to be a history of the Women's Movement, which is a serious thing to take on. I want to write about someone who went through it and how it affected them personally—I want to explore the reverberations. Because I want to understand, and sometimes I understand better by writing. . . .

SUSAN YANKOWITZ

Susan Yankowitz has been writing plays for over twenty years. Her works include A Knife in the Heart, Baby (original version of book, Broadway production, 1983), Qui Est Anna Mark?, True Romances, Slaughterhouse Play, Terminal (a collaboration with the Open Theater), Transplant and The Ha-Ha Play. Her plays have toured internationally. Yankowitz has also written for film and television. She has published several short stories, essays, and a novel, Silent Witness, [1976 by Alfred A. Knopf, Inc. and in 1977 by Vintage.] She is the recipient of two National Endowment for the Arts Creative Writing Fellowship grants, a Rockefeller Foundation Grant in playwriting, a Guggenheim Fellowship, a residency at the Eugene O'Neill National Playwrights Conference and most recently, a National Endowment US/Japan grant to study puppet theater in Japan.

INTERVIEWER: Why aren't we seeing much politically relevant drama on American stages these days?

YANKOWITZ: Well, politics. You can't write political plays here. People shy away from political themes as though they would bring about the very disasters such plays try to examine. Yet British political plays are acceptable in America. David Hare's *Plenty*, for instance.

INTERVIEWER: Your plays are political.

YANKOWITZ: Yes, I've written political plays. But where are they? In my file drawer. Those plays don't get produced. Not even on the regional stages. As a playwright I want to speak not just for myself but for a community. And yet there *isn't* really a community. One of the saddest things in the American theater is that there is not a community of people working in a serious way.

INTERVIEWER: Do you think there is a safe harbor for playwrights to develop their work?

YANKOWITZ: A few pockets, perhaps, but I haven't found them. What we need is an opportunity to work for a few months with a company of actors. Not as preparation for a staged reading, not as a trial, but as part of a creative evolution, in which the only goal is the refinement of the play. That can be of immense value and service to a playwright. But few if any theaters are providing it. The regional theaters are looking for two- and three-character plays that they can put on for a minimum amount of money, that will not offend their audiences, because they're desperately afraid of losing their audiences. . . .

INTERVIEWER: Are you optimistic about the state of the American theater?

YANKOWITZ: I am alternately sanguine and despondent, buoyed and furious. But many people like myself are still passionately devoted to the theater. The doors may be closed to us now, but we will find other doors. I believe there is enough commitment to predict that something must and will change.

INTERVIEWER: How do you feel about the increasing expenses of the theater—high production costs as well as rising ticket prices?

YANKOWITZ: Theater and film are commerce. No other art is commerce in the same way. Large sums of money don't have to be put into a painting in order for it to be hung in a gallery. It doesn't require a great deal of money to write or publish a poem. But in the theater and in film the stakes are so high that money becomes an integral part of the process of having the work realized. I think these stages are corrupting. To the extent that one can separate trade from art, one sees a better form of art emerging. But because trade and art are so tightly entangled, there's no possibility for theatrical art to flourish at this time without a renewed vow of poverty and a divorce from commercialism. We have to band together with like-minded people. That doesn't necessarily mean a woman's theater. It might mean a theater composed exclusively of mothers or of social activists; it might be a dedication to the avant-garde, to finding new forms or to developing an indigenous political theater. But the only way to have any power in the theatrical world is to be independent of commercial interests and to have a small devoted community of one's own.

INTERVIEWER: In England, British women playwrights and directors are attempting to buy a West End theater in order to have artistic control of at least one theater space in London.

YANKOWITZ: That's another point. When you look at who runs the theaters in this country, you see that the majority are run by men. My personal experience has been that women respond to my work much better than men do. In general, a play of mine will get through all the

readers and then a male artistic director, one who has produced misogy-
nistic plays *ad nauseum,* will reject it as "anti-male." It happens time
and again in regional theaters; you get your play up through the woman
who is in second command, and when the script ascends finally to the
top, the person who really has the power is a man, and the man says
no. That's why I think it's a wonderful idea to form a kind of sisterhood
with women in the position of making those final decisions.

INTERVIEWER: Why do you think women respond more to your work?

YANKOWITZ: I've been thinking about it in anticipation of your interview. It's hard for me to understand, because my work, with a few
exceptions, doesn't particularly idealize women nor is it "feminist theater," at least in the narrow sense.

INTERVIEWER: What is the narrow sense of feminist theater?

YANKOWITZ: In the narrowest sense, it's theater whose mission is to
show women in a positive light. It's a kind of hagiography. Which, for
the most part, tends to be destructive of art. Poor feminist plays are, for
the most part, thesis plays, where the writer sets out to show, for instance,
that a woman can be strong in business. That's the writer's purpose and
she writes to that theme. And, as a result, the playwright excludes life,
ambiguity and complexity. I have written such plays myself, and they've
inevitably been bad. Usually I've set out to say something specific about
women—I begin with a conclusion—and the play becomes schematic
and predictable. Imagination and surprise can find no place in these
plays; they're statements, rather than experiences, both for the writer and
the audience. There is a terrible danger in sacrificing art to politics. In
fact, when one's politics are integrated into one's life and thoughts, they
emerge in the art.

INTERVIEWER: Can you give some examples of playwrights with an
integrated sensibility?

YANKOWITZ: Brecht. A figure like Mother Courage is certainly not
an ideal woman, and yet she emerges as a heroic figure. She's torn, she
does low things and she does noble things; she doesn't always behave
admirably. What you see in some feminist work is women who behave
consistently the way we wish we could behave. Let's say that feminists
would agree we would like to be the kind of women who don't depend
upon men and who don't need to please men. Well, I don't know a
woman, feminist or not, who hasn't at some point found herself doing
something to please a man! Maybe she hated herself for it. But that is a
more interesting subject for art, in my view, than to show the woman
who is immune. Because that's not real and therefore doesn't have a
place in art. That's a cartoon. One must value the conflicts. To be a
feminist and an artist at the same time is to say, "Subjects pertaining to

women are worthy of my attention." For example, it is important to look at the *mother* of an assassin, not just the assassin [*Knife in the Heart* 1983]. I suppose that is a feminist element in my work because it's the way I think about things. I look at the women, I'm interested in women. Work which ignores women, or treats them in stereotypic fashion, does not take women seriously.

INTERVIEWER: Caryl Churchill was recently criticized by *The New York Times* [Walter Kerr, Jan. 23, 1983] for presenting a "ruthless," imperfect businesswoman, Marlene, in her play *Top Girls*.

YANKOWITZ: I don't think the issue is how the play is going to be received, because by and large the critics are journalists with slack intellectual standards and a narrow view of the theatrical imagination. We have perhaps five critics whom we can take seriously, in any way whatsoever.

INTERVIEWER: New York critics do have the power to close a production.

YANKOWITZ: Oh, of course they do! But that has to be a separate issue. I don't think we playwrights can really be concerned about the critics. We care, in a secondary sense, but we can't write in anticipation of their reactions. We have to educate them. And maybe they're not educable. That's possible. But that's not something that the playwright has to concern herself with. We have to do the best we can, we must be concerned with writing better plays and finding opportunities to do our work. And if we don't find a typical situation in which to produce our plays, then we have to find an atypical one.

INTERVIEWER: But literary managers, the source of some of those opportunities, often take their cues from the critical reception of a new play. . . .

YANKOWITZ: They do. They do. I agree that in terms of production the power of the critics is a relevant issue. But in terms of the actual work that one does, it is impossible to consider it.

INTERVIEWER: So you feel that maintaining artistic integrity is always more important than gaining productions.

YANKOWITZ: I don't see that there is any choice. I can only write the kinds of plays that I write. That's all. I can't write anybody else's plays. I'm not interested in writing the kinds of plays that are currently applauded by the critics. I would be very glad if the critics applauded me, but I don't want to have to write their version of a successful play. I don't know if I believe it's possible for an artist to change her sensibility to suit the times or to suit the critics. If you are willing to wreak that kind of havoc on your talents, to twist your own artistic values out of shape in order to earn money, how are you going to twist them back? Can you straighten a pretzel once it's been baked? It doesn't seem likely. There are two things. One is success. I would like to be successful, but my *goal* is not success. Even if I beat my head against the wall for the next twenty years (and I probably will), I doubt that when I'm on my deathbed, I'll say, "How I wish I'd written that as a situation comedy!" That's not the way I see the world. Frankly, I don't find meaning in a naturalistic or linear form. From my point of view, it doesn't reflect experience. And it's not a form which I wish to try. That's already a strike against me! I discovered that during an experience in Hollywood with *The Amnesiac* [1980], a screenplay that had been commissioned by an independent producer. I had an idea—a woman who ostensibly has amnesia reinvents herself, and does this by drastic means. I was brought out to Hollywood with my treatment to "pitch the idea." In preparation for this event, I had bought a pair of high-heeled shoes. I literally went out shopping for a pair of high heels so I could have a nice leg to present to the producer. [Laughter] We walked in to the meeting, the producer looked at his watch and he said, "Well, I have a meeting. You have seven minutes." So we pitched this idea. And he said, "It has to be a romantic comedy, it has to end up with the couple reconciled, and it has to be funny." So that's what I tried to do. I don't think I was too successful. I tried to make it funny, and to give it a happy ending. I did it for money, because I was being paid thirty-five thousand dollars, and that was two years for me of living expenses, for three months' work. I didn't think I was corrupting myself. It was a job. And it posed interesting problems for me. But there is no question that had I been writing it for the stage or as a novel, I would have approached the material very differently.

INTERVIEWER: Even so, the ending of *The Amnesiac* is quite ironic.

YANKOWITZ: Well, I try to sneak these things in. One of the things you find in the theater is that the people in management are extremely literal. They don't understand subtlety or irony, they only look at the surface; and if it's satisfactory, they don't look to see its underbelly. Now that's something I try to do, to layer my writing so that one person can understand it one way, and another person can understand it another, and some can understand it in many ways. When my work is at its best, it can be understood on many levels. When I wrote *The Amnesiac* I was saying several different things, and hoping the people in power would notice only the superficial story.

INTERVIEWER: Was the film ever made?

YANKOWITZ: MGM *hated* it. But the independent producer who had brought me there *loved* it. This is another theme of my particular experience as a writer: People are *wildly* divided about my work. They either find my work brilliant or loathe it. Very few people take a moderate position. I can report that with a smile, but in fact it's caused me a lot of grief. I'm only beginning to accept that I will probably always evoke that response.

INTERVIEWER: Going back to craft, how do you achieve these layerings? Is it something evident in a first draft, or something that evolves through rewrites?

YANKOWITZ: Layering is one of the things that interests me in writing altogether, so it's part of the way in which I approach any project. Later, once I understand more about what I'm doing I go back to deepen or enrich a theme or image that may exist in an embryonic form. I take a long time writing. I am prolific, but I spend approximately six hours a day writing. I'd say I write about three drafts for every final script. But each page goes through many drafts. Now it's going to be harder to tell, because I have a word processor.

INTERVIEWER: How does a play begin in your mind? How do you know your material is suited to a play, rather than a novel or screenplay?

YANKOWITZ: Most projects that originate in my mind are either novels or plays, rarely screenplays. Under present conditions, in which the screenwriter has no control over the finished film, writing for the screen is essentially work for hire. From the outset I need to have a sense of form. Certain forms lend themselves naturally to the page and others to the stage. Internal experience, for example, lends itself to novelistic treatment. My novel *Silent Witness* is not at all suited to the theater, dealing as it does with ways of seeing and with alternative interpretations of experience. Anna's consciousness needs to be described, not dramatized. A *Knife in the Heart* could never be a novel. It has to do with a person's functioning in the world. It takes place in the world and not in the head. So I am rarely confused on that score. A *Knife in the Heart* evolved out of two experiences. I had recently given birth to my son, Gabriel, and I was constantly musing about his development and the mystery of personality; I used to go into his room at night, look at him in his crib and think, "What kind of human being is this? What kind of person is developing here?" At the same time—in 1980 and 1981—there was a lot of newspaper coverage on assassins. And I didn't have in mind to write anything about it, it was simply on my mind. Then one day I had a disappointment which caused me to feel very angry and upset. On the bus, later that day, all these inchoate and unconnected questions, thoughts and emotions came together in a series of images: A woman opened door after door and saw her worst fears realized. Those were the opening moments of *Knife*. That's precisely how that play became the form for the anger I was feeling, the sense of doors that wouldn't open, anxiety about my child and about being a mother.

INTERVIEWER: Were you particularly affected by Hinckley [John W. Hinckley, Jr., who made an assassination attempt on President Reagan in 1981], or assassins in general?

YANKOWITZ: By assassins, mass murderers, perpetrations of random violence—all of them. A *Knife in the Heart* was written in the fall that preceded Hinckley's trial.

INTERVIEWER: Did you follow the trial?

YANKOWITZ: Yes. I was fascinated by all the things that corresponded to my character's personality and quirks, even little things. My character, Donald, played the violin. Hinckley played the guitar. Both boys used music as solace and expression.

INTERVIEWER: Were there similar connections between Hinckley's mother and your mother character?

YANKOWITZ: Yes, in some ways. Both women were repressed, lacking in self-knowledge, cool, if not cold. But Mrs. Hinckley had other children; they had turned out fine. Why this one? Why this one? That question haunted me. I was also very affected—again, because I had just had Gabriel—by the Wayne Williams murders in Atlanta, the man who killed young black children. That was even more compelling to me. I kept thinking "How could a man take these little boys and murder them? One after the other. . . ." I imagined the states of mind of all the black children in Atlanta who were now afraid that they were going to be murdered. Ten-year-olds were learning how to shoot guns. All of that was on my mind while I wrote the play.

INTERVIEWER: Why did you set the age of the assassin at twenty-four? Were you making a statement about his generation?

YANKOWITZ: It seems to me that there are increasing hordes of boys who have no place in our society. This is compounded by the celebrity mentality, which makes everyone feel small by comparison. Twenty years ago, it was perfectly respectable for a woman to be a wife and a mother, for a man to be a father with a decent job and the capacity to support his family. That was enough for a boy to aspire toward. Now the pressure is enormous to be "something" or "somebody"—powerful and unique. This results in a climate that covertly admires the assassin as much as the assassinated hero. This widespread adulation of the celebrity is something that fascinates me. It doesn't matter what the celebrity's done. The celebrity could be a maniac or a moron, an anti-Semite or a pornographer, or even Jack the Ripper, it doesn't matter. The celebrity is simply somebody who has accomplished something that sets him apart.

INTERVIEWER: Is there a relationship between worship of the celebrity and a pervasive loss of self-esteem? As the need to revere a celebrity grows does one's own sense of self-value correspondingly diminish?

YANKOWITZ: I think it goes the other way. People lack self-esteem, because they doubt there's anything in them that the society or the family values. Therefore there is an envy and worship of those who *are* valued, a seeking after celebrity to fill the emptiness. I don't think you look at the celebrity and then feel your own emptiness. It starts the other way.

INTERVIEWER: Is there a connection between seeking celebrity and the kids who are joining cults?

YANKOWITZ: I think so. I've written a second novel, *Taking Liberties*, about an actress in the middle of her life and career. She works in a small repertory company in Connecticut and she's never quite been successful. She starts having fits onstage, seizures which resemble epilepsy, and through a series of coincidences becomes involved with a charismatic personality who claims that he can heal her. The book is the story of the way in which she puts herself into this man's power, delivers herself into his hands, and becomes an instrument for him. The theme derives from my interest in cults; I am trying to suggest that the relationship between power and impotence is a major source of the rise in American cults and the search for gurus, an impulse which ultimately leads to a phenomenon like Jonestown. But my emphasis is on one small relationship, which focuses intensely on the issues of authority and free will. It's a very bleak, dark novel. Several editors have felt that the characters aren't sympathetic, and that its bleakness makes it a poor candidate for sales. *Silent Witness*, also a rather dark novel, was published in 1976 [and reissued in 1977]; in today's climate, it is unlikely that that novel would find a publisher. As a result, I am no longer submitting *Taking Liberties* and am considering reconceiving it as a play. I've begun work on the first act.

INTERVIEWER: Is this the first time you have attempted to adapt a piece of your prose into a stage play?

YANKOWITZ: Yes. It's difficult because you have to be able to shake free of the fiction; you have to learn what you can use and what you have to let go of. I expect to have trouble with the second act: I don't think I can resolve it in the way that I resolved the book; it has to go someplace else and I don't yet know where. You can describe certain states of mind very easily in a novel that you can't describe on stage, and you have to find some kind of theatrical or physical equivalent for them.

INTERVIEWER: How did you become interested in cults?

YANKOWITZ: I was interested in emptiness, in people who gravitate from one group movement to another, like Bob Dylan. First it's politics, then it's born-again Christianity, then it's Judaism. They flit from one involvement to another in a desperate effort to become whole. It fascinates me that so many people are willing to relinquish themselves. Educated people, intelligent people, creative people allow themselves to become docile instruments, allow other people to exercise power upon them. I'm trying to find my own connection to this response to authority, so that my work can encompass compassion as well as understanding. But my first response is indignation!

INTERVIEWER: Is the cult phenomenon something particular to our time and our American culture?

YANKOWITZ: It seems to be happening everywhere, but it is worse here. We seem to have an abundance of frightened, isolated people and an equal number of megalomaniacal fanatics who prey upon them. Our culture, with its emphasis on individualism and self-creation, fosters in young people a consuming sense of personal failure in the absence of conventional success, and a corresponding need to find connection— somewhere, anywhere. Because, the myth goes, anyone can become President (or Michael Jackson, or Jane Fonda), the person who doesn't is nothing in his or her own eyes.

INTERVIEWER: It's interesting that some of the same elements that are in your early work, going back to *Slaughterhouse Play* [1969], are also in your recent work: explorations of our relation to authority; the master-slave relationship; the lip service one pays to institutions; and the loss and maintenance of personal identity. We're in a different decade, the issues are taking different forms, but your call to not be seduced by authority has remained a part of your sensibility.

YANKOWITZ: That's the interesting thing about writers . . . I'm sure we all have a psychological predisposition towards certain kinds of material. It may take different forms, but you do find yourself repeating the same themes. Though I often think I'm working on material which is entirely different, I look at it in retrospect and say, "Here I am again." A new theme emerging in my work is that of parent and child. Of course, I'm a parent now, and that experience is generating new feelings and reflections, which connect with the old themes.

INTERVIEWER: Is it difficult to work on that parent-child relationship? Many of the writers we've spoken with have put their mother-daughter material on the back burner.

YANKOWITZ: You see, I have never written from the daughter's point of view. That's interesting, too. You'll notice in drama and fiction that writers, for the most part, identify with the child. Their works are usually written as rebellion against their parents, a need to throw off something from childhood. No matter how old the writer is, when the writer finally tackles this subject, it's usually from the perspective of the child. My inclination, on the other hand, is to write from the point of view of the parent.

INTERVIEWER: [English theater critic] Benedict Nightingale [writing for] *The New York Times* has dubbed American plays that deal with the child struggling for autonomy "diaper drama." ["There Really Is a World Beyond 'Diaper Drama,' " *New York Times*, January 1, 1984].

YANKOWITZ: If I see another family play I might throw up. [Laughter] However, we all know that it is a prototypical American subject, its finest example being *Long Day's Journey into Night*. And all the themes in *Long Day's Journey* are those that American writers have been picking up and using over and over. The theme of the child struggling for independence, just as America struggled for its liberation. The child struggling for an identity separate from that of the parent. The parent who for one reason or another is uncomprehending and unable to recognize the child's distinctive qualities, and the child who suffers and yearns for that respect: *Death of a Salesman*. The child as artist, and therefore separate and different from the family in which it was raised. And then the disruption and reforming of the family unit, a typically American concern.

INTERVIEWER: Do you see America as an adolescent culture?

YANKOWITZ: I don't think we've gotten there yet. We've not yet reached a civilized age, an age either of reason or wisdom.

INTERVIEWER: Are American audiences ready for grown-up themes?

YANKOWITZ: The themes we are discussing are compelling; the ways in which they are executed are not artistically mature. To some extent, of course it's what audiences like to see: their own experiences replicated on the stage. Everybody's come from a family. So everybody is interested in their dynamics and problems.

INTERVIEWER: Your plays are confrontational, you accuse the audience of being partially responsible for the kinds of social inequities that you are portraying.

YANKOWITZ: Yes, it's in all of my work in one way or another. Even *Silent Witness* forces the witness, the reader, to enter into the experience of Anna and make certain choices for her.

INTERVIEWER: Was the development of your interrogatory style connected to your initial work with the Open Theater?

YANKOWITZ: *Slaughterhouse Play* precedes *Terminal* [both plays were produced in 1969]. The fact is that I am interested in questions, and not so interested in answers. I am concerned that the audience take in the question and try to form their own responses.

INTERVIEWER: Did this desire for the audience to "take in the question" naturally grow out of your personal concerns, or were you influenced by other writers who had or have similar goals?

YANKOWITZ: In all writing, influences and inclination meet. I was very influenced by Brecht and also by Artaud. In many ways, these two are quite dissimilar. What you see in my work is a synthesis; what's organic is the impulse that attracted me to these different writers. I *adore* Chekhov. But nothing in my work bears any resemblance to his. Something in me can't encompass his precise and intense human attention to character nor his marvelous, sometimes comic, indirection. I hope that in the course of my development that connection will occur, but it can't be imposed. The particular bond that's made between one writer and her predecessors emerges as the work.

INTERVIEWER: What were you drawn to in the work of Brecht and Artaud? What did they teach you?

YANKOWITZ: I have always been drawn to works that had, first of all, a political dimension, that saw the world and tried to understand a relationship between the individual situation and a condition in the world. And I was drawn to forms which didn't make it necessary to write a story from beginning to end and tie it up in a neat little package for the audience, forms which, although more artificial, are in another sense *more* natural, because they don't *pretend* to be real. These allow you to use the stage as a construct and to make the play a work of art (or artifice) rather than an imitation of nature. That is what attracted me to Artaud and Brecht; in both cases you have an absolute rejection of domestic structures, conventional narrative, the fourth wall. At the moment, I'm fascinated by Japanese theater, and its extreme stylization. Theater is not life and I see no artistic virtue in pretending that it is. What is most exciting to me in theater is what is *not* life, what is exaggerated and metaphorical and invented, works that illuminate life by creating a world of its *own* conventions, not ours.

INTERVIEWER: Are you saying that realism can never be valid as a style, as valid as nonrealistic form, capable of symbol and metaphor?

YANKOWITZ: I'm certainly not saying that it *never* can be, but it rarely seems to. We would also have to define how we understand naturalism or realism. For instance, I don't consider Chekhov a realistic writer. I think his work is very stylized, artificial . . . and artificial is a word of praise from me!

INTERVIEWER: Even though he deals with family?

YANKOWITZ: Yes. But it's not slice-of-life. Because of the language, and the relationship between one line of dialogue and another. I think when the language is successful in my plays, and in other plays that I admire, it is not the language of everyday speech. I fall asleep at plays where I hear conversations that I've heard on the street. That's not what I want to hear in the theater. I want language that in itself is a style, that pays attention to diction and rhythm and vocabulary and silence; language as individual as the characters should be. Dialogue always derives from character. The question is, what do these particular people talk about and how do they do it? What does the form and vocabulary of their sentences reveal about them? How does it relate to the content of their words? Language, in any medium, must have its own idiosyncratic nature connected to character and the atmosphere the writer is trying to create. My language is very textured and literary. It uses puns, allusions and certain poetic techniques: assonances, repetitions, images, compression. Characters do not speak casually or in a conversational mode, even when they're having a conversation. This lets the theatergoer know that he or she is watching theater, not people having conversation. What I'm attempting is a distillation of thought in the particular voice of the character, a condensed expression. I use a good deal of imagery, which is hard to do because the contemporary theater is distrustful of verbal imagery. One of the ways in which I have been able to use it is by trying to refine the monologue form. In a monologue, which is definitely an artificial device, a convention, one is allowed a certain freedom that is difficult to achieve in dialogue. That's one way I'm able to sneak it in.

INTERVIEWER: Your language is also very rhythmic.

YANKOWITZ: Rhythm is very important. I was talking to a friend this morning, an architect. We were discussing the creative process, and I said that most people would think the easiest thing to do in a play is to change a character's name. Now, the writer who is not very developed —and there are many of them represented on our stages—will simply change the name, for example, from Janet to Jane. If it were me, I would have to go through my entire script, and every time I had substituted a monosyllabic word for one with two syllables, I would have to check the rhythm, which is affected by that change. I might want to retain the difference, I might feel that the difference doesn't matter, but I would have to consider it. That's an extremely important part of the way in which I write. I also write for the breath. That's something I learned from the Open Theater. When I started working with the Open Theater, I was a very young playwright, I had just started writing for the theater. My first experiences were in hearing people speak the words. They weren't the words on the page. Actors—like poets who read their work aloud— are concerned with the breath, where the pause comes and how much language can be encompassed, and what the difference is when words occur on an extended breath and when they don't. So the breath is something that I hear when I'm writing. As a result, punctuation is *extremely* important to me. A colon or a semicolon or a comma make a tremendous difference. If somebody changes it, I'm irate. Not because I'm being protective, but because it makes a difference in the way that the line needs to be heard.

INTERVIEWER: This must make it very difficult for you in rehearsal, where a director might say, "Cut that line, we don't need it." Do line cuts interfere with the musical rise and fall of your language?

YANKOWITZ: They might. Sometimes you can delete a line, and although the rhythm is changed, the difference is interesting or illuminating in another, also acceptable, way. But every alteration in language needs to be considered. I had a fight in Williamstown [Williamstown Theatre Festival] over the word *vagina*, a fight that lasted approximately three weeks. In *Knife*, the word *vagina* is used once. The director substituted, without my permission, the word *womb*. I came to rehearsal one day—and I was barred from most rehearsals . . .

INTERVIEWER: Why were you barred?

YANKOWITZ: On principle. Because this director believed that writers don't know what they've written and need a director to demonstrate it to them. He said to me, "Chekhov did not *know* what he had written; he needed Stanislavsky to show him. I am going to show you. If you're at rehearsals, you're going to distract and inhibit me." One day, despite the decree, I walked in and heard *womb*. I said, "Wait a minute. You can't do that." He said, "Well why not? It's the same thing." First of all, it's not the same thing. Anatomically and biologically it is not the same thing. The birth canal and the uterus are not identical. The line is, "The *vagina*! Remember? This is where his head pushed out." Besides that, the word *vagina* has an entirely different quality from *womb*; it is an abrasive word. I wanted an abrasive word, not a poetic one. I didn't want womb. The director and some of the actors made me feel like I was crazy for having a big fight over one word. "What's the difference?" And I kept saying, "There's an enormous difference!" And explaining. The actress who played Mrs. Holt said, "Well, it's an awful word. Isn't there some other one you can use?" I said, "You know the other words. What would you prefer? *Cunt? Pussy?* What would you like?" She didn't say anything after that. But the fact is that *vagina* was the only word that would do there. No other word in the language would have done. Finally they left it in.

INTERVIEWER: Did you ever threaten to withdraw the play over that issue?

YANKOWITZ: No, I didn't. I was very weak that summer. I came up to Williamstown two weeks after an ectopic pregnancy. I almost lost my life, as well as a tube, and a baby. I almost died because I was bleeding internally. And I had a blood count of six. There were many battles to be fought over this Williamstown production and I lost many of them because I didn't have the physical and emotional strength. *Knife in the Heart* has had a very interesting kind of life in some respects, because people privately have been extremely impressed by it and publicly have stamped on it.

INTERVIEWER: Playwright Michelene Wandor has observed in her monograph *Understudies* that when a male playwright is angry and temperamental in rehearsal, he's considered a turbulent, moody artist. However, when a woman behaves in a similar manner, she's considered . . .

YANKOWITZ: Difficult. The word is *difficult*. I know. It's applied to me all the time. Implied in *difficult* is an inability to control you. In my experience, the inevitable power struggle between playwright and director is always exacerbated by the male-female situation.

INTERVIEWER: What do you think are the elements in *Knife in the Heart* that people found frightening?

YANKOWITZ: The major element that's frightening is that it doesn't answer the questions it raises. People constantly are saying, "But why? But why did this happen?" And I reply that the play *is* a question. Certain theories are proposed about why a boy from a seemingly average family commits mass murder, but the riddle is not solved. In my view, it is not a question that I or you or anybody can answer. I felt that posing the question in many forms—cultural, psychological, social, political, historical—was the most interesting approach to take with this play, but it has disturbed a lot of people. All of us have grown up feeling uncomfortable with something left hanging in the air unresolved. We expect it in life but don't want to find it in the theater. The audience is waiting at the end of the play for me to say, "And therefore, this is why it happened." For the boy to break down and say, "My mother never touched me," or for the father to break down on the stand and say, "I beat him when he was two years old! I beat him so hard he . . ." They are waiting for that moment. We do live in a world in which there is random violence on every scale. People need to feel that they can get a grip on it, that they can escape from it, and that it's not going to happen to *them*. If you say it happened because this mother was cold and didn't touch her child, then the woman in the audience can say, "Oh, well. That wouldn't happen to me, because I touch my kids!" If you say it's because the father beat his child, the man in the audience can say, "Oh, well, I don't beat my kid, so he's not going to turn out that way." If you give some kind of an answer, it exempts you from responsibility.

INTERVIEWER: In a way you are saying this is our collective guilt, that we are all a part of the culture which created this violence. . . .

YANKOWITZ: That's what I'm always saying. In everything I do, I'm saying, "Look, this is our world. Look what we've made." Not look what *you've* made. Look what *we've* made. Where does it come from? And how can we change it?

INTERVIEWER: Do you feel as comfortable writing male characters as female characters?

YANKOWITZ: In general I find it difficult to write sympathetic, balanced male characters. For instance, in the first draft of *Knife in the Heart*, Mr. Holt was not at all fully imagined. He was weak, dull, a cipher. Through successive drafts I finally managed to make him a credible human being. It had always been my intention to make him a real flesh-and-blood character; there would be no value in trying to do otherwise.

INTERVIEWER: So the problems you find in dealing with male characters have more to do with characterization than language.

YANKOWITZ: Yes. I remain too distant, too critical; I'd like to inhabit a male sensibility for a while.

INTERVIEWER: Laurie Stone of *The Village Voice* accused you of being "ahistorical," of recreating Iago, the old villain, rather than creating a contemporary political assassin ["Slice of Life," *The Village Voice*, August 30, 1983].

YANKOWITZ: Then she simply misinterpreted it. The play confronts a kind of violence that is typically American. Of course there are political assassinations elsewhere. But political assassinations elsewhere are political assassinations. This boy's act is not political at all. What happens in this country is that the impulse toward self-definition, particularly in young men, expresses itself frequently through an act of violence that may attach to a political figure but has absolutely no political significance. I was frequently criticized because I don't state in the play that this boy is bad. And that he's an aberration and he's terrible and immoral. The critics want me to pronounce a moral judgment. And I absolutely refuse to do it. First of all, if the audience doesn't know that what this young man's done is evil, then we're in deeper trouble than even I believed. No one needs me to make the obvious comment. Further, I don't want to separate Donald from us by making him into an Iago. I want to humanize him so that we can see ourselves in him, can see that he reflects us.

INTERVIEWER: So it could just as easily have been about John Lennon's assassin or . . .

YANKOWITZ: That's right. The play is about somebody who is trying to commit an act which will validate the self. Because our public figures are the ones who attract the most attention, the act often finds its object in a political figure, or a star like Lennon, or somebody in the limelight. This is, in my opinion, a particularly American phenomenon.

INTERVIEWER: Does it have to do with sexual inadequacy?

YANKOWITZ: I suspect it has something to do with a kind of pervasive impotence; maybe sexual impotence is a metaphor for it. Somebody who did a very intelligent, literary review of *Knife* noticed all the phallic imagery in the boy's speech, his monologue: the policeman with the gun, the fireman with the hose, the knife itself. He pointed out a number of images that I had not used consciously. I think he was right. I do see violence as a contemporary expression of male virility. How are men validated by the society? Usually through some act of aggression, whether it occurs in conventional forms, such as ruthlessness in business or through competitive sports, et cetera. One can look at the violent act as a slight curve of the traditional path.

INTERVIEWER: Do you think that a gender bias exists in theater criticism?

YANKOWITZ: Yes. Recently we saw *Fool for Love* [by Sam Shepard] —which we admired—but there you have a case of a dominant male character and a supposedly equal female counterpart. In fact, the female is not equal in any sense. She's not given language comparable in color and richness to the male character, she's not given the stage time of the male character, nor the complexity, the individuality or the passion. It is quite clear that the playwright was fascinated by the man, and endowed him far more fully than the woman. Not one reviewer mentioned that. But if the situation were reversed, and if the play were written by a woman, I assure you that it would have been commented on, and not favorably.

INTERVIEWER: Do you feel that there is a female aesthetic in drama?

YANKOWITZ: I wouldn't say so. I think that the work of women differs tremendously. Women are less conventional, more daring, more willing to reinvent the world. Perhaps that's one reason why we're less successful as a group.

INTERVIEWER: Would you tell us about your experience as a playwright at the Yale School of Drama?

YANKOWITZ: It was a tremendously valuable and creative period for me, the one time in my life when my primary obligation was to write. My teachers varied in their response to my work, and although I received a great deal of praise and encouragement, there was already, even at this time, some uneasiness about the power of my plays and their unusual forms. John Gassner, who was my first playwriting teacher there—though only for a short time—said he had no idea how to evaluate work like mine which broke with traditional dramatic structures. But I learned by writing and by discussions with some of my teachers—like [Richard] Gilman, [Gordon] Rogoff, and [Stanley] Kauffmann—who valued my theatrical impulses.

INTERVIEWER: Did you study theater as an undergraduate at Sarah Lawrence?

YANKOWITZ: I wasn't the least bit interested in theater. I was writing fiction until I graduated and immediately afterward, in 1963, went to India for a year. The man with whom I traveled on his Fulbright was writing plays. I experimented with the form as a sort of discipline—without any commitment—but when I returned to New York, a friend took me to see the work of the Open Theater. They were doing a series of demonstrations at The New School. Their techniques and concerns entirely coincided with my own and I felt, for the first time, that perhaps I had found a vocation.

INTERVIEWER: You take a frequent swipe—sometimes comically, sometimes tragically—at marriage. Now you are married yourself . . .

YANKOWITZ: I think marriage is really, for the most part, a lethal institution in which many women are trapped, suppressed, broken, transformed into drudges, their spirits broken. Herb and I were married in France. The ceremony was performed in French so that we barely understood what was being said. We just said, "Oui!" It was a way of avoiding unpleasant associations. You don't want to feel that you are putting your feet into the Chinese foot-binding shoes. And traditional marriage is clearly that. That is in the plays. That feeling and that warning.

INTERVIEWER: What are you trying to affect in the audience? What do you want to stir in them?

YANKOWITZ: The mind first, and secondarily, the heart. I want the questions of the play to reverberate. That's one thing my work has succeeded in accomplishing, always. At the O'Neill [Eugene O'Neill National Playwrights Conference, Waterford, Conn.] and at Williamstown, people did not come out at intermission talking about dresses or restaurants. People were talking not even about the play, but about the issues that the play raised. And that occurred frequently in the reviews, as well.

Another thing that I'm always interested in is eliminating the barriers between "us" and "them." I want audiences to feel that the world of the play is not separate from their world, their lives. I am saying that you are that woman, you are that boy. You are those black people, you are those white people oppressing those black people. Look at that, look at your own complicity in this, look also at those feelings in yourself that are so close to the feelings that motivate these characters. What person hasn't had the impulse to strike out to do something terrible in order to be taken seriously by the world? And once we say we are very close to it, although we are too civilized to commit the act, let's look at the impulse in ourselves so that we can understand and perhaps find ways of changing the society that incites it. The other thing I believe is that the frontier between the impulse and the act is a very narrow one and that it takes just a little bit of pressure to cross over it. Thank God that most of us live on this side of it, but let's realize that we're infinitely close.

AFTERWORD

It is popularly thought that women playwrights have no tradition. Though we can trace ourselves back as far as Hrotsvitha of Gandersheim—a tenth-century Saxon nun who wrote comedies in Latin to entertain her cloistered sisters—we have yet to find anyone between our Dark Ages dramatist and the actress-writers in Renaissance Italy who contributed to the scenarios of the commedia dell'arte.[1] And things are spotty, to say the least, between those lively theatricals and Aphra Behn (the first professional woman playwright) who caused a bit of a stir on the English stage in the last half of the seventeenth century. Between Behn and Lillian Hellman, it seems our numbers and visibility have repeatedly waxed and waned in strange and interesting cycles. We tend to pop up vigorously and prolifically in times of great social and cultural upheaval, only to disappear again when the tremors calm. In recent years—thanks to the research and writings of Judith Barlow, Rosamund Gilder, Karen Malpede, Honor Moore, Professors Helen Krich Chinoy and Linda Walsh Jenkins, among others—we have begun to uncover traces of those women dramatists who have gone before, and to reevaluate them in our own terms rather than accept male judgment as to their literary significance. These artists have left little behind them in the way of opinion on the craft or the conditions under which they practiced it. The fragments that do remain suggest they shared some of the anxieties of their modern counterparts. Hrotsvitha wrote, "Unknown to all around me, I have toiled in secret, often destroying what seemed to me ill written and rewriting it. . . . I have not submitted the work to any experts for fear that the roughness of style would make them discourage me to such an extent that I might give up writing altogether. . . ."[2] Aphra Behn displays a little more defiance: ". . . had the Plays I have writ come forth under any Man's Name and never known to have been mine, I appeal to all unbyast Judges of Sense if they had not said that Person had made as many good Comedies as any one Man

---

[1]Honor Moore, *The New Women's Theatre* (New York: Random House, 1977). Introduction, pp. xiv–xv.
[2]Rosamund Gilder, *Enter the Actress: The First Women in the Theatre* (New York: Houghton-Mifflin, 1931), pp. 23–24.

451

that has writ in our Age, but a Devil on't the Woman damns the Poet . . ."[3]

Is it possible that our history has been deliberately obscured? Not such a far-fetched notion, really. History has been diddled with before, skimmed over, submerged, rewritten, and otherwise hidden. For example, as a schoolgirl in the British educational system in the mid-1950s, I wasn't taught much about American history or geography. TV had not yet made its way into working-class homes, and kids of my ilk were not given to poring over encyclopedias for entertainment; so that was it. We grew up in ignorance. America was half desert for the cowboys and half Hollywood for Doris Day. The country could have been ten miles wide or ten thousand, for all we knew or cared. In retrospect, one can readily see the reason for this convenient lapse of the British bureaucratic memory. We have always been a bit miffed at losing so prime a piece of colonial real estate (and in such a *rude* way) to a bunch of tax-evading, badly dressed malcontents. A humiliating turn of events, best forgotten.

Since most of life is about territory and power—and the gain, loss, and retention of same—I don't think it's straining the metaphor with excessive willfulness to see the stage as a prime bit of real estate, too. Not only prime but sanctified, with a priesthood as suspicious of women as any religion. And I can't say I blame the chaps for wanting to keep it all to themselves. It makes a lovely platform from which to persuade large numbers of people to one's political and/or emotional point of view. Even if one hasn't got a political point of view to tout (a popular political position these days), or an emotional one to preach (a form of lecturing highly favored by American theater over the political sort), the stage provides an advantageous tower from which to defend the status quo. The drama is, after all, the most public of arts. The most aggressive form of writing. The author lurks unseen with godlike powers, able to shove living, breathing human beings around on stage, able to "bump them off" at will, capable of making us cry or gasp out loud or otherwise embarrass ourselves in front of others. If heretical ideas or unpopular politics are contained in print between book covers, they can be chucked against the wall in the privacy of one's own home. And herein lies the dramatic rub. It has never been acceptable in the past (and still isn't very nice today) for women to make a fuss in public, on or off the stage. So one can understand—if not approve—the tendency to keep the ladies in the pews and out of the pulpit, where they are capable of considerable damage when out of control. The sixties and early seventies were evidence enough of this when women stormed the stage with their fury and mocking

[3]Ibid., p. 195.

humor, making rude noises in public. A humiliating turn of events, best forgotten.

One way of keeping women playwrights out of the theatrical pulpit is to deny their existence altogether. (Some irritable scholars, for instance, have claimed Hrotsvitha was a hoax.) Those playwrights who cannot be denied must be roundly disparaged. The considerable task of denial and disparagement has fallen squarely into the lap of the male critic who has taken up defense of The Holy Real Estate with a suspicious amount of relish. If playwright Honor Moore[4] is on the right track, this may be because male critics are "not ready to see the central events of women's lives as metaphors for their own experience." If these men are *only* able—or only *willing*—to identify with their own gender, there are serious implications here not only for women's theatrical history but for the present and future fate of professional women dramatists. Are male critics sitting insecurely out there in the dark of the audience with a competitive "If you can't join 'em, beat 'em" attitude? And if this is so, what is it that creates such anathema? Questions worth looking into.

This book began as an angry letter to *The New York Times*. Rachel Koenig and I wanted to take Walter Kerr to task for his dismissive review[5] of *Top Girls*, a play by Britain's Caryl Churchill. Churchill is an internationally respected playwright, and more than a little political in her concerns. Mr. Kerr must have slept through or ignored the politics, as nowhere within his article is this profoundly important aspect of her work mentioned, though he finds time to reprimand her for allowing her female characters to be "unpleasant" to one another.

Our letter grew long and unwieldy. And instead we decided to embark upon a book of interviews to try to discover why women's plays are so desperately misunderstood. If Churchill—one of our finest living playwrights—was having trouble communicating women's concerns to male critics, what were the implications for the rest of us? Churchill is certainly equal in skill and output to our own David Mamet. In fact, his play *Glengarry Glen Ross* is not unlike *Top Girls*. It might serve some purpose to compare the two plays.

Churchill is from Britain. Mamet is American. Both are excellent, well-established playwrights of equal artistic stature. *Top Girls* and *Glengarry* ran within approximately a year of each other: the former at the New York Shakespeare Festival and the latter on Broadway. Both plays had one-gender casts, Churchill's all female, Mamet's all male. Both

[4]Moore, op. cit., p. xiii.
[5]*The New York Times*, Arts and Leisure Section, January 23, 1983.

plays begin in a restaurant and move quickly into the contemporary workplace. Both plays are concerned with personal and economic betrayal, both have plenty of conflict and harsh language, both are particularly candid and unsentimental examinations of the destructive quest for power and money. Churchill's females struggle in the job-bartering arena of an employment agency. Mamet's men competitively peddle worthless real estate to hapless buyers. Both playwrights take structural liberties with time and space—Churchill rather more so than Mamet. *Top Girls*, unlike *Glengarry*, opens with a brief flight of imagination into the past. Churchill's leading character, a modern career woman, entertains women of extraordinary achievement from history and literature in a fashionable present-day restaurant. The author allows them to converse across the centuries, matter-of-factly and with wit, about their gains and losses, and the prices paid for breaking with tradition. This historic group is quickly left behind, and the actresses transform for the rest of the play into clients or employees of a modern employment agency. The main character changes from charming hostess to the cool, somewhat ruthless, head of a business. The playwright's message is not complicated: We march into the future dragging our history. If we don't learn from it we may repeat it. We are warned not to become Margaret Thatchers in our race to slice off a piece of the male economic pie.

In Mamet's *Glengarry Glen Ross*, the hard-bitten male realtor characters have learned nothing from Willy Loman in *Death of a Salesman*. Most of them haven't even Willy's weary innocence or good intentions. They are busy repeating their fathers' mistakes, carving away at each other verbally and physically for the Almighty Dollar. The language is tough and authentic (more "fuck"s per page than Churchill) as Mamet warns against the dangers of unbridled Reagan-style competition and the corruption that follows a "business before people" attitude.

Mamet's play was hailed as "powerful and searing." It was awarded a Pulitzer Prize. Deservedly so. The critics shed tears of praise and gratitude in print. Mamet's entire "body of work" was discussed in relation to his shining new creation. The reviewers drew upon the most gladiatorial superlatives in their vocabularies—almost as if writing for the sports page.

On the other hand, Churchill's *Top Girls* was derided by Walter Kerr in the Sunday *New York Times* under the headline ARE THESE FEMINISTS TOO HARD ON WOMEN? (Imagine Mamet's critical analysis under ARE THESE MANISTS TOO HARD ON MEN?) Kerr's article began with the following disparaging remark: "Naturally, most feminist plays up to now have been written by women. Pretty soon, though, I'm afraid the male playwrights may have to take over. *Somebody's* got to be more sympathetic to the women on the job. Certainly, Caryl Churchill isn't very nice to them in her Top Girls." Does Kerr mean "nice," one has to wonder, in the way that Shakespeare's Hamlet is *nice* to Ophelia? Or the manner in which Tennessee Williams's Stanley is *nice* to Blanche Dubois?

There is little in the way of popular forum that provides opportunity to challenge critics and reviewers. *The New York Times*, which holds the professional reputation, income, and future of every playwright in America—and some beyond—in its pages, offers only an irregular column called "Theatre Mailbag" for general readers' letters. This feature might more appropriately be called "The Thrice Annual Theatre Thimble" for all the rebuttal space it provides or fair chance the playwright has to challenge the undeniable power of the critics to destroy years of work. In the *Dramatists Guild Quarterly*,[6] playwright Jeffrey Sweet has properly called for *The New York Times* to grant a more equitable forum for the dramatists. To date there has been no response.

George Bernard Shaw, in his essay "The Technical Novelty of Ibsen's Plays," tells us that after the famed Norwegian shocked England with *A Doll's House*, restoring discussion of morality and ideas to a place of honor on the stage, "Within twenty years, women were writing better plays than men; and these plays were passionate arguments from beginning to end." Sadly, G.B.S. did not tell us who these women were and what they were being so passionate about. But one can hazard a guess that they were having a go at something more than romance and melodrama. Of course, Shaw—critic as well as playwright—lived at a time when it was rather more acceptable, even sporting, for male playwrights to quarrel publicly in print with their critics. John Osborne and Edward Albee, in the last couple of decades, have also (rather less acceptably) battled brilliantly in defense of their politics and innovations. But these authors have been allowed to stand as having had *intelligent* failures. After all, a man may not have adequately defended his social ideas and may be "misguided" politically, but the next ding of his stage bell is awaited with critical breath suitably bated because—like Rommel in the desert, or Lenin in Moscow—he is a worthy opponent. Deadly but exciting. Difficult as the boxing matches of our Osbornes and Albees may be with their critics, the playwrights are, at least, acknowledged. They exist. Women playwrights do not.

How is it that Shelagh Delaney (the lone "angry young woman" in the midst of Britain's postwar "angry young men" writers) has slipped from public view, leaving behind a single, recognized jewel: the classic *A Taste of Honey*? Where is Delaney now? Why is she lost to the stage after so radiant a beginning?

[6]*Dramatists Guild Quarterly*, Spring 1985, pp. 27–30.

From Angelina Grimké's *Rachel* in 1916, to Alice Childress's *Wine in the Wilderness* in 1969, over 125 plays were written by American black women.[7] Could even the most avid theatergoer name more than three? And where are the militant, feminist voices of the last two decades? Is it safe to assume that recently acclaimed playwrights such as Marsha Norman and Beth Henley will be assured a place in history? Women of equal achievement in the past have dropped into relative obscurity despite their Pulitzer prizes.

Professor Helen Krich Chinoy and Linda Walsh Jenkins, in their prodigious work *Women in American Theatre*,[8] devote an entire chapter to the question: "Where are the Women Playwrights?" They list more than six hundred past and present American dramatists in the back indexes, along with bibliographies and copyright dates. Yet, for the average intelligent person, after Agatha Christie and Lillian Hellman, the counting gets rough. Occasional theatergoers will remember Pulitzer Prize—winners Henley and Norman for *Crimes of the Heart* and *'night, Mother*, respectively; they might, when pressed, come up with Lorraine Hansberry for *Raisin in the Sun* and Jean Kerr for some bright Broadway comedies, but then memory begins to falter. Those people who earn their living from theater, in one way or another, are able to recall longer lists: Caryl Churchill, Megan Terry, Ntozake Shange, Maria Irene Fornes . . . uhhmmm . . . Rosalyn Drexler . . . Eve Merriam . . . ahhh . . . let's see, wasn't it a woman who wrote *The Chalk Garden*?[9] Didn't Lillian Hellman win a Pulitzer for something or other?

Contrary to popular misunderstanding, Hellman was never awarded a Pulitzer. But Ketti Frings was. Zoë Akins was. It's a prestigious prize, but hardly a guarantee of a place in theater's Hall of Fame. Five women received the Pulitzer Prize for Drama between 1921 and 1958,[10] yet few people remember them. One has legitimate cause to worry whether, twenty years from now, anyone will be able to recall Henley and Norman or the controversial plays they gave us. I'm not suggesting that there has never been a male playwright whose works have been forgotten. I *am* saying that of all the plays we remember, 99.5 percent of them are by men. And it simply won't do.

Though one applauds and is encouraged by the successes of a few

[7]Victoria Sullivan and James Hatch, *Plays By and About Women* (New York: Random House, 1973), Introduction, pp. xiv–xv.
[8](New York: Crown Publishers, Inc., 1981), reissued in paperback.
[9]Enid Bagnold.
[10]Zona Gale, *Miss Lulu Bett*, 1921; Susan Glaspell, *Alison's House*, 1931; Zoë Akins, *The Old Maid*, 1935; Mary Chase, *Harvey*, 1945; Ketti Frings, *Look Homeward, Angel*, 1958.

women playwrights, one can't help noticing that there is a price to pay for slipping beneath the barbed wire surrounding "the mainstream." There is an air of complacent "Put up, or shut up!" among critics now—a sort of, "No excuse for bitching anymore, girls. Cut the feminist crap and get on with it!" And, indeed, we have. So individually industrious are we that vigilance over hard-won gains has slackened. So busy are we outrunning the label "victim," that we've forgotten our yet-to-be-outdistanced position as "underdog." We congratulate each other that if New York City doesn't acknowledge us, at least we are gaining a foothold out in the regional theaters. And so we are. Institutions such as the Actors Theatre of Louisville, the Hartford Stage Company, and ACT in San Francisco are showing an increasing commitment to dividing their stages between men and women more equitably than in the past. And other houses are slowly beginning to pay more attention to their play selections as women waltz off with major awards from international theater festivals.

But there are still many nonprofit and semicommercial theaters across the country—partially funded by federal, state, and municipal tax monies—that have never produced a play by a woman beyond Christie's *Murder at the Vicarage*. And there are not enough homes for women playwrights that specifically encourage the development and production of drama by women (e.g., Julia Miles's Women's Play Project at the American Place Theater in New York City; Horizons, a group in Washington, D.C., that produces only scripts by women, though they hire men onstage and backstage and play to a mixed audience).

One thing is sure: There is no dearth of good women's plays out there to choose from. I'm convinced after reading hundreds of them of the overall fine quality of the work. Yes, mediocrity exists, as with male work. And it shouldn't be rewarded by virtue of having been written by a woman. But mediocrity, in my opinion, occurs far more frequently, and with no corresponding constraints, in popular criticism. In collecting and absorbing over thirty years' worth of media reviews of women's plays, I've come to the conclusion that the concerns, the irony, the innovations, and intentions of women playwrights are for the most part, woefully lost on the majority of our critics. Gender bias is rampant in the language. With notable exceptions, commentary runs from paternal tolerance to aggressive misogyny. The phrase "soap opera" was used hundreds of times to dismiss women's subject matter. Divorce, generation gaps, infidelity, the hazards of marriage and parenting, are all themes to be found in men's plays as often as in women's. Yet these male plays—Tom Stoppard's *The Real Thing*, for instance, or Peter Nichols's *Passion*—are not described as "soaps" but powerful close-ups of the human condition.

Rachel and I came away from those three decades of reviews with the overwhelming feeling that women playwrights, as with women in other professions, are "damned if they do and damned if they don't"—that they must be twice as good as their male counterparts, work twice as hard for half the praise, less than 10 percent of available grant money and only a 7 percent share of the stage. This last pitiful percentage exactly mirrors those of Britain, Australia, and Canada. British playwright/critic Michelene Wandor, referring to a report on a survey[11] in her preface to *Plays by Women*, Volume 4,[12] says that, of the British women's 7 percent share of all plays produced, nearly half are accounted for by Agatha Christie plays. Wandor remarks that there is nothing wrong with producing plays by Christie. What she feels *is* wrong, however, is that, "such a vital medium . . . represents women writers (and to some degree, by implication, also the 'image' or function of women in plays themselves), in such a scandalous minority way." She quotes directly from the report: " '. . . the more money and prestige a theatre has, the less women will be employed as directors and administrators; the less likelihood that a play written by women will be produced . . . and the less women will be on the boards.' " Wandor states, "There are important professional and aesthetic implications which follow from this. . . ." She suggests that women dramatists are constantly having to work double time in "an uphill struggle" not only for "content and subject matter which has to prove its validity, but for aesthetic satisfaction, technical choices and professional sophistication." The greatest number of women are to be found in theaters that are: " '. . . the least subsidized and least well-equipped, and offer the smallest stages, the smallest audiences, the least predictable and controllable venues, the smallest budgets . . . in other words, the most difficult circumstances in which to produce art.' "

Of course, however successfully one might struggle with theater's pervasive discriminatory sexual and economic politics in the future, one cannot legislate respect in the deeper recesses of the heart. Today, as in the past, women playwrights are rarely, if ever, thought of as having the power or the literary significance of a Miller, a Pinter, Williams, or Albee. And no woman's name is whispered in the long shadows of Brecht, Ibsen, Shaw, or Beckett. In fact, it's been widely held for centuries that females are incapable of "great" drama. As Chinoy relates in *Women in American Theatre*,[13] the critic George Jean Nathan accused Lillian Hellman of having "the generic inability" to master an "economy of emotion." Chinoy goes on to say that producer John Golden, in a 1939 speech—

[11]British Conference of Women Theatre Directors and Administrators, 1982–83.
[12](London and New York: Methuen, 1985.)
[13]Chinoy and Walsh, op. cit., p. 129.

even as he presented a national achievement award to American playwright Rachel Crothers—said, "There are few, if any, great women dramatists—the reasons obvious: They were congenitally good, sweet, tender, loving, shy . . . so protected that they could never have seen the side of life . . . that one should know, see—perhaps, even live, to be a great dramatist."

When Emily Mann wrote with understanding of the "side of life" we are said to be too sweet and shy to know about, she was gunned down with enough critical force (by over a dozen New York reviewers) to make the movie character Rambo pale beside Minnie Mouse. Mann's play *Still Life*, taken from hours of taped conversations with a Vietnam veteran, his wife, and his mistress, dared to suggest a link between domestic brutality and war. The reviewers attacked not just the play itself but challenged the author contemptuously on every level: mental stability, professional competence, psychological maturity, and her politics (her feminism). It was obviously un-American to imply that Fascism begins in the kitchen. As far as I know, only two New York critics came to her defense: Marilyn Stasio of the *New York Post* and Michael Feingold of *The Village Voice*. Feingold went so far as to grapple with his colleagues in print about their embarrassing overreaction. Eventually, *The Village Voice* awarded Mann a prestigious Obie award. And *Still Life* is translated into many languages, performed all over the world, and considered to be a modern American masterpiece.

As for the militant feminist playwrights, they are still out there. Some have maintained their radical politics. Most came to see open confrontation as unproductive. Regardless of where they now place themselves on the political spectrum, they are North, South, East, and West, busy evolving, directing, producing, teaching, and writing plays more prolifically than ever. Many of them (though not nearly enough) are included in this book. Their work continues to be published and produced, year after year, in such small but faithful houses as Manhattan's Theatre for the New City and the Magic Theater in Omaha, Nebraska. Some of them have over fifty plays to their credit. Though they're discussed in some university classrooms, and increasingly written up now in academic and theater magazines, the reviewers, with a few notable exceptions, stubbornly refuse to see them as having "a body of work" comparable to that of Sam Shepard, Lanford Wilson, or David Mamet. They must prove themselves with each new play, as if just starting out. Many of them are branded "feminist" (the word now a pejorative in critical language), whether or not the authors intended to strike a blow for women's rights. If it is the vigorous playwright's responsibility to take a swing at the Establishment now and then, and given that powerful members of

the Establishment are (for the most part) men, then it follows that the
female playwright, if she has any political intention at all, must sometimes
express discontent with men in her work.

Had Shelagh Delaney written A *Taste of Honey*, and its sharp-tongued,
funny antiheroines, after the women's movement instead of before, she
would have been branded a feminist, too. The British playwrights we
interviewed didn't seem to know much about her or whether she was still
writing for the stage. She isn't even mentioned in *British Theatre Since
1955: A Reassessment*.[14] A good example of deliberate erasure of women
playwrights from the record. Some experts say she's a "one-play wonder."
Others claim director Joan Littlewood is really responsible for making A
Taste of Honey into a work of art. Still others say it isn't a work of art at
all. Delaney wrote one other play that I know of, *The Lion in Love*. It
was dismissed by the critics.

I went to see a brilliant film the other day called *Dance with a Stranger*.
The screenplay was by Shelagh Delaney. The writing was as perceptive
and unsentimental as ever, spare as a blueprint, seasoned to perfection
now by the artist's maturity. Theater's loss is cinema's gain.

A couple of years ago, producer Joe Papp sponsored a festival of black
women playwrights. A timely and conscientious project. The black female
voice is heard less and less frequently in the theater these days, as raw
vitality and defiance in women, on and off the stage, grows increasingly
less fashionable. As I write, black playwright Lee Hunkins is preparing
to track down those 125 plays by black women, applying for a grant in
hopes of anthologizing the most exciting of them. She intends to add to
the public record (alongside Hansberry, Kennedy, Childress, Shange,
J. e. Franklin, Vinette Carroll, Micki Grant, and others) such names as
May Miller for *Riding the Goat* (1930), and Georgia Douglas Johnson
for *Plumes* (1926). In her introduction to *Plays by American Women:
1900–1930*,[15] Judith Barlow describes Miller as "one of the most prolific
black women playwrights" and Johnson as winning prizes for her work
as well as "hosting a salon in her Washington, D.C., home that attracted
(and inspired) many of the writers associated with the 'Harlem Renaissance,' a flowering of black arts in the twenties." Sullivan and Hatch, in
Plays By and About Women,[16] assess many of the black women's plays
as angry. We hardly need to ask why. Critics feel that they have heard

[14]Ronald Hayman, (Oxford: Oxford University Press, 1979).
[15]In *Plays by American Women: 1900–1930* (New York: Applause, 1985), the editor, Judith E. Barlow, has recorded both endings to Zona Gale's Pulitzer Prize–winning play,
Miss Lulu Bett (1921).
[16]Sullivan and Hatch, op. cit., p. xiv.

enough "black" problems and "women" problems and "poverty" problems; they are bored by "victims" and impatient with working-class plays
that are invariably described as "melodramas" and summarily dismissed
with predictable, always unflattering references to *Mother Courage* or
Tobacco Road (the only two plays they seem to remember about poor
people). Well, perhaps stories of the dispossessed *are* melodramas. Poor
people truly "ain't got the money for the mortgage on the cow" and
landlords *do* have a way of showing up to evict those behind on their
rent. The issues persist whether or not reviewers are tired of them.

There has been much discussion as to whether men and women playwrights are different. As with men and women in general, they may not
be all that different at the very deepest levels of artistic and personal
experience. We really don't know. But to say that good art is genderless
is more a matter of wishful thinking than hard research. If this were so,
we'd have Hrotsvitha in the Park and the Susan Glaspell National Playwrights Conference.

What we do know is that our society and its institutions treat men and
women differently and continue to pressure both genders for different
behaviors that conform to convention. The theater, as one of those institutions, does the same. Women and men playwrights alike—and the
characters they create—are publicly punished for unacceptable behavior.
Punishment cannot exist without the power of authority. For society this
power is the law and its enforcement agents. In the theater, it is the critics
who police the stage for unacceptable behavior under the guise of aesthetic
judgment. Since women are still more restricted and less valuable than
men in the theater—as in society at large—the possibilities and actuality
of stepping out of line are higher and the consequences more cruel than
for men. And that 7 percent portion of the stage to which we presently
lay claim is constantly at risk. But if half of the plays presented in the
commercial and nonprofit theater were to be written by women, I'm not
sure that much would change beyond more work for actresses. It is only
when the truth is welcome on stage and morality discussed and political
views expressed with flamboyant courage in the manner of a Churchill
or Mamet that things will change. As long as women are censored at all
levels of the theater (and they are), as long as women censor themselves
(and they do), as long as women are damned for not being "very nice"
when they exhibit real behavior while men are applauded for the same,
then there will continue to be two groups of dramatists who reside in
separate worlds: the acceptable group . . . the men; and the subver-
sives . . . the women.

—K.B.

INDEX